THE HOLOCAUST NOW

Contemporary Christian and Jewish Thought

THE HOLOCAUST NOW

Contemporary Christian and Jewish Thought

Edited by
Rabbi Dr. Steven L. Jacobs

Cummings & Hathaway
P · U · B · L · I · S · H · E · R · S

For My Grandparents,
Ella and Leo Jacob:
Married July 29, 1920;
Murdered by the Nazis,
Late 1941 or Early 1942.
With Love.

And for My
Father,
Ralph Albert Jacobs
[May 1, 1921 - September 27, 1981]
The Saving Remnant

The Holocaust Now was originally published in 1993 by the University Press of America, 4720 Boston Way, Lanham, Maryland, 20706, in two volumes – *Contemporary Jewish Religious Responses to the Shoah* and *Contemporary Christian Religious Response to the Shoah*, volumes V and VI, respectively, of *Studies in the Shoah*. These volumes remain in print and are available from University Press of America.

Copyright © 1996 by Steven L. Jacobs

ISBN: 0-943025-92-3

All rights reserved. No part of this work may be reproduced or utilized in any form or by any means, electronic or mechanical, including photocopying, microfilm and recording, or by any information storage and retrieval system without permission in writing from the publisher.

First Printing

Printed in the United States of America by: Cummings & Hathaway Publishers
422 Atlantic Avenue
East Rockaway, NY 11518

For information regarding ordering, call: (800) 344-7579

TABLE OF CONTENTS

Preface xi
   Zev Garber
Foreword xiii
   Rahel Feldhay Brenner

Introduction 1
   Judaism and Christianity After Auschwitz
   Steven L. Jacobs

CHALLENGES TO THE MIND

Auschwitz: Re-envisioning the Role of God 25
   Peter J. Haas
Evil and Existence: Karl Barth, Paul Tillich, and Reinhold
   Niebuhr Revisited in Light of the *Shoah* 53
   Alan Davies
Suffering, Theology and the *Shoah* 71
   Alice Lyons Eckardt
Asking and Listening, Understanding and Doing: Some Conditions
   for Responding to the *Shoah* Religiously 97
   John K. Roth

CHALLENGES TO FAITH

Why? 119
   Bernard Maza
The *Shoah*: Continuing Challenge to Christianity 141
   John T. Pawlikowski
How the *Shoah* Affects Christian Belief 169
   Thomas A. Idinopulos
Voluntary Covenant 185
   Irving Greenberg
A Contemporary Religious Response to the *Shoah*: The Crisis of Prayer 217
   Michael McGarry

The Holocaust Now

Mysterium Tremendum: Catholic Grapplings with the *Shoah*
    and Its Theological Implications 235
    Eugene J. Fisher
In the Presence of Burning Children: The Reformation of Christianity
    After the *Shoah* 263
    Douglas K. Huneke

CONTEMPORARY CHALLENGES

In a World Without a Redeemer, Redeem! 291
    Michael Berenbaum
After Auschwitz and the Palestinian Uprising 303
    Marc H. Ellis
Theological and Ethical Reflections on the *Shoah*: Getting Beyond
    the Victim-Victimizer Relationship 325
    Rosemary Radford Ruether
Revisionism and Theology: Two Sides of the Same Coin 353
    Harry James Cargas
Between the Fires 369
    Arthur Waskow

REFLECTIVE CHALLENGES

The Holocaust: A Summing Up After More Than Two Decades of Reflection 379
    Emil L. Fackenheim
Apocalyptic Rationality and the *Shoah* 393
    Richard L. Rubenstein

CHALLENGE TO THE PRESENT AND FUTURE

Academia and the Holocaust 411
    Alan L. Berger

Notes 425
Glossary 499
Bibliography 521
About the Contributors 535
About the Editor 543

PREFACE

The controversy about the teaching of the *Shoah* as the paradigmatic genocide in American colleges and universities makes me think of the personal anguish of an 84-year-old survivor who studies Jewish Studies and philosophy with me at Los Angeles Valley College, a multi-ethnic public institution located in the eastern San Fernando Valley, California.

His name is Abraham L., and it is his concern as much as any other survivor of the Shoah that convinces me that, by offering State of California *mandated* Shoah education, we are not abandoning our mission as an institution of higher education. To the contrary, we are honoring that commitment.

Abraham [Hebrew for "father of a multitude of nations"] is forever having flashbacks. One moment he is here with the living, and the next he is back in a Nazi concentration camp, dead man walking. A common occurrence can spark traumatic experiences that imprison him. Children at play, electric railway, chimneys become trajectories for a stolen childhood, cattle cars of human cargo, crematoria belching human waste product. Night and day, season in and season out, he breathes the fumes of the "Final Solution," the Nazi annihilation of Six Million Jews. He is forever living the guilt and pain of surviving. A religious man, he pines over "I have been young and now am old; yet I have not seen the righteous forsaken, nor his seed begging for food" [Psalm 3725], recited in the *Birkat Hamazon,* the Grace After Meals.

Nonetheless, he manages to convert his image of captivity into mental stepping stones to escape his private hell. In Yiddish, the language of his murdered *landsleit* in the millions, he asks, how in today's world, where for many the is a nonevent, could the unique intentionality of the Shoah be remembered? And how to make sense of this catastrophe wihtout parallel?

My student's inquiries are instructive, for they put the lie to several of the myths now circulating about the issue of the Shoah at the college level:

Myth No. 1: Students who need Shoah education are the survivors themselves. Typically, these adult returnees are intelligent, competent seniors who simply need skills remediation before they can successfully transmit their story to those who were not there.

xi

The Holocaust Now

Myth No. 2: Shoah affected the Jewish People, so why study the *Jewish* tragedy and not others? Wrong again. The subject of the Shoah, the near total state-sponsored destruction of European Jewry in the bosom of Christendom, and other terrible genocidal acts of the Nazi regime against others, involves us all. Descendants of slaves or victims of colonialism, or of parents interned in detention camps during World War II must learn that they came for the Jews, Sinti-Romani ["Gypsies"] people, communists, homosexuals, and no one cared. This time they'll come for the Hispanics, or the blacks, or the Asians. Multiculturalists must hear the bigoted message of "dislike of the unlike," learn from it, and vow "Never Again" for any of God's children.

Myth No. 3: A number of college, university, and seminary programs may lack the mechanics [i.e. trained staff, funding, library resources, etc.] to offer a class on the Shoah, or the subject matter may be limited in appeal. An irrelevance. Themes from the Shoah can be generalized within topics such as "Studies in Human Values," "Racism and Genocide," "Moral Choices," etc., and taught within the division of social sciences, humanities, and other disciplines. Shoah education should be offered whenever and wherever someone recognizes the need for it. Responsible academics do, and, in this age of tribalism, terrorism, religious intolerance, and ethnic cleansing, we ask if not in developmental education, then where?

There is no shortage of publications on the Shoah, but students' knowledge of religious and theological thinking about the Great Catastrophe remains scanty. Why so? Significant articles are scattered in a wide variety of journals and books and often out of reach and/or too expensive for downsizing library budgets or personal purchases.

Yet *The Holocaust Now: Contemporary Christian and Jewish Thought* is an innovative approach to reverse this trend. Editor Steven L. Jacobs and 19 invited Jewish and Christian scholars reflect on his two questions: *What are the questions which we as religious thinkers should be asking about the Shoah today?* and *What are the answers you yourself would give?* The result is an insightful learning tool to probe hard questions about Judaism and Christianity, defined at Sinai and Calvary and confined by Auschwitz.

A plethora of views, visions, deepthought and disparity characterizes this volume. For some students, this may be disconcerting. So be it. What matters most is Shoah mattes are interpreted by cross-denominational religious scholars. If by this, the reader becomes no longer indifferent, no an amen-sayer, and can now say, "It is my responsibility," we will all benefit. To this end, *The Holocaust Now* offers a blazing beginning.

Zev Garber
Los Angeles Valley College

FOREWORD

*The fact is that the Shoah happened because it
could have happened.*

Harry James Cargas

*....at most only a fragmentary Tikkun is possible.
This is because we are situated in the post-Holocaust world.
We must accept our situatedness. We must live with it.*

Emil L. Fackenheim

The above reflections define the conceptual parameters of this important book. We live in a world in which the inconceivable horror of the *Final Solution* became a reality. This reality has indeliby and critically affected our historical, ethical, and theological perspectives. The exposure of unfathomable evile has called into question humanity's elemental yearning for redemption, or *Tikkun*.

The waning of faith, which forebodes nihilistic cynicism and indifference, motivates the search for a redefinition of the meaning of human existence. Elie Wiesel tells us, "Traditional ideas and acquired values, philosophical systems and social theories - all must be revised in the shadow of Birkenau."[1] This need to revise and redefine underlies the *raison d'etre* of the essays compiled in this volume.

As mentioned above, *The Holocaust Now: Contemporary Christian and Jewish Thought* is an important book. Steven L. Jacobs has put together an excellent selection of writings by prominent scholars, educators, and thinkers. Clearly, the wealth of ideas, the profundity of thought, and the seriousness of the considerations before us makes this volume a very important contribution to the field of Shoah Studies.

The importance of these essays, however, lies not only in the issues that they address, but, perhaps, first and foremost, in the double religious orientation that they represent. The outstanding quality of this book emerges in its premise that the revision and redefinition of values in the post-Shoah world is indispensable for both Jewish and Christian religious thought. That is to say, the *tremendum* of the Shoah brought forth a universal recognition of the need to re-think and re-structure previous attitudes and

The Holocaust Now

convictions, a need that places both Jews and Christians on a spiritual quest.

Furthermore, the *perspective*, rather than the religious identities of the authors, as the guiding principle of the essay arrangement, demonstrates that the quest for redefintion and reform begins in a dialogical situation. The juxtaposition of Christian and Jewish discussions of the Shoah is of essence in a world imbued with Shoah consciousness. It presents an interaction underlined by mutual concern for post-Shoah theology and ethics.

Quite understandably, the responses to the Shoah of both Christians and Jews focus primarily on the issue of Jewish suffering. Can Jews reaffirm their covenant with God who kept silent when their children were burning? Can Christians continue to believe in the redemptive nature of the Christ's suffering in view of the methodically planned and executed genocide of the Jews?

Is it possible for Jews to believe, as Bernard Maza does in his essay, that the Shoah was God's punishment and at the same time the "birth pangs of the Messiah," which brought forth the birth of the Jewish State? Is it possible for the Christians to accept the views of Pope John Paul II and of Cardinal O'Connor, quoted in Alice Eckardt's essay, that "the Jewish enriched the world by their suffering" which is "conjoined with" the suffering of the Crucifixion?

These attempts to comprehend the affliction, to explain the inexplicable annihilation place the suffering in pre-Shoah theological frameworks. Such an approach which fails to confront the horror of the Final Solution highlights the theology of refusal to apply redemptive properties to the suffering of Jews in the Shoah.

The theologians who break away from the conventional explications of suffering argue that no extent of mystification or attenuation of Shoah suffering is acceptable. They claim that the pain of the Shoah victims needs to be confronted and recognized. This uncompromising position impels re-thinking and re-statement of the very foundations of both Christian and Jewish theologies of redemption.

Let us recall briefly the concepts of redemptive history as proposed by the pre-Shoah Jewish philosopher Walter Benjamin and the post-Shoah Christian theologian Johannes Baptist Metz. Benjamin claims that history can be redemptive only if it is "retroactive," that is, conscious of the past of the defeated, the persecuted, the afflicted.[2] Metz follows in Benjamin's footsteps arguing that salvation lies in the "memory of suffering." Only the consciousness of past suffering may bring forth the redemption of "dangerous" freedom.[3]

As the theologians - the Christians John Pawlikowski and the Jewish Irving Greenberg - demonstrate in this volume, the unmediated and unalleviated consciousness of the Shoah is "dangerous" indeed. The memory of Shoah suffering enforces a redefinition of God's authority and the revision of the role of humanity vis-a-vis divinity. In Greenberg's view, Shoah consciousness establishes a "voluntary covenant," whereby the human beings become "senior partners" in their relationship with God.

Forward

In Pawlikowski's view, the "commanding" God is replaced by a "compelling" God, to whom humanity is drawn, but no longer summoned.

The "danger," however, does not lie in the departure from the traditional view of the omnipresent divine. The post-Shoah perception of disempowered God does not suggest loss of faith. On the contrary, it obliges the individual to reaffirm faith by accepting the "dangerous freedom" of the ethical bondage.

The propositions of the "voluntary covenant" and of "compelling" God place the responsibility for the world on the individual. In the aftermath of the Shoah, humanity, rather than divinity, is accountable for history. In both thinkers' reassessments of morality in the post-Shoah world, the consciousness of suffering has transmuted theology into ethics. The ethical freedom of the post-Shoah individual lies in his or her responsibility towards the world.

The prominence of the ethical aspect in post-Shoah theology emerges throughout the book. It is especially pervasive in those articles, or sections of articles, which discuss the applicability of the lessons of the Shoah to the contemporary world. These texts are preoccuped with prevention of future events of human mass destruction. The argumentation is based on the premise that, in the aftermath of the Shoah, an awareness of the distinction between the history of human societies and the evolutionary history of nature is of absolute essence.

The so-called "Social Darwinism" applies the law of biological evolution to the multiracial, multicultural, multireligious structures of human communities. "What happens," as Peter Haas tells us, "is a scenario in which diverse races....are engaged in a natural struggle for the survival of the fittest." Scientific racism reinforced by uncurbed technological development deprives humanity of its humaneness. This is the lesson that the Nazi ideology and the implementation of the Final Solution have taught us.

As responsible human beings, we must remain conscious of the horrifying implications of the social struggle for domination. It is therefore imperative to rethink modernity's orientation or racial evolution which brought about both the Shoah and the atomic bomb. Otherwise, the race for supremacy may end, as Arthur Waskow contends, in the destruction of the earth. "If we do not see the two fires in relation to each toher, then the fire behind us [of Shabbat] will lose its meaning, and the one that is yet to come will consume us."

Not all thinkers see the implications of the Shoah in eschatological terms of global destruction however. Some apply the lessons of the Shoah to the existing situations of racism, exploitation, persecutions, and discrimination, as they are being inflicted upon vast masses of human beings in today's world.

For example, two leading feminist theologians consider the Nazi ideology of *Untermensch* as the ultimate negative development of Western capitalist society. Elizabeth Schussler-Fiorenza and Rebecca Chopp speak about Western the imperialist ideology of dehumanization which culminated in the event of the Shoah. The feminist

The Holocaust Now

movement condemns the patriarchal construction of Western society and its inherent subjugationof women. The liberation theology movement sees colonialism and its ruthless subjugation of the weak and defenseless arising from the same sources that engendered the Shoah.

The lessons of the Shoah presented in this volume take an even more challenging form of a critical reconsideration of the Israeli-Palestinian conflict. A fascinating meeting of minds emerges in the articles by the Jewish Marc Ellis and the Christian Rosemary Radfor Ruether.

As both thinkers argue, to a considerable extent, the theology of the Shoah has been used, by both Jews and Christians, to explain and justify Israel's occupation of the territories and tis disregard of the Palestinian plight. "Can the new Sinai," Ellis asks, "move beyond militant Zionism and extreme alienation?" "Who," Ruether inquires in reference to the same issue, "is going to be the victim of our liberation? Who is going to be ensalved by our redemption?"

Both theologians claim that the Jewish people cannot become the oppressors of others in the name of the history which oppressed them. Both thinkers argue that recovery from the trauma of the Shoah will actualize neither in an abusive treatment of the other nor in self-righteous self-justification. On the contrary, a self-critical self-reevaluation will lead to a constructive understanding of the legacy of the Shoah. This is the legacy, both thinkers claim, of solidarity and collaboration.

In view of Israel's recent reconsideration of its politics, this volume gains special significance. The hope, indeed the ongoing realization of peaceful collaboration between Israelis and Palestinians, highlights the importance of these essays in today's world's political reality. These are not merely philosophical contemplations and theoretical suggestions of how to mend the world. The evolving peace process translates the concept of human responsibility towards the world into concrete historical events. It thus validates the premise of this book which argues the need to revise and redefine the hypotheses of faith and ethics in the post-Shoah world. The fact that this revision is occurring in the arena of political praxis allows us to become cautiously hopeful about the future.

Rahel Feldhay Brenner
University of Wisconsin-Madison

---

1. Elie Wiesel, "Foreword," in Harry James Cargas, *A Christian Response to the Holocaust* [Denver: Stonehenge Books, 1981], iii.

2. Walter Benjamin, "Theses of the Philosophy of History," *Illuminations* [New York: Schocken Books, 1973], 253-265.

3. Johannes Baptist Metz, *Faith in History and Society: Toward a Practical Fundamental Theology* [New York: The Seabury Press, 1980. Translated by David Smith.], 110.

Introduction

In my own introductory contribution, I attempt to briefly survey and respond to the major Jewish and Christian thinkers who have grappled with the enormity of the *Shoah*, after first having addressed an issue of crucial importance: the question of the theological and/or historical uniqueness of the Shoah. I conclude by enumerating those categories of Jewish religious concern which must be addressed in any attempt to reformulate a relevant and contemporary post-Auschwitz Jewish theology, suggesting, therefore, a preliminary direction for future Jewish thought: [1] God, [2] Covenant, [3] Prayer, [4] *Mitzvah* [Commandment], [5] Celebration of Festival-Calendar and Life-Cycle Events, and [6] Jews and Christians in dialogue.

SLJ

INTRODUCTION

JUDAISM AND CHRISTIANITY AFTER AUSCHWITZ[1]

Steven L. Jacobs

I. Introduction

That the events of the Shoah, specifically the years 1933-1945, which saw the deaths of approximately six million Jews, five million non-Jews, and twenty-million Russians--not to mention untold Allied and German military combatants and civilians--have profound theological implications is patently obvious. That those who, in their anguish and their pain, both Jews and non-Jews, have "chosen" [if that is, indeed, the correct word!] to wrestle with these implications are pitifully few in number should be equally as obvious. Names like Arthur Cohen, Irving Greenberg, Eliezer Berkovits, Emil Fackenheim, Richard Rubenstein, and, of course, Elie Wiesel in the Jewish community; and Harry James Cargas, Alan Davies, Alice and Roy Eckardt, Franklin Littell, Michael McGarry, John Pawlikowski, David Rausch, Rosemary Radford Ruether, and John Roth in the Christian community, are known only to the initiated should, also, be obvious. For both Judaism and Christianity, whose very theological houses are built upon the premise of the God-who-acts-in-history, whatever else we may say of both God and faith, the Shoah is a frontal assault upon both. Might this, then, not be the first theological implication: That the events of the this very limited moment in history would cause such a fundamental and radical restructuring and rethinking of the entire historical understanding of both Judaism and Christianity that we best leave well enough along, save for the few, and get on with our lives, preferring not to deal with those implications rather than consider them?

Such would certainly seem to be the case for both Jews and Christians in the world today. For Jews, the miracle of the modern rebirth of the State of Israel on May 14, 1948, the phoenix literally arising out of the ashes of the Shoah, and its ongoing struggle for survival, have all but preoccupied Jews and Jewish energies, and is, in and of itself, by and large, a redirection of Jewish thinking away from the Shoah. For Christians, the ever-increasing encroachment of both secularism and third-world theologies, fundamentalism and the "electronic gospel," have directed Christian thinkers away from the events of the Shoah, if, indeed, they were truly of primary theological concern in the years following the Second World War. For both communities, the tragic history of relationship, culminating in the events of the Shoah, has distanced both communities from confronting directly the theological meaning of those events, allowing other lures and crises to supplant the two essential questions to which both communities have failed to respond adequately: [1] "Where was God in the Shoah?" and [2] "Where was humanity in the Shoah?" [Additionally, for Jews, "What covenantal relationship now exists between the Jewish People and God in light of the death camps?" And for Christians, "How does Jesus the Redeemer now present himself to an unredeemed world which could, seemingly, countenance a Shoah?"]

Before attempting my own conclusions, it will best serve our purposes to survey, however briefly, those aforementioned thinkers and respond to them individually and collectively. While those so surveyed are by no means all-inclusive, they are, in reality, the major thinkers who have attempted to grapple with the magnitude of the Shoah.

We begin, however, with the following caveat: In light of the Shoah, the post-Auschwitz theological enterprise *must* address these two questions: [1] The historical uniqueness of the Shoah--yes or no? and [2] Irving Greenberg's oft-quoted criterion, "No statement, theological or otherwise, should be made that would not be creditable in the presence of burning children".[2] Rephrased by Cohen, "No God is worth a single child's life. How much the more so untold children?".[3] Commenting on this very idea, Robert Sherwin writes:

> All the wisdom of all the philosophers, said Dostoyevsky, cannot explain the death of one innocent child. How, therefore, to explain the deaths of one million one hundred thousand children? Any statement would be an understatement. Yet the holocaust embraces a basic paradox. It imposes silence but demands speech. It defies solutions but requires responses.[4]

If such is, indeed, true, as I fully believe it is, then we must, likewise, agree with Cohen that:

> Any constructive theology after the 'tremendum' must be marked by the following characteristics: first, the God who is affirmed must abide in a universe whose human history is scarred by genuine evil without making the evil empty or illusory not disallowing the real presence of God before, even if not within, history; second, the relation of God to creation and its creatures, including both, now include demonic structures and unredeemable events, must be seen, nonethe-

Introduction

less, as meaningful and valuable despite the fact that the justification of life and struggle is now intensified and anguished by the contrast and opposition that evil supplies; third, the reality of God in his selfhood and person can no longer be isolated, other than as a strategy of clarification, from God's real involvement with the life of creation.[5]

Let us return, then, to the two caveats prior to surveying those Jewish and Christian thinkers who have had the courage to deal with the Shoah and their attempted reconciliation with their own understandings and their own tradition's understanding of the relationship between God, humanity, and the world.

II. The Theological-Historical Uniqueness of the Shoah

In my own teaching, I use the following definition of the Shoah: "The historically-validated, legalized, bureaucratic marriage of technology and death." This definition is predicated upon my understanding that the event *is* unique, both theologically and historically, in both Jewish and world history, though, to be sure, the result of an historically pre-prepared environment which evolved from generations of Western and Christian anti-Jewish and anti-Judaic sentiment, best summed up in Hilberg's schemata, "You [i.e. the Jews] have no right to live among us as Jews!" to "You have no right to live among us!" to "You have no right to live!"[6]

The very uniqueness of the Shoah marked, perhaps forever and all times, a radical shift in the understanding of who and what the Jew was: Prior to the rise of the Nazis, those who sought to do harm to the Jews--either individually or communally--admitted that the Jew could change by surrendering his or her identity and adopting that of the larger society. In pre-Christian Egypt, Greece, and Rome, one born a Jew could renounce his or her Judaism and take on the coloration of that larger society, and, while he or she may have suffered social discrimination, one or two generations later, all was forgotten and forgiven. In Christian society up until the advent of the Nazis, renunciation of Judaism in favor of Christianity opened doors to integration into a new, non-Jewish world. Again, aside from the Marranos, whose questionable conversions were the source of their affliction, former Jews saw the integration of their offspring one to two generations later. Thus, almost all pre-Nazi Western European societies admitted the possibility of change from formerly Jewish identity to non-Jewish identity, and, with it, a subsequent loss of discrimination and oppression.

For the Nazis, however, this historical understanding of anti-Judaism was, essentially in error. Whatever else we may say of the so-called "racial theories" of the Nazis, they saw no way for the Jew to change. Previous manifestations of antisemitism, then, may be labelled "cultural antisemitism," "social antisemitism," "political antisemitism," and "theological" or "religious antisemitism." Now, for the first time in history, the Jews were confronted with "biological antisemitism." Not what they did, how they behaved, how they practiced their faith and its rituals and ceremonials was at issue, but what they were was the root of all that afflicted the Western world. "Jewishness" was a physical component of the individual, part of the very lifeblood of the Jew, and, thus, could no more be changed that could amputation of limb render the individual a whole human being. "Race-mixing" between Jew and Aryan, according to the Nazis, had to result in an inferiorization and mongrelization of the Aryan race; there was simply no other way to perceive that negative relationship. This shift, then, from non-biological forms of antisemitism and anti-Jewish persecution and prejudice to biological antisemitism marks the Shoah unique on the world scene.[7]

There are, however, those within the Jewish community who do not so regard the events of the Shoah as unique, as there are those within the Christian community who, equally, perceive the events of the Shoah as part of some, as yet unknowable, Divine plan. Daniel Polish writes:

> As we reflect on how to understand God after the 'shoah,' then, I reject the proposition that we treat it as being of a different order of reality from anything that preceded it, thus needing theological responses of a wholly new order. I regard it as being different in magnitude but not in kind, from cataclysms that the people had known before in its history.[8]

I would, however, contend that the concerns of those who reject the Shoah as unique is not with history, but with maintaining the structures of historical Jewish faith as previously presented by generations of Jews. David Weiss, writing in *Sh'ma: A Journal of Jewish Responsibility*, sees the Shoah as a continuation of the sad and tragic story of Jewish persecutions, but not unique.[9] And he is not alone in his thinking! Martin Cohen enumerates those whose response to the Shoah is, even today, to think in historically-traditional terms:

> Thus, Ignatz Maybaum, emphasizing the role of the Jews as the Suffering Servant, views the Holocaust as a divine visitation to being an end to a decaying era and to usher in a new, utopian world. Menahem Hartom explain the Holocaust as punishment for Jewish assimilation and sets the state of Israel as its intended outcome, although the Jewish people 'was not worthy of it by its conduct.' Bemoaning the tendencies to irreligiosity in Israel's secular nationalism, Hartom warns against another retributive visitation.

Introduction

Joel Teitelbaum, leader of the anti-Israel Satmar Hasidim, goes so far as to blame secularist Zionism for the divine visitation of the Holocaust. David Chomsky shares Hartom's faith, but rejects his fear of assimilative trends in Israel. On the contrary, he sees the possibility of the Jews in secular Israel becoming a 'kingdom of priests and a holy people.' Issachar Jacobson hears in the Holocaust a call for Jews to renounce all attempts at rational explanation of its events and to reaffirm their Jewish belief 'to remain people of faith, fearing God and always doing good, for in these ways alone can we grasp something of God's wisdom.'

Similarly, Jacob Rothschild calls on the Jew to rise above the natural human desire for explanation of daily events to a strong and unquestioning faith in human history under the guidance of God.[10]

For the traditionally-minded believer, everything that occurs, occurs as the result of the God-who-acts-in-history. Certainly no event of the cataclysmic proportions of the Shoah escaped Divine attention. All continues to be theologically and historically as it has always been theologically and historically. Jewish and Christian religious responsibility becomes the integration of attempts to fathom the meaning of these events within a God-controlled world. To reject these events as, somehow, outside the purview of the Divine is to reject, consciously or otherwise, the whole theological enterprise as it has historically evolved.

Yet questions abound which admit of no easy answers: [1] Why did this controlling Deity permit these events to take place? [2] Did God, in actuality, so construct these events as a means of punishing an errant Jewish community according to the classical lines of the Covenant? [3] What sin have the Jews committed that warranted such punishment?[11] [4] And, if not the Jews alone, what sin had others--Gypsies; political enemies of the Third Reich; sincere Christians, including clergy--likewise committed that warranted their own horrendous deaths? [5] Did the Deity, in fact, choose Adolf Hitler and his minions to do Divine bidding?

For those who affirm the historically-traditional notions of faith, the only creditable conclusion is that the Shoah is punishment. Whether we like it or not, whether we wish to accept it or not, this notion of God's relationship with humanity answers all relevant questions and remains intact. The Shoah was punishment for sin, though we know not the nature of the sin which merited such punishment. That there are others, Richard Rubenstein most particularly, and even Elie Wiesel, who reject such a notion should be obvious. I would classify myself among them.

In commenting himself on his interview with Dean Heinrich Gruber of the Evangelical Church of West Berlin, himself an avowedly anti-Nazi who suffered physically because of his opposition, Richard Rubenstein experienced the very "crisis of faith" which rendered the historically-traditional understanding of God and God's relationship with humanity passe, which is at the heart of the quest for a relevant, rethought theological response:

> Having commenced with his biblical interpretation of recent history, he could not stop until he had asserted that it had been God's will to send Adolf Hitler to exterminate Europe's Jews. At the moment that I heard Gruber make this assertion, I had what was perhaps the most important single crisis of faith I have ever had. I recognized that Gruber was not an Antisemite and that his assertion that the God of the Covenant was and is the ultimate Author of the great events of Israel's history was not different from the faith of any traditional Jew. Gruber was applying the logic of Covenant Theology to the events of the twentieth century. I appreciated his fundamental honesty. He recognized that, if one takes the biblical theology of history seriously, Adolf Hitler is no more nor less an instrument of God's wrath than Nebuchadnezzar....
>
> If one accepts the doctrine that God is distinctively involved in the history of Israel, the fundamentalist Christian may indeed be right in asserting that the sorrows of the Jews have been inflicted upon them for rejecting Jesus. Whether one is a fundamental Christian or a traditional Jew, it is impossible to regard the sorrows of Jewish history as mere historical accidents. They must in some sense express the will of God as a just and righteous Creator. Either such a God is a sadist who inflicts pain because he enjoys it or he has a reason for the misfortune he inflicts. The only morally defensible motive for a superior to inflict pain on an inferior would be punitive chastisement which has as its purpose altering the victim's mode of behavior. If one takes Covenant Theology seriously, as did Dean Gruber, Auschwitz must be God's way of punishing the Jewish people in order that they might better see the light, the light of Christ if one is a Christian, the light of Torah if one is a traditional Jew.[12]

The Shoah may, also, be perceived as unique because of its very modernity on two accounts: [1] The operative concept of "surplus populations" so well orchestrated in the writings of Richard Rubenstein[13], and [2] The very use of technology which made of the concentration camp process of death the ultimate epitome of the assembly line, to wit:

Introduction

> Efficiency was at its peak in the concentration camp process: In the morning, you stepped off the train. In the evening the corpse was buried or cremated. Clothing was packed away, after having been sorted and repaired, if necessary, for shipment back to Germany. People were killed on an assembly line basis.[14]

The theological implications of both--declaring any population outside the context of human community and the use of technology for totally negative purposes--have not been explored to any great degree by Jewish and Christian thinkers, though Catholic theologian Michael Novak has begun to explore the theological implications of the corporation[15], and Richard Rubenstein himself seems to heading in this direction in his *The Age of Triage*.

Having now, concretely, established the uniqueness of the Shoah as a theological concern, we move, of necessity, to the second pre-concern: That the construction of any valid post-Auschwitz theology must confront the historical reality of evil death, most poignantly, the useless deaths of so many children, Jewish or Christian. Such a theology must wrestle, even unsuccessfully, with the enormity of these deaths--in ovens, in gas chambers, by bayonet or bullet, often in the presence of parents or grandparents, often accompanied by the very adults who represented for these children the only safety and security permitted them in their nightmare world. The death of any child poses enormous theological difficulties, though both Jewish and Christian traditions continue to affirm the reality of the God-who-acts-in-history when confronted with such. The deaths of one million children below the age of twelve, and an additional one-half million if we raise the age to eighteen, is a double frontal attack to which neither has responded, even inadequately.

III. Jewish Thinking About the Shoah

We begin, most appropriately, with Elie Wiesel's *Night*, most particularly that passage most often viewed as the fullest literary expression of the theological dilemma:

> One day when we came back from work, we saw three gallows rearing up in the assembly place, three black crows. Roll Call. SS all around us, machine guns trained: the traditional ceremony. Three victims in chains--and one of them, the little servant, the sad-eyed angel.
>
> The SS seemed more preoccupied, more disturbed than usual. To hang a young boy in front of thousands of spectators was no

The Holocaust Now

light matter. The head of the camp read the verdict. All eyes were on the child. He was lividly pale, almost calm, biting his lips. The gallows threw its shadow over him.

This time the Lagerkapo refused to act as executioner. Three SS replaced him.

The three victims mounted together onto the chairs.

The three necks were placed at the same moment within the nooses.

"Long live liberty!" cried the two adults.

But the child was silent.

"Where is God? Where is He?" someone behind me asked.

At a sign from the head of the camp, the three chairs tipped over.

Total silence throughout the camp. On the horizon, the sun was setting.

"Bare your heads!" yelled the head of the camp. His voice was raucous.

We were weeping.

"Cover your heads!"

Then the march past began. The two adults were no longer alive. Their tongues hung swollen, blue-tinged. But the third rope was still moving; being so light, the child was still alive....

For more than half an hour he stayed there, struggling between life and death, dying in slow agony under our eyes. And we had to look him full in the face. He was still alive when I passed in front of him. His tongue was still red, his eyes were not yet glazed.

Behind me, I heard the same man asking:

"Where is God now?"

And I heard a voice within me answer him:

"Where is He? Here He is--He is hanging here on this gallows...."[16]

Rubenstein in rejecting Gruber's conclusions, and along with them the historically-traditional Jewish response, and Wiesel in presenting in starkly dramatic form the very same picture, seem to me to be saying that the previous ways in which we have thought about God, about God's relationship with humanity, in particular the Jewish people, have now become passe, that the very categories of relationship no longer suffice to explain or incorporate into their schema new, contemporary historical evidence that what happened during those dark years is, quite literally, beyond the scope of those understandings. What is now called for are new ways of thinking and understanding the universe and the place of both God and the Jewish people--and Germans and Christians and everyone else--in it.

Introduction

Rubenstein's honest, pain-filled willingness to confront the Shoah directly in theological terms, independent of his conclusions, has called forth his share of critics and defenders: Seymour Cain applauds him for cogently raising the questions he raises, but, equally, argues that his proposals were contradictory and confusing, bordering on the irrelevant.[17] Michael Wyschogrod takes him to task for the very divisiveness within the Jewish community that his writings sew:

> The sin [sic] of Rubenstein is, therefore, that he permits Auschwitz further to divide the Jewish people at a time when survival is paramount if Hitler is not to be handed a posthumous victory, and survival demands unity.[18]

Because Rubenstein can no longer believe after Auschwitz as his ancestors believed, he labels himself a 'pagan', though, to be sure, his paganism is an existential paganism whereby he also affirms his place as a member of the Jewish people who must now rely on their own resources to survive:

> I am a pagan. To be a pagan means to find once again one's roots as a child of earth and to see one's own existence as wholly and totally an earthly existence. It means once again to understand that for mankind the true divinities are the gods of earth, not the high gods of the sky; the gods of space and place, not the gods of home and hearth, not the gods of wandering, though wanderers we must be.[19]

Pagan or not, Rubenstein's break with historically-traditional notions and ideas continues to subject his theology to a veritable "conspiracy of silence" today in institutional Jewish life.

Wiesel, on the other hand, is relatively untouchable. After all, he is, by his own admission, a storyteller, and does not venture into the realms of academic-intellectual discourse confined to philosophy and/or theology. He offers no systematic response to his experiences, but prefers to simply tell the story and energize the moral commitments necessary to prevent repetition, leaving to others their own avenues of responsibility.[20]

A somewhat different tack is that taken by Orthodox Jewish thinker Eliezer Berkovits, author of *Faith After Auschwitz*.[21] For him, the traditional notions of God, Covenant, and Jewish people remain intact. For him, for whatever the reason, always unknown to us, God chose "to turn His face away from us, to hid His face"--perhaps as the ultimate expression of commitment to human freedom--and the resultant perversion of that freedom was the events of the Shoah. Thus, to ask the question "Where was God?" according to Berkovits becomes the wrong question. God is where He has always been: Waiting for faltering humanity to mature in its responsibilities. The question we must ask and continue to ask is "Where was humanity?" and how can that humanity overcome its potential for future repetitions?

What is surprising about Berkovits is the very radical understanding he has of human freedom as, somehow, beyond the arena of Divine accountability, and his acceptance of *hester panim* [God's "hidden face"] as speaking meaningfully to the human condition. The God who cares is, seemingly, willing to maintain His distance even when humanity so desperately needs that involvement and caring for its own salvation. Could it be, then, that having removed Himself from humanity--out of that commitment to human freedom--the Deity is no longer capable, not to mention unwilling, or re-entering into relationship? Berkovits provides us no answer. Also, other than for the initial act of creation which merits thanksgiving, how do we enter into a meaningful relationship with a God who [arbitrarily?] removes Himself? And why bother to do so--since He has seemingly rejected any involvement with the affairs of humanity?[22]

This same question might very well be asked of Irving ["Yitz"] Greenberg who, in his own writings, speaks of a "voluntary covenant" with God in light of Auschwitz. This Orthodox thinker, too, like Eliezer Berkovits, essentially negates all previous Jewish understandings of Covenant, which is perfectly acceptable--except that he wishes to maintain his place within that same Orthodox community which continues to speak in historically-traditional ways. Commitment to the Jewish people, to be involved with the Jewish people and its ongoing struggle for survival, to continue to affirm time-honored religious forms, as well as innovative forms, is not Covenant, no matter how well-intentioned the covenantor. That Covenant of Jewish tradition is predicated upon a God who will provide and protect its adherents so long as they own up to their responsibilities as members of a covenanted community. Now, since we voluntarily have the option of choosing to accept this covenant, we, also, have the option of rejecting that very same covenant, and God may not necessarily be a part of either decision. Stripped to its barest bones, Greenberg's position may only be a more contemporary rejection of the notion of the Shoah as expression of Divine punishment for a people who failed to honor its historic covenant.

Emil Fackenheim, on the other hand, sees no voluntarism at all, though he does not speak in covenantal terms, but, rather, in emotionally-historical ones. For Jews to reject their Jewish identity and merge with the larger culture and society is to grant Hitler and his minions that very victory which was his ultimate goal all along: To make the world 'Judenrein'!

I believe that whereas no redeeming voice is heard at

Introduction

Auschwitz, a commanding voice is heard, and that it is being heard with increasing clarity. Jews are not permitted [By whom?--SLJ] to hand Hitler posthumous victories. Jews are commanded [By whom?--SLJ] to survive as Jews, lest their people perish....They are forbidden [By whom?--SLJ] to despair of God, lest Judaism perish....Jewish survival, were it even for more than survival's sake, is a holy duty.[23]

Emotionally powerful words, indeed--but spoke only to those who have already made the commitment to positively affirm their Jewish selves. The essential problem with Emil Fackenheim is two-fold: [1] For the Jew for whom the Shoah is an "uncomfortable bit of history," at the very least, appeal to it will not build a house of positive Jewish commitments and/or practices; and [2] As the events of 1933 to 1945 recede further and further into history, transmission of those horrific events to succeeding generations becomes even more difficult to teach, and becomes a theological absurdity upon which to affirm Jewish faith. Essentially, the Jewish voice which speaks at Auschwitz speaks to those who have always heard such voices and who continue to incorporate into their own Jewish *weltanshauung* Jewish historical experiences. The newer adherents to Jewish commitment because of such events remain pitifully few.

In brief, then, these are some of the significant Jewish thinkers who today continue to grapple with the theological meaning of the years 1933 to 1945. They have been subject to serious critique, some more than others, some less than others. Before, however, examining my own thinking, let us address those Christian thinkers who have, likewise, attempted to, somehow, deal with the Shoah in light of their own religious traditions.

IV. Christian Thinking About the Shoah

Catholic Gerard Sloyan writes of Christian history:

More than eighteen hundred years of Christian antipathy for Jews for alleged theological reasons were followed by an attempt unique in history to exterminate them. *Whether or not a direct causality can be proved becomes an indifferent matter.* The sequence alone requires that Christians purge from their faith and theology and not merely from their behavior anything that could have led to this demonic outcome. On any reading of Christianity, one would think that the motivation so to act cannot be found in divine revelation.[24]

While agreeing with Sloyan as to the re-examination required of Christianity when confronting the Shoah, I do *not* agree that "causality" is "an indifferent matter." It is the very essence of the challenge to Christian faith: Whether, in point of fact, inherent in Christianity's presentation of itself to the world is an antisemitism potentially so virulent that the right set of historic and environmental factors could bring about a repetition of the Shoah. If such is true, and antisemitism is not yet expunged, then it is only a matter of time before we realize that repetition. If, on the other hand, there is no causality, not foundation on which to build the house, then the examination is one of relationship between the ideas and practices of Christianity and the various aberrations which have been inflicted upon the Jewish people for the past two thousand years. Either way, the task at hand is not easy, nor is it free of pain. But the failure to examine the past is prelude to the future. Irving Greenberg writes:

> Nothing less than a fundamental critique and purification of the Gospels themselves can begin to eliminate Christianity as a source of hatred. What the Holocaust reveals is that Christianity has the stark choice of contrition, repentance, and self-purification or the continual temptation to participate in or pave the way for genocide.[25]

John Pawlikowski, also a Catholic, calls for a re-examination of the Catholic understanding of God and humanity in light of the Shoah, but equally stresses that the Church itself must rethink its relationship with non-Catholics, especially Jews, because of the Shoah. To maintain the kind of successionism and triumphalism that has been part and parcel of Christianity's history is, today, morally wrong and theologically objectionable.[26]

Harry James Cargas, on the other hand, not a priest, is, along with Rosemary Radford Ruether, the most radical critic of the Roman Catholic Church in the aftermath of the Shoah. Calling himself a "post-Auschwitz Catholic," he writes of his "obsession" with the Shoah, and presents sixteen proposals for forging new links between Jews and Catholic Christians, among which are the following:

> [1] The Catholic Church should excommunicate Adolf Hitler.
> [2] The Christian liturgical calendar[s] should include an annual memorial service for the Jewish victims of the Holocaust.
> [8] The Vatican's historical archives for the twentieth-century need to be opened to historians.[27]

Rosemary Ruether, even more a radical theologian than Cargas, calls for a restructuring of Christian thought because her own examination of the texts of Christianity have led her to conclude that, indeed, the Gospels are antisemitic and do contain within them the seeds of historical anti-Judaism. In *Faith and Fratricide: The Theological Roots of*

Introduction

Anti-Semitism, she calls for nothing less than a total re-evaluation and rethinking of the theological relationship between Judaism and Christianity, revolving around a new understanding of Christology as the "key issue" in that relationship.[28] She shares that concern with Michael B. McGarry, whose *Christology After Auschwitz* surveys Roman Catholic opinion subsequent to the Second World War in light of the momentous import of Vatican II, and, hesitatingly, makes some predications as to future directions.[29] He does not, however, go far enough in his own thinking, though he, too, realizes that a rethinking of the place of Christ in Christian theology, most particularly a down-playing of triumphalist successionism, presents enormous problems within all facets of Christianity.

Anglican priest Alan Ecclestone, in his own book *Night Sky of the Lord,* likewise tries to deal, albeit unsuccessfully, with the theological dilemmas for Christianity posed by the Shoah.[30] He calls for the following new agenda for the Christian community, like the others noted previously: [1] an acknowledgement and understanding of antisemitism; [2] the abandonment of anti-Jewish theology; [3] "the recovery of the Hebraic understanding of the creation and the nature of human life"; [4] "the religious significance of Jesus"; and [5] "the problems [sic] posed by the State of Israel". While his book is an attempt to expand upon his agenda, his desire for Jews to rethink Jesus and discover worth in him nullifies his desire to further dialogue. His difficulty, like so many, appears to be the difficulty in accommodating within a Christian world-view an equally-valid expression of the God-human encounter of which Christ has no part, as well as a general unwillingness to deal with the raw notion that Christianity *may* have had a direct relationship and responsibility for those pre-1933 events which led to the Shoah.

Protestant thinkers Franklin H. Littell and David A. Rausch have written companion volumes attempting to explore the meaning of the Shoah for non-Catholic Christians: Littell's *The Crucifixion of the Jews: The Failure of Christians to Understand the Jewish Experience*[31] and Rausch's *A Legacy of Hatred: Why Christians Must Not Forget the Holocaust*[32] start from the standpoint of history, acknowledging in the process Christian complicity and responsibility for the events which led to the ovens and the gas chambers of World War II. Though both texts are well-organized and provide exacting documentation for their conclusions, neither Littell nor Rausch have worked through the theological implications of their studies, nor provided a thorough reconstruction of non-Catholic Christianity for their readers. Such continues to remain the primary task for both Catholic and non-Catholic theologians in light of the Shoah.

Seminal to any discussion of antisemitism in a Protestant religious framework has been A. Roy Eckardt's *Elder and Younger Brothers: The Encounter of Jews and Christians*[33] Small wonder, then, that both Eckardt and his wife Alice Lyons Eckardt have turned their attention to the Shoah with *Long Night's Journey into Day: Life and Faith After the*

The Holocaust Now

Holocaust.[34] Calling for a radical rethinking of the Christian faith, the primary focus is the Crucifixion-Resurrection phenomenon as centrally and uniquely decisive. A concise summary of their work to date is contained in an article entitled *"Post-Holocaust Theology: A Journey Out of the Kingdom of Night"*.[35] It likewise represents an excellent summary of the theses, questions, and future directions for serious Christian theologians attempting to integrate the historical event of the Shoah into any Christian post-Auschwitz theology.

Eckardt posits five basic theses essential to any Christian understanding of the Shoah:

> [1] The Holocaust--the Nazis' decision and systematic measures to annihilate all Jews anywhere within their reach, and to remove all evidences of the Jewish presence and testimony--was unique in both world and Jewish history.
>
> [2] At the same time, the Holocaust could not have occurred [I am convinced] without the centuries of Christian teaching ["the teaching of contempt"], ecclesiastical decrees, laws rooted in and justified by the church's theology and urged by church officials, and the ever-growing demonization of the Jew within Christian society.
>
> [3] The Shoah was--and is--an absolute event, because it was meant to be final: an end, an absolute end.
>
> [4] The Holocaust is and must be recognized as a decisive event in and for Christianity.
>
> [5] The Shoah challenges the faithful of both Christianity and Judaism at fundamental levels.[36]

Acceptance of these five theses for the Christian theologian mandates a rethinking of Christianity at its most basic level: At the very point where Christ redeems the world. And yet, except for the thinkers noted above, decidedly in the minority, such calls for rethinking go unheeded and unheard. Even so significant a book as John Roth's *A Consuming Fire: Encounters with Elie Wiesel and the Holocaust*[37] fails to address this troubling question, as I noted in my review of the book:

> Yet even here [in Roth's commentary to Wiesel's *One Generation After*], Roth falls far short in the power of his own witnessing and testimony in response to the question he himself poses, "Jesus--God in Christ--has overcome the world?" If Roth would have us understand the life and death of Jesus as the reaching out of God in order "to give hopeless men a momentary future and even hope for a future," then confronted with Wiesel's child-God on the gallows, he has not achieved

Introduction

his objective. *The Christian theological dilemma of the redemptive Christ versus an unredeemed world which would countenance a Holocaust remains unresolved.*[38]

Having left this central question unresolved, what then are Christians to make of the questions Eckardt herself asks further on in her article:

--How are we to understand a German cardinal's letter sent to his clergy following the November 1938 *Kristallnacht* telling them that this nation-wide attack on Jewish places of worship, businesses, homes, and persons was not a matter for the church or clerical persons?

--How are we to grasp the fact that in the years between 1939 and 1945 the only two references the Jesuit periodical *Civita Cattolica* [published by the Vatican] made to the Jews were in denunciatory ways in connection with the trial and crucifixion of Jesus?

--How are we to countenance The *Christian Century*'s editorial comment after *Kristallnacht* that not only was it "highly inadvisable to let down our [American] immigration barriers" but "Christian....citizens [of the United States] haveno need to feel apologetic for the limitations [on immigration]?"

--How are we to accept that the best Pastor Martin Niemoller was able to say regarding the "alien and uncongenial" Jews was a grudging acknowledgment that "God has seen fit to reveal Himself to the Jew, Jesus of Nazareth," and therefore this "painful and grievous stumbling block has to be accepted for the sake of the Gospels?"

--How are we to appropriate the truth that while the Warsaw Ghetto inhabitants were making their desperate stand against machine guns, poison gas, flame-throwers, artillery, and planes, the Christian part of the city observed Holy Week, and churchgoers paused on their way to or from Easter services to watch as Polish Jews hurled themselves from burning buildings?

--How are we to deal with the reality that on each 28 December during World War II Christians were able to continue blithely commemorating the death of the Holy Innocents at Bethlehem, while showing such little concern, even after the news had reached them, that millions of other innocents were being done to death by a modern Herod at Belsen and Auschwitz?

--And when a rabbi went to a local priest to plead for his intercession with the authorities to stop the deportation of Jews to Auschwitz, or at least to do something to save the innocent children, the cleric's response was: "There are no innocent Jewish children. You are all guilty of the Lord's death, and unless you confess this and enter the church, you will suffer these punishments deservedly." How can we live with this knowledge?[39]

Such poignant questions only jaggedly scratch the surface of the tragic history of Jewish-Christian relationships. Examples abound of Christian indifference and insensitivity to Jewish suffering. Yet, when these very questions are asked by Christians, when sincere and committed Christians learn of such tragic examples, they cry out for response, at the very least a theological response. And, like every other Christian theologian--Catholic as well as non-Catholic--who has wrestled with the profound theological implications of the Shoah, Eckardt considers the following "essentials of such a restructured and revitalized theology":

> First, the church needs to put an end to all teachings of superiority and claims of exclusive possession of the means of salvation.
> Second, the church and its theologians must cease finding comfortable ways of meeting the negation of Judaism built into both its traditions and its own addition to Scripture, the New Testament.
> Closely allied to the foregoing argument that the church must abandon its displacement claims is a third essential corrective: the church must cease once and for all its presentation of the Jewish people as the enemies of God and the children of Satan, as well as the Christ-killers or murderers of God, for the issue is far more than a religious one.
> Fourth, we must stop asserting that the cross constitutes the ultimate in human suffering.
> A fifth point is that the Holocaust not only exposed the extent of the church's anti-Jewish theology, but it also revealed the shallowness of its own devotion to its own ethic.
> There is a sixth point. Is it enough to rediscover the historical Jesus, a *hasid*, or to affirm that it is through this Jesus that we Gentiles have--by a strange process--been brought into the original Covenant with God and Israel?....Can one affirm the Resurrection without at the same time continuing the displacement theology of the church?[40]

Having now presented her theses, asked her questions, and enumerated her "essentials," Eckardt has, in fact, presented the Christian community with its theological agenda for the twenty-first century. That precious few will heed her call, in light of the

Introduction

Shoah and its theological implications, is a continuing tragedy of the first magnitude, one best left to Christians, rather than Jews, to respond.

V. Personal Conclusions

For me personally, as I have indicated at the beginning of this essay, the Shoah is a unique event in both Jewish and world history. Having come to this conclusion growing up in the home of a survivor of the Shoah, meeting other survivors, having studied this phenomenon beginning in my teenage years, having had the opportunity to teach this material on the college and university level, having now written both articles and book reviews dealing with the Shoah, and continuing to research various aspects of the Shoah, I have, also, concluded that it is unique theologically as I have struggled with my own Jewish identity. Certainly for Jews; most particularly for Christians. Having so concluded, I have now committed myself to try and understand both that singular uniqueness as well as the historical and theological implications of the Shoah. What follows, then, are my own theological conclusions which, at the very least, chart for me my own future theological agenda. As one committed to and ordained to serve the Jewish people, I continue to try and reconcile the experiences of Jewish history--in particular one cataclysmic, rupturous event--with the evolving nature of Jewish belief which I now understand to move in a direction significantly different than the historically-traditional notions of the past being emulated, largely without thought, in the present.

[1] I can no longer believe or accept the notion of the God-who-acts-in-history, the very foundation upon which both Judaism and Christianity have built and maintain their faiths. Indeed, I can no longer pray to such a notion of God, for I no longer regard this notion as the true and correct understanding of Divine reality or the Divine-human encounter. Not only did Six Million of my brothers and sisters die during the Shoah, as well as five million non-Jews, but the historically-traditional notion of God also died in the concentration camps which puncture the landscape of Europe. What is now demanded in the realm of theological integrity is a notion of Deity compatible with the reality of radical evil at work and at play in our world, a notion which also admits of human freedom for good or evil without false appeal to a Deity who "chose" [?] not to act because He or She could not act. To continue to affirm the historically-traditional notion of faith in God as presented by the Biblical text and subsequent religious history is to ignore the Shoah with all of its uniqueness and to ignore those who, like myself, continue to feel the pain of family loss, who remain committed to Jewish survival--not because a Deity wills it, but because without this community, we are cut off from even this most fragile of moorings.

[A] A possible source of affirmation of Deity, therefore, in light of my own--and others'--rejection of past notions, lies in the concept of a "limited Deity" who could neither choose nor reject action during the years 1933 to 1945, but, rather, who could not have responded to those humanly-created and crafted processes--even if He or She had wanted to do so. Such a notion, however, must for me be allied with the notion of a Creator-God who, having initiated such a process, prepared an earthly environment wherein so much that has happened historically continues to be possible. Whether this same Creator-God chose to begin this process through the act of self-limitation, or even out of a genuine desire and commitment to human freedom, and cannot now, as evidenced by history, reverse the process is, ultimately, secondary. We human beings are here for however long we now choose to have this planet endure, and no appeal to that Deity--rational or emotional--will now overcome our technological fury should be choose to unleash it. Samuel Pisar, a "graduate of Auschwitz" and author of the book *Of Blood and Hope*, is, indeed, correct, when he writes that the Shoah is a pilot project for the end of humanity.[41]

Here, too, is a theological lesson gleaned directly from the Shoah: The technology which resulted in the deaths of millions in concentration camps and elsewhere has forever shattered the easy appeal to a Deity who will, somehow, curb the limits of human intellect for good or evil and prevent repetition of the Shoah. If anything, the reverse is now possible: Having let the genie of destructive technology out of the bottle of human ignorance, our best hope for survival lies not in the heavens but in we ourselves, in our ability to educate the next generation to evince the same intellectual expertise to creative measures as we have thus far evidenced to destructive measures.

[B] The notion of Covenant, too, now becomes redefined. Greenberg's "voluntary covenant" becomes an option for those who wish to so enter it--as does its opposite, a rejection of the entire enterprise. Covenant with Deity whereby both Divine and human partners agree to certain stipulations in order to maintain harmony and equilibrium is no longer applicable. We can no longer trust God to keep the enemy from crouching at our door--to use the prophetic metaphor--not can Deity trust us not to act in ways that would prove a violation of sacred trusts regarding the living things of our planet. If we are to enter into a covenant in a religious framework, it must now be with each other--as individuals, as communities, as nation-states. Possessing the potential to destroy each other, we must guard against making use of that potential by our willingness to engage in continual dialogue despite our differences as well as our rejection of the value-systems held by others. Just as we would have the Russians and Americans engage in continual dialogue on issues of nuclear arms, so, too, must Jews and Christians, Jews and Arabs, Jews and Germans, Jews and Jews, Christians and Christians engage in continual dialogue with each other. Appeals to Deity will not make such conversation possible. Appeals to each other will.

[C] Prayer, too, must be rethought. Appeals to Deity to correct present situations or to dramatically alter future possibilities will have now become of no avail. Having not responded to words spoken in earnestness and fervor during the long, dark night of Nazism's all-too-successful reign, to expect that same God to respond on a less frightful level to less critical pleas is theological absurdity. Prayer will now have to become an internal plea for recognition that the universe does manifest certain harmonies if we are but receptive to them; that creation allows us more possibilities for human growth than destruction; that aesthetic appreciation of our world enhances our pleasure at being a part of it; that the poetic words of our predecessors, now reinterpreted, likewise increase our understanding of the shared yearnings of all of humankind for peace; that the disciplined gathering of like-minded groups in celebration can help energize us to confront the challenges of our own day; that we need not suspend our intellect nor deny historical realities when we engage ourselves in prayer.

[D] The Jewish notion of *mitzvah* as "commandment" or "Jewish religious obligation" will now have to be reinterpreted. No longer can this concept of Divine commander have merit for those for whom such responsive behaviors merited such sadistic contempt from their Nazi oppressors. Again, Fackenheim's "commanding voice," heard only by those who are already listening, will not be heard by those not already sensitized to their Jewish responsibilities because of the events of the Shoah. Besides, even Fackenheim himself would not have the temerity to maintain that this voice is even remotely akin to the *Bat Kol* of Jewish talmudic tradition, the Divine voice which spoke to the rabbis of the ancient academies in an effort to resolve their disputes. As I have written previously, the only mitavah now incumbent upon the Jew in light of the Shoah is the mitzvah of study, the responsibility to know in order to make informed decisions in this post-Auschwitz age.[42] But the notion of *mitavah* as the religiously-commanded act of Deity to creation, imposed upon the Jewish people by an historically-bound and committed authority structure, is yet another casualty of the Shoah. To include only those who are now willing to maintain those structures is equally as pernicious as excluding those who no longer wish to do so. What is of relevance is those Jews who, freely, are willing to make commitments, who are now willing to practice those forms of historically-traditional behaviors which they themselves find meaningful, both individually and collectively. But to presume guilt towards those who no longer think and act in accord with the ways of the past is to deny the present. The focus must be inclusive rather than exclusive if this people, so devastated by the enormity of its losses, is to again regain its equilibrium given the contemporary pressures with which it is currently confronted.

[E] Celebration, then, of festival-calendar events, as well as life-cycle events, will now have to be rethought, not so much for the specific manner in which they are celebrated, but for the rationale behind their celebration. No more can this or that holiday be celebrated or sanctified for the historically-traditional reasons previously supplied.

The Holocaust Now

No more can given life-cycle events be celebrated for similar reasons. Though the actual practices themselves may not vary one iota from previous patterns of behavior, the whys and wherefores in light of the Shoah now demand a degree of intellectual consistency coupled with theological integrity heretofore unknown in the past. No more can the Passover, for example, be seen as God's liberation of the Jewish people from the slavery and bondage of Egypt when the slavery and bondage of Nazi Germany resulted in the deaths and degradations of so many. No longer can the ritual of circumcision of an eight-day old Jewish male be understood as entering into covenant directly with God when those already committed to that covenant realized its impotence throughout Nazi-occupied Europe. New words are needed to address new realities; if not new words, then new interpretations of old words--not for all, but certainly for those of us for whom the old ways can no longer be maintained or resurrected.

[2] Lastly, a similar agenda must be presented to the Christian communities by the Christian communities and for the Christian communities. For Jews, what must be rethought is the whole notion of God and the Covenant and the Jewish people. For Christians, what must be rethought is the whole notion of God the Father, His Son Jesus the Christ, and the relationship of that Christ to this unredeemed world; and the Christian community to the Jewish people given the history of non-relationship which led to the Shoah, and the relationship which now must exist subsequent to it. Now more than ever, serious, studious, open and honest dialogue is needed between Jews and Christians, not to erase the past but to understand it, and to chart new directions away from its repetition and continuation.

CHALLENGES TO THE MIND

The Holocaust Now

Auschwitz: Re-envisioning the Role of God

Peter J. Haas would have us shift our focus from Divine involvement and/or intervention in the Shoah to humanity's absence of thinking about God and its replacement by "secular, scientific" thinking which allowed such evil to happen. For him, the proper arena is not that of God's involvement—which would have required miraculous intervention on a consistent basis—but, rather, what were the factors and, therefore, implications which led to the empowering of that evil which the Shoah embodies. He, too, raises concern as to the "uniqueness" debate vis-a-vis the Shoah—which he regards as "dangerous" in its theological implications—as well as the inherent danger of reducing the Shoah to a banal expression of recurrent evil.[1]

SLJ

The Holocaust Now

AUSCHWITZ:
RE-ENVISIONING THE ROLE OF GOD

Peter J. Haas

I. Introduction: The Question of Theodicy

For any theologian who contemplates its horror, the Shoah must raise anew the question of theodicy, of the nature of evil in a universe [allegedly] ruled over by a Benevolent Creator God. The absence of any Divine intervention to save the victims of the Nazi fury forces us to ask about the nature, and even relevance, of such a God in the modern, technology-driven world. There have been, of course, a number of attempts by theologians to deal with just these questions. None, at least so far, has found a way of both maintaining the goodness and omnipotence of God while at the same time preserving the utter evil of the Shoah. In the following, I wish to argue that such theologies are bound to fail to convince modern people precisely because they rely on traditional [that is, medieval] concepts about the nature of such a Creator God, and, specifically, how such a God is assumed to interact with the human world.[2] In particular, all envision a God that is active physically in the world. I will suggest in what follows that a more helpful model for dealing with theodicy in the "post-modern" world is to conceive of God's presence being made active discursively or semiotically. Viewed in this way, the Shoah, rather than making the concept of God meaningless, in fact does the opposite: makes God that much more necessary and urgent.

This shift of focus immediately changes how we must frame the question of theodicy. In what follows, I shall be asking not so much why God did not intervene, but how it was that such evil came to be conceived and then empowered. As I shall discuss more fully later on, the idea that we, as moderns, can expect God to interrupt human affairs so as to abort impending evil is not only naive but unworkable. Once the stage has been set for an evil to occur, the most predictable outcome in this world of ours is for that evil to occur. So the question that should occupy us is how people came to adopt evil as a reasoned course of action, rather than why it is that God does not intervene in the process of evil already underway.

In fact, I want to argue that it is precisely the absence of God from the decision-making discourse that may help us to account for such evil as the Shoah.[3] My contention will be that it was only when God was removed as an active force in the shaping of Western thinking that Auschwitz becomes conceivable. In this sense I agree with Elie Wiesel when he claims that the Shoah represents a problem not so much in Judaism as it does in Christendom. It was within Western civilization, after all, that the evil was conceived, discursivized, organized, and managed. And while it is true that much of the intellectual background of the Nazi anti-Jewish thinking was drawn from Christian tradition, and while it is also true that for the most part organized Christian institutions did little or nothing to aid Jewish victims, I think it is wrong to conclude that the Shoah was a "Christian" event. Quite the opposite: it represents, to my mind, the eclipse of Christianity [or more broadly, of religion] as a source of morality in the West. It seems quite clear, at least in retrospect, that during the Shoah most Christian institutions acted as pure secular organizations, despite their claims to the contrary. They, in effect, abandoned the moral field to the scientists, engineers, and bureaucrats of the secular Nazi ideology. God had, in effect, ceased to function as a meaning-generating concept for the bulk of European civilization despite the continuity of Christian bureaucratic institutions. To be sure there were still believing Christians in Europe who never accepted the Nazi version of things and who at times even risked life and limb to defy them. But Christianity as an organizing moral force of a civilization was dead. The secular Nazi ethic won the ability to shape the course of things to come by default. While this loss of God's presence is more of a problem within Christendom than in Judaism, it nonetheless raises important theological issues even for Jews.

My argument shall be in the following that if we continue to allow our future to be governed by the principles of the secular, scientific world, we open ourselves to the same boundless possibilities that opened the way for the Nazi exploitation of the situation in Germany. While reference to God or religious principles is no guarantee in and of itself of righteousness or moral propriety, it at least gives us a language within which to carry on a moral discourse. It gives us control over what we will be willing as a people to tolerate . This lesson it seems to me is an important one for us to bring forth from the Shoah.

II. The *Sitz im Leben* of Shoah Studies

Before explaining my thesis in detail, let me situate my thoughts in their context. My reflections find their place in what might be termed the "third generation" of Shoah studies. The "first generation" includes by and large the studies done up into the sixties. At that time, there was little work done on trying to interpret or account for the Shoah in any other than the most mechanical ways. The interest was on documenting what had occurred. In the decades immediately following the Shoah, the theological questions it raised rarely entered academic discourse. Shoah studies was in the main the specialized area of a few isolated scholars.

A noticeable shift occurred in the late sixties, signalling the beginning of the "second generation" of Shoah studies. It was in fact at about this time that the term "Holocaust" came into general usage. One important academic harbinger of this change was the publication of the first edition of Raul Hilberg's magisterial study *The Destruction of European Jewry*.[4] This study showed that enough data had been achieved for the Shoah to be examined "as a whole" and so take its place in the academy. It was also at this time that the first major post-Auschwitz Jewish theology appeared, in the form of a collection of essays by Richard Rubenstein entitled *After Auschwitz*.[5] In fact, Rubenstein's essays were not so much a theology as a claim that in the wake of Auschwitz there was no need for theology, since Auschwitz made it clear that the idea of God is dead. Along with Hilberg, Rubenstein helped set the academic agenda of Shoah studies for the next twenty years. After Hilberg, the historical task was to carry forward the work of showing how the Nazis conceived, and more importantly controlled, their vast empire of evil. After Rubenstein, the theological task was to reappropriate God, to show that God was somehow still alive and worthy of Jewish respect after the Shoah. The major Jewish "Shoah theologians" I shall discuss shortly all fit more or less into this period.

What I am calling the "third generation" of Shoah studies is just now coming into focus. In his recent book, The *Holocaust in History*, Michael Marrus argues, I believe correctly, that in the last few years, there was evident a growing interest in using our knowledge of the Shoah as a jumping off place for addressing the larger humanistic questions of the modern age.[6] That is, the field of Shoah studies has reached a level of maturity in which the task is no longer the accumulation of additional data, but rather reflections on the data already at hand, and the integration of the Shoah into overall discourse of modern consciousness. As Marrus' book also indicates, this generation is likely to be characterized as well by a reappraisal of some of the conclusions reached in the past.

It seems to me that two general approaches to the interpretation of the Shoah have taken shape up to this point, each with its own implications for how one might approach the theological problems generated by the Shoah. The first treats the Shoah as an utterly unique event; one that was so evil that it forms its own category. The second alternative view sees the Shoah as an example of the cruelty that is implicit in human nature, and of the power of technology to make the exercise of that cruelty possible to an unprecedented extent. On this view, the Shoah, while surely different in degree from other past [and present] atrocities is not to be understood as fundamentally different in kind. Each of these positions, as I have said, establishes fundamentally different perspectives from which to approach the theological questions.

The first view, that the Shoah is unique, is the assumption of most Jewish [and, for that matter, Christian] "Shoah theologians." It is, of course, precisely this view that stands behind Rubenstein's claim that the Shoah points to the death of God. For Rubenstein, this means that after Auschwitz, we are forced to face up to the fact that the older concept of God as an active agent in our world can no longer work: It is dead.[7] We must prepare ourselves to get along in a world without God, relying on the support of the human community for survival.

While not all Jewish theologians have drawn from the unprecedented character of the Shoah the extreme conclusion that Rubenstein has, they have all acknowledged that to some extent the conceptions of God and history that flourished before the Shoah are no longer functional. Arthur Cohen, for example, calls the Shoah a "caesura" in human experience, such that we are forced in its wake to bring all our previous assumptions into question: no theology, no understanding of history, no view of the nature of the human being can remain unquestioned in the shadow of Auschwitz.[8] Emil Fackenheim has likened the Shoah to Sinai, a world-shaking theophany from which new foundational elements of Jewish existence emerge [in this case, the imperative to survive, although I am not sure how really unprecedented that is].[9]

The problem here is that if the Shoah is really that much of a break with the past, then nothing of the past is really relevant anymore, including traditional Judaism. Nothing, as it were, emerges from the black hole of Cohen's caesura. Or to use Fackenheim's more troublesome metaphor, if the Shoah is really "Sinaitic" in implication, then we must wonder if the first Sinai has been rescinded or superseded in whole or in part, and if in part, which part. Fackenheim wants to treat the Shoah Sinai was an addendum to the original Sinai, but that I think begs the question.[10] In all events, I find this whole range of responses dangerous. If the Shoah is really unique, then there is the possibility that it really has no bearing on the rest of human history. It becomes, in essence, an event that stands by itself in a splendid isolation, and so incapable of teaching any lessons applicable to normal history.

The second view, that the Shoah is not ontologically or essentially different from other acts of human cruelty, is a minority position among Jewish theologians. The reason is that this view renders the Shoah somehow trivial, robbing it of any special power to make us rethink the human situation. This attitude toward the Shoah might be summed up in Hannah Arendt's famous phrase, "the banality of evil."[11] Evil, in other words, is just one of those things. I think Arendt had a much different and suggestive meaning in mind, and I shall get back to that in due course. But this popular reading of her saying I think captures the implication of this view of the mass-murder of Jews in Europe. In the end, it is just one more event in the dreary history of humankind.

Since the two positions sketched above encompass the logical possibilities for categorizing the Shoah, the fact that neither approach has been able to sustain a viable

Auschwitz: Re-envisioning the Role of God

theology calls for some reevaluation. My argument, to restate matters, is that the problem lies not in these two approaches, but in the common assumption underlying both. In each case, the theological response has been framed around the question of why God did not intervene. I want to argue, as I have said, that a more fruitful approach is to ask how evil comes to be empowered in the first place. But before pursuing my own argument, a closer look at the results of more traditional theological reflection will be helpful.

It has been a stable element of Western theology that the term "good" reflects an objective reality and that that objective reality is [or is established by] an infinitely powerful creator God. One corollary of this conviction is that evil can in the end not prevail against those cared for by God. Since this creator God is all-knowing and all-powerful, evil can only exist with the acquiescence of this God, and, since this God is also assumed to be perfectly good, it follows directly that this God cannot by nature abide the untrammeled assertion of evil. What appears to us as evil must, therefore, be either [1] deserved, that is just, punishment, [2] part of a larger divine plan that we cannot fully discern or appreciate, or [3] illusory.

There have been theological responses to the Shoah built on this scheme, but they are all disappointing. Some are, in fact, downright pernicious, such as the view that the Shoah was simply a just punishment for Jewish sins.[12] From a Jewish perspective, these attempts to account for the Shoah are simply unworkable. If indeed the child hung by piano wire as described in Elie Wiesel's Night is receiving his just punishment by a good and powerful God, then the terms "good" and "powerful" take on new and horrid meanings.[13] This, is not I think a theology with which to we can live.

Not all responses constructed in terms of this traditional matrix of assumptions are this naive, however. A somewhat more sophisticated response is that of the conservative Christian theologian David Rausch who at least sees in the Shoah a reflection of human evil and a charge to people not to be complacent in the face of evil.[14] The most sophisticated response in this key is that of the Jewish Orthodox thinker Eliezer Berkovits.[15] For Berkovits, there is still a traditional Judaic theological system than can comprehend the Shoah, that of *El Mistater*, the "hiding God." There are times, this theology claims, that the good and powerful God of the universe detaches the Divine self from the world. In a cosmic sense, this Divine distancing has to be seen as a gift, allowing for the full expression of human freedom and initiative. At those times, of course, evil is also free to be unleashed and horrors like the Shoah can occur. Nonetheless, this theological strategy holds, the Divine is never permanently withdrawn, but will eventually reassert its presence and then in some way balance the evil that was done in its "absence." Thus the argument has been made, for example, that the Divine Face was "hidden" during the early part of this century, allowing the Shoah to proceed unhindered. But subsequently the involvement of God again became apparent in the

The Holocaust Now

revitalization of Judaism and especially in the birth of the State of Israel.

Although this approach has some advantages—it takes the evil of the Shoah seriously [It really took place in the absence of the Divine], and it preserves the conviction that God is ultimately is ultimately good and caring—it is not without its problems. There is first of all the question of God's hiding. As I said, this is done to grant humans freedom of action. Horrors like the Shoah, it is said, are simply the price we must pay for freedom. An analogy, I suppose, is to let little children get hurt doing something dangerous so that they can learn by experience. While this makes a certain amount of sense, I think it can be pushed too far. After all, a parent can hardly be expected to let his or her child shoot a neighbor's child in order to teach the danger of handguns. Certainly the slaughter of 11 million people by the Nazis, and the deaths of maybe 35-40 million others in the war altogether, is a brutal way for God to arrange a lesson on the evils of Jew-hatred. It is hard to imagine how we should be expected to face this God again after the Shoah, knowing that it was "allowed" by a Divine act designed to teach people a lesson.

Of course, this strategy has taken that into account. The Divine does eventually reappear in human affairs, and works to achieve some counterbalancing. I guess the analogy would be the parent who, after allowing a child to get hurt or inflict pain on another, steps in to make matters better, taking everyone out for ice cream or whatever. But this does not quite work in the case of the Shoah. First of all, while the resurgence of the Jewish community and the establishment of the State of Israel are surely related to the Shoah [and what in contemporary Jewish life is not?], it is simply incorrect historically to say that the State of Israel is a result of the Shoah, and it is awkward morally to say that it makes up for or compensates [even somewhat] for the suffering of the victims. Nor would this notion of Divine recompense square well with the whole point of the process of *hester panim*, the hiding of the Divine face. If the point is to allow people to suffer and learn from their freedom, then the idea that God will eventually return and make everything comes out okay in the end seems out of character. A consistent application of this theology, it seems to me, would be to allow the Shoah to happen, to let its lessons be learned or not as the case may be, and then let history follow whatever course it will.

In the end, then, these more traditional theological responses to the Shoah turn out to be asking good questions but to be fashioning poor answers. The problem is to determine what alternatives to the traditional axioms are available. In essence, anyone who is dissatisfied with the above is left with the alternative of eliminating one or more of the basic premises of Western theology on which the above is based. That is, one must assume that God is not all-knowing, not all-powerful, or not good. Let us look briefly at the results of accepting each of these options.

The first option, that God is not all-knowing, creates interesting problems. While it might be possible to sustain a theology that holds that God is unaware of all the mundane and essentially trivial details of everyday affairs, it is a much more cosmic claim to say that God was unconscious of the Shoah. If the Deity is susceptible to this kind of unawareness, the we are basically left with an otiose [ineffective, useless, superfluous—Editor] God that has no reliable role in human destiny except maybe in the broadest sense. Nonetheless, this is certainly one way of accounting for the Shoah.

A second possibility is to claim that the creator-God may be omniscient but not all-powerful. Since this seems to be somewhat self-contradictory—if the Deity could create the world, this Deity should be able to control it as well!—this option seems the most problematic. It has a long history in Judaism, however, especially in mystic circles. The Lurianic Kabbalah of the sixteenth century, and its modern-day heirs in Hasidism, claim that while God was omnipotent at Creation, the ability of God to intervene in the Creation has become limited due to a cosmic accident. Evil is a result of this Divine catastrophe and will remain potent until the Divine power is restored through a process called tikkun. While powerful in its symbolism, this view cannot finally reconcile the claim that, on the one hand the Creator-God was omniscient and omnipotent, and on the other hand, that this God was the victim of an unforeseen accident.

One modern attempt to bridge this gap, by making the limitations of Divine power in effect a voluntary or self-imposed move on the part of God, is that of Eliezer Berkovits. We have already discussed his views above and pointed out some of the problems implicit in them.

The third option that God is not good can be easily dismissed. There would be no theological or moral point in worshipping such a deity.

In their classic forms, then, none of these theories is without its problems. It is difficult to see why we should worship, much less have faith in, a God who admittedly has only limited ability to respond to our needs. True the Kabbalists developed a scheme for getting around this through their particular devotions and practices leading to *tikkun*. But without this Kabbalistic technology of manipulating the flow of forces through the *sefirot*, we are left in a rather hopeless position. We acknowledge God's weakness without any countervailing power to overcome that deficiency. Given our own undeniable technological prowess, it is hard to see how a religion based on such a weak and unreliable God can compete for allegiance.

III. Re-Focusing on Evil

I am struck by the failure of all of these approaches to come up with an explanation of the Shoah theophany that makes helpful sense. This suggests to me that the question has to be posed in a different way. It is for this reason that I have chosen to focus not on the failure of God to intervene, but on the nature or source of the evil.

The Holocaust Now

This rephrasing of the question allows me to avoid one of the major difficulties of reflections up to now, namely the assumption that somehow we must account for the lack of God's intervention in the Shoah. It is as if we are perfectly ready to accept the presence of evil but expect that it will always be addressed by God in miraculous ways. This seems to me to be a false premise. We are generally not prepared to assume that God will routinely intervene miraculously in individual human affairs. If I am flying an aircraft which I have failed to fill with sufficient fuel, the plane will crash. This is a simply law of physics. None of us would either [1] expect a Divine miracle to occur, such as a giant hand grabbing the plane and guiding it to a safe landing, or [2] feel that God needed to be blamed or justified for the ensuing and totally foreseeable crash. Acts have consequences and we are perfectly willing to accept that without calling all our theological assumptions into question.

It may be possible to look at the Shoah in the same way, only writ large. The Shoah was, at one level, "only" a series of individual decisions and acts, coordinated to be sure by a bureaucracy, but nonetheless individual acts which as a rule had precisely the outcome anybody would normally expect that they would. A Divine frustration of the Shoah would have involved innumerable miracles: perfectly good equipment that inexplicably would not function in certain cases, trains loaded at point A but arriving empty at point B, resurrections, etc. We expect none of these to occur in our daily routines, and there seems no good reason therefore to expect them at other times. Otherwise the Shoah would have turned into a series of miraculous interventions, utterly outside the range of human experience or thought, followed by a the sudden reassertion of normal physical and historical processes. I think we are being unrealistic to expect that. I grant that the Shoah was unusual in the depth and intensity of its evil, but it does not follow from this that we must demand that the laws of history, physics, etc. come to an end on this account.

On the other hand, it is abundantly clear from the Shoah [as it is from all history], that people exercise considerable initiative over the events of the world. It is, of course, true that the unforeseen or uncontrollable will happen; our influence is not perfect. But by and large the direction of political and economic affairs seems to follow along the channels laid down by human leaders. Certainly on a scale such as that of the Shoah, we seem to be able to shape and sustain an overall dynamic. So our consideration of the meaning of God's absence in the Shoah has to take place in the awareness that in the normal run of things, the force shaping events is human initiative and that God rarely if ever appears directly to reshape entirely what people have wrought. Otherwise the study of history and economics would be meaningless.

The result of these considerations is not necessarily to remove God from the picture entirely, but it is to make the human factor in the creation of evil the center of attention and to diminish our expectation that God must always [by nature, as it were]

Auschwitz: Re-envisioning the Role of God

intervene. God may be benevolent and active in history in some way, but we ought to expect our deeds to bear their natural consequences and build our theologies on that. If we still have pretty good control over events, something every manager takes for granted, then we must be prepared to rephrase how it is that God does interact with this world.

I want to argue, then, that Western culture—and especially modern Western notions of ethics—has developed the unprecedented possibility of empowering and institutionalizing evil. In essence, I wish to argue that the loss of a traditional religious-based ethic, and the emergence of a secular, "scientific" ethic made the conception, and more important, the justification [in moral terms], of the Shoah possible. The Shoah represents, then, a kind of quantum leap in the human ability to institutionalize evil and so, while unique in some sense, is overwhelmingly relevant to us today.

IV. The Nature of Evil

Let me begin by considering the nature of evil as evidenced in the Shoah. I start by returning to Hannah Arendt's haunting phrase "the banality of evil" because I think she had in mind something along the lines of what I wish to propose here. I think her phrase can be taken to mean a number of different things and that it has often been taken in a way that Arendt herself may not have had in mind. Usually the phrase has been understood, because of its context in the Eichmann trial, to be referring to Eichmann more or less personally. That is, that for Eichmann [and others], doing evil had become banal, a matter of unreflective routine. The phrase has a much more powerful message if we take it to mean that evil itself had become banal.[16] That is, for the perpetrators of the Shoah, the evil they were doing was no longer regarded as bad, or at least no longer regarded as worthy of reflection. That is to say, that evil had lost its sting, becoming ordinary and even routine, and so not a matter requiring further reflection.

It is, in fact, precisely this view which I find evidenced in the literature of the Shoah: the casual carrying out of terrible acts of human cruelty day after day by people who in other ways seems perfectly normal and loving. It was certainly not that such people had no conscience; they indicate again and again in their diaries and memoirs that they did. To be sure there were those who knew what they were doing, recognized its evil for what it was and nonetheless enjoyed what they were doing. But I have been struck again and again in reading through diaries by the ordinariness and at times human decency and sensitivity of the authors who in other areas were out-and-out accomplices in mass murder. Somehow, for these people, the evil in which they were engaged had become sanitized, robbed of its horror.

I believe we can account for this neutering of evil in terms of a routine phenomenon in moral discourse. It is a commonplace in moral philosophy that actions take on

The Holocaust Now

a moral meaning only within the context of the specific act and how that act and its context are described. That is, as the description of an act changes, so might our moral evaluation of that act. A killing in a parking lot may appear to us to be a clear-cut case of murder. But if we subsequently learn that the alleged killer was in fact attacked and that he or she shot the "victim" in self-defense, what at first may have struck us as a vicious murder may now seem quite justifiable. In fact, as we add considerations and complications to the story, we can manipulate our hearers to react in certain foreseeable ways. When confronted with a particular situation, then, with all its details and interconnections, conclusions as to what "really" happened and judgments as to the rightness or wrongness of certain actions turn out to be much more complicated that they may have at first appeared. We have all certainly experienced this feature of moral reflection. We can come to know so much about a situation that it is often hard in the end to say who is really at fault, and even what real wrong was committed altogether.

This observation about moral thinking has something significant to tell us about the Shoah. It tells us, I think, that it is possible in theory for the Nazi authorities so to describe the situation that the common audience could come to see the grossest acts of evil as serving a greater good and so justifiable. That is, through appeals to history, science, theology or whatever, the moral meaning of Nazi-inspired atrocities was blurred beyond recognition for the participants. Caught in the descriptive web of Nazi discourse [or what I call in my book "the Nazi ethic"], everyday people simply thought they were doing the right thing. The evilness of their acts was no longer descriptively obvious.

That certain segments of Nazi society should have been immune to this sort of linguistic sleight of hand goes without saying. People constantly exhibit the ability to dissent from the popular ideas of the day. That is why the silence of the Christian community [and the legal and medical professions, to name some other obvious examples] is so striking. But for most people, it seems, the values of the Nazi ethic were simply accepted, and the ensuing evil was quite simply rendered banal, in this second sense.

Before moving on, let me pause to take an example out of our own national experience in Vietnam, for I think this reflects something of a similar dynamic at work. In the context of the war, good clean-cut American young people did commit atrocities on Vietnamese civilians. Rarely was this done, I suspect out of sheer sadism. Often the soldiers were acting out of fear or out of a belief that what they were doing was a necessary evil for winning the war. It is thinkable that at least on some occasions, our soldiers acted out of a sense of higher ideals and within what they thought were the parameters of Western morality. They were facing a savage enemy, the enemy posed not only an immediate threat to their lives and health, but also more indirectly to their country. Both the context of warfare and the context of legitimate self-defense provides a framework in which inflicting death on others is regarded as permissible [if not laudatory] in our received ethic. We can let slide for now the question of whether the soldiers' understanding of the nature of the threat was correct or even warranted. At issue for our received Western morality is the perception of the perpetrator, that is whether or not the moral agent was motivated by proper intentions. If the agent is convinced that a certain situation morally justifies a certain course of action, then that agent, as we generally, regard matters, is required to follow that course of action.

Because the distinction between what people think is required and what an ethic should require is important to my argument, I shall make a verbal distinction between the two. To this end, I will use the word "ethics" and its derivatives to denote the rationalizing process of the actor as she or he makes a decision as to what to do in a particular situation. My claim is that such a decision is ethical provided that the agent has considered general rules of moral behavior, has used moral arguments to arrive at a decision and sees himself or herself as acting in accord with the demands of morality as understood to apply at the moment. I reserve the word "morality" to apply to a more universal judgment as to the overall rightness or wrongness of the act, seen as it were from an outside, neutral position. That is, I use *ethics* to describe the inner dynamics of the decision to act one way or another, and *morality* to judge the character of that decision according to a theoretically constructed standard. My argument will be that many perpetrators, and even bystanders, of the Shoah may have been acting ethically in that they at the time saw themselves serving some higher good which seemed to them to be morally justified. This does not preclude the possibility that we might now find the acts morally reprehensible. All I mean to say is that from the point of view of the moral agent, all we can expect is for the individual to act according to what he or she deems to be the moral requirement at the moment. We may well decide in hindsight that the action was wrong or violated the spirit of morality. My claim, then, concerns not the content of the moral life per se, but rather the status of the decision.

If these remarks are correct, then it suggests how we might deal analytically with the evil of the Shoah and how that evil might be related to God. It first of all makes it possible for us to continue to regard the perpetrators [or at least a good proportion of them] as still operating within the parameters of an ethic. That is, we can treat the Shoah as part of the flow of human events rather than as some sort of unconnected anomaly. Second, still within our universe, the above model allows us to account for Nazi activity in a way other than that it simply was evil for evil's sake. Rather it makes it possible for us to view the perpetrators as what they probably were: more or less ordinary people living in a perverse universe but considering their actions and doing what they thought was the appropriate thing to do given the circumstances. Viewed in this way, the Shoah has a powerful and urgent message for us still today.

It speaks to us today because the above model bears close correspondence to how we experience our own internal moral dialogue. This is not to imply that we are all like Nazis. But it is to say that we have all faced the task of doing something we really would rather not have to do but feel compelled to do for reasons of profession, business, state or some other "greater good." Diaries and other evidences of the Shoah suggest, as I have said, that similar human factors operated in the Shoah.

Let me emphasize before moving on that I do not wish to say that all ethics are equally the same. I recognize that the Nazi ethic established itself, people thought within it in the normal way humans think. I want to shift concern from how the Nazis and their supporters could be such perverse people to the question of how it is that perverse ethics can so establish themselves that ordinary people will regard them as self-evident and then operate in good conscience within them.

This way of framing the problem, I think, leaves us with a sense of both our own power and our own helplessness. In terms of power, it means that human society has the capacity, through the formation of rhetoric, to establish the evaluative discourse within which most people will form their ethical judgments. What Nazism shows us is that the human understanding of right and wrong is not innate and changeless [as the ancients might have supposed], and that this understanding is not strictly rational as so much of Western philosophy has asserted. Rather, human understanding is rooted in how people in groups define and evaluate matters in public. This then is a powerful tool left in our hands. The content of right and wrong, good and evil, are forged by human minds given the materials of our own societies and civilizations. An ethic such as that of the Nazis not only can exist and did exist, but is very capable of existing again. We know now that intelligent, mature people, with access to sophisticated technologies can forge an ethical discourse to their own liking.

This is also, of course, the basis of our feeling of helplessness as well. In effect, the very affirmation of human power to produce such an ethic at the very same time denies that God ought to function as some sort of cosmic umpire who will step in at the appropriate time. We can become trapped in the very web of ethical rhetoric that we spin. In fact, I would argue that is what happened in Nazi-occupied Europe. Perpetrators and bystanders eventually become victims [in some sense] of the juggernaut that they had helped to set into motion. To be sure, some of these musings-after-the-fact may be self-serving. But many also indicate pain, anguish, and guilt; too late perhaps but real nonetheless. There can be no question that the Nazis and their collaborators have had to pay a heavy price for their entanglement in the Shoah even if they were not its official victims. The rhetoric captured even its inventors.

Auschwitz: Re-envisioning the Role of God

V. The Nazi Ethic

To recapitulate the argument up to this point, I have argued that in considering the relationship of God to the Shoah, we seem to hit a dead end if we focus exclusively on the question of why God did not intervene. A more fruitful approach, given the assumption that God generally will not intervene except in the unusual case of a miracle, is to ask how is it that such evil comes about initially. We have also at this point talked about the ability of people to create ethical systems that create accepted definitions of good and evil. The claim is that the Shoah can be accounted for on the basis of these ideas. Nazi Germany created an ethic that defined the killing of Jews [and others] as good. Absent any counter-ethic, and given the usual absence of miraculous Divine intervention in the flow of history, the inevitable happened. To help us understand the origin of evil in the world, then, it will be helpful to examine exactly how the Nazi ethic came into being and how it was able to co-opt other ethics. This will give us a clearer picture of the dynamics at work.

In the case of the Shoah, we have a fairly good idea of the intellectual background of its ethic.[17] This ethic drew largely on three intellectual currents that had become acceptable in German [and European] society in general during the late nineteenth and early twentieth centuries. These are racial antisemitism, social Darwinism, and fascism. I will argue below that the combination of these three strains of thought—one social, one scientific, and one political—created a worldview which could, and did, support an ethic of genocide. I want to discuss this intellectual confluence first. I then need to turn back to the question of what this means for our understanding of God's relationship to the world. I will argue since none of these premises are based on a notion or vision of God, the resulting ethic in effect left no place for God to operate and so made anything [or everything] possible. As I said at the beginning of this essay, this is one of the most striking lessons of the Shoah.

The social strain of thought has to do with anti-Judaism. This is the one thread in the Nazi ethic that has a clear grounding in religion, although by the nineteenth century it had become more or less secularized.[18] The pariah-status according to Jews has a long history in the West, going back to Roman times. This attitude became a stable of Western civilization with the advent and spread of Christianity. Thus by the dawn of the Enlightenment, there was a long-standing and powerful critique of Jews and Judaism built into the social structures of Europe. So powerful was this tradition that it continued into the Enlightenment period, even though the intellectual hegemony of the Christian churches had been broken. Thus Jews still found themselves to be outsiders in large parts of central Europe into the nineteenth and twentieth centuries, although this social exclusion was now based on scientific or secular grounds, not on theological ones. That is, Jews were no longer outcasts because of their religio-mythic crime of

39

decide or because of their failure to acknowledge the truth of Catholic or Lutheran doctrine. Rather, Jews were outsiders now because they were seen as racial or national aliens, people incapable of assimilating into and contributing to true Western civilization. We can already see this change in attitude in the latter part of the eighteenth century when Wilhelm Dohm could argue for extending civic rights to Jews on the grounds that given a chance, Jews could indeed become productive members of German society.[19] His unspoken assumption was that Jewish differentiation was a function of social and cultural forces, not theological ones.

Gradually this social exclusion, freed of its religious mooring, became attached to a much different sort of warrant: scientific racism. By the nineteenth century, European colonial expansion had brought Westerners face to face with societies in Asia and Africa. These cultures were regarded as clearly more primitive than those of Europe. On the one hand, this evaluation was used to justify Western colonial paternalism over the "benighted" natives. It became the "white man's burden" to bring civilization to these masses. On the other hand, the discovery of primitive societies raised the question of why Europe was so much more advanced. What had kept these other areas from attaining the same scientific and cultural achievements as the Europeans? An answer gradually emerged from nineteenth century science. Research in genetics and physical anthropology convinced many scientists that the human species was not homogeneous, but was made up of a number of different sub-species. Each such sub-group had its specific genetic make-up and so its particular abilities. These abilities manifested themselves in the diverse areas of human culture developed by the population in question: language, literature, social organization, art, etc. Thus the relative primitiveness of native societies in Africa or Asia could be accounted for on the basis of racial endowments of the group; its innate "civilizing" ability. In all cases, the level of civilization achieved by a race reflected the limits of its abilities; inferior cultures indicated underlying limits within the genetic group, the race.

This conviction in fact stands behind a number of philosophical and scientific initiatives undertaken in the nineteenth century.[20] These studies not only took the idea of racial diversity seriously, but tended through their results to ratify these assumptions in the popular mind. One good example is the "science" of phrenology, the measurement of the proportions of the human skull. This field emerged out of the simple deduction that if different human populations were in fact different races, and if each race had different genetic endowments, then these should be apparent not only in such hard-to-measure traits as language, literature and culture, but also in quantifiable areas like bone size. The skull was seen as an especially promising source of data since it houses the brain. Thus a complex scientific and pseudo-scientific sub-culture emerged which measured skulls, tabulated different ratios, looked at nose size and compiled impressive piles of data meant to document the existence and relative advance of various racial types.

While natural scientists concentrated on these matters, social scientists concentrated on the cultural attainments of the world's diverse racial groups. For a number of reasons, the most promising cultural traits for this kind of study were taken to be language and literature. Thus racial theorists appropriated the results of philology, the study of language, to illustrate their theories. In essence, the idea was that by charting out how languages are related to each other, one could see how the underlying racial groups of speakers are related to each other. A good example of how intertwined philology and scientific racism became is the case of the "discovery" of the Indo-European family of languages. Philologists by the nineteenth century had sufficiently developed the study of linguistics to be able to create a taxonomy which showed the relationship of a number of diverse European and sub-continental languages. Thus a category of Germanic languages incorporating German, Dutch, and Swedish, for example, could be contrasted to a category of Romance languages such as French and Italian. These, in turn, could be associated with each other over against Indian languages, and both conglomerates could be combined over against completely unrelated languages such as those of the Semitic family [Arabic, Hebrew, etc.]. If languages represent racial groups, it followed, then the filial relations apparent in language should reveal the filial relations among the relevant racial populations. It is just this logic which gave rise to the hypothesis of an ancient Aryan racial group, i.e. the group that "produced" and carried forward the ancient Indo-European language.

The results of all this was raised to the status of a philosophical truth through an appropriation of the writings of the great German philosopher G. W. F. Hegel. Hegel's contribution to nineteenth-century thought was to articulate a theory of historical evolution. In his view, human culture over time traces out a kind of progression in which the spirit of truth is seen gradually to reveal itself. Primitive cultures simply reflect an earlier stage in this progressive self-revelation of the Spirit. On the basis of this philosophy of history, each contemporary civilization can be located at its proper point on the continuum of human cultural evolution, and so its level of civilization is accurately developed.

What made Hegel's ideas attractive was that they seemed to parallel the results of scientific investigations that assumed that human abilities had evolved. This meant that a primitive culture reflected a population that was innately and objectively less developed. Thus, for example, a Hottentot might be taught to speak proper English and to dress like a country squire, but underneath he would still be finally a Hottentot, and that ultimate bedrock of character would always finally make itself known. Thus the differences among diverse populations is real, objective and scientifically verifiable. The relevance for us here is, of course, that Jews, having their own culture, religion, language and facial types, must represent just such a race, and insofar was they are deemed inferior socially and culturally, so, it follows, must they be understood to be innately inferior as well.

It is against this background that the second stream of thought takes on immense importance. I am talking here of a certain view of what we might call social Darwinism. While the nineteenth century scientific view of race clearly established superior and inferior peoples, it did not pass moral judgments on these differences. It was simply a way to create a scientific taxonomy of the diversity of human cultures. But social Darwinism, by positing a scenario in which these races were in conflict, and within which it was the natural order of things for the stronger [and presumably therefore better] to dominate if not destroy the inferior, set the stage for a program of race with its own unique ethic.

It should be noted at the outset that the conclusions reached by the social Darwinist were only distantly related to the scientific work of Charles Darwin himself. Darwin had set out to explain how different species of animals had come to predominate in certain areas while other species of the same genus dominated in other areas. His conclusion was that there was a certain natural variety in any genus, and that those individuals and their offspring that had characteristics that best fit a particular environmental niche would over time come to dominate that niche. In another region, of course, a different pattern of environmental characteristics would be present, and so a different set of characteristics in the population would be selected, so that over the course of generations, we could talk of the emergence of two different species of the same genus.

Social Darwinists began with this basic scheme but added stipulations that radically changed its character. First of all they applied the process of natural selection [or "survival of the fittest" as it became known] not to genetic characteristics but to societies or cultures. In short, they claimed that societies or cultures which were "superior" were naturally destined to dominate or even oust those that were inferior.

It is, of course, quite a jump to go from the process of genetic selection to social conflict. More ominous was the [mis]appropriation of the basic mechanism of "survival of the fittest." For Darwin, this was basically a matter of statistical probability. Individuals better suited to the environment would stand a better change of surviving and of having off-spring that would survive, thus gradually changing the genetic pool. The social Darwinists took the struggle entirely literally. In their view, social groups were in constant physical conflict over who could inhabit a certain ecological niche. The law of nature was that the superior group had to win, and the inferior group must either become subservient or die out. To anticipate where this argument is heading, it was from this a short jump to the assumption that the dominant group had a moral obligation to survive and in the process to eliminate its inferior rivals.

The latent ethical imperative of social Darwinism comes to the surface when it is combined with the scientific racism we discussed above. This combination yields an

Auschwitz: Re-envisioning the Role of God

ethic in which the human genus is understood to be composed of diverse and unequal species that are engaged in an inevitable conflict over who will dominate available resources. It is also the case that for the proper working out of the Spirit, the superior group has, as it were, a moral obligation to win out and dominate or eliminate its rivals. Social conflict of this kind thus is really a matter of literal social life or death.[21] The old medieval theological view of the just war was now resurrected as it were, as a natural struggled to be fought with any means possible to ensure the survival of the superior group.

All that is lacking now for the full ethic of the Nazi worldview to take shape is a theory of how this metaphysical struggle between good and evil is to be translated into politically usable terms. This last component is provided by the political theory of fascism. This theory provides a political program for formulating institutions in light of these modern "insights" into the forces of history. One of the foundational assumptions of this theory is that there is a fundamental distinction between what was called "the nation" and "the state." In technical terms, the nation was the genetic pool or population that is represented in a particular culture. Thus in Europe, the Italians, French, Germans, Slavs, etc., all represent different nations. Their national identity comes out in a variety of expressions: language, law, art, literature, social customs, etc. The state, on the other hand, is a political organization, a government and its various social and cultural institutions. The idea of fascist political theory was for each nation [i.e. genetic or cultural group] to have its own political expression in a state of its own: Italy for Italians, France for the French, Germany for Germans, etc. On the one hand, this could be seen as merely a pragmatic tool for insuring cultural survival—a nation dominated by the institutions of a foreign state might not be allowed to express its national culture fully or freely. There is a more ominous side to this theory, however, when it is combined with the racial conflict theories of social Darwinism. What emerges is a scenario in which diverse races, each organized into a political state, are engaged in a natural struggle for the survival of the fittest. Political tension between states thus takes on a new meaning, and the need to subdue rivals becomes a cosmic moral imperative. Every state, by its very existence, is now seen to be a threat to, and a target of, every other nation [or state] in Europe.

The question, of course, is how is the state to embody and express authentically the real interests of its underlying racial group, its nation. It is at this point that the theories of fascism come into play. The basic idea here is that the state is to be the institutional manifestation of the nation. To achieve this, the state must be governed by a single voice, that of the folk as a corporation. The problem, of course, is how to do this. Democracy might seem an obvious answer to us, but from the point of view of many nineteenth and early twentieth century nationalists, it appeared to be the exact opposite. After all, the point of democracy is to recognize and legitimate a variety of voices and constituencies. The parliaments of European democracies seemed to be in essence arenas within which different national and ideological interests fought things out and learned to compromise their own principles. Indeed, many of the parties in the parliaments had acknowledgedly non-statist interests in mind: socialism, for example, or regional autonomy. So democracy was seen as in fact a form of government that explicitly undercut the creation of a single national voice in the political arena. Fascist thought, therefore, led quite naturally to the idea that the state could be an authentic expression of the underlying nation only if power and initiative were lodged in one individual at the top who was in touch with the character of the folk and could be its sole spokesperson. This person, in essence a dictator, could then form the institutions and laws of the state to reflect in a straightforward and uncompromised fashion the will of the nation.

This notion of politics, combined with the thesis of history as the arena of a natural struggle among the nations for the survival of the fittest, leads directly into the ethic of the Shoah. For any particular nation, the assumption is the highest good is its own survival. This survival must be defended again and again on the stage of history. Further any surrounding nation [or race] must be seen as at least a potential enemy. Every neighboring nation must either dominate you or be dominated by you. So the ultimate good for any nation is to struggle as hard as it can to dominate its potential rivals.

The alternative, according to the ironclad laws of nature, is extinction. The state now has an important role to fulfill. Its job is not so much to protect individual rights as to defend the nation in the "Darwinian" struggle for survival. In this sense, the defense institutions of the state stand at the center of its raison d'etre: the army, police, internal security forces, etc. Conversely, any foreign group that resides within the boundaries of the state must ipso facto be suspect. This includes not only groups of other obvious nationalities, but even people of the state's nationality who have become recruited to other non-national causes, that is, ideologies which question the authority of the state or question the assumption that the highest moral good is the defense by the state of its national or racial interests. Thus political movements such as communism [or international socialism] and religious groups such as the Roman Catholic Church with its international character, or Jehovah's Witness with its allegiance to God placed above allegiance to state, all were seen as natural enemies of the proper fascist state.

In light of the above considerations, it does not take much imagination to see how the Nazis could come to see the Jews as mortal enemies, despite the small number of Jews in Germany, or why the Nazis were so intent on purging Jews from all vital organs of the state, and then finally from the state itself; why there was such dread of international communism, which was seen as linked in some way with the "Jewish race" [so-called "Jewish Bolshevism"]; and how, as the war began to turn against Germany, the "war against the Jews" [to use Lucy Dawidowicz's powerful phrase] became almost hysterically urgent.

Nor, I think, is it hard to see how others could be persuaded to go along with the Nazi program, at least to some extent, given the wide range of scientific, philosophical and historical arguments on which they could draw to validate their interpretation of events. In a country as adrift as was Weimar Germany in many ways, in a country that was mired in a sense of malaise, the appeal of a clear, logical, scientific explanation that also offered a plan to reverse matters should hardly be surprising. And above all, and this is my point, once accepted the general truth of the above interpretation of the human predicament, one could more or less tolerate the Nazi war against the Jews with a clear conscience. In the long run, its serves a higher natural good and so is ethically right as a program. True, it may entail certain injustices or sufferings when applied on an individual level, but so does almost any government program. Resistance was short-circuited further by the fact that to resist meant to posit an alternative view of the world, one that had to deny the entire historical, scientific and philosophical legacy on which the Nazi ethic was based. This few individuals were willing, or able, to do with any degree of self-assurance. That professional organizations could not see the possibility of an alternate ethic, especially professional organizations in fields like medicine and law, and even more so theology, is a more serious problem.

VI. The Role of God, Religion, and Religious Ethics

I now wish to return to the original question concerning the role of God in all this. One of the striking features of the intellectual complex that stands behind the Nazi ideology is its thoroughly secular character. To be sure, it drew its satanic images of the Jew from a massive repertoire of defamations promulgated by the Church. It is even true that many of the early anti-Jewish measures of the Nazis [e.g. yellow badges, ghettos] had been initiated by the Church in the Middle Ages [to include in an indirect way the concern with race in the form of the Spanish Inquisition's concern with *limpieza de sangre*, purity of blood]. Nonetheless, the ideology framed by the Nazis was not a religious system. It claimed, correctly, to be secular and scientific. This is, I think, an important point because it makes the Nazi ethic self-referential in a way that is normally not true of religious ethics. Let me explain.

Although religion and religious ethics are notoriously hard concepts to define, there seems to be a general consensus that one common feature of all religions is their referral at some point to a sacred source of authority. Thus, to take but one example, Little and Twiss in *Comparative Religious Ethics* define religion in part as "a set of beliefs, attitudes, and practices based on a notion of sacred authority...."[22] John P. Reeder's analysis of Judaic and Christian ethics begins at a similar point, claiming that both traditions have in common a sense that a transhuman source causes and legitimates the moral order.[23] It is this transhuman or sacred source that is one distinguishing feature of Jewish and Christian ethics as opposed to a purely secular ethic.

A second distinguishing feature, it seems to me, is the aspect of tradition. By this I mean a sense that the articulation of the ethic must be in some way consistent with what the ethic is understood always to have been. In Western religious ethics, the notion that an ethic is timeless is an important ingredient in ethical discourse. This is not to say that religious ethics do not change, nor is it to say that religious ethics do not reflect their time and place. It is to say, however, that in formulating ethical arguments within a Western religious context, we are concerned with the relationship between what we propose to do now and what has been the accepted norm for our religion in the past. We in general respect the past and want to be able to claim that our own standards are consistent with it. In real terms this does not limit our present options, but it is a feature of ethical discourse or rhetoric which, I am now proposing, is of some importance. This importance lies in the fact that it provides some sort of accepted standard by which to judge the acceptability of proposed change.

It is the lack of these features, I wish to argue, that allowed the Nazi ethic to reach the extremes that it did. In the first place, it could make no reference to a source of morality beyond the physical processes of nature. That is, for the Nazi ethic, the question of right and wrong was reduced to the question of mechanics: how to exploit the laws of nature to certain predetermined ends. Such a question, of course, can be part of any ethical discourse. The problem is that in the Nazi ethic there does not appear to be any room for appeal or consideration beyond this. Once the question of how best to harness the forces of nature has been asked, there remains only the question of specific tactics. Broader reflections on rightness or goodness are ruled out a priori.[24] Ethical discourse, in short, has been reduced to a kind of social science in which the sole value is the physical survival of one side or the other at any cost.

In the second place, there is a lack of historical or social depth in the Nazi ethic, and thus no internal way to achieve perspective on newly-emerging claims. The Nazi ethic, as I have tried to show above, was based on the popular scientific insights of the day. This is, of course, what gave their ethic its aura of truth. But we also know that scientific theories, and more generally the paradigm out of which theories grow, are always to be regarded as hypothetical and ephemeral.[25] Scientific theories are proposed in a sense precisely to be tested and surpassed. They are poor foundations for a permanent and trustworthy ethic. We know that the self-evident truths of yesterday are the quaint curiosities of today, and we ought to be just as sure that the self-evident truths of today hold no pro-mise of eternal validity.[26] But the perspective to achieve that sort of skepticism comes only from historical experience. It is only through knowing the past, or at least being forced to confront its values seriously, that we can break the hold of today's self-evident truths. This is the service provided by traditional religious rhetoric. It may not force us to continue in the conclusions reached in the past, but it at least forces

Auschwitz: Re-envisioning the Role of God

us to consider how more recent proposals might be an improvement or an advance. The problem with a purely secular, scientific ethic is that there is no room for such a perspective; people are in a sense ethically obligated to conform to the apparent demands of the most up-to-date hypothesis. The end result is that in this type of ethic, there can be no appeal made to a source of legitimation beyond what people see as their own immediate good.

In many ways the argument I am making here is similar to the one made by Alasdair MacIntyre in *After Virtue*. In his ground-breaking study of the state of contemporary moral philosophy, MacIntyre argues that in essence much of what passes for ethics today is merely a sort of Weberian utilitarianism. By this he meant that one of the paradigmatic "characters" of the modern world is the manager and that the hallmark of the manager is competence and efficiency in getting the required job done.[27] This is, as it were, the *telos* of the manager, and he displays his virtue by fulfilling the *telos* effectively. The problem, of course, is that in such a case, the worthwhileness of the mission, or the cost of the means needed to accomplish the job are not fully comprehended by ethical discourse. The larger issues of right and wrong are lost to view in the narrow focus needed by the manager.[28]

The point is that with the breakdown of any overarching sense of what the human species is and the loss of any perspective on what the proper *telos* of our deeds might be, ethical thinking has become focused and contextualized. MacIntyre labels this essentially emotivist ethic Weberian because it is Weber who demonstrated most forcefully how one's social role, that is, what one is expected to be or to accomplish, determines one's values. Without an ethic that allows the individual to transcend reflectively his or her social role of the moment, any ethical choice that must be made will perforce be based on whatever theories of the world are then current. In other words, the manager will be able in his or her mind to justify the actions or decisions in question only in reference to the organizational context in which the action or decision takes place.

This narrowing of the base of moral decisions need not be restricted to merely managerial positions in an organization. MacIntyre shows that even major ethical theories of the last several centuries need to be understood in context. What sound like universal descriptions of the moral enterprise are in fact little more than culturally-bound articulations of certain positions which have been expressed as though they were universal truths. Emotivism, to take but one of his examples, is best not understood as a universal ever-applicable theory of the nature of ethics, but is a particular position staked out at a certain time to address a single issue. The problem of misunderstanding begins when, like the bureaucrat's justification, it is abstracted out of its particular institutional or dialogical context and made out to be a universal theory for the definition of all ethical deliberation everywhere and at all times.

The Holocaust Now

It is my contention here that the Nazi ethic is a prime example of where this loss of transcendence in ethical discourse can lead. The Nazi policy toward the Jews, we now know, did not appear full-blown in 1933. Rather, the details of the Nazi policy underwent a long period of incubation and refinement during which time the specific policies, procedures and institutions of their ethic were gradually shaped. It in fact seems that it was not really until the Wansee Conference of January, 1942, that the ultimate policy of extermination through gassing was fully articulated. Up to that point, the policy developed by fits and starts, depending on bureau-cratic infighting, conditions in Germany, the progress of the war and so forth.[29]

To summarize, then, the myriad decisions that were made to plan and then carry out the Shoah on a day-to-day basis were made within a bureaucratic context and, as MacIntyre makes clear, reflect the rather narrow world of the bureaucrat. There was, of course, an attempt to frame the decisions of the bureaucracy in terms of larger ethical principles, and it was these that were supplied by the trends listed above, namely Jew-hatred, Social Darwinism, and fascism. These provided the secular rationale, or rather the secular discourse, for expressing what the bureaucrats had already chosen to do within the constraints of their own positions.

The Nazi ethic then really justifies in universal and scientific terms the particular needs of its own bureaucracy. The values that emerge are based on what the organizational process has already determined to be necessary. The reason that such a bureaucratic discourse could drive the ethical thinking of the entire country, to include its professionals and its religious institutions, is that no [effective] counter-discourse seems to have been available. It was precisely this lack of a more religious, traditional ethic, I maintain, that made the Shoah possible. The bureaucracy under Hitler simply developed policies it felt were necessary to carry forward its mission. Since no higher system of ethical values seems to have been available for judging the mission, the needs of the bureaucracy become by default the community's ethic.

Within this context, the activity of the Nazis and their collaborators makes a certain amount of sense. These people retained their moral sensitivity and their sense of duty to a higher good. What changed, simply, is the nature or the description of that higher good. The content of the older ethic, based on God, was replaced by an ethic defined by bureaucratic need and buttressed by the supposed rational neutrality of science. People could devote themselves to this new ethic with good conscience, feeling that they were still fulfilling their moral duty and serving a higher good. This I think helps account for the apparent devotion so many Germans and others displayed toward their gruesome tasks. They were not moral cripples, they were normal, well-intentioned people who could, and did, do their jobs with dedication and devotion and return home at night to be average husbands and fathers. This is I think why Hannah Arendt resorted to the notion of the banality of evil. Within this ethic, people were simply doing their jobs. The evil we now see was for them not regarded as evil. Had they so regarded it, I contend, they would not have done it so consistently without challenge or revolt. People simply do not do, on the whole, what they really regard to be evil. That seems to me to be part of what it means to call something evil. Rather, by relying on an ethic that was purely contemporary and scientific, people lost sight of the real evil they were doing.

If this view of matters is correct, then a number of conclusions would been to follow. One is that acting ethically is a matter of form rather than content. That is, people can consider themselves to be acting in a good, commendable way regardless of the actual content of their ethic. This is what confounded the Nazis and their cohorts. They thought they were doing the right thing and in many cases at the end of the war were surprised to find that the Americans and British far from being impressed with the German deeds were repulsed. Many Nazis seem to have gone to their graves [or are still alive today] never having fully realized the enormity of the evil they did. The point is that just because one is dedicated to a cause and can call upon scientific and ideological warrants does not mean that they system of behavior is itself moral. It simply means that the behavior is able to be expressed in ethical form.

The second conclusion is that secular theories cannot be relied upon to generate a trustworthy ethic. The scientific [or pseudo-scientific] theories adopted by the Nazis misled them frightfully. They and their followers may have thought they were acting according to the dictates of history and nature. In fact they became the prisoners of a bureaucratic dynamic that I think eventually got out of control In some sense, the Nazi state ended up becoming a prisoner of its own system. They became pawns of the monster they themselves unleashed. Rather than bringing themselves and their country to a new level of security and respect, which was after all the stated goal, they brought their country to the exact opposite. Their reliance on science and political theory betrayed them. The betrayal was possible because the Nazis had no way of knowing when they were being led astray; they had no outside marker or standard by which to fix their position.

A third conclusion has to do with the power of this kind of system of meaning. After all, it engulfed not only the party ideologues, but also people who should have known better, who did in theory at least have an alternate ethic which should have governed their perspective on matters. Most obvious were the professions: doctors, lawyers, professors, etc. These people we would expect to be committed to a set of views that would or should preclude the Nazi ethic. Doctors, for example, ought to have seen through the notion that Jews were a different race analogous to different species in the natural world. After all, the species of the natural world have distinct genetic traits, which is untrue of Jews. Yet doctors not only participated in the Nazi racial warfare, but in fact in many cases were its leaders. And despite the fact that doctors as a matter of professional commitment should be dedicated to relieving human suffering, all too many took the opportunity of the Shoah to perform hideous experiments on unwilling human subjects. As a group they allowed their own professional ethics to be completely overridden.

The same can be said of lawyers. Here again is a group who we would expect would be especially sensitive to the rule of law, and to the impartial application of the law. This group should be especially sensitive to the claim of human rights and due process. However, quite to the contrary, lawyers ended up serving a system that denied just these principles. The reason was strikingly simple. Once the law was so written so as to deprive Jews as a class of human rights, the lawyers could proceed to treat Jews as non-humans and still uphold the highest values of "the law." Like the physicians, they allowed themselves to be reduced to mere practitioners of whatever the law happened to be, not questioning if that was right or wrong. They allowed their moral competence to be restricted to the narrow limits of their professional conduct.

The group that offers the biggest surprise in this regard is the Christian theologians. Here is a group clearly dedicated to a vision of the world diametrically opposed to the Nazi view of matters. This group would also seem to be the least likely to allow itself without further reflection to be reduced to mere functionaries. Their job after all is to think ethics and to challenge the powers that be after the model of the Biblical prophets. That this group too became entirely coopted is one of the big disappointments of the Shoah.

Exactly what we are to make of the impotence of the Christian theologians is hard to know. For one thing, I think, it reflects the very intellectual shift that made Naziism possible in the first place, namely the displacement of religion by science in the mid-nineteenth century. The Nazi ethic, with its scientific and rationalistic basis was able to gain ascendancy precisely because there was no stiff opposition. The religious worldview had withered away under the impact of scientific advance, Church obscurantism, and Higher Criticism.[30] The Church [whether Catholic or Lutheran] continued to exist as an institution, clearly had ceased to function as a moral or intellectual force. Its practitioners no longer were truly dedicated to its own indigenous ethic. They too could become servants of the new Nazi ethic and could learn to fulfill their own religious functions within the universe of discourse fashioned by the Nazi system. They certainly proved incapable, as an estate, of bringing to bear against the development of Nazi Europe any alternative voice, much less a sustained critique.

What this tells us is how easy it is for religion to descend into idolatry. In effect, even the churches in Nazi Germany took their epistemological cues from the secular culture proposed by the Nazis. The bulk of church theology and theologians who supported Hitler did not point to a realm of meaning or moral significance beyond the Nazi construct of the Aryan race. Christianity had been reduced to a series of civil religions, each celebrating the sacredness of its own nationality and none [even the multi-national Catholic Church] arguing from a more global or universal position. The reason I think that the Church men [and women] themselves found the secular ideologies overwhelmingly persuasive.

VII. Summary and Conclusions

My argument can no be summarized as follows: [1] people establish systems of values on the basis of their understanding of good and evil, [2] these values then serve as a basis for persuading masses of people to pursue certain courses of action and to avoid others, [3] that history shows that once people set a certain chain of events into motion, all we can expect is for the natural consequence of that chain of events to occur, i.e., we cannot expect God miraculously to intervene to bail us out. From this it follows that [4] even the worst atrocities can be supported by an ethic if that ethic is able to define genocide or torture convincingly as good for the circumstances at hand. The point, to restate my thesis, is that focusing attention on why God did nor did not perform miracles removes the responsibility from where it really belongs, on the human agents who subscribe to the ethic and then act in accordance with its precepts.

I do not mean to be naive on this point. Religious people have committed their fair share of horrors and atrocities. It is by now a well-rehearsed fact they almost every anti-Jewish measure instituted by the Nazis during their early years had its precedent in the Church's treatment of the Jews: yellow badges, ghettos, expulsions, etc. The mere appropriation of religious symbolism or the invocation of religious rhetoric does not in and of itself guarantee anything. But the acceptance of a religious worldview that demands that people look beyond the temporal thought of the day does offer a stance by which secular ideologies or bureaucratic convenience can at least be confronted and, if necessary, critiqued. It offers the possibility of a moral vision that transcends, or at least is different than, that of the prevailing political ideology of the day. It seems to be that if we do not allow that sort of view into our moral discourse, then we really have no basis for expecting people to counter the next "shoah" on moral grounds. There simply will be no Archimedean grounds upon which to exercise such moral leverage. The Shoah stands in stark testimony to the fact that if no longer moral vision is present, if religious rhetoric is not allowed to offer a voice over against secular purposes and ideologies, then anything is indeed possible.

The Holocaust Now

Evil and Existence

In reviewing the thinking of three prominent Protestant theologians on the subject of evil—Karl Barth, Paul Tillich, and Reinhold Niebuhr—Alan Davies reminds us of the difficulties the religious communities confront when staring directly into the face of radical or cosmic evil epitomized by the Shoah. Both Karl Barth and Paul Tillich began their discussions of evil in the aftermath of the First World War; here the difference ends, however. For Barth, for whom "theology overwhelms history," the gift of the Christ is the optimistic response to the problem of *das Nichtige,* "nothingness." So much so, that he never mentions the Shoah in his magisterial *Church Dogmatics,* and exhibits a "blind spot"—Davies' term—towards not only Judaism, but all non-Christian religions. For Tillich, however, a critical distinction is made between the "daemonic" and the "satanic" in his understanding of evil. National Socialism was daemonic; antisemitism is incontrovertible proof of its daemonism and the Shoah is the fruit of its labors. For Niebuhr, however, wary of the mystical traditions of his German counterparts, and equally at home in the world of historical reality, what is critical is original sin and the failure of contemporary humanity, particularly German humanity, to realize its implications. Ultimately, according to Davies, all three fail to provide a cogent religio-theological explanation of the Shoah, despite the magnificence of their attempts. "The Shoah, in the final analysis, simply defeats both theology and philosophy. Its evil remains a mystery, and no attempt to unravel its threads by searching for the historical causes of antisemitism and mass murder in European culture will ever plumb its ultimate depths."

SLJ

The Holocaust Now

EVIL AND EXISTENCE: KARL BARTH, PAUL TILLICH, AND REINHOLD NIEBUHR REVISITED IN LIGHT OF THE SHOAH

Alan Davies

I. The Growing Realization of Evil

That the mass destruction of the European Jews at the hands of Nazi Germany was an act of monumental evil is manifestly obviously; the Shoah, as Arthur Cohen has written, was the 'Tremendum'.[1] Evil and its mystery, a subject that philosophers and theologians have debated throughout the ages, has acquired new proportions in the twentieth century. My own first encounter with "man's inhumanity to man" came during my boyhood in Montreal, when, in 1945, I came across the first terrible Allied photographs of the newly-liberated Nazi death camps in one of the city's newspapers. My father, believing that I was too young to see such things, had hidden the paper's illustrated section in a closet, but I stumbled on it by accident. To this day, I have not fully digested the horror. Even prior to the Nazi revelations, however, Western society had been greatly altered by the multiple upheavals of the age, and their attendant cruelties. Protestantism, my own religious tradition, had been greatly altered as well, as liberalism was replaced by neo-orthodoxy, with its rediscovery of evil as the great surd in human existence. The new orthodoxy was named after the old orthodoxy [Protestant scholasticism of the late sixteenth and seventeenth centuries] partly because its resurrected the hoary orthodox doctrine of original sin, thereby casting off the treasured assumptions of the eighteenth-century Enlightenment that had dominated theology until "the guns of August" sounded in 1914. Despite this fact, neo-orthodoxy was not a simple restatement of former creeds and confessions; it was also strongly influenced by modern existentialist philosophy, another school of thought that entertained dark notions about the human condition, and its twentieth-century expressions. Evil, therefore, was at the center of Western speculation, both religious and secular, before the 'Tremendum' occurred, although not before its portents were visible on the horizons of European history. Profound theological interpretations of the nature of sin and evil were conceived before their practical enactment in the terrible events of the

Second World War, when the force of sin and evil exploded in full fury. These interpretations deserve to be examined in the context of the Shoah: a tragedy of which two of the three theologians in this essay had little apprehension when they first set their pens to paper.

II. The Power of Nothingness [das Nichtige]

The great Swiss theologian Karl Barth composed the famous section on evil in his *Church Dogmatics* in the immediate post-war years; consequently, he alone thought his thoughts after the terror. It is remarkable, therefore, and, in retrospect, extremely puzzling that this anti-Nazi theologian never refers to the attempted annihilation of the Jews on the part of Nazi Germany in the course of this seminal discussion, although he does allude to the Shoah elsewhere.[2] Had Barth been either an antisemite or a German nationalist, the matter would not be in the least puzzling, but he was neither. In his eyes, antisemitism was a "sin against the Holy spirit"[3], and the National Socialist state with its totalitarian claims was "the Beast out of the Abyss"[4]. What, then, explains the omission? Are his chapters merely the continuation of pre-war reflections, written as if nothing significant had happened between 1939-1945, and thus uninformed by the experiences of his time? Are they merely an exercise in the history of ideas, a metaphysical discussion for its own sake—a defense of the faith against the atheistic philosophers Martin Heidegger and Jean-Paul Sartre? Or is the explanation of a different order? Perhaps the doctrine itself suggests an answer.

As Barth's translators have pointed out, the English language does not contain a satisfactory equivalent to the German *das Nichtige*: "nothingness" is too feeble, since the Barthian power of nothingness is not nothing: "the Nihil," which Otto Weber prefers, has the advantage of a semantic connection with the term "nihilism," with its evil and destructive connotations, but it is not an English word, and, in any case, the Barthian Nihil is deeper and more terrible than philosophical and moral nihilism.[5] For lack of a better alternative, the more familiar term will be employed here. What exactly is it intended to signify? It is intended to signify not merely evil, but [to adopt Immanuel Kant's expression] radical evil, or evil chosen and committed as an end in itself, rather than as a means to another end, because it is grounded in an evil will; radical evil is thus both mysterious and absolute in character.[6] Barth, however, unlike Kant, was a theologian, and not confined by the limits of philosophical language, which must avoid the assumptions and dogmas of religious faith. For the theologian, radical evil moves from philosophy into theology as soon as its mystery and absoluteness are taken seriously, since the characteristics raise essentially religious questions, and religious questions require religious answers. In Barth's theology, radical evil or nothingness is more than the sum total of the many antithetical aspects of the world: non-being, death, darkness, finitude, etc.—in short, the "shadow side" of creation [creation, of course, is a theological, not a philosophical category] that, of necessity, belongs to existence itself.[7] Can there be being without non-being, life without death, light without darkness, infinitude without finitude? Can even these concepts exist without their polar opposites? Indeed, these various "nots" or "frontiers" of creaturely, especially human, existence are not evil in themselves, although, when invaded by the power of nothingness, they become the instruments of evil, and hence easily confused with evil. Real evil, that which Barth designates nothingness, transcends natural evil, lying outside of the created order, being "neither God nor....creature, but possessing reality—a reality of its own—nevertheless"[8]. Nothingness owes nothing to God's will; rather it represents that which God does not will, or the choices that God does not make—all of the malignant possibilities spurned by a good Creator that lurk around the edges of the creation as its travesty and perversion, seeking to annul the divine decree.

> The character of nothingness derives from its ontic peculiarity. It is evil. What God positively wills and performs in the *opus proprium* of His election....is His grace....What God does not will and therefore negates and rejects, what can this be only the object of His *opus alienum*, of His jealousy, wrath, and judgment, is a being that refuses and resists and therefore lacks His grace. This being which is alien and adverse to grace and therefore without it, is that of nothingness. This negation of His grace is chaos, the world which He did not choose or will, which He could not and did not create, but which, as He created the actual world, He passed over and set aside, marking and excluding it as the eternal past, the eternal yesterday.[9]

Nothingness, therefore, which the Biblical era personified in the form of demons, and which the Christian Middle Ages personified as a single immensely powerful devil, is as real as the chaos that constantly overcomes life in a multitude of ways, turning order into disorder. Neurosis, psychosis, the disintegration of the spirit, the destruction of the body, the destruction of the body politic: all of these things are real—why, then, should nothingness, the power that strives to reduce everything to nothing, be regarded as unreal? Nothingness is sin, but, according to Barth, it is more than sin, since sin is a human matter whereas nothingness is more than simply human; in metaphorical and mythological language, it is God's enemy. As God's enemy, moreover, it is a power to be feared and taken seriously, not to be dismissed lightly as a figment of the imagination because demons and devils, interpreted literally, do not exist. In this respect, the modern mind is at a disadvantage, falling victim to rationalistic assumptions that invariably minimize the problem of evil by dismissing any notion that assigns evil any measure of transcendence. Barth does not argue in favor of these demons and devils, but he does not deny their existence either; they, too, are not nothing.[10] They symbolize transcendent evil, and radical evil—evil for evil's sake—is certainly transcendent. Whatever internal problems and contradictions the Barthian doctrine of nothingness may contain, its author cannot be accused of taking too mild a view of his subject in the context of the twentieth century. Even prior to the Shoah, Nazi Germany was the embodiment of nothingness, and doubtless the model in Barth's mind for much of his analysis. Nothingness has the capacity to charm, as did Hitler with his charisma and his mass audiences. Hence many Germans fell under his spell, including many churchpersons, almost including Barth himself, despite the latter's impassioned opposition to the regime: "We were in danger of bringing, first incense, and then the complete sacrifice to it as to a false god."[11]

The Shoah could have been and should have been the theologian's proof-text par excellence. Transcendent evil, mass murder as an end in itself, a delight in indescribable cruelty, the triumph of chaos over order, the victory of the irrational over the rational, the destruction of the spirit as well as the body, the reduction of everything to nothing—in short, all the works of *das Nichtige* in all of their perversity, all were present in superabundance. The power of nothingness scarcely requires further documentation. For this reason, perhaps, so many individuals, past and present, have averted their eyes from the event itself, and engaged in the art of denial; they cannot endure its metaphysical dimensions. Had Martin Heidegger, for example, ever allowed himself to gaze into the true depths of nothingness, according to Barth, he would never have deified "nothing" as the "pseudonym which conceals the Godhead."[12] Nothing, for Heidegger, consequently, is "not a dreadful, horrible dark abyss but something fruitful and salutary and radiant."[13] A philosopher whose thought was colored by the First World War, the greatest of the German existentialists, clearly evaded the lessons of the Second World War, and particularly the lessons of the Shoah. Is it merely coincidence that he found it possible to embrace National Socialism? Like Barth, Emil Fackenheim finds a connection between Heidegger's political sympathies and his ability, even in his old age, to recognize radical evil.[14] Today, the new school of [so-called—Ed.] "historical revisionism" or Shoah denial also refuses to recognize radical evil as a universal possibility. If men such as Arthur Butz in the United States and Ernest Zundel in Canada allowed themselves to encounter nothingness, the nothingness in themselves, their nationalist and racist gods would be shattered, and their personal identities as well.[15] What they fear is not history, but that which history reveals about the human condition. They fear the face of the Nihil.

Barth, of course, was a Christian, and his theology reflects this fact at every turn. In his eyes, even the knowledge of nothingness ultimately depends on a knowledge of God's self-revelation in Christ, or the divine decision against nothingness that, by virtue of its supreme light and glory, illumines the contours of the abyss as nothing else can. This does not mean that only Christians can recognize radical evil; it does seem to mean, however, that only Christians can discern its true spiritual depths. Naturally, Jews are likely to dispute this claim on both religious and historical grounds. Had Barth paid more real attention to the Shoah when he developed his doctrine, he might have hesitated before committing himself to such a dubious and even offensive conclusion. A great blind spot involving Judaism [and, incidently, the other non-Christian religions] mars his entire system.[16] One mistake, moreover, leads to another, and it is not surprising that an interpretation of revelation that excludes the vast realm of religious experience outside the bounds of the Christian faith also excludes the possibility of anything ever challenging its central paradigm. Christ defeated *das Nichtige* on the cross; henceforth, "nothingness is routed and extirpated."[17] Henceforth, it is not to be feared, for its power to annihilate is no more; it possesses the semblance of power—admittedly, a dangerous semblance—but no longer the substance of power: its dominion has ended. God's "yes" to humanity is absolute and irrevocably, and to think otherwise is to deceive ourselves. Most people, of course, including most Christians do think otherwise, regarding the human situation with "anxious, legalistic, tragic, hesitant, doleful and basically pessimistic thoughts," but they are wrong.[18] "Jesus is Victor," and if Jesus is victor, "nothingness has no perpetuity."[19] To be sure, the final revelation of the destruction of nothingness has not taken place; for this reason, non-Christians, post-Christians, and Christians lacking in faith suffer from blindness, mistaking the true state of affairs. That, however, although a sad indictment of our times, does not really matter; truth matters. Nothingness, the "defeated, captured, and mastered enemy of God," is now God's servant, and exists only with God's permission, serving God as an instrument, however unwilling, of the divine will.[20] After the resurrection, even the demons are in chains.

On this note of cosmic optimism, Barth's discourse on evil ends. The optimism is the problem. How, after Auschwitz, can anyone seriously believe that nothingness has lost its dominion, possessing only the semblance of power? Does not history refute Barth? Was it not Barth who was blind to reality, a reality not far removed from his Swiss doorstep? The theologian was no fool; he was thoroughly acquainted with the horrors of his age, and, unlike Heidegger, he did not avert his gaze from the countenance of the Nihil. On the other hand, the character of his theological method, with its stress on transcendence and its suspicion of human experience, including even religious experience, invited a disregard of contemporary historical events as far as the great truths of revelation were concerned. Nazi Germany certainly colored his theology, as the Barmen Declaration that he composed against the German Christians prior to the war obviously demonstrated. This, after all, was the professor who refused in 1933 to begin his lectures in a German university with the required Nazi salute, choosing instead a Christian prayer. His passionate opposition to natural theology in all its forms was inspired by his antipathy to the biological arguments employed by the pro-Nazi theologians and churchpersons who defended the Aryan paragraph. Justifiably he regarded Emmanuel Hirsch's attempt to sacralize the National Socialist revolution as a visitation of the Holy Spirit [*"grossen heiligen Sturm gegenwartigen Volksdeschehens"*] as an outrage[21], and his repudiation of this kind of religious immanence had a great deal to do with his refusal to view history—except, of course, scriptural history—as religiously significant in either a positive or negative sense. As a consequence, as certain critics have noted, much of Barth's thought acquired a decided unhistorical cast, and this is its major weakness.[22] This weakness is apparent both in his failure to mention the Shoah—a manifestation of the power of nothingness *sans pareil* ["without exception"—Ed.]—and in his failure to consider the implications for christology. If Jesus is really victor, why is the devil so visibly out of control? To argue that we suffer merely from blindness, mistaking the true state of affairs, seems insufficient, to say the least. The "Holocaust Kingdom" [Alexander Donat]—the reign of radical evil—is difficult to reduce to a semblance of reality on any ground.

Although Barth's tendency to dwell on the transcendent at the cost of the historical is probably the main reason why he omitted the Shoah from his study of evil, other reasons can be inferred. No one wrote much about the Shoah before 1950; it was too soon, and the realization too difficult to grasp. Moreover, the central principles of Barth's theology were formulated in an earlier era, and, while he was willing to revise his ideas in light of criticism, he never altered their fundamental character. Had he been a younger man, he might have made the "Tremendum" the subject of one of the innumerable brilliant essays that constitute the secondary text of his *Church Dogmatics*, but this was not to be the case. The omission is unfortunate, because it would have deepened his analysis immeasurably, as well as enhanced his image as a Christian theologian whose heart and soul were opposed to antisemitism. Nevertheless, much of what he did write on the power of nothingness remains pertinent to any serious discussion of the nature of evil today. It is also pertinent to the Shoah itself.

III. Paul Tillich: The Demonic

It was during a vacation in Paris in 1926 that Paul Tillich composed his famous essay on the "demonic" [*'Das Damonische'*], thereby giving definitive expression to one of his most distinctive ideas.[23] Art, one of the great passions of his life, is its matrix, since the artists of any society are usually aware of the tremors beneath the surface, which they capture and portray in their works. Art is also concerned with the elements of form and feeling, or the rational and emotional aspects of existence, because it touches the depths and thereby encounters the "holy" or the transcendent in all of its possible configurations, including good and evil. Tribal art especially, as Tillich points out, reveals something in its naivete and primitive power that eludes the Western consciousness and its secular mentality, namely, a form-distorting and form-destroying impulse, and which also has its roots in the holy. "The organs of the will for power, such as hands, feet, teeth, eyes, and the organs of procreation, such as breasts, thighs, sex organs, are given a strength of expression which can mount to wild cruelty and orgiastic ecstasy."[24] These organs are still recognizable—their basic forms are maintained—but with a difference: they are exaggerated and out of proportion, and thus acquire an evil aspect that is at once both religious and alien—the demonic! What art reveals, moreover, is not confined to the artistic realm alone. The demonic is present in the entire history of religion, including the so-called higher religions, and of culture, including the so-called civilizations. It is an illusion to believe that any religion or any civilization can ever escape the demonic and its sinister power; indeed, the more advanced they become, the more subtle and dangerous their distortions also become.

> Holy demonries in a highly purified form exist in the intoxicated laceration-myths and orgies, which re-echo in the sacral sacrifice of the divinity; they exist in the blood sacrifice to the god of earth who devours life in order to create life—the original model of the man-destroying demonry of economics. Holy demonries are present in the cult of war gods, who consume strength in order to give strength—the original model of demonry of war. An outstanding symbol of holy demonry is Moloch, who for the sake of saving Polis devours their first-born—the original of all political demonry.[25]

In Tillich's theology, the demonic and the 'Satanic' are not the same. In one respect, the Satanic is worse than the demonic, since it stands for pure destruction devoid of any creative or positive aspect, i.e., total absolute non-being. In another respect, it is not worse than the demonic, since it contains no form and consequently has no actual existence [to exist requires some measure of form]. If the destructive impulse is completely isolated from the creative impulse, there is literally nothing to destroy, making Satan an empty symbol. Satan, however, in the Biblical and Christian tradition, is not an empty symbol; he is the father of lies and the author of evil—a demonic rather than a satanic function. There is always a "demonic residue" in his character; he is the tempter, but a temptation that lies outside creatureliness is not a temptation "because it contains no dialectics, no 'yes' and 'no'."[26] The prince of demons, according to Tillich, is really "the negative principle contained in the demonic;" otherwise, he is nothing.[27] Not a Satanic Satan, therefore, but a demonic Satan subverts and distorts the good, turning the forms of creation into forms of destruction in which life feeds on life and the kingdom of day becomes the kingdom of night. In religion, the demonic appears as a corruption of the holy: the "Grand Inquisitor" from Dostoevski's great novel *The Brothers Karamazov* who condemns the Christ in order to protect the Catholic Church—the "will to power of the sacred institutions."[28] In the economic order, the demonic appears as a corruption of the process of production, manifesting itself in what for Tillich was the archdemon of modern capitalism, which exploits and starves one segment of society for the benefit of another: a movement that is both creative and destructive at once.[29] In the political order, the demonic appears as a corruption of the drive toward community, producing what for Tillich was the archdemon of modern nationalism, in which nation preys upon nation and in which collective pride swells to inhuman size, with awful consequences for Moloch's victims.[30] Nationalism, like capitalism, with which it is closely linked, is also both creative and destructive at once.

Although social and institutional manifestations of the demonic are terrible enough, its zenith lies in the personal sphere, where the creative and destructive elements of life are elevated to the highest spiritual level. The possessed or twisted personality—the self that is divided against itself—is a source of obvious evil in history, especially when the possessed individual possesses charisma, as so often has been the case. Filled with demonic ecstasy, such persons wreak havoc, because a power from the abyss has gained control over their consciousness, giving rise to the old myth of demon-possession and its modern counterparts; the center of the soul has been invaded, and its rational unity has been shattered. The abyss, a term that Tillich adopted from the seventeenth-century German mystic Jacob Bohme[31], represents the inexhaustible character of the depths of existence, as well as its dark and menacing side. What causes the abyss to erupt is the idolatrous desire to make too much of oneself, confusing the finite with the infinite or the conditional with the unconditional, or the human with the divine. Sin, in other words, unleashes the demonic—"the creative ambition to be like God"—which, of course, in the Biblical narrative, leads to the Fall.[32] The demonic is not identical with sin, since many "sins" do not take a demonic form, but in Tillich's analysis, it is closely linked to the Biblical-Christian concept of sin as a fundamental rebellion against God who sets limits and boundaries in creation. Titanism, or the breaking of these boundaries, contains the seeds of self-destruction, for the self-inflated personality cannot endure; unless grace intervenes and overcomes the demonic, the fate of the fallen creature is sealed. In the end, even the divine acquires the face of the demonic: the "abyss of nothingness" into which everything sinks.[33] Did not Hitler, a demon-possessed man if ever there was one, seek Germany's destruction in the closing months of the Second World War? The nation was not to survive its Fuhrer, once the gods had turned into devils.

As sin is always present, so the demonic is always present, but it tends to express itself visibly more in some periods than in others. The end of an era, as Tillich wrote in one of his post-war books[34], is the dangerous time, since social disintegration—the crumbling of the old systems, old beliefs, and old values—invariably causes the underlying anxieties of life to rise to the surface in the form of a collective neurosis or psychosis. One system of this mood is the inclination to demonize one's enemies, real or imagined, as, for example, Europe demonized the Jews at the end of the Middle Ages and again at the end of the modern era [i.e. the collapse of European civilization into world war, revolution and economic and social chaos]. The National Socialist revolution in Germany was a massive explosion of the demonic in all of its form-creating and form-destroying power during a century of crisis when the world itself seemed threatened with every manner of ruin. Interestingly, to Tillich, a small sign of this ruin was Hitler's "vulgar and barbarous" use of the German language, as the disintegration of language means the disintegration of the human spirit, and a culture capable of producing such a leader must be profoundly disturbed.[35] In *The Socialist Decision* [*Die sozialistische Entscheidung*], a book published on the eve of the Third Reich, he described the demonic aspects of the nation's plunge into a new prometheanism—the mystique of blood, *Volk*, and soil—in an attempt to recover its primordial energies or "powers of origin."[36] The concepts of "blood" and "race," arising from the animal sphere of existence, stir a naturalistic ecstasy that has its roots in a remote tribalism. Modernized in the form of a pseudo-scientific racial theory, these cries from the depths revitalize the soul in a distorted and dangerous fashion. Thus, "the superior power of being of one's own race is affirmed, foreign races and nations are disparaged, and the political and economic claims of supremacy for one's own nation are ideologically justified."[37] Since Judaism, by virtue of its prophetic genius, is the "eternal enemy" of political romanticism and its myths of origin, antisemitism is a necessary and inevitable component of the latter, especially in its Germanic anti-Christian expression.[38] Antisemitism, therefore, in Tillich's eyes, was the final and most deadly proof of the eruption of the demonic in the Germany of his lifetime. So infuriated did he become at the sight of a brownshirt at the University of Frankfort [where he was Dean of the philosophical faculty in 1932], that, we are told, he had to be forcibly restrained by his friends from embroiling himself in serious trouble.[39] National Socialism itself, Tillich believed, might have turned in a creative direction insofar as the movement contained an authentic socialist impulse, but its form-creating potential was devoured by its nationalistic and destructive instincts, so that "a self-annihilating struggle of the European peoples" was inevitable.[40]

If the National Socialist regime was demonic, and if its antisemitism was proof of its demonic character, then the Shoah, the most bitter fruit of the poisoned soil of modern German culture must be regarded as the embodiment of the demonic in its deepest Tillichian sense. The demonic, not the Satanic! To regard the Shoah as Satanic is to eradicate every trace of human causality, transposing the evil to a purely abstract metaphysical plane where its reality disappears. To regard it as demonic, on the other hand, is to relate it to the human condition, where its essential roots surely lie. Anyone who wishes to understand the demonic, Tillich once declared in a post-war dialogue with American students, has only to gaze into the faces of Hitler's storm troopers! "I am not now thinking of the atrocities—they were consequences—but of the totally different human type those faces represent....The troopers belonged to another human category; you felt the absolute strangeness in their completely mechanized and perfectly willing obedience, the fanaticism in everything they did."[41] Evil, the kind of evil that instigates genocide, flows from perverted religion and perverted religious ideals. Did not Adolf Eichmann, Hitler's executioner, regard himself as an "idealist" who had lived his entire life in accordance with Kantian moral law, although, of course, interpreted in Nazi terms?[42] For this reason, at least in his own eyes, he was a misunderstood martyr at his trial—a sacrificial lamb on the altar of duty to the state. Idealism, therefore, at once form-creating and form-destroying, informed by a fanatical racist nationalism with its myth of origin, utterly heteronomous in its submission to authority, not unlike, according to Tillich, the total subjection of Loyola's Jesuits to the Counter-Reformation Church[43], robbed those Nazi faces of their humanity and turned them into ruthless killers. Hitler, intellectually a stupid man, was nevertheless intuitive enough to know that a spiritual vacuum existed in Germany during the Weimar Republic; he also knew how to fill it.[44] Empty spaces do not remain empty for long: demons soon rush in. The Shoah, to which Tillich seldom directly alluded, was the consequence of both an evil ideology and existential estrangement in its most terrible mode. Only if the post-war Germans accept complete responsibility for their demonic actions during the war, he insisted in a public lecture in Berlin in 1953, can the "German problem" be resolved.[45]

It cannot be said of Tillich, as it can be said of Barth, that his theology overwhelms history, causing the lessons of history to suffer neglect. On the contrary, Tillich's thought was profoundly influenced by the historical events of his age, as well as by their effect on the lives of his contemporaries and his own life. The concept of the demonic, with its psychological and religious connotations, owes as much to an experience of human decadence in a dying society as it does to mystical and metaphysical ideas borrowed from long-dead thinkers such as Jacob Bohme and Friedrich Schelling.[46] As Barth was a theologian of the transcendent, Tillich was a theologian of the imminent, and this gives his theology a different character. It saves him from Barth's christological dilemmas, in which everything, including the revelation of evil, is enclosed within the circle of faith, but it exposes him to the opposite criticism: in Tillich, according to Heinz Zahrnt, "God and the world are so interwoven that man can no longer tell the world from God, and can no longer tell God from the world."[47] To be sure, this is a general judgment, and must not be adopted unequivocally; nevertheless, it points to an authentic problem. Form-creation and form-destruction are the two sides of the demonic—the positive and the negative. In what sense, however, can the Shoah be regarded as form-creation?

Was it not rather a manifestation of the purely destructive—in Tillichian language, the Satanic, rather than the demonic? Can any element of anything in the least good or positive be detected in its Satanic depths, any rationale, however perverted, any pragmatic purpose, however wrong? Some historians have argued in favor of a "functionalist" view of the Shoah, seeing it as a massive exercise in problem-solving that moved from one phase to another almost by accident, with Hitler more or less above it all, except as Germany's evil wizard.[48] If they are correct, if the mass murder of the European Jews was essentially the consequence of what sociologists since Max Weber have described as "functional rationality," then seemingly it did contain a rational or form-creating element after all. A bureaucratic machine wildly out of control and acting destructively certainly corresponds to the demonic. No doubt, there is some truth in this depiction, but any attempt to reduce the Shoah to little more than a large-scale case of Weber's social disease inevitably reduces its evil dimensions as well. The abyss disappears, and thus the mystery of radical evil: the Nihil in all its "dread, horror, and darkness"—in other words, in its transcendence. For Tillich, the divine and the demonic were always closely linked; for Barth, they were not. While Tillich was certainly correct in believing that evil must not be abstracted from human causality, the category of the demonic ultimately fails when confronted by a reality in which not even the perversion of the good can be described as present.

IV. Reinhold Niebuhr: Original Sin

Because of its existential and Biblical foundations, Reinhold Niebuhr's understanding of both sin and evil is similar in certain respects to Tillich's doctrine, although the American theologian dislikes the mystical and romantic ideas so important to the German theologian. Bohme and Schelling, Niebuhr believed, both erred in locating the "dark ground" of evil in the Godhead itself, making sin "a consequence of the divine nature."[49] Niebuhr, in fact, distrusted ontological thought in general; invariably, in his view, thinkers of this type [including Tillich] blur the distinction between faith and reason, losing the sharp cutting edge of the symbolic and dramatic language of the Bible.[50] Hence, his point of departure was the Biblical tale of Adam's fall and its parabolic meaning for human existence. Adam falls because the gift of freedom involved him in a profound contradiction: while bound to nature and necessity like the animals, he also knows—as the animals presumably do not know—that he is finite. Standing "at the juncture of nature and spirit," Adam is caught between their insatiable demands[51]; he can become neither pure nature nor pure spirit, but must live in the everlasting tension that they pose. Ambiguity, therefore, marks the human condition, together with tragedy, for it is impossible for a creature who recognizes his/her creatureliness not to attempt to secure himself/herself against the fate that awaits all finite things.

Spirit is not content to perish; thus Adam grows anxious, and seeks a place where he cannot perish, which, of course, he cannot attain because he is Adam and not God. As a result, he falls. His anxiety, however, is not his sin, but merely its "internal precondition," or the "internal description of the state of temptation."[52] The sin is unbelief: a refusal to trust, and consequently the decision to set oneself up as God in lieu of the only true God. Anxiety produces sin, but, like Tillich's demonic, it also produces creative energy, and, indeed, all the works of culture and civilization are the fruits of Adam's determination to overcome the bondage to nature. Nor can the creative and destructive aspects of anxiety be easily separated: "The same action may reveal a creative effort to transcend natural limitations, and a sinful effort to give unconditioned value to contingent and limited factors in human existence."[53] Adam's fall is both upward and downward, and his progeny can never escape this tragic ambiguity: it is the shape of our situation.

The unbelief that lies at the root of all sin not only arises out of this situation, but points to a mystery of evil that precedes human existence itself. Sin rests on sin, and even the temptation that leads to the fall reflects some form of spiritual disorder in the universe prior to Adam. "Before man fell the devil fell."[54] In the Genesis myth, the devil is depicted as the serpent, or an evil principle in the paradisean garden, who plays the role of the tempter. The tempter, however, is also [in later theology] a fallen creature, in this case, a fallen angel: he is Lucifer, son of the morning, who rose in rebellion against the Most High, and, as a consequence, forfeited his exalted state in the heavens. Evil, therefore, is not merely the bad fruit of human sinfulness, although a sinful humanity engages repeatedly in evil actions; it is a dark shadow that falls over our lives from some trans-human zone that no theology or philosophy can really explain or fathom, and that can only be spoken of in a mythological frame. Even Kant, according to Niebuhr, caught a glimpse of this shadow in his doctrine of radical evil, in which he departed from the "moral complacency" of Enlightenment rationalism that otherwise dominates his thought, penetrating "spiritual intricacies and mysteries" in "complete contradiction to his general system."[55] Since a close analysis of sin always discovers these intricacies and mysteries, it still legitimate for Christians to conceive of "original sin," although not, of course, in literalistic terms, after the fashion of an older Christian orthodoxy. Original sin, in Niebuhrian thought, is an existential insight arising form a more profound understanding of the human condition than conventional modern wisdom with its rationalistic bias can achieve. It expresses a "dialectical truth:" we are destined to sin, as Adam was destined to fall, but, like Adam, we are held responsible nonetheless.[56] The power of the tempter is irresistible; however, the tempter appeals to our freedom, so that our freedom, not our bondage to nature, is the instrument of our fall. Our freedom, moreover, is never lost. Indeed, its highest expression, and the "final paradox" of human existence, lies in the discovery of the inevitability of

Evil and Existence

sin, or the triumph of egotism, self-centeredness and the many forms of pride in human affairs.[57] One of these forms—the "pride of power"—leads readily to the kind of naked prometheanism that Nazi Germany, with its "maniacal will-to-power," so perfectly exemplified.[58]

Pride is a sin of the spirit, and the sins of the spirit are always more heinous than the sins of the flesh. The pride of power, in particular, invariably indulges itself at the expense of other life. Nationalism, racism and antisemitism are ideological expressions of both individual and collective egotism, which, when combined with the tremendous might of the modern nation-state, provides a formula for catastrophe, as the Twentieth Century knows only too well. In this fashion, the Shoah and the related atrocities of the Second World War can be seen as the products of original sin in the arena of history, or the deadly harvest of the "pride of nations" run amuck. Niebuhr, of course, was not thinking of the German "Final Solution" of the Jewish problem when he delivered his Gifford Lectures in Edinburgh in 1939, although he certainly had the "daemonic" nationalism of the Third Reich in mind[59]—Edinburgh was actually bombed during one of his lectures[60]—and he was fully aware of current events in Germany. The Final Solution, however, had not yet readily begun. Nevertheless, antisemitism was in the air, and, for Niebuhr, a life-long admirer of Judaism and friend of the Jewish people[61], it represented one of the cardinal evils of the age. "The Nazis," he wrote in 1942, "intend to decimate the Poles and to reduce other peoples to the status of helots; but they are bent upon the extermination of the Jews."[62] To exterminate a people can hardly be regarded as anything but the most extreme of evil deeds by any moral criterion; at the same time, the murderous passions that swept the political and social order in Germany are misunderstood if they are assigned to National Socialism alone. "The Nazis....accentuated but they did not create racial pride."[63] Racial pride, and every other possible expression of radical homogeneity, arises when the ego of a group—any group—is too insecure to permit social pluralism. This insecurity drives its leaders and ideologies in a chauvinistic direction, and the masses soon follow. Consequently, as Niebuhr saw matters, one of the great tasks of civilization is to resist this instinct, employing every stratagem possible "to prompt humility and charity in the life of the majority."[64] Otherwise, Nazi tribal primitivism, or some version of the same phenomenon, becomes a virtual certainty.[65] Hence, it is a serious mistake for the anti-Nazi Western critics of Hitler's Germany to imagine that the crimes of the Third Reich are unique to the Germanic psyche; original sin is universal, and so are its effects.

The universality of original sin, and the mystery of radical evil to which it points, bestows an inconclusive and enigmatic character on the whole of history that contradicts every attempt to see the human epic in neat rational terms. "There are....tangents of moral meaning in history; but there are no clear or exact patterns."[66] We have no choice except to live with this recognition. Faith, however, with its symbols of fulfillment beyond time and space, enables both Christians and Jews to discern the possibility of an ultimate resolution of the antinomies of life, although only in a glass darkly. In the case of Christianity, the central symbol of the cross, in a paradoxical fashion, reveals both the scandalous nature of history—the "abyss of meaninglessness" that crucifies goodness—and the divine mercy that saves us from falling into its depths. If the crucifixion of Jesus was a revelation of this abyss, and of the true character of the world in its depravity and evil, then the Shoah, not the least of the subsequent crimes that have victimized an innocent humanity, both confirms the Niebuhrian vision and supplies it with a new dimension. In the light of Auschwitz, to regard history as lacking in rational coherence and intelligibility, while filled with terror and death, is far from implausible, although Niebuhr did not rest his argument on this event. He could hardly have done so in his Gifford Lectures, and, in his post-World War II writings, his inclination was to see the fate of the Jews in the context of the many disasters and catastrophes of the age. It is not singled out for special treatment; however, it is not minimized either.[67] Evil is evil, and no Christian who understands the degree to which sin is interwoven with the fabric of human existence should be surprised at the diabolical ingenuity and fantastic scope of its inventions. Only the dogmatism of the Enlightenment, and the hubris of modern culture, serve as a barrier, but the unbridled optimism of yesterday has lost, or should have lost, all conviction today. We live in a genocidal world, and there were clues to this fact long before genocide and totalitarianism became the stuff of daily experience. At least one of these clues, according to Niebuhr, lies in the Christian revelation itself.

Whatever else he was, the great American theologian was a realist, and cannot be accused of writing theology as if history did not matter. It was history, and its tragic configurations, that prompted much of his thought, including his doctrine of original sin. Sin and evil were obvious realities; the critical question in Niebuhr's mind was whether an ancient and, from a modern perspective, obscurantist dogma was an appropriate theological setting for a meaningful examination of these realities in the mid-Twentieth Century. In his later years, he decided that his defense of original sin in *The Nature and Destiny of Man* was a "pedagogical error," not because his earlier discussion was invalid, but because modern ex-Christians were incapable of assimilating even the symbolic significance of ancient religious myths.[68] However, despite this failure, original sin, in his opinion, remained "the only empirically verifiable doctrine of the Christian faith."[69] Interestingly, at least one modern Jewish theologian, Will Herberg, has analyzed the human condition in much the same way as Niebuhr, with a similar stress on original sin.[70] Its profundity lies in its compound of freedom and necessity: we are free not to sin, and are therefore fully responsible for our sins; nevertheless, evil constrains us and renders our fall inevitable. The Nazis, in other words, were responsible for the Shoah, and nothing can diminish their responsibility; they acted out of their freedom. At the same time, the Shoah, in the radicality of its evil, ultimately defies rational explanation; there is something transcendent in the magnitude of the crime that points far beyond ordinary human wrongdoing—something that requires the language of mythology, because conceptual language is incapable of capturing its essence. The Nazis were grasped by this strange transcendence, and they became its agents. A tempter of some description whispered in their ears. Dr. Josef Mengele, for example [the so-called "Angel of Auschwitz"—Ed.], a man who certainly tasted of the fruit of the tree of the knowledge of good and evil, appears to have enjoyed the role of God in his death camp selections. In Mengele, a scientist with two earned doctorates, a child of modernity in every sense of the word, Auschwitz was personified, and the myth of the fall assumed a new meaning. Yet Adam is everyman, and everyman stands at the nexus of nature and spirit, subject to the anxiety that is the internal pre-condition of temptation. Mengele, therefore, the quintessential Nazi, cannot be seen as a case apart from the rest of the human race; his tragedy has universal overtones.

Since Niebuhr disagreed with both Barth's theology of the transcendent and Tillich's theology of the immanent, his understanding of evil does not suffer from the major defects of its Barthian and Tillichian counterparts. On the other hand, it can be criticized for failing to explain why sin and evil are not always uniform, and why the tempter does not always succeed in turning the world into Mengele's "univers concentrationnaire." To be sure, there were various special factors to account for the disintegration of Western values in the mid-Twentieth Century, including the rise of nihilism. According to Niebuhr, National Socialism grew on the "soil of despair," a mood that America, unlike Europe, had managed to avoid.[71] Despair, of course, allows all the dark undercurrents of life to flow freely, and homicidal and suicidal impulses to rise to the surface. However, these special factors only beg the question. Our freedom not to sin is still paramount, and if we are fated to sin nonetheless, how is it that some sin more than others? Niebuhr does not answer this question, nor can it be answered within the framework of his theology. In all probability, it cannot be answered at all, but this is another matter. The strength of the doctrine of original sin is also its weakness. Adam is everyman, and everyman sins, and everyman's sin can take the form of murder, and everyman can find himself/herself on the wrong side of the barbed wire at Auschwitz, but, in fact, some Germans, including some Nazis, including even some members of the SS, did not. Why not? Was not Kurt Gerstein everyman, as well as Josef Mengele?[72] Did the tempter whisper less audibly in Gerstein's ear, or was he protected by grace? Here, we trespass on more mysterious ground, and no universalistic doctrine can assist us. Original sin illumines the human condition by explaining why evil—human, not cosmic evil—occurs, but it can never explain why it does not occur. Consequently, even Niebuhr's acute analysis does not do justice to all the paradoxes and illogicalities of life. Is not the Shoah a drama of extraordinary goodness as well as extraordinary evil?[73]

V. Conclusion

For Christians at least, Barth, Tillich, and Niebuhr are all helpful in understanding the "Tremendum." In different ways, the concept of nothingness, the concept of the demonic, and the concept of original sin ring true when tested against an evil that had not occurred when Tillich and Niebuhr composed their definitive statements, and that played no apparent part in the elaboration of Barth's post-World War II theology. This fact, in itself, demonstrates their profundity. None of the three expressions is without its problems: the concept of nothingness is attached to a cosmic optimism that is difficult to reconcile with the raw experiences of history; the concept of the demonic supplies evil—and the Shoah—with a divine ground; and the concept of original sin does not really explain Germany's fall. These deficiencies, however, must not be judged too harshly; it is doubtful if anyone, even today, could succeed where the three great Protestant theologians failed. The Shoah, in the final analysis, simply defeats both theology and philosophy. Its evil remains a mystery, and no attempt to unravel its threads by searching for the historical causes of antisemitism and mass murder in European culture will ever plumb its ultimate depths. Antisemitism is a murderous ideology, but the Nazis did not kill the Jews because they were antisemitic; they killed the Jews because they were evil. Antisemitism was a necessary, but not a sufficient, condition of the Shoah. The antisemitic edifice in Western thought must still be dismantled, but the devil is elusive and full of surprises. Our finitude defeats us, and we must live in fear and trembling.

Suffering, Theology and the Shoah

For Alice Lyons Eckardt, who, together with her husband, A. Roy Eckardt, have assumed central roles in a re-thinking of Protestant theology in light of the Shoah, attempts to find theological meaning in the suffering which occurred during those nightmare years have been found wanting in both the Jewish and Christian religious communities, though, to be sure, some explanations from the past still find currency today [e.g. Ignaz Maybaum]. Her lengthy review of responses to historical suffering and attempts to find positive meaning in suffering in terms of the redemptive process serve as reminders that the "evil that men do" is hardly a new experience. And, while she finds some small measure of comfort in Elie Wiesel's response of protest to that of suffering—reminiscent of Dylan Thomas' well-known poem "Do Not Go Gently into the Good Night"—her critique of Christian theology is profoundly disturbing in its implications for further Jewish-Christian dialogue: "Most of the books of Christian theology still are written and read as if the ghastly murder of six million individuals had never occurred. And those theologians who do mention the Shoah are apt to find a nice little niche for it and then surround it with the same theology that could have been written before 1933 or 1939."

SLJ

The Holocaust Now

SUFFERING, THEOLOGY AND THE SHOAH

Alice Lyons Eckardt

I. Introduction: Planet Auschwitz

The Kingdom of Night with its oppressive greyness, its frightening blackness, and its fire and pall of smoke was a man-made hell on earth. We no longer need Dante or Milton, the Book of Revelation, the lurid paintings of countless artists, Jonathan Edwards' hell and brimstone sermons, or the prophecies of present-day apocalypticists to conjure up the torments of hell to us. For it has all existed here on Planet Earth as "Planet Auschwitz"—a whole universe apart from our own and yet in our midst, directly linked to our world by railroad lines and roads and air-planes flying overhead taking aerial photographs, by the belongings of its victims that were sorted and shipped back to the Third Reich for reuse by its "worthy" citizens, by the products that were turned out of those factories of death: bone meal and ashes for fertilizer, hair for felt cloth and packing insulation, gold torn from the mouths and hands of victims to enrich the bank accounts of the Reich or private SS hoarders.

Moreover, its reality was far worse than the worst imaginings, for its anguish was much more than physical agony [though the extent of that was also beyond the worst nightmarish apprehensions]. From the early stages on, it included the day-to-day torment of parents who found themselves totally helpless to protect their children or their own elderly parents—those dearest to them who looked to them for safekeeping—from humiliation, beatings, exclusion, and the ever-increasing dangers that finally culminated in starvation, shooting, and deportation to the murder camps. In the ghetto stage [a beginning of the process of total annihilation though disguised from the victims], it encompassed the tortuous choice a father or mother sometimes had to make as to which child to give over to a rescuer, or which parent or spouse should receive the precious work permit or hiding place. Or, for a young person, the decision whether to join the partisans in the forests or to try to survive as a non-Jew outside the ghetto. In either case, such action required the youth abandoning his/her family. The anguish involved day by day and hour by hour attempts to decide what was the best action to take, when, in fact, very few options were possible. In the extermination[1] camp stage it could place a person in a literal race of death in which losing meant immediate death but winning meant sentencing someone else to immediate death. It could force a father to make a decision as to whether it was morally permissible to ransom his son from the death barracks when that would mean another man's son being put there in his place.[2] In most cases, of course, an individual was given no opportunity to make any choice for herself/himself or other family members. Nevertheless, uncounted numbers of Jews thought they had such an opportunity on arrival at the death camps and used it to direct a younger sibling, or child, or parent to the line of mothers, children, and elderly, never dreaming that they were thus condemning this beloved individual to immediate death.

The camps of annihilation devised suffering that cannot be imagined by anyone who did not endure it, and that cannot be fully comprehended even by those who did. Ironically, the survivor's return "to the world of the living....makes it impossible for him to believe fully in his own past experience."[3] The reality the victims experienced every minute was that of atrocity, and the "worst" cruelty was always superseded by a still greater cruelty. Their "semi-life" was made possible only by a "hanging on, a resistance of the spirit, a clinging strength one never knew existed even in colossal circus freaks, let alone in the skeletal leftovers" of a tailor, a rabbi, a housewife."[4]

The overwhelming reality of the Shoah is embodied in the enormous suffering it imposed [perhaps even more than in its death statistics]. What are we to take of this suffering? Can our traditional theologies deal with it? Is it to be subsumed under the general category of suffering and evil? Or under God's special requirements of the children of Israel? Or does it defy or challenge earlier attempts to answer the questions raised by inordinate and inappropriate suffering? One answer is given by Andrew Schwartz-Bart in his *The Last of the Just*. "A suffering so great leaves nothing to be redeemed and precious little to forgive or be forgiven." In fact, the Shoah seems to signify for him humanity's faithfulness and God's unfaithfulness.[5]

Hell is conceived of as a "place" or condition where particularly wicked persons receive the punishment they deserve. Justice is seen to be satisfied at last and injustice rectified. For that reason the use of the term "hell" for the Shoah in my opening sentence is inappropriate. For surely we cannot conclude that the Jews of Europe deserved this hell on earth, even though some Jews drew this conclusion, as we will see. [Of course none of the other victims of the camps did either.[6]

Is there any purpose, human or divine, that can justify or compensate for such abysmal agony and despair? Is there any answer that could have given ease to the victims of that can reconcile the still-living survivors or their kin? If an answer cannot satisfy them, dare we let our-selves accept it? Dare we allow it to suffice? But even if some of those who perished and some of those who survived the Kingdom of Night are willing to accept the traditional answers, are we permitted to evade the difficult questions? Does not the history of the way in which Jews responded to various catastrophic destructions require us to propound the questions anew and search for our own contemporary answers? Is this not how we grow in our understanding of God and of human responsibility? Perhaps only the survivors, those who have already experienced the worst that can be dealt out, have the right to cling to the older answers.

To be sure, it may be argued with considerable force that the Shoah raises no new religious questions. The questions had all been raised before—about evil, God's presence or absence, the covenant's continuing existence or its abrogation, repentance or impenitence, forgiveness, martyrdom and self-sacrifice. And, above all, questions about suffering—especially suffering of the essentially innocent and righteous.

But if the Shoah does not produce new questions, it raises all of them with a new intensity, a demand for answers that can take the Shoah reality into account in all of its radicalness. Against the backdrop of such monstrous suffering, such inappropriate death, such widespread complicity and indifference, the traditional answers no longer satisfy many. They suddenly are seen to be as inadequate as the invisible clothing worn by the naked king in the story from our childhood.

Is there perhaps more to the present quandary than a new perception? Has a quantum change taken place? A transmutation of evil into a new and more deadly form of evil, as when deviant cells become cancerous and set out to destroy the body that is their host? Are we required then to deal with this new evil in new ways? At the very least, we are compelled to re-examine the traditional answers our faiths have supplied and on which they relied. Are we afraid that we may find that we have to reject them as deficient or, much worse, even as contributing to the evil that we deplore? Such fear does not permit us, I believe, to ignore the troubling questions or the search for appropriate answers.

II. The Claims of the Past

Both Judaism and Christianity claim there is an objective morality—i.e., an external reality that determines what is intrinsically right and good and what is wrong and evil. Therefore it must shape and define our fundamental values and what ought to be adhered to by the members of the [faith] community. There should be no quibbling over this. Reality and the society's "ought" [values and laws] say, for example, that people must not kill, steal, commit adultery, covet, etc. If they break these divine and social laws, either God or the society will punish the offenders. The Ten Commandments/Tablets of the Law and the moral value system they establish would seem to be a statement of external moral reality, insofar as they are said to originate from God, and therefore to represent the "ought."

But there are additional propositions that are also treated [generally] as fundamental within every social and especially religious community. Within Judaism and Christianity, for example, assertions are made that not only is there purposefulness in suffering but that it has positive and redemptive functions; and that virtue is attached to being among the powerless or oppressed, despite the suffering it may entail, and therefore it will ultimately be vindicated. Then there are Jesus' reported admonitions such as:

> Do not resist one who is evil....if any one strikes you on the right cheek, turn to him the other also. [Matthew 5:39]

> ....if any man will....take your coat, let him have your cloak as well. [Matthew 5:40]

> Love your enemies, and pray for those who persecute you.... [Matthew 5:44]

> Take no thought for your life, what you shall eat; nor....what you shall put on. [Matthew 6:25 & 3; Luke 12:22 & 29]

> Be perfect, even as your Father in heaven.... [Matthew 5:48]

> Judge not, that you be not judged. [Matthew 7:11]

> If your right eye causes you to sin, pluck it out and throw it away. [Matthew 5:29]

Are these to be considered of equal status with the Tablets of the Law? The question of whether these are apodictic [absolute] commands that are divinely undergirded or whether they are more in the nature of *aggadah*—teachings about ethical standards toward which we are to strive—is one of the fundamental arguments within Christian circles.[7] However, generally Christianity has striven to speak of them as absolute commands, even though its representatives and adherents often have acted in quite contrary fashion. [Of course the Torah of the Tablets can also be subjected to hermeneutical treatment.]

If we can utilize Peter Haas' analysis of what constitutes an ethical system and what constitutes morality[8], we need to ask: Are these or similar admonitions and assertions part of foundational morality [an externally existing moral reality]? Insofar as they are claimed to represent something less, an "ethic"—that is, the system of values by which a society actually shapes its behavior? If so, what is the rhetoric of this ethic, and the syntax and semantic of its discourse? What is the nature of the connection between the external moral reality and the ethic being followed? And how has the latter shaped behavior and history?

I am not convinced that the distinction can be a hard and fast one since communities usually insist that their values reflect external reality.

I want to consider one of the basic concepts that are in one way or another fundamental to Judaism and Christianity—suffering [and by extension pay a bit of attention to powerlessness].

Evil and suffering have always been, and doubtless will always be, subjects of great concern, not only to their victims but to any system of thought that postulates a good creator or a purposeful universe. Attempts to explain them are manifold. There is not space to do a thorough survey of these explanations. But I want to examine some of their consequences for both the public rhetoric and the public ethic, including the negative form of that ethic [which usually means as it is applied to "the other"], and for the way they get applied in faith and action.

III. Explanations

Explanations usually tend to put the burden on the sufferers: Either it is their fault [even if no one, except God, knows exactly what sin or wrongdoing has been committed by them or their predecessors!]. Or, it must be borne since God has decreed it in His infinite wisdom. Thus, explanations seek to make a virtue of or assign positive value to something that we instinctively believe to be wrong and evil. The "what is" is justified or assigned legitimacy. [If there is suffering or evil, there must be a reason for it.]

Then the "what is" [the reality] becomes a basis for establishing a system of ethical principles that is intended to determine behavior—what I am calling an "ethic of suffering," [along with an ethic of powerlessness, meekness, non-resistance, etc.].

Some questions that can be raised about the validity and viability of an ethic of suffering and powerlessness include: [a] To what extend have they genuinely been manifested by individuals or the community, especially by the dominant community or those with power and authority? Have these ethics been anything more than an idealized "ought" that have been lauded but ignored—except as something that others are advised to accept? [b] Have they helped the victims or abetted victimizers? In the spotlight of history—especially of our century—have they helped to sustain life and hope, or to foster death and despair? [Have we sold ourselves—or been sold—a faulty bill of goods?] [c] Is there justification for continuing to assert an ethic of suffering [or ethics of suffering and powerlessness, if we need to distinguish between them]? [d] What do the victimized have to say?

The Holocaust Now

If there is sufficient reason to challenge an ethic of suffering and powerlessness, we need to consider whether there are alternative ethics that are retrievable by Christians and Jews that are free of the faults or pitfalls of the prevailing and dominant ethic regardless of whether that ethic is actually practiced or only verbalized.

Without minimizing any of the suffering that in our century has been deliberately and cold-bloodedly inflicted on millions of humans in numerous other situations, we need to pay particular attention to what has been done within our own Western, primarily Christian, sphere since it is here that we can and must test our ideals, our ethics, and our profession of faith by their consequences. And Jews need to make this sphere their primary concern as well, since so much of their past experience has been at the hands of the Christian world, and so much of their present existence and future hope lie within the Western societies.

IV. Jewish Explanations

From the earliest recorded Jewish efforts to understand the rea-sons for the sufferings, defeats, and catastrophes that the covenant people experienced to even the most recent, we find a number of wide-ranging answers: [1] suffering represents deserved punishment; [2] or divine pedagogy: teaching, chastising, disciplining; [3] some suffering is incomprehensible but must be borne since God is trustworthy; [4] the next world will rectify the imbalances of this world; [4a] suffering will increase the reward of the righteous in Paradise; [5] the messianic future in this world will rectify present injustice; [6] suffering of the righteous is to purify and strengthen them, expiate their sins, and bring their faith into action; [6a] it represents "afflictions of love;" [7] natural evil is part of the ordering of, and is for the overall good of, the universe; [8] humans are responsible for causing suffering; [9] it is not the will of God, and God suffers with people; [10] it represents the birth pangs of Messiah and redemption; [11] or, does not represent the birth pangs of Messiah and redemption, and is meaningless [at least to humans]; [12] suffering of Israel is on behalf of others and/or God and therefore is vicarious suffering.

None of these explanations, arguments, or assertions stood alone, but were intermingled and called on by various persons and communities according to their perceived needs. Above all, the conviction of God's absolute justice was firmly held, even during and despite the various assaults on the Ashkenazic Jewish community of Europe throughout the tenth to fourteenth centuries. The testimonies of the martyr-victims of the Crusades not only repeatedly attested that the Holy One's justice must not be questioned, that their own destruction was decreed by heavenly judgment, regardless of their inability to fathom that decree, but they also made use of other traditional explanations. The chroniclers of the events speculated that these victims were the elite of all generations, chosen for their capacity to fulfill the highest duty, in order to "atone for the past deeds of Israel [and] to create a fund of good will for coming generations."[9]

Under the circumstances of unusual suffering the 18th century Poland, the Baal Shem Tov [Founder of Hasidic Judaism—Ed.] and his disciples did not attempt to offer reasons but sought to help their people transcend it, to find joy and even ecstasy in their relationship with God in spite of their plight. But the *rebbes* [Hasidic rabbis—Ed.] went a step further and struggled, on behalf of the people, to breach what appeared to be the closed door of Heaven and to "influence God and move Him to compassion and grace" towards His suffering children.[10]

V. Christian Explanations

The new Christian community had to answer the same difficult questions. Because of its rootedness in Judaism and in the shared scriptures, it came up with many of the same answers: [1] divine punishment; [2] chastisement or warning; [3] disciplining; or [4] a purifying force; [5] suffering leads to hope and assurance via endurance and character[11]; [6] it provides an opportunity to witness on behalf of Christ [thus this suffering allowed for redemptive possibilities that could find merit in the suffering]; [7] it is evidence of divine love; [8] suffering is the result of human disobedience. Some other explanations differed more from Judaism: [9] redemption of suffering will be made only in the next life, hence there are no redemptive possibilities in present suffering[12]; [10] suffering for the elect is part of the "natural order of events" as this world must be destroyed[13]; [11] it offers a contrast by which humans can learn to know and choose good; [12] it is punishment for sin, but only at the social level—that is, it need not be related to a person's sins; [13] natural [physical] evil is attributed to the wisdom of God[14]; [14] it is a corruption of the original creation and is purposeless, therefore only Christ can vanquish it; [15] suffering and evil do not disrupt creation as creation belongs to the Creator; and it is not "spiritually calamitous for persons of faith" who are assured of "eternal peace and justice."[15]

In general, we may say that the Christian emphasis and expectation lay with the hereafter, however near or far of that might be: "after this brief suffering" [I Peter 5:10]. As Carter Heyward has recently written, "the loudest Christian voices have spoken historically of God's justice as characteristic of another time [the eschaton] and/or another place [Heaven]....Christian theology's justification of God—theodicy—has been to direct our attention beyond the here and now...."[16] Moreover, although in several branches of the church, Christian martyrs and saints have a function as vicarious sufferers and therefore intercessors, Christ bears the primary responsibility for redeeming innocent suffering.

By contrast, although Judaism also looks forward to the "messianic age" or the "world to come" when all will be put right, the predominant perspective is that the new age will take place in this world, not in some heavenly abode. Moreover, it is more insistent than Christianity that humanity and God have a mutual responsibility to bring about that perfected world.

VI. Suffering as Redemptive and Its Function as an Ethic

One of the primary ways by which the problem of evil and suffering has been approached is to go beyond explanation and ask more directly whether suffering has any positive function in the process of redemption. The answers to suffering that we have considered so far often touch on this question. But both Judaism and Christianity have additional and more explicit ways of affirming that there is some redemptive force in the suffering of the faithful.

VII. Judaism's Arguments for Redemptive Power in Suffering

[a] *The Thirty-Six Just Ones:* In Judaism a concept developed that there are in every generation Thirty-Six Just Ones[17] whose piety and righteousness sustain the world. This concept has received more attention in Jewish *kabbalah* [mystical literature—Ed.] and folklore than elsewhere. In Jewish folklore, these obscure *lamed vov tzaddkim* [Thirty-Six Just Ones] or "hidden saints" were believed to have special powers which they would utilize to save Israel in times of great peril.

[b] *Binding of Isaac:* More central to mainstream Judaism, however, is Isaac, who for at least two millennia has been assigned a central place as an intercessor or reconciler. The primary lesson drawn from the Genesis account of the "binding" of Isaac was that God does not desire human sacrifice. Thus Isaac saved unnumbered humans from being made sacrificial victims.[18] But other consequences were discerned as well. In time, Isaac came to be seen as the archetypal martyr, and as the lamb of sacrifice who, though "fully and completely offered," was not killed. His sacrificial action, that is, his willingness to be a sacrifice, was held to serve a prior expiation for Israel's sins, God could be asked to remember the *Akedah* [Binding—Ed.] so that He would answer Israel's prayers, deflect His anger against the people, remember the divine mercy, and bring redemption to her. Indeed, Isaac's "sacrifice" would also be a blessing for all peoples.[19]

[c] *Maccabean, Hadrianic and later Martyrs:* In the Biblical telling the readiness of Abraham to obey this most outrageous of divine commands[20] is offset by the angelic intrusion that stayed Abraham's hand. But during the Maccabean period of resistance to Antiochus Epiphanies' efforts to force Jews to abandon their God in favor of the Hellenistic gods, more radical sacrifices were made. Many Jews accepted martyrdom

for themselves and their kin as a way of remaining faithful to the One Holy God of Israel and of sanctifying the Name of God in the presence of idolaters. The stories of a woman [later called Hannah] and her seven sons, and Eleazar come from this time.[21] These martyrs became the paradigm of loving acceptance of suffering to the death for God's sake, even without God's saving intervention.

During the subsequent Hadrianic persecutions, the suffering and death of the Ten Martyrs [all Rabbis] became famous.[22] And the earlier acts of martyrdom were reenacted many times as parents and offspring refused to give in to another attempt to force them to abandon the covenant with their Lord. As recounted in this new setting, the faithful mother comforted her sons by assuring them that they were created in order to "sanctify in the world the Name of the Holy One...." But the mother also recognized that Abraham and Isaac had had a relatively easy testing. And so as her sons prepared to die she admonished them, "Go and tell Father Abraham....You built one altar, but I have built seven altars and on them have offered up my seven sons. What is more: Your's was a trial; mine was an accomplished fact!"[23]

And in the mid-seventeenth century when the Chmielnicki massacres devastated the Jewish communities of the Ukraine and Poland, Nathan Hanover concluded in his chronicle: "if our fate be decreed from Heaven, let us accept the judgment with rejoicing."[24]

[d] *Sacrifice of Isaac:* Surprisingly, however, we find that early in the Common Era, the Talmudic sages began to hold that Isaac was not spared, contrary to the account in Genesis.[25] Some sources said that before the knife was stayed a quarter of his blood was shed "an an atonement for Israel." In others, he was slain and his body reduced to ashes on the altar. In either case, the "blood of Isaac's Akedah" and "the ashes of Isaac" were held to serve "as atonement and advocate of Israel in every generation and advocate of Israel in every generation. And whenever Isaac's descendants are in straits [God], as it were, beholds the blood of his [Isaac's—Ed.] Akedah, and pity fills Him so that He turns away the wrath of His anger from His city and His people."[26]

The readiness of Jews to accept martyrdom as a way out of sanctifying God's Name [*Kiddush Ha-Shem*] became a problem for the Talmudic Rabbis as they sought to sustain Jewish life and faith after the devastation of the Roman wars. They tried to establish conditions under which martyrdom need not be enacted. Perhaps this new attention to the atoning value of Isaac's blood and ashes was, in part, a way of assuring the people that the necessary sacrifice had already been performed and that further ones were not required except under unusual circumstances.

In the generation of the First Crusade massacres, a synagogue poem pointed out that "Once, over one Akedah Ariel [synonym for Jerusalem—i.e. the Jewish people—Ed.] cries out before Thee ," and then asked the agonizing question, "But now how many are butchered and burned!/Why over the blood of children did they not raise a cry?" Despite this question, there were no real protests, no calling attention to "the radical difference between the unconsummated offering [of Isaac] and the offering mercilessly brought to completion [in their own case]." Can this be explained by their having been aware of the ancient tradition according to which the offering was consummated? Certainly the twelfth century poetic interpretation of the Akedah by Rabbi Ephraim and the commentary by Abraham ibn Ezra that "the father 'acted contrary to Scripture,' 'for he slaughtered and abandoned' Isaac on the altar" demonstrate that such an understanding was available to Jews in central and western Europe at the time.[27]

VIII. Christianity's Arguments for Redemptive Power in Suffering

[a] *Jesus' sacrificial and atoning death:* In the first and second centuries of the Common Era, Christianity gave new emphasis to the concept of the atoning function of a righteous one's death.[28] Thus Jesus' sacrificial and atoning death became the cornerstone of Christian faith.

Since Jesus' followers were convinced that his tragic end must have served a purposeful and divinely-ordained end, new consideration was given to the meaning that could be found in the suffering of the innocent: even, in the case of Jesus, the *necessity* of it.

For the apostate Paul, the death of "Christ Jesus" must have been necessary in order to overcome the sin and death that the first human, Adam, had introduced into the world [Romans 5:12-21]. No other means but Christ's "expiration by his blood" would suffice [Romans 5:8; 3:24-25].

Not surprisingly, Second Isaiah's figure of a vicariously suffering Servant of the Lord was appropriated by the Gospel writers and the early church and read as a foretelling of Jesus' role in the divine drama of salvation. The writers of the Synoptic Gospels were intent on "showing how Jesus summed up this whole long tradition of his people by his sacrifice and death."[29]

And just as Second Isaiah had written five and one-half centuries earlier that "it was the will of the Lord to bruise him; he had put him to grief....," so also Paul and the Gospel accounts present Jesus' death and resurrection "as the supreme disclosure of God's love in offering his Son to die, the righteous for the unrighteous, to reconcile a sinful world to its God."[30] [At the same time, Jesus is also presented as one who voluntarily assumed and/or accepted his destiny, even death on the cross.[31]

The Epistle to the Hebrews makes much of the purpose of Jesus' suffering and his sacrificial role: He "learned obedience *through* what he suffered" [5:8]; he offered himself "once for all" as a sacrifice in place of the daily sacrifice at the Temple [7:27]; he "was crowned with glory and honor because of the suffering of death, so that by the grace of God he might taste death for every one" [2:9]; he was made "perfect through suffering [2:10]; he "entered once for all into the Holy Place, taking not the blood of goats and calves but his own blood, thus securing an eternal redemption" [9:11].

[b] *Christian martyrs and emulators of Christ:* Christ's death was a martyr's expiation and his sacrificial love overcame sin and death. But not only for himself: all are "heirs of God and fellow heirs with Christ, *provided* we suffer with him in order that we may also be glorified with him" [Romans 8:17]. [See also II Timothy 2:11-12 and Hebrews 10:8-10.]

By following his example, the faithful will find comfort even in this life *if they endure their trials patiently* [II Corinthians 1:6], and will be approved of by God *if they endure their pain "while suffering unjustly"* [I Peter 2:19, 21]. A second century Hellenistic-Christian sermon affirmed that suffering at the hands of the authorities was "part of a pattern of events in which the people of God....opposed the worldly powers."[32] Sixteenth century Anabaptists went so far as to insist that the Christian pilgrim *must* suffer with Christ. It is not enough to believe that Christ died as an atonement for others.[33]

In any case, "the sufferings of this present time are not comparing with the glory that is to be revealed to us" [Romans 8:18]; "this slight momentary affliction is preparing for us an eternal weight of glory beyond all comparison" [II Corinthians 4:17].

In this way many of Jesus' followers in the first and second centuries were imbued with the conviction that they ought to emulate their Lord. As they suffered with Christ [and he suffered in them], so would they be glorified with him. Once they had "died 'for the glory of Christ,' the martyrs were assured of 'fellowship for ever with the living God'."[34]

But these Christian martyrs had other models in addition to their Christ: the Maccabean martyrs were specifically mentioned by the Christians of Lyon and Vienne who were prepared to die for their faith in 177. There is no question about the significant influence this Jewish martyr tradition come to have on the Christian theology of righteous suffering.[35]

However, as the church gained acceptance and recognition in the Eastern and Western empires, martyrdom became superfluous—except for those Christians who refused to conform to the official orthodoxy! The remembrance of the early martyrs continued as a part of the church's liturgy, iconography, and teaching, but most Christians no longer needed to be prepared to accept the martyr's role. The remembrance did nothing, however, to soften attitudes towards their neighbors who were forced to suffer and be martyred if they wished to remain true to their own faith convictions.

IX. The Jesus and Isaac Traditions

We cannot fail to notice a number of similarities between the [near—Ed.] sacrifice of Isaac and the sacrifice of Jesus as these two events were elaborated upon in the Jewish and Christian communities. In fact, the Church Fathers made a specific connection between the two, seeing the Akedah as a prefiguring of Golgotha: Isaac as the "prototype for the sufferings and trials of Jesus;" Isaac carrying the wood for the sacrificial pyre just as Jesus bore his cross; Isaac as the sheep for the burnt offering and Jesus as the lamb slain for others, even as the Paschal lamb.[36]

From the synagogue's perspective, there are differences between its claims regarding Isaac's [near—Ed] sacrifice and the church's claims regarding Jesus' sacrifice. For one thing, the Rabbis never "set up all salvation and hope of Israel on one man's grace in times gone by." Righteous persons of all times gain merit for the people before heaven. More-over, the Rabbis acknowledged that there are times when the Akedah *fails* to be sufficient due to Israel's iniquities. "There are no merits in perpetuity on high without continuing good action below. Hence, he who cannot find favor through the acts of Torah cannot find favor through the Akedah either....The Akedah Merit proclaims and promises that....the sum of the righteousness of the Fathers is there to add to and complete the reward of sons who engage actively in Torah; and thereby redemption makes haste to come."[37]

By contrast, Augustine spelled out on behalf of the church the absolute uniqueness of the Christ event: it was [and remains] an absolute necessity and revolutionary "reversal of human history."[38] [Ireneaus's view that the Christ event was a *further* evidence of God's grace which *had been present* in the world from the beginning was rejected categorically by Augustine.]

X. A Negative Ethic

The church did not allow for any equivalency in Isaac's "sacrifice" and Jesus' crucifixion [despite the connection it made between the two events], for it used only the Genesis account, that is, the unconsummated sacrifice of Isaac. Therefore it could taunt the synagogue with the fact that Abraham was not forced to abandon his son and Isaac was not required to give up his life, whereas God did make the total sacrifice of His only Son and Jesus' sacrifice was actually carried out. Nor would the church consider any real comparison between the atoning value of Isaac's suffering and the atoning value of Jesus' death on the cross: Isaac's suffering served only Israel and only until the covenant was abrogated and replaced by the new covenant that Jesus established; Jesus' death was a once-for-all sacrifice sufficient for all peoples and all times; only Jesus' death conquered death [through his subsequent resurrection].

Furthermore, since the church, early in its history, came to the view that God had cast off the original covenant people because of their unfaithfulness and had chosen a new people—the people of Christ—the suffering of God's new people was celebrated as faithful testimony to God's truth [as embodied in Christ and in his church]. They suffered as faithful witnesses to God's love and Christ's power to save. But the suffering of the unfaithful—the people of the "old" covenant—was nothing less than deserved punishment for their "hardheartedness and unbelief."[40] Their suffering served as a negative witness, demonstrating what happens to those who reject God's gifts and verifying for Christians that God had indeed rejected His former people.

In this way the theme of the suffering of the righteous was turned into a weapon against the Jewish people who had originated both the concept of righteous suffering and the deed of martyrdom, and who continued to die as witnesses to God [in their own view]. Moreover, adding insult to injury, Christian persecutors often interpreted Jews' willing martyrdom as connivance with the devil.

With considerably more reason Jews also turned the concept of the suffering of the righteous against their Christian adversaries. During the persecutions of the tenth to fourteenth centuries, Jews saw their own martyrdom as suffering on behalf of the true faith whereas the religion whose representatives were forcing this choice on them was seen not only as false but also as contemptuous. The offers to spare them from death in exchange for conversion were rejected with bitter words. Or they pretended to accept baptism in order to have the opportunity to spit at the crucifix.[41]

XI. Responses to Shoah Suffering: Jewish

Since the vicarious suffering of the people Israel as part of God's "secret aim" of transforming the world had become the recurrent theme of Jewish writings from the Middle Ages on, particularly at times of intense Jewish suffering, it is not surprising to find that during and after the Shoah it continued to be expressed [along with many of the other themes, of course].

Rabbi Hirschler, who died in Mauthausen in 1943, is reported to have said, "To us [Jews] the world is like a crucible into which God plunges us in the course of time because we have forgotten Him and have not respected His laws, perhaps for our purification, perhaps for a sacrifice of atonement for the salvation of others. [Therefore,] it may be right and beautiful to suffer beyond one's own sins."[42] Notice, however, the lack of certitude with which he propounds the traditional views, an uncertainty that only partially hides his unspoken questions.

Rabbi Elchanan Wasserman restated the theme of atoning sacrifice with more assurance. As he and others awaited execution at the Ninth Fort outside Kovno [July 6, 1941], he said to his fellow Jews: "It would seem that in heaven we are considered *Tzaddikim* [Righteous Ones—Ed.]. For atonement is to be made with our bodies for *Klal Yisroel* [the world-wide Jewish people—Ed.]. As we do *Teshuvah* [Repentance—Ed.] we should [be concerned] with saving [the souls of] our American brothers and sisters so that they can continue as the *Shearith Israel* [the Saving Remnant]....We go carry out the greatest *Mitzvah* [Commandment—Ed.], *Kiddush Ha-Shem* [Sanctification of the Divine Name—Ed.]. The fire which will burn our bodies is the fire which will resurrect the Jewish people." For Rabbi Wasserman and his brother-in-law, Rabbi Chaim Ozer Grodensky of Vilna, the *churban* [destruction—Ed.] had a "positive meaning: the more evil/punishment, the closer the redemption. Each moment of cosmic catharsis, of suffering, is a moment of messianic entry into history." All of the actors in the drama were "instruments" of God's plan to transform history.[43]

Other rabbis used alternative explanations, such as that Israel's suffering was divine chastisement intended to turn the people back to God. The sin for which they were being punished was variously identified as assimilation, or the idolatry of Zionism[44], or the abandonment of Torah in favor of secularism or socialism. Writing in the Fall of 1939, after the *pogrom* [attack—Ed.] of Kristallnacht [Night of the Broken Glass, Berlin, November 10-11, 1939—Ed.] and the beginning of Polish Jewry's agony, Rabbi Wasserman put the blame on all of the foregoing "sins," and held that the punishment fitted the crime. Nevertheless, he added, the sufferings were all for the sake of reminding Jews of their Jewishness and recalling them to their intended role in redemption.[45]

Contrariwise, Rabbi Issachar Shlomo Teichtal of Budapest in late 1943 came to the conviction that opposition to political Zionism had indirectly contributed to and compounded the tragedy of European Jewry. The purpose of their suffering was to be a stimulant to the Jews in *galut* [exile—Ed.] to return to the Source—the land and his true Jewish self. In this way suffering could be the "prelude to redemption," the beginning of *tikkun* [repair—Ed.], by shattering defective reality.[46]

After the war Ignaz Maybaum also dared to speak of a constructive outflow from the horrors of the Shoah. By God's "severe decree" [*gezirah*], the history of humankind had been thrust into a new age. The old obstructions to progress and community were now removed: the medieval Christian dogma that outside the Church there is no salvation, and the medieval Jewish Codes that "worked on the principle: outside the *din* [law—Ed.], you cannot be a Jew." Now "Jew and Christian meet as equals...." The third churban [his designation for the Shoah] makes possible "messianic progress," just as the two earlier *gezirot* did [when the two Temples were destroyed].

Maybaum was driven to find some such meaning because he "refused to consider the possibility that Jewish history was devoid of meaning." For the Jew, "Auschwitz is the great trial. The Jew is tried, tested, like Abraham at Moriah," but the faithful remnant will pass the test. There was no question for Maybaum but that the six million "died an innocent death; they died because of the sins of other. Western man must, in repentance, say of the Jew what Isaiah says of the Servant of God: 'Surely, our diseases he did bear, and our pain he carried....he was wounded because of our transgressions, he was crushed because of our iniquities' [43:4, 5]. Jewish martyrdom explains the meaning [of this passage]....better than the medieval Christian dogma [of the cross] ever did."[47]

How do survivors of the Shoah respond to the various ways by which Jewish tradition and thinkers have sought to deal with suffering? There is, of course, no way to answer that question definitively. However, Reeve Robert Brenner's detailed survey of seven hundred survivors [camp inmates and those who survived outside the camps], and the effect or non-effect of the Shoah on these persons' religious beliefs and observances is most helpful.

With reference to the thesis that in the Shoah the Jewish people were the sacrifice for humanity's sins, only 11 percent gave affirmative responses. One who did said, "....the good and the best Jews died and the worst lived on. The only way you can make sense out of that is to assume that the one was sacrificed for the other...." But one who disagreed spoke out strongly against any concept of vicarious suffering: "God is not unjust and He is not a Christian God who can offer some third party, Jesus or the Jews of Europe, to die for the sins of others....there is no vicarious atonement in Judaism in a way which would have God sacrifice six million of the innocent for the guilty; nor were they sacrificial lambs, or goats dispatched to the wilderness to absolve the sins of others."

A significant 72 percent voiced the opinion that God was not involved at all and that the destruction was due entirely to human relationships.

Some of the traditional answers were not given by a single survivor in this study: for example, the explanation that evil—the radical evil of the Shoah—is illusory; or the idea that the sufferings of the righteous are "trials of Divine Love;" or that God permits or causes suffering in order to reveal the divine power; or that suffering is God's way of strengthening individuals or refining their nature or purifying their moral character. [The suffering of six million "for the benefit of those that lived? That's insane....What a great injustice to the dead that would be...."]

Not one of the survivors in this study "thought the world-to-come—whether as afterlife, heaven, messianic future, resurrection, or whatever a survivor may conceive—was sufficient alone to make sense out of the Holocaust" [although some believed into a world-to-come]. As one said, "nothing, no possible reward however great which we may be entitled to and which we may receive in a world-to-come can ever compensate for the suffering which we endured in this world."

The single most overwhelming response showed that 98 percent of the survivors in this study rejected the theory that Jewish martyrdom in the Shoah was the result of divine judgment.[48]

Albert Friedlander echoes and reemphasizes this judgment. Any such conclusions are misuses of the Shoah, even if they were made by victims or survivors of the Shoah.

They become "a defense for established position; a substitute for religion, and a substitute for thinking." Just as Jews had to reshape their theology after the previous churban, Jews of today must seek for new understanding. After Auschwitz, Jewish self-definition rejects "imposed concepts" of Jewish destiny "that view Israel as the vicarious/atonement, as a lamb of God or a suffering messiah figure. The *tremendum*....may never be defined as Jewish destiny."[49]

Richard Rubenstein and John Roth agree with Friedlander and Emil Fackenheim and the majority of Brenner's survivors in insisting that while perhaps in some instances the belief that "human suffering may be considered instrumental or redemptive," the "Holocaust defies such hope. No imaginable good-to-come will ever make up completely for what was lost in the Nazi era."[50]

In a profound Jewish theological response to the Shoah and its questions, Andre Neher focuses on the silence of God wherever and whenever it has been felt. He affirms that the testing of Job and of Naomi [and by extension, of the Six Million] is "inauthentic" for, unlike Abraham, they were never asked for any decision or response. A destiny was simply imposed on them; their loved ones were taken from them and destroyed. "Job is alone, cut off from his children by the hurricane of death. And to the end of his experience and of his book, he will remain alone; and though he is given other children, none of his dead children will ever be given back to him....The testing of Job is marred by a failure, that supreme failure which is death."[51] [Compare, if you will, a comment from one of Brenner's survivors: "Ten more wives and a hundred more children will never replace the one beloved wife and the two precious children I lost to the Nazis."[52] And then, Neher protests, we are told, as if the burden of Job's innocent suffering were not enough, that Job was a substitute for Abraham; that God had transferred "all the trials of the combat" from Abraham to his nephew, Job; that Job suffered vicariously for Abraham [as Isaac suffered for Israel, and the Jewish people suffer for the world][53] Why? Because of Abraham's response to God's testing: Neher examines the text and concludes that Abraham decided that he had had enough [even though he had had a choice—whether to obey God's command, and even though Isaac was restored to him]. Having said "Yes" to the test of Mount Moriah, "Abraham could never again repeat his acquiescence, and, in fact, he was not to do so." He decided he was "willing to pay the price of the silence of God" rather than risk another test.[54] Therefore God needed Job.

Does such imposed vicarious suffering help us in our troubling quest for answers or does it only make the task more painful?

And Jews after the Shoah? Almost none of the six million were given any choice; and most [all?] experienced God's silence. Can or will Jews today say "Yes" to the continuation of the covenant relationship with its concomitant possibility of further testing or suffering on behalf of others" Or have they had enough of an ethic of suffering?[55] The answer is neither a simple "No" nor "Yes." In one very important sense, most Jews have said "Yes" by refusing to abandon their Jewish identity and by refusing to opt out of the community. Emil Fackenheim believes that Jews today are responding to the death camps as ancient rabbis would have done—by seeking "to meet the absolute evil of the death camps in the only way absolute evil can be met—by an absolute opposition on which one stakes one's life." As he so tellingly points out, "In the age after Auschwitz, for any Jew to survive as a Jew and *bring up his children as any kind of Jew*....is itself a monumental act of faithfulness." For every Jew today knows that Jews were murdered in Nazi Europe not because of their faith, or lack of faith, but because of the faith of their grandparents. And they cannot know whether their grandchildren will be sought out for destruction for that same reason. No one wishes to prepare a generation of sacrificial offerings; yet no one wishes to collaborate in finishing Hitler's job."[56]

Perhaps the resolution of the dilemma is the one already undertaken: a *willingness to to reaffirm the covenant, in spite of God's silence in the Shoah, as long as they have Jewish sovereignty.*[57] The "Yes" is qualified by this condition. For most Jews are now convinced that martyrdom is no longer the way of sanctifying God's Name or of fulfilling Jewish existence. Therefore, Jewish powerlessness and vulnerability must at last come to an end along with martyrdom. Jews have learned that they will have to make their use of power in ways they dislike as part of the payment for their intention to survive, and to survive as a free people. Jews may have to die defending their right to life as a people but they will die fighting. For what function can martyrdom have when the entire people is being threatened with extinction? Can dead covenant partners witness to God's love or cooperate in perfecting the creation? Is not the covenant meant to be a means of sustaining life? [As the Warsaw Ghetto approached its final demise, a few of the surviving rabbis were troubled by such questions and came to somewhat similar conclusions: the surviving people were to do whatever they could to live as a way of sanctifying God's Name—*Kiddush Ha-Shem*—and preserving the covenant.[58]

As Gordon Tucker puts it, the State of Israel is intrinsic to the "restorative, history-respecting interpretation of redemption." It fits the Biblical meaning of *geulah* [redemption] in the very concrete meaning of that term: a state, a society, in time and history, that makes and is affected by history. It also fits with the Biblical understanding of "salvation" which encompassed the survival of the remnant and the return of those "saved" to their land. The modern State of Israel "is worthy of blessing and is precious because it is a restoration that breathes life into real human beings and into their collectivity. [Moreover, it demonstrates partial redemption is possible and has value.] Redemption need not be 'all or nothing'."[59]

Elie Wiesel is troubled by the traditional answers and tales particularly as they speak of suffering and determine response to it. Although Abraham dared to query

God and remonstrate with Him on behalf of others, he was silent when God told him to make of his son an *olah* [a totally burnt offering]. Why did not Abraham protest on behalf of this innocent son?[60]

Must we not also wonder rather than celebrating Abraham's obedi-ence? By his not protesting in this instance, did Abraham consign his people to being perpetual victims? And even to their being participants in their own victimization? Was it not his silence before God that led the father in Auschwitz on the even or *Rosh Ha-Shanah* [Jewish New Year—Ed.], 1944, not only to conclude that he was prohibited from ransoming his son from the death barracks [because another father's son would be put there in his place], but also to conclude that it was a merit to offer his only son to God as Father Abraham had done?[61]

Wiesel also challenges Job—why did he not carry his protest, his accusations against God, to the end? Why did he suddenly give in? "His resignation as a man was an insult to man....He should have continued to protest...."[62]

The need to protest is one of Wiesel's major themes: protest against human injustice and protest against divine injustice. For Wiesel, failure to protest is a failure to be involved in the divine-human drama: it is a renunciation of responsibility, and thus it enables evil and suffering to prevail.[63] "In those years [of the Shoah], anyone who did not question God was not a true believer....I believe God himself became a question mark then."[64]

Though Wiesel remains within the tradition, he also goes beyond it by pushing the tradition into confronting the revolutionary difference with which it was faced in the years of the Third Reich and which it cannot ignore even now since the precedent has been set. His protests and reworking of the Bible stories are serious and existential attempts to make Biblical faith face that ultimate test.[65]

The precedent of the Shoah requires not only protest to and against God and against any social injustice, but it also requires that the Jewish people cannot ignore the consequences of powerlessness. Wiesel is convinced that "the Jewish people today could not survive physically or spiritually if it were not for Israel." "Israel is the cornerstone, the backbone of Jewish existence everywhere." [In 1970 he also said that he believed that if Israel were to "end in tragedy, it would be the end of the human race....that for the first time man's fate and the Jewish fate have converged....If the world will again try to kill the Jew, it will mean the end of the world."[66]

XII. Responses to Suffering: Christian

How do Christians speak of suffering after the Shoah? Have their thoughts and words been changed at all by that cataclysm in history and human relations? Do they feel any need to change them? Or do they assume that their theology has said the final words on the subject based on their inherited understanding of Jesus death?

Most books of Christian theology still are written and read, and most sermons are preached, as if the ghastly slaughter of six million individuals had never occurred and certainly as if it has no relevance for Christian thought. Those "mainline" theologians who do not mention the Shoah are apt to find a nice little niche for it and then surround it with the same theology that could have been written before 1933 or 1939-1968. On the basis of the theologically-rooted conviction that Christ's experience on the cross encompasses [and even exceeds] all human agony whenever and wherever it occurs, theological constructs do not have to be altered in order to take something new into account for nothing new matters. For such Christians, Auschwitz can be identified as the Golgotha of the Jewish people in the twentieth century without considering whether there are any significant differences in that Golgotha and the original one, or wondering whether Auschwitz has something to say to us about how the church has been interpreting Golgotha all the intervening centuries.[67]

Yet that is exactly what facing the Shoah requires—a recognition that a rupture in history occurred. The German Catholic theologian Johannes-Baptist Metz, who acknowledges the radical demands that the Shoah makes on Christianity, is insistent that Christianity cannot do theology with its back toward Auschwitz; and once facing Auschwitz, it must realize that Christian theology in its entirety must be revised. *"We will have to forego the temptation to interpret the suffering of the Jewish people from our standpoint in terms of saving history. Under no circumstances is it our task to mystify this suffering!"* [68] Robert McAfee Brown agrees: "No theology can encompass this event so that its wounds are closed, its scars healed. The event forever precludes easy faith in God or faith in humanity....Neither faith, I believe, can confront the Holocaust without in some ways being transformed."[69]

If one were to identify Auschwitz with Golgotha, what could the redemptive purpose of six million deaths be? [After all, in the Christian scheme, Christ has already made redemption available to all humanity, so what else can six million "crucifixions" accomplish?"][70] Pope John Paul II and John Cardinal O'Conner have attempted to grapple with that question.

Addressing the Jews of Warsaw on June 14, 1987, the Pope confessed, "We believe in the purifying power of suffering. The more atrocious the suffering, the greater the purification. The more painful the experiences, the greater the hope....You continue your particular vocation [as a saving warning]....This is to be your mission in the contemporary world...." [It would appear that the Pope was saying that the Jewish people will and must continue to suffer according to the divide plan.] On June 25, 1988, after visiting Mauthausen, the People further observed that "the Jews 'enriched the world by their suffering' and their death was like the grain which must fall into the earth in order to bear fruit, in the words of Jesus who brings salvation."[71]

The Holocaust Now

Cardinal O'Conner confesses that he approaches the agonizing question of the Shoah within the context of his own theology of suffering. He is convinced that "the crucifixion and its enormous power continue mystically and spiritually in this world in our day, and will continue until the end of time. Christ....continues to suffer in His Body, the Church [and through the Church in all people]....quite, quite really. And this suffering has a purpose and an effect [on other persons elsewhere in the world], as does ours if we conjoin it with His, if we 'offer it up.'" Because of its effect [in the case of Christ's suffering, the "salvation of souls"], it is a gift to the world. Consequently, "if the suffering of the crucifixion was infinitely redemptive, the suffering of the Holocaust, *potentially conjoined with it*, is incalculably redemptive."[72]

Two questions arise: How is the Jewish suffering in the Shoah to be conjoined to Christ's on the cross? [Can the suffering of those long since dead be offered up by someone else on their behalf?] And what if it was not then [or is not now] offered up? Although an unknown number of Jews went to their deaths affirming their trust in God, certainly a larger number of the victims would not have done so given the circumstances under which they perished, or would not even have been in a condition to do so, and certainly not with the name of Christ on their lips. Is their suffering then non-redemptive and hence meaningless? What is their fate? Is this theology consigning them to an even greater invisibility and non-being than the Nazi killers sought to achieve? Using Metz's dictum, we must ask whether the Cardinal's back is not turned to Auschwitz even though he thinks he is facing it?

Are Christians such as O'Conner *asking Jews* of today to offer up their own pain [as survivors, relatives of victims, or vicarious sufferers of Hitler's obsessive hatred]? Does this mean their having to be accepting of that pain because of it having a possible positive effect somewhere in the world? Can such victims believe that? Is asking for such a response not further burdening those already victimized or intended for victimization? Would it not be more appropriate for such churchpersons to urge that their own community take on [in whatever ways are possible] the pain of the victims and survivors and vicariously bear that pain as fellow sufferers? Not in order to offer it up—which would be presumptuous—but simply by sharing the pain and fear perhaps slightly to alleviate it for the people of suffering.

But there are additional and perhaps even more troublesome questions raised by such a theology of suffering:

[1] Does it actually work? Does one person's suffering really alleviate someone else's condition, as Cardinals O'Connor and Cushing believe? If the amount of pain experienced in the Shoah really were to make a difference, should not the world be on a mountain peak of tranquility and joy? [In point of fact, the reality of the world condition is the exact opposite: The expertise of torture and mass killing has been exported

and appropriated globally by individuals and political groups ready to murder for the sake of power or some ideology.] If someone were to respond to this objection by saying that the fault was that of the victims for not "offering up" their suffering, that person would be wrong insofar as we know that many numbers of the Shoah victims did exactly that in their own way of ultimate trust. But more importantly, such an observation would fault persons for not doing something that they had little or no basis for believing would be effective. Moreover, it would place an unendurable [and inexcusable] burden on the very people who suffered in extremis, not to mention the insuperable burden on anyone who might face such extremities in the future.

[2] Does the concept of vicarious suffering really help? Does one or more person's suffering really atone for the sins of others, as both Christianity and Judaism have affirmed? We have no way of proving that it does. Perhaps we need to ask whether the suffering of one should vicariously benefit another?[73] Is not the recognition of personal and group responsibility the most significant aspect of any kind of rehabilitation and betterment of society? And is not the acceptance of responsibility undercut by theologies of vicarious suffering?[74]

[3] Can we consider "Auschwitz" [the Nazis' whirlwind of mass destruction] in the same category as other suffering? Lawrence Langer points out that the Nazis removed any "exemplary" possibilities from the victims' sufferings and deaths when they cut them off from any appeal "for sympathy, status, or justice [or from] martyrdom." In the circumstances of "Auschwitz" the very word suffering is inappropriate; atrocity is more correct. "The Nazi evil not only subverted good as we know it; the forms it took poisoned the possibility of a redemptive suffering to counteract the moral paralysis it generated."[75]

Terrence Des Pres insists that in such extremity death can never be a victory. "The luxury of sacrifice—[i.e.] the strategic choice of death to resolve irreconcilable moral conflicts—is meaningless in a world where any person's death only contributes to the success of evil."[76]

XIII. Against Finding Meaning in Umerited Suffering

There is a danger in all efforts to find meaning in unmerited suffering—not just that of the Shoah. Just as the concept of martyrdom can be a veil to mask the reality of death, so we may be obscuring unacceptable agony by a veil of good results.

How much of the effort to give suffering a purifying or redemptive power is a result of our not knowing how else to cope with it? Trying desperately to make something good come out of evil? Trying to provide ourselves with reassurance that pain is not meaningless and that evil will not have the last word? And how much of the commendation of the meek and powerless is a result of our not wanting the status quo upset, or of fearing the uncertainty of change?

Instead of speaking about rediscovering the capacity to suffer, or about God's indebtedness to His people for allowing divine forbearance with human sin to persist[77], would we not be more advised to listen to the witness and warning of some contemporary spokespeople among the Blacks, women, Hispanics, poor, tortured [along with the victims and survivors of the Shoah]?[78]

Along with survivors of the death camps, these victims of oppression insist that suffering does *not* ennoble, does *not* provide moral stature or spiritual depth or refined sensibility. It does *not* make a person superior or more authentic than a non-sufferer. [In fact, many feel that they can never fulfill their potential to be human *because of* what they have been subjected to.] These people tell us that as long as we try to comfort ourselves or others with ideas about the positive effects of suffering—including a redemptive function—the less we will be inclined to reject it as the evil it is, and the less we may be inclined to fight against it.[79]

Similarly, these oppressed groups are insistent that powerlessness, and the admonition to find ultimate justification in their oppressed condition, is evil. In Des Pres' words, "In a landscape of disaster....where people die in thousands, where machines reduce courage to stupidity and dying to complicity with aggression, it makes no sense to speak of death's dignity or of its communal blessing."[80]

XIV. God's Pathos/Suffering

Does it help to say that God suffers because of the pain inflicted on Her/His human children, and suffers *along with* those persons? It appears to me that the only benefit in such a view can come from two realizations. The first would be the acknowledgement that *suffering is not part of God's will* or *wish for the creation;* that it is the reverse of what God intended. Therefore, all attempts to find God's beneficent action in any event involving suffering would be incoherent with the divine will.

The second would be a recognition that God's suffering represents the continual threat of destruction and dissolution that faces humankind. Of all the attempts to consider alternative ways of understanding the divine-human relationship and the theodicy question I find Hans Jonas essay "The Concept of God after Auschwitz" particularly appealing and perceptive [as well as succinct]. He has suggested that we recognize that God has been a *suffering* God who is altered from the moment of creation; is a *becoming* God who is altered by what happens in the world; is a *caring* God who is involved with what He cares about; is an *endangered* God who has risked Himself and thus made Himself vulnerable to human events. These events *leave their mark on God*. The cries of "the gassed and burnt children of Auschwitz, of the defaced, de-humanized phantoms of the camps, and of all the other numberless victims of the other man-made holocausts of our time" must now hang over our world "as a dark, mournful, and accusing cloud" and eternity must look down upon us "with a frown, wounded itself and perturbed in its depths." In turn, won't there always be "some resonance to that [heavenly] condition" in our own earthly condition?[81]

XV. Concluding Thoughts

Humans have a tendency to make comparisons and fit new happenings into existing thought patterns. But a contemporary Christian scholar argues that the "Holocaust and all other holocausts which followed in its train or preceded it....have rendered all our previous explanations of suffering either obsolete or insufficient." And death camp survivors attest to the "utter irreconcilability" of their experience with any "prior consoling system of values." Similarly, their anguish "teaches nothing about developing an enduring attitude toward suffering that might eventually lead toward some form of healing, forgiveness, or redemption. The atrocities they beheld or endured were *beyond suffering, as they were beyond the framework of conventional theodicy.*"[82]

The ineradicable problem of the Shoah will not let us rest. We may be better advised to let it remain an unanswered question, forever troubling us, so that we do not hide the warning that it provides and do not obscure the mystery of evil to which it should make us ever more alert. At the same time, since it would be criminal to make the Shoah an event so totally apart from our world that it has nothing to say to us, the troubling questions it raises should make us rethink our traditional answers and propositions about suffering [and punishment]. We also need to be careful about the rhetoric we use about suffering [especially of others] in contrast to the reality by which most of us lead our own lives, so that the way we respond to the oppression and suffering of others will be coherent with what our own instinctive reactions would be were we in their shoes.

The Holocaust Now

Asking and Listening, Understanding and Doing

For John Roth, the construction of a proper methodology with which to approach the Shoah is predicated upon four interwoven acts: asking the right questions, listening for the right words of God, understanding those words, and doing that which is required to mend the world. For him [and for others], it is the works of Elie Wiesel which have yielded those all-important insights of understanding and doing which frame the above-mentioned responsibilities, insights such as the importance of questions over answers, particularly the question of "why;" the inter-relationship of language to life; the "sins" of passivity, indifference, neutrality, and inactivity; the importance of protest against evil and injustice; and the demand for an accounting even from God because one is involved in the human community. As with a number of other contributors, Roth cannot divorce theology from ethics, either before, during or after the Shoah.

SLJ

The Holocaust Now

ASKING AND LISTENING, UNDERSTANDING AND DOING: SOME CONDITIONS FOR RESPONDING TO THE SHOAH RELIGIOUSLY

John K. Roth

I. Introduction

> "I pray to the God within me that He will give me the strength to ask Him the right questions."—Moshe, in Elie Wiesel's *Night*.

Born in Turin, Italy, a Jew named Primo Levi took his degree in chemistry from the university there in 1941. He was arrested two years later for resisting fascism. Deported from Italy to Auschwitz, Levi was sent to Monowitz, one of the main camp's many forced labor satellites. Liberated in late January, 1945, he eventually found his way back to Italy, resumed his career as a chemist, and also became an acclaimed author who wrote about the Shoah with an honesty that few others have matched.

Only once did I meet Primo Levi and hear him speak. He gave the featured address at the annual Shoah commemoration in my hometown, Claremont, California. On that occasion, as on so many others, he showed himself to be life-affirming. And yet, on that night, as on so many others, darkness shadowed Levi's words as he reflected on memory. In what was apparently a suicide attempt, a fall down a stairwell in April, 1987, cost him his life.

Primo Levi's best-known book about the Shoah is *Survival in Auschwitz*. It is a classic memoir about his year there, which Levi called "a journey towards nothingness."[1] Although Levi's writings speak about many things, rarely do they say much directly about God. *Survival in Auschwitz*, however, contains a striking exception to that rule. It came to mind almost immediately when, as a philosopher and a Christian, I began to craft this essay about asking and listening, understanding and doing, which are crucial conditions for responding religiously to the Shoah, the Nazi attempt to annihilate Jewish life root and branch, and to destroy millions of others whom the Nazis took to be *lebensunwertes Leben* ["life unworthy of life"].

As Levi describes it, the scene that came to my mind took place on a Sunday after-

The Holocaust Now

noon in October, 1944. All the prisoners in Levi's part of the camp were ordered to their crowded quarters. As in all the huts—Levi's was number forty-eight out of sixty—everyone received a "card with his number, name, profession, age and nationality" and obeyed the order to "undress completely, except for shoes."[2] Levi and his comrades then waited for the "selection." It would sentence some to the gas chambers. Others would be reprieved to work a while longer.

Levi's account goes on to describe how the SS "inspectors" eventually reached hut forty-eight to process his group. The procedure was as random and capricious as it was quick and simple. One by one, each prisoner ran a few steps and then surrendered his identity card to an SS man who, in turn, passed the card to a man on his right or left. "This," writes Levi, "is the life or death of each of us. In three or four minutes a hut of two hundred men is 'done,' as is the whole camp of twelve thousand men in the course of the afternoon."[3] Not quite "done," however, because in the part of the camp where Levi worked, it usually took two or three days before those "selected" actually went to the gas.

Meanwhile, the prisoners could figure out whose card went left, whose went right, and what the difference meant. Thus, Levi continues by noting what he observed that evening, after the meager portion of soup had been served and devoured, and how he felt about what he saw and heard:

> Silence slowly prevailed and then, from my bunk on the top row, I see and hear old Kuhn praying aloud, with his beret on his head, swaying backwards and forwards violently. Kuhn is thanking God because he had not been chosen.
>
> Kuhn is out of his senses. Does he not see Beppo the Greek in the bunk next to him, Beppo who is twenty years old and is going to the chamber the day after tomorrow and knows it and lies there looking fixedly at the light without saying anything and without even thinking any more? Can Kuhn fail to realize that next time it will be his turn? Does Kuhn not understand that what has happened today is an abomination, which no propitiatory prayer, no pardon, no expiation by the guilty, which nothing at all in the power of man can ever clean again?
>
> If I were God, I would spit at Kuhn's prayer.[4]

II. Asking

Another Shoah survivor, Elie Wiesel, writes in ways akin to, but also quite different from, Primo Levi's. For example, at the beginning of his classic memoir, *Night*, which details Wiesel's experiences as a manchild in Auschwitz at fifteen, he introduces one of his teachers. His name was Moshe, and the year was 1941. Although the Shoah was under way, it had not yet touched Wiesel's hometown of Sighet in what was then Hungary. One day the twelve-year-old Wiesel asked his teacher, "And why to you pray, Moshe?" His teacher replied, "I pray to the God within me that He will give me the strength to ask Him the right questions."[5]

Together, Elie Wiesel and Primo Levi might make one consider that "the right questions" include asking God: "Did You spit at Auschwitz?" "In particular, did You spit at a prayer of thanks offered by one who 'has not been chosen'?" To those questions others might be added: If God did spit at Auschwitz, if God did spit at a prayer of thanks offered by one "who has not been chosen," did God do more than that? And if, in either case, God failed to spit, did God do anything else instead?

Care should be taken before one even considers responding to such potent questions, for they may be beyond answering, even by God. Elie Wiesel suggests as much in one of his gem-like dialogues. Following another "selection," Wiesel invites meditation on some last words between a mother and her daughter:

> Where are we going? Tell me. Do you know?
> *I don't know, my little girl.*
>
> I am afraid. Is it wrong, tell me, is it wrong to be afraid?
> *I don't know; I don't think so.*
>
> In all my life I have never been so afraid.
> *Never.*
>
> But I would like to know where we are going. Say, do you know? Where are we going?
> *To the end of the world, little girl. We are going to the end of the world.*
>
> Is that far?
> *No, not really.*
>
> You see, I am really tired. Is it wrong, tell me, is it wrong to be so tired?
> *Everybody is tired, my little girl.*
>
> Even God?
> *I don't know. You will have to ask Him yourself.*[6]

The Holocaust Now

The Jewish theologian, Irving Greenberg, applies—perhaps even to God—a telling principle when one considers "answers" to "the right questions" raised by the Shoah: "No statement," he contends, "no statement, theological or otherwise, should be made that would not be credible in the presence of....burning children."[7] That criterion—could any other be more demanding?—makes every statement problematic. In the Presbyterian church where I worship, for example, it is customary for the reader of Scripture to begin with an admonition to "listen, listen closely for the Word of God." What do we Christians hear, what should we hear, if we "listen, listen closely for the Word of God" after the Shoah?

A sound response to that question deserves deep and thoughtful consideration. But surely, at the very least, it directs us Christians toward repentant responsibility that changes and corrects anti-Jewish elements in the Christian tradition that helped to create what Primo Levi rightly called "an abomination." Heeding such a call—Christian Scripture would say it entails being "doers of the Word, not hearers only" [James 1:22]—will not by any means set everything right, but it is an imperative shirked at everyone's peril, including God's.

The latter point deserves emphasis because of a principle stressed by Emil Fackenheim, another leading Jewish thinker. Adolf Hitler, argues Fackenheim, should have no "posthumous victories."[8] Fackenheim makes that point in relation to Jewish faithfulness after the Shoah. Fully comprehended, it becomes an imperative for Christians, too. For Fackenheim shows that social reality decisively includes Christianity, even, indeed perhaps especially, after Auschwitz. As a Jew, he is convinced that the world's mending requires not only Christianity's elimination but its reconstruction. That reconstruction depends on asking the right questions and on listening for the right responses. It also depends on understanding that becomes doing what is right.[9]

As a Christian, one reason I go to church is that I hear things there that I do not hear elsewhere. A case in point involves a poem included in a recent sermon by my Pastor, John Najarian. The poem's author was Rainer Maria Rilke. He did not live to witness the Shoah's consuming fire, but, in 1899, this German-speaking writer penned a verse worth hearing after Auschwitz. Listening to it with post-Shoah ears, the poem's premonitions anticipate some Jewish and Christian voices among the defenseless who perished under the Nazis. Rilke may speak, too, for those Jews and Christians living after Auschwitz who try to be faithful to Emil Fackenheim's principle that Hitler shall have no posthumous victories.

> What will you do, God, when I die?
> When I, your pitcher, broken, lie?
> When I, your drink, go stale or dry?

I am your garb, the trade you ply,
you lose your meaning, losing me.

Homeless without me, you will be
robbed of your welcome, warm and sweet.
I am your sandals: your tired feet
will wander bare for want of me.

Your mighty cloak will fall away.
Your glance that on my cheek was laid
and pillowed warm, will seek, dismayed,
the comfort that I offered once—
to lie, as sunset colors fade
in the cold lap of alien stones.

What will you do, God? I am afraid.[10]

Responding to the Shoah religiously is an awesome task. Properly, it can cause one to be afraid. "I would like to know where we are going," Elie Wiesel writes for his little sister, who, in all of her life, has never been so afraid and never shall be again. Her "we" may include God as well as humankind. But if Christians and Jews can muster the right determination, the answer may not be "To the end of the world, little girl. We are going to the end of the world." Instead, the response might be, "We are going to mend the world." That, I believe, is the direction that should map the asking and listening, the understanding and doing, that are basic conditions for responding to the Shoah religiously. To consider in more detail how that mapping might work, Christians especially can profit by listening to Jewish voices. Elie Wiesel's is an example.

III. Listening

Elie Wiesel insists that the essence of being Jewish is "never to give up—never to yield to despair."[11] Keeping that imperative is anything but easy, as *Twilight* shows. Its story does so by exploring "the domain of madness," which is never far from the center of Wiesel's consciousness, and by illuminating, in particular, Maimonides' conviction—its serves as the novel's epigraph—that "the world couldn't exist without madmen."[12]

Arguably the most complex of Wiesel's novels, Twilight defies simple summary. One of its dominant themes, however, emerges when Raphael Lipkin's telephone rings at midnight. This survivor of the Shoah, now a university scholar, hears an anonymous voice denouncing Pedro: "Professor, let me tell you about your friend Pedro. He is totally amoral. A sadist. He made me suffer. And not just me, there were many others."[13] Pedro is Raphael's friend indeed. More than once he has saved Raphael from the despair that repeatedly threatens to engulf him.

They first met in September 1945. Raphael had returned to Rovidok, the Eastern European town that had once been his home. There, on Sabbath afternoons well before Pedro had entered Raphael's life, he initially encountered madness. Raphael would go to the town's asylum to visit an old man who had become his friend. Although Raphael did not understand all the old man had to say, his friend's impassioned vision never left him. Some time later, an encounter with madness of another kind—it, too, never left him—invaded Raphael's Rovidok. Germans occupied that place in September 1939. Raphael was among those who had to watch them hang an old Jew—it seems the victim was Raphael's friend from the asylum—for resisting the occupation.

This death was but the first of many losses Raphael witnessed in Rovidok and elsewhere. All too soon nothing remained for him there. That town could never be his home again. So Raphael left with Pedro, who worked for a clandestine Jewish organization that helped survivors. Pedro's help was more than physical. Akin to Raphael's old friend from the asylum, he taught the young Lipkin: "It may not be in man's power to erase society's evil, but he must become its conscience; it may not be in his power to create the glories of the night, but he must wait for them and describe their beauty."[14]

Much later, the midnight calls keep coming. What's more, the caller seems to know too much. Eventually suggesting where the "truth" about Pedro can be found, the calls lure Raphael to upstate New York. There a Dr. Benedictus—only gradually does Raphael sense that, in spite of his name and calling, this "healer" may be the malevolent caller—administers the Mountain Clinic. It "caters to patients, men and women—mostly men—whose schizophrenia is linked in some mysterious way, to Ancient History, to Biblical times."[15]

Raphael seeks the truth about Pedro as he encounters persons who think they are Biblical characters such as Adam, Cain, the Messiah, and even God. Their madness, which is rooted in an inability to come to terms with humanity or God after Auschwitz, is compounded for Raphael by the attempt that is underway to discredit Pedro. Thus, Raphael edges toward the abyss that awaits him: "What am I to do?" Raphael asks a Pedro who is both there and not there. "To whom shall I turn for a little light, a little warmth? Madness is lying in wait for me and I am alone."[16]

The madness that lies in wait for Raphael would destroy him, and, if he were truly left alone, Raphael might succumb to it. Perhaps that is what the telephone voice intended by calling Pedro into question and Raphael toward despair. Recognition of that possibility, recollection that "Pedro taught me to love mankind and celebrate its humanity despite its flaws," renewed realization that Pedro's "enemy is my enemy"—such forces rally Raphael's resistance.[17]

Asking and Listening, Understanding and Doing

By reaffirming a summons to save, Raphael's battle against madness that destroys does not ensure a tranquil equilibrium. A different kind of madness, the moral madness without which the world could not exist, is the prospect instead. "The caller tried to drive you out of my life," Raphael tells the absent Pedro. "He failed. Does that mean I've won? Hardly. I cry into the night and the night does not answer. Never mind, I will shout and shout until I go deaf, until I go mad."[18]

Twilight is not the first time a man named Pedro has appeared in Elie Wiesel's novels and provided saving inspiration. Differing from his namesake in *Twilight* because he is not Jewish, another Pedro is a decisive presence in *The Town Beyond the Wall*. This novel, the one most closely linked to *Twilight*, begins fittingly with an epigraph from Dostoevsky: "I have a plan—to go mad."[19] It also starts at twilight and under circumstances that can drive one to madness that destroys.

Once Michael's home, Szerenszevaros ["the city of luck"] is now in the vise of Communist victors over Nazi tyrants. Secretly returning to see whether anyone can be found, Michael stands before his former home. Ages ago, a face watched silently there while Jews were sent away. The face, seeking a hatred from Michael to match its own hidden guilt, informs the police. Michael finds himself imprisoned in walls within his past, tortured to tell a story that cannot be told: there is no political plot to reveal; his captors would never accept the simple truth of his desire to see his homeland once more; his fried, Pedro, who returned with him, must be protected.

Michael holds out. He resists an escape into one kind of madness by opening himself to another. His cellmate, Eliezer, dwells in catatonic silence. But Michael hears and heeds the advice that he knows his fried Pedro would give him: "That's exactly what I want you to do: re-create the universe. Restore that boy's sanity. Cure him. He'll save you."[20]

What of such a plan? *Twilight*, as well as *The Town Beyond the Wall* and some thirty more of Wiesel's books, follows *Night*. All of *Night*'s sequels, in one way or another, explore ways in which the world might be mended. Nonetheless, we know that in the order of things dawn, day, and especially twilight leave night close by. Yet even if, as Wiesel contends, "everything to do with Auschwitz must, in the end, lead into darkness," questions remain concerning what that darkness might be and whether the leading into darkness is indeed the end.[21] For if *The Town Beyond the Wall* concludes with Michael's coming "to the end of his strength," it also ends with "the night....receding, as on a mountain before dawn."[22] Similarly, as *Twilight* moves toward night, "from far away, a star appears. Uncommonly bright...."[23]

Twilight and *The Town Beyond the Wall* are both about friendship, another theme that is never far from the center of Wiesel's vision. Both Michael and Raphael have friends named Pedro. In each case, Pedro serves as a special kind of teacher. These relationships transcend the physical limits of space and time. Even when absent from

The Town Beyond the Wall or from *Twilight*, the two Pedros are very much present for their friends. Michael and Raphael take courage from the challenging encouragement that each one's Pedro provides.

Michael and Raphael have learned from the men named Pedro. What they have discerned resonates with lessons I am trying to learn as a Christian and a philosopher who seeks to ask the right questions and to listen so that understanding follows and becomes doing what is right. Considering further, then, the authorship of Elie Wiesel as it moves from *Night* to *Twilight*, with journeys to *The Town Beyond the Wall* and meetings with Pedro among the multitude of encounters in between, here are ten of his major insights—two sets of five that focus first on understanding and then on doing. Simple and yet complex, complex and yet simple, each point is central, I believe, to Wiesel's way of thinking and living. None of the insights is an abstract principle; all are forged in fire that threatens to consume. For those reasons these themes from Wiesel have integrity, credibility, and durability that make them worthy guidelines for all seasons.

IV. Understanding

Elie Wiesel seeks understanding—but not too much. While wanting people to study the Shoah, he alerts them to the dangers of thinking that they do nor can or even should know everything about it. While wanting people to meet as brothers and sisters, he cautions that such meetings will be less than honest if differences are glossed over, minimized, or forgiven. While wanting humankind and God to confront each other, he contends that easy acceptance is at once too much and too little to accept. Wiesel's understanding is never facile, obvious or automatic. Nevertheless, its rhythm can be learned. Five of his movements follow.

1. "The Holocaust demands interrogation and calls everything into question. Traditional ideas and acquired values, philosophical systems and social theories—all must be revised in the shadow of Birkenau."[24] The first lesson Wiesel teaches is that the Shoah is an unrivaled measure because nothing exceeds its power to evoke the question "Why?" That authority puts everything else to the test.

Whatever the traditional ideas and acquired values that have existed, whatever the philosophical systems and social theories that human minds have produced, they were either inadequate to prevent Auschwitz, or, worse, they helped pave the way to that place. The Shoah insists, therefore, that how we think and act needs revision in the face of those fact, unless one wishes to continue the same blindness that eventuated in the darkness of *Night*. The heeded revisions, of course, do not guarantee a better outcome. And yet failure to use the Shoah to call each other, and especially ourselves, into question diminishes chances to mend the world.

    2. *"The questions remain questions."*[25] As the first lesson, Elie Wiesel does not place his greatest confidence in answers. Answers—especially when they take the form of philosophical systems and religious dogmas—make him suspicious. No matter how hard people try to resolve the most important issues, questions remain and rightly so. To encounter the Shoah, to reckon with its disturbing "Whys?"—without which humanity itself is called into question—that is enough to make Wiesel's case.

    Typically, however, the human propensity is to quest for certainty. Wiesel's urging is to resist that temptation, especially when it aims to settle things that ought to remain unsettled and unsettling. For if answers aim to settle things, their ironic, even tragic, outcome is often that they produce disagreement, difference, division, and death. Hence, Wiesel wants questions to be forever fundamental.

    People are less likely to savage and annihilate each other when their minds are not made up but opened up through questioning. The Shoah shows as much: Hitler and his Nazi followers "knew" they were "right." Their "knowing" made them killers. Questioning might have redeemed them as well as their victims.

    Wiesel's point is not that responses to questions are simply wrong. They have their place; they can be essential, too. Nonetheless, questions deserve lasting priority because they invite continuing inquiry, further dialogue, shared wonder, and openness. Resisting "final solutions," these ingredients—especially when they drive home the insight that the best questions are never put to rest but keep us human by luring us on—can create friendships in ways that answers never can.

    3. *"And yet—and yet. This is the key expression in my work.*[26] Elie Wiesel's writings, emerging from intensity that is both the burden and the responsibility of Shoah survivors, aim to put people off guard. Always suspicious of answers but never failing for questions, he lays out problems not for their own sake but to inquire, "What is the next step?" Reaching an apparent conclusion, he moves on. Such forms of thought reject easy paths in favor of hard ones.

    Wiesel's "and yet—and yet" affirms that it is more important to seek than to find, more important to question than to answer, more important to travel than to arrive. The point is that it can be dangerous to believe what you want to believe, deceptive to find things too clear, just as it is also dishonest not to strive to bring them into focus. His caution is that it is insensitive to overlook that there is always more to experience that our theories admit, even though we can never begin to seek comprehension without reasoning and argument. And so Elie Wiesel tells his stories, and even their endings resist leaving his readers with a fixed conclusion. He wants them instead to feel his "and yet—and yet," which provides a hope that people may keep moving to choose life and not to end it.

4. *"There is a link between language and life."*[27] The Shoah was physically brutal. That brutality's origins were partly in "paper violence," which is to say that they depended on words. Laws, decrees, orders, memoranda, even schedules for trains and specifications for gas vans and crematoria—all of these underwrite Wiesel's insistence that care must be taken with words, for words can kill.

Wiesel uses words differently. He speaks and writes to recreate. His words, including the silences they contain, bring forgotten places and unremembered victims back to life just as they jar the living from complacency. Doing these things, he understands, requires turning language against itself. During the Nazi era, language hid too much: Euphemisms masked reality to lull. Rhetoric projected illusions to captivate. Propaganda used lies to control. All of those efforts were hideously successful. In our own day, as Wiesel points out, we bid farewell by saying, "Relax." "Have fun." "Take it easy." Seemingly innocuous, such language is certainly a far cry from words possessed by genocidal intent. And yet innocuous words may not be as innocent as they seem. They are likely to distract and detract from needs that deserve concern and care.

Language and life are linked in more ways than words can say. After-Auschwitz-priorities nonetheless enjoin that words have to decode words, speech must say what speech hides, writings must be unwritten, and set right what has been written. None of this can be done perfectly once and for all. The task is ongoing, but only as it is going on will lives be linked so that "and yet—and yet" expresses hope more than despair.

5. *"Rationalism is a failure and betrayal.*[28] Although Elie Wiesel is hardly an enemy of reason and rationality, he does stand in a tradition that takes reason to have no function more important than assessing its own limitations. And yet Wiesel's critique of reason is grounded somewhat different from that of philosophers such as David Hume or Immanuel Kant. Theirs' depended on theory. Wiesel's rests on history and on the Shoah in particular.

The Shoah happened because human minds became convinced that they could figure everything out. Those minds "understood" that one religion had superseded another. They "comprehended" that one race was superior to every other. They "realized" who deserved to live and who deserved to die. One can argue, of course, that such views perverted rationality and mocked morality. They did. And yet to say that much is to say too little, for one must ask about the sources of such perversity. When that asking occurs, part of its trail leads to reason's tendency to presume that indeed it can, at least in principle, figure everything out.

With greater authority than any theory can muster, Auschwitz shows where such rationalism can lead. Wiesel's antidote is not irrationalism; his rejection of destructive madness testifies to that. What he seeks instead is the understanding that lives in friendship—understanding that includes tentativeness, fallibility, comprehension that looks for error and revises judgment when error is found, realization that knowing is not a matter of fixed conviction but of continuing dialogue.

V. Doing

Elie Wiesel's lessons about understanding urge one not to draw hasty or final conclusions. Rather his emphasis is on exploration and inquiry. It might be objected that such an outlook tends to encourage indecision and even indifference. To the contrary, however, one of Wiesel's most significant contributions runs in just the opposite direction. His perspective on understanding and on morality is of one piece. Thus, dialogue leads not to indecision but to an informed decisiveness. Tentativeness becomes protest when unjustified conviction asserts itself. Openness results not in indifference but in the loyalty of which friendship is made and on which it depends. Wiesel's doing is demanding, but it, too, has a rhythm that can be learned. Here are five of its movements:

1. *"Passivity and indifference and neutrality always favor the killer, not the victim."*[29] Elie Wiesel will never fully understand the world's killers. To do so would be to legitimate them by showing that they were part of a perfectly rational scheme. Though for very different reasons, he will not fully understand their victims, either; their silent screams call into question every account of their dying that presents itself as a "final solution." But Elie Wiesel insists that understanding should be no less elusive where indifference—including its accomplices, passivity and neutrality—prevails. Too often indifference exists among those who could make a difference, for it can characterize those who stand between killers and victims but aid the former against the latter by doing too little, too late.

Where acting is concerned, nothing arouses Wiesel more than activating the inactive. This goal is illustrated in his play, *Zalman, or the Madness of God*. Inside the Soviet Union, an old rabbi, his assistant Zalman, a doctor, a daughter, a grandson, and a son-in-law, the chairman of a synagogue, and the rest of a fearful congregation—along with the troupe of observers—actors—are confronted by choices imposed upon them by an oppressive government intent on forcing them into silent submission. Traveling visitors from the West—some Jewish, some not—wish to witness Russian Jews at prayer. Concerned about appearance, government officials decide to permit the visit, but warnings are issued to the local Jews. There must be no disturbances, no protests, nothing to suggest discontent. Almost everyone is willing to go along. The old rabbi, however, provoked by Zalman or the madness of God, chooses differently. He breaks the silence and testifies to the suffering of his people.

It is a dramatic scene, but nothing changes much—at least on the surface—except that futility gains some ground. The government investigates; the Jews' anxiety increases for a time. No plot is discovered, and fear subsides to a more normal level. The doctor dares to seek out the visiting actors to drive home the protest made by the rabbi. Unfortunately, they have already gone their way silently. Although the possibility remains that the rabbi can have a significant relationship with his grandson, his family may be more lost to him than ever, and there is no assurance that the madness of his moving protest has not pushed him into a permanent disorientation that will be useless, Zalman begins to doubt that his provocation was worth the pain and disintegration and emptiness it has caused. Madness compounds itself.

Such is the strand of hopelessness that runs through this drama. Yet threads of hope are intertwined with that strand. Slim though they may be, those threads direct one to the power of a challenge that resists indifference, passivity, and neutrality by saying: The rabbi must not be left alone; his sacrifice must not be in vain. Indifference makes such threads delicate and fragile. Passivity and neutrality show them to be more easily ignored or forgotten than carried forward into action. And yet the possibility they contain provides the premise on which Wiesel's unwritten third act awaits is post-Shoah direction.

2. *"It is given to man to transform divine injustice into human justice and compassion."*[30] Abraham, Isaac, and Jacob—along with Adam and Eve, Cain and Abel, Joseph, Moses, and Job—this time they are not patients in Twilight's Mountain Clinic but Biblical "messengers of God." Seeds of error, deception, and guilt were born with Adam. Bias, favoritism, hurt feelings, vengeance, and murder form the tale of Cain and Abel. Promises, tests, obedience, trust, survival, hope—these did not add up to a world of rationality and justice for Abraham and Isaac, but they exist.

Jacob fought to secure a blessing, and the world has shaken to the core trying to understand its nature and what it might portend. Wily Joseph escaped the jealousy of his brothers, worked his way to the top, handled Potiphar's wife beautifully, made himself a Just Man. His success was too much; unfairly, his people paid the price. Leadership and the law—these things associate with Moses, but even this man—closest of all to God and his people—glimpsed the future from so far away that he had to wonder. As for Job, maybe life had been unfairly good to him and so his testing was to be commensurate.

Like Wiesel himself, these Biblical messengers understood that human thought and action have enacted and exacerbated too many of the threatening portents that accompany the freedom to choose that makes existence human. They also wrestled with the fact that human existence neither accounts for nor completely sustains itself. Their dearly-earned reckoning with that reality led them to a profound restiveness. It revealed, in turn, the awesome injunction that God intends for humankind to have hard, even impossible, moral work until and through death.

One may not see life the way those Biblical messengers saw it. Whatever one's choices in that regard, it is nevertheless as hard as it is inhuman to deny that injustice too often reigns divine and that moral work is given to us indeed. Elie Wiesel presumes neither to identify that work in detail for everyone nor to insist, in particular, where or how one should do it. Those are the right questions, though, and he wants one to explore them. That exploration, he urges, is not likely to be done better than through the Shoah lenses. Enhancing vision sensitively, they can help to focus every evil that should be transformed by human justice and compassion.

3. *"If I still shout today, if I still scream, it is to prevent man from ultimately changing me."*[31] While "and yet—and yet" may be the key expression in Wiesel's writings, a close contender could be phrased "because of—in spite of." Here, too, the rhythm insists that, no matter where one dwells, there is and must be more to say and do. On this occasion, though, the context is more specific, for the place where "because of—in spite of" becomes crucial is the place where despair most threatens to win. So because of the odds in favor of despair and against hope, in spite of them, the insistence and need to rebel in favor of life are all the greater. And not to be moved by them is to hasten the end.

How this understanding's logic works in tandem with doing can be illuminated further by noting Wiesel's observation that many of those freed from the Nazi camps believed that the world must not have known about them. Disabused of that naivete, some still clung to the idea that if they told what had happened, the effect would be sobering and transforming. That hope, too, proved illusory, for the story has been told, responsibility has been assessed, and, if anything, the Shoah is more widely a part of human memory than ever. The labor, however, has not been sufficient to check the violence, suffering, and indifference that waste life away. Instead, the threats of population riddance and nuclear destruction persist. Not even antisemtism has been eclipsed.

At times, Wiesel hints that humanity's eventual destruction is to be the price—as yet unpaid—for Auschwitz. That counsel of doom will not be his last word, however, as is evidenced by *The Testament*. This novel traces the odyssey of Paltiel Kossover, a character who represents hundreds of Jewish intellectuals condemned to death by Joseph Stalin in 1952. The Shoah does not stand center stage in *The Testament*, but, as is usual in Wiesel's writings, casts its shadow before and after all the action. This book, moreover, contains Wiesel's most fundamental answer to the question he must face repeatedly, a question that elicits a response incorporating the rhythm of "because of—in spite of:" Have things gone so far that memory and protest rooted in the Shoah are futile?

Arrested and questioned, Paltiel, whose name means "God is my refuge," expects to disappear without a trace. He is encouraged by his KGB interrogator to write an autobiography in which, the official hopes, the prisoner will confess more than he does by direct questioning. Kossover can sustain his life by writing about it, but he has no reason to think his testament will ever reach anyone he loves. Even less can he assume that his telling the tale of his own experiences will in any way influence history. Still, he tries his best, and what his best amounts to involves an ancient story—often repeated by Wiesel—that serves as The Testament's prologue.

It speaks of a Just Man who came to Sodom to save that ill-fated Biblical place from sin and destruction. Observing the Just Man's care, a child approached him compassionately:

> "Poor stranger, you shout, you scream, don't you see that it is hopeless?"
>
> "Yes, I see."
>
> "Then why do you go on?"
>
> "I'll tell you why. In the beginning, I thought I could change man. Today, I know I cannot. If I still shout today, if I still scream, it is to prevent man from ultimately changing me."

Kossover does not escape the Soviet prison, but his testament finds a way out. It reaches and touches the poet's son. Stranger things have happened in our day, and thus Wiesel insists, again by way of analogy, that the enormous loss of the Shoah is not all that remains. A future still awaits our determination, especially if the rhythm "because of—in spite of" is heard, understood, and enacted.

4. *"As a Jew, I abide by my tradition. And my tradition allows, and indeed, commands, man to take the Almighty to task for what is being done to His people, to His children—and all men are His children—provided the questioner does so on behalf of His children, not against them, from within the community, from within the human condition, and not as an outsider."*[32] Some of Elie Wiesel's most forceful writing involves tales of the Hasidim. Many features impress him as he traces this Jewish movement from its flowering in eighteenth-century Europe to its presence in the death camps and to its surprising influence in a world that came close to destroying Hasidic ways completely. One of the rhythms of understanding and doing stressed by Wiesel derives, at least in part, from an Hasidic

Asking and Listening, Understanding and Doing

awareness of the relationships between "being for" and "being against."

As Wiesel portrays its Eastern European development, Hasidism combines a genuine awe of God with direct and emotional reactions toward God. It found God eluding understanding, but also as One to whom people could speak. The Hasidim argued with God, protested against God, feared, trusted, and loved God. All of this was done personally and passionately, without compromising God's majesty and beyond fear of contradiction. Levi Yitzhak of Berditchev, for example, understood his role as that of attorney-for-the-defense, reproaching God for harsh treatment of Jews. Joining him was Rebbe [Rabbi—Ed.] Israel, Maggid [Story-teller—Ed.] of Kozhenitz, the author of one of Wiesel's favorite Hasidic prayers: "Master of the Universe, know that the children of Israel are suffering too much; they deserve redemption, they need it. But if, for reasons unknown to me, You are not willing, not yet, then redeem all the other nations, but do it soon!"[33]

Nahman of Bratzlav holds another special place in Wiesel's heart. Laughter is Nahman's gift: "Laughter that springs from lucid and desperate awareness, a mirthless laughter, laughter of protest against the absurdities of existence, a laughter of revolt against a universe where man, whatever he may do, is condemned in advance. A laughter of compassion for man who cannot escape the ambiguity of his condition and of his faith."[34] And one more example, Menahem-Mendl of Kotzk, embodied a spirit whose intense despair yielded a righteous anger and revolt so strong that it was said, "a God whose intentions he would understand could not suit him."[35] This rebel embraced life's contradictions both to destroy and to sustain them. Short of death, he found life without release from suffering. At the same time, he affirmed humanity as precious by living defiantly to the end. Wiesel implies, too, that Mendl hoped for something beyond death. His final words, Wiesel suggests, were: "At least I shall see Him face to face." Wiesel adds, "We don't know—nor will we ever know—whether these words expressed an ancient fear or a renewed defiance."[36]

Love, mercy, challenge, irony, laughter, anger, rebelliousness—Hasidim's spirit and Elie Wiesel's have them all but with a difference than transforms. Anything can be said and done, indeed everything must be said and done, that is *for* children, women, and men. Wiesel understands this to mean that a stance against God is sometimes enjoined. But he hastens to add that such a stance needs to be from within a perspective that also affirms God. Otherwise we run the risk of being against humankind in other ways all over again. Those ways include succumbing to dehumanizing temptations which conclude that only human might makes right, that there is human history as we know it and nothing more, that, as far as the Shoah's victims are concerned, Hitler was victorious.

For....against: the rhythm involves taking stands. Spiritually, this means to be against God when being for God would put one against humankind. Spiritually this also means to be for God when being against God would be against humankind by siding with forces that tend, however inadvertently, to legitimize too much the wasting of human life. Wiesel and his Hasidim are fiercely humanistic. Their humanism, however, remains tied to God. The lesson here is that, without enlivening and testing those ties, and, in particular, their ways of being for and against humankind, a critical resource for saving life and mending the world will be lost.

    5. *"By allowing me to enter his life, he gave meaning to mine."*[37] Another of Elie Wiesel's novels, *The Oath*, tells of a community that disappeared except for one surviving witness. It is a tale about that person's battle with a vow of silence. Azriel is his name, and Kolvillag, his home in Eastern Europe, was destroyed in a twentieth-century pogrom prompted by the disappearance of a Christian boy. Ancient animosity renewed prejudice. Prejudice produced rumor; rumor inflamed hate. Accused of a ritual murder, Azriel and his fellow Jews were soon under threat.

    Not unlike *Twilight*'s old madman from Rovidok, a strange, mystical member of the community—Moshe, whose character and voice are felt, one way or another, in so many of Wiesel's writings—surrenders himself as the guilty party though no crime has been committed. However, he does not thereby satisfy the authorities and "Christians" of the town. Madness intensifies. The Jews begin to see that history will repeat, and they prepare for the worst. Some arm for violence; most gather strength quietly to wait and endure.

    Permitted to speak to the Jews assembled in their ancient synagogue, Moshe envisions Kolvillag's destruction. He knows the record of Jewish endurance, its long testimony against violence, but this seems to have done little to restrain men and women and even God from further vengeance. So Moshe persuades his people to try something different: "By ceasing to refer to the events of the present, we would forestall ordeals in the future."[38] The Jews of Kolvillag become Jews of silence by taking his oath: "Those among us who will survive this present ordeal shall never reveal either in writing or by the word what we shall see, hear and endure before and during our torment!"[39]

    Next comes bloodshed. Jewish spirits strain upward in smoke and fire. Only the young Azriel survives. He bears the chronicles of Kolvillag—one created with his eyes, the other in a book entrusted to him for safekeeping by his father, the community's historian. Azriel bears the oath of Kolvillag as well. Torn between speech and silence, he remains true to his promise.

    Many years later, Azriel meets a young man who is about to kill himself in a desperate attempt to give his life significance by refusing to live it. Azriel decides to intervene, to find a way to make the waste of suicide impossible for his new friend. The way Azriel chooses entails breaking the oath. He shares the story of Kolvillag in the hope that it will instill rebellion against despair, concern in the place of lethargy and indifference, life to counter death.

The oath of silence was intended to forestall ordeals in the future. Such forestalling, Wiesel testifies, must give silence its due; it must also break silence in favor of speech and action that recognizes the fatal interdependence of all human actions. "By allowing me to enter his life, he gave meaning to mine." Azriel's young friend echoes the lesson that Elie Wiesel has shared so generously with those who listen closely for what he has to say. Rightly understood, that listening—and the asking it provokes—becomes a mandate for doing unto others what Azriel did for the boy he saved.

A Postscript

"And why do you pray, Moshe?" Responding to the Shoah religiously entails listening, understanding, and then acting in ways inspired by Moshe's reply to Elie Wiesel's asking: "I pray to the God within me that He will give me the strength to ask Him the right questions." In that spirit let these words from a sixteenth-century English hymn provide an ending that is just the beginning:

> God be in my head,
> And in my understanding;
> God be in mine eyes,
> And in my looking.
> God be in my mouth,
> And in my speaking;
> God be in my heart,
> And in my thinking.
> God be at mine end,
> And at my departing.
>
> Amen.

The Holocaust Now

CHALLENGES TO FAITH

The Holocaust Now

Why?

Bernard Maza's essay, unique to this collection, is an attempt by an Orthodox Jew and Rabbi to deal with both the Shoah and an interpretation of the Jewish Religious Tradition which sees the "hand of God" in all things and events. For Maza, the Biblical prophet Ezekiel holds the key to a correct understanding of the Shoah, especially Chapter 20, verses 32 and 33, along with Ecclesiastes Chapter 1, verse 5. The Almighty *used* the Shoah as a means whereby an errant Israel, falling away from its true destiny of commitment to Torah, might be brought back to its responsibilities. The "birth pangs of the Messiah," as evidenced by the rebirth of the State of Israel as a result of the Shoah, now becomes the beginning of Redemption for Jews the world over. Difficult and problematic as this position is for non-Orthodox Jews to accept, it does remain true to Orthodox Judaism, and, likewise, attempts to address the horrors of the Shoah from that vantage point.

SLJ

The Holocaust Now

WHY?

Bernard Maza

In my book *With Fury Poured Out: A Torah Perspective on the Holocaust*[1], I explained "why the Shoah?" In this essay I will lay out before the reader a brief review of the explanation: How did I arrived at the explanation? What aspect of "why" did I explain and what aspect of "why" did I not explain? Why I explained what I did and why I did not explain what I did not? And, since the explanation bears upon the future of the Jewish people, how does the developing history of the Jewish people since the writing of the manuscript conform to the explanation?

I. The Rising and Setting of the Sun

King Solomon said in Ecclesiastes, "The sun rises and the sun sets".[2] The *Talmud* declares that sentence to be a prophecy. The Torah always will have a central source from which it spreads to the world. It may be a central place like the *Bais Hamikdash*, the Holy Temple. Or it may be a person who teaches Torah from wherever he may be, like Samuel who travelled from city to city teaching the words of the Almighty wherever he went.

When destiny decrees that the Torah will pass from that central course, "the sun rises" first in a new central source before "the sun sets" in its passing central source. In the words of the Talmud, "when Rabbi Akiva was dying, Rebbi was born. When Rebbi was going to die Rav Yehudah was born....before the sun of Eli was extinguished the sun of Samuel shone."

This was true through all of history. The noted historian Solomon Grayzel writes in his *History of the Jews:*

> One of the most remarkable facts in the history of the Jews is that they have never been without a central leadership....Even before the one center realized that it was destined to give up the leadership of the scattered Jewish people, the next was developing the ability to resume

The Holocaust Now

where the former was leaving off.

This was true in all Jewish history. But every intelligent human analysis of Jewish history in the twentieth century pointed to the certainty that the prophecy was soon to lose its truth. In every country of major Jewish settlement, Torah was in steep decline.

The citadel of Torah in the twentieth century, the light of Torah to the world, was Eastern Europe—Poland and its neighboring countries: Hungary, Rumania, and the Baltic States. In the early part of the twentieth century came disturbing signs that the youth were leaving their parents' values and their way-of-life. They were pursuing Socialism and Zionism and rejecting Torah. At first the pace of the change was slow. But as the twentieth century progressed the rate of Jewish youth leaving the Torah life was accelerating. Their parents, the Rabbis, the established community tried desperately to stem the onrushing tide. But by the decade of the 1930's, the elders were overwhelmed. The youth were leaving the Torah at an increased rate. The outlook for the future of Torah in Eastern Europe was dark. The sun of Torah was setting in its source.

In the Soviet Union, since the Communist Revolution of 1917, there was spiritual desolation. There was no Jewish education or Jewish anything permitted. And there was a willing Jewish youth to help the Communist Revolution accomplish its designs. In the 1930's in the Soviet Union, where there was once world-renowned Torah scholars and millions of Torah-true Jews, there was nothing except an almost invisible fossilized remnant of the old generation.

In the early twentieth century, millions of Jews left Eastern Europe to come to the inviting shores of America. Most of them were Torah-observant, and they established a vibrant Jewish community in the United States. There were many synagogues, *mikvaot*[3], *yeshivas*[4] and *kosher* establishments. But in spite of their dedication they were losing their children. The Jewish youth loved America. They rejected their parents' way of life as "European" and they scorned their Torah values as "old-fashioned." They were leaving their parents' life-style in droves. In the United States in the 1930's, very few of the youth walked in step with their parents.

In Palestine, for thousands of years, even after the destruction of the Holy Temple and Exile of the Jews from the Holy Land, there was always brave Torah-true Jews who settled in the *Yishuv*, the settlement. They guarded the holiness of the land with dedication. But early in the twentieth century, Zionism of a secular-nationalistic persuasion inspired the youth of Europe. They led the *aliyah*, immigration, of Jews to Palestine, bringing hundreds of thousands of non-Torah observant Jews to Palestine, greatly outnumbering the Torah-minded Jews. Nowhere was the sun of Torah rising. The prophecy of King Solomon seemed to be coming to an end.

The Talmud tells of the gathering of the people of Israel at Mount Sinai to receive the Torah. The Torah states, "And they stood underneath the mountain." The Talmud

Why?

[B.T. Sabbath 88a] comments:

> Said Rav Avdimi, the son of Chama, this teaches us that the Holy One, Blessed be He, tilted the mountain over them like unto a barrel and said, 'If you accept the Torah good! And if you do not, there shall be your burial place!'

And the Talmud says:

> Said Rabbi Simeon, the son of Lakish, 'What is the meaning of the passage, 'And it was evening and it was morning that sixth day'? It teaches us that the Holy One, Blessed be He, made a condition with all that He created and said to them, 'If the people of Israel accept the Torah which will be given on the sixth day of [the month of—Ed.] *Sivan*, good! And if not, I shall return the world to the state of void and emptiness!'

The Talmud teaches us that the existence of the Jewish people and of the world is dependent upon the fulfillment of the Torah, which is the plan of the Almighty for the conduct of the world. The people of Israel are the bearers of the Torah. When the Jewish people accept and fulfill their function, the Almighty blesses the world with prosperity and peace. Would the Jewish people not fulfill their function and not accept and carry the Torah, the Almighty might discontinue the existence of His creation.

In the twentieth century, the sun of Torah was setting all over the world. What was going to happen to the Torah? To the Jewish people? To the world?

Since the destruction of the Holy Temple, and for all of the centuries of Exile which followed, the people of Israel have recited the following prayer in their morning services:

> Look down from the heavens and see that we have fallen to shame and ridicule among the nations. We have been considered as sheep led to slaughter, to kill, to destroy, to beat, and to shame. But, in spite of all this, Your Name we have not forgotten. Please do not forget us.

The Jewish people, wandering in the Exile, moved from country to country suffering persecution wherever they went. They made their homes in the country that accepted them, stoically suffering abuse and persecution for as long as that country accepted them. When that country tired of its own hospitality and they were expelled, the Jews made their way to another country where they faced the same fate.

The Holocaust Now

The liturgy cited above describes, with pathos, the pathetic heroism of the long-suffering Jew. The power that gave them the strength to persevere, to hope, and to survive, was their faith that the Almighty would not forget them as they did not forget the Almighty.

For generations their faith remained firm, their loyalty to the Torah unswerving. And the generation of 1939, as earlier generations, was steady and undoubting.

But human beings have their limits and the Jewish people had reached theirs. The Jews of succeeding generations could no longer bear to be the shame and ridicule of nations, as a sheep led to slaughter. They wanted to be like the other nations. They would forget the name of the Almighty.

The prophet Ezekiel has said:

> And that which ascends upon your spirit shall not be, that which you say, 'let us be like the nations, like the families of the lands, to serve wood and stone.' [20:32]

In the twentieth century that which Ezekiel had prophesied was coming to pass. There was ascending upon the Jewish people the desire to be like all other nations.

But it was the will of the Almighty that the Jewish people, the bearers of the Torah, would not forsake the Torah. The present generation of righteous would not be the last. The ambition of the coming generation to be like all the nations of the world would not be.

The Almighty knew that the oppression of the Jewish people had to end or the sun of Torah would set. The Jewish people had to be redeemed and returned to the Land of Israel. Only in the Land of Israel would they find freedom from the suffering that was inevitably their lot in the lands of their exile.

When they would be returned to their land and the burden of oppression lifted from their backs, the heaviness would be removed from their hearts. When their hearts and minds would be free, they would seek and find themselves. The *pintele yid*, the spark of Judaism that is in the heart of every Jew, would be awakened. The sunshine of Torah would rise.

This was therefore the moment in the Divine history of the Jewish people that the Almighty judged to be the time for the beginning of the process of Redemption.

The Talmud describes the process of Redemption. There are four stages in the process. They are: Redemption from oppression, ingathering of the exiles, the restoration of Jerusalem, and the crowning of the Kingdom of David, which is the Kingdom of the Almighty.

The prophet Ezekiel has said:

Why?

>As I live says the Lord that only with a strong hand and an outstretched arm, and with fury poured out will I be King over them. [20:33]

The road to the Kingdom of the Almighty, beginning with redemption from oppression, would be preceded by "fury." Not just fury, but a fury of unprecedented magnitude - a "fury poured out."

In the twentieth century the Almighty decreed the unfolding of the prophetic process. It meant the coming of the fury. It meant the Shoah. The Almighty, the Guardian of Israel, hid His Face and He did not protect His people from the evil that was lurking in the hearts of His enemies.

The Shoah came. The hatred that was inside the hearts of the enemies of the Almighty and His people burst out in an explosion of unmatched savagery. And in the midst of the savagery, before the eyes of the murderer, came to life the most incredible saga of sacred heroism ever displayed by a people.

6,000,000 Jews were burned in the flames. Millions of them were marched to the woods to dig their own graves in which they died from the bullets of Nazi machine guns. Millions more were marched to meet their death in the gas chambers. And while they dug their graves and while they went to the gas chambers, they sang and danced. Their hearts were filled with love and their mouths filled with praise of the Almighty Who decreed their deaths.

They scorned the murderers. What power did they have over their souls! They sang *Ani Maamin*, "I believe," and *Sh'ma Yisrael*, "Hear O Israel"—in affirmation of their belief in the Wisdom and Mercy of the Almighty, the Lord of the Universe, to Whom they entrusted their souls.

The following account is related by M. Prager in *Tnuat Hachasidut Bitkufat HaShoah*:[5]

>When the murderer Globotchnik came to Lublin at the end of 1939, he commanded that all the Jews be gathered together in an empty field at the end of the city. When all the Jews assembled, trembling with fear, he announced that everyone should start singing a happy *Chassidic* song.
>
>Someone in the frightened crowd began to sing the sweet Chassidic song "Lomer Zich Iberbeten Avinu Shebashamayim," "Let us Make Up, Our Father in Heaven." But the song did not catch on. At once Globotchnik commanded his troopers to beat the Jews who were not following his orders. The Nazis swooped down upon the Jews and began to beat them mercilessly. Suddenly a loud clear voice rose up in

song. "Mir Vellen Zei Iberbeten Avinu Shebashamayim," "We Will Outlive Them, Our Father in Heaven," singing the same Chassidic melody. In a second, the song caught on. Everyone began singing and then they all joined together dancing a stormy, whirling dance before the eyes of the murderers. The Jews were so intoxicated with feelings of hope and faith that Globotchnik stood there bewildered and confused and began to scream with a shrill voice, "Stop! Stop at once!"

As they waited for their salvation, they went on with their lives as Jews, finding courage, hope, and even joy in their Jewish heritage. They studied Torah and observed Jewish practices. Neither suffering, nor pain, nor fear of death discouraged them.

The following account was related by Zalman Kleinman at the Eichmann trial and published in *Ani Maamin* by Mordecai Eliav:

> One day as I was lying on my bunk in the children's ward in Auschwitz. I saw a guard carrying a big rubber hose, going to whip someone. I jumped from my bunk to see whom they were going to whip. The guard went over to one of the bunks. The boy that was lying there already knew what was coming and he was waiting. The guard said, "Get down." He came down and bent over. The guard began to whip him.
>
> I and the boys who gathered around watched and counted. The boy did not cry, did not shout, did not even sigh. We were astonished, we did not understand....and the whipping went on. He had already passed twenty-five lashes; as a rule we were given twenty-five lashes. He passed thirty. When he passed forty, he turned the boy over and began to whip him on his head and on his legs. The body did not groan, did not cry, nothing....a boy of fourteen and he did not cry.
>
> The guard angrily finished fifty and left. I can still see this great red blotch that streaked the boy's forehead from one of the blows of that rubber hose.
>
> We asked the boy why he was whipped. He answered, "I brought some prayer books to my friends. It was worth it." He did not add a word. He got up, went to his bunk and sat down.

Yaakov Kurtz in *Sefer Ha'aidut*[6] tells of the time during the holiday of *Succos*[7] when he saw an old Jew sitting in a *succah* and singing *z'mirot*[8] in a loud voice. He entered the succah and asked the old man if he realized the great danger of what he was doing. The old man shook his head this way and that and continued to sing. After a while he turned to him and said, "What can they do to me? They can take my body but not my soul. They have no authority over the soul. Their power is only in this world. Here they are powerful. But in the Other World they are powerless!"

The following event, related by Rabbi [Ephraim] Oschry in *Churban Lita*[9], took place in the Kovno Ghetto:

> On the eleventh day of Tammuz 5701 [Sunday, 6 July 1941—Ed.] a group of great Rabbis were gathered in the ghetto of Kovno and were studying Torah. Suddenly the gates were burst open and a group of Lithuanian fascists sprang into the room. They were all deeply engrossed in their study and ignored the intruders. When the murderers saw that no one was paying attention to them, they began to fire their revolvers, and the Rabbis trembled and arose....
>
> The order was given: "Line up! Come with us!"
>
> The Rabbis understood what the order meant. They stood in line. While they were getting ready to march, Rabbi Elchanan Wasserman turned to the prisoners and said, "It seems that in the Heavens they have seen amongst us great righteous men, for they want us with our lives to bring forgiveness upon the people of Israel. We must therefore repent now, immediately, on this spot, for time is short. We must remember that we will surely sanctify His Name. Let us go with heads held high and let no imperfect thought enter it lest it blemish our sacrifice. We are now fulfilling the greatest commandment, to sanctify His Name. The fire which will consume our bones is the fire that will give birth again to the Jewish nation."
>
> Thus they marched, the march of the holy. With pride and honor they went to bring forgiveness to the people of Israel. Thirteen of the elders of Israel, and at their head the great holy Rabbi Elchanan Wasserman, were killed that day....

The sanctity of the Shoah martyrs pierced the heavens, and the Almighty redirected the course of Jewish history. The process of Redemption began to unfold.

On May 6, 1945, World War II ended. The Shoah was over. A pitiful remnant of Jews emerged from darkness to freedom. But their freedom was not pure light. Where were they to go? They would not go back and make their homes in the countries which were the graveyards of their loved ones. The image of their neighbors and countrymen laughingly participating in their murder swam before their eyes like a nightmare.

They emerged from the Shoah left with nothing but a dream. That dream was Palestine, the Holy Land, the Promised Land of the Jews. They waited in the Displaced

The Holocaust Now

Persons Camps until they were ready to leave for Palestine.

They walked through countries and climbed over mountains, always hounded by the British who were determined to prevent the refugees from settling in Palestine. They tracked them through Europe, scouted their boats, stopped them before they could dock. They boarded the boats and took off the passengers, peacefully or forcefully. And many of the boats were turned back to Europe.

In the book *Illegal Immigrants Cross the Seas*, one of the immigrants who made it from Italy to Palestine describes the feelings of the refugees who participated in the escape:

> We escaped through Czechoslovakia, through the plains of Hungary, through the snow-covered mountains of the Alps, and through the sun-drenched land of Italy. We crossed borders and wire fences. The darkness of the night covered us. We disguised ourselves in various ways. We used every means to get to the seaports from where we could got to the Promised Land.
>
> We know that many long days of waiting are ahead of us. Days of wandering in strange ports will be our lot before we reach the miraculous day when we take our first step towards *aliyah* [immigration—Ed.]. We surely will sail in a small boat, one of those boats which sail the seas with assumed names and strange flags. Many days we will sit crowded below the decks, and the stink of the rats and the salt water will choke our throats. The British birds of prey will follow us threateningly. But the hour will come, and through the dark clouds we will see the harbors of Palestine. And our eyes, red from sleepless nights, will be fixed upon the shores of the Promised Land and our hearts will beat.

Vienna was the stopping point for thousands of Jews wandering through Europe. Dr. Garcia Granados who was a member of the United Nations Special Committee on Palestine describes the visit of the Committee to the Rothschild Hospital in Vienna in 1947:

> Little by little, as we began slowly to explore this incredible building, it dawned upon me that I was in the presence of one of the greatest shames of modern times. We began with what had once been a hospital ward. Beds were placed head to feet almost completely filling the room and where there were no beds, there were cots and mattresses. There was no place for people to stand and so all of them either sat or

lay on their beds.

We moved through other rooms in which every possible inch of space was similarly taken by cots and mattresses occupied by men, women, and children. Some lay on the floor.

Hundreds of people swarmed in the corridors. I could scarcely push my way through. In the courtyards hundreds more men and women were camping. There was no room for them inside. Wherever I looked men, women, and children were sitting or trying to sleep curled up on the earth. I descended to the basement of the hospital. It had been divided into large windowless rooms. After our eyes became accustomed to the gloom, we realized there were scores of people lying there. Huge pipes, part of the water system, crisscrossed the ceiling, and from them clothes were spread to dry.

The heavy odor seemed to permeate my being. I felt I was going to be sick....By a tremendous effort, I pushed my way through the people to the door. There I found the Iranian alternate Dr. Ali Ardelan. His face was haggard. He said in a trembling voice, "This is a crime against humanity. I never thought I would witness anything like this." I crossed the doorway and ran to a window opening on the courtyard. I remained there for two or three full minutes breathing deeply and sick at heart for all mankind.

The plight of the Jewish people and the same of the Shoah aroused the sympathy of the world. On November 29, 1947, the General Assembly of the United Nations, aided by an unusual demonstration of agreement between the United States and the Soviet Union, voted for the establishment of a Jewish State.

On May 14, 1948, the government of Palestine proclaimed its independence as the Jewish State of Israel. On May 15, 1948, the British handed over the authority for the government of the State of Israel. The Jewish people were free to return to their Promised Land.

After World War II, along with the gathering hope for the birth of the State of Israel, and its subsequent independence, a new spirit of hope, pride, and self-respect came over the Jews of the world. The sun of Torah began to rise in the United States and in Israel.

No longer were Torah-minded parents losing their children. Their children were joining them to live a Torah-true life. And the parents who were not Torah-minded were, surprisingly, sending their children to Torah Day Schools and learning to become Torah-observant. Many parents were returning to Torah step-by-step with their children.

Before 1939, in all of the United States, there were a handful of Torah elementary schools and Yeshivos teaching Torah to approximately 5,000 Jewish youth. In 1985, there were over 500 *Yeshivos* and Day Schools teaching Torah to well over 100,000 students.

And in Israel, whereas in 1939 there were about 20,000 students learning in the Torah elementary schools and Yeshivos, in 1985, there were more than 150,000 students in the Torah elementary schools and 50,000 in the Yeshivos.

The prophecy of Ezekiel includes three phases: first, "that which ascends upon your spirit;" second, "with fury poured out;" and third, "I will be King over you" [20:33].

Ezekiel prophesied, first, that there will be a time when, although the Jewish people will be pure and devoted to the Almighty, there will come upon the spirit of the Jewish people, the desire to be like other nations. The youth will feel the urge to leave the Torah. In 1939 the prophecy was exactly correct. The desire of the youth was abundantly clear. They were dreaming to be like other nations.

The prophecy speaks then of the second phase. The desire of the new generation will be arrested by the "fury poured out." There will follow a period in Jewish history when they will be caught in the destructive power of the "fury poured out," a fury of monumental devastation.

The Shoah was a tragedy which surely reached the dimensions of the "fury poured out."

The final phase of the prophecy is that as a result of the Shoah, "I will be King over you." The process leading to His Kingdom spans an unspecified number of years. And, as Ezekiel prophesied, the process began directly after the Shoah, with the rebirth of Israel and the resurgence of Torah.

The Shoah and its effects were the fulfillment, in our day, of the prophesy of Ezekiel and the beginning of the process leading to the Kingdom of the Almighty.

II. The Truth of Ezekiel's Prophecy

The explanation of the Shoah advanced above came to me from a conversation with Mr. Abraham Aharon Rimler while we were walking home from the synagogue on the Sabbath in the early 1970's.

Mr. Rimler was born in Poland. As a young man he was trapped into the Shoah and taken to a concentration camp. We spoke often about his life in Poland. On that Sabbath he said to me, "Don't think that the religious Jews in Poland were not having any problems with their children. More and more of them were leaving the synagogue and their parents' way of life to join Zionist organizations and all sorts of clubs."

I was taken aback by the statement. It was a totally unexpected remark.

Ever since I studied the Talmudic commentary on the prophecy of Ezekiel about

Why?

"the fury poured out," it struck me that the prophet may very well have been referring to the Shoah. But that possibility was rejected by me, as it would be immediately rejected by every American Jew. For, as every American Jew knew, in the twentieth century in Eastern Europe the Jewish people boasted a citadel of Torah which was among the strongest in modern Jewish history.

The Jews in Eastern Europe were famous all over the world for their Torah scholarship and dedication. Eastern Europe was the center of famous Yeshivos headed by world-renowned *Roshei Yeshivos*[10], with thousands of devoted students studying the Torah day and night. It was the home of great Rabbinic community leaders and of Torah-observant Jews living in the legendary cities and *shtetlach*.[11] In the twentieth century, Eastern Europe throbbed with Torah living. How could the prophet Ezekiel be referring to this period as being a time when there was "ascending upon the spirit of the Jewish people the desire to be like the other nations" [20:32]?

But when I heard the statement from Mr. Rimler and I recovered from my disbelief, I thought, "If it were really so and not just a personal, mistaken observation, and if the Eastern European youth were actually leaving their parents' way of life, and if the same were true in the other centers of Jewish living in the world, and if their elders, the generation then existing, were still loyal to the Torah up to and during the Shoah, and if after the Shoah, and, as a result of the Shoah, Israel was born, and if, after the Shoah, there was a reverse in Torah loyalty in any center of Jewish population, then the "fury poured out" would have been the Shoah."

I studied the history of the Jewish people in the twentieth century researching every one of the points I indicted above. I found that in all the history of the Jewish people at that time in all of the world there was not one iota of inconsistency with the prophecy.

I studied dozens of shtetlach in Eastern Europe. Most shtetlach of Eastern Europe had compiled Memorial Books describing the life in their *shtetl* before the Shoah. In all of them the pattern was the same. The youth were searching for new horizons. I studied the big cities with large Jewish populations. The pattern was the same. Growing numbers of young people were leaving the Torah life of their parents. And it was also true that in every place the problem was concentrated completely on the youth. Their elders were all of one voice, loyal and true to the Torah.

I studied the major centers of Jewish living in the world. Every-where the pattern was the same as in Eastern Europe, but worse. The youth were leaving or had already left the influence of their parents. Many cut themselves off from their parents' life-style so sharply that hardly an impression was left. In the Soviet Union Jewish life seemed to be already gone. In America and in Israel the youth were going their own way and it would be long before the Torah of their elders would be forgotten.

I studied the Shoah and it was true as the prophecy declared. The martyrs died proclaiming the Kingdom of the Almighty.

And I studied the period after the Shoah. What the prophecy predicted was true beyond all doubt. The Kingdom of the Almighty was being established over the people of Israel. The re-birth of Israel after the Shoah, and clearly linked to the Shoah, meant that the Almighty was returned from His Own Exile to the seat of His Kingdom. And there could be no doubt that after the Shoah and the birth of Israel, Torah education and Torah observance took a giant step forward.

I began to write my book. And while I was writing I knew I was making historical predictions. The coming of the Kingdom of the Almighty is a process. It begins with freedom from oppression and continues to the complete Redemption. All the while Torah will be growing until the realization of the prophecy of Isaiah, who declared, "All the world will be filled with the knowledge of the Almighty as water fills the ocean bed" [11:9]; and the fulfillment of the prophecy of Zachariah, who said, "And it shall be that the Almighty will be King over all the world. On that day, He will be One and His Name will be One" [14:9].

According to the explanation offered, it meant that there would be a continuing, uninterrupted growth of Torah in our day. I knew that the truth of the explanation was being tested even while I was researching and writing. Sure enough, the figures kept going up from year to year.

In the mid-1970's when I began my study until the mid-1980's when I completed my writing, the figures rose steadily. In the United States in 1975, there were 427 Torah Day Schools with approximately 80,000 students. In 1985, there were 500 Torah elementary schools with 100,000 students. In Israel, in 1975, there was approximately 100,000 in the Torah elementary schools. In 1985, there were close to 200,000 students.

Since I completed writing the book, and as of today's writing, the figures have gone up again. In 1990, in America, there were 560 Torah elementary schools with 120,000 students and in Israel there were approximately 275,000 students in the Torah elementary schools.

In analyzing Jewish history in the twentieth century, I linked the prophecy of Ezekiel to the prophecy of King Solomon, who said, "The sun rises," and then, "the sun sets"[12], meaning that before the sun of Torah sets in its central source, there will be a new sun of Torah rising somewhere in a new central source. This implies that during the transition from one center to another, the brilliant sun of the past shall be replaced by a sun which, though destined for future brilliance, is still small.

Therefore, while the rising sun of Torah is growing in brilliance, there are, sadly, places of darkness and shadow which it may not ever light up. Many Jewish lives would never be brightened by the sun of Torah. Would the sun of Torah rising in America and Israel come to the Soviet Union?

At the time of the writing of *With Fury Poured Out*, I did not conceive of the possi-

Why?

bility that Torah would ever enter the Soviet Union. I could not imagine that the Jews of the Soviet Union, so engulfed in the darkness of Atheism and Communism, would ever accept Judaism. And I could not believe that the powers of the Soviet Union would ever let the Torah in or the Jews out. I did not include anything about the Soviet Union in the rising sun of Torah.

But the Almighty is the God of Compassion, and He did not forsake the Jews of the Soviet Union. He included them in His Promise. The Almighty directed the course of the Jews of the Soviet Union to bring them back to Him.

In October, 1990, an interview was held with Yaakov Gorodetsky, the famous "refusenik" and activist from Leningrad. Gorodetsky is today the Director of the International Commission of *Sh'vut Ami* ["Redemption of My People"—Ed.], which is the primary institution for the religious absorption of Soviet Jews in Israel.

Gorodetsky, who was harassed by the KGB since he applied to go to Israel in 1980, was finally "expelled." He left for Israel in 1986. There, in Israel, he and his wife became Torah observant.

At the interview Yaakov discussed the beginnings and the development of religious awareness in the Soviet Union. He was asked what event was the inspiration that sparked the return to Torah among Soviet Jews. Unhesitatingly, without equivocation, he named the Six-Day War [of 1967—Ed.].

Up until the Six-Day War, the Jew of the Soviet Union carried his Judaism like a badge of shame. His papers were different than the identification papers of all other citizens. His "nationality" named no region in the Soviet Union, as did the documents of others. His "nationality" was Jewish. He was scarred and was regularly the victim of a beating by his "friends." He felt apart from, and beneath, the citizens of the Soviet Union.

But, Gorodetsky said, in 1967 with the lightning victory of Israel in the Six-Day War, the word "Jew" took on a new meaning. The Jews looked at themselves with pride. They saw themselves as members of a proud and strong nation. Gorodetsky declared that after the miraculous victory, the Jews said, "We are also men of courage and strength like the mightiest of nations. The Jew is somebody."

The new interest of the Jew in his Jewishness began to take movement in the late 1970's. A leading figure in the movement for return was Rabbi Alexander Miller who was disciple of the world-renowned Torah leader, the *Chofetz Chaim*, of blessed memory. He sat and studied in the *Bais Medrash* [Jewish school—Ed.] in Moscow. Several students gravitated to him. Among them was Eliahu Eses.

Eses began to spread Torah among his friends. He organized classes in his home, braving the watchful eyes of the KGB. He influenced his friends to learn Torah, to teach Torah, and to organize classes in their [own] homes. Soon there were groups of 15-20 students learning Torah in various homes.

The Holocaust Now

At the same time that Torah activity began to spread in the Moscow area, a similar movement was taking place in the Leningrad area. In 1977 Grisha Wasserman, a successful electrical engineer, author and lecturer, became disillusioned by antisemitism in the Soviet Union. He became inspired with a desire to learn about Judaism. He visited the only synagogue in Leningrad. There he befriended an old man who surreptitiously helped him learn Torah.

He began to organize classes in his home. In 1981 he started with three students. In 1985 he had about 15 students and each of them had 15 of their own, all of them between the ages of 18-25. Grisha travelled all over the Soviet Union, teaching and lecturing, to arouse the interest of the Soviet Jews to Torah study.

By the end of the 1970's, the seeds of Torah had taken hold in the Soviet Union.

Torah established a foothold in the Soviet Union because of a combination of factors. The first was the inspiration of the Six-Day War. Torah was given added impetus by the "refuseniks" who became inspired with Israel and would not submit to the powers of the Soviet Union who refused to let them go. The publicity they received, and the sympathy that was aroused among their fellow Jews and the world, did much to kindle Jewish feelings in the Soviet Union. And antisemitism spread by the government and quickly communicated to the masses brought home to the Jews of the Soviet Union the fact and the circumstances of their Jewishness.

In the 1970's the doors of the Soviet Union were temporarily opened for Jews to emigrate to Israel. Tens of thousands were permitted to leave. Among them was the "refusenik" Shimon Grilius who had become religious in prison. When he came to Israel he became a leaders in bringing Torah education to the Soviet immigrants. He founded Sh'vut Ami, the primary center in Israel for religious absorption of the Soviet Jews.

In the mid-1980's *glastnost*, a period of radical change, came to the Soviet Union. With it came to the Soviet Jews a measure of freedom to learn about Judaism and to emigrate to Israel. In 1987 the disintegration of Communism and a new freedom for the people of the Soviet Union brought a great upsurge of antisemitism. The combination of antisemitism and the almost unlimited freedom for the Soviet Jews to emigrate to Israel made for a flood of immigration of Soviet Jews to Israel.

There were now Torah institutions and organizations ready to help the Soviet immigrants in Israel to adjust to a Torah way of life. They were ready to help those still remaining in the Soviet Union to get a taste of Judaism.

Rabbi Abraham Binsky, Director of *Shoreshim* ["Roots"—Ed.], the organization for religious absorption of Soviet Jews in America, is today on leave from *Sh'vut Ami* in Israel which he serves as Director of Absorption Services. In an interview held in October, 1990, he described the activity of Sh'vut Ami. Rabbi Binsky said that they began their activity at the airport. They help the newcomer to find jobs and housing. Sh'vut

Why?

Ami conducts seminars and home study groups all over Israel. In Jerusalem alone their seminars are attended by about 500 people. On the Passover of 1989, about 1,000 people attended a week-long seminar on Jewish history and religion. Sh'vut Ami also encourages the Soviet Jewish immigrant to undergo circumcision when necessary. In the past several years they have influenced some 2,000 men to undergo circumcision.

Sh'vut Ami has a yeshiva attended by approximately 100 young men. The Yeshiva is producing the rabbis and teachers for the Soviet Jewish community. Thousands of Jews who no longer before hardly knew the existence of the Torah have been exposed to Torah and Jewish religious practice.

The figures for the number of Soviet Jews studying Torah in the Torah elementary schools of Israel are as yet unknown. But without doubt there are today thousands of Soviet Jewish children attending regular Torah schools in Israel.

Torah not only reached the Soviet Jews in Israel. It came to the Soviet Union. Where before there was nothing, today there is something alive and spirited. There are synagogues and yeshivos in several cities in the Soviet Union. There are two Yeshivos in Moscow and Jewish schools in Leningrad, Riga, Kiev, Vilna, and other major cities.

The following article, written by Michael Winerip, appeared in *The New York Times* of October 31, 1990. The article tells about Steven Springfield, a Jew from Latvia who left Riga for America in 1947. Mr. Springfield returned to Riga as a tourist last fall:

> It was astounding for him, like visiting a nightmare by the light of day. The spookiest was the Jewish school he had attended in the 1930's. In that same building, now crumbling, a new Jewish school had opened on September 1, 1989. Judaism was repressed so long that the founders expected 100. 500 applied.

The *Jewish Observer* of November, 1990, includes an article entitled "From Kiev with Hope," written by Yehoshua Weber. There he describes the dramatic changes in the spirit and the growth of Torah Judaism in Kiev:

> Focusing on the emerging vitality of one community, Kiev might help bring the religious potential of Soviet Jewry into clearer perspective. Nine months ago....Rabbi Yaacov Bleich, a young American, was appointed the official Rav of Kiev. In the short period of time since then, he and his indefatigable Rebbetzin have spear-headed a quiet revolution among a number of Kiev's 100,000 Jews.
> Under the Bleichs' tutelage, remarkably successful day and sleepaway camps, staffed by energetic young American were organized for both boys and girls. Three hundred wide-eyed children were treated

to four weeks of fun and sports, which included potent exposure to *tefillin, davening, zemiros* [singing—Ed.], and *kashrus* [dietary laws—Ed.]

Hundreds of parents hastened to register their children in Kiev's brand new *Talmud Torah* [for boys—Ed.] and *Bais Yaacov* [for girls—Ed.]....The parents of a hundred children have some how gathered the courage to withdraw their children from the state school system and have entrusted the religious and secular educations of their children to the vicissitudes of an incipient, non-registered Talmud Torah.

....Two hundred and fifty other children are enrolled in a Sunday Torah program, while another fifty attend a more intensive daily after-school program....Twenty budding *talmedei chachamim* [students—Ed.] spend their entire day in an advanced all-day yeshiva.

The *melamdim* [teachers—Ed.], *mohelim* [ritual circumcisors—Ed.], and *shochtim* [ritual slaughterers—Ed.] who came to Kiev....were deluged by an unexpected large number of requests for *brissim* [ritual circumcisions—Ed.].

I had the *zechus* [merit—Ed.] to teach groups of adults in Kiev for a period of three weeks this past summer. A hundred to one hundred-fifty people religiously attending daily classes, many of them sitting through three consecutive two-hour lectures!

The Soviet Jews came to Israel as fast as the planes could take them. And Israel welcomed them with love. In 1990 200,000 Jews came and 300,000-400,000 are expected in 1991. Where before there was darkness for the Soviet Jews, today there is new light and opportunity. As yet, only a small fraction of them have been brought to Torah Judaism. But as the process of Redemption marches along, the numbers rise steadily. The Jews of the Soviet Union will, with His help, join their brethren in the Kingdom of the Almighty.

III. For What Purpose?

The question "Why?," which is the theme of this essay, has several aspects to it. One can direct the question "Why?" at the cause of an event. "Why?" would then mean: "What caused you to act in such a manner?" Or it could be direct at the effect: "To what purpose have you acted in such a manner?"

Ezekiel prophesied why the Shoah would take place both from the aspect of the cause and of the effect. Ezekiel proclaimed what would be the problem in the twentieth century which the Almighty would judge was to be corrected by the Shoah. And

Why?

Ezekiel prophesied what would take place after the Shoah and would correct the problem.

But though the question "Why?" was explained by Ezekiel from these two aspects, there remains another aspect of "Why?" which may trouble the witness to the Shoah: Why did the Almighty choose to permit the Shoah to be the instrument to achieve the desired effect?

In the book of Genesis, the Torah related the event of the Binding of Isaac, the final and ultimate test of Abraham's readiness to serve the Almighty. The Lord says to Abraham, "Please take your son, your beloved son Isaac, and bring him as a burnt offering upon the mountain which I will show you" [22:2]. Abraham arose in the morning, hurrying to fulfill the Will of the Almighty with love.

The test of the Binding of Isaac is the ultimate test not only because he was being called upon to sacrifice his beloved son. It was the supreme test because that command seemed to contradict everything that Abraham believed and everything that he was teaching to the world. He believed with all his soul in the Truth of the Almighty and this command seemed to contradict His Truth. For, the Almighty had promised Abraham, "From your son Isaac shall come forth your eternal seed." And here, the young innocent Isaac was being sent to his death by the Almighty.

Abraham dedicated his life to teaching the world that the Almighty, the Creator of heaven and earth, is the God of Compassion Who blesses mankind with goodness and kindness. And behold, Abraham is called upon by the Almighty to perform an act of seeming cruelty.

In the liturgy of *Yom Kippur*[13], the poet tells the story of the Ten Martyrs, the great classic epic of martyrdom that took place during the days of the Roman Empire about two thousand years ago. And thus says the poet:

> These will I remember, and my soul will pour out. Evil men have swallowed us and eagerly consumed us. In the days of the tyrant there was no reprieve for the ten who were put to death by the Roman government....
>
> "Give us three days," they said, "so that we may ascertain whether this has been decreed from heaven. If we are condemned to die, we will accept the decree of The One Who is All-Merciful."
>
> Trembling and shuddering, they turned their eyes to Rabbi Ishmael, the High Priest, and they asked him to pronounce the name of God and ascend to the heavens and learn whether the decree was issued from God.
>
> Rabbi Ishmael purified himself and pronounced the name of God in awe. He ascended to the heavens, and inquired of the angel robed

The Holocaust Now

in linens, who said to him, "Accept the judgment upon yourselves, you beloved and pure, for I have heard from behind the curtain that this is your fate."

Rabbi Ishmael descended and related to his friends the word of God. Then, the evil man commanded to slay them with force. And two of them were taken first for they were the leaders of Israel, Rabbi Ishmael, the High Priest, and Rabbi Shimon ben Gamliel, the President of Israel....

They did not question the Judgment of the Almighty; they did not complain. They wanted only to know whether "this has been decreed from heaven." If so, they would accept it with love. Or was their fate still hanging in the balance in Judgment before the Almighty. If that were so, they would pray and beseech the Almighty for compassion. Rabbi Ishmael ascended to the heavens. He was told that the decree from Heaven was sealed. He went down to the earth and informed his colleagues. They accepted their fate. They trusted in the Perfect Judgment of the Almighty and no questions left their lips.

But the Torah tells us that Moshe[14] did ask "Why?" Let us proceed to examine the question of Moshe, what he asked, and why he asked it.

The Torah tells us of the following events that took place before the Exodus, and the ensuing dialogue between the Almighty and Moshe.

The Almighty heard the cries of the people of Israel and decided to take them out of their bondage. He called on Moshe and told him to go to Pharaoh and tell him that the God of Israel said to let His people go into the desert and celebrate a holiday in His Name. Pharaoh refused the request, saying to Moshe that the children of Israel want to sacrifice to their God because they are lazy. He thereupon ordered that their work be increased. He commanded that they no longer given the straw to make the bricks and that they should themselves have to gather all the necessary quantities of straw. But the number of bricks that they had to provide each day would be maintained. When the Israelites could not meet that order, they were beaten by the slave masters who shouted, "Why did you not complete your quota of bricks as you did yesterday and the day before?"

When Moshe saw what had resulted from his mission he said to me:

"Why have You done harm to this people? Why have You sent me? From the time that I came to Pharaoh to speak in Your Name, he has dealt harshly with this people, and You have not saved them."

In the sentence quoted, the Hebrew word for the question "Why" differs. In the first sentence, the word is *madua*. In the other sentence, it is *lamah*. *Targum Onkelos*[15] translates each of them differently. In the earlier sentence, "Why did you not complete

Why?

your quota of bricks?" Onkelos translates *madua* as *mah dein*, meaning "What is this?" In the sentence "Why did You do harm to this people?" Onkelos translated *lamah*, why, as *l'mah dein*, which means "to what is this?"

There is a clear distinction between these two question.

Mah dein, meaning "what is this," is aimed at the act. What is the explanation of the act?

It may question the cause, or the justification, or it may be a request for clarification. The word for this question is *madua*.

L'mah dein means "to what is this." The question is directed at the effect. To what effect was this act done?

The word for the question of Moshe is *lamah*. Moshe, the leader of Israel, had the duty to pray for his people. He therefore need to know the effect that the Judgment of the Almighty would have upon the people so that he could pray to have it changed. Thus, when the Almighty sent him to Pharaoh to send the people of Israel out of Egypt and instead of sending them out Pharaoh intensified the slavery, Moshe complained to the Almighty and asked, "Why did You do harm to this people? Why did You send me?"

Moshe asked of the Almighty "What is the effect that You intended to happen when You sent me? Was it not to save the people?" Moshe did not question the wisdom and justice of the Judgment. Rather, he beseeched the Almighty to bring another effect to His people and bring to them an immediate salvation.

The history of the Shoah is the history of the Binding of Isaac repeated six million times. Six million martyrs died, not with complaints, not with questions, but with love and faith. They recited *Sh'ma Yisrael*, "Hear O Israel, The Lord our G-d, the Lord is one." They died proudly proclaiming their love for their Father, the King of the Universe. And they died singing *Ani ma'amin*, "I believe with perfect trust in the Faith and Promise of the Almighty."

Leaders of Israel were like unto Moshe, speaking of the effect that they knew would come from the death of the martyrs. So did the holy Rabbi Elchanan Wasserman who spoke to the Jews of Kovno as they were ready to march to their deaths. He said to the assembled prisoners:

> We are now fulfilling the greatest commandment, to sanctify His Name. The fire which will consume our bones is the fire that will give birth again to the Jewish nation.

We have said that the question *lamah* is aimed at understanding the effect of an action. The question *madua* is aimed at understanding the action.

When one asks "Why did the Almighty choose to permit the Shoah to be instrument of the desired effect?" one questions the wisdom of the action. The question asked of the Almighty is *madua*, and this question the Torah does not ask nor answer. When Moshe was confronted by an Act of the Almighty which he sought to understand, he did not ask *madua*. He asked only *lamah*. He did not question the act. He questioned only the effect.

The following comment by the classic Talmudic commentator Maharsha[16] in the section Brachot[17] will help us understand why Moshe limited his questioning of the Almighty to the effect.

The Talmud states that when the Almighty appeared to him in the Burning Bush, Moshe did three things for which he received three corresponding blessings. The Torah says, "And Moshe hid his face for he feared to gaze at the Almighty." He "hid his face" and "he feared" and "he did not gaze at the Almighty."

The Maharsha explains the three meritorious qualities of Moshe evident in that passage. He writes that a human being hesitates to come close to the Almighty for three reasons. One, he has an instinctive reverence for One so Great and Awesome and does not step forward to stand close to Him. Secondly, he recognizes the limitations of man and hesitates to analyze the concepts of the Almighty lest he err. And third, he understands the infinite nature of the affairs of the Almighty, and knows that man cannot truly understand them.

At the Burning Bush, "he averted his eyes," meaning "he did not delve into the Ways of the Almighty," for he "feared" his own inadequacy and "he did not gaze at the Almighty" for he realized the infinite nature of the Ways of the Almighty.

The Torah is a "Book of Life," a guide to the human being. It teaches him how he should conduct himself for the peace of his body and soul. It teaches man the qualities of the Almighty so that he should emulate them in his conduct.

But, it does not teach man to judge the affairs of the Almighty. In the *Sh'moneh Esray*[18], recited on the Day of Judgment, we proclaim the Almighty as "the King of the Judgment," meaning "the Only King of all Judgment." The Almighty has relegated the judgment of the world to Himself.

We are consoled with the knowledge that the 6,000,000 martyrs have taken their places in the presence of the Almighty in Heaven. We praise Him and thank Him for the blessings which came to the Jewish people after the Shoah. We sanctify Him for His Judgment of Truth, for He is the True Judge. We pray that we, and all His people, be blessed with His favor of peace forever..

The Shoah: Continuing Theological Challenge for Christianity

For John Pawlikowski, for whom the Shoah represents "the ultimate expression of human freedom and human evil," the question now remains whether or not there exists any significant role for God in its aftermath in the construction of a moral schema with which to prevent the reoccurrence of radical evil. Surveying the major Jewish and Christian thinkers, including many less well-known, he finds both communities have not devoted sufficient discussion to any role for God, and would substitute the notion of the "compelling God" for that of the "commanding God." He likewise finds meaning both in the centrality of humility in the post-Shoah world and in the "theology of divine vulnerability," and would, following McGarry, Ruether, and others, present the need for a reformulation of Christology, cautioning us ever that the appropriate uses of power—political, religious, military, economic—must be addressed in any meaningful contemporary Christian or Jewish theology.

SLJ

The Holocaust Now

THE SHOAH: CONTINUING THEOLOGICAL CHALLENGE FOR CHRISTIANITY

John T. Pawlikowski

I. Setting the Context

What follows is an attempt by one Christian scholar to confront some of the overarching theological challenges posed by the Shoah which we are gradually coming to understand as an epochal event in the history of Western society, including the Western church, with decided implications for the future of all of humanity. It is truly an "orienting experience" for contemporary human existence, to speak in the words of Irving Greenberg. We shall probe the Shoah's impact on our sense of God, the Christ Event, the church, morality, and theological methodology. But as we undertake this necessary task of theological and social analysis, we must never let our minds and hearts stray very far from the memory of the six million Jews, including one million children, who were annihilated simply because they were Jews, nor of the up to five million Poles, Rom people, Gays, mentally and physically incapacitated and others who joined them in victimhood as part of the Nazi effort to purify humanity. Likewise, Christians must never lose sight of the fact that the Shoah continues to strain Christian credibility. While contemporary scholarship has adequately documented that the Shoah was primarily parented by currents within certain modern secular philosophies and by social theories which at their core were often profoundly anti-Christian, little doubt remains that classical Christian teaching and preaching constituted an indispensable seedbed for the success of the Nazi effort. Even a scholar such as the late Uriel Tal, who strongly argued for the predominance of secular [and anti-Christian] antisemitism in the genesis of Nazism, continued to underscore the pivotal contribution of the Christian tradition. He insisted that Nazi racial antisemitism was not totally original when subjected to careful analysis. Rather, traditional Christian stereotypes of Jews and Judaism were clothed in new pseudoscientific jargon and applied to specific historical realities of the period. In summation, Tal says that "racial anti-Semitism and the subsequent Nazi movement were not the result of mass hysteria or the work of single propagandists. The racial antisemites, despite their antagonism toward traditional Christianity, learned much from it, and succeeded in producing a well-prepared, systematic ideology with a logic of its own that reached its culmination in the Third Reich."[1]

Christianity cannot equivocate regarding its responsibility for the spread of Nazism if it is to enter authentically the continuing debate about the broader theological implications of the Shoah. Achieving such authenticity clearly will involve a commitment to the full and final purge of all remaining antisemitism from its theological statements, catechetical teachings, and liturgical expressions. The church must likewise be willing to submit its World War II record to a thorough scrutiny by respected scholars. Ultimately, it cannot avoid confronting the question of a fellow inmate posed to Alexander Donat, author of *The Holocaust Kingdom:* "How can Christianity survive the discovery that after a thousand years of its being Europe's official religion, Europe remains pagan at heart?"[2]

Not raising the specific issues involved with the Christian response to the Shoah in no way is meant to convey the impression that they are of secondary importance. On the contrary, they remain absolutely central and critical for any meaningful encounter with this whirlwind of evil that so engulfed European civilization in our century. It would be presumptuous for any Christian to treat the overarching theological issues of the Shoah without first having addressed forthrightly the question of Christian culpability during the Nazi era. Having attempted to discharge this moral responsibility in other writings[3], the following reflections will concentrate on more generalized theological concerns.

II. A New Human Condition

In the final analysis the Shoah represented the beginning of a new era in human self-awareness and human possibility over which hung the specter of either unprecedented destruction or unparalleled hope. With the rise of Nazism the mass extermination of human life in a guiltless fashion became thinkable and technologically feasible. The door was now ajar for an era when dispassionate torture and the murder of millions could become not merely the act of a crazed despot, not just a desire for national security, not merely an irrational outbreak of xenophobic fear, but a calculated effort to reshape history supported by intellectual argumentation from the best and brightest minds in a society. It was an attempt, Emil Fackenheim has said, to wipe out the "divine image" in history. "The murder camp," Fackenheim insists, "was not an accidental by-product of the Nazi empire. It was its essence."[4]

The fundamental challenge of the Shoah lies in our altered perception of the relationship between God and humanity and its implications for the basis of moral behavior. What emerges as a central reality from the study of the Shoah is the Nazi effort to create the "superperson," to develop a truly liberated humanity, to be shared only by a

The Shoah: Continuing Theological Challenge for Christianity

select group, namely, the Aryan race. This new humanity would be released from the moral restraints previously imposed by religious beliefs and would be capable of exerting virtually unlimited power in the shaping of the world and its inhabitants. In a somewhat indirect, though still powerful, way the Nazis had proclaimed the death of God as a guiding force in the governance of the universe.

In pursuit of their objective, the Nazis became convinced that all the "dregs of humanity" had to be eliminated or at least their influence on culture and human development significantly curtailed. The Jews fell into this "dregs" category first and foremost. They were classified as "vermin." The Nazis could not imagine even a minimally useful role for Jews in the new society to which they hoped to give birth. The Polish and Romani peoples as well as gay persons and those suffering mental or physical disabilities were also looked upon as polluters of the new level of humanity envisioned by the Nazis. While proper distinction between these victims and the Jewish people needs to be maintained because, with the possible exception of the Rom community [or "Gypsies"], none were slated for the same kind of wholesale extermination that was to be the ultimate fate of the Jews, they, too, were considered obstacles to the advancement of human consciousness to new levels of insight, power and self-control. Their extermination under the rubric of humankind's purification assumes a theological significance intimately related to the Jewish question. Regrettably the non-Jewish victims are generally ignored in the emerging theological reflections on the Shoah whether by Christian or Jewish scholars.[5]

Uriel Tal captured as well as anyone the basic theological challenge presented by the Shoah. In his understanding, the so-called "Final Solution" had as its ultimate objective the total transformation of human values. Its stated intent was liberating humanity from all previous moral ideals and codes. When the liberating process was complete, humanity would be once and for all rescued from the imprisonment of a God concept and its related notions of moral responsibility, redemption, sin and revelation. Nazi ideology sought to transform theological ideas into exclusively anthropological and political concepts. In Tal's interpretation of the Shoah the Nazis adopted a kind of "incarnational" ideology, but not in the New Testament sense of the term. Rather, for the Nazis, "God becomes man in a political sense as a member of the Aryan race whose highest representative on earth is the Fuhrer."[6]

Tal's research led him to conclude that this new Nazi consciousness emerged only gradually in the decades following World War I. Its roots, however, were somewhat earlier. It was undeniably related to the general process of social secularization that had been transforming Germany since the latter part of the nineteenth century. Its philosophic parents included the Deists, the French encyclopedists, Feuerbach, the Young Hegelians, and the evolutionary thinkers in concert with the developing corps of scientists who, through their many new discoveries, were creating the impression that a triumphant material civilization was on the verge of dawning in Western Europe. In the end, Tal argued, "these intellectual and social movements struck a responsive chord in a rebellious generation, altered the traditional views of God, man, and society, and ultimately led to the pseudo-religious, pseudomessianic movement of Nazism."[7]

III. The Post-Shoah Theological Dilemma

The principal theological problem raised by the Shoah is how does humankind properly appropriate the genuine sense of human liberation that lay at the heart of Nazi ideology without surrendering its soul to massive evil. However horrendous their legacy, the Nazis were correct in at least one respect. They rightly perceived that some basic changes were underway in human consciousness. The impact of the new science and technology, with its underlying assumption of freedom, was beginning to provide the human community on a mass scale with a Promethean-type experience of escape from prior moral chains. People were starting to perceive, however dimly, an enhanced sense of dignity and autonomy far more than most of Western Christian theology had previously conceded. Traditional theological concepts that had shaped much of the Christian moral perspective, notions such as divine punishment, hell, and divine wrath and providence were losing some of the hold they had exercised over moral decision-making since Biblical times. Christian theology had tended to accentuate the omnipotence of God which in turn intensified the impotence of the human person and the rather inconsequential role played by the human community in maintaining the sustainability of the earth. The Nazis totally rejected this previous relationship. In fact, they were literally trying to turn it upside down.

Michael Ryan has emphasized this direction of Nazism in his theological analysis of Hitler's *Mein Kampf*. For Ryan, the most striking aspect of the "salvation history" found in this volume is Hitler's willingness to confine humanity in an absolute way to the limits of time. In the Hitlerian perspective humankind must resign itself to the conditions of finitude. But this resignation is accompanied by the assertion of all-pervasive power for itself within those conditions. The end result of all this was the self-deification of Hitler who proclaimed himself the new "Savior" of the German nation. It is this Hitlerian mindset that allows us, in Ryan's judgment, to term *Mein Kampf* a "theological" treatise. In the final analysis, in Ryan's words, Hitler's worldview "amounted to the deliberate decision on the part of mass man to live within the limits of finitude without either the moral restraints or the hopes of traditional religion—in this case, Christianity."[8]

The challenge facing theology after the Shoah is to discover a way whereby the new sense of human freedom that is continuing to dawn might be affirmed but channeled into constructive rather than humanly-destructive purposes. The understanding of the God-human person relationship must be significantly altered in light of the Shoah. The intensified sense of power and human enhancement that the Nazis championed as a *novum* of our age needs to be acknowledged as a crucial and inescapable element in the ongoing process of humanity's salvation. There is simply no way of reversing the consciousness of a profound readjustment in the nature of the divine-human relationship. That is why the mere repetition of Biblical images and precepts is insufficient as a response to the Shoah. Contemporary humanity perceives itself in a far more liberated condition relative to divine power and authority than the authors of the Biblical texts could ever imagine. There exists today an awareness of dimensions of the Genesis notion of co-creatorship which the Biblical world was unable to grasp in any way. As the moral philosopher Hans Jonas has reminded us, we constitute the first generation with the responsibility for insuring the future of all forms of life in the universe. No previous generation had in its grasp the possibilities for massive destruction that are open to us. In the past, nature had sufficient recuperative powers to heal whatever wounds humanity's capitulation to evil might inflict. This is no longer so to the same extent. That is why, while it is important to consider the Shoah separately so as to properly illustrate its profound distinctiveness as a historical and theological event, it is equally necessary to establish a link with the other shattering experience of World War II—Hiroshima. In one sense, the two events are of a significantly different order; but, in another, as expressions of the newly-found power of humanity to destroy, they remain profoundly intertwined.

The question at hand is whether post-Shoah theology can develop an expression of God and religion which will help prevent the newly-recognized creative power of humanity from being transformed into the destructive force unveiled in all its ugliness during the Nazi era. Put another way, can post-Shoah humanity discover a relationship with God which will provide warrants for the use of its vast new power to shape itself and the creation it has inherited? This fundamental issue has been basically ignored by most Christian theologians up till now.

Reflections on the divine-human encounter in light of the Shoah have emerged in the last decade or so as one of the central theological discussions in Judaism. Unfortunately, as David Tracy has regretted, no parallel development has occurred within Christian theological circles. Few church theologians, says Tracy, are focusing on the ultimate religious question for all believers, including Christians—the problem of God—which, as Schleiermacher perceptively insisted, can never be treated as one among many doctrines but must pervade all other statements of belief. In this regard, Tracy is convinced that "Jewish theology, in its reflections on the reality of God since the *Tremendum* of the Holocaust, has led the way for all serious theological reflection."[9]

IV. Post-Shoah Approaches to God

Theological discussion about God in light of the Shoah has generated a variety of viewpoints among Jewish scholars. It is impossible to treat them in a comprehensive fashion in this discussion. Hence we will focus on a select number of figures whose writings has proven influential in the past several years.

The basic division among Jewish scholars has come over the question of how central a role the Shoah should assume in the contemporary reconstruction of Jewish belief. Most Orthodox Jewish scholars have tended to downplay the Shoah as a major turning point in the understanding of the divine-human relationship. While they remain acutely sensitive that the annihilation of six million innocent men, women and children has traumatized the Jewish People, they hold fast to the belief that the experience ultimately can still be incorporated into classical religious categories of evil. A few Reform Jewish scholars such as Eugene Borowitz have likewise de-emphasized the Shoah has a theological issue in favor of the more traditional concern in Reform Judaism with the problem of how belief in God is to be reconciled with what enhanced awareness of human autonomy in modern times.

David Hartman remains an articulate, creative spokesperson for the above point of view. In a number of writings, including the book *A Living Covenant: The Innovative Spirit in Traditional Judaism*[10], he opts for the contemporary renewal of traditional covenantal religion, rather than the Shoah, as central to the generation of the faith commitment required to guarantee Jewish survival. Adopting a position similar to that advocated by the Christian ethicist James Gustafson about humankind's inability really to know God ultimately intends for creation, Hartman stresses the development of a new faithfulness to Torah observance as the only way of assuring communal survival and a measure of meaning in a frequently chaotic world. The Shoah was certainly a part of this chaos. And its continued remembrance is vital. But in no way should it provide the basis for contemporary belief. For Hartman, "Auschwitz, like all Jewish suffering of the past, must be absorbed and understood within the normative framework of Sinai." Jews will mourn forever the memory of the victims, but they "will build a healthy new society because of the memory of Sinai."[11]

There is reason to show some sympathy for the stance of Hartman and his colleagues. No post-Shoah faith expression can totally divorce itself from the covenantal experience and promises. And to the extent that Hartman means to direct his remarks against those in the Jewish community who would use the Shoah as a basis for the development of a chauvinistic nationalism in the midst of the current Israeli-Palestinian crisis, he deserves applause. Yet, in the final analysis, Hartman's position falls short because of his inability to grasp that the reality of the Shoah no longer allows us to

The Shoah: Continuing Theological Challenge for Christianity

speak of covenantal faith in the same way as did the Biblical or Rabbinic traditions. The Shoah was not merely the most extreme example of the classical theological problem of evil. It had burst asunder the traditional position. To confine our response to the Shoah to the renewal of covenantal faith as Hartman prescribes would be to endanger human survival. For we would remain unprepared to deal with the magnitude of the power and consequent responsibility that has come into the hands of humanity. And failure on the part of humankind to recognize these new post-Shoah realities may allow this power to pass once again into the hands of a new class of Nazis. The frontispiece to Alexander Donat's *The Holocaust Kingdom*, based on Revelation 6:8, poignantly reminds us of that continuing potential: "And I looked, and behold a pale horse and his name that sat on him was Death, and Hell followed with him. And power was given unto them over the fourth part of the earth, to kill with sword, and with hunger, and with death and with the beasts of the earth."

Among those Jewish scholars who have argued for major theological re-interpretation of the divine-human relationship in response to the Shoah the names of Richard Rubenstein, Emil Fackenheim, Arthur Cohen and Irving Greenberg stand out. Brief attention will be given to the first three followed by a somewhat more detailed discussion of Greenberg's approach.

Rubenstein's volume *After Auschwitz*[12] caused a great stir in Jewish circles when it first appeared. Its boldly stated claim that the Shoah had buried any possibility of continued belief in a covenantal God of history and that, in place of traditional faith, Jews must now turn to a creed of "paganism" which defines human existence as wholly and totally an earthly existence shook the foundations of Judaism. When the dust had somewhat settled, the prevailing opinion was that Rubenstein had gone much too far, a point that he himself seemingly acknowledges [at least implicitly] in some of his more recent writings. Today, Rubenstein's position seems somewhat closer to a mystical approach to God. The cosmos is no longer as cold, silent, and unfeeling a reality as he projected in *After Auschwitz*. As John Roth presumably writes in the volume co-authored by Rubenstein and himself, "Today, Rubenstein would balance the elements of creativeness and love in the cosmos somewhat more evenly with those of destruction and hate than he was prepared to do in 1966. What has not changed is his affirmation of a view of God quite different from the mainstream view of biblical and rabbinic Judaism and his rejection of the notion that the Jews are in any sense a people either chosen or rejected by God."[13]

Whatever else may be said in judgment about Rubenstein's initial or more refined perspective, he is credited by a number of fellow scholars with at least one major contribution. Steven Katz, who rejects Rubenstein's original summons to "paganism," is a case in point. He considers Rubenstein "absolutely correct" in his judgment that classical categories of evil no longer are convincing relative to the God-human relationship when confronted by the immensity of the Shoah.[14]

Fackenheim, Cohen and Greenberg, in their approaches to the post-Shoah divine reality, stop far short of Rubenstein's total rejection of a covenantal God. But, despite some significant differences among them, they speak with unified voice regarding the need for a major restatement of this relationship in light of the Shoah.

In his numerous writings, but especially in the volume *The Jewish Return into History*[15], Emil Fackenheim states his conviction that the image of God was destroyed during the Shoah. Our task today, a mandate incumbent in a special way upon the survivors of the Shoah, is to restore the divine image, but in a way that conveys a sense of a new curtailment of God's power in comparison with past images.

Arthur Cohen picked upon on this same theme, but used more philosophically-oriented language to make his point. In *The Tremendum: A Theological Interpretation of the Holocaust*[16], Cohen pointedly rejected the continued viability of any image of God as the strategist of human history. A post-Shoah God can legitimately be perceived [and must be perceived if radical evil is to remain in check] as "the mystery of our futurity, always our posse, never our acts. If we can begin to see God less as an interferer whose insertion is welcome [when it accords with our needs] and more as the immensity whose reality is our prefiguration, whose speech and silence are metaphors for our language and distortion, whose plenitude and unfolding are the hope of our futurity, we shall have won a sense of God whom we may love and honor, but whom we no longer fear and from whom we no longer demand."[17]

Turning now to Irving Greenberg, we find that his language about the effects of the Shoah on the divine image are not as blunt as those of Fackenheim's, but he shares the conviction that a major readjustment is required of our statement of the force of the covenantal obligations upon humanity in light of the Shoah. "The Nazis," he says, "unleashed all-out violence against the covenant...." Their program for the 'Final Solution' involved a total assault on Jewish life and values. For Greenberg, "the degree of success of this attack constitutes a fundamental contradiction to the covenant of life and redemption."[18]

The reality of the Nazi fury forces a thorough reconsideration of the nature of moral obligation upon the contemporary Jewish community and seemingly by implication upon all those other believers [Christian and Muslim] who in some way regard the Sinai covenant as foundation for their faith expression. For this covenant has called Jews as witnesses to the world for God and for a final perfection. "In light of the Holocaust," insists Greenberg, "it is obvious that this role opened the Jews to a murderous fury from which there was no escape. Yet the Divine could not or would not save them from this fate. Therefore, morally speaking, God must repent of the covenant, i.e., do *teshuvah* [repentance—Ed.] for having given his chosen people a task that was unbearably cruel and dangerous without having provided for their protection. Morally speak-

The Shoah: Continuing Theological Challenge for Christianity

ing, then, God can have no claims on the Jews by dint of the covenant."[19]

The end result of any serious reflection on the Sinai covenant in light of the Shoah experience, as Greenberg sees it, is simply the disappearance of any "commanded" dimension on the part of God. "Covenantally speaking, one cannot *order* another to step forward to die."[20] Any understanding of covenantal obligation must now be voluntary: "One cannot *order* another to go on a suicide mission. Out of shared values, one can only ask for volunteers....No divine punishment can enforce the covenant, for there is no risked punishment so terrible that it can match the punishment risked by continuing faithfulness to the covenant."[21]

The voluntary nature of the post-Shoah covenantal relationship unquestionably heightens human responsibility in the eyes of Greenberg: "If after the Temple's destruction, Israel moved from junior partner to true partner in the covenant, then after the Holocaust, the Jewish people is called upon to become the senior partner in action. In effect, God was saying to humans: you stop the Holocaust. You bring the redemption. You act to ensure that it will never again occur. I will be with you totally in whatever happens, but you must do it."[22]

My basic response to the post-Shoah reflections of Fackenheim, Cohen and especially Greenberg is that, despite some reservations, they provide the basic parameters within which we need to understand the God-human relationship today and its connection with the foundations for contemporary morality. For one, consciousness of the role of the human community in preserving human history from further eruptions of radical evil akin to Nazism has been greatly enhanced, as all three have rightly insisted. Humanity find itself after the Shoah facing the realization that "future" is no longer something God will guarantee. Survival, whether for the People Israel or humanity at large, is now more than ever a human proposition. In their differing ways, Fackenheim, Cohen and Greenberg have made this fact abundantly clear. And we need to be profoundly grateful for that. They have clearly confronted us with the post-Shoah reality that any simplistic belief in an interventionist God of history was buried in the ashes of Nazi Germany. Preventing massive human destruction is now far more evidently than before a burden primarily incumbent upon the human community. We must learn to save ourselves from future instances of holocaust, nuclear or otherwise. We are summoned to answer "right now" to D.H. Lawrence's plea, "God of Justice, when wilt Thou teach them to save themselves?"[23] We no longer have the luxury, fact it would be the height of human irresponsibility after the Shoah, to imagine that God will do it in response to simple petitions of prayer. Perhaps because of the freedom God has granted humanity he cannot do it. It might be added here that a fruitful source in our search for a post-Shoah vision of God that would strengthen the human role in the process of salvation might be the Jewish mystical literature with its notion of divine self-constriction in the act of creation.

The Holocaust Now

But despite my gratitude to Fackenheim, Cohen and Greenberg their prescriptions for God-belief after the Shoah are not wholly satisfactory in the end. They would appear to have left humanity too much to its own whims after the Shoah. They have not adequately explored whether God continues to play a significant role after the Shoah in the development of a moral ethos within humanity that can restrain radical evil. The role they have in fact assigned to God is not potent enough.

V. Moving Toward the *Compelling* God

The post-Shoah theological vision must be one that recognizes both the new creative possibilities inherent in the human condition as well as the utter necessity for this creative potential to be brought under the sway of an encounter with the living and judging God. Only such an encounter will direct the use of this creative potential away from the destruction represented by Nazism. We need to find a way of articulating a notion of a transcendent God which can counterbalance the potential for evil that remains very much a live possibility in the contemporary human situation. In other words, we shall have to recover a fresh sense of transcendence to accompany our heightened sense of human responsibility after the Shoah. This is something basically absent from the reflections of Fackenheim, Cohen and Greenberg. Men and women will once more need to experience contact with a personal power beyond themselves, a power that heals the destructive tendencies still lurking within humanity. The newly-liberated person, to be able to work consistently for the creation of a just and sustainable society, must begin to sense a judgment upon human endeavors that goes beyond mere human judgment. Such a sense of judgment is missing in Fackenheim's emphasis on human restoration of the divine image, in Cohen's language about God as our "posse," and in Greenberg's notion of the voluntary covenant, as valid as each notion is in itself.

The Shoah has shattered all simplistic notions of a "commanding God." On this point, Fackenheim, Cohen and Greenberg are perfectly correct. Such a "commanding" God can no longer be the touchstone of ethical behavior. But the Shoah has also exposed humanity's desperate need to restore a relationship with a "compelling" God, compelling because we have experienced, through symbolic encounter with this God, a healing, a strengthening, an affirming that buries any need to assert our humanity through the destructive, even deadly, use of human power. This sense of a compelling Parent God who has gifted humanity, whose vulnerability for the Christian has been shown in the Cross, is the meaningful foundation for any adequate moral ethos after the Shoah.

Some have suggested that "compelling" may be too strong a replacement adjective for "commanding" in speaking about the post-Shoah God. Perhaps they are right. Perhaps "compelling" does tip the scales too much back towards a pre-Shoah vision of

The Shoah: Continuing Theological Challenge for Christianity

divine reality. These critics have offered the alternative of speaking of a "God to whom we are drawn" which admittedly is more cumbersome than "compelling." This inherent and enduring "drawing" power of God would substitute for pre-Shoah models which emphasized God's "imposition" upon humanity.

At this point, the "compelling" vocabulary seems preferable. But whatever image eventually wins the day, the basic point must be made that post-Shoah humanity needs to rediscover a permanent relationship with God who remains a direct source of strength and influence in the conduct of human affairs.

In speaking of the need to rediscover a "compelling" God, I believe I am close to the stage Elie Wiesel has reached as he has probed the depth of the Shoah these many years. Despite the remaining ambiguities, despite the apparent divine failures in covenantal responsibility, atheism is not the answer for contemporary humanity according to Wiesel. After we have exhausted ourselves in protesting against God's non-intervention during this period of night, we still are unable to let God go away permanently. Any attempt, Wiesel insists, to make the Shoah "fit" into a divine plan, any belief that somehow we can imagine a universe congruent with it, renders God a moral monster and the universe a nightmare beyond endurance. But, theologian Robert McAfee Brown, has put it, "....for Wiesel and for many others the issue will not go away. He must *contest* with God, concerning the moral outrage that somehow seems to be within the divine plan. How can one affirm a God whose 'divine plan' could include such barbarity? For Wiesel, the true 'contemporary' is not the modern skeptic, but the ancient Job, the one who dares to ask questions of God, even though Wiesel feels that Job gave in a little too quickly at the end."[24]

Wiesel hints that after all is said and done the Shoah may reveal that divine and human liberation are very much intertwined and that, despite continuing tension, both God and humanity yearn for each other as a result. In consequence of this linkage, Wiesel is prepared to say that human acts of justice and compassion help to liberate God, to restore the divine image as Fackenheim has phrased it. Job, says Wiesel, "did not suffer in vain; thanks to him, we know that it is given to man to transform divine injustice into human justice and compassion."[25] But they also show the need for God's continuing presence, for the human person who claims total freedom from God will not likely pursue such a ministry of justice and compassion for very long. So the human person is also liberated from the corrupting desire to cut all ties to the Creator.

At this point the inevitable question must be posed: How can this "compelling" God serve as the ground of contemporary morality? Strange as it may seem, the Shoah provides us with some assistance in responding to this question. For if the Shoah reveals one permanent quality of human life, it is the enduring presence of, the continuing human need for, symbolic affirmation and communication. What Reinhold Niebuhr called the "vitalistic side of humanity" has not been permanently obliterated. But increasingly in the West, it has been relegated almost exclusively to the realm of play and recreation. The Enlightenment and its aftermath caused a bifurcation in Western humanity which has catapulted reason to a place of overwhelming dominance in the self-definition of the person. All other human dimensions tend to be relegated to an inferior position. In this setting, ethics has become too exclusively rational a discipline and far too dominated by the scientific mentality. The liberals in Germany were powerless in fighting Nazism, not because they did not care, but because they naively assumed that the masses would respond to mere rational moral argumentation. The Nazis were far more perceptive in recognizing the centrality of the vitalistic in human life.

Recovery of abiding contact with the personal Creator God first revealed in the Hebrew Scriptures is as indispensable a starting point for social ethics in the post-Shoah era as recognition of our enhanced co-creational responsibility for the world. The two go hand-in-hand. Any attempt to construct a social ethic for our age by merely assuming the continued reality of this divine presence, however, will not succeed. Neither will efforts built around natural law, Kantian rational consistency models or psychoanalysis provide the requisite moral grounding. The kind of post-Shoah relationship between God and humanity pivotal for the development of social morality in our time will come only through divine-human encounter in worship and prayer. The failure of nearly all contemporary forms of social ethics to deal constructively with the role of symbols, especially liturgical symbols, in fostering social morality, to recognize how crucial they are for overcoming the prevailing one-dimensionality infecting Western society has left us with an increasingly barren public morality.

We may not need to return to the tradition of medieval morality plays. But we desperately need to understand that without liturgy and prayer there is no real way of overcoming self-centeredness and the destructive use of power evidenced in the Shoah save for the kind of spiritless centralization of authority proposed by Robert Heilbroner in his *An Inquiry into the Human Prospect*.[26] Psychoanalysis can uncover humanity's neuroses. But by itself it cannot fully heal. Sacramental celebration and prayer are crucial to this end. God is a Person experienced through symbolic encounter. This revolutionary revelation of the Hebrew Scriptures and the New Testament remains a touchstone for a sound social ethic for our society.

Much more could be said about the God-problem in light of the Shoah. But in the interest of addressing several other issues, we shall end the discussion at this point and turn to the question of Christianity.

VI. Christology and the Shoah

In the almost quarter century since the Second Vatican Council passed its historic declaration on the church and the Jewish People in its document *Nostra Aetate*, consid-

The Shoah: Continuing Theological Challenge for Christianity

erable progress has been made on the constructive restatement within the church of the theological relationship between Christianity and the People Israel. Individual theologians both in Europe and America have led the way, but some important developments have occurred in official ecclesiastical pronouncements as well. Paul van Buren, Franz Mussner, Clemens Thoma, A. Roy [and Alice L.] Eckardt and Peter von der Osten-Sacken, to name but a few, have made extremely important contributions in this regard. My own volumes *Christ in Light of the Christian-Jewish Dialogue*[27] and *Jesus and the Theology of Israel*[28] are modest attempts to survey recent theological developments and propose the outlines of a new theological model. This model is grounded in several key convictions. They are: [1] that the Christ Event did not invalidate the Jewish faith perspective; [2] that Christianity is not superior to Judaism, nor is it the fulfillment of Judaism as previously maintained; [3] that the Sinai covenant is in principle as crucial to Christian faith expression as the covenant in Christ; [4] that Christianity needs to reincorporate dimensions from its original Jewish context as an integral part of its creed; and [5] that the "uniqueness" of the Christ Event, a limited "uniqueness" at that, consists primarily in the enhanced understanding of the linkage between humanity and divinity and its impact on salvation expressed through what Christians have termed "Incarnation." Whether this new Christian-Jewish relationship is best expressed through the notion of a single covenant notion, as most ecclesiastical documents and some theologians such as van Buren propose, or a double covenant model as Mussner and I would have it, remains an open question. What is not debatable is that in light of the Shoah the church's moral integrity will not allow it to retain the classical supercessionist models of the relationship which generated antisemitism for centuries and which, while not the primary cause of the Shoah as was argued earlier, nonetheless played a decisive role in stimulating public acquiescence to the 'Final Solution'.

Johannes Baptist Metz in particular has stressed the church's responsibility to adjust its basic Christological formulations insofar as they impinge on the fate of the Jewish People in response to the Shoah. He proposes three theses as indispensable for theological reflection in the church in this post-Shoah era: [1] "Christian theology after Auschwitz must—at long last—be guided by the insight that Christians can form and sufficiently understand their identity only in the face of the Jews;" [2] "Because of Auschwitz the statement 'Christians can only form and appropriately understand their identity in the face of the Jews' has been sharpened as follows: 'Christians can protect their identity only in front of and together with the history of the beliefs of the Jews';" and [3] "Christian theology after Auschwitz must stress anew the Jewish dimension in Christian beliefs and must overcome the forced blocking-out of the Jewish heritage within Christianity."[29] Certainly Metz is moving in the right direction in his strong advocacy of these three theses. However, he still needs to apply them much more specifically and in much greater detail to an exposition of the meaning of God and

Christ for contemporary Christianity than he has done to date.

Metz is not alone in his failure on the above point. It is generally true of most of the theologians who have undertaken a re-examination of the traditional statements of the Jewish-Christian relationship. While they may be consciously responding to the Shoah through their efforts in this regard, they do little to relate their new Christological statements directly to the Shoah experience and its impact on the God question. And yet, as David Tracy has rightly reminded us, the God question, not the Christ question, is the ultimate theological issue for Christians. A case in point is Paul van Buren who has undertaken the most comprehensive restatement of the covenantal links between the church and the Jewish People yet available. Even in his most recently volume, his constructive Christological statement, fails to treat of the Shoah in any significant way.[30] Rubenstein and Roth are on target in their criticism of van Buren's otherwise monumental contribution on this score.[31]

A few Christian theologians have tried to take up the specific challenge posed by the Shoah for Christological understanding. Lutheran ethicist Franklin Sherman has uncovered in the Cross of Christ "the symbol of the agonizing God." The only legitimate Christology for Sherman in light of the Shoah is one that sees in the Christ Event the revelation of divine participation in the sufferings of people who are in turn summoned to take part in the sufferings of God. "We speak of God after Auschwitz," Sherman insists, "only as the one who calls us to a new unity as between brothers—not only between Jews and Christians, but especially between Jews and Christians."[32] For Sherman, Christ crucified becomes the symbol of the agonizing God. Sherman laments the fact that this symbol of the Cross has become such a source of division, rather than reconciliation, between Jews and Christians throughout history. For, in fact, the Cross points to a very Jewish reality—suffering and martyrdom.

An Israeli Catholic scholar, Marcel Dubois, O.P., moves in a vein somewhat parallel to that of Sherman.[33] While acutely conscious of the difficulty Christians have in setting the reality of the Shoah within the context of a theology of the Cross, and recognizing that such a linkage may appear as an obscenity to Jews whose sufferings in the Shoah the church helped to perpetrate, Dubois nonetheless feels that this is the direction in which Christian theology ought to move: "....in the person of the suffering servant there appears to take place an effable change. Our vision of Jewish destiny and our understanding of the Holocaust in particular depend on our compassion; the Calvary of the Jewish people, whose summit is the Holocaust, can help us to understand a little better the mystery of the Cross."[34]

Douglas Hall is yet a third Christian theologian focusing post-Shoah Christological interpretations around the Cross. His reflections on the Nazi period of night have left him convinced that only a theology of the Cross can express the thorough meaning of the Incarnation today. This Christological emphasis alone establishes the authentic divine-human link implied in the Word becoming flesh by highlighting the solidarity of God with suffering humanity. Such a Christological direction establishes a soteriology if solidarity which sets up the Cross of Jesus as a point of fraternal union with the Jewish people, as well as with all who seek human liberation and peace. Thus, for Hall as for Sherman, Jesus becomes a potential source of union rather than exclusion between Jews and Christians in this post-Shoah era. "The faith of Israel is incomprehensible," says Hall, "unless one sees at its heart a suffering God whose solidarity with humanity is so abysmal that the 'cross in the heart of God' [H. Wheeler Robinson] must always be incarnating itself in history. Reading the words of Elie Wiesel, one knows, as a Christian, that he bears this indelible resemblance to the people of Israel."[35]

The most comprehensive treatment of the Christology-Shoah link thus far appears in the writings of Jurgen Moltmann, especially The Crucified God. He interprets the Shoah as the most dramatic revelation to date of the fundamental meaning of the Christ-Event—God can save people, including Israel, because through the Cross he participated in their very suffering. To theologize after the Shoah would prove a futile enterprise in Moltmann's view "....were not the Sh'ma Israel and the Lord's Prayer prayed in Auschwitz itself, were not God himself in Auschwitz, suffering with the martyred and murdered. Every other answer would be blasphemy. An absolute God would make us indifferent. The God of action and success would let us forget the dead, which we still cannot forget. God as nothingness would make the entire world into a concentration camp."[36]

Moltmann adds that the "theology of divine vulnerability" that emerges from a reflection on the Shoah has deep roots in both rabbinic theology and in Abraham Joshua Heschel's notion of *divine pathos.*

This "theology of divine vulnerability" clearly provides an important starting point for a post-Shoah Christology. For one, it establishes the close link between Christology and the more fundamental God-problem. It likewise opens up the whole question of dual responsibility—divine and human—during the Shoah. Too often, as Elie Wiesel has noted, the onus has been placed exclusively on God's shoulders. The Shoah, let it be said clearly, remains a challenge to any overly positive interpretation of human capacity. The Cross emphasis in Shoah theology exposes us to the notion that God had to pay a price during the Shoah for the freedom accorded humanity in the original act of creation.

But there are aspects to a Shoah theology centered on the Cross that leave the sensitive Christian uneasy. Certainly the propriety of the linkage comes into some question when we consider the significant Christian complicity in the Nazi effort. A. Roy Eckardt is especially strong on this point, arguing that it approaches blasphemy to make such a claim. He also believes that "in comparison with certain other sufferings, Jesus' death becomes relatively non-significant." Another danger Eckardt sees in the Cross

Christology model is that it may generate an exaggeratedly "powerless" plan for human living within a religious context that could result in the annihilation of both Jews and Christians.[37] Additionally, Christian theology has always described the Cross as a voluntary act on the part of God and of Jesus. And the Cross can be properly interpreted in a redemptive fashion only when viewed as the culmination and consequence of Jesus' active ministry. The Shoah was neither voluntary nor part of a redemptive mission in any sense. Finally, some doubts have also been raised whether the theology of divine suffering found in Jewish religious thought is as similar to the Shoah Cross theology as Moltmann and Sherman claim. This remains an open question in need of further exploration.

In the final analysis we have to say that Sherman, Hall, and especially Moltmann are collectively responsible for an important breakthrough in understanding the direct connection between the Shoah and Christology. But their perspectives need to be incorporated into a somewhat broader vision, something I have tried to do in my own writings. Understanding the ministry of Jesus as emerging from the heightened sense of divine-human intimacy that surfaced during the Pharisaic revolution in Second Temple Judaism, the Christological claims advanced by the Church in light of that ministry become an expression of a new sense of how profoundly humanity is intertwined in the divine self-definition. The ultimate significance of this Christology lies in its revelation of the grandeur of humanity, a necessary corrective to the demeaning paternalism that often characterized descriptions of the divine-human relationship in the past.

In my view the fear and paternalism previously associated with the statement of the divine-human relationship were at least partially responsible for the attempt by Nazism to produce a total reversal of human meaning, to hearken back to Uriel Tal's analysis, and finally "overpower" the Creator God. Incarnational Christology can help people recognize that they share in the very life and existence of God. The human person remains creature; the gulf between humanity in people and humanity in the Godhead has not been bridged. But it is also clear that a direct link exists; the two humanities can touch. The human struggle for self-identity vis-a-vis the Creator God has come to an end in principle, though its full realization still lies ahead. In this sense one can truly say that Christ continues to bring humankind salvation in its root meaning—*wholeness*.

With a proper understanding of the meaning of the Christ Event men and women can be healed; they can finally overcome the primal sin of pride, the desire to supplant the Creator in power and status that was at the heart of Nazism. Critical to this awareness is the sense of God's self-imposed limitation as manifested in the Cross. This is where Moltmann's theology becomes absolutely critical, if still incomplete. People now see, through Christ, that their destiny is eternal in their uniqueness and individuality.

The Shoah: Continuing Theological Challenge for Christianity

God will not finally try to absorb them back totally into the divine being. In fact, it has become apparent that God must allow men and women this degree of eternal distinctiveness and freedom of action in order to reach full maturity, to become finally and fully God. This is a viewpoint that bears at least some similarities to the notion of divine self-constriction in the Jewish mystical tradition spoken of earlier.

What I am claiming is that the Shoah represents at one and the same time the ultimate expression of human freedom and of human evil—the two are intimately linked. The initial divine action of creation constituted the liberation of humanity from its total encasement in the Godhead. The Creator God acknowledged that there is need to let go part of divine humanity in the development of divine creative potential. But that part of God's humanity that now assumed an independent existence was faced with the task of establishing its own identity. At times, particularly during the Nazi era, there arose a strong desire to supplant the Creator. Here lies the roots of human evil. But until the modern age, fear of divine punishment kept such desire in check. But the Enlightenment, Nietzsche and contemporary movements for human liberation have changed all that. People began to shed the fear of divine retribution that had controlled human behavior in the past. The Nazis clearly believed they had become the final arbiters of right and wrong. This new sense of freedom, this growing Prometheus Unbound experience, in Western society, coupled with unresolved identity problems, resulted in a catastrophic plan of human destruction in Nazi Germany.

The ultimate assertion of human freedom from God in our time that the Shoah represents may in fact prove the beginning of the final resolution of the conflict. When humanity finally acknowledges the destruction it is capable of producing when it totally rejects the Creator, as the Nazis did during the Shoah, when it recognizes such rejection as a perversion not an affirmation of human freedom, a new stage in human consciousness may be dawning. We may finally be coming to grips with evil at its roots, the centuries-long struggle of the human community to work out its identity by overcoming God. The power of evil will wane only when humankind develops along with a sense of its own inherent dignity because of its links with God through Christ, a corresponding sense of humility occasioned by a searching encounter with the devastation that absence of such humility can occasion. A sense of profound humility evoked by the experience of the healing power present in the ultimate Creator of human power—this is crucial for human survival. On this point of humility as a central response to the Shoah experience I join hands with the ethicist Stanley Hauerwas in his reflections on the event even though we part company on several other of its implications.[38]

Only the integration of this awareness of humility into human consciousness will finally overcome evil and neutralize eruptions such as the Shoah in which humanity tries to "elevate" itself above the Creator. This necessary human self-realization will come more easily in light of the understanding of divine vulnerability manifested through the Shoah in such dramatic fashion. It is no longer "ungodly" to express dependence upon others—the Creator has done it. The full maturity vital for the humane exercise of human co-creatorship requires the assertion of this interdependence to which the Nazis were blind.

Let me add that the ultimate personal healing resulting from a proper understanding of Incarnational Christology must also be tied, for full wholeness and salvation, to the sense of communal interdependence revealed by the Sinai covenant. Here is where the two aspects of the required post-Shoah reformulation of Christology intersect. Any post-Shoah significance for Christology must be stated in the context of Christianity's renewed appreciation of its continuing bonds with the Jewish tradition and the Jewish people. It must also be said that at this point in human history the believing Jew and the believing Christian will likely develop their post-Shoah reflections in somewhat different ways. The Incarnational Christology approach discussed above is meant as the response of a Christian theologian for members of the church. There is no claim that a theological response to the experience is impossible save through Christology. This appears to be a trap into which Moltmann has wandered in *The Crucified God*.

VII. Ethics After the Shoah

In our previous discussion of the God question in light of the Shoah two major components of any discussion about ethics came to the forefront. The first had to do with how can God truly serve as the ultimate ground for ethics in this post-Shoah age. The second issue, intimately related to the first, revolved around the need for a greater recognition of the vitalistic dimension of human life and its role in ethical behavior. This also involved the recognition that if God were to provide moral grounding for the vitalistic dimension of humanity, this would have to be done through symbolic encounters with God, principally in community worship. While more can certainly be said about each of these topics, we shall move on to some other issues at this point. Related to our discussion of ethics in this section will also be a consideration of the Shoah's implications for theological methodology. As will be seen very quickly, the methodological issues and the ethical questions inevitably impact upon one another.

One important result of the increased theological reflections on the Shoah has been an enhanced appreciation for the significance of history. Its events, including the Shoah, must be taken with great seriousness in any considerations of fundamental theological and ethical beliefs. David Tracy has spoken of how such encounter with the Shoah has personally convinced him of this need which will inevitably demand some alteration in previous theological positions in both Christianity and Judaism. He identifies with the call for a post-Shoah return to history found in the writings of Irving Greenberg and Emil Fackenheim. His exact words are these: "We Christian theologians have honestly

The Shoah: Continuing Theological Challenge for Christianity

come to terms with historical consciousness and historicity; we have developed a theological hermeneutics where the subject matter—the event itself—is once again allowed to rule in theological hermeneutic; we have recognized the *Sach-Kritik* that the religious event itself demands. But we have not returned to history—the real, concrete thing where events like the Holocaust have happened, where events like the state of Israel do exist."[39]

Johannes Baptist Metz, following up on his three fundamental theses discussed previously, speaks in a similar vein as Tracy. For him, any statement made by Christian theology in our day, any attempt to find meaning for life after the Shoah, must be considered "blasphemy" if it fails to meet the test of this *historical* event. All post-Shoah Christian theology must be rooted in historical consciousness and in the realization that salvation can be achieved only in alliance with Jews within history: "But this means that we Christians for our own sakes are from now on assigned to the victims of Auschwitz—assigned, in fact, in an alliance belonging to the heart of saving history, provided the word "history" in this Christian expression is to have a definite meaning and not just serve as a screen for a triumphalist metaphysic of salvation which never learns from catastrophes nor finds in them a cause for conversion...."[40]

Two leading feminist theologians, Elisabeth Schussler-Fiorenza and Rebecca Chopp, have also given special attention to the significance of history for theological reflection after the Shoah. Schussler-Fiorenza insists we cannot speak of the suffering of the victims of the Shoah as a "theological metaphor" for all human suffering. Instead, that suffering "must be named in its political particularity. The ideological heart of Nazi-fascism was racism, its ideological catch-word was '*Untermensch*,' the less than human, the sub-human being."[41]

Nazism for Schussler-Fiorenza represented an extreme example of the Western capitalistic form of patriarchy, with origins in Aristotelian philosophy and subsequent mediation through Christian theology. The same ancient philosophical system, imported into Christian theology by Thomas Aquinas and others, that first subjugated women as people with "subhuman" nature combined with religiously-rooted bigotry and a new bio-theology to produce the Nazi cataclysm throughout Europe. Overcoming Biblical and theological anti-Judaism thus becomes the first step in the complicated, rather wrenching process of cleansing Western society of its patriarchal basis.

Rebecca Chopp lays particular stress on the profound connection she perceives between Shoah literature and liberation theology, a relationship she terms unique among Western religious writings. Both in her judgment create new theological space which in turn forces upon Christianity a fundamental reconceptualization of its theology. Christian theology must grapple not merely with individual suffering, but even more with mass suffering. Liberation theology and Shoah literature equally interrupt and disrupt Christianity and Christian theology with the question and the quest "who is this human subject that suffers history?"[42]

Chopp goes on to add that both liberation theology and Shoah literature force us to understand history not merely in terms of abstract notions of evolution or process but primarily in terms of the suffering realities of that history caused by various forms of human exploitation. The history that now must be the basis of theological reflection is not abstract history, but the history of human victims. And the voices and the memory of the tortured, the forgotten, and the dead must become primary resources for Christian anthropology. And, while Chopp does not explicitly articulate this position, one could surmise that she would identify with the direction taken by Schussler-Fiorenza and Tracy, namely, that Biblical anti-Judaism with its inevitable dehumanization of concrete Jewish persons opened the way for Jewish suffering in the Shoah and for the suffering experiences under imperialist colonialism to which liberation theology has been responding.

The argument being advanced by Tracy, Metz, and Chopp about the significance of human history and ethics in all religious statements after the Shoah was actually surfaced in a preliminary form some years earlier by the Austrian Catholic philosopher Friedrich Heer. He insisted that the church's failure to challenge the Nazis in any effective way is symptomatic of how the church has dealt with other manifestations of evil, in particular war and the possibility of a nuclear holocaust. For him, the main problem springs from the church's withdrawal from history: "The withdrawal of the church from history has created that specifically Christian and ecclesiastical irresponsibility towards the world, the Jew, the other person, even the Christian himself, considered as a human being—which was the ultimate cause of past catastrophes and may be the cause of a final catastrophe in the future."[43]

As Heer sees it, antisemitism is the product of a longstanding and deepseated cancer within Christianity that began to grow in its classical period. The disregard on the part of Christians for the well-being of the Jewish people throughout history, especially between 1918 and 1945, can only be understood as part of a general disregard for humanity and the world. He attributes this attitude to the dominance in Christian theological thinking of what he calls the "Augustinian principle." This attitude views the world under the aspect of sin and ultimately leads to a sense of fatalism and despair about the world. Heer remains convinced that this fatalistic tendency constitutes every bit as much a danger today as it did in the period of the incubation of Nazism. In fact, he argues that millions of contemporary Christians share the responsibility for preparing the suicide of the church and of humankind in a new holocaust which may be brought about by nuclear warfare while the churches remain silent bystanders: "There is a straight line from the church's failure to notice Hitler's attempt at a 'Final Solution' of the Jewish problem to her failure to notice today's and tomorrow's endeavors to bring about a 'Final Solution' to the human problem. The murder of millions of Jews during the Hitler era anticipated the murder of millions and perhaps hundreds of millions of human beings who would die if the great war returned—a war that could only end in mass murder and genocide."[44]

The only cure for this centuries-long pattern in Christianity, according to Heer, is to abandon the "Augustinian principle" and replace it with a return to the Hebrew Bible's roots of Christ's own piety and even to older roots—namely, to the original faith of Israel in which people felt themselves to be both God's creatures and responsible partners in the development of the earth.

There are two reservations I have in connection with this call for the return to history. First of all, it must be sensitive to the profound changes in the nature of the God-humanity relationship introduced by the Shoah. I am not sure that Heer has recognized this. Neither have the liberation theologians on whose writings Rebecca Chopp heavily relies. Secondly, this return to history must be accompanied by new explorations into human consciousness, especially the extent to which consciousness harbors the roots of power and evil. None of the Jewish or Christian thinkers we have examined have adequately probed the link between history and human consciousness. We cannot ignore the Freudian/Jungian revolution in our reflections on the Shoah experience. A sustainable ethic after the Shoah will require a new appreciation of the profound connection between history and human consciousness with respect to both human and divine activity. History after the Shoah, as David Tracy has underscored, will revolve not so much about events as about persons, in particular those who, for whatever reason, society has declared to be "non-persons." And part of the process of probing the linkage between history and human consciousness in this post-Shoah era will involved coming to see how the life process in which we all share is seriously harmed by such declarations against certain groups or individuals.

Another important implication for post-Shoah theological interpretation has been suggested by Darrell Fasching. It is directly tied to Tracy's emphasis on post-Shoah history as the history of non-persons. Fasching insists that Christian faith must now be *chutzpah* [brazenness—Ed.] faith, to borrow an important term from the Jewish tradition. It must be a faith that, like the covenantal faith of the Hebrew Scriptures, understands the God-humanity relationship as one of mutual trust and *challenge*. Irving Greenberg has correctly insisted, according to Fasching, that the post-Shoah age allows humans ultimate refuge neither in the sacred or the secular. Rather, continuing in the tradition of chutzpah, both God and humanity need to be questioned. For Fasching, authentic faith after the Shoah can be discovered by one measuring rod along—the deed. True believers are those who decry the creation of "non-persons" and work to make such declarations untenable in society. If this faith model had prevailed in Nazi Germany, Fasching is convinced we would have never witnessed the apostasy of so many Christians and the so-called "German Christian" movement would have gone nowhere.

The primary lesson of the Shoah in the mind of Fasching is the centrality of chutzpah faith for human survival. He is convinced that "the world can no longer afford the luxury of unquestioning faith. Unquestioning faith is pagan faith. Unquestioning faith is a nearly universal characteristic of religion throughout the world. Virtually all forms of religion have asked followers to sacrifice their will and surrender themselves to higher reality. And all faith that asks for a total surrender of will is finally not only pagan but demonic, even if it is faith in Jesus or the God of Jesus. For all such faith is a training ground for fanaticism which blurs the distinction between God and the state and leads to the dehumanization of the chosen victims of the state. The only authentic faith is a questioning faith, a faith prepared to call even God into question. The difference between God and the idol is that idols will brook no dissent. The test of authentic faith is the possibility of dissent against *all authority* in the name of a human dignity which reflects the image of God."[45]

Fasching's contention deserves serious consideration since it is obvious that many Christians supported the Nazi state out of a sense that faith demanded obedience to civil authority. There are examples, however, of Christians with a rather conservative piety not unlike that criticized by Fasching who risked their lives to the point of death in defiance of Nazi policies. And the liberal Christian record terms of social protest during the Nazi era is not outstanding, to say the least, even though liberals had cast aside many of the elements of traditional Christian piety which Fasching holds to be centrally responsible for generating what he calls mass Christian apostasy during the Shoah period. But, in my judgment, he is on to something quite important in his insistence on the primacy of chutzpah faith after the Shoah even if his claims require some adjustment.

Intimately connected to the above two issues is the question of power. For there are those who regard the rejection of all forms of power by the human community as absolutely critical for the realization of human dignity while other commentators on the Shoah take a directly contrary stand—the judicious use of power is unquestionably necessary for the prevention of any future outbreaks of the massive human annihilation that was the Shoah. Neither the Christians nor the Jews with whom we have interacted in this essay have as yet satisfactorily handled this difficult question. Irving Greenberg has undoubtedly been the most direct in positing the relationship between power and the Shoah, although it has entered Richard Rubenstein's more recent writings as well. For Greenberg it would be immoral to abandon the quest for power. "Power inescapably corrupts," he writes, "but its assumption is inescapable after the Holocaust." The only option in the post-Shoah world that will enable us to avoid the repetitions of the human degradation and evil of the Nazi period is to combine the assumption of power with what Greenberg terms the creation of "better mechanisms of self-criticism, correction and repentance." Only in this way can we utilize power "without being the unwitting slave of bloodshed or an exploitative status quo."[46]

Greenberg is correct in stressing that a willingness to use power is indeed a central demand of the Shoah experience, so long as long-established forms of entrenched power in society with the perduring power to create "non-persons" remain intact. A meaningful religious ethic cannot totally reject the use of power in principle at this moment of history, though it certainly may responsibly determine that certain configurations of power [e.g. nuclear weaponry] are totally immoral even when a threat to continued human survival looms large. In this regard, serious questions need to be raised about the argument put forward by Christian ethicist Stanley Hauerwas that *humility* must be our primary moral response to the experience of the Shoah. Our vision of the post-Shoah God must be one which excludes any divine underwriting of human pretensions but rather stands "capable of calling us from our false actions of power and control."[47]

Though I would join Hauerwas in underlining humility as a crucial post-Shoah human virtue, I am unwilling to grant it the same pre-eminence. Hauerwas fails to take seriously enough the human co-creational role after the Shoah. This failure could prove decisive in the effort to prevent further designations of groups as non-persons on a mass scale. His emphasis on humility without enhanced responsibility could result in people of faith becoming bystanders rather than central actors in human history.

The more recent attempt to reflect on the meaning of the Shoah-power relationship from a Jewish perspective has come from Marc Ellis in several works.[48] Ellis is openly critical of Greenberg's perspective, though he extends this critique to other major Shoah thinkers including Fackenheim, Wiesel, and Rubenstein: "The dynamic balance between Holocaust and empowerment found in their analyses of the Holocaust is lost when they enter the realities of the post-Holocaust world. Empowerment, almost without restraint, becomes the watchword. Greenberg's analysis of the State of Israel as the answer to the Holocaust, as *the* sign of deliverance, as the redemption out of nothingness destroys the balance. The Jewish people recently liberated from the hell of Nazi Germany can become, in some minds, reluctant heroic warriors charting the historic course of redemption in a hostile world. Though the forms of oppression vary, the world remains essentially the same—hostile to Jewish interest and survival."[49]

As a Christian ethicist viewing this internal Jewish debate [which admittedly has implications far beyond the Jewish community], it appears to me that both make critical points. What Greenberg is ultimately saying, as I see it, is that after the Shoah we cannot rely on divine intervention in human history to protect us, even if we consider ourselves a covenanted people. The Shoah has shattered the foundations of any such divine-human perspective. And post-Shoah morality must respond to this unparalleled situation. The Jewish community, and by implication all of human-kind, must assume a far greater responsibility for its continued survival. And this can only be accomplished through the judicious use of power accompanied by the development of self-correcting mechanisms for preventing unwarranted application of this power. Ellis, on the other hand, is strongly convinced that Jewish survival, human survival, after the Shoah can be ensured only if Jews tie their destiny to other oppressed peoples of the world, not to the current power elite. And he leaves little doubt that he would include the Palestinians within the ranks of the oppressed.

Greenberg makes another important point in his reflections on power in my judgment, even though he may do it somewhat obliquely. Power assumes such an important ethical role for Greenberg because of his affirmation of the traditional Jewish priority of community survival over individual human rights. Catholic ethicist David Hollenbach has noted that this remains a distinctive characteristic of both classical Jewish and Islamic ethics.[50] We in the West have been conditioned for the past several centuries to accord the highest place to individual human rights in our vision of public morality. The general Middle Eastern approach, rooted in a strong sense of community identity, makes us terribly uncomfortable. But somehow we are going to have to incorporate better this classical Jewish/Islamic vision into our overall moral scheme, without totally sacrificing our cherished commitment to individual human rights, if we are to deal fairly with the power question as it pertains to the current situation in the Middle East.

I believe Ellis has put power aside far too easily. On this basic point, my support goes out to Greenberg. But, while endorsing the basic thrust of Greenberg's ethic of survival, I have serious difficulties with many of the concrete ways he interprets it in his most recent essay on the subject, "The Ethics of Jewish Power."[51] Though in an earlier publication on the subject he called for the creation of "better mechanisms of self-criticism, correction and repentance" as the only way to employ power "without being the unwitting slave of bloodshed or an exploitative status quo"[52], his application, or more precisely non-application, of this rule to Israeli activities in the West Bank/Gaza since the start of the Intifada is both puzzling and quite disturbing. At best, one sees an extremely superficial use of this moral principle as Greenberg discusses particular military activities. Little or none of the moral agonizing recognized by Greenberg in the original essay is present in this "uprising-era" piece. Such an evident lack of sensitivity gives some credence to Ellis' claim that Greenberg in the end transforms the Shoah into a mandate for Jewish survival at any cost.

In addition to the questionable nature of some of Greenberg's specific judgments from a post-Shoah moral perspective, there are three overarching omissions in his approach. The first is his failure to ask whether there might not be significantly more responsible ways of pre-serving public order. Even some Jewish supporters of Israel acknowledge that terrible mistakes were made from the standpoint of peace-keeping operations. New techniques have been developed which the Israeli army chose to ignore. Secondly, and far more importantly, Greenberg fails to realize that preserving public order is not usually best accomplished through the heavy hand of power alone. The words of the leading Catholic thinker Romano Guardini written out of personal experience of the Nazi era need to be weighed seriously by Greenberg: "In the coming epoch, the essential problem will no longer be that of increasing power—though power will continue to increase at an even swifter tempo—but of curbing it. The core of the new epoch's intellectual task will be to integrate power into life in such a way that man can employ power without forfeiting his humanity, or to surrender his humanity to power and perish."[53]

Finally, nowhere in "The Ethics of Power" does Greenberg make an abiding commitment to pursue a peaceful resolution of the current conflict with the Palestinians—an essential ingredient of any current evaluation of Israel's use of power in the necessary maintenance of public order in the West Bank/Gaza. Devoid of such clear commitment, the misapplications of power that have been part of the Israeli-Palestinian relationship since the *Intifada* assume an even greater moral seriousness.

There are other theological and ethical issues that continue to be part of the overall religious discussion of the Shoah. To bring this essay to a close, I would simply like to mention some of them without elaboration. They include the issue of the role of religion in the public sphere. Reflecting on the Shoah some Christian writers such as Franklin Littell and Clyde Manschreck have warned that a Nazi-like commitment to "naked state sovereignty" can easily take hold in nations where religious influence has been totally excluded from the public culture.[54] Franklin Littell has also been influential in the recently developing effort to establish criteria for an "early warning system" for genocide and holocaust.[55] Lastly, there has been an ongoing discussion, intensified by recent research, into Christian understandings of the meaning of the church. Did a certain vision of the church as inherently tied to a conservative political order for its own survival make it possible for Christians to come to regard Jews as "unfortunate expendables" [Nora Levin] or "outside the universe of moral obligation" [Helen Fein] when that survival was threatened?[56]

The centrality of the issues discussed above give ample evidence of the Shoah's continuing relevance for theology in our time. The event was the child of many of the forces most influential in the shaping of contemporary Western culture. And these forces are alive in nearly every part of the world, making the Shoah something far more than a Western phenomenon even though that was its actual locale. Any faith perspective that believes it can avoid the issues raised by the Shoah or summarily dispense with them is opening itself up to self-destruction. Both Christians and Jews for their own well-being, for their mutual enrichment, for the safety and sustainability of creation, must continue to wrestle with them even though we many never penetrate the veil of darkness that covers the event.

How the Shoah Affects Christian Belief

In re-examining the theological implications of the Shoah for Christian faith, Thomas Idinopulos raises two questions of radically different perspective and proceeds to further clarify them in his essay: [1] What if Christ's atoning death did not defeat sin, but, rather, led to more crucifixions, more sin, as evidenced by the playing out of history itself? Does not its very power, therefore, lay in its defeat rather than in its victory, and, thus, continues to serve as a warning to and for all humanity? And [2] What is the proper interrelationship between literature and history, art and the Shoah? Can those who write and create this "literature of atrocity" truly illumine, and thereby improve, the human condition, and avoid repetition—the very goal of sanctified Christian and Christ-like [and Jewish] existence?

SLJ

The Holocaust Now

HOW THE SHOAH AFFECTS CHRISTIAN BELIEF

Thomas A. Idinopulos

I. Introduction: Christian Antisemitism and Anti-Judaism

If there is one thing we learn from history, it is that the forces which shape human destiny are slow in building; that when they finally burst forth with all their capacity for making and unmaking the life of humanity, one is saddened to realize how little they were understood, how poorly perceived in their beginnings. Antisemitism is one such force. The oppression of the Jewish people in the past 2,000 years is connected to the disdain for Jews that one finds in the catechism, preaching and teaching of Christian churches from earliest times. If a history of Christian theological anti-Judaism did not exactly "cause" modern racial antisemitism, unquestionably it helped to prepare the way.

It has been the habit of Christian theologians in recent years, especially since the Shoah, to treat antisemitism less as a matter for which Christians as Christians ought to regard themselves as guilty, much more as an expression of racial idolaters posing as Christians. However, the record of Christian thought makes unmistakable the hostility to the Jew in the canonical Gospels, in the sermons of such church fathers as John Chrysostom, Saint Jerome, and Augustine of Hippo, in the edicts of Christian emperors and the policies of influential popes and bishops, in the later writings of Martin Luther, in the ambivalent postures of theologians as recent as Karl Adam and Karl Barth. What one learns from this record is that subtle, powerful, essentially murderous inner-connections exist between Christian self-witness and political oppression of Jews. As Jules Isaac [the French Jewish historian who pioneered in research demonstrating the connection between Christianity and antisemitism] put it, "without centuries of Christian catechism, propaganda, vituperation, the Hitlerian teachings, propaganda and vituperation would not have been possible."

It is important to keep two things in mind when we address the Shoah. The first is conveyed by the striking assertion of Elie Wiesel, "....the Holocaust teaches nothing." I interpret Wiesel to mean that after we have patiently read through the history books and considered the explanations, we must not be surprised if we are brought back in disbelief to where we began, with an awful sense of the dark, impenetrable mystery of the event. For when the killers were average, law-abiding citizens who carried out their deeds impersonally, with little or no hatred for their victims, when the crime proved so massive that the names of the victims were erased by the abstractness of the number 6,000,000, when one cannot consult the grisly details of the crime without experiencing a revulsion mixed with rage, fright and shame—when one is thus confronted by the truth of the Shoah, one cannot help but realize that there are but two impenetrable mysteries for human contemplation: the depth of evil and the will of God.

The second thing to keep in mind in turning to the Shoah is the matter of respect, what I should like to call—existential respect. There are pure and impure ways to read about the Shoah. We must resist the temptation to rend our study of the Shoah a convenient and unceasing vehicle of blame and praise. For it is quite simply true that no amount of moral judgment on the part of the living can in any way rouse the dead or return a shred of the humanity ripped from them. It seems to me that moral perception of the past proves sound only when it is tied to the present; in other words, what the living should learn from the dead is something of truth worth living for. This is what I mean by existential respect. The dead retain their secrets. A suffering so great leaves little to understand, nothing to be redeemed. It is we the living who write the books, the words are ours, and we shape them in the hope that the past, with all its tragic mystery, can illumine the experiences of our lives here and now.

The great truth we have to learn from the Shoah is how to keep the human spirit alive; it is also the central truth to the matter of education in America. The evil of the Shoah was not a dark, Satanic evil of the medieval imagination; it was a modern evil, technological and antiseptic, "a vast crater of emptiness opened up by a betrayal of spirit." The alternative to spirit is chaos. Chaos prevails when human beings conform to their own techniques and inventions, turning themselves into objects, divesting themselves of individual self-identity. Here the spirit of humanity withers and dies, the spirit which ennobles intelligence with sensitivity and often inspires a human being to act courageously. When chaos replaces spirit, intelligence is put to insensitive uses, moral restraint crumbles, institutional safeguards of life and liberty are abolished, creating a situation which makes anything and everything possible, including wholesale death.

II. Studying the Problem

There are two major areas of scholarly inquiry which seek to establish the relationship between the history of Christianity on the one hand, and the developments of anti-Judaism and antisemitism on the other, a relationship which culminates in the twentieth century destruction of European Jews under Hitler. There are many scholars who have concentrated their attention on the role of Christian institutions, among them James Parkes, Alice and Roy Eckardt, Franklin Littell, and Guenter Lewy. A second line of inquiry, focusing more specifically on Christian scriptures and doctrines, was pioneered by the French historian, Jules Isaac, and developed more recently by John Oesterreicher, Alan Davies, Gregory Baum, Edward Flannery, Fred Bratton, and Rosemary Radford Ruether. The unifying aim of all this research is to document, clarify, and explain the extent of Christian guilt vis-a-vis Judaism and the Jewish people. I should like to make it clear that my paper is not intended to be a contribution to this research. It has a different aim: the Shoah in its specifically *theological* implications for Christian faith. I will not take up here the historical question of Christian ideas and actions in their connection to crimes against Jews; the focus of my attention is the constructive, theological question of the Shoah as it affects or should affect Christian belief.

If one examines the works of the most influential Christian theologians who wrote before, during, and after the Second World War, one will find references to the Shoah, but no extended discussion of the matter, nothing that takes the form of an essay. Karl Barth, Rudolf Bultmann, Emil Brunner, Paul Tillich, Karl Rahner, Teilhard de Chardin, Reinhold Niebuhr: none of them felt compelled by the events of the Nazi tyranny to re-examine the fundamental principles of their theologies. In the generation that followed these giants, some American religious thinkers startled the public in the 1960's by announcing the death of God. Here one would have expected that the connection would have been made with the Shoah. But the opposite happened. The "death-of-God" was interpreted by Thomas Altizer, William Hamilton, Harvey Cox, and Paul van Buren, not as a symbol of historical disaster, but as an injunction for Christians to break their ties with tired, discredited institutions and doctrines, and confidently to create new history as free, secular, mature men [and women] of the modern world. Not unexpectedly, it took a Jew, Richard Rubenstein, to remind his Christian colleagues [It always seems to take a Jew!] that the "death-of-God" means, what in essence Nietzsche said it meant, the breakdown of human culture witnessed in the catastrophes of history.

It does not surprise me that it took a Jew to make the connection between the death of God and the Shoah, thence to remind Christians that the death of God should be an occasion not for joy but for lamentation. I am afraid that the Shoah strikes Christian theologians as it strikes all other Christians, as a particularly Jewish subject, not just in the obvious sense that overwhelming numbers of Jews were involved in the event, but in the deeper sense which should trouble everyone, that whatever questions are raised by the Shoah, whatever institutions, values, beliefs are to be re-examined in the aftermath—these are matters about which properly Jews alone should concern themselves. There is in this, of course, the ordinary, inescapable element of human indifference; we really do not weep over the suffering death that touches not us but others. But I also recognize in the indifference the profound difficulty, perhaps impossibility, for Christian theology to risk confrontation with the worst disaster of Jewish history, indeed, to risk confrontation with great disasters afflicting many human communities throughout history. I will attempt to account for this.

III. Suffering and Indifference

Saint Paul, in his letter to the Romans, writes that "God....shows his love for us in that while we yet sinners Christ died for us." And he concludes, "Since, therefore, we are not justified by his blood, much more should we be saved by him from the wrath of God." [Romans 5:8-9, Revised Standard Version] It is uncertain if Paul was the first Christian to proclaim the conquest of sin in and through Jesus Christ, but he was unquestionably the most influential for all subsequent Christian thinking, starting with the Gospels, whose Passion narratives are constructed on Paul's view of the Cross's victory over sin and death. However, "realistically" the Christian recognizes the facts of human sinning since the death and resurrection of Christ, he seeks to bring his moral assessment of history into harmony with the Cross's victory and its message of accomplished redemption. This holds true even of the most liberally-oriented American Protestant thinkers. One distinguished American thinker who struggled to reconcile his own keen sense of the brutality of human history with the message of accomplished redemption drew an analogy from Second World War history. He argued that Christ's defeat of sin was like the Russians' defeat of the Germans at Stalingrad: there would be more fighting, but the decisive battle had been won, the tide of the history turned.[1] Would that it were true! It would be good to believe that history were like a great war where Christ could win the decisive battle. But if history shows anything, it shows that Christ did not win but rather lost the decisive battle, not once, but over and over again.

It is reasonable to ask, "What would remain distinctive of Christian belief if somehow incontestable proof were provided in history that Christ's cross did not defeat sin, but rather led to more crosses, more sin?" From a Jewish point of view, this is precisely what happened in Jewish-Christian relations. Nevertheless, one must acknowledge that Christian redemption is a matter of faith which, as a religious faith, strengthens, not weakens, in adversity. The Christian is bidden to draw closer to Christ precisely in response to the worsening corruption of the world. One recalls that the Rabbis, upon the destruction of the Second Temple, urged Jews to grow stronger, not weaker, in faith, for God himself had brought about this disaster as punishment for sin. Thus for the Christian, no less than for the Jew, the central truths of faith are revealed by God himself; they are *a priori* truths, established independently of history, faithfully adhered to in spite of history. I will not presume to speak of Judaism, but in the case of Christianity, this "a priorism" of faith leads to a homogenization of sin, a certain flattening out of human guilt.

The Christian doctrine of redemption makes it clear that Christ died for all human beings, whatever their sins, however great or small. No distinctions are made or should be made in human culpability, in the magnitude of guilt. The medieval symbol of purgatory was an insightful, if vengeful, acknowledgement of the differences in wickedness. But Martin Luther and the Reformers, led by Paul's words, "All have sinned and fallen short of the Law," did away with these differences. The liberalization and secularization of modern Western culture completed the process begun in the sixteenth century, by not only doing away with the differences between sin, but by doing away with sin itself.

In this homogenization of sin, in my judgment, stemming as it does from the gospel of the victorious cross, that often leads Christian theologians to utter the words Auschwitz and Hiroshima in one breath. I believe there is an authentic way to associate the two events, to compare the way in which each is an expression of the modern tendency to commit what Camus called "administrative murder," wherein human beings are regarded as objects to be cleanly and neatly disposed of by way of "a few freight trains, a few engineers, a few chemists." [Andre Schwarz-Bart] But there is also an unauthentic linking of Auschwitz and Hiroshima, to suggest that one crime is no worse than the other. When this assumption is made consciously or unconsciously, the Christian is "off the hook." If he is persuaded to believe that Auschwitz is no worse than Hiroshima, then he can treat the destruction of six million Jews and one million Gypsies as another instance of universal evil: which really means that he does not have to treat it in its particularity, to look at it right there where all the terror, all the truth lies.

IV. Jacques Maritain

Jacques Maritain, the French Roman Catholic philosopher, might well be regarded as an exception to the prevailing pattern of Christian indifference vis-a-vis the Shoah. Shortly before the Second World War, in 1938, he authored an essay detailing the rise of antisemitic actions from one European country to another; it is a remarkable statement, containing a presentiment of the extermination of Europe's Jews. Discussing the savagery loosed on German Jewry by the Nazis in reprisal for the assassination of one of their diplomats by a Jew, Maritain concludes with this observation:

> ....when we learned these things, we thought that truly armed men can do precisely what they will with unarmed men, we thought that we must thank the National Socialists for not having decreed that all Jews today—and tomorrow, all Christians who prefer to obey God

rather than men—be simply reduced to ashes by the most scientific means; for in the world today who can stop them.[2]

The full truth of the expressed "reduced to ashes by scientific means" unfolded like a shroud in the next seven years, a truth not wasted on Maritain. If the facts of the Shoah did little to shake his belief in the victorious cross, they did seem to expose him to ambiguities about the relationship between suffering and salvation. In order to appreciate the change, one must note Maritain's attitude toward Judaism before the war, comparing it with what he later said.

In an essay of 1937, "The Mystery of Israel," Maritain refers to "the basic weakness of the mystical communion of Israel," which is "its failure to understand the cross, its refusal of the cross." He also speaks of the passion or historical suffering of the Jewish people:

> It is the passion of a scapegoat, enmeshed in the earthy destiny of the world and in ways of the world mixed with sin, a scapegoat against which the impure sufferings of the world strike back, when the world seeks vengeance for the misfortunes of its history upon what activates that history. Israel thus suffers the repercussion of the activation it produces, or which the world feels it is destined to produce....[3]

When one looks beneath the involution of the writing, one recognizes that the author repeats the argument of the ancient church fathers: The Jewish people, in rejecting Christ, antagonizes the Christian world, thereby bringing down on itself calamity and woe. The clear implication is that if the Jewish people accepts the message of the victorious cross, if Israel ceases to be Israel, antisemitism will stop, Jewish suffering will cease.

It is impossible to know if the events of the Second World War and the Shoah made Maritain recognize that Christian triumphalism is a greater case of antisemitism than Jewish rejection of Christ. What is clear is that, after the war, Maritain seems somehow more realistic in his attitude toward suffering, particularly Jewish suffering. There is the first hint that some suffering is unexplainable, useless, serving no higher, no greater purpose. In an essay of 1946, which takes its title from Jesus' eighth beatitude, "Blessed are they that suffer persecution for justice's sake: for theirs is the kingdom of heaven," Maritain speaks of the classical Christian equation between suffering and salvation. Those who choose to suffer in imitation of Christ's cross, share his victory, inheriting the kingdom of heaven. But what of those who do not so choose: Indeed, what of those who were never permitted a choice? After reciting instances of Nazi atrocities, including references to the destruction of the Jews, Maritain asks:

> Where lay the consolation of these persecuted innocents? And how many others died completely forsaken. They did not give their lives; their lives were taken from them, and under the shadow of horror. They suffered without having wanted to suffer. They did not know why they died. Those who know why they die are greatly privileged.[4]

What is significant about this statement is its spirit: it represents that rare instance in which a Christian thinker felt compelled to search within his own theological system for a specific answer to the specific question raised by the knowledge of manifestly useless suffering. What is remarkable is not the answer given, but the honest facing of the question.

Reflecting on the meaningless suffering of innocent people, Maritain speaks differently of the relationship between Jews and Christians. Now they constitute a kind of fellowship of suffering. "Like strange companions," he writes, they "have together journeyed along the road to Calvary." He continues, "The great mysterious fact is that the sufferings of Israel have more and more distinctly taken the shape of the cross." Here the point is no longer Jewish suffering caused by the rejection of Christ; there is a new emphasis on the Jew's sharing of Christ's cross as the result of this innocent, unjustified suffering. Perhaps it is only that—a change of emphasis, not an essentially altering of the mind. One cannot be sure.

Maritain concludes his essay by suggesting that those who suffer and die without consolation are one with Christ precisely at the point of Christ's own dereliction, his own despairing agony on the cross. He goes on to argue that if they are one with Christ in dereliction, they are one with him in the grace that rises victorious from the cross. And he concludes with these words, "It's in the invisible world, beyond everything earthly, that the kingdom of God is given to these persecuted ones, and that everything becomes theirs." It is just where Maritain addresses himself to the question of useless suffering that I see the implications of Elie Wiesel's works for Christian theology: pointing to dereliction, not to victory, as the authentic, universal, and perennial meaning of Christ's cross.

V. Elie Wiesel

The writings of Elie Wiesel have great implication for Christian faith, but not because one can find in them answers to theological questions. What one finds is a deepening of the question. But is this not the power and genius of the artist—to deepen the question?

When one seeks to understand the role of the Shoah in Wiesel's early works, one must constantly bear in mind that the Shoah never appears as an event simply as such, but rather is transmuted by the imagination into a sensibility through which the author speaks. Thomas Lask, *The New York Times* literary critic, put his finger on this when he says, "There is surprisingly little physical horror in [Wiesel's] books. It is the mind that is outraged, the spirit that is degraded. When an emaciated father gives his bowl of soup to his starving son, when a naked mother covers her child's body with her own against the expected spray of bullets, pain and death pale before the suffering and humiliation in these events."[5]

Through the exercise of imaginative writing, Wiesel transmutes the historical and physical events of the Shoah into a moral and spiritual event. The finest example of this is one of the first in Wiesel's books, the description of the burning children in *Night*. In the way he builds his recollection of the event on the refrain "Never shall I forget....," feeling is intensified, physical horror is transmuted by a moral and spiritual perception. His words take the form of both a curse and a prayer, a form shaping the style of his later writing. Wiesel understands that the ultimate crime of the Shoah was the crime against the spirit. "Guilt was not invented at Auschwitz," he writes, "it was disfigured there." In Wiesel's own effort to restore a sense of guilt about this event, he gives a clue to the relation between literature and history, art and the Shoah. Art restores us to the realm of the particular and human, what is in essence an inhuman or "abstract" event. Let me clarify this.

Anyone who wishes to write clearly, perceptively and persuasively on the stories whose theme is the Nazi destruction of European Jewry should begin with one honest, if painful, admission. We human beings are drawn to stories of concentration camp events out of the same mixture of fascination and repulsion which we experience in reading of the torment and anguish of other human beings, whoever they are, whatever the circumstances of their misfortunes. No one should deny these feelings in himself. In facing the pain, suffering and death of others, we face ourselves. Dostoyevsky, who was as good a psychologist as he was a story-teller, understood these feelings. He once accused his fellow Russian writer Turgenev of cowardice for refusing to witness a public execution of a murderer. In his biography of Dostoyevsky, David Magarshak writes that Dostoyevsky

> would have watched, open-eyed and pale-face, the chopping off of a criminal's head as he did the tearing off of heads of sparrows as a boy—so as to experience [as he put it] 'during the very process of torture a sort of inexplicable pit and the consciousness of one's inhumanity,' the sort of 'cruel sensuality' to which as he declared....'almost everyone on earth' was prone and which was 'the only source of almost all the sins of mankind.'[6]

"Inexplicable pity....the consciousness of one's own inhumanity:" these perceptions directed Dostoyevsky's portrayal of the tortuous lives of crime, guilt and suffering led by his most famous characters. In my judgment, it is the same combination of inexplicable pity before abject suffering and a sense of one's own inhuman capacity for cruelty that influences the artistic imagination of Elie Wiesel.

VI. Shoah Literature as Art

One should not underestimate the difficulty in achieving critical appreciation of Shoah literature. When the traditional conventions or forms of literature are applied to events of great historical catastrophe, there is the tendency for morality to overwhelm art, or worse, for art to be judged by morality. With respect to the Shoah, one can rightly ask if art can illumine pain, suffering and death of this magnitude? Should art even dare to portray such misery? This is not an easy question to answer. It is the question in back of Theodor Adorno's famous dictum "to write poetry after Auschwitz is barbaric" [a dictum, incidentally, which Adorno himself as a writer did not follow]. Should one not feel ashamed to seize the suffering of so many, to transform it through the artistic imagination into creation of beauty and pleasure? Adorno writes that "the so-called artistic representations of naked bodily pain, of victim felled by rifle butts, contains, however remote, the potentiality of wringing pleasure from it."[7] This might indeed be so, unless that in tearing the veil from the unspeakable, art, as perhaps nothing else, makes us sense that of which Dostoyevsky spoke—"inexplicable pity....the consciousness of our own inhumanity." If there is a truth to art, as I believe there is, then it consists of the way in which art's distinct forms can be wielded to reveal what is hidden, to illumine our experience to make us see what we cannot otherwise see or are afraid to see, to touch us at the points at which we share a common life, a common humanity. There are, after all, major differences in technique and vision between, on the one hand, the depiction of "cruel sensuality" which exposes us accurately to ourselves, and, on he other, the depiction of "cruel sensuality" which whets our appetite for more cruelty, teaching us nothing; it is the difference between the spiritual and the salacious, the difference between art and pornography.

George Steiner, the American literary critic who is in part influenced by Adorno, asks whether language itself breaks down when employed to depict events of such enormity, of such appalling ugliness. "The world of Auschwitz," he writes, "lies outside speech as it lies outside reason."[8] There is considerable truth in this statement. Those who have had the patience to study the matter recognize that the destruction of six million human beings, methodically, without passion, was not an act of blood lust or vengefulness, or even of simple hatred. Lacking these elements, it is virtually impossible to discover a motive for such murder, and without motive, there is little basis for rational comprehension. But the facts are there and what one learns from them leaves him speechless. It is precisely to these facts that Steiner contends that silence not language is the only legitimate response to the Shoah.

But any careful examination of the best of Shoah literature suggests that Steiner's maxim, "Auschwitz lies outside speech as it lies outside reason," has not been wasted. For artists like Wiesel in *Night*, and Andre Schwarz-Bart in *The Last of the Just*, do not so much portray the Shoah itself, as an objective historical event; they seek rather to convey the personal experiences of individual human beings, caught up in fantastic events beyond their control, beyond even their comprehension, and most especially to record their own deepest feelings about these events. There is an inescapable biographical aspect to Shoah literature. An effect is made to depict the Shoah from the side of the victim, more precisely, from the side of the survivor. Little attention is paid to the assassins, to their motives, or the politics behind them. Moreover, in the delicacy with which they treat their subject, in the effort at intimate detail, at restrained narrative, in the absence of melodrama, in the consistent refusal to introduce judgment, whether in praise or condemnation, in the effort to describe actions accurately, in the wish above all to search for moral and spiritual depths amidst vast emptiness—in all this I sense in Wiesel [and also in Schwarz-Bart] precisely that quality of silence which Steiner says is the only respectful response to the Shoah. The writings of these two authors do not really conform to the "literature of atrocity"—a category introduced by critic Lawrence Langer.

Let me return for a moment to Steiner's statement that "the world of Auschwitz lies outside speech as it lies outside reason." He concludes with this thought: "To speak of the *unspeakable* is to risk the survivance of language as creator and bearer of humane, rational truth. Words that are saturated with lies or atrocity do not easily resume life." In Steiner's judgment, Auschwitz is an event which brings to an abrupt halt the movement of the creative spirit that has shaped Western civilization. Until the Shoah, writers were able to discern in suffering something of significance, something they could mold in relation to the dreams and illusions and tragedies of human life. But after the Shoah, one is confronted by a suffering so abysmal, that nothing, literally nothing can come from it, nothing that is instructive and creative, nothing redemptive and healing. The manufacturer of death produces only statistics and you cannot make poetry of statistics. Eric Kahler understands this when he writes that "The most frightening aspect of our present world is not the horrors in themselves, the atrocities, the technological exterminations, but the one fact at the very root of it all: the fading away of any human criterion...."[9] And, of course, if the human criterion fades, so does the artistic imagination. In this respect, I fully share the view of Adorno and Steiner that one must create artistic beauty out of the Shoah, not because the Shoah was evil, but because it was abstractly evil, so inhumanly evil. In this same vein, Wiesel says, that the Shoah teaches nothing. This is a significant statement. For I view the major achievement of his early works, the creation of a style in which what is by nature mute is given a *kind of voice*—not its own voice, but a kind of voice. As Wiesel said of his own writing, he writes not with words, but against words.

The literature that has arisen from the ashes of the Shoah has as its unifying purpose the translation of the abstract into the particular. It takes the number six million and divides it into the story of the living, suffering and dying of individual souls. It seeks to discern within abject despair an ultimate significance which can revive the spirit, so that a human being can face the truth and not turn away from it in disgust. The best of this literature avoids judgment, whether by praise or condemnation. Like much other literature, it salvages something of worth from the wreckage of human history. As art, it does not aim to propagate the truth. The aim of art, Joseph Conrad once said, is to speak "to our capacity for delight and wonder, to the sense of mystery surrounding our lives; to our sense of pity and beauty and pain." And this the literature of the Shoah does. Investing with significant form the raw materials of human experience, it gives us on the outside a relation to what is deeply hidden and mysterious. By steady reflection not so much on the truth as on the shape and feel of the truth, this art succeeds in discerning a profound human tragedy within the crushing mediocrity of the evil it depicts.

If, as most agree, the Shoah cannot be wholly or easily or ever understood, I do not believe that art provides some sort of special understandings where other efforts fail. But then it is not the purpose of art, as such to *understand*. The significant form—that is, the *meaning*—which art bestows on the raw materials of experience is compounded of imagination, intelligence, feeling and sheer craftspersonship. This does not mean that art makes us understand what may not be understandable. Nevertheless, what is not understood is shaped by human hands and minds; impenetrable evil is penetrated with meaning. And we who attend to what Wiesel has artistically accomplished, are by virtue of our own imagination, feeling, intelligence and appreciation of craft, put into intimate relationship, as he has been, to what we do not understand. Thus, the mystery of the Shoah is not dissolved; it is deepened, made to be part of our lives.

VII. Wiesel and Christianity

The one scene in Wiesel's works to have the greatest implication for Christian faith is the hanging of the three Jewish saboteurs in *Night*. Here Wiesel, precisely as an artist, deepens immeasurably the theological question—"Did Jesus succeed in saving the world by the shedding of his blood?"

The Holocaust Now

The SS seemed more preoccupied, more disturbed than usual. To hang a young boy in front of thousands of spectators was no light matter. The head of the camp read the verdict. All eyes were on the child. He was lividly pale, almost calm, biting his lips.

The gallows threw its shadow over him.

....

The three victims mounted together on the chairs.

The three necks were placed at the same moment within the nooses.

"Long live liberty!" cried the two adults.

But the child was silent.

"Where is God? Where is He?" someone behind me asked.

At a sign from the head of the camp, the three chairs tipped over.

Total silence throughout the camp. On the horizon, the sun was setting.

"Bare your heads!" yelled the head of the camp. His voice was raucous. We were weeping.

"Cover your heads!"

Then the march past began. The two adults were no longer alive. Their tongues hung swollen, blue-tinged. But the third rope was still moving; being so light, the child was still alive....For more than half an hour, he stayed there, struggling between life and death, dying in slow agony under our eyes. And we had to look him full in the face. He was still alive when I passed in front of him. His tongue was still red, his eyes not yet glazed. Behind me, I heard the same man asking:

"Where is God now?"

And I heard a voice within me answer him:

"Where is He? Here He is—He is hanging here on this gallows."

I do not know if Wiesel consciously employed images from the story of Christ's crucifixion to tell his own story. Perhaps it does not matter. The same formal elements are there: three Jews, each accused of crimes, one a youth and the symbol of innocence, all forsaken by God. I have been told that some Christian theologians interpret this story as a Jewish vindication of the Christian belief of salvation through Christ's cross. I interpret this story differently. It seems to me a parody of the Christian teaching of the Cross. Christians never teach the cross without also teaching the empty tomb. The Christian story of the cross does not end in defeat, but in victory, in resurrection. But there is no empty tomb in Wiesel's story, no resurrection; the story of the cross ends not in new life, but with more death. What this story suggests is that if the world waits to be healed, if God and humanity wait to be reconciled by the blood of a young innocent

Jew in the twentieth century, as in the first century, perhaps salvation is not worth the price. Dostoyevsky sensed something of the same when he had Ivan Karamazov say to Alyosha, "....I renounce the higher harmony altogether. It's not worth the tears of....one tortured child...."

If Wiesel's story is a parody of the Christian theology of the victorious cross, it is also a penetrating insight into the perennial truth of the cross. For each day of the earth's history, countless, unnamed human beings suffer their crosses unwillingly and die without hope. The Gospel writers wrote of the empty tomb because they sincerely believed that Jesus was the Messiah and rose to heaven upon his death. But in telling their story, they did not overlook one of the deepest, most human episodes in Christ's Passion. They wrote of Jesus' disciples fleeing the scene of his arrest in mortal fear of their own lives. It is a marvelous symbol of the simple truth that no human being chooses his cross gladly; rather, he suffers it in humiliation and defeat. Wiesel communicates this truth in the history of the hanged boy, thus symbolically joining the Shoah victims to all the victims of history.

The same truth is obscured for Christian theologians by their insistence that despite the evidence of history, that the cross ended not in defeat but in victory. But the sixteenth century Christian painter Matthias Gruenewald seems to have understood it differently. In Gruenewald's Isenheim altarpiece, we are given to see the distinctly human reality of Jesus' Cross. Jesus is nailed to pieces of wood, suffering torments that will bring about his death, a wretched figure alone and forgotten. In this depiction of the Crucifixion, there is no effort at softening, at blurring, at using the soft blues and warm pinks that idealize what is hard and real. There is no stretching and smoothing of the body to make it appear fully and lovely, to give it that strangely erotic appearance that one finds in the abominable crucifixion art hanging everywhere in Christian institutions. In Gruenewald's picture, there is twisted sinew, the bones are bruised, the body pallid, the head hangs limply from the shoulders, the open mouth exudes the odor of impending death. There is all about the air of humiliation and defeat. What Gruenewald depicts in his portrait of the Crucifix-ion is the crushing truth of common suffering.

Gruenewald depicts in his painting what Wiesel expresses in his story: that it lies within the power of art to take the muteness of suffering and give it voice, to proclaim a kind of gospel which speaks of human suffering, a suffering in which one recognizes both God's helplessness in the world and man's imaginative efforts to respond to that helplessness.

The Holocaust Now

Voluntary Covenant

For Irving Greenberg, "voluntary covenant" begins with the self-limitation of God and, therefore, the participation of humanity in creating a "perfect" world. Rabbinic tradition essentially reinterpreted the Torahitic covenant with God, especially after the destruction of the Second Temple in the year 70 C.E. Now, in light of the Shoah, that covenant with God can no longer be morally commanded. Jewish have now become "senior partners" in this covenantal relationship by, realistically, *voluntarily* recommitting themselves to covenant with God as evidenced, for example, by the recreation of the State of Israel after the Shoah, and must now assume total responsibility for their actions and behavior.

SLJ

The Holocaust Now

VOLUNTARY COVENANT[1]

Irving Greenberg

I. Redemption, Human Freedom and the Covenant

The central teaching of Judaism is redemption. *Yahadut* teaches that the world and the life which emerges within it are grounded in the infinite source of life and energy which we call God. As the continuum of life unfolds, the emerging life becomes more and more God-like—more and more valuable, more and more responsive to others, more and more free. Animals have soul qualities, but humans reach the level of being an image of God[2]—the highest level of holiness except for the Divine itself.

The intrinsic nature of God is beneficent, giving and pulsing with life. Therefore, the life which is growing in the ground of the Divine will continue to grow until all of its possibilities will be fully realized and perfected.[3]

However, the present condition of the world does not appropriately support the fullness of the image of God. There is poverty, sickness, oppression, and degradation. Death itself is the ultimate denial of life and its dignity. But reality is not neutral; it is rooted in a loving transcendent God who cares. Therefore, it cannot remain indefinitely oppressive and valueless. Some day all this will be corrected—the world will become the paradise it was meant to be. Even death will be overcome so that life/holiness will be fully upheld. In this messianic time, death will be defeated not only prospectively, but retrospectively through resurrection. Only then will the divine nature underlying reality be truly manifest.

Judaism makes an even more remarkable statement. God respects human freedom. Although God yearns for this messianic consummation and promises that it will be, God will not force humans to be perfect. By a process of voluntary self-limitation [covenant], God allows humanity to participate in the process of creating a perfect world. Underlying this process is the concept, the reality, of covenant. God's first covenant is with humanity as a whole. Never again will God bring total destruction on the world even if it is evil. Total destruction is so intimidating that is incompatible with human freedom and dignity. The divine acceptance of humanity's flawed quality allows humans the margin to go on even if evil wins out temporarily. Yet the Divine remains committed to, and yearning for, the attainment of the final perfection. Therefore, God does not surrender the capacity to punish or reward. God only yields the right to force and overwhelm the human.

From the Divine perspective, the great danger in the grant of freedom is that humans may exercise their freedom by settling for a reality which is less than the final perfection. Given the limits of reality, the power of inertia, the force which oppressors maintain, there is real danger that some status quo, far short of the final perfection, will triumph. God is caught between the freedom given to humans and the ultimate dignity which God wishes to be the possession of all humans. Yet forcing the final freedom is not the way to have people become free.[4]

This logic leads God to a second covenant with Abraham and the Jewish people. This Jewish covenant makes possible reconciliation of the conflict between the Divine respect for human dignity and respect for human freedom. God first singles out Abraham; later the entire Jewish people accepts this covenant. They promise that they will testify, model a way and teach the world the goal of final perfection. The Jews will not settle for less; they will not fully join humanity until the redemption comes. Instead they will challenge; they will testify "not yet;" they will debunk all absolutes because there are not but God. The Divine promise is that this is not a totally quixotic mission—redemption will come to be. The divine promise is that God will be Israel's God throughout the way; that as long as this people carries on this purpose and keeps its Divine connection, it will remain alive to carry it out. Knowing that the Jews will permanently represent that party of final redemption, the Divine is willing to release all of humanity to exercise its freedom. Thus, the Jewish covenant is a blessing for all the families of the earth and is part of a covenant with all humanity. "....if you will obey Me faithfully and keep My covenant then you will be My treasured possession of all the nations. Indeed all the earth is mine but you will be a kingdom of priests [i.e. ministering to all nations, connecting them to the Divine] and a holy nation to Me."[5]

Respect for human freedom means that Israel too must make concessions to reality. The Way of Judaism upholds the principles of the ultimate human condition—to the extent that it is possible now. Jews are commanded to treat others with as much justice and kindness as present parameters allow—and a bit more. Thus the *halakhah*, although it is the way to perfection, makes many compromises along the way—from eating meat at the ritual pole to slavery, war and the status of women at the ethical pole.[6] These concessions are part of the process of redemption. They will be overcome ultimately but, on the way, they are affirmed. Any covenant that respects freedom must allow for process.

Because redemption will not be achieved in one generation, the Torah is not only a covenant between God and Israel, but also a covenant between generations. It is of-

Voluntary Covenant

fered to those "present here standing with us today before the Loving God, our Lord and also to the one who is not here with us today."[7] By taking us its task, each generation joins the past and carries on, until the day that the hopes of all will be fulfilled. If one generation rejects the covenant or fails to pass it on to the next generation, then the effort of all the preceding and future generations is lost as well. Each generation knows that it is not operating in a vacuum; what precedes it makes its work possible, just as its successors will make or break its own mission. Thus, the covenant is binding not just because it is juridical—that is, commanded—but because others continually accept its goal and become bound to its process.

However, there is a catch again—a Divine Catch-22 as it were. If Israel's freedom is respected, then there is a danger that Jewry will sell out along the way. The Jews are only human; they were not chosen because of superior, innate goodness any more than they were because of any numerical greatness.[8] Therefore, who shall be witness to the witnesses? What guarantee is there that Israel will not yield to moral fatigue along this endless way?

Preventive mechanisms operate on both sides of the covenant. On the Divine side, God is more 'active' with Israel, holding the people to the standard by a visible process of reward and punishment designed to teach the people to uphold the covenant. This is the theme not only of the Pentateuch [viz., rain and long life are rewards for obedience] but also of the historical books of the Bible.[9] On the human side, since Israel may waver, some element of coercion or enforced loyalty is necessary to take up the moments of moral slackness. The covenant is sealed into Jewish physical existence, and thus is experienced in part as 'involuntary'.

The great symbol of the involuntary covenant is circumcision; once the covenant is carried in the flesh, it is hard for the Jew to assimilate, i.e., to 'pass' as an uncovenanted one. The Jews journeying to redemption may be compared to Ulysses about to pass the Sirens. Knowing that the Sirens' music is beautiful and indeed irresistible, waiting to hear it yet knowing that to draw near the sound is to inexorably smash the ship and scuttle the voyage. Ulysses has himself lashed to the mast. No matter how seductive the music, nor overwhelming the urge to go to the Sirens and live [or die!] with them, he cannot do so because he is bound without escape. Circumcision is the physical mark that prevents Israel's escape into the mass of humanity. Even when the spirit is weak, the flesh forces some willing or unwilling testimony, imposed at an age when the child cannot accept or reject circumcision is a powerful symbolic statement that all Jews[10] are bound by birth and stand for the covenant whether or not they are in the mood to witness, or are spiritually heroic enough to actually practice the higher level of behavior which faithfulness demands.

This is far from a perfect solution to the problem. Circumcision is not an absolute barrier, and with enough effort Israel may succeed in overcoming this obstacle to assimilation. In addition, if the covenant is only a burden then it will become hateful. And Jewish behavior may become so deviant from the covenant as to outweigh and contradict the verbal or symbolic testimony. Instead of bearing witness, Jews could disgrace and degrade the Divine Name and make the covenantal testimony non-credible. Nevertheless, since the covenant is carried in the flesh, and the existence of the people is, in itself, a statement of Divine Presence and concern, then every Jew—even one who sins or whose behavior is not up to par—carries the message.

Other dynamic aspects of the covenant model are central to Jewish history and religion. From this concept also stems the Jewish vision of God as pedagogue—teaching Torah to Israel and the world. If goodness cannot be imposed by power, then humankind must be educated toward perfection. Teaching becomes the special role and concern of God. Indeed the special covenant with Abraham and the revelation at Sinai are part of the process of teaching humanity. For teaching purposes, God is the ultimate model. The imitation of God becomes the basis of ethics.[11]

The Jewish tradition also asserts that the covenant binds God. The Divine is not merely the source of the Torah but is also bound by the covenant's terms. Form this principle stems the Jewish tradition of arguing, indeed going to trial, with God. The task of the religious person is not only to obey God, but to represent the human claims in the covenant. A teacher and/or a parent, however warm or responsive, cannot truly enable the student/child to grow unless he/she is prepared to be available in some committed way as a reliable and consistent model. Thus Divine acceptance of human freedom becomes irrevocable—unless the covenant itself is revoked. Since humans are limited, the final perfection will come slowly, and only through partnership of humans and God. Of course, once God is bound then God too becomes dependent on the partner, Israel, for the final achievement of the goal. As this implication emerged in history, it was initially resisted both by Prophets and Rabbis who feared that God's ultimate power would be undermined by such a view.

The Divine is saddled with an erratic covenantal partner. God must ask repeatedly—every time the Jews fail—is the game worth the candle? Is this partner too frail a reed on which to lean? Is Israel too weak or incorrigible to carry this burden through history? The logic of respect for freedom is to accept the Jews' limitations, but the urge to change partners is strong. The temptation to shift is expressed in Exodus 32:40 when God struggles with the idea of wiping out Israel and starting again with Moses. Before the initial covenant, the Divine exercised this tactic by wiping out humanity with the Flood and starting again with Noah. In the Biblical stage of the covenant, after every catastrophe, Jews asked themselves whether the Divine has lost patience. Was God upholding the covenant by punishing Israel or was God rejecting Israel as the covenantal partner?

The dynamics of these interacting aspects of the covenant model account for the pattern of the unfolding of much of Jewish religious history and development. My contention is that the concept of covenant has been transformed as it has unfolded under crisis, that we are living in such a moment of crisis and transformation now, and that there are possible models of past response that we can apply to the present.[12]

II. The Covenant in History

A. The First Destruction and Exile

Since Judaism affirms that the final perfection will take place *in history*, Jewish triumph and Jewish liberation tend to raise the credibility and persuasiveness of the redemptive hope and the covenant itself. Indeed the core event of the covenant and of Jewish religious history is the Exodus, the paradigm of God's redemptive action. Yet great tragedies or defeats shake the confidence in the coming of the final redemption. The persuasiveness of imperfection and evil overwhelm the frail evidence of redemption [the memory of the Exodus]. When the First Temple was destroyed, the very sanctuary of God had been violated, a seemingly impossible feat as long as the Divine Presence was there. But because the prophets perceived that Israel's sinfulness justified the Destruction, the catastrophe proved not that God abandoned them—or that other gods triumphed over God—but that God was punishing the Jews for their failure to live up to the covenant. The punishment was educational, a way of conditioning the Jews that obedience to the covenant benefits them. And, like circumcision, punishment 'forces' Israel to live up to the covenant.[13]

However, a deeper crisis grew out of the intensity of the Destruction. Possession of the Land was the symbol and guarantor of the validity of the covenant—yet the Jews were forced from the Holy Land. Then the covenant itself might have been forfeit! If the evil of the Israelites had so angered God, might not God have totally rejected the Israelites? In a sense, the Destruction was a test of what the covenant idea itself implied. Was it a utilitarian or functional covenant in which the Divine Partner had now decided to cut losses or was it fundamental to God's being, a plan that could not forfeit? The classic expression of this issue is found in Hosea and the story of Gomer, the unfaithful wife. In Hosea's experience, the Divine instruction to claim back the heartbreaking adulterous wife overrides the *halakhic* rule to divorce her. Similarly, after the rage, the hurt, the jealousy, the wrestling with rejection, comes God's anguished affirmation: "How shall I give you up, Ephraim? How can I surrender you, Israel?"[14] The prophets come to see that the Divine love was so total as to override laws and logic—and any notion of Divine limited liability in the covenant.

Ezekiel [37:11] gives a similar report. Jews were saying: "Our bones are dried up, and our hope is lost; we are cut off." The implication that the Jews are dead grows out of the fear of forfeiting the covenantal promise of eternal existence for this people. The prophetic answer that God will not abandon the covenant no matter how many times the Jews break it was decisive on this score. "Yet for all that, when they are in the lands of their enemies, I do not reject them, nor do I abhor them to finish them off and thus to break My covenant with them, for I am the Loving God, their Lord." These consoling words at the conclusion of the curses [Leviticus 26:44] became so normative that the concept of a Divine rejection of the covenant was ruled out in later Jewish writings. The punishment-for-sins theory became dominant in prophetic literature, the only trace of an alternative theory of destruction being Isaiah's theme of Israel as a suffering servant, i.e., suffering for the sins of others.

B. The Second Destruction and the Unfolding of the Covenant

The crisis of the Destruction of the Second Temple was even greater. The wound was so deep that it could not be healed without a transformation of the relationship within the covenant.[15] Christian Jews concluded the covenant was broken. Jesus' life therefore ushered in a New Covenant and his followers left the Jewish community. The Sadducees and others insisted that the covenant was unchanged and the Temple had to be rebuilt so that the traditional covenant channels of worship, grace, and forgiveness could be reopened. The Rabbis, however, concluded that fundamentally the covenant was a pedagogical model. God, as master pedagogue, had raised Israel to a new point: in the Destruction was a call to Jews to a new level of covenantal relationship. God had 'constricted' or imposed self-limitation to allow the Jews to take on true partnership in the covenant.[16] While the word *shutafut*, partnership, appears nowhere in the Bible, it is a motif in Rabbinic literature.

Many other conclusions follow. The Second Destruction means the end of prophecy; direct revelation is inappropriate in a world where God is *not* manifest. Yet even as the Divine Presence becomes more hidden, it becomes more present; the widening ritual contact with the Divine goes hand in hand with the increased hiding. The synagogues which are more 'secular' than the 'sacramental' Temple are located everywhere. They take over the central role in Jewish cult that was formerly invested in only one location, the Holy Temple in Jerusalem where there was a uniquely *manifest* Divine Presence. The Rabbinic emphasis on Talmud Torah and on Jewish learning bespeaks the internalization of religious awareness and understanding which is needed to perceive the hidden Divine Presence. This level of perception is appropriate and necessary for a more mature partner in the covenant. An enormous expansion of *halakhic* models in living follows, an expansion described by scholars as the application of Temple holiness standards to daily, more secular, settings. Blessings and ritual purifications articulate the presence of the hidden Divine everywhere and sensitize the practitioner to 'see' that Presence. In the same way, the Rabbis stress that when one performs acts of kindness,

Voluntary Covenant

the *Shechinah* [Indwelling Presence of God—Ed.] is present. The Divine Presence is there when one visits the sick, or makes love, or when one is modest, or when one honors the aged.[17] Other actions: arrogance[18], sexual immorality[19], or perversion of justice obscure or remove the Divine Presence.[20]

The interpretation of the Destruction as a call to greater responsibility in the covenant underscores the role of God as teacher, what Maimonides later described as the pedagogical model in the tradition. Talmud Torah, i.e. study, becomes the central religious act: "Talmud Torah equals all the others [*mitzvot*]."[21] The holiday of the giving of the Torah, observed in the Pentateuch, is articulated in the *Torah She B'al Peh* [Oral Law]. The Rabbis' liturgy for *Shavuot* [Festival of Weeks—Ed.] constitutes a symbolic renewal of the covenant at Sinai. Learning becomes equivalent to the Biblical ritual acts; for example, the study and recitation of sacrifices is equal [in efficacy] to the act of bringing the sacrifices.[22] God portrayed repeatedly as learning and teaching Torah: "In the first three hours [of the day] the Holy One Blessed be He sits and studies Torah....what does God do in the fourth quarter of the day? Sits and teaches Torah in the house of the Rabbis."[23] Learning becomes a form of imitating God.[24]

Without using the formal term of 'Revelation', a term not really in their vocabulary, the Rabbis interpret the Destruction as revealing both the new role of God and the new responsibilities of Israel in the covenant. But the shift from manifest intervention to hidden Presence brings out further implications of the covenant model about which the Rabbis feel ambivalent. Punishment are somewhat mechanical forms of pedagogy. In a sense, they also operate as external reinforcement, much as external Revelation operates. This was less problematic in an age when sparing the rod was considered pedagogy. But still, the best pedagogy would seem to be one that elicits internal response by the pupil—a system in which the teacher serves as model rather than enforcer.[25] Explaining the Destruction as Divine punishment for sins is not as adequate an explanation as before. This remains the dominant explanation, in part because it is also an important defense against the claim that the Destruction is a rejection of Israel as covenant partner. However, there is a significant expansion of an alternate interpretation. The Divine Presence does not so much punish Israel in the Destruction as its suffers alongside Israel.[26] The Divine does not so much punish Israel with Exile as it goes into Exile with Israel: "Where [Israel] went into Exile, the Shechinah when with them....to Egypt....to Babylon...."[27]

Finally, if the Shechinah is hidden, then awareness of the Presence will be more dependent on Jewish actions. The Rabbis were both attracted and concerned by this implication: "You are My witnesses," says the Loving God, "and I am Lord. [Isaiah 43:12]. The Rabbis comment on this verse: "When you are My witnesses, I am the Lord; when you are not My witnesses, I am not, as it were, Lord."[28] "When Israelites do God's will, they add strength to the Mighty on High....when the Israelites do not do

God's will, they weaken, as it were, the great strength of the One who lifts them up...."[29]

C. New Roles in the Covenant

Out of the Rabbinic understanding of the Destruction of the Temple came a fundamental transformation of roles in the covenant. The promise and goal remained the same—God and Israel. The Divine Presence became at once more shielded and more present; the Jews' role became more active. God's will was no longer revealed through prophets, ongoing messengers carrying out Divine instructions, but rather through the judgments of the Rabbis. These judgments grew out of the past record of instruction [i.e. the Scriptures and salient precedents][30] which Rabbinic wisdom then applied to the present situation.[31] Since individual judgments differed, decisions were reached by majority rulings. Such decisions were considered authoritative, and equivalent to a word from God. Hence, formulation of the blessing concerning God, "Who sanctifies us in His commandments and commanded us to...." is recited even over Rabbinic injunctions. True, the Rabbis offered a Biblical justification for such an application of the blessing: God "commanded us" by instructing us to listen "to the judge [Rabbi] who will be in those days" [Deuteronomy 13:9-11].[32] While this can be understood mechanically, at a deeper level the Rabbis were asserting the authority of the covenantal way. The generations that follow must have the authority to apply and adapt the covenant in their days or we will not reach the final goal. If one accepts the goal, then every future judge's ruling has the authority of the One whose commandments initiated the way.

Still, the Rabbis were modest in their ideology. They saw themselves as inferior in authority, not empowered to judge the Torah or revise it according to their lights. Their authority is rather as the continuers of the way. Nonetheless, they did not shrink from the responsibility to bring the Torah and the Jewish people through the next stage on the way to Redemption. Thus, they interpreted the law of the rebellious son[33] as theoretical, not actual.[34] They restricted the process of capital punishment so narrowly that two Rabbis said that with one more twist they could prevent any capital punishment from ever being applied.[35] They permitted a woman to testify to her own husband's death lest she otherwise be "anchored," unable to ever marry again. They improved the terms of divorce and the financial protection for women in marriage beyond those in the Torah.[36] In truth, they even suspended the laws of the Torah, although they did not believe that they had the authority to repeal them. After the Second Destruction, the ordeal of the *sotah*, the wife suspected of unfaithfulness, was set aside by Rabbi Yohanan ben Zakkai on the grounds that there were so many cheaters that the ordeal was no longer effective. I suggest that this is a halakhic consequence of the loss of the *manifest* Divine force. The sacramental efficacy of Divine power evident in the Temple

Voluntary Covenant

[i.e. the swelling of the faithless woman's belly] was no longer available.[37]

The mixture of authority and modesty of the Rabbis is also consistent with the unfolding of the covenant model. For the Rabbis, Scriptural commandments had primacy of place because they set the ultimate goal: Scriptures are the foundation of authority for everything that follows. Furthermore, while God was perceived as self-limiting, God was still commanding and active; Scriptures, with their record of an earlier more intense role for God, retained primacy. Although the prophet Samuel was manifestly more noble, more learned, more 'miraculous' in power than earlier judges, the need to proceed through history gave "Jeftah in his generation [as much authority] as Samuel in his."[38] By extension, the Rabbis had all the authority they needed. Indeed, the decisions of the Rabbinic Court were studied and used in the Heavenly Court.[39] An erroneous setting of the calendar, or, according to some, even an erroneous interpretation of the Torah, is still accepted on High.[40] Since the covenant is the way to final perfection, the Torah had to take into account the flaws and limits of human beings.[41] Thus there is room for addition, extension, and perfection of the Torah. In our generation, Rabbi Joseph B. Soloveitchik expressed the ultimate logic of this position: the scholar is co-creator of Torah, just as by their actions, human beings become co-creators of the universe.[42]

The Rabbis had a powerful sense of both the continuity and discontinuity in their role. The classic expression of this dialectic is the Rabbinic tale of Moses in Rabbi Akiva's Yeshiva. When Moses came to visit, he could not understand the Torah that was being taught there. He grew faint, presumably from embarrassment and grief that his teaching had been left behind. Then, when a student asked from whence Akiva's teaching is known, and was told: It is tradition from Moses at Sinai, Moses is calmed and consoled. We cannot dismiss this text with Mordecai Kaplan's patronizing view that the Rabbis were so ignorant of method that they undertook radical revisions in an unselfconscious way. Nor need we accept the traditionalist view that everything to be said in the future was already said at Sinai. Rather, the Akiva story is parallel to the Talmudic passage that "whatever a tried and true student [*talmid vatik*] will some day innovate was already told to Moses at Sinai."[43] There is conscious recognition of novum in the aphorism, but the new is in fact fully continuous and identified with what Moses was given at Sinai. The novum too is part of the process of the covenant. As part of the way to perfection, a new ruling has all the authority of the covenant with which it is identified and whose goals it seeks to realize. Kaplan has reversed the truth and dismissed the Rabbis as intellectual 'yokels' who have no consciousness of method because of the modern tendency to underestimate the past.[44] The Rabbis understand well that they are developers and conservers at the same time. Development is not the same as revision, reform, or rejection.

Another analogy may shed some light on this view. In the New Testament's Gospel of Matthew, which is written in a Hebrew Christian setting, contemporaneous with the emergence of the post-Destruction Rabbinic view, Jesus says in the Sermon on the Mount: "I am not come to destroy [the Law and the Prophets] but to *fulfill* [them] for verily I say unto you, 'til heaven and earth pass, one jot or one tittle shall in no wise pass from the law, *'til all be fulfilled.*"[45] Yet in the very same speech, he calls for going beyond previous standards. We know that the Hebrew Christians also operated out of a covenantal model. They believed that the new covenant was the unfolding of the old. The Destruction convinced them that the new covenant succeeded the old. Although it led them out of the Jewish community, they were being very Jewish in their thinking in applying the model of the revelation message in their historical event.

The unfolding of the covenant involved a transformation of the partner people and their observance, but not a repudiation of the covenant as it had been up them. One should not push the parallel between Rabbinic and Hebrew Christian views too far because in one key, decisive way they parted company. Convinced by the Destruction of the Temple and the failure of subsequent attempted rebellions, especially the messianic Bar Kochba revolt, the Christians decided that a New Covenant had been born. The Rabbis, however, concluded that the covenant had been renewed; the was rebirth, not new birth.[46]

D. The Renewal of the Covenant

The claims of the Rabbinic interpretation of the covenant is articulated in a classic Talmudic passage which, despite its notoriety, had been taken too lightly. In it, the Rabbis hint at a second acceptance of the Torah.

> "They stood at the bottom of the mountain" [Exodus 19:17]. Said Rav Avdimi bar Chama bar Chasa: this teaches that [coming out of Egypt] the Holy One Blessed be He clapped the mountain over them like a tub and said: If you accept my Torah, good; if not, this will be your burial place. Said Rav Acha bar Yaacov: from this we can derive a legal "out" from the Torah [i.e. if we fail to observe it we can plead that this covenant was taken under coercion and is not legally binding—See Rashi, loc. cit.]. Said Rava: nevertheless [it is binding] for they accepted it again in the days of Ahashuerus, as it is written, "the Jews established and took upon themselves" [Esther 9:27], i.e. they [re-established what they had already taken upon themselves.[47]

Why is the Sinai Covenant acceptance labeled 'coerced' in this passage? *Tosafot* [Talmudic commentaries—Ed.] is disturbed by this view and points to other, seem-

Voluntary Covenant

ingly voluntary acceptance of the Torah found in the Pentateuch such as the Israelite response "we will do and we will listen" [*na'aseh v'nishma*] and the covenant ceremony on Mounts Gerizim and Eyval.[48] Rabbeinu Tam suggests that at Sinai the Jews were pressured by the awesomeness of the Revelation—that "because it comes by Divine Speech [i.e. Revelation] therefore it is coerced, but in Ahasuerus' time they accepted it out of their own will [*mi-da'atam*—literally of their own mind or judgment] out of love of the miracle.[49] But is not appreciation of a miracle also coercive? I would suggest that the Talmud understood that the Covenant of Sinai was not coercive *when it was given*, as witness the Israelite affirmation "we will do and we will listen," etc. However, living after the Destruction, after the Divine ceased manifest interventions, in retrospect, the overt Divine salvation which backs the Sinai offer of covenant is perceived as coercive, if for no other reason that the gratitude in the heart of the saved ones obligates them to accept. The miracle of Purim is not coercive because unlike the Exodus miracles, it is hidden. Purim occurs after the Destruction of the Temple. The name of God is nowhere mentioned in the Book of Esther. The Purim miracle of salvation from genocide can be explained away as natural, achieved by imperfect humans using morally arguable methods. The recognition of the hidden Divine hand in all this is the insight which shows the Jews have come of age. They have reaccepted the covenant of Sinai on the 'new' terms, knowing that destruction can take place, that the sea will not split for them, that the Divine has self-limited and they have additional responsibilities.

If we take the Talmudic story to its ultimate logic, it is even bolder; it says that were Jews living only from the covenantal acceptance at Sinai, the Torah would not be fully binding after the Destruction. Post-Destruction Jews are living under the command of the Torah by dint of the reacceptance of the Torah at Purim time. The covenant of Purim is also a covenant of redemption, but it is built around a core event that is brought about by a more hidden Divine Presence acting in partnership with human messengers. Yet the covenant of Purim does not replace Sinai; it renews it.

Later the Talmud completes the circle of interpretation in an extended comparison of Moses imposing the covenantal oath on Israel to the oath taken by a litigant in a legal case. The Talmud says:

> We know that the commandments are binding on those who stood at Sinai; from whence do we know that future generations and future converts [are bound]? Scripture tells us [not only with you do I establish this covenant....but] with those who are not here with us today [Deuteronomy 29:1-4].

Thus the Talmud holds that the covenant is open, is offered to all who choose to join in it in the future, and is binding on them by that acceptance. Then the Talmud asks:

> From whence do we derive that commandments which will be innovated in the future such as reading the *Megillah* [are binding]? Scripture tells us "[the Jews] established and took upon themselves" [Esther 9:27]. they [reestablished what they had already taken upon themselves.[50]

In this passage, the authority of Rabbinic ordinance is based on the reaccepted covenant, the Purim renewal of the redemptive way. The authority of the Rabbis ultimately stems from their role in taking up the covenant and leading the way on this portion of the covenantal journey to redemption.

E. The Authority of the Rabbis

If the authority of Rabbinic ordinance stems from its role in carrying out the covenant further, then it is as binding as anything in written Scripture to anyone who accepts the covenant and its goals. Indeed, insofar as a Rabbinic law may move us closer to the covenantal goals, it may be more binding than Scripture. When Rabbinic law goes beyond the Torah law and brings us closer to the ultimate goal of the woman also being in the image of God, i.e., of infinite value/equal/unique, its authority becomes even more compelling than its predecessor sources.

This view is a change in my own thinking, and is contrary to two classical modern theological responses. Under the impact of modern values, various nineteenth century thinkers, seeking to clean up the halakhah and to bring it closer to the contemporary state of moral, intellectual and ethical judgments, tried to distinguish between Scriptural and Rabbinic ordinances. Scripture contained the universalist, prophetic Judaism; Rabbinic tradition was the later set of accretions—a literature in which legalism, particularism, and ritualism had run riot. In this same spirit, many secularists, especially Zionists such as Ben Gurion, tried to recover the pristine Biblical Judaism and to reject the Rabbinic, Diaspora traditions. These views fail to take history seriously. Ironically, despite their surface humanism, they end up glorifying God and failing to grasp the extraordinary shift in the covenantal partnership which is represented in Rabbinic Judaism. Implicit in these views is a loss of hope that the covenantal mechanism can respond to the crisis of modernization. Thus many Reformers felt impelled to reject law and legal process in order to assert the freedom needed to clean up moral problems in the tradition, as well as to develop new models and values for the new conditions. Ironically enough, despite their present-mindedness, they missed the radical openness of the covenant to further events in history. After all, Jeremiah spoke of a new [renewed] covenant and of a day when people would swear not by the God who brought up Israel out of the land of Egypt but of the God active in a later redemption.[51] This same blind spot blocked Reformers from considering Zionism favorably, yet the later redemption of which Jeremiah spoke was that of bringing Israel back to the land of its ancestors. Thus the Enlightenment thinkers failed to recognize the transfer from the Divine to the human realm of religious function and of leadership in developing the law which was at the heart of the Rabbinic vision and achievement. Yet this increased role for human beings in the covenant constitutes an empowerment and a bestowal of dignity which is the true goal of modern culture.

This is also contrary to the other classic position which evolved under modern influence. In defense against rapid change and reform, Orthodoxy developed an ideology denying that any development or change ever took place in the halakhah. In further defense against change, there has been a strong tendency to deny any overall goal or telos to the Torah by halakhah by rejecting any attempt at a rationale of mitzvot and by eliminating the study of Bible and philosophy. Instead, Orthodox ideology offered a juridical view of the covenant. The Law is commanding and binding because God ordered it. Human judgment itself must be sacrificed wherever it comes into conflict with the authority of the tradition. In the extreme version, the Rabbis are seen as "tape recorders," replaying words that were in truth said thousands of years ago. In the more moderate forms, the Rabbis are glossators, footnoters, judges who can expand or underscore existing patterns but whose authority must remain that of epigones. The range of the process is perceived as having been further restricted by later decisions such as the closing of the Talmud or the acceptance of the *Shulkhan Arukh* as the universal authority. While there is support for this view in the ahistorical tendencies of later Rabbinic Judaism, I submit that this is essentially a lockjaw view of the tradition caused by the traumatic infection of modernization. This view is particularly inappropriate because it denigrates the Rabbis' achievement, and occurs in an age where another unfolding of the covenant is taking place. The final irony is that the divisions between Orthodox, Conservative, Reform, and Reconstructionist [or at least between Orthodox on the one hand and the latter three, on the other] appear to be at a peak at a moment when they are all being challenged, and even by-passed, by a new covenantal transformation.

III. The Age of the Voluntary Covenant

A. The Shattering of the Covenant

When the Nazis came to power, they began a devastating assault on the Jewish people. As other nations and peoples failed to resist, the attack broadened. An unprecedented decision was taken to kill every last Jew in the world—for the crime of being. In 1941 the phase of mass murder began.

As the attack developed, the Nazis unleashed all-out violence against the covenant as well. The values and affirmations of the covenant were totally opposed, indeed reversed, even as the covenant people were killed. Jewish holy days were violated with roundups, *Aktionen,* selections and evil decrees. The Warsaw Ghetto was enclosed on Yom Kippur, 1940. Deportations from Warsaw to Treblinka death camp at the rate of 6,000, then 10,000 a day were begun on Tisha B'Av, 1942. The final destruction of the Ghetto was scheduled for Passover, 1943. Public prayer was prohibited in Warsaw in 1940. Keeping the Sabbath became impossible because forced labor was required on that day. Education was forbidden; newspapers were closed; libraries confiscated.

The assault on Jewish life and values became total. *Einsatzgruppen* [shooting squads] were deemed too slow, too costly, too problematic. The search for cheaper, swifter killing methods led to use of Zyklon B gas, an insecticide, in the Auschwitz gas chambers. To bring the cost down, the amount of gas used was cut in half the summer of 1944. This doubled the time of agonizing death, a death marked by asphyxiation, with damage to the centers of respiration, accompanied by feelings of fear, dizziness, and vomiting. Jews were impressed into service to round up other Jews for transport. The alternative was death or being sent themselves. Parents were pitted against children and children against parents for survival. A food ration of 800 calories per day was established in the ghettos, in a climate where working people need 3,000 calories per day. But the amount of food needed to supply even the official caloric standard was never delivered. Kosher slaughter was banned.

The degree of success of this attack constitutes a fundamental contradiction to the covenant of life and redemption. In Kovno, pregnancy was prohibited on pain of death. In Treblinka and Auschwitz, children were automatically selected for gassing upon arrival [except for some twins and others selected for medical experimentation]. The Jewish covenant pledges that human life is of infinite value. As the killing frenzy intensified, thousands of Jewish children were thrown directly into the crematoria or burning pits in Auschwitz to economize on gas. Still another time, the gas chambers were full of adults, so several thousand children were gathered and burned alive. This *sonderkommando* prisoner testified about this as follows:

> When one of the SS sort of had pity upon the children, he would take a child and beat the head against a stone before putting it on the pile of fire and wood, so that the child lost consciousness. However, the regular way they did it was by just throwing the children onto the pile. They would put a sheet of wood there, then sprinkle the whole thing with petrol, then wood again, and petrol and wood and petrol—

Voluntary Covenant

and then they placed the children there. Then the whole was lighted.[52]

"Could there be a more total despair than that generated by the evil of children witnessing the murder of other children....being absolutely aware that they face the identical fate....there is now a Godforsakenness of Jewish children that is the final horror."[53] Does not despair triumph over hope in such a moment?

Since there can be no covenant without the covenant people, is not the covenant shattered in this event? In Elie Wiesel's words: "The Jewish people entered into a covenant with God. We were to protect His Torah, and He in turn assumes responsibility for Israel's presence in the world....Well, it seems, for the first time in history, this very covenant is broken."[54] Or as Jacob Glatstein put it: "We received the Torah at Sinai/and in Lublin we gave it back/Dead men don't praise God/The Torah was given to the Living."[55] In response to the Destruction of the Temple the Talmudic Rabbis said: *"Mi Kamocha ba'ilmim HaShem?"* ["Who is like You among the silent, O God?"] instead of *"Mi Kamocha ba'elim HaShem?"* ["Who is like You among the mighty, O God"][56] Today would they not say what Glatstein said?

By every logical standard, Wiesel and Glatstein are right. The crisis of covenant runs deep; one must consider the possibility that it is over. Had the Shoah stood alone, would not affirmations of the covenant of redemption appear to be mockery or illusion?

A. Roy Eckardt was pointed to yet another dimension of the crisis. In retrospect, the Divine assignment to the Jews was untenable. In the covenant, Jews were called as witness to the world for God and for a final perfection. In light of the Shoah, it is obvious that this role opened the Jews to a murderous fury from which there was no escape. Yet the Divine could not or would not save them from this fate. Therefore, morally speaking, God must repent of the covenant, i.e. do *teshuvah* for having given His chosen people a task that was unbearable cruel and dangerous without having provided for their protection.[57] Morally speaking, then, God can have no claims on the Jews by dint of the covenant.

The fundamental shift in the nature of the covenant can be put yet another way. It can no longer be commanded. Covenantally speaking, one cannot order another to step forward to die. One can give an order like this to an enemy, but in moral relationships, one cannot demand the giving up of the other's life. One can ask such a sacrifice, but one cannot order it. To use another image of Elie Wiesel's: When God gave us a mission, that was all right. But God failed to tell us that it was a suicide mission.[58] One cannot order another to go on a suicide mission. Out of shared values, one can only ask for volunteers. Similarly, God can no longer enforce or educate for the covenant by punishment. The most horrifying of the curses and punishments threatened in the Torah for failing to live up to the covenant pale by comparison with what was done in the Shoah. All Jews now know that by being Jewish they expose not only themselves but their children and even grandchildren to ultimate danger and agony.[59] No Divine punishment can enforce the covenant, for there is no risked punishment so terrible that it can match the punishment risked by continuing faithfulness to the covenant. If the Jews keep the covenant after the Shoah, then it can no longer be for the reason that it is commanded or because it is enforced by reward or punishment.

B. The Assumption of Covenant

But do the Jews keep the covenant? There were a significant number of suicides among survivors who so despaired that could not live on without their lost loves, lost families, lost faith. Still others converted or ran away from the Jews to assimilate and pass among the Gentiles and so tried to shake off the danger and pain of being a Jew. But the overwhelming majority of survivors, far from yielding to despair, rebuilt Jewish lives and took part in the assumption of power by the Jewish people. For many of them, refusal to go anywhere but Israel meant years of waiting in DP camps, or a miserable risky trip in crowded, leaky, and unseaworthy boats to Israel or internment in refugee camps in Cyprus and Mauritius. Was there ever faith like this faith?

The Jewish people overwhelmingly chose to recreate Jewish life, to go on with Jewish testimony after the Shoah. What is the decision to have children but an incredible statement of hope, of unbroken will to redemption, of belief that the world was still to be perfected—so that it is worth bringing a child into this world. When there was no hope, as in Kovno or Warsaw in 1943-44, the birth rate dropped precipitously to a ratio of less than 1 to 40 deaths. Logically, assimilated Jews should have gone even further with assimilation once they heard about the Shoah for thus they could try to rid themselves of the dangers of being Jewish. Instead, hundreds of thousands of them opted to become more Jewish. Committed Jews have responded by the largest outpouring of charity and concern for other Jews in history. Observant, learned Jews have recreated yeshivot and Torah study so that today more people study Torah/Talmud full time than ever before in Jewish history, and that includes the Golden Age of Spain and the heyday of East European Jewry.

By every right, the Jews should have questioned or rejected the covenant. If the crisis of the First Destruction was whether God had rejected the covenant, then the crisis that opens the third stage of the covenant is whether the Jewish people would reject the covenant. In fact, the bulk of the Jews, observant and non-observant alike, acted to recreate the greatest Biblical symbol validating the covenant, the State of Israel. "The reborn State of Israel is the fundamental act of life and meaning of the Jewish people after Auschwitz....The most bitterly secular atheist involved in Israel's upbuilding is the front line of the Messianic life force struggling to give renewed testimony to the

Voluntary Covenant

Exodus as ultimate reality."[60]

What then happened to the covenant? I submit that its authority was broken[61] but the Jewish people, released from its obligations, chose voluntarily to take it on again. We are living in the age of the renewal of the covenant. God was no longer in a position to command, but the Jewish people was so in love with the dream of redemption that it volunteered to carry on its mission.

When the Jewish people accepted the covenant, they had no way to measure what the cost might be. The *Midrash* repeatedly praises the Israelites' response to the offer of the covenant, "We will do and we will listen,"[62] as amazing. As the cost of faithfulness increased, the Jews might have withdrawn and cut their losses. In fact, in this era, their faithfulness proved unlimited. Their commitment transcended all advantages of utilitarian considerations. They had committed their very being.[63]

In Soloveitchik's words, the covenant turned out to be a covenant of being, not doing.[64] The purpose of the Jewish covenant is to realize the total possibility of being. It is not like a utilitarian contract designed to achieve limited ends where, if the advantage is lost, the agreement is dropped. The Jewish covenant is a commitment, out of faith, to achieve a final perfection of being. Faith sees the risks but knows that without the risks the goal can never be realized. Covenanted living, like marriage or having children, is an open ended commitment, for the risks are great and one never knows what pain, suffering, danger or loneliness one is taking on. Faith in the final perfection involves seeing what is, but also what could be, precisely because life is rooted in the ground of the Divine and we do have a promise of redemption. Out of this faith comes the courage to commit.

The crisis of the Shoah was that not in their wildest dreams did Jews imagine that this kind of pain and destruction was the price of the covenant. Nor did they realize that the covenant might unfold to the point where God would ask them to take full responsibility and unlimited risks for it. Yet, in the ultimate test of the Jews' faithfulness to the covenant, the Jewish people, regardless of ritual observance level, responded with a reacceptance of the covenant, out of free will and love. For some, it was love of God; for others, love of the covenant and the goal; for others, love of the people or of the memories of the covenantal way. In truth, it hardly matters because the three are inseparable in walking the covenantal way.[65]

If the covenant is not over, then what does the Shoah reveal about the nature of the covenant? What is the message to us when the Divine Presence was in Auschwitz, suffering, burning, starving, yet despite the most desperate pleas, failing to stop the Shoah?

The Divine Presence need not speak through prophets or Rabbis. The Presence speaks for itself. If the message of the Destruction of the Temple was that the Jews were called to greater partnership and responsibility in the covenant, then the Shoah is an even more drastic call for total Jewish responsibility for the covenant. If after the Temple's destruction, Israel moved from junior participant to true partner in the covenant, then after the Shoah, the Jewish people is called upon to become the senior partner in action. In effect, God was saying to humans: You stop the Shoah. You bring the redemption. You act to ensure that it will never again occur. I will be with you totally in whatever you do, wherever you go, whatever happens, but you must do it. And the Jewish people heard this call and responded by taking responsibility and creating the State of Israel. Thereby, the people took power into its own hands to stop another Shoah as best it could.

The decision to create a Jewish state is also a decision to create a society and social reality in which Jews and Jewish values direct the fundamental decisions. For two thousand years, the Jewish witness to the world could only operate on the verbal level, indirectly, influencing the forces which moved the world such as Christianity, Islam, Western culture. Now Jewish actions can directly affect the historical destiny of the world. Now Jews can construct a society that can affect others by example. Israel, as a Jewish-run reality, can exemplify the joint process of human liberation and redemption. For example, Israel represents an agricultural society that utilizes limited resources, transforming desert into fertile, productive land, thus offering the way for the world to overcome poverty and hunger. Israel serves as a model of an open, educational society taking a population from pre-modern poverty and passivity and creating from it a people that assumes responsibility and increases its dignity without losing is past and its values. This is what Israel has done in part with its Oriental Jewish migration. Both these models are particularly significant for the Third World where the bulk of humanity struggles with the problems of poverty, fatalism and renewal of social institutions.

Of course, the politics of oil and world rivalries have isolated Israel and reduced its influence. Also, Israel itself is far from perfect and has only partially succeeded in these models. However, these limitations are congruent with the shift from powerlessness and ideal existence to exercise of power and the conquest of reality. Reality is recalcitrant and flawed, and all triumphs are partial and equivocal. It is also true that many Israelis accept the call to prevent another Shoah, but do not accept the commitment to create a redemptive model society. In a situation of voluntary covenant, there cannot be one goal imposed from above. Rather those who accept the calling must persuade and influence the others to take part in the process.

The Jewish tradition itself has been less helpful than it could be because traditionalists have not fully taken up the challenge of the new covenantal role for Israel. Religious leaders have spent must energy trying to rebuild the pre-Destruction reality rather than sanctifying the new every day. Sometimes people say that they would respond if only they were to receive clear prophetic instruction.[66] But the revelation of our lifetime is so veiled and ambiguous that there is little certainty and few clear, unassailable responses. This very lack of clarity is consistent with the voluntary nature of the covenant and the new maturity of the people Israel. Anything clearer might be coercive. The redemption will become obvious only retrospectively when the Jewish people recognize it as such. Jews must take a more active role in discerning the covenant's presence and in realizing its goals. Then will the Jewish people truly have come of age in the covenant.

C. Was the Shoah Necessary?

The recognition that consciousness of the voluntary covenant grows out of the experience of the Shoah may lead to misunderstanding. This insight may be interpreted as an affirmation of the Shoah.[67] Some have argued: Without the catastrophe, there would have been no State of Israel. Therefore, the Shoah is a necessary sacrifice or blood-letting that paves the way for redemption. Similarly, some may think that since the maturation of the covenant comes out of the Shoah, the disaster was necessary. Some may also believe that this unfolding of the covenant is an explanation of why the Shoah happened or even some rationale for it. I reject these possibilities.

There can be no rationale for the Shoah. If anyone offers such, you may be sure that the explanation has domesticated or denatured the Shoah. The explanation is no explanation but rather some plausible tale about a sanitized and selected version of the Shoah which has little to do with reality.[68] There can be no historical or sociological or military explanations of how the Shoah actually operated and what factors enabled the Nazis to carry out the mass murder so successfully. Such explanations are necessary if for no other reason that the need to prevent a recurrence. But that is a far cry from explaining the 'why' or the essence of the event.

The same must be said about the development of the voluntary covenant. In retrospect, the voluntary stage is implicit in the covenantal model from the very beginning. Once God self-limits out of respect for human dignity, once human free will is accepted, the ultimate logic is a voluntary covenant. As Soloveitchik writes: "The very validity of the covenant rests upon the *Juridic-Halakhic* principle of free negotiations, mutual assumption of duties, and full recognition of the equal rights of both concerned with the covenant."[69] The full dignity of the human partner can only emerge when that partner takes full responsibility. Any state less than that is encouragement to dependence out of weakness. Residual punishment is coercive and erodes the moral insight of the human partner. In a voluntary covenant, there is a deeper dependence—that of relationship, love, self-expectations based on the model of the other—but it is a dependence out of strength. The ultimate logic of parenting is to raise children to meet life's challenges, but to sustain them with a continuing presence and model, not with continual interference or rescue from problems. Further analysis suggests that in every covenantal relationship, the partners must ultimately choose between equality and force. True love can only exist when the imbalance of power has been overcome by redistribution of power, or, in God's case, by a binding renunciation of using the imbalance.[70]

This redistribution of power was the underlying thrust behind modern culture's empowering of the human being. In retrospect, this is what Zionism sought to do to the Jewish covenant starting in the nineteenth century. Thus there were positive reasons and forces operating before the Shoah to bring Jews and humanity a higher level of responsibility for redemption, just as there were 'secularizing' trends preceding the Destruction of the Temple. Nevertheless, most traditionalists and modernists failed to see this new dynamic of power as operating within the covenantal framework. Many concluded that the true purpose of modern culture was to reject the covenant or slay the covenantal partner for the sake of human liberation. In significant measure, this misconstruction is directly implicated in the emergence of pathological forms of total human power unleashed in the modern forces which reach a climax in the Shoah itself. In a counterpart error which was the mirror image of that of modern total secularists, religious groups interpreted the covenant to demand human subservience or passivity and opposed the emergence of the new level of human responsibility. However, now that the Shoah has occurred, it is no longer possible to delay the emergence of the new level.

There is no good in the Shoah, only a tragedy which forces us to face up to an issue and a responsibility which was long coming. The Jewish response to the Shoah, as to the Destruction of the Temple, is the act that crystallizes and energizes this transition. The Shoah is not a necessary *quid pro quo* for anything. It is the shock that almost destroys the covenant. It continues to degrade God and educate humans to savagery and destruction. However, thanks to the power of human love and faith that will not yield the dream of redemption, the Shoah can be fought, and perhaps its effects can be overcome in history. This is the struggle that is now going on.

IV. Implications of the Voluntary Covenant

A. The Promise of Pluralism

The total assault on Judaism and on the Jewish people was an attempt to stamp out the covenant, the witness, and, ultimately, the presence of God who is the Ground of life and the covenantal hope. Therefore, the very existence of the Jewish people is a fundamental statement that the covenant is ongoing. The survival of the Jewish people in a world full of enemies, where the model of the Shoah is circulating, is in itself testimony to the existence of a hidden God whose awesome, if invisible, force is evidenced in the ongoing life of the Jewish people.[71] The renewal of Jewish living through having

Voluntary Covenant

children, and restoring human dignity constitute the creation of images of God.[72] These images point to the God of whom they are the image; they are the best, most indelible testimony to God in a world where total evil has triumphed in recent times. Such witness could not be given without profound wells of faith and hope to draw upon the individual Jews who live this way. Finally, the Jewish people, by recreating the State of Israel and rebuilding the land, has given the witness which shows the world that God lives and the covenantal hope is not in vain. All Jews who elect to live as Jews makes these statements whatever their self-definition and official behavior.[73]

It makes no essential difference if the Jews involved consciously articulate the covenantal hope or express a belief in God who is the Ground of the covenant. The witness is given by their actions. Actions speak louder than words. People who profess God but gas men, women, and children or burn them alive are atheists whatever their words may be. People who profess to be atheists or to be without hope yet who actively uphold the covenant, even at the cost of their lives, betray their true position by their actions. If anything, their denials only add to the hiddenness of the Divine. Therefore, their theological language is the appropriate one for this time, more appropriate than those who go on speaking as if God were visible and fully performing under the previous terms of the covenant.

In the age of voluntary covenant, every person who steps forward to live as a Jew can be compared to a covert insofar as a convert, one who voluntarily opts to be a Jew, must make certain commitments and express certain beliefs. Then the classic conversion ceremony may guide us to contemporary Jews' proper affirmations. Through the conversion pro-cess, the convert testifies that although the Jews are driven, tormented, and persecuted to this very day, the convert still wants to be a Jew, that is, wants to offer the testimony of hope anyway. The convert learns the unity of God and the denial of idolatry; the analogue in our time is the affirmation of God's presence which is witnessed by Jewish existence itself.

The convert must affirm some of the weighty commandments/obligations of a Jew and some of the lighter ones. In this generation, all who opt to live as Jews automatically state their readiness for martyrdom, not only for themselves but for their children and grandchildren as well. There can be no 'weightier' commitment than this. A decision to live in Israel, and to a lesser extent a commitment to support it, constitute acceptance of the mitzvah to witness, to build a redeeming social reality, even to bring the Messiah. The appropriate range of 'lighter' commandments/obligations to be undertaken can be explored or debated between the denominations. But morally speaking, the simple observance of all of the classical mitzvot can hardly be the only option offered under the covenantal definition.[74]

While the covenant is now voluntary, birth into it remains an important statement. By being born a Jew, a person summons up all the associations and statements implicit in Jewish existence, including the Jewish testimony to a God who cares. One may opt out by refusing to live as a visible Jew, by trying to escape the fate of a Jew, by trying to deny. However, if one chooses to continue living as a Jew, one makes all the fundamental affirmations implicit in Jewish existence. This is true even if one does not use the officially articulated ways of making one's statements such as bearing witness to creation through Shabbat [Sabbath] observance or expressing the Messianic hope through prayers such as *Aleinu*.

As long as the covenant was involuntary, it could be imposed from above in a unitary way. This corresponds with the image and role of revelation in the Biblical period, which includes unequivocal command and visible reward and punishment for obedience and disobedience. With the shift in covenantal relationship which characterizes the Rabbinic era, the revelation becomes more hidden, more subject to pluralist interpretation. Focus on reward and punishment shifts from the worldly toward the other-worldly hidden realm.

In the new era, the voluntary covenant is the theological base of a genuine pluralism. Pluralism is not a matter of tolerance made necessary by living in a non-Jewish reality, nor is it pity for one who does not know any better. It is a recognition that all Jews have chosen to make the fundamental Jewish statement at great personal risk and cost. The present denominations are paths for the covenant-minded all leading toward the final goal. The controversy between them will not be whether God has commanded these ways. Conservative, Reform and secular Jews can freely concede the dimensions of past commandments, but insist nevertheless that these are no longer effective or optimal ways of achieving the goals. Orthodox Jews, even the ultra-right who uphold every past observance or *minhag* [custom], will recognize that their commitment to observe the entire tradition constitutes a voluntary acceptance, one which can be modeled but cannot be *demanded* of all. Thus, they can be faithful to the full authority of the halakhah, accepting the challenge of modeling it and making it credible and persuasive to *Klal Yisrael*, while respecting the incredible other types of commitment and contributions which other Jews are making. Such an admission would only confirm the phenomenology of Jewish life as it is now being lived. It would be morally and humanly liberating without yielding the hope of moving Klal Yisrael into the classic paths of halakhah. Of course, the psychology of Orthodoxy currently will not be receptive to this approach, but such an obstacle is not a problem of principle or integrity. Rather, it is a function of human limitations, community and political needs, all of which can be dealt with tactically.

It would be unreasonable and, considering the varieties of religious experience and sociological circumstance, unwise to expect total religious unity. There can still be ongoing controversies and policy differences between the denominations. But the members of all the groups have committed their total being to be witness to the cov-

Voluntary Covenant

enant by living as Jews. The recognition of this overarching unity enables us to adjudge these controversies as being "for the sake of Heaven."[75] In the Talmud, the school of Shammai and the school of Hillel often gave diametrically opposite rulings. Yet they affirmed that both views are "the words of the living God,"[76] precisely because they recognized the underlying unit of their common assumptions about the nature of God and Revelation. The unity which was destroyed in the modern period is restored in the common recognition of the voluntary covenant.

Groups can go on judging and trying to persuade each other to change, but the criteria for resolution of the conflict will be the ability to reach the goals of the covenant, including contemporary effectiveness and transmissibility. Orthodoxy might concede that a particular practice is not effective today. However, they continue to accept it as binding out of respect for past generations and their role in the covenant. Out of the sense that this generation is only a way station on the long covenantal road, they can accept temporary ineffectiveness of a practice in one moment in order to have the resource available in another. The definition of being Orthodox might be accepting the models of the past as binding out of recognition of the incredible, Divine power in them, and being bound by the process of the covenant, a process seen as inseparable from is goals and content. Then the differences with non-Orthodox Jews are tactical, and others' faithfulness to God and to the covenant can be admitted without undermining Orthodox affirmations. Once the validity of the others is recognized, the shortcomings or faults in the halakhic system can be admitted, and, to the extent possible, corrected. As long as the legitimacy of the others is not recognized, many problems will be denied and possible solutions rejected on the grounds that to change would give aid and comfort to the "enemy."

By the same token, Reform, Conservative, and secular Jews would waive the modernist criteria that justify their positions. This means that every part of the tradition may present itself for serious consideration to be judged by the same criteria of consistency with the covenant, transmissibility and effectiveness. Any new approaches developed by these Movements will also be reviewed by the same criteria. Some changes may be judged as concessions legitimated by the need to successfully negotiate the covenantal paths, and they are subject to repeal or redirection if the situation changes. New paths or models may be as sacred or more sacred that then inherited ones if they are deemed closer to the covenantal values or more effective in attaining them. It follows from this, however, that both reform and tradition are aligned along a continuum of attempts to live by the covenant. Reform behavior is not antinomian, but is distinguished from traditional Judaism by the giving of different weights to different covenantal values. The increased "heavier" role of women in Reform is an affirmation of the covenantal promise of redemption and ultimate dignity for women as well as men, rather than a rejection of the commandments or roles for males in tradition. Feminist corrections of the halakhah are an attempt to move more urgently toward the covenantal goal of humankind being in the image of God, which implies equality for women, rather than a rejection of the concept of obligation or of the traditional feminine positive roles.[77]

Once disagreements take place within the bounds of the common risk and dream of Jewish existence, the groups might take on or set aside a common practice for the sake of unity, beyond the merits of the practice itself. Each group would be committed to use all its resources and methods to reach out and enable the others to live in good conscience with the same model or at least not to disrupt or shatter the others' ways where they differ. At least all groups would recognize the element of risk and creativity in trying to be faithful to the covenant at a moment when new roles and new institutions are emerging. Since whatever models of service are offered tend to be projections of past experience, there is a tendency in transition times to offer the familiar even when something new or original may be needed. At moments of transformation there is the risk of a faithfulness that misdirects, even as there is a risk of excessive novelty and betrayal of the tried and true methods of the covenant. Each group should welcome the insights and criticisms of the others as necessary correctives, sources of perspective in a fluid and unformed situation in which all want to do the right thing but fear falling short.

B. Human Co-Creativity in the Covenant

Although obedience is the natural response in an involuntary covenant, nevertheless the principle of mutual obligation stimulated the Jews to engage in controversies with God throughout history. The greater the degree of human partnership, the more frequent and profound is the role of humans in challenging God to live up to the covenant. In an age of voluntary covenant, humans have all the more right and obligation to represent the covenantal goals and values to God. Humans must take responsibility, both for the goals and the consistency of the means with the goals. Since humans are being called to take full responsibility in action for the realization of the covenant, they cannot escape the responsibility to judge the means and methods available to pursue the goals. Those who are entrusted with a task, and who take full responsibility for its realization, must be allowed discretion to achieve the goal. This delegation of authority is all the more justified in light of the Jewish faithfulness to the covenant, exemplified by the voluntary reassumption of the covenant in this generation despite the obvious risks involved.

The urgency of closing any gap between the covenantal methods and goals is greater in light of the overwhelming countertestimony of evil in this generation. The credibility of the covenant is so weakened and so precariously balanced that any internal element that disrupts or contravenes its affirmations must be eliminated. So savage was the attack on the image of God that the counter response of reaffirmation must be extraordinary. Any models or behavior patterns within the tradition that demean the image of God must be cleansed and corrected at once. The hope of breakthrough toward perfection is higher in a generation which feels the obligation to match the extraordinary outburst of evil with a countervailing upsurge of good. Therefore, there is motivation and sufficient authority even among the Orthodox to correct the tradition or move it toward its own goals of perfection. The authority to change grows out of loyalty to the tradition and to the covenantal goals.

Part of the response must be to identify covenantal values and make judgments on the relative weight to be assigned to each. In the past, it has been argued that any judgment in conflict with established tradition is improper. Since the word of God is self-validating, change, by definition, must be based on appeal to outside criteria and is therefore invalid. With increased human responsibility and greater hiddenness of God and of Revelation, the exercise of judgment not only by Rabbis but by a wider variety of people becomes urgent. One cannot pass the buck to tradition. The responsibility for getting to the final perfection is squarely on this generation. It must exercise the responsibility with humility and self-criticism, but faithfulness requires that judgments be made.

Since the State of Israel is the central vehicle of Jewish power, self-defense and redemption-building, its needs should be given greater religious weight, perhaps rated as a matter of life or death. Some will object that this runs the risk of idolatry vis-a-vis the state. Both traditionalist and liberal Jews might conclude that the danger of idolatry is the overriding concern. Other traditionalist and liberal Jews might pursue a policy stressing the State's needs while taking action to avoid idolatry. Either decision would be good, particularly as it grows out of a wrestling with the actual situation, rather than out of the routine party lines of conflicting forces in modernity and tradition. The treatment of women, of the handicapped, and of Gentiles in the tradition are other examples where Jewish utopian values are in conflict with the present reality. These value concessions to reality must now be challenged even if we agree that they are Divinely normative. The challenge, the defense, and the final resolution should not follow present party lines, but should explore the best ways of advancing the covenantal goals. Indeed, side by side experiments may be the right prescription until we sort out the best ways. In an experimental situation, either a more traditional or more innovative *modus operandi* becomes a creative and helpful foil for the other position, so that pluralism becomes a source of strength.

C. Messianic Time

Classically great destruction so challenges the affirmations of the covenant that it creates an urgent anticipation of a countervailing achievement of redemption. Nothing less can restore the credibility of the way. An event as massively devaluing as the Shoah needs an event of Messianic proportions to restore the balance. Voluntarily taking up the covenant, then, means taking up the challenge of Messianic breakthroughs. The expectation of great redemption is further nurtured by the incredible nature of the creation of Israel, which is heralded in the tradition as the harbinger and necessary condition for the Messianic fulfillment.

Why, then, has this generation hesitated to speak in Messianic terms? Partly it is due to the need to speak modestly after such a triumph of evil; partly the hesitation is due to the triumph of modernity and its rational, limiting style which has a chilling effect on Messianic expectations.[78] And why has the Messianic principle, when applied, been such a poor guide to action? The invocation of Messianic associations for David Ben Gurion was essentially a political trick to gain new immigrant votes for the very people who were proceeding to strip the *Sephardim* of their traditional values and give them the short end of the social stick. In the case of the *Gush Emunim*, the Messianic models have led to a devaluation of security and other realistic considerations and sometimes to a down-grading of the dignity of Arab concerns and needs on the West Bank.

I submit that these ills grow out of a failure to grasp the nature of the Messianic in the era of voluntary covenant. A Messiah who is triumphant and does it all for Israel would be utterly inappropriate in such an age. The arrival of such a Messiah would be morally outrageous, for the Messiah would have come at the wrong time. As Elie Wiesel has written, if any Messiah is going to redeem us by Divine strength, then the time to have come was during the Shoah. Any Messiah who could have come and redeemed us, and did not do so then but chooses to come now is a moral monster. Wiesel is right: it is too late for the Messiah to come.[79] *Therefore we will have to bring the Messiah.* Bringing the Messiah is the crowning response to the Divine call for humans to take full responsibility in the covenant. A Messiah who needs to be brought can only be partial, flawed, hidden.[80] Such a model of the Messiah may dampen the dangerous tendency to exercise utopianism, not to mention antinomianism, implicit in the end-time. At the same time, the model assigns new urgency to achievements of justice and peace, to coming closer to vegetarianism[81] and the full dignity of other humans, to witnessing more openly and more universally even as we prepare to become one with the world.

D. Responding

In a situation of fundamentalist transformation, playing it safe is tempting, but dangerous. The familiarity of the response gives consolation and a false sense of security in a bewildering vortex of change. However, there is a real risk of acting like the Sadducees at the Destruction of the Temple. Upholding the familiar, insisting that it is the only authoritative way, may leave one totally invested in recreating the status quo. When the status quo does not return, exhaustion and death of the spirit follow.

The alternative is to incorporate the new events and the new situation, first into understanding and then into the covenantal way. This process may lead to mistaken judgments ranging from premature Messianism to present-mindedness to loss of a coherent sense of the past. Taking action is risky; not taking action is risky. The appropriate response is to act, with anxiety, with conflict, with fear, but to act nonetheless. The first step is to incorporate the new event into the traditional way of life and into Jewish memory. *Yom HaShoah* and *Yom HaAtzmaut* [Israel Independence Day] must become central holy days of the Jewish calendar. Their 'secular' nature and grass roots origin are appropriate to the new era of holiness in which humans take responsibility for sanctification and redemption. The ambiguity of the days, and the fact that their sanctity is open to challenge, is an expression of the hiddenness of the Divine in the new era.

Many other commandments emerge from the new reality. The model/mitzvah of pilgrimage both to the scenes of the Shoah and to Israel, and the telling of the tale in secular settings including film, books and other media are the new secular liturgical acts. A range of acts of justice and restored dignity, which flow from these events ["You were slaves, you were in ghettos, you were in camps, therefore you....you were freed, you were outsiders and taken to the Promised Land, therefore you...."], are the ethical counterparts of this liturgical development. Both types of acts are part of the expansion of the covenantal round of life to incorporate the new experiences. The accounts of these events and the lives and the models that grow out of them constitute a new Scripture and a new Talmud.[82]

The redemption event of this era, Israel, the Scriptures which are being written, the spiritual leadership of this new age will be even more secular, more 'naturalistic,' more flawed than in the Rabbinic Era, as is appropriate given the greater hiddenness of God. Every act of life be-comes potentially holy, the locus of the hidden Divine Presence. Not only are special days such as *Shabbat* and prohibition of work ways of sanctification, but work itself properly done is a religious act. Work as the expression of the commandment *lashevet* [to settle the world]—work as the creation of an infrastructure for human dignity, work as the exercise of the human capacity for power and control which are part of the image of God—will become a halakhically holy enterprise.[83] Thus, every day and not just one out of seven can become a holy day.

The holiness of sexuality can be expressed not only the prohibition or in *mikveh* [ritual immersion], but in the acts of love themselves. Sexuality as communication, as the revelation of the image of God in me, as the discovery of the image of God in the other, as affirmation of the pleasure of life, as a joyous vehicle of creating life becomes the continual expression of holiness. The Torah commands the Jewish people: '*Kedoshim tih'yu*' [Be holy!].[84] In a classic commentary, Nachmanides defines holiness above and beyond specific ethical and ritual commandments as fulfillment of the Talmudic dictum, '*kadesh atzm'cha b'mutar lach*' [Sanctify yourself in the areas which are permitted][85], go beyond the letter of the law and exercise restraint in those areas which are permitted.[86] The concept of secular sanctification suggests that holiness in the permitted is achieved not only by extending prohibition, but by directing action and spirit toward the covenantal goal.

Much of the expression of holiness can be accomplished using the existing models of *b'rachah* [blessing], selection, and sharing. Some of this expansion may come from heightened consciousness and developing inner attitudes and perceptions of holiness. Thus the voluntary covenantal model reaches a climax. In such moments, it begins to approximate Jeremiah's promise of a new covenant written on the heart.[87] However, this renewed covenant does not reject law or form, nor does it repudiate or supersede the original covenant. The voluntary covenant is built on the involuntary covenant; it continues and moves toward the final goal.

Contemporary Jews will have to explore the liturgical sources and models that can nurture a holiness that is at once more subtle and more elusive. The great covenantal symbol, circumcision, reflects the involuntary nature of the covenant. It also 'excludes' women and makes their representative function relatively less central.[88] In the new era, the symbol of the voluntary covenant may well be the revival, side by side with circumcision, of the *brit bayn habetarim*, the covenant between the pieces.[89] This was the original covenant ceremony, the conversion ritual of Abraham, the first non-Jew to become a Jew. He entered this covenant voluntarily before he became circumcised and permanently marked. Women can enter into the covenant between the pieces equally with men. This ceremony symbolizes that in the era of voluntary covenant, all are bound equally, i.e. all have voluntarily committed themselves to this incredible and dangerous task.[90]

Modern history has shown that democracies can ask for and elicit more total sacrifices from their citizens than even the great tyrannies can dare demand of their people. This encourages us to hope that the age of voluntary covenant will be marked by more encompassing religious life, greater commitment to justice, and an overall higher level of spiritual achievement by the Jewish people. The age has already started with un-

Voluntary Covenant

precedented spiritual heroism in the response to the Shoah. One may pray that we be worthy—and that the best is yet to come.[91]

The Holocaust Now

The Crisis of Prayer

Reflecting upon the title of this volume, Michael McGarry enjoins us to consider two paralleling responsibilities: [1] the internalization of the memories of the Shoah by those who experienced it first-hand, a "sacred trust" for Christians, especially Catholics, and for Jews; and [2] a re-thinking of the role of prayer in our post-Auschwitz world as it related to the fate of God, the very meaning of community, and the very purpose of worship within the Church itself. Summarizing his own thoughts, he writes, *"Christians" contemporary religious response* to the Shoah is to pray for the Jews, not supposing that an interventionist God will reach out to support them—that possibility was shown to be futile in Auschwitz; rather they do so in order to align themselves with the intentionalist God who has chosen the Jews as God's very own and stands with them in their suffering, in their triumph, and in their calling."[1]

SLJ

The Holocaust Now

A CONTEMPORARY RELIGIOUS RESPONSE TO THE SHOAH: THE CRISIS OF PRAYER

Michael McGarry

I. Introduction

In an address in Sydney, Australia, Pope John Paul II reminded his hearers that "this is still the century of the Shoah."[2] Many other events besides the Shoah might be marshalled forward to characterize the past hundred years: the introduction of mass communications, the era of possible nuclear annihilation, the beginning of space exploration, or the shrinking of the planet into the "global village." In a most profound sense, however, the cloud of the Shoah hangs over the Western Hemisphere and eclipses even those other epoch-making events. The Shoah is the reference point, the historical *caesura*, the *mysterium tremendum* of the century.[3]

For the religious person, the Shoah stands as a particularly difficult moment. It is a radically "re-orienting event" for both Christian and Jew; it has become the overarching reference point for personal and theological self-understanding. The purpose of my remarks in this essay, therefore, are to reflect as one religious person, a Roman Catholic, on some dimensions of this epochal event as we approach the third millennium. I do not suggest or give this unique event religious meaning as such; I do not even suggest to find religious meaning within it. Rather, I propose to take the title of the original volume—*Contemporary Christian Religious Responses to the Shoah*—quite literally and to meditate with the reader on some of its aspects. I do not propose to give a survey of what others have seen as the religious responses; those have been done quite competently and completely.[4] My aim is to reflect thoughtfully on, first, what it means to be a *contemporary* person thinking about this subject, and, second, what *religious* [not philosophical or even "professionally theological"] responses might be, specifically the crisis of prayer after the Shoah.

II. Some Dimensions of Contemporary Reflections on the Shoah

While attending the very significant "Remembering for the Future" Conference at Oxford, England, in the Summer of 1988, I pondered the demographics of the other attenders. Most of them, it appeared to me, had been alive, even adults, during the Shoah years. For them, "remembering" was the primary category for grasping it. They sought desperately to cling to those years lest they be lost to future generations by irresponsible forgetting. This sense of "remembering" was heightened by the presence of many survivors who chillingly prefaced their remarks with "I remember when...." As a community forced over a few days, committed to a corporate remembering process, they offered compelling testimony which seemed to be almost a sacred trust to then be handed on to the next generation.

At the same time, I noticed a not insignificant number of young scholars like myself who sought to absorb the memory of the survivors. For this younger generation, the goal was not so much to keep a memory alive as it was to make someone else's memory their own. Or, to put it another way, they were seeking to solidify individual memories into a corporate memory, whether that be of the Jewish people, the Christian community, or people of Western Civilization. They—we—felt strongly that "remembering" this episode in our century was an urgent mission, not only to escape trivializing the six million Jews who were executed, not only to avoid marginalizing the five million others who were obliterated in the Nazi attack, but to insure that such a memory will act as a bulwark to prevent such genocide from happening again.

To reflect a *contemporary* response to the Shoah, it seems to me that we must recognize the critical moment before us: We are at the threshold of the post-survivor period after which there will be no living voice to say what the Shoah was like, no voice to correct the record, no witness to corroborate the evidence about horror of The Night. Now is that fragile moment when a generation passes on a personally-owned, and often individually experienced, memory into the minds and hearts of the generation which must first learn the memory and then make it its own.

Some other unique dimensions of this moment are to be recognized in the controversies surrounding the building of the National Holocaust Memorial Museum in Washington, D.C. These disputes revolve, in part, around the following question: who owns the Shoah—the survivors, who are fewer and fewer in number? The survivors' children—who have pledged to their parents never to mislay their legacy? The educators of the future—who may wish to use the Shoah for their own agenda and exposition of "its lessons?"

However we answer the question as to who owns the Shoah, *our* moment witnesses the erecting of Shoah Memorials now to be found in almost every major city in the United States, dozens of sites in Europe, and a few sites in Israel.[5] What is one to

The Crisis of Prayer

make of this contemporary development? What does it, then, mean to be surrounded by these memorials while, at the same time, the reality and meaning of the Shoah, once missing from our historical and religious courses of study, are increasingly finding a place, even a place of honor, in our curricula?[6]

At the same time, while the Shoah seeks it rightful place in American civic and educational life, a confluence of other powerful Jewish concerns emerges: the lower birth rate of American Jews, the worrisome dilution of Jewish commitment through intermarriage, the ongoing anxiety for Israel's security, and the emerging wonderment at the wisdom and the tactic of using the Shoah as the reference point for Jewish life into the 1990s. There are other concerns which characterize our contemporary situation. So at the very time when a generation is asked to pass on the memory and the lessons of the Shoah, these other concerns are calling it into question or diverting its energy.

As a comparison for dilemma, one may well recall the generation who grew up in the United States after the Great Depression: their fiscal habits were marked by frugality, measured vision, and dogged work. The next generation, despite multiple warnings from those who had struggled out of poverty so heroically, look for quick, professional ways of making money, often quite unconcerned about the long term effects of their way of life. Analogously, Jews who emerged from Auschwitz's ashes forged new lives and helped to create national policies which secured their freedoms. Now they often find a new generation who does not appreciate the battles that have been won for them. This new generation sometimes sees the focus on the past as morbid and the wrong center of gravity for the Jewish people. For many of them, "never again" does not carry the emotional anxiety of what less vigilance caused their grandparents' generation. In other words, the hard won victories of a certain generation are taken for granted by the next. At the same time, the contemporary generation—those who learn of the Shoah rather than remember it, who must be vigilant on the basis of the warnings of others and not because of a gut wrenching experience of their own—must find ways to make this event of the century their own.

In this situation, the Jewish community has its work cut out for itself, but the Christian community may find its tasks even more difficult. For many Christians, the Shoah does not even register in their universe of moral concern. Many think it should be shrugged off as an event from another generation, on another continent, and perpetrated by barbarians now extinct. For them to "remember," to learn about the time when the Christian community failed its Jewish brothers and sisters and, indeed, itself seems like an almost impossible and unfair burden.[7] The challenge for Christians [and I must be even more particular—for Catholics] is to situate the Shoah squarely within their own history, even as they study it within larger world history. This is a delicate task because post-World War II American Catholics, educated in a post-Vatican II Church,

221

do not respond well to appeals to guilt or even global responsibility. They eschew, for better or worse, anything which hints of "guilt-tripping," and they have been forged, like other Americans, in a very individualistic climate which makes historical and relational ideas difficult to grasp, must less appreciate.[8]

The Roman Catholic Church has begun to educate its members about the Shoah, at least in terms of official directives. In 1985, a very important Church document counselled that religious "Catechesis should....help in understanding the meaning for the Jews of the extermination during the years 1939-1945, and its consequences."[9] The challenge, then, for the Catholic Church is to heed its own guidance on the inescapable necessity of studying the Shoah, not just for better Christian-Jewish relations, but, more importantly, for better and more authentic self understanding.[10]

Emil Fackenheim has written that we are all "*situated* in the post-Holocaust world. We must accept our situatedness. We must live with it."[11] Together, Jews and Christians of this contemporary generation—from different perspectives and for different reasons—must come to grips with our post-Shoah situation. They must study a history free of ideological distortions, one which invites not only remembering and grieving but also commitment and courage. The danger abides, however, that the ecclesiastical directives might become a burial place rather than a spur to such a process. Thus the task of making the Shoah part of collective Catholic memory, while intended and promised, has only just begun.

III. A Contemporary Religious Response

My organizing principle in considering the dimensions of a contemporary *religious* response to the Shoah may be something of a surprise in a "scholarly" article. That is, I suggest that prayer—the believer's and the Church's articulated relation with the Creator—is a prime casualty since and because of the Shoah and thus needs to be addressed.[12] And this not simply for academic interest: prayer imposes itself as an existentially insistent question related to the fate of God, the meaning of community, and the purpose of worship within the Church.

In reading other articles of this genre, one often gets the impression that the fate of God in and after the Shoah does not matter much to the writers. Rather, they describe, quite antiseptically, what theologically and rationally has happened to God because of the Shoah. One seldom gets the impression that the writers care much personally because they themselves are not all that affected. Without giving up a systematic approach, I hope to avoid such a distancing from my subject. What I mean by "distancing" may be compared to the difference between the journalist's account of a woman losing her husband in an automobile accident and the description *by the widow* of the ache she feels at her husband's absence. And so, I hope that my addressing the religious response to the Shoah through the prism of prayer may be seen as a more personal exploration of mourning God lost through the "accident" of the Shoah. And that God, not coincidentally, is a spouse—the spouse of the Jewish people [Hosea 2], the spouse of the Church [Ephesians 5:25-30]. My reflections, therefore, are not the dispassionate notes of the learned "observer of the religious scene." Rather, I hope to speak as one whose passionate "spouse God" has been perhaps mortally wounded or revealed to be less than faithful within that tragic darkness in Christian and Jewish history known as the Shoah.

My starting premise is that prayer, the believer's fundamental activity, has been shattered by recognizing the Shoah as *part of Christian history*.[13] From my perspective, these questions need to be addressed, and they constitute the outline for the rest of this essay.

A. What did prayer mean in the Shoah world?

B. How does prayer's Addressee—God during and after the Shoah—resemble the God revealed in the Hebrew and Christian Scriptures?

C. What might our prayer be in the post-Shoah world?

A. What Did Prayer Mean in the Shoah World?

The contemporary crisis of prayer looks for clues to its solution by first asking what prayer might have meant *within* and *during* the Shoah. And, as one would expect, this question arises in different wordings and urgency for the Jewish and Christian communities.

During the Shoah, most Jews found their prayers fruitless. They screamed out to the God of their ancestors for the Nazi onslaught to be reversed; they cried out to be saved. They wailed at God that He would deliver them from the plague of forced evictions, family ruptures, burned synagogues, and dreaded boxcars to death. Prayer, for most of them, seemed not to find responsive ears. Many felt their access to the Divine had been somehow severed. Many others felt even that the God of their ancestors had been unmasked as nonexistent. Roth and Rubenstein describe it as follows:

> For if Auschwitz made it no longer possible to trust God's goodness simply, it made questions about God and wrestling with God all the more important. Wiesel has been heard to say: 'If I told you I believed in God, I would be lying; if I told you I did not believe in God, I would be lying.'[14]

Other Jews, too small in number, felt that their petitions had indeed been answered through escapes, rescue, family reunions, or release for their children. These Jews regarded the [and sadly few] righteous Gentiles almost as messengers from a merciful God who hid them in blackened cellars or offered them asylum from the catastrophe's fury. And prayers of gratitude were offered.

From still others, unanswered prayers, regardless of results, rose with energy and enthusiasm. Fackenheim recalls the Hasidim at Buchenwald who purchased [with four rations of bread] confiscated tefillin [phylacteries—Ed.] with which they "prayed with an ecstasy which it would be impossible ever to experience again in....[their] lives." This act of faith Fackenheim calls a kind of resistance, responding to God's command to live, to live as Jews. The Hasidim, by their prayer, refused the Nazi redefinition of their identities and their dignity.[15]

In the end, however, one has to say that the vast majority of Jewish prayers in the Shoah appear fruitless. Indecent, it would be obscene to enter into some sort of accounting exercise, weighing, on the one hand, those whose desperate prayers for escape were followed by exhausted prayers of gratitude with, on the other hand, the millions whose prayers dissipated as surely and as quickly as the smoke from the crematoria. This, indeed, would be grisly bookkeeping. But what does one do with either of these prayers? Where does one go? Are the survivors' prayers of gratitude meaningless babble because so many other co-religionists were annihilated? At very least, one must honor the faith and dignity of those Jews who prayed during and after the Shoah by not dismissing them as naive fools. Indeed, in our own dilemma, the prayer within the Shoah might be the very foundation for the possibility and meaning of prayer now. To paraphrase Fackenheim's kabbalistic [i.e. mystical—Ed.] principle, perhaps "prayer here and now is meaningful only because prayer then and there in the Shoah was actual."[16]

For Christians, similar questions arise. First, the Christian experience of the Shoah was that of seeing God's Chosen abandoned, even as many of them prayed for survival and deliverance. From a distance, Christian's beheld God's first Chosen threatened with annihilation, and God did not come to their rescue. They saw God's elect stunned by the wall of God's silence. The sensitive Christian must ask, "I claim that the Jews' God is my God and where was my God?"

A second Christian question arises: "What about *their* prayer in the Shoah world?" Again we turn to Fackenheim who recalls the time when a simple invocation for the Jews took on prophetic character and caused the death of one Christian leader. This prayer was that of Domprobst [Prior] Bernhard Lichtenberg who offered liturgical intercessions for the Jews in Berlin's Hedwigkirche. His prayers were marked by two critical characteristics: they were *public* and they disclosed a possible counterforce to

The Crisis of Prayer

the Nazi death machine. As Fackenheim notes, had Christian Europe joined in sincerity and in chorus with Lichtenberg to pray for the Jews by name, "they would have caused the collapse of the kingdom of the Antichrist."[17]

Third, if only a few German Christians uttered public intercession for the Jew, what were American Christians praying about during World War II? Surely it was not concentrated on the plight of the Jews in the Nazi onslaught. Numerous scholars have chronicled American preoccupations during the Second World War.[18] Understandably, Americans focused on defeating the Axis powers, which defeat would entail the end of the concentration camps. Thus, Americans prayed for victory even as they knew of so much suffering on the part of the Jews and other persecuted peoples.

Fourth, to complete the inquiry about prayers *during* the Shoah, one has to ask the terrifying question, "What kind of God were the Germans and their collaborators imagining when they prayed for victory?" A God who helped the good overcome the bad? A God who took sides in international conflicts? What flowed through the religious imagination of some SS guards as they bounced their infant on their knee on Saturday, went to Church on Sunday, and returned to work on Monday? Of what possibly could they have been thinking when they prayed? I have found no answers to this dreadful question in my research; I am even afraid to come across any.

These reflections about the prayer life of those who invoked God during the Shoah are very disturbing to those of us who pray for deliverance from war and other harmful threats. But whatever else one might say about the God to whom all these people prayed, in the end this God did not seem strong enough

[1] to transform the majority of German and Austrian Christians into people who would refuse to take part, directly or indirectly, in the extermination of Jewish people;

[2] to move Roman Catholic leadership to do more to influence Axis nations to cease persecuting the Jews;

[3] to save six million of His First Chosen.

Which brings us to the next major question....

The Holocaust Now

B. How Does Prayer's Addressee—God During and After the Shoah—Resemble the God Revealed in the Hebrew and Christian Scriptures?

Whatever else they said, Biblical writers depicted God as radically and directly involved in history.[19] In the Hebrew Scriptures, God is repeatedly credited with changing history's course for the sake, and/or at the beckoning, of His beloved, the Jewish people. Oftentimes historical events were depicted as the consequence of the people's action. When they had been faithful to the covenant, God rewarded the people's goodness. When they turned to other gods or ignored the widow, orphan, or poor, God punished them. Perhaps more accurately, one might say that in the wake of a calamity—as, for example, a flood, drought, or attack of locusts—the people sought the cause of God's anger disclosed in those events. This theme of Divine retribution constitutes one important theme in the Hebrew Scriptures. One readily thinks of examples: Isaiah 8:5-8; Baruch 2:22 ff; Hosea 13:7-15; Ezekiel 11:1-13; Amos 3:2; Noah, and many others. [This theme, obviously, is not missing from the New Testament; cf. Luke 13:34, 19:41-44; Matthew 11:20-24; etc.]. Indeed, some contemporary Jews have sought to explain the Shoah precisely as God's chastisement because European Jews had not been faithful to God, and therefore God allowed more than one-third of them to perish.[20] Most Jews [and Christians] vehemently reject this interpretation, particularly before the inexcusable fact of the one and a half million children tossed into the crematoria's flames. A God who would cause—even allow—such to happen ceases to be a God in whom to believe.[21]

One cannot leave this notion of Divine retribution, however, without adverting to certain Christian tendencies to interpret in general Jewish misfortune to God's punishment for various infidelities. The Christian Scriptures themselves predict great Jewish calamity for not following Jesus. Most obvious is the way Gospel writers interpreted the destruction of the Second Temple as a sign of God's wrath for the Jews' "unbelief" at the time of their messianic visitation. Most Scripture scholars today would read Gospel threats of destruction and scattering as predictions *ex eventu*, prophecies made after the fact in the polemical situation of the early Christian community asserting its superiority after the Jewish calamity. This line of reasoning, however, one must leave behind in the wake of the Shoah. Rosemary Radford Ruether is correct where she states, "By applying prophetic judgment to 'the Jews' and messianic hope to 'the Church,' Christianity deprived the Jews of their future."[22] This penchant for applying all Hebrew Scripture prophecies of destruction to the Jews and all those of blessedness to the Church needs to be seen as part of the very teaching of contempt which provided part of the atmosphere which made the Shoah possible.

Despite the uselessness of Divine retribution as a viable description of God's hand

The Crisis of Prayer

in the Shoah, Christians can retrieve from their religious heritage a different, more productive Divine portrait. This is the image of a God who is said to "abandon"--not punish—his beloved.

Christians can perceive abandonment by God most dramatically in the very life of the Jew Jesus. Christians believe that Jesus was God's "beloved son" [Mark 1:11]. The Gospel writers recount numerous events and words which attest to Jesus' intimacy with the Father, most notably his almost unique "abba" experience.[23] But this same believed Chosen One experienced abandonment from his God during his agony in Gethsemane [even as he desperately implored God to deliver him][24] and his subsequent crucifixion on Golgotha.

Ironically, the Shoah may be the event which suggests that Gethsemane and Golgotha require an interpretation different from that of the tradition. We concluded at the end of Section A that God-within-the-Shoah was limited insofar as God did little more for the Jews strangling in the Nazi vise than God did for "his only begotten son" seized by Roman despots. The tentative, correct disclosure of Gethsemane and Golgotha, then, is not that God could have saved Jesus and did not, but that God was *unable* to save him....just as God was unable to save his first chosen, the Jewish people, during their agony. I am not saying that God put a kind of strait jacket on His/Her own loving, rescuing arms at the time of the Agony or the Shoah. Rather, each event reveals that long before either, God created humans in such a relation to Him/Herself that God would respect their freedom, even to the point of appearing impotent in rescuing His beloved. By creation's prior arrangement, the Creator could not intervene since the history's interim course had been handed over to human responsibility.

Other parts of the Scripture speak to God's way in creation. The author of Genesis describes how God, in mysterious wisdom, chose to create humans in freedom. Indeed, the second creation story in Genesis hints at the self-determined limitation of God who did nothing to prevent Adam and Eve from swiftly using their freedom for evil, with all its tragic consequences.

Or one can see in the Book of Job this same insight about the God refraining from intervention in human adversity. Whether this wisdom parable is about God's patience, faith, or Divine absence[25], God's answer to Job's desperate plight is framed in a litany of creation language:

> Where were you when I laid the
> foundation of the earth?
> Tell me, if you have understanding,
> Who determined its measurements—
> —surely you know!

***

The Holocaust Now

> Or who shut in the sea with doors,
> when it burst forth from the womb;
> when I made clouds its garment,
> and thick darkness its swaddling band?
> —Job 38:4-5, 8-9 [RSV]

The answer to Job's current strife is to be found not in some explanation about good deeds rewarded, infidelity punished, but in reflection on God's role in the very moment of creation. God says to Job, in essence, "This is the way I created the world and you have to remember: I am God and you are not. My non-interventions in your sorrow have their explanation in creation. *This is the way things are.*"

Similar to God's absence from Job are God's role during the Flood, during the Exile, during the Crucifixion, and during the shoah. Human implorings could not move God to renege on a "policy of non-intervention" in order to turn around these and other catastrophes. From the very beginning the consistent Biblical message reveals that God would not, could not, intervene, even when such could have saved the people from harm or from themselves. The creating God, strange to say, made Him/Herself semi-impotent by the very act of creating the free human being. Rather than becoming an instant rescuer, God chose the more puzzling course of imparting His/Her *intentions* about creation through the Torah and, Christians must add, Jesus. And this would have to suffice. Regarded more positively, however, one may say that God fashioned a partner through creation. This perspective is similar to Paul van Buren's:

> [We Christians] lacked the audacity to see God precisely in the suffering and failure of the cross. God steps back to leave us free to work His will, if we will, and suffers with us in all our failures. Therein lies the power and majesty of His infinite freedom, that He is free in the fullest power of personal love to hold back, to sit still and to suffer in agony as His children move so slowly to exercise in a personal and loving way the freedom which He has willed for them to have and exercise.[26]

In a profound and frightening way, God chooses to depend on humans for God's purposes in creation. It is our responsibility to live before Him according to His will.

Or, as Etty Hillesum's words, written shortly before she was taken to Auschwitz, more poetically affirm: "And yet I don't think life is meaningless. And God is not accountable to us for the senseless harm we cause one another. We are accountable to Him!....[It has been a] hard day, a very hard day....But I keep finding myself in prayer.

The Crisis of Prayer

And that is something I shall always be able to do, even in the smallest space: pray....And if God does not help me to go on, then I shall have to help God."[27]

As I have already indicated, for the Christian, Jesus' *praying for deliverance* at Gethsemane relies on the same Biblical God who was unable, by prior creation arrangement, to rescue His beloved. Jesus, seeing the almost inevitable consequence of his threat to the Romans[28], prayed to be spared execution. As the faithful Jews, he begs for rescue....indeed his last cry from the cross acknowledged his feeling of God's abandoning him [Mark 15:34]. The God who was absent in so many ways in the crises of Israel was absent again in the cry of His Chosen.

I am quite aware that many will find this comparison exceedingly improper, even monstrous: that is, the comparison between the death at Roman hands of one seemingly failed prophet and the systematic and inexorable crush of the Nazi slaughter of six million, including one and a half million children. However, the single, but crucial point I wish to make is *for Christians* to see that *the God of Jesus* is the same God of Abraham and Sarah, of Moses and Miriam....who is *the same God revealed*, by absence and silence, *in the* Shoah. It is not as if God had physically and regularly intervened in history for centuries before 1933 and stopped; rather the God of the Hebrew Scriptures and of the New Testament has always been experienced and *believed in* through God's absence.

It must be admitted that the theme of God's absence and silence is not completely new. Rubenstein and Roth write at careful length what many have written on "the silence of God."[29] What I suggest that goes beyond their report is that, not only is God's absence not new in the Shoah, it is a fundamental mode of the Biblical God's way of being since, and because of, the creation.

But God was not completely absent from Auschwitz. Most eloquently, Elie Wiesel describes the search for the Absent One in the camps. As the SS hanged two adults and one young boy, all inmates were forced to watch:

> The three victims mounted together on the chairs.
> The three necks were placed at the same moment within the nooses.
> 'Long live liberty!' cried the two adults.
> But the child was silent.
> 'Where is God? Where is he?' someone behind me asked.
> At a sign from the head of the camp, the three chairs tipped over. [The observers were forced to gaze closer.] Then the march past began. The two adults were no longer alive. Their tongues hung swollen, blue-tipped. But the third rope was still moving; being so light the child was still alive....
> For more than half an hour he stayed there, struggling between

life and death, dying in slow agony under our eyes. And we had to look him full in the face. He was still alive when I passed in front of him. His tongue was still red, his eyes were not yet glazed.

Behind me, I heard the same man asking:

'Where is God now?'

And I heard a voice within me answer him:

'Where is He? Here He is—He is hanging here on this gallows....'[30]

This is no distant echo from the God of Job, the Psalms of lament, and the God of Jesus' crucifixion. Commenting on this oft-quoted passage, German Lutheran Jurgen Moltmann said, "Any other answer would be blasphemy....To speak here of a God who could not suffer would make God a demon. To speak here of an absolute God would make God an annihilating nothingness. To speak here of an indifferent God would condemn men to indifference."[31] Besides Moltmann, many other commentators have put the experience of God-within-the-Shoah under the rubric of Divine suffering.[32] But God as suffering with the Chosen or as absent/silent at the catastrophe of the beloved are not contradictory; indeed, they are two expressions of the same lived experience. That is, "Where is he? Where is God when God's beloved are suffering?" God is with them, silent *and* suffering.

On a more theoretical plane, Chicago Catholic theologian John Shea offers a very helpful construct for systematizing this discovery of God's Biblical and Shoah resemblance. Shea distinguishes between the "interventionist God" and the "intentionalist God." The former is the God who is naively and unreflectively believed to change the course of nature and history by directly but intermittently interrupting the workings of the world. This God is said to cure cancer, bring rain, and save people from accidents. After the Shoah, a Deity who could have rescued the six million and did not is hardly the God who would turn around a single person's lung cancer. Such a God seems to be totally without credibility. And, as we have intimated above, such a description of God may well be a misreading of much of the Hebrew and Christian Scriptures.

The "intentionalist God" is the Creator God who fashions the cosmos in a particular way. Through a relation with this God, the Jewish people first and the Christians later came to understand that God's purpose in creation is to serve life and justice. Scripture's function has less to do with what God has done to change history as to show God's concerns.

> The [Biblical] story of hope and justice is a tale of God's heart not his hands. Paradoxically, for our age, the [Biblical] stories of the intervening God do not reveal his *modus operandi* but the concerns which obsess Him....The story of hope and justice chronicles the values of the

Biblical God.[33]

The Biblical God's values are known through both the commandments and narratives of the Hebrew Scriptures and, for the Christian, the commandments and stories of Jesus. For the latter, the prime locus for Jesus' intention is his answer to the lawyer's question, "What is the greatest commandment?" Jesus replies that it is to know that God is one and God we must love with all our hearts and mind; a second is likened to it, to love our neighbor as ourselves. [Luke 10:25-28] In narrative form, the center of gravity is the Last Judgment scene in Matthew 25 where Jesus asserts that when one feeds the hungry, clothes the naked, or visits the imprisoned, one is indeed doing so to Christ himself. These are the values of the intentionalist God revealed in the Hebrew Scriptures and the New Testament.[34]

Finally, in thinking about the resemblance between the Biblical God and God during the Shoah, it would be incomplete to reflect only on God's silence or absence. One must return also to those extraordinary moments of liberation remembered in our respective traditions. In the Jewish tradition, most significant is the Exodus wherein Moses' experience of God was so overwhelming and immediate that he was empowered to lead a reluctant people out of more than four hundred years of slavery through forty years' journey to the land "flowing with milk and honey." Without being glib or simplistic, without implying that the Shoah was the price to be paid, the rebirth of Israel may be seen as another such liberation. On the Christian side, one must return, of course, to Jesus' resurrection. However one might explain its historicity, the resurrection of Jesus is the Christian way of saying that, in the end, the self-imposed limitations of God's acting in history are themselves limited. The final creative act of God is to embrace creation, never finally leaving it to ruin. For the Christian, the Resurrection is the cause and foundation of hope that life is not meaningless, short, or without final vindication. Here I do not wish to compare, much less equate, Jewish and Christian views of the afterlife or the teleological meaning of the cosmos. The point simply is that both traditions cling to these corporate memories which reveal God both as limited and as finally victorious.

C. What Might Our Prayer Be in the Post-Shoah World?

According to St. Augustine, "The best disposition for praying is that of being desolate, forsaken, stripped of everything." Surely the Shoah world provoked such disposition. And in the circumstance of the Buchenwald Hasidim and Domprobst Lichtenberg, we overheard prayers that spoke out defiantly against the rumble of the death machine. The post-Shoah world, too, is replete with broken lives and pained voices, echoes of the Shoah. Today, to become aware of the Shoah—in a time when it has to be learned before it can be remembered—is to attend to the cries of those in the camps, of those mothers torn from their children, and those babies' bloodcurdling screams quickly extinguished by lapping flames. It is to allow those voices to sensitize us to contemporary suffering. Contemporary prayer is not a matter of substituting concern for the Shoah with concern for contemporary events. Simply speaking, it is to reckon with our "situatedness" of living in a post-Shoah world in order to get in touch with the purpose of the "intentionalist God" who has made us partners in creation.

Often in such articles about "God after the Shoah," one reads a survey of what theologians have to say about the fate of God in and after the Shoah. These articles are eminently important, and I owe much to their insights. But I suggest the wisdom of the aphorism, "Those who take religion seriously should beware of those who take it professionally," applies quite poignantly here. Has one been "desolate, forsaken, stripped of everything" enough to be terrified at the possibility of losing one's God? Has the Christian Church allowed the experience of the Shoah to seep into its soul deep enough to pray to the God revealed therein, which we have discovered to be the same God revealed in Hebrew and Christian Scriptures? Can one turn oneself over, even a little, to feel empathically the desolation of a survivor? Although his faith seemed to have been destroyed by the flames of the Night, Elie Wiesel argues that he had to continue his dialogue-feeling-like-monologue with God:

> Master of the Universe, I know what You want—I understand What You are doing. You want despair to overwhelm me. You want me to cease believing in You, to cease praying to you, to cease invoking Your name to glorify and sanctify it. Well, I tell You: No, no—a thousand times no! You shall not succeed! In spite of me and in spite of You, I recite the *Kaddish* [Memorial Prayer—Ed.], which is a song of faith, for You and against You. This song You shall not still, God of Israel.[35]

From a very different place on the Christian side, French Reform theologian Jacques Ellul has relentlessly pursued the question of the crisis of prayer for the modern person.[36] In a world racked by enormous tragedy, including the Shoah, Ellul candidly admits, "It is futile to pretend that prayer is indispensable to man. Today he gets along very well without it. When he does not pray he lacks nothing, and when he prays it looks to him like a superfluous action reminiscent of former superstitions. He can live perfectly well without prayer."[37] After dismissing various reassuring views of prayer [self-discipline, to obtain favors, to obtain consolation, to express resignation, and so forth], Ellul concludes that the only reason for praying in the modern age—or any age, for that matter—cannot be found in rational justifications in the world or in seeking God's enlistment to develop one's projects. What does one do when one is "desolate, forsaken, stripped of everything?"

> No, at those times I have in fact to cling to 'a reason' outside myself, objective, which I find compelling, which pushes me along, in other words, like a hand in my back forcing me ahead, constraining me to pray. It is the commandment which God in his mercy has granted to make up for the void in my heart and in my life. 'Watch and pray;' that is the sole reason for praying which remains for modern man.[38]

Like the survivor, for Ellul, there is no guarantee that prayers will be answered....or even that they will be listened to. One does not question the commander. One obeys, not out of simple duty or compulsive reaction, but simply because of the personally addressed command from the Creator God heard through the Jewish and Christian traditions.

Whether, like Wiesel, a Jew must pray after the Shoah so as not let God "off the hook," or whether, like Ellul, one must pray after the Shoah because the personal command to do so has not been retracted, one might be left with a simple, but profound, conclusion. After the Shoah, one can pray to the Creator God who has unleashed humankind into freedom, one can utter entreaties to the Deity because the Buchenwald Hasidim, draped in *tefillin* [phylacteries—Ed.], danced during the Shoah. Today, Christians must pray Domprobst Lichtenberg's prayer because cruelly too few Christians even whispered it during the Shoah. With the Domprobst, we Catholics must pray *publicly* "on behalf of the Jews and the poor concentration camp prisoners." Lichtenberg stated at his trial, "I told myself that only one thing could still help, namely, prayer....for the Jews."[39] By praying with him, albeit sadly belatedly, Christians align themselves with the intention of our Creator God that the Jews survive, that they survive as *Jews*.

Here, then, the first and second parts of our essay come together. *Christians' contemporary religious response to the Shoah* is to pray for the Jews, not supposing that an interventionist God will reach out to support them—that possibility was shown to be futile in Auschwitz; rather they do so in order to align themselves with the intentionalist God who has chosen the Jews as God's very own and stands with them in their suffering, in their triumph, and in their calling. Prayer is the way, then, for believers to keep reminding themselves of God's creative will so they will live according to it. Frighteningly and lovingly, since the Shoah, it is clear that there is no other way for the world to be influenced by God than through the lives of God's creatures. As van Buren reflects:

> That the Creator should so love His creatures as to make His own

heart's desire depend upon their longing to fulfill His plan bespeaks a love that surpasses understanding. That the Creator can choose to make us creatures His co-workers means that He, in His freedom, has chosen to make Himself our co-worker....He suffers in His own right over our failure to recognize that when we are most fully taking responsibility, we are only cooperating with Him who is most fully present and active when we are fully present and active.[40]

And now, if enough Christians recite the Domprobst Lichtenberg's prayer, God's will may be done. It has been revealed in creation and in the covenant, and tenderly left in our hands. God's will is that the Jews survive as Jews.[41] Already the Good Friday liturgy directs Catholics to pray that the Jewish people "may continue to grow in the love of....[God's] name and in faithfulness to his covenant."[42] It is a prayer we desperately wish the Christian community had uttered loudly and with conviction in 1935. Today it is a prayer which must be seared into the regular, public prayer of the Church.

Mysterium Tremendum

For Eugene Fisher, "remembering" [*anamnesis* in Greek; *zikkaron* in Hebrew] is a primary category of bridge-building between the Catholic and Jewish communities and leads him directly to a "theology of praxis," whereby he enumerates those categories of theology which now need be rethought in light of the Shoah: [a] forgiveness and reconciliation, [b] repentance, [c] the uniqueness of the Jewish experience in the Shoah and its meaning for Catholic [and other] Christians, [d] suffering, [e] the State of Israel, [f] hope, [g] love, and [h] Catholic teaching about the Shoah. Basing himself on contemporary post-Shoah events [e.g. Bitburg, Kurt Waldheim, the Auschwitz convent], which themselves are nevertheless pain-filled and difficult, he suggests possible directions and avenues of thought which may, possibly, transcend the barriers which seemingly presently exist, and offers new directions for increased dialogical understanding.

SLJ

The Holocaust Now

MYSTERIUM TREMENDUM: CATHOLIC GRAPPLINGS WITH THE SHOAH AND ITS THEOLOGICAL IMPLICATIONS[1]

Eugene J. Fisher

I. Introduction: Anamnesis and Zikkaron

To speak of the Shoah, its witnesses remind us, is an impossible task. How can one encapsulate in words the absolute horror of the deaths of millions? Is not the very attempt to find meaning, even religious meaning, in such an event somehow blasphemous?

Yes. But not to speak may be worse. It would be, in the words of Emil Fackenheim, to commit the final blasphemy, to allow Hitler the posthumous victory of having silenced forever the voices of the prophets.

Judaism and Christianity are religions of remembering, of *anamnesis* and *zikkaron*, of wrestling out of the tragic vagaries of history the meaning to guide our divinely-covenanted peoples on the path toward hope. As Daniel Polish in a moving article arguing the possibility of "Witnessing God after Auschwitz" has said: "To be silent is a sin, doing violence to the Jewish imperative to remember. No, we must speak of the Shoah.... Had the generation of the Exodus been allowed the final say in understanding their experience, we would have found no redemption in it....[Only their] humiliation, despair, and terror."[2]

If there was a temptation to silence in the dialogue between Jews and Catholics in the face of the intractable realities of the Shoah, that silence has been shattered by the increasingly vocal controversies between our two communities in recent years. Even as Pope John Paul II on April 13, 1986, became the first Bishop of Rome since St. Peter to visit a synagogue, the seeds of those controversies were developing: the process of beatification of Edith Stein was moving toward its conclusion; a small group of Polish nuns were working to turn into a modest convent the interior of an abandoned theater adjacent to the infamous death camp at Auschwitz-Birkenau; and Kurt Waldheim, former General Secretary of the United Nations, was being proposed as President of Catholic Austria.

All three actions touched on the Shoah and thus on a memory sacred to the Jewish people today. Jewish nerves, rubbed raw by centuries of persecution, and the Jewish soul, scarred by the agony of the loss of one third of its entire people just fifty years ago, cried out with sincere anguish, an outcry of pain and accusation that threatened the rip apart the still delicate fabric of the new relationship Catholics and Jews have been weaving in patient dialogue for over twenty years in this country and throughout the world.

Despite the rhetoric, however, the fabric of our relations has not torn. Rather, in Rome and New York, Washington, D.C. and local parishes and synagogues throughout the country, Catholics and Jews continue to listen to one another's fears and hurts, breaking through, I believe, to a truer and deeper dialogue than ever before.

Catholic theologian David Tracy, following Arthur Cohen, fittingly describes the Shoah as "theologically the tremendum of our age."[3] Numerous Christian as well as Jewish thinkers have grappled in the wake of the Shoah with the implications of the Shoah for their respective theologies.[4] My point in this paper is not to rehearse that literature, but, rather, to focus on the more specific issues of misunderstanding and mistrust raised to the surface of our relationship by the recent controversies and their attendant rhetoric, and on how Catholic theology has and can react to it all. The present paper should be seen, then, not so much as an exercise in systematic theology, though organized thematically, as a "theology of praxis," seeking to draw out of recent events in Catholic-Jewish relations some of the underlying dynamics pertinent especially to a Catholic response to the Shoah.

Of necessity, then, rather more attention will be given to official Catholic documents and especially to the pronouncements of Pope John Paul II than might be typical of an academic approach to Shoah studies. But I believe that this Pope, perhaps more than any other, can show us the way to move beyond the blockages of the past toward reconciliation. Finally, though I have picked a major theme or two for each controversy, the reality is that most of the issues are present in each, with the concerns and misperceptions consequently intensified over the whole period.

II. Bitburg, Waldheim, and the Theology of Forgiveness

The first event, though not one primarily between Jews and Catholics, revealed an ongoing misunderstanding by Catholics of Jewish teaching and Jewish spirituality. So pervasive is this misunderstanding that it needs to be addressed before proceeding any further. This is the issue of forgiveness, a variation of which was heard also during the Waldheim affair.

Reacting to Jewish outcries over Bitburg, many Christians [not just Catholics] were heard to ask: "What's the matter with Jews? Hasn't there been enough on the Shoah? Why can't they forgive after all this time?" Underlying such plaints, at times quite explicitly, is one of the most ancient elements of the "teaching of contempt" against Jews and Judaism. That is the belief that Judaism [the "Old Law"] preaches justice and vengeance, while Christianity, following the teaching of Jesus, especially the Sermon on the Mount, proclaims mercy and forgiveness. The ironic fact that Christians over the centuries, because of our oppressive treatment of Jews, have needed far more forgiveness from Jews than they need from us, is seldom noted by Christian critics of "vindictive" Judaism.

But do Judaism and Christianity hold two entirely different, antithetical understandings of the theology of forgiveness as so many Christians presume? What, exactly, are Jews saying to us underneath the often hurtful rhetoric thrown at us via the media? The 1974 *Vatican Guidelines*[5] remind us that:

> The Old Testament and the Jewish tradition founded upon it must not be set against the New Testament in such a way that the former seems to constitute a religion of only justice, fear and legalism, with no appeal to the love of God and neighbor.

As with the law of love [Matthew 22:34-40, which reiterates the commandments of Deuteronomy 6:5 and Leviticus 19:18], Jesus' saying on love of enemies in the Sermon on the Mount [5] [Matthew 5:43 ff] draws on Jewish sources. In point of fact, there is no command in the Hebrew Scriptures or in rabbinic tradition to "hate your enemy." Instead we find:

> Do not rejoice when your enemy falls, and let not your heart be glad when he stumbles! [Proverbs 24:17]

> If your enemy is hungry, give him bread to eat; if he is thirsty, give him water to drink. [Proverbs 25:21]

Rabbinic tradition in turn commented upon and reinforced these Biblical sayings:

> Rabbi Hama bar Hanina said: "Even though your enemy has risen up early to kill you, and he comes hungry and thirsty to your house, give him food and drink. God will make him at peace with you."

> Rabbi Simeon bar Abba said: "The verse [Proverbs 17:13] means that if a man returns evil for evil, evils shall not depart from his house...."

> Rabbi Nathan said: "Who is the most powerful? Whoever wins

the love of his enemy."

Jewish tradition here is not total pacifism, as the minority position within Christianity would interpret and apply Jesus' words. Rather its theme, as in the High Holy Days of *Rosh Ha-Shanah* [Jewish New Year—Ed.] and *Yom Kippur* [Day of Atonement—Ed.], is reconciliation, the great Jewish theme stressing the reconciling power of divine love over hatreds: "God will make peace with you."

Like the commandment to "love your neighbor as yourself" [Leviticus 19:18], acts of loving kindness [*hesed* in Hebrew] toward one's enemies are considered in Judaism to be part of Biblical law: "If you see the ass of one who hates you lying under its burden, you shall help to lift it up" [Exodus 23:5]. Rabbinic tradition commented:

> A person goes along the road and sees that the ass of an enemy has fallen under its burden. The person goes over and gives the enemy a hand to unload and reload....Then they go over to an inn and the ass driver thinks: so and so loves me so much, and I thought he hated me. Immediately they talk with one another and make peace. [Midrashic commentary to Psalm 99:4; underlying its sentiments may be Amos 3:3: "Can two wander together without becoming one with one another?"][6]

If Judaism holds such a rich theology of forgiveness and reconciliation, the persistent Christian critic may still ask, why the outbursts over Bitburg and Waldheim? In the former case, Bitburg, the answer lies in the nature of the event itself: the Christian President of the United States and the Christian Chancellor of Germany got together over the graves of Nazi SS troops to forgive each other for acts of war. Jews were neither consulted nor invited to participate. The fact of the Shoah, therefore, was ignored. Trivialized. Not allowed to interfere with "more important matters of State" between the two countries. Jews were not to be present to forgive—or even to tell their story—which is one reason why the United States Catholic Bishops' Conference, along with so many other non-Jews, urged the President to cancel the event.

III. Waldheim and the Theology of Repentance

The Jewish perception of a trivialization of the Shoah, of judging the systematic murder of six million innocents to be of such little present moment that it should not give pause to current affairs of state, also played a significant part in Jewish reactions to the granting of a papal audience to the President of Austria. Again, numerous Catholic voices could be heard calling on Jews to forgive Waldheim, whose crimes on the scale of Nazi butchery, after all, were not that great even he had based his career on lies about his relatively minor role in the Germany army.[7]

Again, let us look at little deeper into the rhetoric. What were Jews trying to tell us Catholics about the significance, to them and to us, of the audience? While I believe that the papal audience was justifiable for reasons of state that were given by the Holy See and because Mr. Waldheim, who has not been convicted of any criminal charges is the duly-elected head of a democratic state and should be considered legally innocent until proven guilty, I also believe that we Catholics need to listen very closely to what has been said to us in this affair.

The Jewish accusation against Mr. Waldheim, if I understand it correctly, was not so much that he was a major war criminal of the Shoah, an Eichmann or a Klaus Barbie, but that he appears to remain entirely unrepentant about his arguably minor role in mass murder. This note of unrepentance was present in almost all of the Jewish statements of protest against the audience. It effectively challenges Catholics who would criticize Jews as "unforgiving" over the incident. Forgiveness, in Christian theology no less than in Jewish theology, requires repentance. While no human being can fully plumb the depths of Mr. Waldheim's heart to sit in judgment on his soul—only God can do that—still, his public posture and his grudging admissions of the truth as each new piece of evidence against his original story came out, has left the impression that he has not yet fully, at least in public, come to grips within his own conscience with the enormity of the evil perpetrated against the Jewish people and against humanity by the Nazi death machine of which he was certainly a part.

What Jews are saying in essence, then, is no more and no less than what the prophets and Jesus said to the world in earlier generations: "Repent and sin no more!" It is a timeless and timely message. For Christians to speak of reconciliation with Jews in this, as the Pope has rightly called it, "the century of the Shoah," we must take the first step, repentance, a *heshbon ha-nefesh*, an accounting of the soul. I believe we have begun to do this, in the Catholic community most clearly through the declaration of the Second Vatican Council, *Nostra Aetate*, and in the remarkable progress [not well known enough in the Jewish community, I fear] in implementing the Council's mandate in Catholic teaching and preaching in all levels of the Church's life, especially, perhaps in this country.[8]

Still, the words that Cardinal Eichinger of Strasbourg addressed to the Second Vatican Council retain their urgency for all Christians today:

> We cannot deny that not only during this century but also during past centuries crimes have been committed against the Jews by the Sons and Daughters of the Church....We cannot ignore that during the course of history, there have been persecutions and outrages against

the Jews; there have been violations of conscience as well as forced conversions. Lastly, we cannot deny that up until recently, errors have insinuated themselves, too frequently, into preaching and into certain catechetical books in opposition to the spirit of the New Testament. In going back to the sources of the Gospels, why not draw sufficient greatness of soul to ask forgiveness in the name of numerous Christians for so many misdeeds and injustices?[9]

Pope John Paul II affirmed this attitude of repentance when he said to Catholic representatives of Episcopal Conferences meeting in Rome in 1982:

> Certainly, since a new bough appeared from the common root 2,000 years ago, we know that relations between our two communities have been marked by resentments and a lack of understanding. If there have been misunderstandings, errors and even insults since the day of separation, it is now a question of overcoming them with understanding, peace and mutual esteem. The terrible persecutions suffered by the Jews in various periods of history have finally opened many eyes and disturbed many hearts.[10]

IV. Pope John Paul II and the Uniqueness of the Jewish Witness to the Shoah

On June 14, 1987, the Pope met with representatives of the tiny remnant of the Jewish community of Warsaw. This address, I believe, provides a spiritual and theological basis for a Christian reflection on the Shoah. Decrying the "terrible reality" of the attempted extermination of the Jewish people, "an extermination carried out with premeditation," the Pope noted that "the threat against you was also a threat against us [Polish] Catholics," though "this latter was not realized to the same extent." The Pope clearly acknowledges here the uniqueness of the Jewish tragedy even while affirming the enormity of Polish Catholic suffering at the hands of the Nazi death machine:

> It was you who suffered this terrible sacrifice of extermination; one might say that you suffered it also on behalf of those who were likewise to have been exterminated.

The Pope also addressed the uniqueness of the Jewish witness to the Shoah, saying that "because of this terrible experience, you have become a loud warning voice for all humanity....More than anyone else, it is precisely you who have become a saving warn-

Mysterium Tremendum

ing." A saving warning. Such words, to Catholics, are theologically pregnant, reminding us of the "saving warnings" of the prophets themselves. Drawing out this point, which takes the Shoah very seriously I believe as a *mysterium tremendum*, a "sign of the times" through which Christians may discern something of God's plan of salvation for all humanity, the Pope made a significant step in developing a Catholic theology of the Shoah and of Judaism's continuing unique role as the Chosen People of God:

> I think that in this sense you continue your particular vocation, showing yourselves to be still the heirs of that election to which God is faithful.
> This is your mission in the contemporary world before the peoples, the nations, all of humanity, the Church. And this Church, all peoples and nations feel united to you in this mission.

"Particular vocation" and "mission," of course, are part of the Catholic vocabulary of election and covenant. Here, very clearly, the Pope is framing an understanding of the continuing salvific validity of the Jewish people as God's people. It will be noted that the Pope reaches the universality of the Jewish witness to the world [and to the Church itself!] only through full acknowledgement of Jewish particularity. The mission of the Church in the world, its proclamation to the world, does not absorb Judaism's mission and witness. Rather, the Church united itself to that ongoing Jewish vocation which it acknowledges as divinely willed, and, indeed, an essential part of God's plan of salvation for all humanity.

It will also be noted that the Jewish witness to the Shoah is entirely a *post-Christian* vocation, not dependent on the teachings of the "Old Testament, but considered valid *on its own*, which is to say Jewish terms, even though coming to be considerably after the close of the New Testament period. So far as I know, this is the first time, the Church, whether Catholic or Protestant, has pointed to a specific aspect of Judaism's post-New Testament role in the history of salvation, giving concrete theological substance to the Second Vatican Council's general theme, as articulated in the 1974 "Guidelines," that "the history of Judaism did not end with the destruction of Jerusalem, but rather went on to develop a religious tradition rich in religious values." In the Pope's words in Warsaw, paying heed to the particular witness of the Jewish people today concerning the significance of the Shoah "helps me and all the Church become even more aware of what unites us in the disposition of the Divine Covenant." The story of the people Israel, today no less than in Biblical times, remains a story, with all its tragedies and hopes, that is a "light to the nations." Israel remains God's people. And Israel's story remains one that the Church, in developing its own theological visions, must address.

V. Cardinal John O'Connor and the Theology of Suffering

The Pope's Warsaw address raised also a theological issue given great prominence in the press during Cardinal John O'Connor's trip last January to Israel. That is the Christian theology of suffering. Coming out of Yad Vashem [Israel's Shoah Memorial—Ed.] in Jerusalem, Cardinal O'Connor gave an interview in which he mentioned that in a certain sense the Jewish suffering of the Shoah may be considered a "gift" to humanity.

Cardinal O'Connor's statement was jumped upon and denounced by Jewish leaders, I think unfairly, even before he returned to New York. This, then, is a case where the Jewish community has the responsibility to listen closely to what Catholics are saying, and to come to understand the Christian theological categories involved before reacting to it with denunciation in the press.

No devout Christian, I believe, can go to Yad Vashem, see there the moving evidence of the horrifying loss of innocent Jewish lives and the monstrous evil that the Shoah represents, and not be challenged to the core of his or her spiritual life. Inevitably, this will take the form of reflection upon the suffering of another Jew, Jesus of Nazareth, whose death, and we believe, resurrection is the bedrock for us of all our faith and hopes.

To us, the death of that Jew at the hands of Israel's Roman oppressors two millennia ago frames our very understanding of reality, all that we are and hope to be as Christians. To us, it is our essential mysterium tremendum. Out of despair can come hope, out of death renewed life. That Jesus' death is a divine gift bringing all humanity closer to God's love is the central paradox, the central mystery of Christian faith. Because of it we can proclaim with joy Adam's [which is to say humanity's] fall into evil, "O felix culpa!" "O happy fault!" We can, we believe, most deeply, discern some meaning, some hope in all human suffering.

If this sense of hope amidst despair is true because of the death of one Jew long ago, Christians will inevitably ask themselves, might it not also be true, and much more so, of the deaths of six million Jewish women, men, and children consigned to the most diabolical hell humanity has ever created for itself?

This is not to equate the suffering and death of the one with the sufferings and deaths of the six million. Such an equation would be monstrous. Nor is it to seek to absorb the deaths of the six million into the theological categories developed by the Church to articulate its faith that the death of Jesus, and therefore death itself, has some purpose, that there is reason to hope even in the face of the most awesome evil, evil understood as a mysterium tremendum. It is more simply, and more profoundly, to struggle for the theological insights, the words, to help us cope with the awesomeness of the Jewish tragedy in ways that can link its significance to our deepest spirituality as Christians. Such attempts as Cardinal O'Connor's, then, should not, I believe, be viewed as either theologically flippant or as an attempt to subsume Jewish experience into Christian categories. Flawed as they are, and all attempts to derive significance from the Shoah, meaning from such massive, senseless tragedy, will be to some extent flawed by our incapacity as finite creatures to express in words what must be said, the attempts to use these words derived from the central mystery of the Church itself, must be seen as sincere and honest offerings of the Christian heart.

Pope John Paul II, in Warsaw, after proclaiming as a Pole and as a head of the Catholic Church, that Jews suffered in the Shoah "on behalf of those who were likewise to have been exterminated" had Hitler's plans been allowed to fulfill themselves on all non-Aryans, stated:

> We believe in the purifying power of suffering. The more atrocious the suffering, the greater the purification. The more painful the experiences, the greater the hope.

I suspect that many Jews today will find religious references such as "purification" and the "purifying power of suffering" applied to the Shoah to be somewhat mystifying, though they have solid precedent in the Hebrew Scriptures and close parallels with mystical Jewish literature through the ages.

Some Jewish thinkers, such as Elie Wiesel and Emil Fackenheim, feel that no theological framework can be adequate to absolute horror. For Wiesel, Jews can still utter the *Ani ma'amin* ["I still believe...."—Ed.] of traditional faith in the coming of the Messiah, but never in the same sense as before. Now, there is always tension. Nothing, not even Israel reborn can justify those deaths. And still one prays—for to be a Jew is to pray: "Ani ma'amin, Isaac. Because of Belsen. Ani ma'amin, Jacob. Because of and in spite of Maidenek. Pray to God. Against God. For God."[11] For Fackenheim, the Shoah holds no salvific meaning. The deaths of so many must remain meaningless. There is only the commanding Voice, in one sense a new revelation, in another sense not, adding a 614th commandment to the Torah's 613: survive. But the Jew is commanded not just to survive, but to survive as a Jew, i.e. as a moral person in full historical consciousness and perpetual remembrance of the six million. Martyrdom, the traditional *Kiddush Ha-Shem*, "sanctification of the Name," is overtaken, exhausted of meaning, fulfilled, ended in the deaths of the innocent multitudes.[12] The Martyr has a choice: convert or die. The victims of the Shoah only died. None of the classical theological categories or images can any longer be considered authentic.

Fackenheim follows Buber in stressing that God cannot be replaced by theological "concepts of God," but must be encountered in the crucible of history. He accepts the reality of Biblical revelation, and challenges us to grapple with it in the tragedies of contemporary events. Fackenheim rejects Martin Buber's notion of a contemporary [and by implication temporary] "eclipse of God." "The God of Israel cannot be God of either past or future unless He is still God of the present."

The questions of theodicy and the meaning of suffering, of hope out of despair, life despite death, are raised by the Shoah for Christians as well as Jews. And for us Christians there is an addition challenge. Bishop James Malone of Youngstown, Ohio, speaking to the National Workshop on Christian-Jewish Relations, put the distinctive Christian problem this way:

> Acknowledgement is due that all too many Catholics were, in fact, among the executioners of death-camp inmates. But equally to be acknowledged are the millions of Catholics and thousands of their clergy who were themselves victims of death-camp executioners. Part of the Christian tragedy is that untold numbers of Christians lost their lives attempting to shelter Jews. Part of the Christian tragedy, too, is that Christians were numbered among the executioners and among the victims. At one and the same time, Christians were both oppressor and oppressed.[13]

Similarly, the Holy Father has stated that "reflection upon the Shoah....impels us to promote the necessary historical and religious studies on this event which concerns the whole of humanity today....There is no doubt that the sufferings endured by the Jews are also for the Catholic Church a motive of sincere sorrow, especially when one thinks of the indifference and sometimes resentment which, in particular historical circumstances, have divided Jews and Christians" [John Paul II, August 8, 1987].

VI. The State of Israel and the Theology of Hope

Running like a blue thread through the white heat of Jewish responses to Cardinal O'Connor's trip to Israel and to the Waldheim audience, and indeed through all of the dialogues between our communities, is the Jewish insistence on full diplomatic recognition by the Holy See of the State of Israel. An exchange of ambassadors, the Jewish community is telling us, would be symbolic of the Church's acknowledgement of the Jewish people's right to self-identity. Without going into details on the reasons of the Holy See's posture on the diplomatic question, I would like to raise what for me is the deeper issue: What can the Church say of the rebirth of a Jewish State in *Eretz Yisrael* [Land of Israel—Ed.] theologically?

Interestingly and not coincidentally, this issue is linked in Catholic reflection as in

Mysterium Tremendum

Jewish reflection with the theological question raised by the Shoah.

For many Jews, Fackenheim among them[14], the religious dimension of the Shoah has its sole, if only partial, resolution in the rebirth of the State of Israel. The survivors of the death camps chose life over death, hope over despair, and so founded a nation, tiny and insecure but their own, where Jews could be Jews, religiously and morally, and where the Jewish spirit could rediscover itself in the wake of the destruction of much of its traditional patterns of thought.

This is why for Jews, even those who live in other lands, the Land of Israel represents so crucial a part of religious survival. It is not solely a place of refuge, a place which, if it had existed in 1939, would have meant that much of European Jewry could have been saved. It is more deeply a sign [a 'sacrament' if we were to apply Catholic terminology] that moral life, the life to which Jews are called in covenant, remains possible after the absolute evil that was Auschwitz.

Irving Greenberg, building on Fackenheim, puts it this way:

> To raise a Jewish child today is to bind the child and the child's child on the altar, even as Father Abraham bound Isaac. Only, those who do so today know that there is no angel to stop the process and no ram to substitute for more than one and one-half million Jewish children in this lifetime. Such an act, then, can come only out of resources of faith, of ultimate meaningfulness-of Exodus trust....The reborn State of Israel is this fundamental act of life and meaning of the Jewish people after Auschwitz. To fail to grasp that inextricable connection and response is to utterly fail to comprehend the theological significance of Israel....
>
> The real point [of Israel] is that after Auschwitz, the existence of the Jew is a great affirmation and act of faith. The re-creation of the body of the people, Israel, is renewed testimony to Exodus as ultimate reality, to God's continuing presence in history proven by the fact that his people, despite the attempt to annihilate them, still exist.[15]

The Pope, speaking spontaneously to Jewish leaders in Castelgandolfo on September 1, 1987, himself used the paradigm of the Exodus in meditating upon the source for hope that through divine grace good can be discerned even after the awesome evil of the Shoah.[16] In Miami, the Pope acknowledged officially for the Church not only the existence of the State of Israel but the Biblical source for Jewish attachment to it and the "inextricable connection" between Israel and the Shoah as well:

> Catholics recognize among the elements of the Jewish experience

that Jews have a religious attachment to the Land, which finds its roots in Biblical tradition. After the tragic extermination of the Shoah, the Jewish people began a new period in their history. They have a right to a homeland, as does any civil nation, according to international law. 'For the Jewish people who live in the State of Israel....we must ask the desired security and the due tranquility that is the right of every nation.'[17]

The meaning of Israel is a message of hope, not only for Jews, but for all peoples of faith throughout the world. Tragedy, however seemingly implacable, need not lead us to abandon the struggle for survival in a post-modern world. Nor does the nature of our survival need to be merely petty or self-serving. One can survive and still strive for the betterment of others. The cycle of victim and oppressor can be broken.

Israel thus exists as a burst of hope rising out of despair; as an affirmation of life spoken amid the vivid memories of death; as a cry of joy hurled in the face of doom; as a statement of love that survived an abysmal hatred.

The very existence of Israel can thus be a symbol of hope and faith for all struggling peoples. The Jewish people, descendants of those who lived through the first Exodus, have seen its meaning reaffirmed in our time. The Exodus serves as a powerful sign to all of the possibilities of true liberation from oppression. This is a fact which calls for profound reflection. To every person of faith it is a fact which elicits a response of faith, a renewal of our commitment to the best in our own traditions, and a deep sense of confidence in the ultimate meaningfulness of God's creation.[18]

VII. Edith Stein, the Auschwitz Convent, and the Theology of Love

In a famous rabbinical tale, a master asks his disciples if they love him. "Of course," they reply. "Then what hurts me?" "We do not know," they respond in some confusion. "If you loved me," the master concludes, "you would know what hurts me."

Catholic-Jewish relations after the Shoah, it can be said, is in somewhat this same situation. Catholics profess their love, but do not always understand the immense trauma of the Shoah for the Jewish people. Jews, struggling with their own grief, are not always aware of the pain their rhetoric can at times cause Catholics.

In late 1987, Rabbi Daniel Polish published an editorial entitled "A Painful Legacy: Jews and Catholics Struggle to Understand Edith Stein and Auschwitz."[19] In it, Polish attempts to articulate how Jews perceived and why they reacted the way they did to the news [not always accurately presented in the media] of Edith Stein's beatification and the establishment of a small Carmelite convent adjacent to the site of the major Nazi death camp in Poland.

Mysterium Tremendum

Polish first captures the sense of perplexity among many Catholics to the Jewish outcry in the two cases: Are not, Catholics ask, the beatification of a Catholic and the establishment of a convent internal Church matters? Should not these symbolic gestures on the part of the Church to join its voice to that of the Jewish people in prayerful memory of the six million be acknowledged by Jews as sincerely motivated Catholic efforts to heal the wounds of the past and to heed the Jewish people's own call to the world to remember the Shoah?

"How difficult we must seem to Catholics to make sense of," Polish comments, "in both cases we [Jews] responded to what one could construe as expressions of fellow-feeling, even solidarity." Polish has it right. Catholics are confused, and hurt, by Jewish rebukes in these matters, and especially by the tendency on the part of some Jewish commentators to call into question the sincerity of the intentions of Catholic authorities, often without even first asking what the Catholic motivation might have been, but simply presuming an evil intent.

But before lapsing into righteous indignation on our part, we Catholics need to listen a bit more carefully to understand the very real fears that underlie the Jewish rhetoric that has caused so much pain over the last months. These fears are [and as a Catholic I can only say this with a profound sense of sadness and contrition] all too solidly founded in our history. Again, Rabbi Polish helps us to move beyond harmful rhetoric to the deeper sensitivities involved: "At the heart of the Jewish response to the beatification of Edith Stein is the perception that it has the effect of legitimizing efforts to promote conversion among the Jews."

From a Jewish point of view, Polish writes, it is very difficult to distinguish the Catholic Church's veneration of a Jewish convert and the blatantly proselytizing activities of extreme fundamentalist groups such as the "Jews for Jesus" and the "Messianic Jews." Catholics would quickly respond that such Jewish fears are groundless. As the Bishops' Committee for Ecumenical and Interreligious Affairs of the National Conference of Catholic Bishops [NCCB] stated on the occasion of the beatification itself:

> Catholic respect for the integrity of Judaism and for the ongoing validity of God's irrevocable covenant with the Jewish people is solidly founded on our faith in the unshakable faithfulness of God's own word. Therefore, in no way can the beatification of Edith Stein be understood by Catholics as giving impetus to unwarranted proselytizing among the Jewish community. On the contrary, it urges us to ponder the continuing religious significance of Jewish traditions, with which we have so much in common, and to approach Jews not as potential 'objects' of conversion, but rather as bearers of a unique witness to the Name of the One God of Israel.[20]

The Holocaust Now

The intent of the Church is seen in Pope John Paul II's repeated insistence on his homily during the beatification ceremony on May 1, 1987, that Edith Stein died as 'the daughter of a martyred people....a Jew....a daughter of Israel' and 'at the same time' a Catholic martyr who was sent to Auschwitz by the Nazis in reprisal for the strong public protest issued by the Catholic bishops of the Netherlands against the deportation of Dutch Jews.

The Pope's careful phrasing acknowledges clearly the uniqueness of the Jewish tragedy as well as the obvious fact to the Nazis neither Jewish nor Catholic tradition held any authority. To the Nazis, Edith Stein was simply one more Jew to be murdered with bureaucratic efficiency. No more, no less than the rest of the six million. Catholics, then, according to the Bishops' statement cited above:

> ....see the beatification of Edith Stein as a unique occasion for joint Catholic-Jewish reflection and reconciliation. In honoring Edith Stein, the Church wishes to honor all the six million Jewish victims of the Shoah....Catholic veneration will necessarily contribute to a continuing and deepened examination of conscience regarding sins of commission and omission perpetrated by Christians against Jews during the dark years of World War II.[21]

This Catholic intent and predicted effect, one may say, is almost precisely the opposite of that feared by the Jewish community as articulated by Polish. It is at this point as well that our consideration in dialogue of Edith Stein merges with differing perceptions of the Auschwitz Carmel convent. Polish accurately reflects widespread Jewish opinion, I believe, when he states that Stein's beatification and the move by the Carmelites into the abandoned theater adjacent to Auschwitz are seen "as part of a pattern of Catholic actions....leaving the impression that the Catholic Church is trying to appropriate the Holocaust as its own."

Such an allegation will come as a surprise to Catholics, especially those not involved in dialogue with the Jewish community. Polish explains that for Jews the Shoah is a *tremendum*, "filled with import as any event in our millennia-long experience." Just as the Exodus, the Babylonian exile, and the destruction of the Jerusalem Temple were part of the sacred history of the Jewish people, "so do we perceive this tragedy wrought upon the body of our people as an intrusion of God, ineffably, into human history—a *sanctum* for us."

As the Catholic Church appropriated into itself the Sacred Scriptures and sacred story of Israel, Polish argues, and as it has continued to absorb "the very location of temples, shrines, and sacred graves of the various native traditions and cultures it has displaced," over the centuries, so, too, is it "appropriating the Holocaust—this *sancta* of the Jewish people—to itself." The essence of Catholic tradition, a tradition symbolized by the crucifix, Polish states, is to discern the transcendent meaning and "redemptive potential" of suffering. Having been born in an appropriation of the Jewish experience of suffering and redemption, Polish implies, it may be "inevitable" for the Church [and not necessarily with invidious intent] to wish to take as its own this latest chapter in the ongoing Jewish story. But in the process the particularity of that story as Jewish is once again lost, once again put to another, Christian purpose.

However, in neither case, would these very sincere Catholic expressions of reverence for Jewish victims have had the desired effect—the subsuming of the Shoah into Christian categories—that Polish and many in the Jewish community for whom he speaks seem to fear. Rather, they would and were intended to have the effect of supporting the Jewish particularity of the Shoah against those who would trivialize the Shoah, such as the Communist government of Poland, which seeks to universalize it, and the neo-Nazi revisionists who seek to deny it. They would stand as perpetual challenges to the Christian conscience and reminders of the evils of antisemitism and, indeed, of the ancient Christian "teaching of contempt" so strongly condemned by the Second Vatican Council and repeatedly by Pope John Paul II.

While the Edith Stein debate has died down as it has become apparent that her beatification has not led to any increased proselytism of Jews by Catholics, the Auschwitz convent has become increasingly controversial.

On February 22, 1987, four European Cardinals, including Franciscus Macharski of Krakow, committed the Church to moving the convent "within two years." When the anniversary came and went in 1989, with no ostensible movement on the part of the Carmelites, Jewish protests began.

These protests, in turn, have triggered Polish Catholic protests, since Auschwitz is also a major Polish symbol of the millions of Polish Catholics murdered during the Nazi occupation. While these arguments have real merit and need, I believe, to be brought into the dialogue between Catholics and Jews, so that the latter might begin to understand some of the deep pain experienced by the former, the issue for Catholics should not be who is "right" but what is the proper course of healing love.

Reverend Stanislau Musial, Secretary of the Polish Bishops' Commission for Dialogue with the Jews, answered the underlying question when asked whether he thought that "the Polish people are psychologically prepared to accept" moving the convent:

> The decision to move the Carmelite convent was the fruit of a dialogue. Some might ask whether this dialogue with the Jews was unilateral and....led to hasty concessions....However, the Catholic representatives did not enter into the [1987] talks in a calculating way. A

sincere dialogue took place, conducted in a spirit of love and respect for all. Only this kind of dialogue can bear fruit.[22]

Cardinal Macharski, confirming the Church's intention to proceed with the move, but not committing himself to a specific timetable, put the matter even more succinctly and profoundly. The Church's renunciation of its rights to the present location, he said, is "a demand of charity, not of justice."[23]

In other words, while they may be arguments on both sides [a convent outside the camp, after all, hardly represents a "appropriation of Auschwitz/Birkenau even if that were its intent], there are times for argument and times, in dialogue, for the simple response of love when confronted with another's very genuine pain. The Shoah, properly understood, reaches that bedrock level of what Christianity is all about: love. Christian acknowledgement of the reality of the other's deepest anguish is, as in the rabbinical tale, the beginning of love, of an understanding that is concrete in its actions and the opposite of sentimentality. One loves with healing deeds, not with hollow words.

VIII. Can Christians Teach About the Shoah?

The question posed here is deceptively simple. It is, in reality, a set of questions, each more difficult than the last. Some of them, at least the beginning ones, are:

— What is the Shoah?

— What is there about the Shoah that makes it distinctive?

— What challenges, religious, moral, historical, and social does it raise for the educator?

— Why can or should there be a distinctively *Catholic* educational response to the Shoah, as suggested by the 1985 Vatican Notes and even more strongly by Pope John Paul II in his address to the Jewish community of the United States in Miami, on September 11, 1987?

— What is the proper educational and catechetical goal for Shoah education in a Catholic setting?

In this section, I shall try to respond to these and related issues in a preliminary fashion, hoping to provide at least some ground for the larger discussion which must be initiated within the Catholic educational community and between that community and its counterparts in the Jewish community.

1. What is the Shoah and what makes it distinctive?

By the Shoah, I mean here specifically the Shoah, the events leading up to and including the Nazi decision to exterminate the entire Jewish population of Europe, even at the expense of the German war effort itself.

Why not other events? The Armenian genocide, for example? Or the equally devastating [in terms of numbers] Nazi slaughters of the Slavic population of Eastern Europe? Or Stalin's or Cambodia's massacres of their own populations? All of these deserve in their own way the title "genocide." Why could not any one of these or anyone of a hundred other ancient and modern examples serve just as well in the classroom to raise the question of human inhumanity and the reality of human evil?

In response, I would first agree that such questions are quite valid. An honest educational approach ought to be inclusive rather than exclusive. One must not fall into the trap of pitting the victims of Nazi and other brutality against one another. Each and every human being is of infinite worth, formed in the image of God. One does not, cannot, morally, try to tote up on some gruesome quantitative scale the pain and suffering of individuals or groups to see which was "worse" or "more deserving" of our compassion. Such judgments can be made by God alone. So, yes, it is quite appropriate, even necessary in Shoah education to speak of the suffering of non-Jews, of Poles and Slavs, Gypsies and resistance fighters, Seventh Day Adventists and homosexuals. God, the Bible teaches us, hears the cries of all. The Divine suffers with the suffering of all human beings. On this level, no valid distinctions are permitted between the pain of one and the pain of another. Each human being is of infinite worth to the Creator of all.

Yet, there is something about the Shoah, the Jewish suffering of the Shoah, that enables, even impels us to see in it a paradigm for the sufferings of others, not more urgent or more serious or "more" anything, but in itself distinctive, arresting, compelling.

I suspect that both the Christian and Jewish communities today recognize the reality of this affirmation, even as both of our communities experience immense difficulty articulating why we feel this way. Part of the answer may lie in what has been called, whether helpfully or not, the "uniqueness" of the event. Both the scope [relatively speaking] and the method and manner of the process of the enslavement and mass murder pose historical and theological challenges that are nowhere else quite so clearly raised. Nowhere else has racial genocide been so integrally woven into the ideological fabric of the state as in Nazi Germany. In no other case have the potentials for the evil of bureaucracy, modern technology, "objective" science, and higher education itself been more starkly revealed.

This is a negative revelation, certainly, but it is also a necessary one for our time. In the summer of 1987, as we have discussed above, Pope John Paul II returned to his native Poland, meeting in Warsaw with the tiny remnant of the once great Polish-Jewish community. He spoke there of the particular Jewish "witness" to the Shoah as a "saving warning" to the world and to the Church itself. The Pope linked this Jewish witness of Jewish suffering directly to the ancient prophetic witness, insisting on its distinctive, unique significance. To this Jewish witness, which, if heard, can be a saving witness for the Church and for the world, he stated, the Church can only "unite" with its own witness.

This is startlingly unprecedented language to hear from a Christian, no less from the Pope himself. The Church's saving proclamation "united" to that of another people, another proclamation, another saving witness? Yet the Pope has reaffirmed this Warsaw statement, referring to it time and again since then. He means it. We Catholics should, I believe, attend carefully to it.

2. Why the Jews?

This is a double-edged question which brings us closer to the heart of the mystery. The Jews, the Church has proclaimed with ever-greater clarity since the Second Vatican Council, not only were but are chosen by God to be a "light to the nations." They remain, now no less than before, "the Suffering Servant" of God. Given this clear and "irrevocable" divine calling, Christians cannot but strive to respond to the Jewish suffering with the eyes of faith. It addresses us, because of our very belief in God's Word, in a way that we cannot but seek to relate it to our own mystery as Church.

I will not here attempt to detail what a proper Catholic theological understanding of the Shoah might be like. I will only affirm as strongly as I can that one must be developed by us today. This is a clear mandate for us as Church, as ourselves "People of God." For we, too, in God's Spirit" are, in a very real way, in the line of the prophets.

I cannot, then, fully answer "why the Jews?" here. The answer, if there is one short of the *eschaton* [end of days—Ed.], is for the Jewish people themselves to utter. It is for us, as Church, to support that utterance, to attend to it, to listen and to respond to it in reliance on the Holy Spirit and Christ's salvific love for al

3. The Shoah raises distinct spiritual, moral and social
challenges.[24]

It took place in the heart of "Christian Europe." Christians were both among its victims and chief among its perpetrators [even if many of the latter are most accurate!-

described as apostates].

On the one hand, this trenchant reality questions the basis of Western civilization as we know it. How could this monstrous event happen in "civilized" Europe in the twentieth century? Where were the limits, the moral restraints, the laws? How could civilization move from the repressive [but sadly familiar from Christian history] legislation of Nuremberg in the early 1930s to Auschwitz and Bergen-Belsen in less than a decade? The people that ran the death camps, that put in commercial bids to build the crematoria and provide the gas pellets for the death chambers, were not illiterate savages, not a "golden horde" of Mongols or Huns, but the graduates of the finest institutions of higher learning the world had known to that day. Stepped in Christian culture, they returned from a day of systematic, dispassionate murder of women and children to listen to Bach and Beethoven, and perhaps to read Goethe and Schiller. They were scholars and scientists, doctors and writers. Many had Ph.D.s and other advanced degrees.

If the best of our education, the heights of our culture, could not make them hesitate to participate in such ultimate depravities as whole-sale, calculated murder, of what benefit, really, is education? What reliance can we place upon it? Education itself, I believe, must raise and respond to these questions today.

4. The Shoah and the Church

But if the Shoah raises chilling questions regarding our comfortable assumptions about twentieth century "civilization," it raises equally hard challenges regarding our understanding of religion and God. Many of the perpetrators saw themselves as "good" Christians, Protestants and Catholics. How could they? What was missing [or, more chillingly, present] in the Christian education they had received for centuries that allowed them to remain blind to what they were doing? Or indifferent to what others were doing in their name?

Many scholars point here to the ancient Christian "teaching of contempt" against Jews and Judaism as providing a negative framework, though not the direct cause, for the ease with which Hitler scapegoated the Jews. Without the medieval "demonization" of the Jews, they argue, modern racial antisemitism would not have been possible, much less so successful politically in Europe.

I believe there is truth in these assertions, uncomfortable as they are, though distinctions must be made. If the teachings of Christian preachers and Church leaders, bad as they sometimes were, were a sufficient cause for genocide, that would have happened, as many of these same scholars also point out, long before when the Churches had direct political power in ancient, medieval and Reformation Europe to implement their theology. But it did not happen then. Not for hundreds of years that their power held sway. It took the breakdown of that ecclesial authority, and with it the breakdown of its moral restraints by the Enlightenment and the "secularization" of Europe, to make possible the Shoah.

In medieval Christendom, Jews *in extremis* could always convert and survive. Often enough, they were able successfully to appeal to canon law and to the popes for legal protection or direct intervention to save them. But the Shoah, in our time, reveals how fragile civilization can be without such moral restraints. Secularity, no less than religion, it turns out, can have a dark side as well as a beneficial one. Interreligious and religious/secular dialogue, I would affirm, is not just a luxury in view of such awesome realities. It is a vital necessity for human survival as we approach the Third Millennium of the common era of Christian-Jewish interaction in history.

5. What, then, is the goal of Catholic teaching on the Shoah?

Again, I cannot here give a complete outline. This is up to Catholic educators themselves to develop. But I can give some indicators of directions to follow. An educational goal, as I see it, is not simply to expose evil, but to attract students to the good, to "act justly" as the prophet would say. It is not simply to list horrors, though confrontation with the horrors of humanity's inhumanity is necessary. Antisemitism is sinful—mortally so. This is a commandment for our generation and for all Christian generations that follow us.

But acknowledging evil is not in itself the point of Catholic catechesis [education—Ed.]. It is merely the counterpoint. Our educational goal, rather, is, first, to clarify for the students the deep challenges to our society and to our religion that the fact of the Shoah raises, and, second, to provide for students a structured and hope-filled environment within which they can begin to grapple with the issues of evil and goodness that the first of the crematoria cast in such painfully sharp relief.

The ultimate lesson of the Shoah for the believer is not evil but the mystery of the good, not despair but hope. Given the most implacable system ever devised for the destruction of the human spirit, how did so many [albeit relatively few] manage to maintain a sense of humanity in a world filled with corruption? What motivated those who risked their own lives to save Jews? How did so many [relatively and absolutely] of the victims maintain religious belief in the face of ultimate horror? Why did so many Jews go into the gas chambers singing the ancient Hebrew chant, Ani ma'amin [I believe....]? How were the survivors able to emerge from the camps and build new lives? Bear a new generation of the Jewish people? Build a new nation—the State of Israel—out of the ashes? In short, our teaching strategy must be one of hard challenges. It is one that accepts and cherishes the Jewish witness to us as Christians, that realizes in the Jewish witness a "saving warning" and, paradoxically, a saving hope as well.

IX. Conclusion

Finally, I would like to alert readers to three recent official documents of the Church that are pertinent to Shoah education. These are one statement of the Holy See and two issued by committees of the National Conference of Catholic Bishops.

All three of these documents need to be read within the context of the reassessment of official Catholic thought regarding Jews and Judaism begun by the Second Vatican Council.[25] Although the Second Vatican Council's declaration on the Jews, *Nostra Aetate, No. 4*, was very much precipitated by the Catholic reaction after the Shoah, it was not until 1974, in its implementing document for Nostra Aetate[26] that this crucial context for the Conciliar debate was first officially acknowledged at this level:

> ....the step taken by the [Second Vatican] Council finds its historical setting in circumstances deeply affected by the memory of the persecution and massacre of Jews which took place in Europe just before and during the Second World War.[27]

It was not, in turn, until 1985, that the *Notes* issued by the same Committee[28] for the first time universally mandated that Catholic religious education [properly, "catechesis"] "should help in understanding the meaning....of the extermination [of Jews] during the years 1939-1945, and its consequences," though Pope John Paul II had begun addressing the subject in some depth even earlier.[29]

It can be said, then, that many of the themes and issues first raised at scholars' conferences on the Shoah over the years are only now becoming embedded in the official teaching of the Roman Catholic Church. The other side of this same statement, of course, is that these crucial themes are becoming embedded in the very heart of the teaching of the Church, filling the catechetical "gap" left by the concurrent attempt to remove the vestiges of the old, pernicious "teaching of contempt" against Jews and Judaism condemned by the Second Vatican Council.

While perhaps relatively slow to act, the Church's institutional memory is long, and, once committed, correspondingly deep.

The first statement to which I draw your attention is primarily historical and moral, though it does rebut rather effectively one lingering element of the theology of contempt, the pernicious dichotomy between so-called Jewish particularity and Christian universalism. Both elements are to be found in both traditions, of course, as the document rightly points out.

The Pontifical Commission on Justice and Peace statement, "The Church and Racism," is, in many ways, a remarkable document for the Holy See to issue. It offers a survey of "racist behavior throughout history" that does not seek "to gloss over the weaknesses and even, at times, complicity of certain Church leaders....in this phenomenon," but rather analyzes the growth of intergroup antipathy to its apotheosis in modern antisemitism. Indeed, it calls antisemitism "the most tragic form that racist ideology has assumed in our century," citing specifically the Shoah in this context. [Section No. 15]

Nor does "The Church and Racism" shirk from including the Christian teaching of contempt in its pre-history of modern racial antisemitism, acknowledging that "within 'Christendom,' the Jews, considered the tenacious witnesses of a refusal to believe in Christ, were often the subject of serious humiliation, accusations and proscriptions" [Section No. 2]. It distinguishes, properly, this *religious* polemical stance from modern racial ideology as it appeared in the eighteenth and nineteenth centuries. It devotes a major section to the development of National Socialism in the twentieth century, citing it as "responsible for one of the greatest genocides in history." "This murderous folly," the statement continues, "struck first and foremost the Jewish people in unheard-of proportions," thus acknowledging the historical uniqueness of the Shoah, while also calling to memory Nazism's genocidal attacks "on the Gypsies and Tziganes and also categories of persons such as the handicapped and the mentally ill."

The Holy See's document recalls the stern opposition to these Nazi policies by Pope Pius XI [which has never been a subject for scholarly contention] and by Pope Pius XII [which has, though perhaps unfairly]. "The Church and Racism" is a timely statement that will be immediately of use to Catholic teachers not only in history, but in ethics and religion courses as well, providing them with the beginnings of a framework for the development of Shoah education on all levels, as Pope John Paul II called for during his visit to Miami on September 11, 1987.[30] I say "beginnings," because the Holy See's document on the Shoah, also promised by the Pope in Miami, is still forthcoming. This latter will be drafted, however, as is most appropriate, only after "serious studies" on the subject have been undertaken jointly by Christians and Jews through the mechanism of the International Catholic-Jewish Liaison Committee.[31]

The two American documents were issued by different Committees of the United States Bishops' Conference. It June of 1988, *Criteria for the Evaluation of Dramatization of the Passion*, by the Bishops' Committee for Ecumenical and Interreligious Affairs, was published in both Spanish and English. This document centers on depictions of Christ's death and spells out, in some detail, how it can be portrayed dramatically without having the implication, as in the past, of "collective guilt" of Jews for Jesus' death.[32]

In this, as with the second document to be discussed below, one can see how the Church is moving into a new stage in its implementation of Nostra Aetate's effort to eradicate antisemitism from Catholic teaching, reaching even the level of local passion plays and media presentations.

The second document, *God's Mercy Endures Forever: Guidelines on the Presentations of Jews and Judaism in Catholic Preaching*, published January, 1989, is a statement by the NCCB Committee on the Liturgy. Designed for homilists, it covers the entire spectrum of the Church's liturgical calendar. Bishop Joseph P. Delaney of Fort Worth, who chairs the Bishops' Committee on the Liturgy, begins his Preface to the document with the following words:

> Even in the twentieth century, the age of the Holocaust, the Shoah, the "scouring Wind," God's mercy endures forever.
> The Holocaust drew its fiery breath from the ancient, sometimes latent, but always persistent anti-Semitism which, over the centuries, found too large a place within the hearts of too many Christian men and women. Yet, since the Holocaust and since the Second Vatican Council, Christians have struggled to learn the reasons for such irrational and anti-Christian feelings against that special people for whom "God's mercy endures forever," to deal with those feelings, and to overcome them through knowledge, understanding, dialogue, and love.[33]

The purpose for these liturgical guidelines, Bishop Delaney continues, is thus "to see to it that our [Catholic] liturgical celebrations never again become occasions for that anti-Semitic or anti-Jewish sentiment that sometimes moved the liturgy in the past."[34]

Drawing on the 1974 Vatican *Guidelines*, the 1985 Vatican *Notes*, and a wealth of recent liturgical and Biblical scholarship, *God's Mercy* offers historical perspective and hermeneutical clarification to Christian preachers. It begins by noting the "Jewish roots of the Liturgy," not only Biblically but also in the synagogue and post-Biblical Jewish forms of worship. It rejects explicitly the false notions "that the New Covenant 'abrogated' or 'superseded' the Old, and that the Sinai Covenant was discarded by God and replaced with another" [Section 6], as well as the *deicide* [God killer—Ed.] charge [Second 7].

God's Mercy denounces "triumphalism" and instead frames a positive understanding of the Gospel message that affirms unequivocally the Church's teaching about Christ while affirming also the continuing validity of God's covenant with the Jewish people. It does this, it should be noted, on specifically Christian theological grounds:

> The Christian proclamation of the saving deeds of the One God through Jesus was formed in the context of Second Temple Judaism and cannot be understood thoroughly without that context. It is a proclamation that, at its heart, stands in solidarity with the continuing Jew-

ish witness in affirming the One God as Lord of history. Further, false or demeaning portraits of a repudiated Israel may undermine Christianity as well. How can one confidently affirm the truth of God's covenant with all humanity and creation in Christ [See Romans 8:21] without at the same time affirming God's faithfulness to the Covenant with Israel that also lies at the heart of Biblical testimony? [Section 8]

God's Mercy tackles the often-abused "fulfillment" theme of the Advent liturgy, noting that the Biblical prophecies are not to be understood as "merely temporal predictions," but are also "profound expressions of eschatological hope." They are "fulfilled" [i.e. irreversibly inaugurated] in Christ's coming, but preachers must also note that "the fulfillment is not completely worked out in each person's life or perfected in the world at large." Hence, it concludes, "with the Jewish people, we await the complete realization of the messianic age." [Sections 11-12]

Similarly, *God's Mercy* affirms traditional Christian applications of Biblical texts, such as typology, but notes that such interpretations, while valid, do not exhaust the "unfathomable riches" and "inexhaustible context" of the Hebrew Bible. The association of the *Akedah* [the Binding of Isaac] with Christ's sacrifice, for example, is a natural one for Christians. But this does not invalidate traditional Jewish applications of the same Biblical text, from which Christians can continue to learn. [Section 14]

In these areas, I believe, *God's Mercy* is moving toward a positive, non-triumphalist form of Christian anamnesis ["memory"] within the very understanding of the Church's worship. Since, for Catholics, *lex orandi* is indeed *lex credendi*, the significance of such liturgical hermeneutics is quite apparent.[35]

God's Mercy, as does the Vatican *Notes*, stresses that the conflict scenes in the Gospel between Jesus and "the Pharisees" often reflect later Christian-Jewish disputes "long after the time of Jesus" [Sections 16-20], and, like the BCEIA *Criteria*, takes particular care with the passion narratives of Holy Week [Sections 26-28]. The document concludes with a summary listing of nine "general principles" applicable to all homilies throughout the year. I would like to see this list posted on the bulletin boards of every Catholic seminary, parish rectory, and school faculty lounge in the country.

Finally, the Bishops, for the first time that I know of in any official Church statement at this level, recommend joint Jewish/Christian Memorial Services for the victims of the Shoah and offer specific examples of prayers to be said at Mass on the Sunday closest to *Yom Ha-Shoah*:

> 29. Also encouraged are joint memorial services commemorating the victims of the Shoah [Holocaust]. These should be prepared for with catechetical and adult education programming to ensure a proper

spirit of shared reverence. Addressing the Jewish community of Warsaw, Pope John Paul II stressed the uniqueness and significance of Jewish memory of the Shoah: 'More than anyone else, it is precisely you who have become this saving warning. I think that in this sense you continue your particular vocation, showing yourselves to be still the heirs of that election to which God is faithful. This is your mission in the contemporary world before....all of humanity' [Warsaw, June 14, 1987]. On the Sunday closest to Yom Ha-Shoah, Catholics should pray for the victims of the Holocaust and their survivors. The following serve as examples of petitions for the general intercessions at Mass:

—For the victims of the Holocaust, their families, and all our Jewish brothers and sisters, that the violence and hatred they experienced may never again be repeated, we pray to the Lord.

—For the Church, that the Holocaust may be a reminder to us that we can never be indifferent to the sufferings of others, we pray to the Lord.

—For our Jewish brothers and sisters, that their confidence in the face of long-suffering may spur us on to greater faith and trust in God, we pray to the Lord.

The Holocaust Now

In the Presence of Burning Children

For Presbyterian Douglas Huneke, Irving Greenberg's working principle to which he alludes in the title of his essay "In the Presence of Burning Children," has not produced "a radical, systemic institutional reformation of Christianity in Europe or America." After examining "The Ten Points of Seelisberg" [Switzerland, 1947] and their contemporary implications according to the following schema: [a] the Jewishness of Jesus [#1, #2, #3, #10]; [b] love of God and one's neighbor [#4]; and [c] theological antisemitism [#5, #6, #7, #8, #9], for him, the theological agenda of post-Shoah Christianity still must be framed by three tasks: [1] examination and repudiation of Christian antisemitism, [2] analysis of the theological and social implications of the Nazis' murder of the Jews; and [3] a "re-ordering" of education for both laity and clergy. Significantly, at the heart of his essay Jesus the Christ still remains as the model to be emulated, based on his exhaustive study and interviews with those Christians who were themselves "rescuers."

SLJ

The Holocaust Now

IN THE PRESENCE OF BURNING CHILDREN: THE REFORMATION OF CHRISTIANITY AFTER THE SHOAH

Douglas K. Huneke

With Admiration for Sergey Lyozov, Christian, Shoah Scholar, and Opponent of Antisemitism, Moscow

I. In Their Presence

Throughout history, warriors have reserved special terrors for mothers and children. Early in the history of Israel, Elisha prophesied that when Hazael became King of Syria, he would "....dash in pieces their [Israelite] little children and rip up their women who were with child" [II Kings 8:12]. The brutality of Hazael's soldiers pales next to the record of Hitler's SS. It became a routine Nazi practice, particularly among the *Einsatzgruppen* [mobile killing units], to snatch an infant from its mother and, before her eyes, smash her child's head against a wall, or impale an infant on a bayonet, or execute a mother and child together. When I wrote the biography of Herman F. Graebe, a German railroad engineer who rescued hundreds of Jews in the Ukraine, Graebe described carefully and with tremendous emotion how the strength of his decision to rescue Jews and, later, to testify at the Nuremberg trials, was solidified when he witnessed his co-nationals smashing infants against pillars and impaling them on bayonets. His vivid accounts recalled a painting that hangs in the administration center of the Israeli Shoah memorial, Yad Vashem. It depicts a battered infant lying askew in the corner of a stone wall, a trail of blood begins mid-wall and traces the child's passage to the ground.

A. At Watch on Buchenwald's Perimeter

In spite of its setting, on a hill looking out over a lush and beautiful valley and beyond to the historic city of Weimar, Buchenwald is a desolate memorial to the Jews who were murdered there. On the north perimeter of the camp, outside the rusting

The Holocaust Now

barbed wire, is a thick stand of poplar trees. Just inside the wire fence are memorials to the Soviet prisoners of war, Communist anti-Fascists, and Jews who were exterminated by the Nazis. In 1976, as I stood reading the monuments, my eyes caught a movement near the fence. A woman with a wizened face, wearing a long black coat and bandanna, paced in the small clearing between the poplars and the once-electrified fence. Keeping a discrete distance, I watched this woman walk up and down the fence line. Her body bent and contorted as she moved; her arms flew up in the air and then drove down toward the ground. She twisted her hands as if in deep, agonizing grief and her lips moved as if praying or conversing. This ritual continued for several hours each of the days that I was visiting the camp.

Why was she there? What past torments compelled her presence on this mountain? Had someone she loved been tortured on the infamous whipping block? Was she mourning the death of a parent or husband who was led into the gassing rooms only to exit through the chimney? Was she mourning the death of her child? Who could wipe away the horrible vision, the haunting eyes of the small ones in Buchenwald's special children's camp? Has she walked hundreds of streets and scanned bundles of Red Cross photographs searching for the face of her child? Alone now, does the Mourner's *Kaddish* [Jewish memorial prayer—Ed.] cross her lips? Does she find solace in her prayers?

The Shoah covers its students with a shroud of pained silence, surrounds them with unanswerable questions, and casts them into haunting, wordless encounters. It is painful to see the faces, to look into the wide, vacant eyes of the nine hundred little children who survived Buchenwald's gas chambers. It is worse for those who survey the endless enlargements for a single recognizable family trait. The source of this woman's anguish remained a mystery; her sorrow and prayers were private by her choice. An invisible wall blocked the visitor from the survivor. So I kept a discrete distance, reciting the Kaddish under my breath, and prayed for wizened old women in long black coats and bandannas.

B. A Defiant Prayer at Majdanek

The suffering of mothers and children confronted me in a powerful way again at the former extermination camp, Majdanek, in Lublin, Poland. There was a large, grassy field at the entrance to the camp. As I left the Visitors' Office and walked along the promenade to the main camp monument, I passed three women peacefully pushing their babies in strollers. Near them, on a curved park bench, in the shade of a tree, sat another woman who gazed into the camp serenely, a baby nursing at her breast. Beyond them, the sky was split by the largest and most imposing Polish monument to the victims of Nazi terror. In the distance, antiquated, but perfectly preserved guard tow-

In the Presence of Burning Children

ers cast long shadows across tall barbed wire fences and swaying pine trees hid the camp from its nearby neighbors.

While the eyes of her nursing infant stared gently and contentedly at her, she looked out at a universe that betrayed the tranquility of the moment: the barracks [cramped and stagnant], disinfection showers [public undressing], barbed wire [calculated ravaging of the spirit as parents and children were separated violently], gas chambers [the dash, shaved and naked, under flailing truncheons to the release of death], crematorium chimney [gross, posthumous examinations for jewels and money]. How could this woman nurse her child under such a dark cloud of history? Why did these women come to this place? Certainly there were other places infinitely more pastoral and certainly easier to reach from Lublin's town square. Then it struck me: They brought the consummation of sexual love, the new gift of their wombs, and paraded defiantly at the edges of the citadels of death. The nursing mother brought the most vulnerable symbol of life and peacefully sat before death's kingdom, proclaiming:

> See! Look at my baby—You shall
>   never smash another one against a wall!
> Look! My breast, full of milk—you will
>   never cause another woman's breast to wither and
>   dry!
>   I am
>   here to declare to you that you shall
>   never again separate children from parents!
> You imposed death, but I gave life—
>   I live beyond you! Against you!
> They were innocent women and children—not a danger to you;
>   now,
>   I am
> a threat to your memory because
> I exist and
> I create beyond your life and death.
> For the souls of women and children who knew your whips,
>   your humiliations, your terrors,
>   I am!
> For my child and for 1,500,000 children
>   I offer the warmth and nourishment of my breast,
>   the rich milk of human love and hope.
> Do you see me?
>   I am here!

The Holocaust Now

> I am nursing!
> In spite of you, because of you,
> I am!

II. A Fatal Alliance: Nationalism and Triumphalism

The sense of hope that I drew from the women's presence and their defiance of death is tempered by Adolf Hitler's declaration in *Mein Kampf*: "Today I believe that I am acting in accord with the will of the Almighty Creator: by defending myself against the Jews, I am fighting for the work of the Lord."[1] Hitler's sense of a "holy war," joined with the growing and militant nationalism that took root in the fertile soil of racism, permeated nearly every level of ecclesiastical leadership, and profoundly influenced the life of the German churches. Prominent theologians gave special credibility to this nationalistic way of uniting God's Word with the theory of the *Volk*, sounding more like the emerging political preacher of hatred and division than ministers of the Gospel. An example is a lecture in 1937 by Lutheran theologian, Paul Althaus, who has been described as a distinguished and influential figure in German theology at that time:

> As a creation of God, the Volk is a law of our life....We are unconditionally bound to faithfulness, to responsibility, so that the life of the Volk as it has come down to us not be contaminated or weakened through our fault. We are bound to stand up for the life of our Volk, even to the point of risking our own life....Our life in our Volk is not our eternal life; but we have no eternal life if we do not live for our Volk. This is not a question of the absolute value of the Volk, but of our absolute obligation to the Volk.[2]

In an apparent attempt to discredit the then newly-released Theological Declaration of Barmen [1934], Althaus signed the *Ansbacher Ratchlag*, which included the following lines underscoring a theological and ecclesiastical support for Hitler's holy war:

> In this knowledge we as believing Christians thank God our Father that He has given to our Volk in its time of need the *Fuhrer* as a pious and faithful sovereign, and that he wants to prepare for us in the National Socialist system of government 'good rule,' a government with discipline and honor.
> Accordingly, we know that we are responsible before God to assist the work of the Fuhrer in our calling and in our station in life.[3]

Only a small remnant of theologians, pastors, and church leaders publicly challenged the blatant linking of the law of God with the laws of the German state and the nationalistic fervor of the Volk. Those who dared to publicly disapprove were quickly silenced by the Reich and most paid with their lives. The majority of German Christians remained secure in their silence. The others turned their words to the service of the Reich and continued on a course that legitimated the bonding of German nationalism and Christian triumphalism. The effect of this silence and the unification of nationalism and triumphalism opened a fatal new chapter in the history of Christian antisemitism and gave tacit legitimacy to those who were preparing the design for Hitler's "Final Solution."

A. Fatal Loyalties

Could these theologians and preachers have known that Hitler and his colleagues took the fearful silence of the many and the support of the complicit as a license for genocide? Could they have known that their words might afford special encouragement to men like Pastor Ernest Biberstein? Biberstein, a student of theology and for eleven years a parish minister, commanded the brutal and efficient *Einsatzkommando* 6 in *Einsatzgruppe* C.[4] Could they have imagined that their words and activities would be taken as a sign permitting well-educated, religious men and women to put Jews to death in mass graves, in sealed chambers, in silent forests; to smash children against walls or force them to be held in front of their mothers so that two persons might be dispatched by one bullet—a strange economy of death in a universe devoted to death?

Could they have foreseen that a young survivor of Auschwitz would one day bear witness to the systematic institutionalization of Nazi horrors against women and children, to the end result of unchecked racism, nationalism, Christian triumphalism, and antisemitism?

> Not far from us, flames were leaping up from a ditch, gigantic flames. They were burning something. A lorry drew up at the pit and delivered its load—little children. Babies! I saw it—saw it with my own eyes....those children in the flames. [Is it surprising that I could not sleep after that? Sleep had fled from my eyes]....
> Never shall I forget that night, the first night in camp, which has turned my life into one long night, seven times cursed and seven times sealed. Never shall I forget that smoke. Never shall I forget the little faces of the children, whose bodies I saw turned into wreaths of smoke beneath a silent blue sky.[5]

In 1943, a year after Auschwitz opened, Althaus learned for the first time that German soldiers were routinely killing civilians in occupied lands. That revelation reportedly repulsed him, but not so much that he was provoked by the offense nor compelled morally to speak out against the killings or the Reich. Instead, he and the others knowingly continued to place their words and ministries in the service of genocide.

III. The Geography of Genocide: In Their Presence

Drawing a lesson from the silence of the majority of the German churches and from the active complicity of theologians, preachers, and ecclesiastical bureaucrats, Rabbi Irving Greenberg drafted a "working principle" to guide Jews and Christians who probe the implications of the Shoah: who seek a humane, informed, and faithful response to the victims and survivors. Greenberg's "working principle," given wide public voice for the first time in 1974, is the foundation for a long ignored, but essential radical reformation of Christianity after the Shoah. In light of the impotence of most of Christianity before the Nazis, his words must be understood to be the definitive mandate for post-Shoah Christianity:

> Let us offer, then, as working principle the following: No statement, theological or otherwise, should be made that would not be credible in the presence of burning children.[6]

A post-Shoah Christian theology, if it is to have integrity and credibility, must begin at the edge of a mass grave, at the entrance to a gas chamber, beside a bloodstained wall, in the presence of burning children.

A. Agenda for Post-Shoah Christianity

The agenda for post-Shoah Christianity has remained virtually unchanged since the Nuremberg Tribunal weighed the evidence and pronounced its verdict on genocidal crimes against humanity. The tragedy is that the presence of burning children did not bring about a radical, systemic institutional reformation of Christianity in Europe or America. The post-Shoah agenda is framed by three central tasks: first, a careful study of the origins of and a full repudiation of Christian antisemitism which found its complete and most violent expression between 1933 and 1945; second, a thorough analysis of the theological and social implications of the Nazi destruction of European Jewry; and finally, a re-ordering of theological education for laity and clergy to the end that the church never again acts freely and destructively on triumphalist beliefs, is not a perpetrator of antisemitic or other divisive teachings, nor a willing partner conforming to the political, social, or theological directives of ill-intentioned authorities.

B. The Seelisberg Paradigm

In August, 1947, the Third Commission of the International Emergency Conference of Christians and Jews met in Seelisberg, Switzerland. French historian Jules Isaac provided the commission with a study document entitled, "The Rectification Necessary In Christian Teaching: Eighteen Points."[7] Isaac's paper served as the basis for the final statement of the conference, "The Ten Points of Seelisberg."[8] The Commission distinguished itself by its very early date relative to the end of the war, by the participation of Protestants and Catholics, and by the decision of the Commission to have Jews review and comment on the various points. The very factors that distinguished the work of the Commission appear to have worked against its noble purposes. The meeting may have brought forth its product too near the end of the war and the beginning of a generalized public awareness of the horrors of the Shoah. In 1947, survivors were still slowly piecing their daily lives back together and few had begun to process what they had lived through or plumb the Shoah's implications. Those who spoke of the unspeakable offered their testimony to a world that had no means to comprehend the brutality and immensity of the "Final Solution." More importantly, survivors quickly discovered that words were inadequate for their experience.

Also in 1947, Protestants and Catholics did not have a familiar basis for dialogue and common pronouncement. It was most likely too early for institutional Christianity to make the necessary connection between centuries of antisemitism and the work of the camps. Another indication that the Seelisberg document was premature is the absence of any reference to the Shoah. This is most surprising considering that many participants knew that Isaac's wife and daughter had died in a concentration camp. None of these observations are intended to diminish the importance of the Seelisberg Points, but rather to indicate why the points did not lead to the changes imagined by the participants.

The drafters of the "Ten Points of Seelisberg" were visionaries who sensed the urgent need for what Paul van Buren would describe twenty-eight years later:

....at least a few Christians have begun to realize that a reconsideration of what Christians have been saying about Judaism and of Christian-Jewish relations must lead to a reconsideration of Christianity itself....Theology can shut its eyes and pretend that the Holocaust never happened and that Israel doesn't exist. Theology has shown itself capable of such blindness before! But if there are prospects for serious theology, for a theology not hopelessly blind to matters that pertain to the heart of its task, then the

The Holocaust Now

time has come for a reconsideration of the whole theological and Christian enterprise of the most radical sort.[9]

Mindful of the presence and witness of burning children, I shall now examine several of the Seelisberg points as the basis for the study and repudiation of Christian antisemitism. The implications of the "Ten Points of Seelisberg" may yet serve to launch a radical reformation of the whole theological and Christian enterprise.

C. The Challenge of the Shoah to Christianity

The first three and the tenth points of the Seelisberg document address the Jewishness of Jesus and his movement by affirming that "it is the same living God who speaks to us all" through the Hebrew and Christian Scriptures[10]; that "Jesus was born of a Jewish mother" in the lineage of David and lovingly embraced "his own people and the whole world;" identifies the first followers of Jesus as Jews; and the tenth point calls Christians to keep from speaking of the "first members of the Church as if they were not Jews." Tragically, centuries before and during the time of the Shoah, the vast majority of theologians and preachers rejected out of hand or ignored the truth of these points. The few preachers and theologians who did attend to these details met strong resistance. In their important study of the Shoah, Richard Rubenstein and John Roth recount the time when, in December, 1933, Reformed theologian, Karl Barth, preached a sermon entitled, "Jesus Christ was a Jew." This courageous message predictably caused a rift in the membership of the church. Shortly thereafter, Barth wrote a member of the church, "anyone who believes in Christ, who was himself a Jew, and died for Gentiles and Jews, simply cannot be involved in the contempt for Jews and ill-treatment of them which is now the order of the day."[11]

The implication of the first three Seelisberg Points is that Christian antisemitism and any harmful or destructive acts which follow from it are, by definition, fratricidal attacks upon the history of God's covenantal relationships [the Hebrew and Christian Scriptural record of the covenants], upon those who live under God's unaltered promises [Jews], and, ultimately, upon the Creator of the universe. The prophetic texts in Hebrew Scripture and the Christian Gospels portray clearly the God who shares fully the wholeness and humiliation, suffering and joy, freedom and bondage of the covenant peoples. If Jews suffered and died at the hands of Christians during the Shoah, God, who identifies fully with God's people, suffered and died, as victim of these same Christians. God was murdered with each and every Jew who died during the Shoah. This is to say that those baptized believers whose antisemitism led them to be silent, complicit, or active participants in the Shoah were guilty not only of antisemitic fratricide, but also of Deicide. Any form or expression of antisemitism, no matter if it is fatal or subtle, must be regarded as an expression of Christian self-hatred that has the capacity to destroy those who practice it and those who are its targets of abuse, including God who is never divided from God's people.

The presence of the God whose fate is inextricably bound to the fate of the covenant peoples finds a powerful statement in Elie Wiesel's memoir. At Buna, three inmates, two adults and a child, were to be hung as suspected saboteurs. Jews in the camp were forced to watch as ropes were placed around the necks of the adults who shouted, "Long live liberty!" The child was silent, but behind Wiesel a voice asked, "Where is God? Where is He?" The child was slow to die and Wiesel concludes the account:

> For more than half an hour he stayed there, struggling between life and death, dying in slow agony under our eyes. And we had to look him full in the face. He was still alive when I passed in front of him. His tongue was still red, his eyes were not yet glazed. Behind me, I heard the same man asking: "Where is God now?" And I heard a voice within me answer him: "Where is He? Here He is--He is hanging here on this gallows...."[12]

A Protestant theologian in the mid-1970's, perhaps moved by Wie-sel's experience at Buna, expressed a Christian understanding of the link between God's fate and the fate of God's people. He wrote that the most compelling contemporary image of the Passion is of a Jew hanging crucified on an electrified barbed wire fence at Auschwitz. A theology that dares to separate God from God's people; that denies or diminishes the promises of God to humanity; that ignores or contributes to the suffering of others; or that fails to perceive in the suffering of another human being, the pain and suffering of God, has failed to comprehend the pathos communicated by the prophets and the commitment of God in the various covenants.

D. Two Faithful Remnants Honor a Commandments

The fourth of the Seelisberg Points calls Christians to remember that the "fundamental commandment....to love God and one's neighbors" is contained in the Hebrew Scripture and confirmed by Jesus, and is "binding upon both Christians and Jews in all human relationships, without any exception." In Elie Wiesel's novel, *The Oath*, the narrator describes the thoughts of Moshe the madman:

> He knew that nothing justifies the pain man causes another. Any messiah in whose name men are tortured can only be a false messiah.

The Holocaust Now

> It is by diminishing evil, present and real evil, experienced evil, that one builds the city of the sun. It is by helping the person who looks at you with tears in his eyes, needing help, needing you or at least your presence, that you may attain perfection.[13]

Not all German Christians followed a false messiah or the political preacher of hatred and division. A faithful remnant actively and publicly resisted the rise of National Socialism and Adolf Hitler. Some created and signed the Theological Declaration of Barmen, while others preached against the idolatry, falsehood, and folly of nationalism. Many of their stories are memorialized in the book, *Dying We Live*, edited by Helmut Gollwitzer. In his forward to the book, theologian Reinhold Niebuhr described these religiously-motivated dissidents, lovers of spiritual and civic freedom, as "Revelations of the heroic heights to which the human spirit may rise when it is informed by 'grace,' a power that transcends the sense of duty and that is infused into those lives which have a sure hold of the meaning of human existence, which transcends their own lives and survival...."[14]

A second remnant of Christians, a distinct minority numbering fewer than ten thousand persons among the millions of people living in all of Central and Eastern Europe, responded directly to the tears, the need for help or at least offered the presence described by Moshe. These women, men, and children intervened personally and directly on behalf of desperately endangered Jews, dissidents, peasants, and others. The rescuers of Jews embodied the practice of a Christian faith called for in the fourth Seelisberg Point and grounded in the Biblical teachings to "love your neighbor" and "care for the sojourner in your midst." These Christians defied laws, endangered themselves and their families, and successfully resisted the combined forces of culture, nationalism, state authority, and misguided theologies. Their actions answered in the affirmative Cain's question, "Am I my brother's keeper?" and removed any limitations or barriers to the lawyer's question in the Gospel of Luke, "Who is my neighbor?"

Most of the rescuers were unlikely characters who did not stand out in their religious, social, vocational, or political settings. For the most part, they were common people who performed their daily routines until some act of brutality or the arrival of a frightened stranger, a survivor, galvanized their compassionate spirits and propelled them into activities that most others were unwilling or unable to consider. In spite of almost insurmountable odds and dangers, they managed to act honorably in an evil era. They were not perfect nor was that their goal, and they did not see themselves as heroic. On the contrary, they were people who simply remained faithful and human. A person does not fulfill the Biblical mandates to love one's neighbor and care for the sojourner without certain predispositions and skills which are structured on a radical understanding of faith. A warning is in order. As the case of Pastor Ernst Biberstein, commander of a mobile killing unit, dramatically illustrates, it is not sufficient to have a formal theological education and an articulated faith based on Biblical values and teachings. Those values and teachings are useless unless they can be translated into behaviors that protect, sustain, and sanctify human life.

In 1980, I began a study of the moral and spiritual development of Nazi era rescuers. In the succeeding years I interviewed rescuers and those whom they saved, and conducted case studies in the archives of the Department of the Righteous at Yad Vashem. The findings significantly influence the practical application of the fourth Seelisberg Point.[15] Nazi-era rescuers had a discernible spirit of adventurousness. These people were risk-takers in multiple, overlapping areas of their lives. They were not, however, reckless or impulsive. Numerous rescuers reported that they engaged in elaborate planning procedures and calculated their actions carefully in order to maximize security and reduce the risk to the people they were helping. A Dutch rescuer who was an award-winning skier is an example. He regularly waited for nightfall and then skied the route he would take the next morning with refugees. Skiing entails certain risks which are magnified when the conditions become extreme, as when this rescuer skied in the dark. He did this to be certain that military snow patrols had not moved into the area he and the Jews would be traveling, thereby minimizing the risks to everyone.

Nazi-era rescuers had an intense identification with a parental model of moral conduct. Virtually all of the rescuers in my study reported a close, significant relationship with one or both parents who acted morally, who made use of a decidedly moral vocabulary, and who actively practiced their values in the presence of their children. Numerous rescuers recall that their parents based their moral teachings on religious concepts and frequently quoted one or more passages from Hebrew and Christian Scriptures that illustrated and supported their beliefs and actions. There was also a useful and practical folk wisdom or common sense of quality about the moralizing. One rescuer reported that the Bible lessons his father frequently read to him dealt with kindly behavior and how to get along with people and life. Another rescuer told how his father connected the feeding of strangers and the care of widows and orphans with the Biblical mandates for such behavior.

A significant factor disposing Christians to act altruistically was a religiously-inspired non-conformity that was linked to Biblical directives to compassionately care for those who are vulnerable, disenfranchised, and who suffer oppression and injustice. A Dutch rescuer summed up the matter of religiously-inspired non-conformity when she explained the foundation of her altruistic actions by quoting Saint Paul's admonition in Romans 12:2, "Be not conformed to this world, but be transformed to a completely new way of thinking so as to know what is the good and acceptable and perfect will of God." She went on to say that, "For me to kill or betray Jews would have been to conform to evil. I had no choice but to follow God's will and save Jews from the

The Holocaust Now

Nazis."

Religiously-inspired non-conformity coupled with the social ethics of the Christian Scripture became intellectual mandates to intervene on behalf of desperately endangered people. A German rescuer noted that his interventions, which he justified using Biblical passages, afforded him an important and comforting sense that there was consistency between his religious beliefs and how he lived his life. We have already seen the discontinuity that existed for those who made a connection between nationalism [*das Volk*] and Christianity. The effect of the discontinuity led to conformity, complicity, silence, and indifference. Their allegiance was to a transitory and inhuman political order rather than to the ethical and spiritual teaching of their faith.

Many Nazi-era rescuers had sophisticated empathic imaginations. The essence of the empathic imagination is the ability to place oneself in the actual situation or role of another person and actively visualize the long-term consequences of the situation of that person. The so-called "Golden Rule" of Matthew 7:12 is the Biblical model for the empathic imagination, "Do unto others what you would have them do unto you." The German rescuer Herman Graebe had one of the most effective empathic imaginations of the rescuers I interviewed. It was nurtured by his mother who always asked him in situations of moral choice, "Fritz, what would you do?" Her questions were neither idle nor rhetorical.

Graebe's empathic imagination served him at the edge of a mass grave in Dubno, Ukraine, where he watched his contemporary, an anonymous, naked Jewish man point to the sky and speak to his son moments before the two descended a ledge in the mass grave and were murdered. In Graebe's empathic imagination, he and his own young son became the two Jews standing before the pit. Forty years later, Graebe vividly remembered thinking at the time what he would say to his son if they had been the ones waiting to be murdered. As he walked from the scene, heartsick, his mother's question crossed his consciousness: "And Fritz, what would you do?" Graebe went on from this encounter to establish a successful rescue network in the Ukraine.

Rescuers were quite adept at hospitality. They removed endangered people from intensely hostile environments, offering them a respite from the forces that sought their destruction. They shared food, drink, warmth, rest, protection, and presence. Hospitality is the specific training ground of religiously-motivated altruism. Henri Nouwen, a Roman Catholic theologian, has written the following description of this quality:

> In a world full of strangers, estranged from their own past, culture, and country, from their neighbors, friends, and family, from their deepest self and their God, we witness a painful search for a hospitable place where life can be lived without fear....That is our vocation, to covert the *hostis* into a *hospis*, the enemy into a guest and to create

the free and fearless space where brotherhood and sisterhood can be formed and fully expressed.[16]

Finally, rescuers of Jews had all learned to confront and manage their prejudice. Entrenched and culturally validated stereotypes of Jews determined the political, social, and legal actions that resulted in centuries of dehumanizing attitudes, injury, or death. When such stereotypes are set aside in deference to a greater consideration of human dignity or a more egalitarian worldview, the effects of prejudice and brutality can be avoided. Moral parents, humane Biblical teachings, and a worldview that enabled the rescuers to interpret the persecution of Jews as morally repugnant all contributed to the containment of prejudice.

It must be noted that there were very few communal rescue efforts during the Nazi era. Communal rescues were orchestrated by religiously-based groups with credible and inspiring leaders. It is clear from the few examples of communal rescue [i.e. Le Chambon and Assisi] that compassionate interventions leading to the protection of victims will be most successful when there is a community of like-minded persons with an organized ethic that supports such interventions. Institutional Christianity reaps a justifiable condemnation when it fails to prepare people to act in a pro-human manner or fails to build both an ethic and a structure that protects human life and ensures the dignity of persons.

Nazi-era rescuers are models for the mandate set forth in the fourth Seelisberg Point: they had the skills and predispositions that empowered them to love God and their neighbors. Any form of religious or secular education that fails to take Nazi-era rescuers into consideration has abandoned the past, neglected the present, and risks defaulting on a faithful and humane future.

E. Additional Challenges to Christianity Today

The remaining five points of the Seelisberg document address important specific forms of theological antisemitism. Point five calls Christians to avoid "disparaging Biblical or post-Biblical Judaism" in order to extol Christianity. This common form of triumphalism holds that Christianity is the fulfillment and completion of Judaism and incorrectly concluded that all covenants between God and the Jews were breached and, therefore, revoked. Christianity is seen by those who accept this flawed line of reasoning as superior to Judaism. This reasoning has served historically as the basis for countless evangelistic "missions to the Jews." No Christian who stands in the presence of burning children would dare to seek the conversion of Jews. Such a Christian must struggle with the contradictions implicit in speaking of a God of love whose followers were the architects of mass murder and genocide; of a covenantal God who did not save the covenant people, who did not extinguish the flames or dispel the gas or vanquish the adversaries. These irresolvable contradictions will quench the evangelistic fervor and humble the triumphalist spirit of any believer who stands before the Shoah.

The implication of the fifth Seelisberg point is harsh, but it must be said. Christians who pursue the conversion of the Jews fail to hear the screaming, tortured anguish of the victims, they fail to comprehend the fragile rebirth of post-Shoah Judaism, and they fail to confront the powerful questions about God and faith and promise that arise from the ovens and mass graves. Whether acting out of a mistaken benevolence or self-righteous triumphalism, these Christians seek to do to the Jews spiritually what Hitler sought to accomplish physically.

The sixth, seventh, and ninth Seelisberg Points are closely related. The sixth point confronts the issue of using the word "Jews" in the context of "the enemies of Jesus," and the words "the enemies of Jesus" to identify the whole of the Jewish people. It should be noted that the Gospel according to John frequently employed the "collective term 'the Jews' in a restricted and pejorative sense to mean Jesus' enemies."[17] The drafters of the Ten Seelisberg Points preferred to keep the warning unlimited, but the Gospel of John does pose the greatest difficulty for exegetes and preachers who wish to eliminate this problem. The seventh point urges Christians to "Avoid presenting the Passion in such a way as to bring the odium of the killing of Jesus upon all the Jews or upon the Jews alone." The drafters correctly note that the Jews were not the only ones demanding Jesus' death, that they alone were not responsible. The point ends with a lengthy and impassioned plea for responsible religious education that avoids inflaming believers and leading them into "an undiscriminating hatred of the Jews at all times, including those of our own day." The ninth point challenges the perpetuation of the "superstitious notion that the Jewish people is reprobate, accursed, reserved for a destiny of suffering."

Much of the legacy of the hatred of the Jews can be traced to the teaching of the church that Jews were and continue to be responsible for the crime of Deicide in the crucifixion of Jesus. For centuries, clergy and theologians have solidified their power by distorting the historicity of the crucifixion. They have deflected responsibility from a few Jewish leaders who worked in concert with the political leaders of the Roman occupation government to a transhistoric collective Jewish responsibility. This dishonesty was the fertile soil in which the seeds of the Shoah were planted early in the development of the church. Even Hitler tried to capitalize on this fatal harvest when, in *Mein Kampf*, he asserted that Jesus' attitude toward Jews was displayed at the end of a whip in the Temple. Hitler concluded that the Jews sealed Jesus' fate on the cross to protect their business interests and he compared Jews of his day with those who arranged Jesus' death.[18]

In his study paper for the Commission, Jules Isaac asserted that "those who had him [Jesus] arrested and sentenced, the chief priests, were representatives of a narrow oligarchic caste, subjugated to Rome and detested by the people...."[19] The Seelisberg drafters elected to avoid placing blame anywhere. In retrospect, this is a serious shortcoming. It is not possible to avoid the question of responsibility for the crucifixion, just as it is irresponsible to tolerate the willful and fatal distortion of history. Ellis Rivkin has written a persuasive volume in which he offers a political, social, and religious challenge to the charges of Deicide leveled against the Jews. Addressing the confluence of events leading to the death of Jesus, Rivkin writes:

> The times were no ordinary times; the tempests, no ordinary tempests; the bedlam, no ordinary bedlam; the derangements, no ordinary derangements. The chaos that gave birth to a charismatic like Jesus was the very chaos that rendered clarity of judgment impossible....Everyone was entangled within a web of circumstance from which there was no way out....The emperor sought to govern an empire; the procurator sought to hold anarchy in check; the high priest sought to hold his office; the members of the high priest's sanhedrin [governing council—Ed.] sought to spare the people the dangerous consequences of a charismatic's innocent visions of the kingdom of God, which they themselves believed was really at hand....
>
> It is in this maelstrom of time, place, and circumstance, in tandem with impulse-ridden, tempest-tossed, and blinded sons of men, that the tragedy of Jesus' crucifixion is to be found. It was not the Jewish people who crucified Jesus, and it was not the Roman people—it was the imperial system, a system which victimized the Jews, victimized the Romans, and victimized the Spirit of God.[20]

Jews were not the enemies of Jesus nor of the emerging church. To blame all Jews in all eras for the crucifixion and to use the death of Jesus to justify the centuries of inhumanity that culminated in the Shoah is to completely fail to understand the meaning of Jesus' death on a Roman cross. The message of the cross proclaims the end of imposed, officially sanctioned death. For Christians, the crucifixion and resurrection compose an inseparable unit of belief that bears witness to the love of God overcoming corrupt power and defeating death in all its myriad forms. The crucifixion and resurrection are a direct challenge to the systems that perpetuate oppression, anarchy, and faithlessness.

On the basis of distorted historical accounts and a misunderstanding of the meaning of the crucifixion, Christians have fallen into the erroneous belief that Jews and Judaism are, in the words of Seelisberg Point Nine, "reprobate, accursed, reserved for a destiny of suffering." Christians who subscribe to this belief have taken God's place and substituted their own moral and eternal judgment on Jews for God's more compassionate quest to be reunited with the covenant people. In the words of Seelisberg Point Eight, these Christians refer to limited, suspect "scriptural curses" and elect to hear only "the cry of a raging mob, 'His blood be on us and on our children!'" Seelisberg and Ellis Rivkin find agreement in Jesus' response to his fate. After indicting the imperial system of Rome which victimized Jews, Romans, and the Spirit of God, Rivkin concludes:

> And Jesus understood. Twisted in agony on the cross—that symbol of imperial Roman cruelty and ruthless disregard of the human spirit—Jesus lifted his head upward toward God and pleaded, "Father, forgive them; for they know not what they do."[21]

The Ninth Seelisberg Point does not directly address the humiliation and suffering experienced by Jesus during the process of the crucifixion, but does caution that misrepresentation of the Passion can lead to timeless, indiscriminate hatred of Jews. Jules Isaac warned in his study paper that the cruelty was a result of the normative procedures in Roman executions and certain excesses by Roman soldiers. The emphasis on the suffering of Jesus, a central motif in many observances of the Passion, has contributed to the anger many Christians have felt toward Jews. This has been most notable in the Holy Week pogroms that terrorized Jews over the centuries. Careless rendering of history and inaccurate ascription of responsibility for the crucifixion resulted in vigilante-like revenge.

Christians who claim that Jesus' humiliation and suffering was without comparison, risk perpetuating through this hyperbole, a contempt for Jews who had no part in the crucifixion and who would not have participated in it had they lived in Jerusalem at the time. It is inappropriate and terribly insensitive to compare suffering. The suffering of one person does not negate or justify the suffering of another person. The only faithful response to suffering is to oppose and transform it. It is faithless and cynical to exalt the humiliation and suffering of Jesus to legitimate violence against Jews and attacks upon Judaism. Christians who do so must stand in the presence of burning children and say to them that their humiliation and suffering does not compare to Jesus' suffering on the cross; that their suffering is not real suffering.

The implications of Seelisberg Points five through nine judge institutional Christianity whenever it uses Jesus to isolate, torture, and kill Jews. Those Christians who believe that Jews are the enemies of Jesus and the church for all time, who blame Jews for the crucifixion, who hear the cry "his blood...." and ignore the prayer "Father, forgive them....," and who replace God's mercy with their judgment, must stand in the presence of burning children and say to them, "You deserve this fate because you and your ancestors crucified Jesus and because you have crucified him anew by refusing to accept him as your messiah."

IV. The Unfinished Agenda: A View from the Parish

For its time, the Ten Points of Seelisberg were bold and visionary. Forty-two years later, with the specter of burning children still before us, their cries still echoing in our ears, Seelisberg commands implications that should ignite a revolution in theological education, preaching, and teaching, and in the daily lives of believers. Burning children, tortured mothers, and gassed fathers should be the source of heretofore unimagined questions about the nature of God and covenant. They should be the reason behind a transformation of education that begins by examining the moral and humane uses of knowledge. They should disrupt and challenge not only Judaism, but values-neutral humanism, and the religion that turned murderously on its own roots. Gas chambers and crematoria should be relentless witnesses against unquestioned obedience to authority, uncritical conformity to nationalistic and triumphalist ideologies, and unconditional loyalty to a state or ruler.

My students at the University of Oregon helped me to understand why such changes come so slowly and they showed me that there was both a tremendous will to confront the implications of the Shoah and a profound and costly transformation awaiting those who examined their lives and futures in the presence of burning children. The struggle of one student illustrates the will and the cost, not only for academics, but any who allow their lives to be challenged by the Shoah. She was a pre-med major when she enrolled in my class on the literature of the Shoah. Her view of medical practice was only informed by an idealistic understanding of the Hippocratic Oath. All of the students read a history of the Shoah and a variety of books by survivors. At the end of the course, the students were required to submit a paper in which they addressed the implications of the Shoah relative to their vocational aspirations. She read sections from several volumes on the medical experiments at Auschwitz. Her innocent view of medicine and humanity was overturned by the Nazi medical doctors who conducted the experiments. Having confronted the dark side of her calling, she wrote of the awareness and fragile hope arising from her painful studies:

> As a pre-medical student and scientist, any future avenue I might take will require that I look closely at how I will apply my knowledge. I must be aware and cautious of possible inhumane uses of my knowledge and research. I hope I will be strong enough to use my knowledge for the benefit of the human community.

The Holocaust Now

If my personal experience and that of the majority of my students can be generalized, Christians and their religious institutions that undertake such a confrontation must expect that it will send crushing seismic waves through the structures of their lives and most likely shatter the paradigms with which they have built their values and worldviews. That cost will be seen as a small price to pay for standing in the presence of, truly listening to, and changing because of the experience of victims and survivors. Historically, Christianity has made important advances based on reform movements that sought religious and human freedoms, protection of human life and dignity, and civic responsibility. Once past the initial wrenching and pain, I expect that a genuine encounter with the Shoah would give Christianity a just and humane footing from which to enter the next century and the courage and strength to join with post-Shoah Judaism to confront the powerful forces of death at work in history.

A. The Difference the Shoah Makes: Loyalty

What shall be different because we begin our theology and live our faith in the presence or burning children? One antecedent contributing to the role of Christianity in the Shoah was the misplaced loyalty of many leading theologians, clergy, and laity. Instead of a complete commitment to Jesus and his compassionate and humane teachings, the loyalty of these Christians was to a religiosity that almost uniformly submitted to the emerging political order, to nationalism, and to the Volk. A Christian is called to follow Jesus exclusively and seek to know and hold fast to Jesus' teachings and the commandments [the Decalogue and Jesus' commandment to "love the Lord your God....and your neighbor as yourself"]. This loyalty is the essential security for believers who live in periods of great insecurity, turmoil, and evil. When one is faced by malevolent authorities, this loyalty is the liberating source of critical thinking and constructive suspicion [as contrasted to cynicism which robs people of power and causes them to disengage from difficult situations in which there are great social pressures to conform, competing interpretations, and ambiguous outcomes]. This loyalty will lead Christians to actively resist those laws—both civil and church laws—strategies, programs, and officials that foster mistrust and division, that contribute to injustice and oppression, that ultimately lead to the destruction of human life. In order to measure the effects of Christian loyalties, one need only contrast the misplaced loyalty, the failure of critical thought and constructive suspicion, and the fatal equivocations of theologians like Paul Althaus and Ernst Biberstein with the unambiguous commitment and courage of theologians like Dietrich Bonhoeffer and clergy like Martin Niemoeller [and those whose lives are memorialized by Gollwitzer].

In the Presence of Burning Children

B. A Problem of Obedience

A concomitant to misplaced loyalty was obedience to ill-willed authorities. When their religious commitment was diluted and their spiritual and ethical grounding was eclipsed, many Christians found themselves bereft of the resources with which to question or resist the directives and policies of the Nazis. Challenged by the murderous acquiescence of Nazi soldiers to their leaders, Stanley Milgram reached a chilling conclusion in his study on obedience to authority:

> ....ordinary people, simply doing their jobs, and without any particular hostility on their part, can become agents of a terrible destructive process. Moreover, even when the destructive effects of their work become patently clear, and they are asked to carry out actions incompatible with fundamental standards of morality, relatively few people have the resources needed to resist authority.[22]

Institutional Christianity did not help its adherents understand that loyalty to Jesus and obedience to the Biblical mandate to sanctify and preserve life have irreversible significance. A tragic lesson of the Shoah was the wide-spread failure of the seminaries and churches to ready the preponderance of the faithful to recognize and resist the evils of the National Socialist movement. Worse than that, it failed baptized believers who experienced no incongruity between their faith and the acts of burning children, shooting women into a mass grave, and gassing whole families. A politically astute remnant of Christians whose commitment led them to resist National Socialism did not establish their own laws, but rather followed a greater mandate, God's law of grace and love. These Christians knew that for their obedience to God, they must be prepared to spend years in prison, as Niemoeller and others did, or even to die, as Bonhoeffer and others did.

Nazi era rescuers, like the Christians who resisted the political rise of National Socialism, stand in stark contrast to those who were silent, complicit, or active participants in the Shoah. The rescuers had minimal ambiguity about their allegiance to Jesus and his teachings, no uncertainty about the Biblical origins of their resistance, no naivete about the possible consequences of their actions, and no confusion about their responsibility for others. Milgram concluded from his study on obedience to authority that: The disappearance of a sense of responsibility is the most far-reaching consequence of submission to authority."[23] Those who could not resist ill-willed authority, passed responsibility to the representative of authority, saying, in effect, "I only did what I was told to do," or "I was only following orders." They were also unable to assume responsibility for the fate of their victims because their loyalty had shifted its locus from a

Biblically-based ethical and humanitarian commitment to concern for satisfying fully the demands of the authority figure.

By contrast, Nazi era rescuers operated in a universe of Christian and humanitarian obligation that was without boundaries or limitations. The most moving example of this was a Polish woman who with her family hid thirteen Jewish refugees on their farm. A neighbor betrayed them for a reward. Warned that the Nazis and militia were enroute, they were able to send the Jews into the forest. When the soldiers could find no hidden Jews, they shot the woman's husband and eldest son as a warning to those who might consider giving aid or comfort to Jews. The next morning, before she had buried her loved ones, this woman had a new group of refugees hiding on the farm. By the end of the war she had saved forty-two more Jews. The course of the war turned against Germany and in the retreat soldiers were separated from their units. Many of the stragglers were killed by partisans or civilians. This woman hid several young German soldiers, and, in order to protect them, sent them on their way wearing the clothing of her murdered husband and son. She explained that the foot soldiers were innocent of the killings at her home or of Jews and that they should not suffer because of their leaders. Her behavior gives profound new meaning to Jesus' admonition "to love your enemies."

It must be noted that rescuers did not subscribe to a sentimental standardless altruism. After the war, rescuers actively sought justice for the victims of Nazi crimes against humanity. Herman Graebe's testimony, read before the Nuremberg Tribunal, set the tone for the trials and he spent the years until his death in 1986 pursuing War Criminals who evaded justice and challenging historical revisionists who denied the reality of the Shoah.

C. Christians With and Without Church Support

It is interesting to note that nearly half of the Nazi-era rescuers in my sample described themselves as post-institutional Christians. They emphasized that they considered themselves to be "good Christians" who read the Bible and were spiritual and prayerful, but could not bring themselves to attend church or did so only faintheartedly and occasionally because, during the war years, they did not receive the support or encouragement of the church. Two examples will illustrate their concerns. A Polish woman who lost her life saving Jewish children did not return to the church after her priest refused to provide her with baptismal certificates for the children. A devout German rescuer disdained the Lutheran tradition after his pastor refused his request for help in hiding Jews. A number of rescuers indicated that they did not turn to the churches for help because, as one rescuer put it, "I did not even think of the church as a place to look for support of my efforts." The implication of this finding is that many of the most faithful, moral, and compassionate people were driven out of the very institution that should sustain their values and work! What is to become of the individual churches that discourage altruists, but not the indifferent and not the killers?

A significant counterpoint to those who became post-institutional Christians are those who found strength and support within their parishes. A Dutch woman who saved some forty Jews is an example of the many. I spent several days interviewing her at Yad Vashem. During the second day of interviews she began looking at her watch. Several times I inquired about her fatigue or other commitments she might have. Finally, this eighty year old woman said, "I have truly enjoyed my time here, the reunions with those I love, but I am anxious to return home. You see, I am the coordinator of refugee settlements for my church and tomorrow we are welcoming two families who have lived on the South China Sea for months. I think I need to be there even though I am scheduled to remain here for another week." With strong loyalty to Jesus, clear values, an active religious life, and the ongoing support of her church, this woman, like so many others, continued to be a caring and helpful person.

The Nazi-era rescuers revive a healing view of humanity, they lift up the cause of kindness and human dignity, and they redeem our weakened hope for the future. Those who study the Shoah and live in the nuclear age must understand what enabled the rescuers to act as they did and realize that their actions did not come about ex nihilo, but rather were learned, grounded, rehearsed, and affirmed in ways that ensured their continued refining and practice. Our schools, colleges, universities, seminaries, churches, and synagogues cannot give less than that to their peoples. It is imperative that these primary institutions of society understand the work of the rescuers as an antidote to the tremendous death instinct at work in our times.

D. The End is the Beginning

I am compelled to end where I began, asserting that the location from which Christian theology and ministry must start and conduct their work is in the presence or burning children. If this is not the beginning point, I fear that theology and ministry will fail to prepare believers to resist the compartmentalization of labor, knowledge, and society which encourages reliance on external authority; the debilitating threats of thermonuclear war; the ravages of Apartheid; the new breeds of totalitarianism; the resurgence of racism, nationalism, and religious triumphalism; and the attraction of a self-interested indifference to the momentous problems and opportunities leading the world into the new century. If theology and ministry begin with the Shoah, the new paradigm which is birthed will restore hope and vision, loyalty and obedience. Then Christians will be better able to confront powers and principalities with constructive suspicion; to respond to the cries for help from torture cells around the globe and to the supplications of refugees from Central America, Southeast Asia, and the Eastern Bloc; and to resist those forces which deprive people of dignity, freedom, and life.

E. What the Shoah Reveals

The presence of burning children was a unique revelation to Christianity. It revealed that much of the Christian understanding of God was embarrassingly meager, untested in the face of murderous suffering, and often sublimely individualistic and self-serving. It revealed that before, during, and after the Shoah, much of what was heard from pulpits was "civil religion" which lacked relevance and the prophetic passion for justice and dignity. Civil religion neither challenged the political will of those in power nor commanded a humane response to the atrocities. Accompanying this revelation that religion and government had crafted a separate peace, which virtually eliminated the ability of the church to have an influential or moderating voice in politics and government. The Protestant origins of this unofficial concordat can be traced to 1525 when Martin Luther sided with the landlords and governors in the Swabian Peasant Revolt. Luther wrote and circulated a polemic entitled, "Against the Robbing and Murdering Hordes of Peasants," in which he attacked the peasants for abandoning their loyalty to their rulers, under the banner of Jesus. In 1933, Luther's treatise was placed in certain jail cells occupied by Germans who questioned or opposed the policies of the Reich. The message to dissenters was clear: loyalty to the state was paramount. It is little wonder that Christian leaders did not actively disassociate themselves from dependence on the state and state privileges.

The Shoah revealed the prevalence of the "cheap grace" Dietrich Bonhoeffer warned of in 1937 when he wrote:

> Cheap grace is the deadly enemy of our church....The sacraments, the forgiveness of sin, and the consolation of religion are thrown away at cut prices. Grace is represented as the Church's inexhaustible treasury, from which she showers blessings with generous hands, without asking questions or fixing limits. Grace without price; grace without cost![24]

He went on to describe the opposite, "costly grace:"

> Such grace is costly because it calls us to follow, and it is grace because it calls us to follow Jesus Christ. It is costly because it costs a life, and it is grace because it gives man the only true life. It is costly because it condemns sin, and grace because it justifies the sinner.[25]

In the Presence of Burning Children

Evangelical theologian Helmut Thielicke wrote a critique of post-war church services, that was certainly accurate for the war years as well, "Despite the times, from many pulpits we heard only very conventional, pallid sermons which did not reach men's hearts and left them cold. We seemed to be denied a prophetic awakening."[26]

Not everything that the Shoah revealed was negative. It revealed that in the absence of a powerful prophetic voice there was, once again, a remnant who refused to abdicate their faith and their humanity. In the histories of Judaism and Christianity, very often it is the faithful remnant that preserves and saves the hour, redeems the community, restores hope, and lights a way into the future. Post-Shoah Christianity can begin its rebuilding on the foundation of the loyalty, freedom, spiritual values, egalitarian worldview, compassion, and courage of Christian dissenters, victims and martyrs, rescuers, and drafters of such declarations as Barmen and Seelisberg.

F. Final Thoughts

Two concluding observations seem necessary as I review what I have written. First, I have assumed throughout that the Shoah is a uniquely Jewish experience in history and that its implications and lessons are universal. Politicians, peace activists, environmentalists, revisionists, and others have co-opted the name associated with Hitler's genocide, "the Holocaust," without sensitivity to the offense and pain this corruption of language causes. To speak of the "Holocaust" in relationship to anything other than the Jewish experience under National Socialism is a clear indication that the one so employing the term has not stood in the presence of burning children. The term "the Holocaust" does not belong to the world, but if there is to be a future free of such suffering, its implications and lessons must belong to the world.

Finally, Helmut Thielicke observed that in post-war Germany, "Instead of preaching of repentance and salvation, we had the proclamation of a collective guilt and a hysteria of self-accusation which was in need of psychological understanding rather than having any theological justification, and this led to a hardening of men's hearts."[27] While I do not agree that collective guilt and the hysteria of self-accusation have no theological justification or lesson, I am painfully aware of the way in which people's hearts can be hardened when they read about the Shoah ["read about" as contrasted to "learning from" its victims and survivors]. This chapter contains what may appear to some to be harsh conclusions bluntly stated. It is not my intention, estimable reader, to create a defensive barrier to the very reformation I seek, nor to be discordant or judgmental. I long for a greater reformation of Christianity than has occurred since 8 May 1945. It is my great love for Christianity and the church and my restrained hope for the future, not only of the church, but also the human family, that moves me to impatience and candor. It is also the case that for twenty years I have not found an acceptable or

The Holocaust Now

polite way to say what I feel must be said in the presence of burning children.

    I recently came upon the poetry of Wendell Berry. There is one particular poem that has become my prayer as I continue to probe the Shoah. I wish I had had it earlier and share it for those contemplating beginning or who are mid-course in the reformation.

>....These times we know much evil, little good
> To steady us in faith
> And comfort when our losses press
> Hard on us, and we choose,
> In panic or despair or both,
> To keep what we will lose.
> For we are fallen like the trees, our peace
> Broken, and so we must
> Love where we cannot trust,
> Trust where we cannot know,
> And must await the wayward-coming grace
> That joins living and dead,
> Taking us where we would not go—
> Into the boundless dark.
> When what was made has been unmade
> The Maker comes to His work.

CONTEMPORARY CHALLENGES

The Holocaust Now

In a World Without a Redeemer, Redeem!

For Michael Berenbaum, the lesson of the Shoah is clear: The world is an unredeemed place and will [forever?] continue to remain so. While critical of the fervent messianic pretensions and predilections associated with militant Orthodox Judaism, particularly in Israel, the ongoing task of humanity is not to wait for—or believe in—the coming of the Messiah [*beviat ha-Maschiach*], but to take upon itself the responsibilities to act as redeemers ["It is too late for the Messiah. The God who was silent then should be ashamed to act now."] Indeed, if the world possesses any possibilities at all of redemption, they will come about by dint of human effort and not by appeals to religious faith.

SLJ

The Holocaust Now

IN A WORLD WITHOUT A REDEEMER, REDEEM!

Michael Berenbaum

I. Israeli Zionism and Orthodox Messianism

The easiest affirmation I make as a Jew is that this world has not yet been redeemed. The evidence is so overwhelming—especially after the Shoah—that the point is just not worth arguing. This world has not been redeemed.

Jewish have been making the very same point since the beginning of the common era. We have been denying the Christ in its various forms, including Jesus of Nazareth, the nation-state, and, most recently, the Soviet state.[1] Yet the attraction to the Christ is equally strong, and, at moments, the yearning becomes most intense.

Even though it is much more difficult to believe in the Messiah and in redemption than to deny their presence in this world, Jews have striven for the redemption in diverse forms of religious life ranging from military revolution to quietistic piety. In the past, we have embraced for brief periods of time false Messiahs, often with disastrous results. From Bar Kokhba[2] to Sabbatai Sevi[3], the lure of a Messianic figure has been dangerous. Yet to resist this religious infatuation has been equally difficult.

Were one attempting a history of contemporary Judaism three decades ago, as did Arthur Hertzberg in his anthology on Zionism *The Zionist Idea*,[4] one could have written with confidence that, for the modern Jew, Messianism has become secularized, and only in its secular form has it achieved a modicum of success.

Certainly Zionism was built—directly and subliminally—on the Messianic impulse of the Jewish people. Theodor Herzl was received in Eastern Europe with the enthusiasm of a Messianic leader—secularized but Messianic nonetheless. The rabbinic leadership that resisted Herzl understood the true implications of his mission. They taught that Zionism was a human usurpation of divine prerogatives, an anti-religious revolution in Jewish life. Herzl, too, misjudged the character of his movement. He soon found himself forced to be mindful, if not respectful, of the Messianic impulse of the masses of Jews who would settle for nothing less than the historic land of Israel. They rejected the Uganda proposal approved by the Zionist leadership.

The Holocaust Now

Zionism, Marxism, Freudianism, and even some aspects of Reform Judaism imply a secularization of the Messianic impulse, and, hence, its limited realization. However, over the past thirty years, the greatest Messianic movements have been seen as the non-secular and anti-secular religious movements that have arisen in Israel and shaped a Messianic politics of settlements in Judea and Samaria and conflict with Arabs and between Jews.

These Messianic movements have been joined in recent years by an intensified Messianic urgency among Lubavitch Hasidim, who may be concealing or slowing revealing the Messianic role of their current Rebbe, Menachem Mendel Schneerson, now reaching his mid-eighties. Childless, he is without an apparent heir. Quite often, his followers in Israel will be awakened in the middle of the night and sent scurrying to the [Western] Wall to pray, and thus, according to believers, many disasters have been averted. Lubavitch Hasidim live with a considerable sense of agitation and those of us with contacts in the movement know that over the past few years, some followers have even spoken openly about the Rebbe's Messianic role.

There is considerable division within Orthodoxy as to the meaning of the modern State of Israel. In some quarters, Zionism is still condemned as anti-Jewish, a human abrogation of God's role to bring about the redemption. Nothing galls these leaders more than to see the Jewish people led by a brazenly unobservant and secular leadership. *Neturei Karta* and the followers of the Satmar Rebbe are the most notable adherents to this doctrine, but there are others and their presence within the religious community, and especially within the world of the *Yeshivot*, is prominent. Recently, they have sought to embarrass the State by attracting as converts—penitents—the elite fighters of the Israel Defense Forces [IDF], its pilots.

Rabbi Joseph Dov Baer Soloveitchik, the acknowledged dean of Yeshiva University Orthodoxy [which was once known as "modern Orthodoxy" and more recently as "centrist"], has written of the modern State of Israel as *kol dode dofek*, "the knock of my beloved".[5] The State is, perhaps, a manifestation of the Divine Presence within Jewish history. The evidence of God's presence is slight—only a knock—yet quite suggestive, but Soloveitchik is reluctant to stretch the evidence or to speak of the immediate implications of that Presence.

In the early years of the *Yishuv*, the first Chief Rabbi of Palestine, Abraham Isaac Kook, compared the Zionist enterprise to the building of the ancient Temple—even the least pious of workers was able to move about freely on the entire Temple mount, including the Holy of Holies, the most sacred site in the consecrated Temple. The Holy of Holies could be entered only once a year and only by one man: On Yom Kippur, the High Priest would enter this most sacred site only after a period of penitence and cleaning as prescribed in the a demanding ritual. So, too, Kook ruled, to build the new Holy of Holies, it is permissible to work with secular Jews until the moment of its consecration.[6] Kook thus bridged the gap between the Yishuv and non-Zionist Orthodoxy, granting only transient legitimacy to the early pioneers. He did conceive of the Zionist endeavor as *reishit tzemichat geulateinu*, the "first flowering of our redemption," language that was later incorporated into the official prayer for the State authored and sanctioned by Israel's Chief Rabbis. Kook's vision of redemption was gradual, proceeding by this worldly and rather unorthodox means and linked directly with the Land of Israel. Kook made peace with the necessity of Zionism even while he denied its longevity.

Some students of Kook, such as the late Zvi Yaron[7], argue that Kook's chosen metaphor was more designed to appease the Orthodox than to make a directly theological statement, but it seems clear that he never accepted the legitimacy of the Zionist enterprise in an ultimate sense, as a permanent and acceptable way of sustaining the Jewish future.

The tension in Kook's initial position has come back to haunt his followers, most especially his late son Rabbi Zvi Yehudah Kook, who became the spiritual force behind the settler movement, many of whose members were trained in his Yeshiva, Merkaz Harav.

Two events intervened, the twin revolutions of modern Jewish history, the Shoah and the rise of the modern State of Israel. Elsewhere, I have written of the revolutionary impact of both events, and these writings need to be repeated here. Suffice it to say, that no generation of Jews has lived history quite as intensely as ours, save, perhaps, the ancient Israelites who went from Egyptian servitude to the Event at Sinai, and spent the next forty years attempting to understand precisely what had happened. No future Jewish theology will be credible without grappling with both the Shoah and Israel. And certainly both loom large in the imagination and identity of every Jew.

The Shoah remains in the background for Rabbi Zvi Yehudah Kook and his disciples. Yet even for them—no less than for the post-Shoah theologians—Auschwitz poses serious theological dilemmas. Unwilling to forsake their belief in God and Torah, Zvi Yehudah Kook and his followers are forced to reunderstand the timetable of history. The Shoah is thus approached as *the* apocalyptic event, the great battle between the forces of good and evil, between Gog and Magog. An event of such magnitude forces thinking to a different level of interpretation. Apocalyptic catastrophe sets the stage for the redemptive events of Israel.

While for many secular Jews, 1948 marks a turning point in Jewish history, *the* event of modern Jewish history for the younger Rabbi Kook and his *Gush Emunim* disciples is not the foundation of the modern State with its secular Declaration of Independence, but the miraculous victory of 1967, the reunification of Jerusalem, the restoration of the Temple Mount to Jewish rule, the return of that same Jewish rule to the ancestral lands of Judea and Samaria, and the religious resurgence that followed this mammoth victory. Thus, the *Hallel* Psalms will be recited on the 28th of Iyar, *Yom Yerushalayim*, on the day of the reunification of Jerusalem, but not on the 5th of Iyar, *Yom Haatzmaut*, Israel's Independence Day.

I vividly recall the sixth day of the Six Day War, the Shabbat on which the war ended. On Friday evening, we gathered in the old Hillel House building on Balfour Street in Jerusalem. The synagogue was filled with student soldiers, many enjoying a few moments of free time, ready to being the *Kabbalat Shabbat* Service, when the then-President of Israel, Schneur Zalman Shazar, walked in accompanied by the then-Chief Rabbi of the Israel Defense Forces, General Shlomo Goren. Naturally they were invited to speak. Goren, who was to introduce the President, spoke of Shazar as the first President of a unified Jerusalem and of an Israel restored to its land. He also declared that, on Monday, Shazar would be the first to greet the Messiah of Israel as he rode down Jaffa Street in Jerusalem. Goren had had a busy week. He had blown the *shofar* at the [Western] Wall on Tuesday; he had flown to the Sinai on Wednesday and again blew the shofar from atop one of the hills which we had declared the site of the theophany. And while anything was believable in the euphoria of Jerusalem on June 10, 1967, Goren seriously believed that the Messiah would arrive imminently. He was not alone. And in twenty years, the ardor of some has only intensified.

In contrast, Shazar spoke in measured, poetic tones. Known for his long-winded, sermonic addresses, Shazar was uncharacteristically brief and crisp. "All my life," the Israeli President—a fellow traveller though not a disciple of Lubavitch—whispered, "I prayed, 'clothe yourself with the garments of majesty, O Jerusalem', and today I lived it. *"Rav lach sevat beamek habachah,* 'you have sat enough in the valley of tears'" he said with tears in his eyes, paraphrasing the words of Lecha Dodi. His expectations, unlike those of Rabbi Goren, were modest and simple. His joy intense yet sober. Shazar reflected that day, the other dimension of the victory: the sober, cautious realism of those given to fervor but not to Messianic abandon.

The tensions between his views and Goren's persist to this day within religious circles.

Yonina Talmon has argued that Messianic movements are never the product of catastrophe alone. They are born of the imbalance between expectation and reality, of the disappointments that follow a period of sustained hope.[10] During the past half century, Jews have endured quite a buffeting. Victims of the epitome of inhumanity in a governmentally-sponsored and systematically-structured mass genocide, we have also witnessed the flourishing of hope with the rebirth of the Jewish people in its ancestral land only three years after the destruction. Yet even the history of the State has also been characterized by cycles of despair and hope—war and armistice, then war and triumph crowned by the return to Jerusalem, followed by an enormous explosion of energy and enthusiasm and then followed by two devastating wars less than a decade apart. Attacked on the most solemn day of the Jewish year, Israel lost 2,500 soldiers in the Yom Kippur War along with a sense of its invulnerability. Nine years later, it lost one fifth as many men, but something almost as important as well—confidence in the righteousness of its cause, the wisdom and integrity of its deeds.

Religious Messianism in Israel is nourished by social realities. In Israel there are four parallel—separate but equal—school systems, a secular Jewish school system, a religious school system sponsored by the State, an ultra-Orthodox system sanctioned by the State but with minimal governmental involvement, and an Arab school system. Almost without exception, religiously-observant Jews attend a religious school system. They also belong to religious youth movements and can serve in the Army in a program that permits them to both study at Yeshiva and engage in army study at one and the same time. Thus, Israeli Orthodox youth are raised in self-segregated societies designed to preserve their religious world-view. Often they reach their early twenties without encountering secular peers with a cognitively dissonant world-view. Increasingly as well, they live in neighborhoods segregated according to religious observances: ultra-Orthodox enclaves, religious neighborhoods, and secular areas.

For the better part of a half century, the ideology that dominated Israeli society and provided it with its core of values was secular Zionism. During the past twenty years, the motivating power of this world-view has waned as the four basic promises of secular Zionism remain unrealized despite the incredible triumph of the State of Israel. Secular Zionism has promised normalcy, independence, an end to Jewish vulnerability, and the ingathering of the exiles. Yet Jewish life continues to be abnormal and the State of Israel remains abnormal as a state among the nations of the world. "A nation set apart," rather than "a people like any people" defines the reality of contemporary Israel. So, too, Israel received independence precisely as the world has become interdependent and the sovereign state finds itself interdependent with the Diaspora—whose demise Zionism had predicted—for financial and political support, and interdependent, if not dependent, on the United States for an economic, political, and military lifeline.[11]

Furthermore, power and sovereignty have not ended Jewish vulnerability; they have altered the means by which we combat our vulnerability. An unanticipated sense of vulnerability persists. Finally, while Israel has absorbed more than two million immigrants, over the past twenty years, the number of *yordim* has exceeded the number of *olim*. There are more Israelis in New York than in Jerusalem. And Israelis increasingly come westward for an encounter with cosmopolitan culture just as American Jews come as pilgrims to Israel in search of their Jewish roots. Mutual exchange rather than absorption has characterized Israel's relations with the North American Diaspora. So total has been the collapse of the secularist Zionist vision that Zionism is often treated as a term of derision rather than a lofty ideal.[12]

The Holocaust Now

Militant nationalism and religion have stepped into the vacuum created by the decline of Israel's civil religion of secular Zionism. Both never expected normalcy nor did they fully believe that Jewish vulnerability could be ended. They never sought to be integrated into the world, but rather to stand apart from the world—either by necessity or because of a national religious vocation. In the movement of Gush Emunim, they have fused into a Messianic, nationalist movement.

II. The Theology of Yehuda Amital

Perhaps the most interesting—though not necessarily the most influential—theological exposition of the Messianic religious Zionist perspective was presented by Rabbi Yehuda Amital, the head of Yeshivat Har Etzion, a Talmudic academy set in the rebuilt Etzion block destroyed by the Jordanians in 1948. Amital's *Hamaalot Mamaakim, Ascent from the Depths,* is a slim, powerful collection of addresses on the religious meaning of war and his speeches to the Yeshiva students on the meaning of the hour.

From the Six Day War, Amital argues, we learned that war can serve a redemptive purpose, since, without any desire on Israel's part, and following a specific request to King Hussein that Jordan stay out of the war—the Jewish people were restored to the city of Jerusalem and all the sacred sites. Although the Yom Kippur War at first appears to be an anti-redemptive manifestation of history, the opposite may be the case in so far as Israel's military victory was greater than in 1967.[13]

The choice of the Yom Kippur as the day to begin the war, Amital reasoned, was an implied attack on Jews and Judaism—an assault by Islam against the Gold of Israel—yet the Western nations were the real losers of the war. The false Western God—the god of technology—was clearly addicted to oil and cheap supplies of energy. Israel's massive victory against powerful armies and overwhelming odds was a great act of divine salvation, Amital told his students. The purpose of the war was to mold and purify the Jewish people into a spiritually pure unit able to withstand the pressures of the Messiah's footsteps. He called for a reintensification of efforts, a deepening commitment that is equal to Messianic stakes.

Amital was politically astute in his assessment of the West, yet stubborn in his refusal to see the war as stemming from real grievances and fought for military/diplomatic purposes. He returns to the language of a pre-secularized warfare, a language sanctioned by tradition yet one which classical Zionism sought to overturn. He has further immunized his disciples and their fellow travellers from responding to political pressures, viewing all such compromises as a retreat from a divinely-mandated task.

Amital's position is even more interesting because he moderated his views after the war in Lebanon. Given the militant patriotism of the *hesder* Yeshiva students [those to divide their army service between the Yeshiva study and military duties], they vol-

In a World Without a Redeemer, Redeem!

unteered for the elite units of the IDF often replacing or serving alongside Labor Zionism's elite, the *kibbutzniks*. In Lebanon, for the first time, Yeshiva students were on the front lines and suffered disproportionately high casualty rates. Amital's response was bold. He told his students that Jewish responsibilities to the Land of Israel must be balanced by a commitment to the Torah of Israel and the people Israel. If the former is emphasized to the exclusion of the other commitments, then the future of Israel is misconstrued. While the war in Lebanon may have hardened many positions, it moderated at least one. Amital was immediately ostracized by his former political allies.

III. Catastropic Implications and the Shoah

It is understandable that a non-secularized Messianic striving in contemporary Israel has led to idealism and self-sacrifice. It has also led to terrorism and to fundamental assaults on Israeli democracy and the rule of law. It sustains a climate in which apocalyptic politics can become the norm for a significant segment of society and apocalyptic politics in a nuclear age is a sure prescription for catastrophe. Given the scope of such serious and disciplined Messianic movements, we must again understand the full implications of the Messianic impulse.

After the Spanish Expulsion, the religious response to catastrophe took the form of Lurianic Kabbalah, which deepened our understanding of exile and made more difficult, though also more concrete, the task of redemption. According to Lurianic Kabbalah, exile was ontological—part of the primordial experience of creation.[14] The divine sparks were scattered by a cosmic catastrophe. And redemption was gradual, almost painfully slow, acts of *tikkun*, of restoration, reuniting one by one the divine sparks with their source.

If such was the response to Expulsion, what then should be our response to the Shoah? It is too late for the Messiah. The God who was silent then should be ashamed to act now. Jews can no longer affirm what Gershom Scholem called the anti-existentialist posture of Messianism.[15] Both Gush Emnunim and Lubavitch have joined secular Zionism and American Judaism in their commitment to a religious and political life of activism. They have become active in forcing the "hand of God"[16]. Jews can no longer wait for God but must become the initiator. On this we concur.

Yet, while it may also be too late for redemption in a global sense, but it is certainly not too late to redeem.

Emil Fackenheim returned to the Lurianic tradition when he sought to describe the post-Shoah reality of life. Where Rabbi Isaac spoke of *shevirat hakelim* [the breaking apart of the vessels—Ed.], Fackenheim writes of the rupture and returns to the image of tikkun, translated as "mending" rather than restoration, to describe the aftermath of the rupture.[17] The garment may be sown whole, but the original rent remains even after tikkun. It will never become whole again in an unbroken seamless fabric. On Purim, 1967, three months before the war, Wiesel described Auschwitz as the breaking of the covenant established at Sinai.[18] Richard Rubenstein's image was even starker: Auschwitz was nothing less than the death of the God of history—at least within the experience of the believer.[19] In my own work, I have preferred the image of the void, absence where presence has been.[20] Other radical images of the Jewish condition have also been offered. As with the generation after the Expulsion, we live at a time of shattering, of broken vessels, where the reality of exile—of non-redemption—is decisive.

Our response must be equally clear. After the rupture, mend, Fackenheim tells us. The possibility of mending—even the model of mending—was offered amidst the darkness, so we know what has to be done. Mend the rupture, he exhorts us.

Unlike Maurice Friedman[21], I believe that Wiesel offers no more compelling image of the redemptive task that when he writes in *The Town Beyond the Wall*:

> To say 'I suffer, therefore I am' is to become the enemy of man. What you must say is 'I suffer therefore you are. Camus wrote somewhere that to protest against a universe of unhappiness you had to create happiness. That's the arrow pointing the way: it leads to another human being and not via absurdity.[22]

So, too, he wrote in 1967:

> In a world of absurdity, we must invent reason, we must create out of nothingness. And because there is murder in the world—and we are the first to know it—and we know how hopeless our battle may appear, we have to fight murder and absurdity and give meaning to the battle, if not our hope.[23]

While in his later work, Wiesel may flirt with the Messiah and return to traditional language with intensified urgency, the task of redemption has been reduced to a human scale. God has been replaced by the human image, "the image of a people who have routed defeat and survived in community, in celebration, in solidarity, in hope, in despair, in pain and in violence."[24]

In my own religious life, the Sabbath plays a much more significant role than the Messiah because the Sabbath is part of the week, in dialogue with the week, a foretaste of what can be, a moment of redemption that points back to the world rather than away from it. And the Sabbath does not make promises that it cannot keep.

In *Evil and the Morality of God*, Harold Schulweis has suggested a predicate theology. Instead of speaking of God, we speak of godliness and instead of speaking of redemption, Schulweis suggests, we go about the business of redeeming, deed by deed, person by person, spark by spark. The Messiah is therefore neither a person nor an event, but a series of actions that heal, save and console, that create hope after despair and empower the powerless and redeem the oppressed rather than consecrate those who have arrived.

I do not believe with a complete faith in the coming of the Messiah, but while he/she tarries, I will strive to redeem every day until....

Perhaps God will surprise us. Perhaps not. But the human task is clear and the Jewish task is our covenant with history and with memory made more urgent by what we have experienced and more poignant by the longings of generations.

A decade ago I wrote: "perhaps for Wiesel, to be a Jew after Auschwitz is to hope for a Messiah and to work for a Messiah while knowing full well that the hope is for naught."[25] Over the past decade, it has become less true of Wiesel and more and more true of my own life especially as I grow increasingly fearful of the politics of those who would work for a Messiah in the traditional sense. I remain convinced that the task is both necessary and vital—but only if it grounded in the sober realism of the work that is not redeemed nor likely to be. From the Shoah we can learn the urgency of the task. From Messianism in contemporary Israel, we must learn the dangers of religious infatuations. From our Lurianic forebears, we can learn much about modesty and humility—and also about the duration of the struggle.

The Holocaust Now

Marc Ellis' challenging and provocative essay criticizes Shoah theology for not going far enough in its legitimate concern for Jewish survival, dealing as it does only with the Jew as victim and for becoming a political "tool" in the hands of both the Israeli and American Jewish communities. Like Rosemary Radford Ruether in Volume II, "Theological and Ethical Reflections on the Shoah: Getting Beyond the Victim-Victimizer Relationship," he focuses on the newly-empowered State of Israel and its supporters in the American Jewish community, both of which he chastises for only learning *Jewish* lessons of victimization from the Shoah and ignoring the legitimate and rightful claims of the Palestinian people. In so doing, however, he reasserts the role of theology as questioner of the *meaning* of historical events, painful though the events may be, and the implications to be derived therefrom.

SLJ

The Holocaust Now

AFTER AUSCHWITZ AND THE PALESTINIAN UPRISING

Marc H. Ellis

I. Introduction

The decisive victory of Israel in the June 1967 Six Day War crystallized certain trends in Jewish theological understanding. In a sense, the war itself heightened the dialectic of Shoah and empowerment present in Jewish life since the discovery of the death camps and the emergence of the State of Israel. Many Jews felt that a revolution in theological thought was needed to match the revolutionary change in the Jewish condition characterized by the loss of European Jewry, the shift in diaspora Jewish power to North America, and the reality of a Jewish state. After the Six Day War, that revolution was accompanied by Shoah theologians who, in despair and courage, chartered a theology that is now normative for the Jewish community throughout the world.[1]

In the years after the 1967 war, Shoah theology, as pioneered by Elie Wiesel, Emil Fackenheim, Richard Rubenstein, and Irving Greenberg, was radical and incisive. It named the collective trauma the Jewish people had experienced as *a*, or often as *the*, formative event of Jewish history. Though diverse and often at odds with one another, Shoah theologians generally juxtaposed the Shoah with the Biblical origins of the Jewish community to pose the question of God's fidelity to a covenanted people. Among other ideas, they challenged the Rabbinic tradition both in its theological analysis of the diaspora condition and the type of leadership, or lack thereof, it provided in the Shoah. At the same time Shoah theologians critically analyzed the other side of modernity with its landscape of mass dislocation and mass death.[2]

If the formative event of the Shoah made necessary retrospective probing of traditional Jewish understandings in the theological and political realms, it also called for the development of a framework for sustaining Jewish survival in the present. Shoah theologians understood quite correctly that the Shoah was the most disorienting event in Jewish history. Thus in the midst of broken lives and shattered faiths, Shoah theologians began to articulate a future for the Jewish people.[3]

Herein lies the genius of the Shoah theologians: they understood that the prospective search need be as radical as their retrospective probings. Within the radical questioning of past and future, the Jewish people would continue to need a sustaining faith, but Shoah theologians recognized that this would no longer be overtly theological in the present. Hence, in order to survive in the face of a disorienting event, Shoah theologians had to redefine what it meant to be Jewish. The ancient definition of a practicing Jew as one who engaged in study, ritual, and observance of the Law was no longer adequate, and Shoah theologians knew it. At the same time, they also understood that religious affiliation or non-affiliation after the Shoah was an insufficient test of fidelity to the Jewish people. What Shoah theologians offered instead was a framework to integrate diverse experiences and outlooks into a strong solidarity with the future of the Jewish people. No longer would the primary commitment to synagogue, to liberal/radical politics, or to an assimilationist indifference suffice. Instead, Shoah theologians broached a broad and energetic commitment to the commands of the Shoah experience: memory, survival, and empowerment, especially as embodied in the State of Israel. It was these commands that allowed for the continuation of the people so that at some point in history, there would be a context for the resolution of the questions posted by the Shoah. In a sense, Shoah theologians gathered the people together for the only kind of Sinai experience possible after the Shoah.[4]

The new Sinai, in gathering Jews of different persuasions into a transformed covenant, demanded a radical probing of the diverse worlds Jews lived within, including the worlds of Christianity and modernity. Indictment of historical Christianity was simple enough, at least in its overt institutional capacity; apathy toward, complicity in, and solidarity with the murderers was the order of the day. The "righteous gentiles" were clearly a minority to be mentioned, though often in passing and surely as exceptions. The collapse of European culture and values, the need to emphasize the dark side of the ideology of progress, the failure of the democracies to respond to massive Jewish refugee populations—these were more difficult issue to face. Modernity, as a promise to the world of human betterment and freedom, and especially emancipation for the Jewish people, needed a radical analysis as well. Thus, Shoah theologians confronted a dual crisis of massive proportions involving the shattering of the Jewish people and modernity.

Just as they responded to the crisis of Jewish life by creating a framework for solidarity among the Jewish people, Shoah theologians responded to the crisis of modernity by envisioning a solidarity for those consigned to the other side a century of progress. Richard Rubenstein and Irving Greenberg have crystallized this struggle to articulate a theological thesis for our time: "The passing of time has made it increasingly evident that a hitherto unbreachable moral and political barrier in the history of Western Civilization was successfully overcome by the Nazis in World War II and that henceforth the systematic, bureaucratically administered extermination of millions of citizens or

After Auschwitz and the Palestinian Uprising

subject peoples will forever be one of the capacities and temptations of governments." They explained further that the "victims ask us, above all, not to allow the creation of another matrix of values that might sustain another attempt at genocide." The terrible tragedy of the Shoah thus lay in the future as much as in the past.[5]

By the mid-1970s Shoah theologians had addressed the crisis of the Jewish people and modernity, proposed a framework for solidarity among the Jewish people and others suffering around the world, and thus had outlined the essential dimensions of Shoah theology as we inherit it today. Shoah theologians had succeeded in the task that faces all theology: to nurture the questions that allow us to understand the history in which we are participating and creating. Yet it was at this moment, the time when Shoah theology became normative for the Jewish people, that its critical edge became elusive. Shoah theology was succumbing to that to which all theologies inevitably succumb: it no longer could address the questions critical to the history the Jewish people were creating. The reasons for this failure are complex and beyond the scope of this essay. Suffice it to say here that Shoah theology emerged out of a situation of powerlessness that demanded a mobilization of psychic energy and material activity toward empowerment; the dialectic of Shoah and empowerment acted as a counterbalance and a critique of weakness and empire. However it did not have within it a way of analyzing power once it had been achieved. Because of the experience of Shoah, the theology lacked objectivity regarding power in Jewish hands. It could not and does not address the case of Jewish empowerment.[6]

In fact, as the situation in Israel changed over time, with expanded borders, two decades of occupation, the invasion of Lebanon, and an increasing role in global arms sales and foreign policy intrigue, Shoah theology's dialectic remained as it had crystallized at the moment of the 1967 triumph. What did change was its emphasis on empowerment. The critical role of the Shoah diminished. We might say that in this process the Shoah became the servant of power, called upon to legitimate activity that hitherto was seen as unethical, even immoral. Jewish in the United States were in the most difficult situation of all diaspora communities: maintaining highly visible support of Israel and creating the climate for an expanded American role in support of that state as necessary for its survival while being relatively powerless to affect Israeli domestic and foreign policy, even when in profound disagreement.[7]

As Shoah theology lost its ability to enter critically into the contemporary situation of the Jewish people, its reliance on empowerment became more and more obvious. A strange paradox ensued that continues today: a theology that poses the most radical religious and ethical questions functions politically in a neo-conservative manner. Not only are the most articulate Shoah theologians neo-conservative in their political stances; they help to legitimate the shift of Jewish intellectuals from the left to the center and right of center on the political spectrum. Even Shoah theologians with previous liberal credentials bear analysis: by the 1980s Irving Greenberg, who wrote so eloquently about the prophetic call of the victims of the Shoah in the 1970s, was essentially supporting the re-emergence of American power under Ronald Reagan. At the same time, he warned against the misuse of the prophetic to undermine the security of the State of Israel: "There is a danger that those who have not grasped the full significance of the shift in the Jewish condition will judge Israel by the ideal standards of the state of powerlessness, thereby not only misjudging but unintentionally collaborating with attempted genocide." The subliminal if not overt message is clear: those who dissent carry a heavy burden, even to the point of creating the context for another Shoah.[8]

II. Memory as Burden and Possibility

For many Jews, especially since the Palestinian uprising and its brutal suppression by the Israeli government, the burden of proof has shifted. Instead of criticizing dissenters as Shoah theologians are wont to do, more Jews are beginning to analyze the politicized use of the Shoah as a way of crushing dissent and mobilizing the community to repress Palestinian aspirations to human dignity and justice. If Shoah theologians recognized and articulated the Jewish desire to cease to be victims, others are recognizing a similar Jewish desire not to oppress another people. Though this has not as yet reached a theological articulation, criticism of the politicized used of the Shoah in relation to the State of Israel may lead to such a theology. In short, recent discussion of the Shoah beyond Shoah theology opens up the essential choice before the Jewish people: if the memory of suffering is to be a burden to us and to others or a possibility for healing and justice.

In a recent essay Phillip Lopate, a Jewish essayist, reopens what for Jews is an extremely emotional subject. He begins with a most provocative title: "Resistance to the Holocaust." Lopate's intention is less to speak of the atrocities of the Nazi era, which are to his mind "enormous and unforgivable," than to address the cultural, political, and religious uses to which the disaster has since been put. Born after World War II, but before the term "Holocaust" had become commonplace, Lopate as a child heard "concentration camp; gas chambers; six million Jews; what the Nazis did .' Some might see it as an improvement to use a single designation for the event. Yet for Lopate, placing a label on such suffering serves to tame the experience. As use of the term Holocaust became more common in the mid-sixties, Lopate found it to have a self-important, almost vulgar, tone: "Then, too, one instantly saw that the term was part of a polemic and that it sounded more comfortable in certain speakers' mouths than in others; the Holocaustians [sic—Ed.] used it like a club to smash back their opponents....In my own mind I continue to distinguish, ever so slightly, between the disaster visited on the Jews and the 'Holocaust.' Sometimes it almost seems that 'the Holocaust' is a corporation headed by Elie Wiesel, who defends his patents with articles in the Arts and Leisure section of the *Sunday Times.*"[9]

Taken in a certain context, Lopate's words seem almost too easy. Yet it is clear throughout that he is participating in the most ancient of Jewish practices: refusing idolatry insofar as the Shoah, or the use of it, become crystallized, untouchable, almost a God. What suffers, of course, when everything is reduced to the Shoah or analogous to the Shoah is the ability to think through the issues that confront the Jewish people. As Lopate notes: "The Hitler/Holocaust analogy deadens all intelligent discourse by intruding a stridently shrill note that forces the mind to withdraw. To challenge the demagogic minefield of pure self-righteousness from an ironic distance almost ensures being misunderstood. The image of the Holocaust is too overbearing, too hot to tolerate distinctions. In its life as a rhetorical figure, the Holocaust is a bully."[10]

The Shoah as a bully can also become Shoah as kitsch. The Israeli author Avishai Margalit explores this theme in an essay titled "The Kitsch of Israel." According to Margalit, kitsch is based on an easy identification of the represented object; the emotion evoked in the spectator comes simply from a reference to the object. Although genuine art always maintains a distance from the represented object, thus involving the spectator in interpretation and allowing a variety of perspectives to emerge, the idea of kitsch is to arouse a strong emotion from the spectator's relation to the original object. Thus, in the Jewish context, a glimpse of Masada, or the Wall, or the Temple Mount is enough to move the "Jewish heart," and the marketing of Israel takes full advantage of these images. Kitsch can also be politicized and become, in Margalit's terms, part of a state ideology whose "emblem is total innocence." The image of the Israeli soldier and the Wailing [i.e. Western—Ed.] War are two such items of kitsch, evoking easy emotional identification with the important secondary understanding of a beleaguered nation. Of course, as Margalit points out, the opposite of total innocence is total evil: "The innocent and pure with whom we sympathize have to be relentlessly protected from those plotting their destruction."[11]

For Margalit, however, the place that should be furthest from such easy emotion, Yad Vashem, the Shoah memorial in Israel, has, paradoxically, become an element of state kitsch. He cites a recently dedicated children's room, pitch dark with tape-recorded voices of children crying out for their mothers in Yiddish. As Margalit remarks, this kind of kitsch even a "kitschman of genius" like Elie Wiesel would find hard to surpass: "The real significance of this room is not its commemoration of the single most horrible event in the history of mankind—the systematic murder of two million children, Jewish and Gypsies, for being what they were and not for anything they had done. The children's room, rather, is meant to deliver a message to the visiting foreign statesman, who is rushed to Yad Vashem even before he has had time to leave off his luggage at his hotel, that all of us here in Israel are these children and that Hitler-Arafat is after us. This is the message for internal consumption as well. Talking of the P.L.O. in the same tone as one talks of Auschwitz is an important element in turning the Holocaust into kitsch."[12]

Margalit reports that with the outbreak of the Palestinian uprising, when criticism from within and outside Israel has reached its peak, the increased evocation of Shoah memories is noticeable. Included is a Shoah quiz show, shot in Poland, on which young Jews are asked questions relating to the massacre of Jews in Europe. For each correct answer two points are awarded. Applause is forbidden as being in bad taste. Margalit's conclusion: "Against the weapon of the Holocaust, the Palestinians are amateurs. True, some of them have adopted their own version of Holocaust kitsch, based on the revolting equation of the Israelis with Nazis and of themselves with Nazis' victims; but as soon as operation 'Holocaust Memory' is put into high gear by the Israeli authorities, with full-fledged sound-and-color production, the Palestinians cannot compete. The absence of the main actor and the stage queen, Begin and Golda, is certainly a loss for political kitsch, but a new star has risen, Benjamin Netanyahu ['Arafat is worse than Hitler.'], and prospects are now bright—nothing will make us cut the kitsch."[13]

Increasingly in Israel, the Shoah is seen in a similar light, as an event that is consciously manipulated by the state and it leadership. This is the theme of Boaz Evron, an Israeli writer and commentator, in his essay "The Holocaust: Learning the Wrong Lessons." For Evron, two terrible things happened to the Jewish people over the last half-century: the Shoah and the lessons learned from it. The ahistorical interpretations of the Shoah made deliberately or out of ignorance have become in Evron's mind a danger both to the Jewish people and to the State of Israel for the following reasons: The term "Holocaust" is rhetorical and ambiguous; it exists without historical reference and thus has become indefinite and movable, almost exempting one from understanding it. "The murder of the Jews in Europe," though not as galvanizing, more accurately reflected and locates a historical event in which there were murderers and those who were murdered. Such an even become worthy of historical investigation and is lifted from the mystical pseudo-religious. By analyzing the historical context, Evron finds different lessons to be drawn from the event than Shoah theologians do. For example, Evron points to the basic assumption that the Nazi policy of mass murder was directed almost exclusively against Jews. The facts speak differently: Gypsies and three million non-Jewish Poles were murdered, and millions of Russian prisoners of war and forced laborers were murdered as well. The enslavement and extermination of the Slav people was almost a possibility for the Nazis. For Evron, antisemitism served as "catalyst, as the focal point of the extermination system" that was destined to become a central and permanent institution of the Third Reich.[14]

Thus the Nazi murder of the Jews was unique only in preparing the world for the institutionalization of extermination. The argument presented as a corollary, that the Jews of Palestine were saved by Zionism, is also false: they were saved by the defeat of the Nazis at El Alamein and Stalingrad, which prevented the Nazis from conquering Palestine and exterminating the Jewish population. The lesson of the Shoah is therefore different: "The true guarantee against ideologically-based extermination is not military power and sovereignty but the eradication of ideologies which remove any human group from the family of humanity." For Evron, the solution lies in a common struggle aimed at overcoming national differences and barriers rather than increasing and heightening term, as strong trends within Israel and Zionist movement demand.[15]

There were many reasons why the historical presentation of the murder of the Jews in Europe was rejected for an ahistorical view summarized in the word "Holocaust." According to Evron, the Germans were interested in this because it limited, in a sense, their liability. Instead of focusing on the systemic and expanding possibilities of a system of extermination, a focus that might have kept alive the feelings of fear and suspicion after the War in Germany's neighbors, limiting the memory of the Jews and the Shoah enabled Germany to more easily reintegrate itself into the world of nations. The Western powers were also interested in this insofar as it allowed them to wipe the slate clean and begin to rebuild Germany as a barrier to Soviet expansion.[16]

The "Jewish monopolization" of the Nazi experience was also welcomed by Jewish leadership in Israel and in the Diaspora, as a way of strengthening German guilt, thus continuing and increasing the amount of compensation payments for survivors, and as a way of mobilizing world support, moral, political, military, and financial, for the Jewish state. For Evron, this new and creative policy of inducing moral guilt was a prime reason for the Eichmann trial. It shifted the tragedy out of the past and made it a basis for future preferential relationships. And as importantly, this policy became a blueprint for relations with most Western Christian states, especially the United States; they were to support Israel on the basis of guilt rather than self-interest.[17]

Evron sees the ramifications of this policy to be enormous. In the first place, it contravened an aim of the Zionist movement to normalize the status of the Jewish people and reduced Israel to the "level of an eternal beggar." Henceforth, Israel survives on the "six million credit" instead of, like any other country, on developing and marketing its energy and skills. Living off its past, Israel exists, like the Shoah, in an ahistorical context, thus avoiding economic and political confrontation in the real world. Paradoxically, a renewed feeling of isolation grows as the adulation of the survivor Israel increases. The policy also generates what Evron considers a moral blindness: because the world is out to get Israel in the present and in the future, any links with oppressive governments and any oppression of non-Jews within and around Israel can be justified.[18]

The Shoah can also be used as a powerful tool by Israel and Jewish leadership in the United States to organize and police the Jewish community. Diaspora Jews, for example, are made to feel guilty for not having done enough to prevent the Shoah; at the same time the message is conveyed that Israel is threatened with annihilation. The message is clear: unequivocal support for Israel prevents a second Shoah. Evron sees the image of the Shoah past and Shoah future as so important to Israel and American Jewry that the reality of Israel's strength is submerged in myth:

> When you try to explain to American Jews that for many years to come we will be stronger than any possible combination, that Israel has not, in fact, been in danger of physical annihilation since the first cease-fire of the War of Independence in 1948, and that the average human and cultural level of Israeli society, even in its current deteriorated state, is still much higher than that of the surrounding Arab societies, and that this level rather than the quantity and sophistication of our arms constitutes our military advantage —you face resistance and outrage. And then you realize another fact: this image is needed by many American Jews in order for them to free themselves of their guilt regarding the Holocaust. Moreover, supporting Israel is necessary because of the loss of any other focal point to their Jewish identity. Thus, many of them resist the suggestion that the appropriate aim for Israel is to liberate itself from any dependency on outside elements, even Jewish ones. They need to feel needed. They also need the "Israeli hero" as a social and emotional compensation in a society in which the Jew is not usually perceived as embodying the characteristics of the tough, manly fighter. Thus, the Israeli provides the American Jew with a double, contradictory image—the virile superman, and the potential Holocaust victim--both of whose components are far from reality.[19]

The equation of Arab hatred of Israel with the Nazi hatred of Jews, for Evron, arises logically out of the ahistorical quality of the Shoah. The Nazis, who created an irrational hatred of the Jews so as to justify the system of mass extermination, are likened to the Arabs, who, according to Evron, have a quite rational reason for opposing Israel as a powerful enemy that has expelled and displaced over a million of their compatriots. The difference between an illiterate Palestinian refugee and a highly trained SS trooper is blurred beyond distinction, and the defense of the country in the Six-Day War and the Yom Kippur War becomes less an integral part of the sovereign political existence than a stage on which the destiny of the Jewish people is played out. Identifying Palestinians with Nazis, as the continuous reminder of the Shoah does, leads to hysterical responses rather than reasoned policy. These parallels have serious moral consequences as well. Because the choices presented to Israel are not realistic—only Shoah or victory—Israel becomes free of any moral restrictions, because any nation that is in danger of annihilation feels exempted from moral considerations that might restrict its efforts to save itself. For Evron, this is the rationale of people who argue that everything is permitted because the world wants Israel's destruction. "They do not hesitate to recommend the most drastic steps against the non-Jewish population in Israel. Although it is a serious comparison to make, it is worth remembering that the basic Nazi claim justifying the slaughter of Jews was the 'Jewish conspiracy' to destroy the German nation." Evron concludes that Israeli and Jewish leadership, caught up in an ahistorical world, threaten to become victims of their own propaganda. They draw on a bank account continuously reduced by withdrawals. As the world moves on there are fewer who remember the Shoah, and those who do, including the Jews, become tired of it as a nuisance and a reflection of a reality that does not exist: "Thus the leadership, too, operates in the world of myths and monsters created by its own hands. It has created this world in order to maintain and perpetuate its rule. It is, however, no longer able to understand what is happening in the real world, and what are the historical processes in which the state is caught. Such a leadership, in the unstable political and economic situation of Israel today, itself constitutes a danger to the very existence of the state."[20]

III. Solidarity with the Palestinian People

With Lopate, Margalit and Evron we come full circle. In the beginning, the Shoah necessitates empowerment; the misuse of the Shoah generates doubt about the use of Jewish empowerment to close off dissent and oppress another people and ultimately may even endanger empowerment itself. Critique of the politicized use of the Shoah reasserts the dialectic of Shoah and empowerment rescues the Shoah from becoming subservient to an empowerment which takes on a life of its own. To a profound degree, the reassertion of the dialectic of Shoah and empowerment returns us to the original question first posed by Shoah theologians: the future of the Jewish people. But if this question came to articulation in the miraculous victory of the 1967 War, hence Shoah and empowerment, the question of the future of the Jewish people today is raised within the confines of present history and thus includes the Palestinian uprising and the aspirations of the Palestinian people. In sum, though enormously complex and with tremendous ramifications, the dialectic of Shoah and empowerment must today broaden to include a solidarity with the Palestinian people. Thus the step beyond the impasse of Shoah theology and the critique of its politicized use lies in a paradoxical embrace of those whom we as Jews have oppressed.

The Holocaust Now

What does this solidarity with the Palestinian people mean today? What are the foundational visions which may shape this concept of solidarity into flesh and blood reality?

The first step, of course, is to abandon the two-rights understanding, as if the question of Jews and Palestinians is a symmetrical one. Whatever one wants to argue from the Jewish side vis-a-vis Jewish history—our difficult history in Europe which gave rise to Zionism and the culmination of that history in the Shoah, which provided the final impetus for the birth of the Jewish state—the effect for Palestinians has been brutal, even catastrophic. A. B. Yehoshua, the Jewish-Israeli novelist, writes that the "concept of historic right has no objective moral validity when applied to the return of the Jewish people to its land." Rather, as a committed Zionist, Yehoshua argues that the Jewish people have a "full moral right to seize part of *Eretz Yisrael* [the Land of Israel], or any other land, even by force," on the basis of a right he calls the survival right of the endangered. His underlying proposition is as follows: "A nation without a homeland has the right to take, even by force, part of the home-land of another nation, and to establish its sovereignty there." Thus Yehoshua, unlike most Jews, admits of what might be termed a "necessary theft," [a] "moral invasion," as it were. But to hold the Palestinians responsible for resisting that theft or to expect them to accept it is in Yehoshua's eyes ridiculous, as is the extension of that theft to the rest of historic Palestine, that is the possible annexation of the occupied territories. For Yehoshua, the basis for the Jewish right is the seizure of a part, and thus if Jews intend to extricate themselves from the "situation of a people without a homeland by turning another people into a nation without a homeland, our right to survival will turn to dust in our hands."[21]

Whatever one thinks of Yehoshua's foundational argument that the survival of the Jewish people is linked to a territorial sovereignty—a position that should be probed in a deep way by Jewish thinkers—his two-rights position moves well beyond the typical expression of Jewish innocence and Palestinian demonism. Though his book bears the English title *Between Right and Right*, his argument speaks of Jewish necessity, the dispersal of Palestinians, and the rights of Palestinians to resist. Thus the title might be better rendered as *Between Jewish Necessity and Palestinian Rights to A Homeland*. Accordingly, it could be that the formation of Israel was necessary in its historical moment and at the same time wrong vis-a-vis the Palestinian people. The original sin [sic-Ed.] was European antisemitism, not Palestinian resistance to a Jewish state. But even here, if one accepts Yehoshua's analysis of historical necessity in seizing only a part of the land, the framework he maintains is strictly separatist. That is, the necessity of survival, the formation of a Jewish state, is extended beyond the historical moment into a relentless future: to survive physically and culturally Jews must be separate in their own land for the remainder of world history. The moral invasion is to flee the fire and to build a new home among others who have fled the same fire. Those who fled the

After Auschwitz and the Palestinian Uprising

Jewish fire must re-build their own homes somewhere else.[22]

Here the "two state" position, while seemingly progressive, needs to be questioned within the framework of solidarity. The entire burden of proof is placed on the Palestinians. For example, the two-state position as argued by most Jews, including Yehoshua, places primary responsibility on the Palestinians to, among other things, demonstrate their ability to live peacefully with Israel, to renounce their fundamental claims of sovereignty over all of Palestine, to guarantee a demilitarized state with Israeli security positions within Palestine and the right of Israeli invasion if militarization occurs. At the same time, it also limits forever the size of Palestine to one-fifth its original land mass in the least fertile part of Palestine. Among other things, it assumes, at a foundational level, that Israelis should be afraid of Palestinians but Palestinians have nothing to fear from Israelis, a position that many Palestinians in their diaspora find surprising, if not untenable.[23]

Though a two-state solution may be the only practical possibility at the moment, it falls far short of the solidarity requisite to the crisis which confronts both sides. Most Jews, for instance, see the two-state solution as a way of ridding themselves of the Palestinian "problem" demographically and morally. Give them their state and Jews are free of a possible Palestinian majority, hence the preservation of the Jewish state; Jews are also morally cleansed of having expelled, beaten, tortured, and murdered Palestinians, thereby protecting the purity of the Jewish soul. The position is clear as Amos Oz, the Jewish-Israeli novelist describes it: granting a divorce between Jews and Palestinians. The image is equally clear: separate Jewish and Palestinian states with a wall so high that Jews will never have to see another Palestinian. Palestinians will be banished from Jewish history.[24]

The desire to preserve, or rather reassert, Jewish innocence by banishing the victims of Jewish oppression is understandable and inadequate. It allows Jews to retreat from this confrontation with Palestinians and within themselves as if the bloodshed had not occurred. By allowing Jews to see themselves in their pre-state identity, they ignore the brutality of which Jews are capable, thus ignoring Jewish post-state reality.

That recent Jewish history is covered with blood through our contemporary oppression of Palestinians is a lesson absolutely necessary for Jews as a people. We cannot come to grips with our recent history unless we see the Palestinians now as intimate to our self-identity and capabilities as a people. That is, the victims of Jewish power are as intimate to us as we are to those who oppressed us. Confronting the Jewish abuse of power is impossible without the physical preservation of Palestine in our midst, and the prospects of Jewish healing both in its trauma of European mass murder and in its trauma of beating and expelling another people cannot be worked out alone.

Progressive proponents of the two-state solution seek to banish the bad Jewish conscience in a way that delays the future with the history Jews have created. Thus a genuine Jewish progressive position is dependent on moving beyond the State of Israel and the State of Palestine into a genuine vision of confederation which allows both autonomy and integration of Jews and Palestinians. Of course, this also leaves open the possibility of a Palestinian return to parts of Palestine that would be closed off in a two-state scenario. If genuine solidarity is to be gleaned, then the Palestinians have a right to be healed of their own trauma of displacement, thus allowing a new perspective on their own catastrophe. Only a Palestinian right to return can authenticate what the Palestinian educator, Muhammed Hallaj, has described as the interlocking destiny of Jews and Palestinians. In short, the argument for a reality of Jewish and Palestinian life together in historic Palestine moves beyond the typical Jewish concern for Jewish purity and innocence by envisioning a future which recovers the deepest ethical impulses of the Jewish people in confrontation with the reality of Jewish history.[25]

But arguing from the Jewish perspective does not in the least diminish the Palestinian recovery by placing it solely with the Jewish framework. The Palestinian future is for Palestinians authentic and self-generating. Their desire or refusal to live with Jews is of course their decision to make within the context of Palestinian history. Jewish life as interlocking with Palestinian life is an absolute necessity from the Jewish perspective, but is, in my view, entirely optional from the Palestinian perspective of living on the other side of Jewish power.

Solidarity with the Palestinian people moves beyond romanticization and demonization. Solidarity with the Jewish people in Europe was an ethical and practical necessity not because all Jews were beautiful but because Jews as a people were innocent. As documented by many Jewish historians, the Jewish ghettos had heroes, ordinary citizens, criminals, and collaborators. The behavior of Jews towards other Jews ran the gamut of great charity to unbridled brutality, and, of course, everything in between. And the Palestinians are no doubt similar in regard to their complexity, and, in this situation, their innocence. Hence, Jews often want it both ways: a retroactive demand of rescue of all Jews during the Shoah, coupled with no discussion of Jewish internal realities outside the framework of innocence. Similarly, they reject any connection between Jewish rescue and Jewish behavior just a decade after the Shoah, or even today, but find it surprisingly easy to take to task Palestinians with regard to the policies of the Palestine Liberation Organization, an example being the Palestinian reaction to Iraq's invasion of Kuwait, and anything that seems to compromise Palestinian innocence from a Jewish perspective. They also constantly link the Palestinian struggle for liberation with the policies of a future Palestinian state, as if the unknown future should determine the level of support for the current struggle. Thus, as Jews, we rightly shift the burden of proof to those who oppressed us, but, in a strange twist now continually shift the burden of proof to those whom we are oppressing.[26]

After Auschwitz and the Palestinian Uprising

To accept this analysis is to radically change the Jewish perception of the Israeli-Palestinian conflict, from two rights to wrong and right; from aberration to continuity; from the need for "corrections" to a radical critical evaluation. As important, and as difficult, is the radical reevaluation of Jewish self-understanding these statements imply. Israel is not innocent, and neither are we: our claims on suffering are now forfeited. Our claim to chosenness, even in a secularized form, has become irritating rather than compelling. Israel is not redemptive; and neither is our empowerment. Instead, Israel, and for that matter the politicized use of the Shoah, is a burden to the Palestinian people and to the Jewish people as well. The question of Israel and the remembrance of the Shoah so central to Jewish identity have become something other than expected and so have we. Is it possible to see ourselves as a people organized to destroy another people without radically reevaluating who we have become as a people? And, if we have betrayed our suffering, and our empowerment is built on the blood of others, where are we to turn in order to reconstruct a way of being Jewish in which we can recognize our own faces and hearts and realize the deepest impulses of the Jewish people?

This is the task before us, one that will need the skills of politics, ethics and theology to successfully realize. In Emil Fackenheim's analysis of the imperatives of the Shoah in 1968, he emphasized the need for sheer survival of the Jewish people in order to face the questions of Jewish history and a possible Jewish future. Today, just [a little more than] two decades later, in a way that Fackenheim could not then and does not today understand, in a momentous inversion, the survival of the Palestinian people provides the possibility of a Jewish future. There is not doubt what the German Catholic theologian Johann Baptist Metz had in mind when he envisioned the future of Christians and Jews after the Shoah in these words: "We Christians can never go back behind Auschwitz: to go beyond Auschwitz, if we see clearly, is impossible for us by ourselves. It is possible only together with the victims of Auschwitz." In light of the Palestinian uprising, these words assume new meaning relative to the common journey of Jew and Palestinian. For Jews the challenge might be stated thusly: "We Jews can never go back behind empowerment; to go beyond empowerment, if we see clearly , is impossible for us by ourselves. It is possible only with the victims of our empowerment, the Palestinian people."[27]

IV. Toward A Jewish Theology of Liberation

The inclusion of the Palestinians in the historic drama of the Jewish people is to recognize our responsibility within empowerment and to realize that the test of a people's maturity and judgment is the ability to critically evaluate the history it has created. To seek empowerment after a history of victimization is natural and good; to create a new set of victims ultimately undermines that empowerment. Simply put, the destiny of Jew and Palestinian is intimately connected.

Though there are many strands of the Jewish tradition to be looked at in this regard, the most obvious and ancient is the theme of liberation. And while having political, economic and cultural dimensions, the theme of liberation has always been a basic theological question as well. The Israelites, in becoming a people, also chose a God who would be with them in their struggle for liberation. A crucial phase in this struggle and choice was an atheism toward theologies which held these diverse tribes in subjugation. Thus the Israelites said a profound "No" to political and religious ideologies which enforced injustice and a "Yes" to political and religious realities which led toward liberation. Of course, in the struggle for liberation new forms of oppression, both internal and external, appeared. The prophets were those who called attention to the tendency toward internal and external oppression. Social and political relations within and outside the nation of Israel were, according to the prophets, key to the question of the relation of the people to God.[28]

What is suggested here is not a return to the Biblical God as related in the Exodus and Sinai; Shoah theologians have correctly pointed out the new Sinai needed after the Shoah. But the need for a remembrance of Jewish suffering and for Jewish empowerment is hardly in a theological sense sufficient in and of itself. The triumph of a militant empowerment can only lead on the one hand to an angry and expansionist religious fundamentalism, as we have seen markedly in Israel, and on the other a continuing and militant alienation from the Jewish community by a majority of Jews. In short, the broken tension of suffering and empowerment is not only leading to the oppression of the Palestinian people; it is leading to a civil war within the Jewish community. The triumph of religious fundamentalism and alienation from the Jewish community may lead to the end of the Jewish tradition, or the development of a new Judaism almost unrecognizable to those born in the first generation after the Shoah.[29]

The theological challenge is therefore straightforward: Can the new Sinai called for by Shoah theologians move beyond militant Zionism and extreme alienation? The challenge in turn poses a further question: Can we in the Jewish community move toward a healing of our own wounds without binding the wounds of others, wounds that we have caused? Does not the task of Jewish theology rest in this challenge and question? And if we approach this challenge and question, mindful of our history and tradition, is it not here that the reality of liberation might take hold?

We know at least two roads, from the negative side, which will not yield a serious approach to liberation? the maintenance of our innocence and the proposition that Israel is redemptive. In fact, our experiences tell us something different. As it turns out, in the concrete reality rather than our wishful imaginings, where we as Jews have power we do most every-thing that has been done to us. Though the claim is that we

After Auschwitz and the Palestinian Uprising

were forced into things by our enemy [a claim made by most everyone who has power], the reality is something different. Historically vis-a-vis the Palestinian people, Israel has been and continues today to be expansionist and oppressive. Our innocence on this essential point, of course, does more than mask the facts; it helps preserve our sense of ourselves as victims *which we are decidedly not today*. A radical critique of Israel thus serves as a challenge to an essential part of Jewish identity, the perception of ourselves as victims. The sense of victimhood and innocence then reinforces the Jewish sense of powerlessness and isolation, even if we are more powerful than at any time in the last two thousand years, and, at least in the West, more accepted and integrated than ever before. In a strange twist, Shoah theology must state boldly that we as Jews are no longer innocent and in this way confront our own self-perception with the reality of our situation.[30]

At some point, and the sooner the better, Jews will also have to admit that Israel is not redemptive. A central aspect of Shoah theology and Jewish identity is tied to the dream of redemption as embodied by Israel, but the realities contradict the dream. As it turns out Israel is a state like any other; it has, for example, selfless public servants and corrupt political officials. Israel has corporations and prisons, white collar crime and prostitution. Aspiring to democracy, at least for its Jewish citizens, Israeli society, like most societies, has well-defined social and economic classes as well as a social order which exhibits widespread cultural and racial discrimination. Israeli occupation forces do essentially what all occupation forces do: they repress, displace, deport and torture the people whom they occupy. In one sense the discussion of Israel as a state, society, and occupying force seems elementary, but Jewish discussion, especially within Shoah theology, rarely, if ever analyzes Israel in this way. Israel is a dream of redemption, but the reality is something different.[31]

At another level Jews within and outside of Israel know the other side of Israel. For years, before the latest influx of Soviet emigres forced to come to Israel, more Jews have left Israel than emigrated to it. The estimated number of Israelis in permanent residence in America and Canada, for example, is at least five hundred thousand and may approach one million people. Considering that the Jewish population of Israel is just over three million people, this is a large percentage of the Israeli population which has sought homes in other countries. And how many Jews from the United States have emigrated to Israel and stayed there? Despite the rhetoric the number is almost too small to mention: some fifty thousand Jews from the United States over more than four decades, a figure which does not include the number who have returned. Interestingly, of the four most prominent Shoah theologians, only one, Emil Fackenheim, lives in Israel, and this after his retirement. Shoah theologians are representative of the Jewish population at large: choosing to live outside of Israel. The point here is simple if it was not obfuscated by Jewish theology: Jewish people contradict the notion of Israel as redemptive with their bodies, which remain elsewhere. We do not as a people seek to live in what has become an isolated garrison state. Despite our theological ruminations, Jews, even after the Shoah, choose to live in Western democratic secular states as equal partners with non-Jews.

The addition of solidarity to the dynamics of Shoah and empowerment can only come by moving beyond innocence and redemption and therefore into a critical reevaluation of recent Jewish history and our own choices within it. But if our identity is bound up with the sense of innocence and redemption, even if we know differently, what is there on the other side? If we accept loss of innocence and understand that Israel is not redemptive, where and who are we as Jews? What, then, is our identity if it is no longer based on innocence and redemption?

The difficulties here are many and the reason we cling to this identity, despite all evidence to the contrary, lies within this difficulty. All of this has come upon us too suddenly: the Shoah, then Israel, then our realization that we are no longer victims and that Israel has become something other than we expected. In the larger sense, we have become something other than we expected or that our theology tells [us] we are. We might say that a new Jewish theology must begin with a celebration that we are no longer victims and a lament that we, like others, have created victims. That is, our call for redemption has become a form of domination over others and ourselves. We are weighed down by the burden of our history and our aspirations. Boldly stated, the memory of the Shoah and the State of Israel have become burdens to the Jewish people. The question is whether we are going to continue to labor under this burden and burden others with it, or choose another path: to see our suffering and the limits of our empowerment as a path of solidarity toward other struggling peoples, including and especially, those who labor under our power, the Palestinian people. Using our history of suffering and our new-found power as an opportunity for solidarity rather than as a blunt instrument of oppression, paradoxically opens up the possibility of healing the Jewish trauma of the Shoah.

Here lies before us the question of liberation, less in a final drama of messianic redemption than in a mature struggling with the limitations and beauty of life, with the suffering and hope of humanity and our small but significant contribution to the human future. Does the Shoah lead to a small garrison state, if you will an empowered ghetto, or to a difficult embrace of the world which rejected us? Hidden here is the explosive question of whether the world has changed, whether for instance Western Christians have been transformed from enemy to friend. But one suspects that though the behavior of Christians toward Jews has changed dramatically, the Jewish image of the Christian as enemy has hardly changed at all. Is this because if Jews recognize that Christians can transform themselves from enemy to friend, we might also have to admit that we have transformed ourselves from victim to oppressor? Do we seek to freeze the world at the moment of Shoah because it serves our purpose of remaining, at least in our own mind, victims and innocent? Does our present sense of chosenness revolve around this claim of ultimate victims, and does our perceived status in the world directly relate to this claim? To see ourselves always as victims, of course, perpetuates our brokenness and our isolation. Is this what we want to bequeath to our children? And if this ultimate victim status allows a blank check to Israeli power, will we have any tradition worth inheriting?[32]

Perhaps it would be better to simply admit that the experience of Shoah has led us to the conclusion that only a new form of Judaism, based on statehood and power, can help navigate Jewish survival in a hostile world. Surely then we must admit to the formation of a Constantinian Judaism which, like Constantinian Christianity, links religion and state power, where religion, granted its realm of freedom, agrees to bless the state and legitimate state power. Whether we want to admit it or not, Shoah theology has assumed this posture: it is a theology in service of the state. In Constantinian Judaism the religion continues and becomes even more publicly evident. Rabbis are produced in great number and the synagogues become more expensive and beautiful. Unfortunately, these elaborate synagogues, like the Medieval Cathedrals of Europe, sacrifice depth even as they gain their symbolic public importance. Judaism continues but the bottom, as it were, drops out: the ethical commands praised in prayer are in reality practiced less and less and more often transgressed. In fact transgression, rather than aberration, is woven into the structure of Jewish life. This is, the logic of Jewish state power in Israel is the elimination of Palestinians from Jewish life and therefore is embedded in the very structure of the state. If this logic is not critically confronted then it must be declared off-limits to critical discourse. To a large extent this has already occurred. Silence is assumed, then counselled. If silence is broken and reality spoken publicly, penalties can range from social ostracism to excommunication from the Jewish community.[33]

Yet Constantinian Judaism is always reminded through text and tradition that a Jewish ethical inheritance remains, and that those ethics are part of a covenant once accepted at Sinai. A corollary is that the covenant remains even in periods of the eclipse of God and that at these times it is even more urgent to seek out others beyond the Jewish community for solace and strength. The main thrust of the Jewish tradition in a sense becomes even clearer in light of the Shoah and Israel, that is the movement toward community and away from empire. The temptation of empire is a warning of dislocation and fragmentation and a reminder of the possibility of community.

The original Sinai seems to have embodied this temptation and possibility: leave empire [Egypt], form community [Sinai], tend back toward empire [Solomon], be reminded of community [prophets]. Thus the Israelites were called from empire to community and soon it was realized that the test was the people's tendency toward one or

The Holocaust Now

the other, and that somehow the question of God was intimately involved in this choice. Can we today place the realities of Shoah and Israel within the dialectics of community and empire? And might the question of God be related to this choice? Or put more subtly, is it possible to approach the question of God after the Shoah if we decide, light of our domination, to dominate another people? Or does the possibility of the question of God take on new form if after the Shoah and Israel we again choose community, especially with the Palestinian people? Thus the preservation of Palestinians in our midst involved the possibility of our healing, as related earlier, but also may allow us to approach the question of God in a different way. If in feminist parlance the personal is political, the political is also theological. There is a Jewish community, beyond a warrior God and an empty secularism, beyond the conquest of another people and a convenient silence, and that position is found in the pursuit of community.

Within the claims of innocence and redemption, within the tendency toward empire, there are voices who assert that community is the only way forward for the Jewish people, and that within this path the possibility of liberation arises. And strangely enough this voice was sometimes spoken within the ultimate empire, the death camps, much more clearly that it is today. Within Constantinian Judaism one hears, as a subversive witness, the voice of the Dutch Jew, Etty Hillesum, who, despite the possibility of escape, accompanied her own people to Westerbork and then Auschwitz. In Hillesum we find hope for a world beyond suffering, that indeed Jewish suffering might become a clarion call for community. In her March 21, 1941, diary entry, Hillesum writes of forgiveness as a way of refusing to hate even the enemy. Her solidarity with the Jewish people extends to those caught up in a system that dehumanizes and in effect murders the conquerors as well.

> What a bizarre new landscape, so full of eerie fascination, yet one might also come to love again. We human beings cause monstrous conditions, but precisely because we cause them we soon learn to adapt ourselves to them. Only if we become such that we can no longer adapt ourselves, only if, deep inside, we rebel against every kind of evil, will we be able to put a stop to it. Aeroplanes, streaking down in flames, still have a weird fascination for us-even aesthetically-though we know, deep down, that human beings are being burnt alive. As long as that happens, while everything within us does not yet scream out in protest, so long will we find ways of adapting ourselves, and the horror will continue. Does that mean that I am never sad, that I never rebel, always acquiesce, and love life no matter what the circumstances? No, far from it. I believe I know and share that many sorrows and sad circumstances that a human being can experience, but I do not cling to

them, I do not prolong such moments of agony. They pass through me, like life itself, as a broad, eternal stream, they become part of that stream, and life continues. And as a result all my strength is preserved, does not become tagged on to futile sorrow or rebelliousness.

And finally: ought we not, from time to time, open ourselves up to cosmic sadness? One day I shall surely be able to say to Ilse Blumental, "Yes, life is beautiful, and I value it anew at the end of every day, even though I know that the sons of mothers, and you are one such mother, are being murdered in concentration camps. And you must be able to bear your sorrow: even if it seems to crush you, you will be able to stand up again, for human beings are so strong, and your sorrow must become an integral part of yourself, part of your body and soul, you mustn't run away from it, but bear it like an adult. Do not relieve your feelings through hatred, do not seek to be avenged on all German mothers, for they, too, sorrow at this very moment for their slain and murdered sons. Give yourself all the space and shelter in yourself that is its due, for if everyone bares his grief honestly and courageously, the sorrow that now fills the world will abate. But if you do not clear a decent shelter for your sorrow, and instead reserve most of the space inside you for hatred and thoughts of revenge-from which new sorrows will be born for others-then sorrow will never cease in this world and will multiply. And if you have given sorrow the space its gentle origins demand, then you may truly say: life is beautiful and so rich. So beautiful and so rich it makes you want to believe in God.[34]

Two years later on July 3, 1943, just months before her deportation to Auschwitz, Hillesum concluded with the hope:

All I wanted to say is this: The misery here is quite terrible; and yet late at night when the day has slunk away into the depths behind me, I often walk with a spring in my step along the barbed wire. And then time and again, it soars straight from my heart-I can't help it, that's just the way it is, like some elementary force-the feeling that life is glorious and magnificent, and that one day we shall be building a whole new world.[35]

The Holocaust Now

Theological and Ethical Reflections

For Rosemary Radford Ruether, whose own work *Faith and Fratricide: The Theological Roots of Anti-Semitism* [1974] may be perceived equally as "foundational" as that of Richard Rubenstein's *After Auschwitz: Radical Theology and Contemporary Judaism* [1966], in delineating the need for the centrality of a reformulated Christology in light of the Shoah, her current re-examination of both Jewish and Christian thinkers reveals a critique not previously encountered among Christians: the use of Shoah theology as a means of Jewish empowerment in American and in Israel, particularly with regard to the Palestinians. Here, Ruether moves beyond the Shoah in focusing on the Jewish People now as "normal human beings, capable, like any other people, of taking power in a dominating way and using it to make victims of other people." The questions she asks—"Who is going to be the victim of our liberation? Who is to be enslaved by our redemption?"—are, in essence, part of her theology of consistent universalism, not allowing either the particularism of Jewish thinking or the philosemitism of Christian thinking, either fundamentalist or liberal, to erect barriers to a reality leading to disengagement of Jews, Christians, and/or Arabs.[1]

SLJ

The Holocaust Now

THEOLOGICAL AND ETHICAL REFLECTIONS ON THE SHOAH: GETTING BEYOND THE VICTIM-VICTIMIZER RELATIONSHIP

Rosemary Radford Ruether

I. Introduction: Redemption Through Genocide

In the midst of the Second World War, Adolf Hitler, leader of the German people, conducted a systematic campaign to exterminate European Jewry. This genocidal campaign was directed at all Jews, on the basis of what was presumed to be a shared racial nature. It did not matter if the Jew was male or female, infant or elderly, culturally assimilated into German or other European societies or set apart by traditional Jewish dress, speech and way of life, secular or religious. Even if the Jew was a convert to Christianity did not finally matter, although there was some distinctions made on this ground at first. For Hitler and Nazi ideology, a Jew was a Jew. All belonged to one racial nature, which Nazism regarded as inimical to the national 'purity' of the Aryan race.

In Hitler's paranoid worldview these two races, Aryan and Jew, were set apart, not simply as superior and inferior types of human beings, but as ontologically opposite species of good and evil. The Aryan was exalted above the merely human to the heroic; the Jew was sunk below the creaturely to the pestilent and the demonic. To exterminate the Jew was, in Hitler's mad fantasy world, to redeem the Aryan from the dangers of 'contamination' by a disease of mental, moral and physical weakness and to inaugurate the Third Reich, the Germanic millennial age of undiluted virility.

This crusade of redemption through genocide almost succeeded. Six million Jews were annihilated. This meant not only more than one-third of the Jews of the world at that time, but also ninety percent of the rabbis and religious scholars of Eastern and Western European Judaism. The Shoah pulled up an entire culture by the roots. Although individuals may survive from these communities of European Jewry and return to live in small numbers in places like Warsaw or Amsterdam, the cultural communities of Jewry that existed in these cities before the Second World War can never be reconstituted. The Nazi Shoah was more than the killing of a large number of individuals. It was *ethnocide,* the effort to destroy a people as a cultural entity.

The more traditional Jews of the Eastern *shtetls* [villages—Ed.] were the least likely to escape. Although remnants of these people with their traditional culture may have been transplanted to America or to Israel, a void has been left in the heart of the human community of peoples that can never be filled. Like the extinction of one of the species of creation, when a national community is exterminated, a distinct and irreplaceable part of reality has been destroyed, never to be restored.

This enormity happened in the 'heartland' of Western Christian Europe: the land of Goethe, Beethoven, and Mozart; of Kant, Hegel and Schelling; of the founders of modern Christian theology, Schleiermacher, Ritschl and Troeltsch. Germany was the center of the Christian Enlightenment, from which flowed the classics of modern European literature and music, philosophy, theology and Biblical studies. It happened with the passive acquiescence or active collaboration of most European Christians and with no decisive protest from church leadership, Catholic or Protestant.

Many individual Christians sought to save their Jewish neighbors at the risk of their own lives, but official church leadership did not mobilize in united protest. Even the Confessing Church in Germany, under the intrepid leadership of theologians like Karl Barth and Dietrich Bonhoeffer, were primarily concerned to protest against a Nazi 'cultural Christianity' and failed to focus on Nazi antisemitism as an issue.[2]

II. From Story to Theology

For both Jews and Christians in the post-War period, the Shoah throws the viability of their religious traditions into question, but in quite different ways. Yet it took more than two decades for theological reflection on the Shoah to begin to be articulated, and for Jews and some Christians to recognize that theological business as usual could not continue after this fissure had opened up in the world.

For almost two decades there was virtual silence from theologians, Jewish or Christian. Perhaps this was because, before there could be Shoah theology, the Shoah had to be articulated as story. Meaningless chaos must be shaped as meaning, even if only as the meaning of meaninglessness, the speaking about the unspeakable. Elie Wiesel's first book, *Night,* was published in Yiddish in 1956 and became available in French in 1958 and in English in 1960.

The first Jewish religious thinker to name the Shoah as a major crisis for traditional Jewish theology was Richard Rubenstein in the mid-1960's. Rubenstein, a non-establishment Jewish religious scholar, published his foundational book, *After Auschwitz: Readical Theology and Contemporary Judaism* in 1966. In this volume, Rubenstein questioned the very possibility of faith in God after the Shoah.

Theological and Ethical Reflections

Emil Fackenheim, a German Jew transplanted to Canada courtesy of British internment camps for German refugees, had been writing primarily on Hegel and religious philosophy, with no reference to the Shoah. As he himself admits in an article published in May, 1970, in *The Christian Century*, before 1967, he was "at work on a theology that sought to show that nothing unprecedented could call into question the Jewish faith—that it is essentially immune to all secular events between Sinai and the Messianic days."[3] Fackenheim took up Rubenstein's challenge and began to write about the possibility of religious faith after the Shoah.

Rubenstein, in a reply to this article by Fackenheim, also published in *The Christian Century* [July 29, 1970], said that Fackenheim was the first Jewish theologian to "agree with me concerning the unique and decisive character of Auschwitz for Jewish religious life." Rubenstein said "at the time I wrote After Auschwitz, one could search through almost everything written by contemporary establishment [Jewish] theologians without finding the slightest hint that they were living in the same century as Auschwitz or the rebirth of Israel."[4] [There is an unconscious irony in the appearance of this exchange in a journal named *The Christian Century*, for this journal was given this name in 1900, in order to signify the expected triumph of Christianity in the twentieth century.]

By the early 1970's the Shoah had become a key theme of theological reflection for Jewish and Christian theologians. In 1974 a major conference, held at Saint John the Divine Cathedral in New York City, brought together the leading Jewish and Christian thinkers that had made the Shoah a central lens for viewing and revisioning their religious traditions.[5] For Jews, particularly for American Reform Jews, the Shoah would become the new normative theology, central to modern Jewish identity. For Christian theologians a focus on the Shoah was more the specialty of a few thinkers rather than a central paradigm. But it was increasingly incorporated into the thought of major Christian theologians.

This difference is understandable [if not excusable] since the Shoah challenged traditional Jewish and Christian religious self-understandings in quite different ways. For Jews, the Shoah, as an attempted extermination of Jews as a people, the central issue was theodicy. If God is in charge of the world, and is the God who elected Israel as his people, how could such an event take place? Is faith in the God of Jewish self-understanding still possible after Auschwitz? If not, what is the nature of Jewish collective identity?

For Christianity the issue was less the existence or goodness of God than the goodness and redemptive value of Christianity. If Christianity played a major role in fomenting the Shoah, how can Christians continue to affirm the redemptive essence of Christianity? For Christians the issue was the culpability, not only of Christians, but of key Christian doctrines, in this evil. Christology was the central problem for a Christianity after the Shoah. If faith in Jesus as the Christ, the Messiah of Israel, was a major ideological factor in promoting anti-Judaism in Christian cultures and societies, is such a belief still tenable?

III. Jewish Shoah Theology

For Richard Rubenstein, Auschwitz brings to an end the possibility of belief in the God of traditional Judaism. This God was understood as the Lord of History, providentially in charge of historical events and directing them to an ultimately redemptive end. Belief in the God of providential guidance of history demands a theodicy to justify the ways of God to humanity. The question of theodicy is how evil is possible if God is both good and in charge of history. If God allows evil, then God is not wholly good. But if evil happens because God cannot prevent it, then God is not wholly omnipotent.

Classical theodicy tried to solve this conundrum by declaring that there are hidden reasons for God's permission of evil. Out of evil God brings final good, although His full design is hidden from our eyes. The traditional strategy of the Jewish tradition for explaining the evils that befall the Jewish people is to assert that these evils are punishment for sin. God is chastening His people. When they learn from this chastening and repent of their sins, becoming wholly obedient to God's commandments, then redemption and blessings will follow.

A minority tradition supplemented this interpretation by a martyr theology. Through its sufferings the people of Israel is atoning for the sins of its people, perhaps the sins of all people. Exemplary figures, such as prophets and holy teachers, could be seen as playing the paradigmatic role in this work of atonement. Christianity took its interpretation of Jesus's atoning suffering and death from this martyr theology of first century Judaism.[6]

For Rubenstein no such rationalization of evil as a means to future good can justify the enormous unjust suffering of the Shoah or vindicate divine justice and goodness in the light of so many innocent Jewish victims. No possible sins could justify such vast destruction of Jewish people, people selected only because they were Jews, without regard to any actual particularities of either morality or immorality. If God could be imagined as willing the 'final solution' of destruction of the people of Israel, how can such a God be the God of Israel? The Shoah breaks the link between the God of Israel and the people of Israel as God's chosen people.

For Rubenstein a God who could will the destruction of the Jews in punishment for even the greatest sins cannot be claimed as good. If such a God exists, then He is a cosmic sadist. One cannot honor or hope in such a God, but only recoil from Him in horror. According to Rubenstein, God is dead after Auschwitz. Henceforth Jews must cease to look beyond immanent historical events for meaning and justice, in an effort to make sense out of senseless evil. There is no divine plan that will work out for the best in the end. Such faith in God must be renounced, rather than attempting to justify God's justice in the face of the Shoah.

Rubenstein also believed that Jews should abandon the idea of their special election or chosenness. They should cease to see themselves as paradigmatic of humanity in relation to ultimate reality. Such notions of Jewish specialness have created cycles of self-inflation, gentile jealousy—expressed either as hostility or as over-identification with Jews—and cataclysmic violence against Jews, leading to crises of Jewish self-doubt. Jews made the mistake of allowing gentiles to 'overhear' this concept of Jewish chosenness and thereby to wish to identify with it.

Rubenstein sees Christianity as the major example of this tragedy of a gentile identification with the Jewish concept of divine chosenness. By attempting to claim this idea for themselves, they must deny this status as still intact for Jews. Christian antisemitism is the negative side of a competitive Christian relationship to Jewish self-understanding of divine election.[7] Rubenstein would affirm Jewish particularity, but as one particularity among others. Jews are unique as every people in their own way are unique. Rubenstein, in these remarks, seeks to 'normalize' Jewish identity, as one cultural community among others.

In keeping with his Freudian interpretation of collective psychology, Rubenstein views civilization pessimistically. In a subsequent book, *The Cuning of History*, he denies the uniqueness of the Shoah. The Shoah should be seen as an extreme expression of a general trend in modern bureaucratic and technological societies and sovereign states.[8] While modernity has brought the human capacity to express technological skills to the highest level or prowess, it is at the same time perfecting the techniques of mass murder.

The Nazi extermination of the Jews did not happen through outbreaks of irrational passion, but was the bureaucratic realization of an ideological theory. The technological metropolis is moving, more and more, toward this finale as necropolis, the annihilation of the human through objectification. Rubenstein speaks of himself as becoming a political conservative, suggesting that it would be better to avoid preserving too many redundant people through liberal humanitarianism that the state will feel the need to annihilate.[9]

However, underneath Rubenstein's pessimistic account of history and technological civilization there lurks a romantic impulse to break free of historical alienation and return to identification with spontaneous libidinal 'nature.' The Jew of historic rabbinic Judaism, with his belief in a transcendent God of commandments, rewards and punishments, is the alienated Jews, a type of the alienated 'man' of civilization. This Jew was in a state of exile or estrangement from his own embodiment, both from his own body and from the natural world around him.

But, lurking underneath this ethical Jew, with his self-estranging system of law and his punishing God, there remains the natural Jew, longing to be integrated into the rhythms of nature, the circling seasons and the life cycle. This natural or 'pagan' Jewishness Rubenstein sees as derivative from the Canaanite background of ancient Hebrew religion. This paganism Judaism repressed but also preserved in its festivals, by imposing a historical meaning upon the earlier festivals of the agricultural year.

It is through this Freudian lens that Rubenstein interprets the antinomian elements in Zionism over against rabbinic Judaism. Rubenstein's views of Zionism seemed to have been particularly influenced by a fringe Canaanite Movement in Zionism which saw the return from exile as a reclaiming of the pre-Jewish Canaanite identity.[10] The return to the land expresses a desire to return to spontaneous relation to the body, both one's own body and its sexuality and to the embodiment of the community in its own national land. The Israelis with their agricultural dances are reclaiming the peasant Hebrew underneath the law-bound urban Jew.

Rubenstein, in his book *My Brother Paul*, also interpreted Christianity, specifically Pauline antinomianism, in terms of this desire to escape from civilization and its discontents.[11] Such a return to the body also shifts the understanding of the divine. The Jew returned from self-estrangement rediscovers the real deity of nature which Judaism rejected, not the Lord of history, but the cosmic Matrix, the devouring primal Mother from which all things spring and to which they return at death.

This concept of the divine Matrix as the real deity of nature coincides with Rubenstein's description of himself as a 'Catholic' rather than a 'Protestant' Jew. What binds him to Judaism is not its ethical commandments, but rather its cultic life, built on the old agricultural festivals. These are the rituals that bind a community together through collective experiences, not in order to solve the human dilemma of good and evil, but rather to comfort one another in shared affliction in the midst of ultimate meaninglessness.[12]

While other Jewish thinkers agreed that the Shoah must be seen as a major challenge to traditional Judaism, Rubenstein's reading of this crisis through a post-Freudian interpretation of rabbinic law as repression infuriated most Jews. Although Emil Fackenheim agreed with Richard Rubenstein that the Shoah had created a crisis for traditional Jewish theology, he vehemently disagreed with Rubenstein's Freudian outlook and his demythologizing of Jewish election. For Fackenheim, it is blasphemous to say that the Shoah is one expression among others of "tendencies of Western civilization in the twentieth century."[13]

As Fackenheim developed his own approach to Shoah theology, he would reject all comparisons between the Shoah and other events of modern mass violence, such as the genocide of American Indians, the enslavement of African Blacks, with its results of mass death, the violence of the war in Vietnam or the bombing of Hiroshima and Nagasaki.

For Fackenheim the Shoah was an evil of a different order than any other human evil. It is evil without remainder or purpose, evil for evil's sake. It stands out beyond all other relative evils as unique, as absolute evil. The Shoah also calls Jews back to Jewish uniqueness and particularity, from all desires to be assimilated into generic universals of human progress. Jewish faith must be rebuilt by recommitment to this unique Jewish status of chosenness and its ongoing continuation.

It is by raising Jewish children after the Shoah that Jews reaffirm their faith in the continuing life of the people Israel. By raising Jewish children Jews refuse to give new victories to Hitler.[14] This is a conscious and collective commitment. It carried over also to the state of Israel. By committing oneself to the defense of the state of Israel one expresses one's determination that the people Israel shall survive as a nation.

Such commitments to Jewish survival, for Fackenheim, have critical theological significance. Through dedication to Jewish survival, the eclipsed face of God can be restored. The relation between God and Israel has been reversed. Where once the existence of God guaranteed the existence of Israel, today the continued existence of the people Israel guarantees the existence of God. For Fackenheim Jewish survival makes no distinctions between religious and secular Jews. Such distinctions were abolished by the fires of Auschwitz. Simply by continuing to affirm themselves as Jews, by raising Jewish children to continue to affirm themselves as Jews, Jews witness against Satan. They overcome the triumph of Satan in Hitler's death camps, and so prove that the bond between God and the Jewish people is stronger than the power of Satan.

Fackenheim does not dispute Rubenstein's assertion that one cannot construct a theodicy of the Shoah itself. The Shoah eclipses the presence of God and cannot be justified by any redeeming purpose. But the presence of God can be restored through the redemptive acts of Jewish familial and national survival. For Fackenheim, the ongoing existence of the State of Israel became the primary means and expression of this redemption of the God of Israel.

In an essay entitled "The Holocaust and the State of Israel: Their Relation," Fackenheim constructs a theological connection between the two which is total and unbreakable. This is not a relationship of moral causality. Fackenheim would not say that the state of Israel happened because of the Shoah, either in the sense that God allowed the state of Israel to come about to redeem the Jewish people from the Shoah, or in the sense that the world community supported the emergence of this state as recompense for the Shoah. Rather the relation between the two realities is established by the continuous and total response of Jews themselves.

By total commitment to the defense and security of the state of Israel, Jews negate the threat to their existence of the Shoah. This relation between the state of Israel and

The Holocaust Now

the Shoah must be exclusive, undiluted by any other concerns for general human goods and evils. As he put it "the heart of every *authentic* response to the Holocaust—religious or secular—is a commitment to the autonomy and security of the state of Israel."[15]

For Fackenheim the founding of the state of Israel is "the beginning of the dawn of our redemption."[16] In traditional rabbinic thought the Jewish people would be restored to their homeland by an act of divine intervention in history, the coming of the Messiah. This coming might be spurred on by religious acts of prayer, repentance, and strict observance of Torah. Fackenheim concurs with modern Jewish thinkers, such as Rabbi Abraham Isaac Kook, who not only emphasize the efficacy of human redemptive acts in bringing about the Messianic times, but abolish distinctions between religious acts and secular acts such as land settlement.[17]

Human effort, in effect, can overcome divine inaction and make the beginning of redemption within history. Fackenheim believes that the heroic acts that have gone into the founding of the state of Israel cannot be explained by human causation within ordinary historical developments. There is a miraculous element to such extraordinary efforts that could reunite a people scattered all over the world, rent apart by centuries of cultural separations, which could revive an ancient language and make it a modern national language and create a powerful state capable of defending itself against overwhelming odds. Such heroic acts are, for Fackenheim, proof that Zionism is a theophany of the Jewish collective will "in touch with the Absolute."[18]

Fackenheim makes a direct symbolic identification between resistance to Hitler, resistance to the Arabs and resistance to Satan. For Fackenheim the Arabs are the current manifestation of Satan that seek, like the Nazis, the extermination of the Jewish people. By fighting the Arab enemies of Israel, one reverses the victories of Satan, of Hitler, of the past. In his essay Fackenheim paints two complementary pictures of the Jew face to face with absolute evil in the form of the Shoah. One is the calm, dignified rabbi who insists on praying the *Kaddish* [Memorial Prayer—Ed.] for his flock before the Nazis begin to shoot them down in their mass grave. The second picture is that of a Jewish butcher who leapt out of that grave and sunk his teeth into the throat of the Nazi officer, hanging on until the Nazi died. These two redemptive acts complete one another; the one is that of transcendent goodness in the face of absolute evil, the other is that of the absolute will to refuse to let evil have the final victory.[19]

For Fackenheim, the Israelis today represent, in collective form, the will power of the butcher who leapt out of the grave, while the Arabs are the collective manifestation of the Nazi officer into whose throat they sink their teeth. Through this determination to defeat their enemies, Jewish powerlessness is overcome, and Jewish redemption is inaugurated. Even in the midst of the Shoah, the flame of Jewish will to live sprang up, foreshadowing the will made powerful in the state of Israel.

Theological and Ethical Reflections

For example, in 1943, Mordecai Anielewicz, a leader of the Warsaw ghetto uprising, perished in the flames, satisfied that Jewish passivity had been breached and Jewish self-defense had begun. That same year a kibbutz in Palestine was named for him. Five years later a small group of members of Kibbutz Yad Mordecai [Yad=hand—Ed.] held off the Egyptian army in a battle critical for the survival of the Jewish state. In this event Fackenheim sees the spirit of the Warsaw uprising resurrected and present in the battle of Israelis against the Arabs that threatened their state.[20]

Other Jewish thinkers, in their response to the Shoah, were not willing to make such a total and exclusive relation between the negation of Auschwitz and the new power of the state of Israel, nor to sever the redemption of the Jews so completely from concern for the redemption of human communities. The writings of Irving Greenberg in the mid-1970's became the leading example of a more balanced approach, freed from the extremes of both Rubenstein and Fackenheim. His talk, "Cloud of Smoke, Pillar of Fire: Judaism, Christianity and Modernity after the Holocaust" was the keynote address of the Saint John the Divine conference in 1974.[21]

In this address Greenberg discussed the challenges to both traditional Jewish theology and traditional Christian theology by the Shoah. Both Judaism and Christianity, he said, were religions of redemption. Both hope that the evils of human history will be finally overcome by divine redemptive action. Both base their hopes that life will win over death, good over evil, on foundational paradigms of redemption in the past that shape subsequent ways of life and self-understanding.

For the Jews, the foundational paradigmatic event is the exodus from slavery in Egypt and the giving of the covenant on Sinai. For Christians it is Easter, the revelation of the resurrection of the Crucified One. In the light of Easter, the crucifixion is remembered, not as meaningless evil, but as an act of divine atonement for human sin. Both religions insulate themselves from further crises of meaning or revelations of God by living between this foundational paradigm and the expected fulfillment of messianic deliverance at the end of history.

The Shoah challenges both of these Jewish and Christian strategies of insulation from history. For Jews the Shoah threatens the basic faith in a God who has entered into a covenant with the Jewish people. There can be no covenant if their is no covenant people. There can be no God of the covenant if that God could will or allow the people of the covenant to be exterminated.

But the Shoah offers an even more devastating challenge to Christianity, for Christians have not been innocent victims, but collaborators with the Shoah. Christianity was the major source of the 'teaching of contempt' for Jews and Judaism that was translated into secular terms by Nazi racial antisemitism. Christianity did not only hope for a future deliverance from evil, but believed that it had already received the downpayment on the messianic advent in Jesus's death and resurrection. But a Christianity which could use its faith in Christ to foment hatred against Jews, leading to pogroms and to Nazi attempted genocide, is a creed whose claims to possess the beginnings of redemption through this same Christ has lost credibility. Belief in Jesus as the Christ has become a font of evil, not the beginning of redemption.

Greenberg also perceives in the Shoah a challenge to modern secular messianism as well, the redemptive claims of the Enlightenment, of scientific rationalism and liberal universalism. These secular gods of modern civilization failed in the death camps. The claims of progress through science and technology were turned into a means for racist destruction. Science provided the tools for mass murder. Nor did world Jewry rise to the occasion, according to Greenberg. Jews outside of Europe [in America] proved more concerned about their well-being in their own country than with rescuing their threatened sisters and brothers in Europe.[22]

The failure of human projects of redemption, religious and secular, is experienced as an absence of the divine presence in the modern world. We live in the time of the silence of God. For Greenberg this divine absence and silence does not justify a denial of God's existence. Greenberg speaks more in the mystical language of Elie Wiesel, rather than the demythologizing language of Richard Rubenstein. We have entered into a time of profound silence that no longer knows how to speak adequately about God. The test of adequate language about God has become the burning children of the crematoria. Today any statement about God or about religious truth must be tested by the light of the burning children. Any religious statement that cannot be uttered in the presence of these innocent victims cannot be uttered at all.

For Greenberg the Shoah has shattered all certainties about how God is acting in history. Today we can only have 'moment faiths' that spring from the tentative human acts of redemptive concern. New ways of speaking about God must grow experimentally from such concrete human redemptive acts. Greenberg wishes to speak cautiously of what such acts are, not with the tones of absolute commands issued from Sinai characteristic of Fackenheim. Humans have to demonstrate by real actions on behalf of life that faith in human goodness is still possible. Through building up signs of commitment to life, one can also begin to posit that there is a divine life and goodness that is stronger than evil and violence.

In 1974 Greenberg saw commitment to the state of Israel as one such sign that hope is possible. This shows that Jews have arisen from the Shoah to affirm their collective survival. The state of Israel also brings to an end all those efforts to snuff out Jewish collective life that began 1900 years ago with the Roman victory over the Jewish national uprisings and their destruction of Jerusalem. But, unlike Fackenheim, Greenberg wished to balance concerns for the welfare of Jews in Israel with concerns for the welfare of Jews through the world in the diaspora. He also wished to balance particularity and universalism, concern for Jewish welfare with concern for welfare of others.

Jews today, together with people of all human religious and secular cultures, have to seek to overcome the denigrating stereotypes that denied full and equal human dignity to one another. "This," Greenberg says, "is the overriding command and essential criterion of religious existence today," not to create another matrix of inter-group hostility that could lead to another genocide. Only by joining together in the work of rehabilitation of the image of God in the face of other human beings can we also rehabilitate the presence of God in our midst in history.[23]

Not all major Jewish thinkers, however, were willing to concede the claim that the Shoah had created a major crisis in faith in the God of Israel and the continuing claims of that God on Jewish life through the Torah. Orthodox Jewish theologian, Eliezer Berkovits, would say that the main question raised by the Shoah is not "Where was God?" but, rather, "Where was man?" Berkovits, in his 1973 volume *Faith After the Holocaust*, explained the possibility of radical evil in history by the nature of God's creative act of a reality separate from Godself.[24] In creating the world God makes a voluntary withdrawal of divine omnipotence from the sphere of creation in order to make room for human freedom and choice.

The Shoah is the extreme example of the human misuse of freedom to make evil choices, rather than good choices. But this extreme example of the human capacity to choose evil does not disturb the fundamental framework for the Jewish understanding of God and the path to which God calls us.

Other less traditional Jewish religious thinkers who had come out of the anti-war movement of the 1960's, such as civil rights activist turned religious thinker Arthur Waskow, sought to make connections between the Shoah and the threat of nuclear war. Waskow seeks to restate the moral and mystical connection between Jewish particularity and universal humanity by seeing the Jewish people as a paradigmatic people who have gone ahead of the rest of humanity and tested the threat of annihilation that now looms over all humanity in nuclear war.

Waskow's symbolic linking of the fires of Auschwitz and the fires of the holocaust that threaten us all in nuclear weapons even suggests a martyr role for the Jewish victims of the death camps. God, in some sense, 'planned' the Shoah to avert the ultimate holocaust from humanity as a whole. By entering the incinerator first and demonstrating its effects, the Jewish victims call all people into solidarity to avoid the "fire next time" that will destroy us all.[25] Such mystical connections in Waskow's thoughts are strained. Can such speculations that the Jews are God's chosen avante garde, to avert humanity's threatened destruction, pass Greenberg's test of religious assertions utterable in the presence of burning children?[26]

IV. Christian Shoah Theology

Christian responses to the Shoah have been slower to develop than Jewish ones. As mentioned before, Christian theologians who have made the Shoah a central theme of their thought remain isolated individuals; they have not become a theological movement. It is true that church bodies, both Catholic and Protestant, have felt the need to respond collectively to the Shoah. During the Second Vatican Council, in the first half of the 1960's, there was a major discussion of how the Shoah must impel Catholic Christianity to take a critical look at its heritage of anti-Judaism.

In the document on the relation of the Catholic Church and other religions, the section on relations to the Jewish people specifically repudiated the ancient Christian charge of deicide. The death of Jesus was said to be the particular responsibility of certain Jews and gentiles in the first century. It is also a paradigm for all humanity's apostasy from God. But there can be no inference from the death of Jesus of any special or inheritable guilt of all Jews.[27]

Protestant responses to the Shoah have focused on the question of mission to the Jews. This was central to the statement of the German Evangelical Church issued in 1975.[28] This statement confessed the historical complicity of Christianity with antisemitism. It also made a link between antisemitism and anti-Zionism. Not only must Christians oppose antisemitism in their own nations, but they must also support the independence and security of the state of Israel. Such support for the state of Israel is not simply a recognition of a human need of the Jewish people, like all people, for a secure homeland, but it is an event in the salvation history of the people of God.

Such a statement suggested that the return of Israel to its national homeland was, in some sense, a fulfillment of prophecy and the beginning of redemption. Yet this German Christian statement failed to reject the thesis of the superior salvific status of Christianity. It did not reject mission to the Jews, but remained committed to the idea that full salvation for the Jews awaits their conversion to Christ. Thus, by implication, the return of the Jews to the Holy Land remains linked with a Christian messianic scenario of a final victory of Christ.[29]

A number of Christian denominations have developed statements on Jewish-Christian relations that seek to repudiate antisemitism. They have also developed educations programs and revisions of liturgical and catechetical material to purge their teachings of negativity to Jews and Judaism.[30] Yet, generally speaking, such revisions of Christian thought, to purge it of antisemitism, have not seen the Christian view of God present in Christ as deeply shaken by such revisions.

For those Christian theologians who have taken the Shoah and the critique of Christian anti-Judaism as central themes of their thought, the issue of Christology has been the critical problem. Is it possible to continue to believe that Jesus is the Christ, the fulfillment of the Jewish hopes for the Messiah, and yet purge Christianity of antisemitism?

In the book which I published in 1974, *Faith and Fratricide: The Theological Roots of Anti-Semitism*, this question of Christology was central.[31] As I put it in that volume, is it possible to affirm that Jesus is the Christ without at the same time teaching a negated and supercessionary relation to Judaism, as an incomplete faith that failed to accept its own 'fulfillment' in Christ? In that book I defined antisemitism as the "left hand" of Christology. The negation of Judaism is the shadow side of the affirmation that Jesus is the Christ. This relation goes back to the earliest roots of Christian faith. The two are interwoven already in the New Testament.[32]

Christian symbolism constructed a series of negations of Jews and Judaism: Judaism as the 'old' covenant, superseded by the church as the new covenant; Judaism as an ethnic particularistic religion, superseded by Christianity as a universal, inclusive religion; Judaism as outward letter, external conformity to law, in contrast to Christianity as spirit, as obedience to God informed by inward spiritual power or 'grace.' In each of these theological dualisms Christian self-affirmation of its superior and higher spiritual status is built on a corresponding negation of Judaism as its incomplete or even antithetical 'other.'

Christian theology was built from its earliest days, as a break-away Jewish sect that became gentile, on a competitive relation to Judaism over who is the true and final chosen people of God. This religious rivalry was translated in the fourth century, when Christianity assumed power as the favored religion of the Christianized Roman empire, into a series of ecclesiastical and imperial laws that relegated Jews to a permitted but despised status in Christian societies. It is this fifteen centuries of theologically-based hostility to Jews, incarnated in political, social and cultural systems in Christian societies, that is the background of modern European antisemitism.

Foundational doctrines of Christian faith, their belief that Jesus is the Messiah of Jewish hope and that the Church is the New Covenant, the New Israel, that supercedes the old Israel, are the ideological matrix out of which European antisemitism emerged. Thus Christian purgation of antisemitism must struggle both against the effects of its teaching in social antisemitism, but also it must grapple with these teachings themselves.

In the concluding chapter of that volume I outlined what I saw where the key shifts in the interpretation of Christian theology, particularly in Christology, necessary to overcome theological anti-Judaism. I suggested that the key to a Christology without antisemitism is a theology of hope that sees Jesus's messianic identity as proleptic and contextually limited, not as absolute, universal, final and fulfilled. Both of these two steps, to be proleptic and to be contextually limited, are necessary to a reinterpretation of Christian hope without its antisemitic shadow side.

By proleptic, I mean that the experience of Jesus as messianic announcer, crucified by his antagonists in his Jewish and Roman imperial contexts, resurrected in hope, anticipated, but does not fulfill, our final deliverance from antagonistic relations. We can affirm the truth of our hope of that prophetic announcer of God's coming redemption. But the fulfillment, the overcoming of violence and injustice, are as much ahead of us today as they were ahead of that popular Jewish teacher two thousand years ago. Christians as much as Jews struggle with an unresolved history, holding on to our past paradigmatic experience as the basis of our hope that evil will not have the last word and God will win in the end.

But it is not enough to simply admit that salvation is incomplete. Christians must also accept the contextually limited relevance of their theological symbols and the historical experience on which they are based. Remembering Jesus, his life and death, are the breakthrough experiences that found our particular people, the Christian people. They are the paradigms drawn from our interpreted experience that mediate hope in the midst of adversity to us. But this does not mean that they are the only paradigms that may do this. Other people with other collective memories continue their struggle for redemption on other grounds; among them, the Jews, for whom Jesus's life, death and anticipated coming again did not become the normative paradigm and who continue to found themselves efficaciously on the Exodus and the Torah as their memory and their Way.

This explication of antisemitism as deeply intertwined with Christology was generally welcomed by Jews, for whom this thesis was somewhat obvious. Jews had long experienced Christian violence toward them as rooted in the assertion that they are "Christ-killers." Many Christians who had been involved in Jewish-Christian dialogue were at first antagonized by this thesis, wishing to see antisemitism as more peripheral rather than central to Christian doctrine. However, several other Christian writers have made the revision of Christology, in light of the Shoah, central to their writings.

One example of this rethinking is the writings of husband-and-wife pair, A. Roy and Alice L. Eckardt, in recent books such as *Long Night's Journey into Day: Life and Faith After the Holocaust* [1982] and *Jews and Christians: The Contemporary Meeting* [1986].[33] For the Eckardts, a full and adequate Christian response to the Shoah necessitates fundamental revisions in the interpretation of Christian teachings. All notions that Judaism has either an inferior understanding of ethics or an incomplete capacity to redeem vis-a-vis Christianity must be decisively rejected.

The Eckardts believe that Christianity must rethink the basic understanding of Jesus's resurrection and the claim that Jesus is the Messiah of Israel. Jesus cannot be said to have risen from the dead in a physical sense [and there is no other way to interpret this original Christian belief] or to be in an already achieved messianic status because the world is still unredeemed.³⁴ The Eckardts take seriously the Jewish view that the coming of the Messiah does not refer simply to a changed spiritual relation to God [as Christianity has tended to see this], but to a decisive shift in human relations that begins the conquest of historical evil. Since this obviously has not happened, it is impossible and indeed meaningless to say that the Messiah has already come.

Jewish rejection of Jesus as the Messiah is not unfaithfulness, but faithfulness to the God and to the understanding of the messianic advent of their tradition. Jews have remained faithful both to the one covenant that God made with them and also to a realistic and wholistic understanding of redemption. This understanding of redemption does not split the spiritual from the physical, the personal from the social, as Christianity has generally done.

This unification of the religious and ethical with the social and the political is, for the Eckardts, a central insight that Christianity needs to relearn from its Jewish 'elder brother.' Although they do not say so, one might see in liberation theologies such an effort by Christians to reclaim the social realism of the Hebrew prophetic tradition. The Eckardts, however, see this reunification of the spiritual and the political as a central element of Jewish self-understanding that Christians must accept, if they are to understand the importance of the state of Israel for contemporary Jewish thought, both religious and secular.

The Eckardts do not want to make absolutist claims for a relationship of Jewish peoplehood to a divinely-given land in Palestine. They say, rather, that no people has an absolute claim to anything. All human claims to states or land are partial and relative. They would strongly reject the sort of fundamentalist Christian Zionism that assimilates a Jewish return to the Holy Land into a Christian dispensationalist eschatology, for by saying that such a return is necessary as part of the fulfillment of prophecy and an ultimate conversion of the Jews to Christianity. They characterize such a theology as antisemitic, since the formation of a Jewish state is celebrated only as a stepping stone to Jewish conversion, the annihilation of the unconverted and the triumph of Christ.³⁵

While seeking to avoid "territorial fundamentalism," the Eckardts typically characterize any criticism of the policies of the state of Israel, whether from Palestinians or other Arabs, or from Christian peace activists, such as Quakers, as motivated by antisemitism. They see all criticism of Israel as springing from a hostility to Jewish empowerment and self-determination.³⁶ They say that "the worst fate that can befall any people is to be bereft of political sovereignty."³⁷ Jews have a right to a state because every people have a right to a nation-state, to national self-determination.

To reject a Jewish state is an expression of an antisemitic ideology that believes that only the Jews, of all the world's peoples, are to be homeless and powerless wanderers and to lack a home [state] of their own. For the Eckardts the Jews do not have a special

The Holocaust Now

God-given right to a state different from other people. They have the same right to a state as other people, for a state is the basis for defending one's national existence against one's enemies.

A somewhat different view of the relation of the state of Israel as a solution to antisemitism is taken by Franklin Littell, whose long commitment to struggle against Christian antisemitism is expressed in his book, *The Crucifixion of the Jews* [1975].[38] Littell's theology springs from the Anabaptist free church tradition of radical rejection of church-state amalgamation.[39] The authentic calling of the Christian church is to remain a counter-culture that must stand in tension with and prophetic critique of all worldly systems of power. The church is a community set apart from the state to witness to an alternative, redemptive lifestyle of God's messianic age. This Kingdom lifestyle is characterized by pacifism, egalitarianism and communal sharing.

Littell uses this Anabaptist critique of Christendom in his battle against Christian antisemitism. He was influenced in this particularly by the Barthian theological attack on German Christianity as 'cultural Christianity.' For Barth, the essence of the Christian failure to oppose Hitler was its sellout of the Gospel to a pagan nationalism and idolatrous sacral state.[40] Littell sees the Jews of Medieval Europe as better preserving this counter-cultural ethic, as a people set apart, without power in Christian theocratic states.[41]

However, these free church principles come out oddly in Littell's thought when he turns to the necessity for Christians to give absolute support for Israel as a Jewish state. Such a state he sees as an essential component of Jewish identity. Like the Eckardts, Littell sees the nature of the Jewish people as a wholistic social and political community, not just a spiritual peoplehood divorced from political expression. One of the fundamental mistakes of Christianity is this spiritualization of peoplehood. Littell identifies this communal nature of Judaism with the necessity of a state.

Unlike the Eckardts, Littell gives special or unique status to this Jewish right to a Jewish state. The right of the Jews to a state is not simply a particular expression of a universal right of all people to a state. Rather the Jewish people have a unique right to a state on this particular land. God has chosen the Jewish people as a unique community and promised them this particular land. Thus, only for the Jews is there a valid fusion of spiritual and political identity, of peoplehood, land and political sovereignty. The Jews are set apart from all other people as the only people whose ethnic identity has been mandated by God and who have been given a land in which to express their national identity.[42]

Even more than the Eckardts, Littell scores any criticism of Israel, whether from Arabs or from Quakers, as antisemitism. He also identifies any opposition to a Jewish state as a lingering expression of an ideology that decrees powerlessness and misery for Jews as divine punishment and sees Jewish empowerment as a threat to this ideol-

Theological and Ethical Reflections

ogy.[43] Littell also condemns Islam as an extreme example of a false sacral political order that fuses religion, culture and state. He claims that Israel as a Jewish state challenges the idea of an Islamic state.[44] It is hard to know what Littell means at this point, if Israel is itself a divinely-mandated theocratic state. An Islamic and a Jewish Torah-state would seem more to be rivals in the Middle East, with similar ideas of religious law and theocratic politics.

One of the most systematic efforts to rethink Christian theological claims in the light of a sorry history of Christian antisemitism has come from Episcopal theologian Paul van Buren. Van Buren is developing a four-part *magnum opus*, *A Theology of the Jewish-Christian Reality*, three volumes of which have appeared: *Discerning the Way* [1980]; *A Christian Theology of the People Israel* [1983], and *Christ in Context* [1988].[45]

Van Buren's theology is deeply shaped by Protestant Neo-orthodoxy. Neo-orthodoxy rejected the liberal universalism of nineteenth century Enlightenment theologians, like Schleiermacher. The doctrine of original sin was taken with radical seriousness. All human beings are fallen and have lost any natural connection with God. This view of the human condition leads to a positivist Christological monism. Only through Christ is their authentic revelation of God and redeeming relation to God. Such a view left no room for a positive evaluation of non-Christian religions. Judaism, at best, could only have a preparatory role in the economy of salvation. But, without faith in Christ, the Jews remain in darkness.[46]

Van Buren has transferred this monistic idea of historical revelation to God's covenant with the people Israel. God [the only God that Jews and Christians know] has made Himself known in only one way, as the God who chose the people Israel as His people.[47] The covenant of God with Israel at Sinai is God's foundational and normative work at the center of creation and the redemption of creation. All other work of God in history [it is not apparent in van Buren that God is at work in nature at all] flows exclusively from this one elect center.

Van Buren uses the metaphor of light and darkness for the relation of this one revelatory center, the covenant of God with Israel, to the gentile world. He draws his use of this metaphor, not only from Christian theology, but also from Jewish messianic Kabbalism.[48] The covenant of God with Israel is both the one place where the true God is revealed and also the center from which creation is being healed from its brokenness. The Gentile, lacking any natural relation to God, is by nature sunk in darkness, both spiritually and morally. Gentiles exhibit the godless nature of humanity as idolatrous and morally perverse. The Gentile, then, is the 'natural' human or 'pagan.'[49]

God, however, is not only the God of Israel, but the creator and redeemer of all nations. God has chosen to reach out to the gentiles through His covenant with Israel. Israel is called to be God's unique people, walking in the Way of Life which God has given them in the Torah. But Israel is also called to be the light to the nations, to communicate its revelation of God and the healing of the nations to the gentiles. This extension of the covenant of God with Israel to the nations is specifically the role of the Christian Church.

Christianity, or the Christian Church, is not a 'new covenant' of God with a new people, which supercedes the covenant of God with Israel. That covenant is eternal and unchangeable. Rather, the Christian church is an extension of the one covenant of God with Israel to the gentiles. The dispensation of salvation to the gentiles is, in a sense, a new work of God in history, but in a strictly auxiliary and dependent relation to the sole covenant of God with Israel.[50]

Van Buren completely rejects the title of Christ for Jesus. Jesus was not the Messiah of Israel.[51] The appropriation of this title for Jesus is an error that manifests how deeply Christianity misinterpreted its own mandate. Jesus is central for Christianity, but not as Messiah of Israel, or as the basis of a new covenant superceding that of Israel. Jesus is the paradigmatic expression of the extension of the covenant of God with Israel to the gentiles. Jesus is where Israel is summed up in one person and given to the gentiles. The gentiles plug into the covenant of God with Israel through their relation to Jesus as Israel-for-us. Jesus is central to the salvation of Christians [gentiles connected to God's covenant], but Jesus is unnecessary for the salvation of Jews, who are the primary possessors of this covenant.[52]

By seeing itself as a 'new covenant,' superceding the covenant of God with Israel, Christianity fell into error, cut itself off from its Jewish roots and therefore lost the source of the authentic interpretation of its mission. This error was compounded by an antisemitic teaching of contempt for Jews and Judaism. Christianity responded with hostility when Jews refused to accept this false concept of Jesus as the Messiah and the Church as the New Israel, superceding the Jewish people. Christians called on the Jews to abandon faithfulness to the Torah in favor of a new way of salvation through Christ alone.

Such a gospel of Christ could only be rejected by the Jews with a resounding 'No!' This rejection of the Christian gospel is not unfaithfulness, but rather the expression of the faithfulness of the Jewish people to its God. Christians must come to recognize Jewish rejection of this type of Christian gospel as a witness to truth, recalling the Christian church to its true identity and mission.[53]

The culmination of Christian self-deception, expressed in hostility to Jews, was the Shoah, the effort to destroy the Jewish people entirely, so that all memory of their negation of a secularized Christian triumphalism could be erased. Van Buren parallels the crucifixion of Christ and the Shoah, Golgotha and Auschwitz. Both represent the power of Satan, or the evil impulse that resists God's love. But they are also the places where God Himself entered into history and was present in the suffering of the faithful man of Israel, Jesus, and in the suffering of the people of Israel.[54]

Theological and Ethical Reflections

The state of Israel is a resurrection sign, the sign that God's faithfulness to life against death perseveres. By aligning itself in solidarity with the Jewish remembrance of the six million, but also in support for the state of Israel, the Church participates in this saving hope on the other side of the horror of human resistance to God.

> In so far as the Church seeks to enter into the Jewish memory of the six million, in so far as the Church shares with Jews the determination that there shall never be another Holocaust, in so far as the Church holds most dear the Jewish State as one precious affirmation of Jewish life after so many deaths, it plays a minor part in the affirming of those dead that their death is not the ultimate fact for them, that God's cause for his people continues.[55]

Once the Christian church has returned to its true, auxiliary relationship to the covenant with Israel, then Israel will be able to recognize and claim the Christian Church as its own vehicle for its mission to the gentiles. Heretofore, it has not been able to do this because of Christian hostility and misinterpretation of its relationship to the people Israel. The Christian church and its teachers must humble themselves and become disciples of the Jewish tradition in order to regain their true place in God's economy of salvation.

The central expression of Jewish faithfulness to their covenant with God is faithful obedience of the commandments of the Torah. The core of the Christian false gospel was the effort to invalidate the Torah as mere legalism with salvific efficacy. Van Buren believes that Christians do not need to observe the Torah because Jesus is their Torah. But the Torah remains central to the ongoing response of Israel to its covenantal relation to God. Jewish apostasy is non-observance of Torah.[56]

God's covenant with Israel includes the promised land. The land has been given by God to Israel in perpetuity, whether or not they are actually present in it. No other people, whether they have dwelt there for centuries or millennia, have any true right to this land. Jewish presence in the land normatively takes the form of a Jewish state. Such a Jewish state cannot be like other states. It is called to a higher destiny, not only to be an exemplar of all other nations, but also the place where creation itself is being healed. The Jewish state is the beginning of the redemption of creation, the overcoming of fallen creation's resistance to God manifest in Golgotha and Auschwitz.

The Jewish state must realize its redemptive nature by becoming a Torah state. This is why Israel cannot be governed by a secular constitution. It is called to take on the full yoke of the Torah as its law in order to fulfill its redemptive task, both for itself and for the healing of creation.[57] By implication, this also means encouraging the state of Israel to become fully a theocratic state, where the commandments of Torah are enforced as state law. The fact that most Israelis are secular and vehemently antipathetic to further extensions of the power of the rabbinate over their lives apparently does not concern van Buren.

The true Jew is the Torah-observant Jew. The non-observant Jew is not only apostate from God's command's, but threatens the redemption of creation that flows from Torah observance. Thus it is for the sake, not only of Jews, but of all creation to encourage Jews to become Torah-observant. Van Buren's ideas of becoming Torah-observant center on things like food and Sabbath laws. There is no acknowledgement at all that there is any injustice involved in the relation of the state of Israel to the Palestinians, whom van Buren calls "the strangers in the land," and that doing justice to the Palestinians might be a part of becoming faithful to the Torah.[58]

The role of the Christian church is to extend the revelation of God in the covenant with Israel, and the healing work of God in and through Israel, to the nations. Christianity does this by preaching the Gospel, rightly understood, to the nations. This is the 'good news' that, in Jesus, God has extended the covenant with Israel to them. Christianity should also render service to the people Israel, both in atonement for its past sins of antisemitism and also as an expression of its authentic subsidiary relation to Israel. It should do this by becoming an extension of the Anti-Defamation League, combatting antisemitism among gentiles.

Christians should also raise money for the defense of the state of Israel and defend Israel against all anti-Zionist criticism. All suggestions that the state of Israel is less than just in its relation to the Palestinians, or in its relations to third world nations, are simply lies, according to van Buren.[59] Christians should learn the truth [presumably from the government of Israel] and take it upon themselves to combat such calumny.

Christian Shoah theologians as a whole are concerned to combat Christian antisemitism, to define and remove the roots of this antisemitism in Christian theology. However, Rosemary Radford Ruether and Paul van Buren represent opposite strategies for defining and uprooting the theological source of Christian antisemitism. Van Buren wishes to do this by monocentric particularism. The one true God of creation and redemption is available through only one people in whom He is revealed, and in one land through which His redemptive intent is manifest. Redemption of the nations and the rest of the world is an extension of this one covenant, in a strictly subsidiary relation to it.

Rosemary Radford Ruether, by contrast, would solve the dilemma of Christian competitive negation of Judaism, and other religions, by moving to a consistent universalism which would allow every human culture, and its quest for truth and justice, to have its own validity. God as the center of creation and redemption is not manifest through only one center, through one people and one land, but as the center for all peoples and all lands, defined in distinct and different ways. Christianity is just as

Theological and Ethical Reflections

relative and particularistic as Judaism; it is not the universal truth over against ethnocentric particularism.

The relation between the universal and the particular cannot be found by universalizing one particular people and their culture, either as a Judaism extended to all the world through the Christian Church, as van Buren would have it, or by a universalizing of Christianity in a supercessionary relation to Judaism. Each human cultural community has its own particularity and limits. It must enter into dialogue with other cultural communities, both as peers and as 'others,' whose various world visions are not reducible to one language. One universal culture or religion is neither possible nor necessary.

Yet, in order to live in peace and justice on one planet, the different human cultures and religions need to find concrete ways of affirming their mutual respect for one another. There also must be some working consensus on what justice and human rights mean as the basis of an international rule of law by which all people must be judged in their treatment of others, both within and between their national communities.[60]

V. Post-Shoah Theology: Jewish and Christian

Although Shoah theology began to be articulated less than twenty-five years ago, by the end of the 1980's it was heading into an impasse. Its credibility as a fruitful avenue of theological and ethical thought is in jeopardy. This, in my opinion, is because it has become too uncritically a tool of Jewish empowerment, in America, but especially on behalf of the state of Israel, discarding any moral critique of the possible misuse of such power.

Christian Shoah theologians particularly have tended to compensate for antisemitism by a hyperbolic philosemitism that is unwilling to allow that Jews in power can be like anyone else in power; namely, abusers of power. Such compensatory philosemitism betrays an unwillingness on both sides, Jewish and Christian, to accept that Jews are normal human beings, capable, like any other people, of taking power in a dominating way and using it to make victims of other people.

The imagery of former powerlessness and victimization is constantly rehearsed to claim that such use of power is necessary for 'survival' and that, without more weapons and more land, 'another Holocaust' is around the corner. Anyone who suggests that the time has come to concede human rights and some areas of national self-determination to the Palestinians who remain in the present occupied territories are accused of desiring this future Shoah and being opposed to the rights of Jews to defend themselves from annihilation.

With the fourth largest army in the world, including nuclear armaments, and after months of concentrated military, economic and cultural assault on an unarmed Palestinian people, this rhetoric of survival has lost its credibility. It is time to say *Yesh G'vul*, 'there is a limit,' in the slogan of the Israeli army reservists who refuse to serve in the occupied territories. Jews have had a tragic history of powerlessness and victimization, but this history does not justify the victimization of another people, the Palestinians, a people who have had little to do with that past history of Jewish oppression, but who have become the main victims of Jewish power in Israel.

In mid-June, 1989, Lieutenant-General Dan Shomron, Chief of Staff of the Israeli Defense Forces, warned rightist politicians that the Palestinian uprising could not be resolved militarily, "short of mass deportation, or starvation and genocide."[61] Shomron himself did not suggest that such military measures should cease in favor of political negotiations, but went on to recommend harsher measures against uprising leaders, such as doubling the length of administrative detention and expulsion without trial. That a term like "genocide" could be used as one of the 'options,' in what is increasingly being termed in Israel "the final solution to the Palestinian question," is an indication of how far Jewish power in Israel has moved into the shadow of its worst antithesis.

A younger Jewish theologian who has sought to find a way forward from this impasse of a Shoah theology is Marc Ellis. In his book, *Toward a Jewish Theology of Liberation*, Ellis seeks to rescue Shoah theology from its misuse as a tool of abusive power, particularly in relation to the Palestinian people.[62] Ellis affirms the original insights of Jewish and Christian Shoah theology. In theologians like Irving Greenberg the deep probing of the questions of divine power and presence in history led to tentative ways of affirming life and hope through a concern for all threatened life.

But, increasingly in the 1980's, Greenberg's own thought became focused on the justification of Jewish empowerment as an end in itself, impervious to the possibility of serious ethical failing.[63] Ellis affirms Jewish empowerment as good and necessary to rescue Jews from abject vulnerability. But he asks the Jewish community to take ethical responsibility for the use and abuse of this power, to stop using the rhetoric of past powerlessness to cover up present power and to refuse to face the possibility that they, too, like any other people, can become abusers of power.

Ellis sees a parallelism between a Christian abuse of its theological and political empowerment by victimizing the Jews, and the current Israeli victimization of Palestinians. A similar parallelism was suggested by Yeheskel Landau, Israeli founder of Religious Zionists for Peace, *Oz V'shalom*. In his reply to my paper at a conference at Bethel College, Newton, Kansas [April 10, 1989], Landau compared my earlier book, *Faith and Fratricide*, and my recent book *The Wrath of Jonah*, by saying, "Rosemary is very consistent. In her previous book she showed how antisemitism is the left-hand of Christology. In her new book she has show how anti-Palestinianism is the left-hand of Zionism."

Theological and Ethical Reflections

Ellis believes that, just as Christians after Auschwitz could find no authentic basis to reclaim the moral content of their tradition, and to go forward, except through solidarity with the Jewish people, so Jews, both in Israel and in the Diaspora cannot reclaim the moral basis of their tradition today for the future except by reaching out in solidarity with the human and national rights of he Palestinian people. Ellis quotes the Catholic theologian Johannes Baptist Metz's statement:

> We Christians can never go back behind Auschwitz. To go beyond Auschwitz, if we see clearly, is impossible for us by ourselves. It is possible only together with the victims of Auschwitz.[64]

Ellis paraphrases this statement for Jews today:

> We Jews can never go back behind empowerment. To go beyond empowerment, if we see clearly, is impossible for us by ourselves. It is possible only with the victims of empowerment.[65]

Ellis calls for a new framework for Jewish theology capable of a positive future. Shoah theology, emerging from reflection on the death camps, represents the Jewish people only as they were then, helpless and suffering. But it does not and cannot speak to the people the Jews have become--powerful and often oppressive.[66]

Shoah theology, Ellis says, spoke radically about the question of God in the midst of a threatened annihilation and argued rightly for Jewish empowerment. But it lacks the framework to face the costs of that empowerment. It has not ethical guidelines for a Jewish state with nuclear weapons, supplying military arms to authoritarian states, such as Guatemala, unjustly expropriating the land and houses of Palestinian peasants and torturing resisters to the occupation.

The new framework for theology that Ellis delineates is a theology of solidarity with the Palestinian people. This is not simply a generic call for solidarity with all victims. Rather it demands that people in power take responsibility for the particular victims of their particular power. Jews are not simply to flee back again into general humanitarianism which pays no attention to who they are in particular. Rather, by taking responsibility for who they are as a particular people at this time in history, they also have to take responsibility for that people who their power has victimized most specifically, namely, the Palestinian people.[67]

For Ellis, this theology of solidarity means a de-absolutization of the state of Israel. This does not mean a disregard or abandonment of the state of Israel by diaspora Jews. Rather, there must be a more mature relationship to it. As Jews in the Diaspora need to de-absolutize the power of gentiles to make room for their own equal rights as citizens, so in Israel they need to de-absolutize the redemptive claims of the Jewish state in order to make room for Palestinian civil rights within Israel and Palestinian national rights along side Israel.[68]

As Ellis was defining what he saw as a post-Shoah theology of solidarity with the Palestinians, a parallel theology was being developed by Palestinian Christian theologian, Naim Ateek. In his 1989 book *Justice and Only Justice: A Palestinian Theology of Liberation*, Ateek showed how militant Zionist use of the Bible as the basis for expropriating land where Palestinians once lived has thrown the validity of the Bible, particularly the Hebrew Scriptures, and its God, into question for Palestinian Christians. Palestinians experience themselves as the victims at the expense of the other. Each have to concede space to live to the other and to be able to forgive each other's past misdeeds. Each have to learn to enter into the perspective of the other. Israelis claim they need security, and Palestinians say they seek justice, but neither security nor justice is possible for one without the other. Israelis need to acknowledge that security for them is possible only through justice to the Palestinians. Palestinians need to realize that justice will be possible for them only through acknowledging Israeli fears of insecurity, even if these fears appear irrational to a disarmed, landless and stateless people, suffering under Israeli military might.

A post-Shoah theology, in effect, must critically examine the shadow side of all monistic theologies of liberation and redemption. We must ask "Who is going to be the victim of our liberation? Who is to be enslaved by our redemption?" A theology of solidarity beyond the victim-victimizer relation must seek a path of hope freed from this shadow side. Whenever the Messiah of one people triumphs only by cursing another people; whenever our promised land is claimed by expropriating the land of an earlier people, whether ancient Canaanites, modern Palestinians, Indians in America, or Blacks in South Africa, not only is redemption incomplete, but the seeds have been planted for new evils, new holocausts.

Christians and Jews, Israelis and Palestinians, must recognize that power constructed as domination over others always creates violence, injustice and hatred. Christians have been amply guilty of this in the past, both toward Jews, toward other peoples whom they have conquered and colonized and toward each other. The very possibility of power, much less oppressive power, is new to Jews. It is difficult for them, perhaps, to change rhetorical gears and to deal with the fact that they, too, cannot only gain power but use it unjustly.

Marc Ellis has suggested the moral health of the Jewish community demands this shift to a new self-understanding that accepts responsibility for the costs of power. Dialogue and solidarity between Christians and Jews today cannot be based solely on the innocent victim-guilty victimizer relation of the remembered pogroms and death camps. It must be a mutually self-critical collaboration of peoples, both of whom know that they are capable of abuse of power. Each are seeking to regain their prophetic voice toward injustice, both in their own societies and in relation to each other.

This, I think, also means that Jews and Christians must overcome their antagonism to Arabs and to Muslim people. They must extend their dialogue to the Muslim world and the Arab people as well, without in any way being blind to the parallel tendencies to violence and competitive domination in that culture as well.

In all such relations we must seek a conversion that shifts from an ethic of competitive power, in which the victory of one is possible only through the defeat and humiliation of the other. We must seek a theology and ethic of co-humanity that fosters a quest for mutual justice between neighbors who must learn to live together in one land and on one earth. This quest must curb the tendencies of all three monotheistic faiths to foster triumphalistic self-affirmation through hatred and negation of the others. It must call forth and develop the best of all three religious traditions, Judaism, Christianity, and Islam, of compassion, forgiveness and mutual regard for the neighbor as oneself.

The Holocaust Now

Revisionism and Theology

Harry James Cargas' essay responds to the contemporary phenomenon of those who would deny the very historicity of the Shoah, seeing in its "politicization" by "pro-Zionist Jews" [and others] an attempt to win support for a beleaguered Israel. He cites three "reasons" by these "historical improvisationists"—preferred term—attempt to undermine the historical validity of the Shoah: "First, they wish to undermine the state of Israel; second, they wish to contribute to a resurgence of anti-Judaism; finally, they appear to want to rehabilitate the reputation of the Nazis." After presenting what he believes to be their arguments and demolishing them in the process, he next presents a brief history of Western Civilization's anti-Jewish journey, including that of the Church, thus forcing us to contemplate this so-called "historical revisionism" as an outgrowth of that which preceded it, namely centuries of antisemitic acts, thoughts, and writings. Sadly, in so doing, he forces us to diminish our naivete that such an absurdity could spring *de novo* on the world scene, and, therefore, obliquely, challenges the Christian [and Jewish] religious communities to rethink the long-range and extended implications of their theologies.[1]

SLJ

The Holocaust Now

REVISIONISM AND THEOLOGY: TWO SIDES OF THE SAME COIN?

Harry James Cargas

I. Introduction: Who Are These Persons?

It is not easy to think about the people who try to tell us that the Shoah never occurred. How should we speak of these men [there seems to be no women who are publicly advocating this position]. Do we call them liars? Shall we label them fools? Are they mad? Is it just that they are haters? Are they unbelievably stupid?

We may be tempted to treat them casually, even with mockery. After all, they are advocating that which is ridiculous. Intellectually, they are less than infants. They could be looked upon as partners in denial with members of the Flat Earth Society, and who have as much relevance. But while we tend to think the Flat Earth Society charming, knowing that many of its members cling to it for diversion and fun, no such description can be applied to the people who give themselves the respectable title of "Revisionist Historians." They are, rather, "Improvisationist Historians," men intent on distorting truth, on spitting on the graves of the dead—through the manipulation of evidence.

All historians select from the data available. But all decent historians make some attempt to approach the raw material of history with a certain detachment, a certain objectivity, a certain integrity. We do not find this to be the case with the Improvisers.

An outline of their charges gives us an idea of just who they are, just what these liars and/or fools and/or madmen and/or haters stand for. Or rather, what they stand against. Clearly, they oppose the continued existence of the state of Israel. They are so obsessed with the destruction of that political entity that they will attempt the most illogical, inane kinds of argument in order to support their illogical, fraudulent history.

The Shoah—that massacre of nearly six million Jews and uncounted others at the hands of the Nazis and their collaborators in death camps deliberately designed for such a satanic purpose—never happened. Such is the Improvisationists' most sensational absurdity. They focus exclusively on the Jewish deaths, insisting that either they never occurred or that the numbers are greatly exaggerated. At most, some

The Holocaust Now

Improvisationists offer a figure of 200,000 Jewish deaths—"only 200,000" in their words—nearly none the result of deliberate murder but rather from typhus and other diseases. But never do these fictioneers refer to the figures of the non-Jewish dead. What of them? Are their tragedies to be taken as accurate, only the numbers of the Jewish dead to be questioned?

But then, if the Shoah never was, why spread such a lie? The bogus historians tell us that the whole story is a giant conspiracy on the part of the pro-Zionists who wanted to make the world sorry for what was done to Jews. A post-war universal guilt would thus be a convenient basis from which Zionists would labor for the establishment of the state of Israel. So it seems a few Zionists came together and developed this fanciful tale about the Shoah and got every Jew in the world—*every Jew in the world*—to go along with the deceit. They are telling us that 18,000,000 Jews, 18,000,000 People of the Book, people whose very historical roots are in a profoundly moral tradition, that 18,000,000 Jews all agreed to a tremendous hoax. This would include, of course, many Jews who are *not* Zionists; this would have to include the Jews who are anti-Zionist. This would even have to number the Jewish survivors of Auschwitz and Buchenwald and Dora and Bergen-Belsen who are *anti-Zionist*. 18,000,000 Jews agree to the Big Lie. Indeed!

Add to this the fact that after the Second World War, Nazis and other Germans admitted to the atrocities done in the concentration camps. The Germans collaborated, the Improvisationists offer, because by doing so they guaranteed themselves Allied economic support in rebuilding their war-torn nation. "This means," the Allies said to the defeated Germans, "we French and Russian and British and American and other peoples are all of us pro-Zionists and we are all deliberately lying about the Shoah. We will help German economic recovery only if you Germans, too, join this otherwise incredible plot." And the Germans, according to feigned history, did so. The evidence for this: there is not one shred.

The reason, of course that the Allies were forced in cooperation with the Zionists was simple: continued Jewish control of the media. Can we imagine how Jews dominate the [former—Ed.] Soviet press, for example? Are the Improvisationists looking at the world media currently—that same media which they continue to claim is controlled by Jews. Former Defense Minister Ariel Sharon was unaware that the American press is managed by Jewish interests. Former Minister Menachem Begin did not think the French press is operated by Jews. A definite hostility can be detected towards the Jewish invasions of Lebanon by the media which, later, in much smaller print, corrected gross errors of fact in reporting events in Lebanon—errors which did not reflect glory on Jews. And what is the evidence that the disguised historians show us to prove Jewish control of the media? There is not one shred.

One must notice, also, the Improvisationists' determination to make us believe that

Revisionism and Theology

the Soviets, too, went along with the Zionist plot about the Shoah. The Soviets, whose armaments surround Israel even today in such a threatening manner, were pro-Zionists and to this day have not let the cat out of the bag regarding fabrication. The evidence that the Soviets were in on the game: there is not one shred.

There is indeed a plot connected with the Shoah. But this conspiracy has naught to do with the Zionists, with the victims, with the Allies. A plot has been hatched by the Improvisationist Historians who would like to plant doubts in our minds regarding the truth, the pain, the suffering, the anguish, of the Shoah.

Nazi eyewitnesses of the most expert variety have testified to the horrors of the murders of millions of people in death camps. [One million of these were Jewish boys and girls not yet in their teens.] Rudolf Hoess, the commanding officer at Auschwitz, made a personal confession so enormous that he may be the one person in all history who might accurately say, "I directed more murders than anyone else who ever lived." Adolf Eichmann's testimony likewise was damning proof of the Shoah. Many, many other Nazis corroborated the truth of the massacres. The Improvisationists claim that these witnesses were coerced into convenient confessions. Their proof: there is not one shred.

II. Fantasy Extraordinaire

For a moment, let us imagine a contemporary world in which these fakers of history are correct. Let us pretend with them that the Shoah never occurred. What would it mean if they were right in saying that the deaths of millions of Jews never happened?

First, of course, it would mean that one awful lot of people are lying. And lying magnificently! You can compare the stories of Auschwitz survivors who have never met and they jibe, right down to the little, least significant details of existence in the death camp. Former inmates from Czechoslovakia, Poland, Norway, and other countries, people who have never heard of each other, corroborate each other's account, to a kind of perfection. That can only be described as "magnificent lying."

Think, too, of the Nazis who, at the Nuremberg War Trials, supported the lies of the Zionists—even before the Zionists invented them! Rudolf Hoess appeared to spill his guts in his confession which became the autobiographical book, *Commandant at Auschwitz*. This by the man who said, "I personally arranged the gassing of two million persons between June-July, 1941, and the end of 1943." The Improvisers would have us believe this man is a *liar*—not a killer!

Adolf Eichmann would also have to be transformed from a murderer to one who slaughtered words rather than people. Here is Eichmann's own somber recollection:

> I was sent by my immediate superior, General Muller....He liked

to send me around in his behalf. I was, in effect, a traveling salesman for the Gestapo, just as I once had been a traveling salesman for an oil company in Austria. Muller had heard that Jews were being shot near Minsk and wanted a report....they had already started, so I could see only the finish. Although I was wearing a leather coat which reached almost to my ankles, I was still very cold. I watched the last group of Jews undress, down to their shirts. They walked 100 or 200 yards—they were not driven—then they jumped into the pit. It was impressive to see them all jumping into the pit without offering any resistance whatsoever. Then the men of the squad banged away into the pit with their rifles and machine pistols. Why did that scene linger so long in my memory? Perhaps because I had children myself. And there were children in that pit. I saw a woman hold a child of a year or two into the air, pleading. At that moment all I wanted was to say, "Don't shoot, hand over the child." Then the child was hit. I was so close that later I found bits of brain splattered on my long leather coat. My driver helped me to remove them. Then we returned to Berlin.

These words could not be true according to history mocked—although they helped get Eichmann executed.

Historians galore participated in the great lie. We can name writers of such stature as Hugh Trevor-Roper, William L. Shirer, and Arnold Toynbee [none Jewish and the last named considered by some to be anti-Israel] who contrived a plot about the Shoah with the rest.

The Vatican, too, had to go along with the forgery of history. Catholic priests were everywhere. These clergypersons would have been able to see so very much. And, of course, Rome had been accused of failing to help Jews in their hours of desperate need. Pope Pius XII has been singled out particularly for harsh criticism concerning his so labeled "great silence," his alleged non-intervention on behalf of Jews during World War II. If ever the Catholic Church needed a defense for moral failure, some feel, here is the issue. Yet the Vatican never chose the easy way out. The moral center of world Catholicism could have saved itself serious embarrassment by merely telling the truth: Why should the Church have acted? There was no persecution of Jews; there was no Shoah. The fact that no Pope has offered this defense shows just how deeply that Rome is allied to the Zionist plot. [The fact that the Vatican does not officially recognize the State of Israel cannot be discussed here because it does not fit in with Improvisationist data.]

Many other liars could be mentioned, including all of those—*all of those*—Allied officials who participated in the various war crimes trials after the war, particularly those at Nuremberg. All judges, all prosecutors, and all lawyers would have to have been corrupted by the Zionists, and that, according to this view of synthetic history, is what happened.

And there are countless more prevaricators, but let us just consider one other group, the Shoah survivors who became parents. Victims who outlived the death camps tended to marry survivors. A shared, almost unutterable experience, tended to bring such coupled together. But in order to promote the Zionist myth, they all had to lie to their children about grandparents. They had to tell their infants that they had no grandmothers and grandfathers—all for the promulgation of Israel. What are Jewish holidays like in the homes of survivors of the Shoah? *They are lonely. Their families are abbreviated.* We have to wonder what the survivors did with their fathers and their mothers.

Arthur Butz, in his Improvisationist book *The Hoax of the Twentieth Century*,[2] gives us a hint of how Jewish families reacted to the opportunity to advance the Shoah myth. This hero of the contemporary neo-Nazis writes that some Jews were sent to labor camps to help the German war effort. Then we read these words:

> In many cases deported Jewish families were broken up for what was undoubtedly intended by the Germans to be a period of limited duration. This was particularly the case when the husband seemed a good labor conscript; just as German men were conscripted for hazardous military service, Jews were conscripted for unpleasant labor tasks. Under such conditions it is reasonable to expect that many of these lonely wives and husbands would have, during or at the end of the war, established other relations that seemed more valuable than previous relationships. In such cases, then, there would have been a strong motivation not to re-establish contact with the legal spouse.

Think of it! Many Jews who were married preferred not to return to their original families. Clearly Mr. Butz here destroys the myth of closeness of Jewish families. [Butz has done much service for the Improvisers, by the way. Among his more brilliant analyses is his insight into the use of Zyklon gas at Auschwitz. Far from denying its availability, Butz informs us that Zyklon gas was "used as an insecticide at Auschwitz." So Zyklon was employed to help Jews, not harm them, he tells us. He fails to document his claim, and he cannot defend the enormous quantities of "insecticides" ordered, but these are minor failings.]

The Holocaust Now

III. The Shoah Could and Did Happen!

Let us continue to look at the world as *if* the Shoah never happened from another point of view: even if the Shoah had not occurred, *it could have*. The climate had been created, for centuries, which made a Shoah possible. There was a Shoah, so obviously it was possible. But we should look very keenly at what created an atmosphere which permitted, and more, *encouraged* a massacre of the proportions we know. Here is a paragraph from a book I published in 1976:

> Adolf Hitler, a baptized Catholic who was never excommunicated by Rome, implemented a policy of total destruction because, and only because, he was able to. Only because people willingly cooperated in individual and mass murders. Who, for example, were the architects who designed the ovens into which people were delivered for cremation? Who meticulously executed the plans for the efficient gas chambers into which naked men, women, and children were herded to die? Who originated the design for the camps, those models of economical, technological destruction? Which firms bid on the contracts to build the camps, the gas chambers, the ovens? Who bribed whom to win the coveted contracts, to gain the chance to make a profit and serve the Fuhrer by erecting houses of death and torture? Which doctors performed experiments on Jewish victims? Who shaved their heads, and all bodily hairs, to gain materials for clothes and rugs? We've heard of lampshades made from Jewish skins, of soap made from Jewish bodies, of enforcers throwing Jewish victims—most of them dead, but not all—into huge pits, of brutal guards crushing babies' skulls with rifle butts, and shooting aged and unhealthy Jews who couldn't keep up on forced marches, and making naked Jews stand for hours in freezing weather for either convenience or amusement. Who were these tormentors? What of the train engineers who guided the cattle cars packed with starving, dying, dead Jews to locales of internment? And what ordinary citizens of many European nations who, as the death trains passed through their communities, would throw bits of bread into the cattle cars to be entertained by watching famished Jews fight over the food in an agonizing display of attempts at survival?

What led up to these possibilities? Historically the picture is devastating. We can find seriously anti-Judaic passages in the words and acts of the Romans: Cicero, Seneca, Tiberius, Democritus, Trajan, Caligula, Quintilian, Juvenal, Tacitus—a list much too long.

Then came the Christians. Not all, numerically perhaps not even many. And yet *far too many* Christians of influence had terrible and *erroneous* things to say about that general group of people called "the Jews." Here follows only a sketch of a very tragic history of our inhumanity toward each other. And we recall as we reflect on this, not only must we be aware of the atrocities committed against Jews, we should also be conscious of what violence these words of Christians have done to the teachings of Jesus, the Jew. Here is Father Edward Flannery from his excellent book on Christian anti-Semitism, *The Anguish of the Jews*[3]:

> The first Christian Church, full of zeal and fervor, was a Jewish church in leadership, membership, and worship; and it remained within precincts of the Synagogue. But as the universalist implications of the Gospel message [not yet fully written] made themselves felt, a series of developments gradually brought this arrangement to an end. In the tones of a prophet, Stephen charged the people and their leaders with infidelity to Moses as well as to the Messiah [Acts 7:2-53]. By private revelation, Peter was instructed to accept the demi-proselyte, Cornelius, into the Church without committing him to the Law [Acts 10]. The council of the apostles at Jerusalem decreed that gentile converts were not to be held to the legal observances [Galatians 2; Acts 15:11]. Finally, at Antioch, Paul confronted Peter, insisting that while Jewish Christians might practice the Law, faith in Jesus Christ was necessary and sufficient for salvation [Galatians 2:11-21]. This was the final disposition of the matter. Judaeo-Christianity, thus rejected, was destined to become a snare to Christian and Jew alike and a source of conflict for both Church and Synagogue.

Early Christian-Jewish hostility grew and some Jewish persecution against Christians took place, although it was comparatively insignificant, mainly reactionary. Soon, a nearly two millennium assault on Judaism began. Ignatius of Antioch required that no Christians could keep the Jewish Sabbath. He claimed that the prophets of Israel were not truly of the Jewish religion but were Christians before their time. Nils Dahl has written that "The simplistic doctrine that Israel was rejected and the Church chosen to be a new people of God is not really found within the New Testament, although it is adumbrated in some of the later writings." However, Rosemary Radford Ruether in *Faith and Fratricide*[4] insists that the Church won historical existence for herself by negating Judaism and claiming to supersede the historical existence of Israel. Ruether claims that a new Christology offers a way out of anti-Judaism for Christians.

The Holocaust Now

But back to the historical thread. Saint Justin was probably the first to claim that the Jews had to suffer because they killed Jesus. This is both bad history and bad theology and has been proven to be so repeatedly by theologians, but the errors have persisted through the centuries with all their tragic effects.

In the third century, Saint Cyprian insisted that "Now the peoplehood of the Jews has been cancelled." The next century gave us Saint John Chrysostom:

> How can Christians dare "have the slightest converse with Jews, "Most miserable of all men" [Homily 4:1], men who are"....lustful, rapacious, greedy, perfidious bandits." Are they not "inveterate murderers, destroyers, men possessed by the devil," whom "debauchery and drunkenness have given them the manners of the pig and the lusty goat. They know only one thing, to satisfy their gullets, get drunk, to kill and maim one another...." [1:4]. Indeed, "they have surpassed the ferocity of wild beasts, for they murder their offspring and immolate them to the devil" [1:6]. "They are impure and impious...." [1:4].
>
> Their Synagogue? Not only is it a theater and a house of prostitution, but a caravan of brigands, a "repair of wild beasts" [6:5], a place of "shame and ridicule" [1:3], "the domicile of the devil [1:6], as is also the souls of the Jews" [1:4, 6]. Indeed, Jews worship the devil; their rites are "criminal and impure," their religion is "A disease" [3:1]. Their synagogue, again, is "an assembly of criminals....den of thieves....a cavern of devils, and an abyss of perdition" [1:2; 6:6].
>
> God hates the Jews and always hated the Jews [6:4; 1:7], and on Judgment Day He will say to Judaizers, "Depart from Me, for you have had intercourse with My murderers." It is the duty of Christians to hate the Jews; "He who can never love Christ enough will never have done fighting against those [Jews] who hate Him [7:11]. "Flee then, their assemblies, flee their houses, and keep far from venerating the synagogue because of the books it contains in it" [1:5]. "....I hate the Synagogue precisely because it has the law and prophets...." [6:6]. "....I hate the Jews also because they outrage against the law...."

Many other saints and church leaders could be quoted from this point on, but more than enough has been indicated already to illustrate what needs to be said here.

But there were more than words—actions based on those words. Forced baptism became a practice. Jewish children were taken from their parents, baptized and not returned to their homes. This was done in spite of condemnations of such acts by popes. Another ugly chapter is that of the Crusades, still pointed to with pride in the

Revisionism and Theology

current *Catholic Encyclopedia*, it should be noted. Next came charges of Ritual Murder. They seem to have begun in the 12th Century. Ritual murder was first said to be the sacrifice of a Christian victim, by Jews, usually a child, during the Christian Holy Week, for religious purposes. All over Europe, for centuries, such absurdities were claimed and many Jews were massacred, raped, had their homes pillaged and destroyed. One such event took place behind the Iron Curtain just a few years ago. A Catholic priest and historian, a Father Vacandard, has established that not a single case of Ritual Murder has ever been proven—not one, not ever.

Pope Innocent III's Fourth Lateran Council ordered that Jews and Saracens had to wear distinctive clothing. This was seven and a half centuries before the Nazis forced the Jews to wear yellow stars. The Talmud was burned by Christians, and, in 1298, about 100,000 Jews were killed in Germany and Austria because of the unfounded allegation that a Jew—one Jew—had desecrated a communion host.

Then came one of the most tragic eras in Christian history, the Inquisition. Set up only to root out heresy among Christians, it was, as we know, turned against Jews as well. There is no need to give accounts of torture and executions at this point—the story is too familiar.

Then came the Reformation. Things did not get better for the Jews. Here are the words of Martin Luther. And remember: this is not a quote from some Nazi officer caught up in the spirit of trying to rid the world of Jews:

> First, their Synagogue or school is to be set on fire and what won't burn is to be heaped over with dirt and dumped on, so that on one can see a stone or chunk of it forever....Second, their houses are to be torn down and destroyed in the same way....Third, they are to have all their prayerbooks and Talmudics taken from them....Fourth, their rabbis are to be forbidden publicly to praise God, to thank [God], to pray [to God], to teach [of God] among us and ours....And furthermore, they shall be forbidden to utter the name of God in our hearing; no value shall be accorded the Jewish mouth [Maul] by us Christians, so that he may utter the name of God in our hearing, but whoever hears it from a Jew shall report him to the authorities....Fifth, the Jews are to be deprived totally of walkways and streets....Sixth, they are to be forbidden the lending of interest and all cash and hold of silver and gold are to be taken from them and put to one side for safekeeping....Seventh, the young, strong Jews and Jewesses are to have flail, axe, and spade put into their hands.

The story gets no better. In 1700, Johann Eisenmenger published *Judaism Unmasked* which has been an inspired encyclopedia of anti-Juda-ism until now. Names of people pronouncing anti-Judaic sentiments include Schleiermacher, Fichte, Goethe, Marx [himself born a Jew], Voltaire, Diderot, Spinoza [another Jew], Hegel—what a long list! Then in 1884 came Arthur de Gobineau's *Essay on the Inequality of the Human Races*.[5] Jews, in the author's view, were distinctly inferior to German Aryans and Hitler's policy of destroying Jews was based in great part on de Gobineau's errors.

In Germany itself, the nation was saturated in anti-Jewish atmosphere, and few people spoke out on behalf of the vilified. From 1925-1927, over 700 racist anti-Jewish newspapers were published throughout the country. Even in children's books, passages such as this could be read: "Without solution of the Jewish question/No salvation of mankind."

The Jew was blamed for the loss of World War I, for Germany's economic woes, for being of impure blood and literally for being less than human. Adolf Hitler came onto the scene proclaiming that "by defending myself against the Jew, I am fighting for the work of the Lord." It was said of Der Fuhrer that "God had manifested himself not in Jesus Christ but in Adolf Hitler." The Minister for Church Affairs in Germany in 1937 urged that "A new authority has risen as to what Christ and Christianity really are—Adolf Hitler." The same man, Hans Kerrl, even went beyond this when he postulated that "As Christ in his twelve disciples raised a stock fortified into martyrdom, so in Germany today we are witnessing the same thing....Adolf Hitler is the true Holy Ghost!"

IV. Where Do We Go From Here?

Indeed, the climate was prepared. The fact is that the Shoah happened because it could have happened. It was not an effect of a one-time satanic interference in human events. *The Shoah was centuries in the making.* The responsibilities are enormous and widespread. Jews born in 1942 had been condemned in 342 and 1542 as well. And those who deny that the genocide took place are, indeed, participating in this ignominious continuity which helps to grant victories to the Nazis beyond their graves.

Why do the Improvisationist/Historians ply their sham trade? The answer may be seen as threefold: First, they wish to undermine the state of Israel; second, they wish to contribute to a resurgence of anti-Judaism; finally, they appear to want to rehabilitate the reputation of the Nazis. Willis Carto, a treasurer for Liberty Lobby, has written that Hitler's defeat was America's defeat. Austin App blames the United States for starting the Second World War and for fighting on the wrong side.

Actually, however, this turns out not to be too surprising. Here is part of a letter, written to U. S. Chief of Staff George Marshall by Dwight Eisenhower when he was the Supreme Commander of the Allied Forces in the European Theater. After visiting the newly-liberated camp at Ohrdruf, Eisenhower wrote:

Revisionism and Theology

> The things I saw beggar description....The visual evidence and the verbal testimony of starvation, cruelty, and bestiality were so overpowering as to leave me a bit sick. In one room there were piled up twenty or thirty naked men, killed by starvation; George Patton would not even enter. He said he would get sick if he did so.. I made the visit deliberately, in order to be in a position to give *first-hand* evidence of these things if ever, in the future, there develops a tendency to charge these allegations merely to "propaganda."

Eisenhower somehow anticipated the appearance of nay-sayers in the future. But the most meaningful blow rendered against the bastardization of history by the Improvisationists occurred at an International Liberators Conference held at the State Department in October, 1981. I participated in the meeting and witnessed what I am about to relate.

Death camp survivors and those who freed them were among 500 men and women from fourteen nations who gathered in Washington for the emotion-laden assembly. Included were former soldiers, war correspondents and medical personnel from Russia, Poland, Czechoslovakia, France, Israel, Great Britain, Denmark, the Netherlands, Norway, Switzerland, Belgium, Canada, New Zealand, Yugoslavia, and the United States. All gave witness to what they saw upon liberating Auschwitz, Buchenwald, Bergen-Belsen, and Dachau. In so doing, they put an end to the lie of the pseudo-history of the Improvisationists.

Among those who testified to the truth was Soviet Lieutenant Vassily Petrenko, hardly with any Zionist purpose in mind. Yet Petrenko, who led the liberation of Auschwitz, did indeed acknowledge the truth of the death camps.

The evidence was so overwhelming that Polish Brigadier General Franciczek Skibinki noted that "With every hour of this conference we are convinced that we came at the right time to the right place." The distinguished British jurist Colonel G. I. A. D. Draper urged that all nations adopt laws making it a crime to advocate the claim that the Shoah never occurred. He received an ovation for that remark.

Those who doubt the truth about the annihilation of more than a third of the world's Jews are either liars, fools, mad, haters, stupid, or a combination of these. The plethora of evidence presented at the Nuremberg War Crimes Trials is certainly enough to convince any reasonably rational person. So are the histories, the eyewitness accounts by Shoah survivors, the confessions by the Nazis. To question the reality of the Shoah ought to be unthinkable.

In his book *Vatican Diplomacy and the Jews During the Holocaust*[6], 1939-1943, a Catholic priest at Seton Hall University, John Morley, documents so much that condemns the Improvisationists. He quotes Catholic communiques from at least seven nations—letters, memos, directives, etc.—which affirm that high Vatican officials did indeed know what was happening to Jews through Europe. And what was happening was indeed horrendous, nearly unimaginable. The Vatican had hardly been a source of strong Zionist support. The documents which Father Morley quotes were not written to help establish the state of Israel. Anyone who says the opposite is a liar.

Even the Arabs today, many of whom feel that the Israelis are intruders on Arab territory, do not deny the Shoah.

In October, 1982, speaking at Webster University in Saint Louis, Dr. Hatem Husseni, the Palestine Liberation Organization's Deputy Observer to the United Nations, talked about the deprivations of his people since the recognition of Israel. He *compared* their suffering to those of the Jews during the Shoah. Dr. Husseni is hardly part of a Zionist conspiracy.

I myself am not a Zionist. [Nor am I anti-Zionist.] I teach, write, and speak about the reality of the Shoah as a Christian failing—as the greatest Christian tragedy since the Crucifixion of Jesus. My basic purpose is to explore how so many persons in Christian nations could have acted in so un-Christian a manner, whether they were active persecutors or merely neutral observers who just "didn't want to get involved." I do not do work on behalf of the State of Israel. I do my work because I am obsessed by the fact that millions upon millions of mothers, grandparents, babies, fathers, doctors, laborers, teachers, rabbis, clerks, secretaries, and others were murdered by thousands of men who were baptized in Christ. I want to know how this can be true.

And, tangentially, I want to know about the pornographers as well. Who are they? How dare they write and speak their filth! Listen to the titles of the works they offer for sale:

Christ is Not a Jew
Our Nordic Race
The Negro and World Crises
A Gallery of Jewish Types
I. Q. and Racial Differences
Proof of Negro Inferiority
Who Brought Slaves to America
[Which pretends to prove that Jews
were responsible for the slave trade]
The South's Part in Mongrelizing the Nation
White Man Think Again!
Etc., etc., truly *ad nauseum*

Indeed, there is a conspiracy concerning the Shoah! But the plot was not hatched by Zionists to support the legitimization of Israel; nor do Soviets, Yugoslavs, anti-Zionist Jews, Vatican officials, and so many others I've quoted—including members of the PLO—join in any scheme to take territory away from Arabs.

   The only conspiracy about the Shoah is entered into by the nay-sayers, those who take the blood of Hitler's victims willingly on their hands. They are the conspirators, they are those who make a forgery of history, who manipulate, contrive, counterfeit, fabricate, and mock not only the facts, but all people as well. We are poorer, as a human race, for their existence. Their only contribution has been, by prompting a reaction, to cause the Shoah to be the most validated, documented tragedy of all time. But the problem has absolutely nothing to do with whether or not the Shoah happened. The problem has to do with our response to the Shoah. What have we learned from that awesome event? What are we going to do about it?

The Holocaust Now

Between the Fires

For Arthur Waskow, critic of so much of contemporary American Jewish society, whose little essay is "midrashic poetry" [i.e. interpretive Scriptural commentary], the analogy between the Biblical text and the Shoah is an obvious one: We are living in the period "between the fires" of Auschwitz and possible thermonuclear conflagration. Unless we learn to affirm life right now through the process of "making Shabbat" [i.e. Sabbath pause], there will be none to affirm any kind of future whatsoever—nor any seed planted for future generations to record what comes next.

SLJ

The Holocaust Now

BETWEEN THE FIRES[1]

Arthur Waskow

I. Introduction

I am writing during the week of the Torah portion called *Lekh L'kha* ["Go forth," Genesis 12:1-17:27—Ed.]. In the midst of the portion [Genesis 15] there is the eerie story of how the wandering Abram—not yet Abraham, nor yet our forbearer—experiences the Covenant between the Fires. He has come in spiritual agony, fearful that for him and Sarai there will be no next generation. He places the divided bodies of several sacrificial animals in two rows. They flame up in a "smoking furnace." He stands between the first, and there falls upon a "thick darkness." He slips into a profound trance. In it he becomes a partner in the Covenant of the Generations: he and Sarai will have seed, and they will live in the land bounded by the Jordan and the Sea.

Abram has created a kind of "Shabbat in space." In one direction there is a fire that represents the candles that begin Shabbat; in the other direction, there is a fire that represents the *Havdalah* candle that ends Shabbat. But what makes the space between these two into a Shabbat-space is that Abram experiences and accepts in it the Dark of Mystery. Shabbat is the emblem and the practice of Mystery. In it we recognize that although we feel sure we know exactly what to do next and feel driven to do it, in fact we do not know what comes next—since there is in life a mysterious element. And so on Shabbat we do nothing, and celebrate the fact of not-knowing with joy, not fear or anger. From our plunge into this Mystery we learn new paths.

Abram lets the mysterious darkness come into himself. He "rests"—not merely pausing, but letting the Mystery absorb him. And so there wells up in him the Covenant that extends through time to future generations. In recognition that this Shabbat is one in space, he receives a promise of a holy space—the Land that is infused with Shabbat.

How does this speak to the meaning of the Holocaust? *We are the generation that stands between the fires*—behind us the smoke and flame that rose from Auschwitz, before us the nightmare of the flood of fire and smoke that could turn our planet into

The Holocaust Now

Auschwitz. We come, like Abram, in an agony of fear that for us—for all of us—there may be no next generation.

II. The Challenge

What will transform the Fire that lies before us? What will turn it into a light that enlightens rather than a blaze that consumes? What will make possible for us the covenant of generations yet to come?

The first teaching of this story is to see the Holocaust as both unique and non-unique: to see its fire reflected in a giant mirror that could dwarf even its unprecedented horror. To see ourselves living not *after* the Fire, but *between* the Fires. And to see a profound connection between them, not mere accident.

The second teaching of the story is to make this time between the Fires into a time of Shabbat: a time of affirming and celebrating Mystery, a time to pause from the project of modernity and let a new path emerge from the mysterious darkness.

Let us explore these two teachings in more depth. What does it mean to experience and connect these two fires?

Both of them flame up from the sparks of modernity. The dark sparks, struck on the granite face of History by the dark side of modernity. There are two ways of talking about this: one uses God-language, the other History-language. Let us start with the second—the one that modern people are used to—and then to see whether we learn something more from talking God.

Over the millennia the human race learns, empowers itself. Learns to organize larger and larger societies, more and more complex patterns. Learns to make itself, and then reaches a whole new stage—learns that it is remaking itself. Breaks from the embedded traditions of the past. Decides that there are no mysteries to be celebrated, only ignorances to be conquered.

The human race creates modernity. Learns the workings of the planets, the stars, the Galapagos turtles, drosophila, DNA, the proton, the id, the working class, the historical dialectic. Reunites the two lost supercontinents. Abolishes smallpox. Sets foot on the moon, makes deserts bloom. Changes the chemistry of the oceans, puts every human voice throughout the earth in touch with every other, makes five billion people, brings down the center of the stars to burn and freeze the earth.

And along the way, as a byproduct, it makes possible the Holocaust. Before modernity, pogroms—but not a Holocaust. Only the social organization of a modern bureaucracy, only telephones and radios, only railroad trains, only Zyklon B, could make an Auschwitz possible.

But why was it the Jews who became the target of this runaway modernity?

In the language of modernity, we can say that history put the Jews of Eastern Europe into the most vulnerable position possible when confronting a human race that was drunk on its new-made "modern" power. The Jews were a stateless people. A non-military people. A *prototype people.* What is it Elie Wiesel says? That in the face of nuclear annihilation the whole earth is Jewish—like the Jews who faced the Holocaust. Why [say I]? Because now *everyone is a stateless person.* Every people, even every government, has been disarmed. Because in the face of Planetary Auschwitz Camp I [the U.S. nuclear "arsenal"], the Soviet Union has no weapons of defense—only the threat of Planetary Auschwitz Camp II. And vice versa. "To provide for the common defense" is the deadest letter in the American Constitution.

The holy people, the stateless people, the people who had only the Talmud for a Constitution and rabbis for police—they died the soonest. But they point the way for all of us.

We have been talking the language of modernity. I think this language is necessary, but I do not think it is sufficient. If the Holocaust Past and the Holocaust Yet-to-Come are cancers of modernity, then some other language, some language that encompasses and transcends modernity, is necessary. I propose that this language is God-language. But not the old God-language. God in a new key, a new name, a new sensing. For the old God-language was itself transcended, reduced, relativized, by the leap of modernity.

The Hassidic Rebbe of Chernobyl gave us a hint, two hundred years ago. He taught that we must see the world as God veiled in robes of God so as to appear to be material. Alz iz Gott. All is God. Our job is to unwrap the veil to discover that our history is God, our biology is God, our....is God.

In this way of speaking, the Nazi Holocaust and the Bomb are byproducts of the Divinization of the human race.

Even the Holocaust—it is all right to tremble as you read this, for I am trembling as I write it—even the Holocaust was an outburst of light. Those who say we cannot blame God for the Holocaust are only partly right: it was the overflow of God, the outbursting of light, the untrammeled, unboundaried outpouring of Divinity, that gave us Auschwitz....and may yet consume the earth.

Start back, before the Holocaust. Imagine the God Who stood outside the world, but let a spark of Godness flare up in every human being. And over millennia of slow human history, let the spark catch into a glowing coal—into a sense of God, the Presence, hovering almost among us, almost within us, not quite beyond us.

And then, in the burst of light that is the modern age, the coals burst into flame. Powers once felt to be Divine are now infused into human beings. Powers like the ability to make a revolution [it was God Who made the Exodus from Egypt]. Like the ability to create new species. Like the ability to destroy all species. Flame by flame, the human race in the modern age incorporates into itself the powers that we once called

Divine.

And now in this God-language, why the Jews? In this kind of language, the God Who chose us from outside history at Sinai is still choosing us from inside History. We are God's canary-people: the people God sends down the mineshaft first, to test out whether the air breathes ecstasy and revelation or is full of carbon monoxide. If we keel over....

Now God knows, we all know: the air is heavy with poison.

III. Why the Jews?

Why us, how did we get chosen? From *inside* history—the history that made us the first stateless people is the history that chose us to be the canary-people. No more mysterious than that—but that is plentifully mysterious.

So was the Holocaust inevitable? Were the Nazis God's own arm, in a paroxysm not of punishment—not at all this time "for our sins"—but of untrammeled power striking down its holy victim? Did God forget to put on t'fillin [i.e. phylacteries—Ed.] one morning and the unbound Arm of the Almighty....?

Wait a minute, *damn* your midrashic poetry, are you saying so many babies and so many bubbes [Grandmothers—Ed.] died because God was coming deeper into the world? How good can such a God be? Very good; but not totally good. Very good, despite and because of the evidence of the Holocaust, because it was the surge of enormous God-power to do good in the world that made it also possible to do such enormous bad in the world. And very good because the teachings from God, about God, teach and taught the human race how to prevent the Holocaust. And very good because the teachings left us free to choose. But not totally good—or we would have used our freedom better.

I do not believe that Auschwitz was inevitable—but the Divine Insurge made it very hard to avoid. I do not believe that the looming Planetary Auschwitz is inevitable, but rather than the Divine Insurge is making it very hard to avoid. Indeed it is a little less hard to avoid because we have already experienced the Nazis. The fact that our canary-people keeled over is one of the weightier rocks that we can roll into the path of the juggernaut. Maybe the most we can hope to gain from Auschwitz is not perfect security for the State of Israel, not the end of anti-Semitism as a Christian dogma, not *Mashiach* [Messiah—Ed.], but indeed just "never again"—just the minimum, never again.

I do not mean Kahane's "never again the Jews." That one is easy to refrain from doing. Why bother with the Jews again, who needs to prove that *one is possible?*—But *never again, not the whole earth,* now *that* remains to be proved. The Universal Auschwitz, now *that* is an eternal monument still waiting to be erected by some Super-Hitler who will not even mind that no one will remain to be horrified by his monument. So the warning of "never again?" The warning to the rest of us to prevent such a Super-Hitler,

Between the Fires

that may remain as the one decently useable product of the Holocaust.

I am not saying that God sent the Holocaust and murdered the Jews in order to warn the planet. I would say, instead, that God and only God made the Holocaust immensely possible; God also made the Holocaust avoidable; we chose. If we can learn from the Holocaust not to destroy the earth, then we could have learned from the murder of Abel not to do the Holocaust.

Why did Abel die? Because the curse of Eden was work-work-work-work until you die. Exhaust yourself. Shabbat comes into the world to reverse the curse of Eden.

What is the teaching? The teaching is to pause. The teaching is to make Shabbat. That teaching is to put a boundary, a loving limit upon the unbridled. God-energy that is bursting its way into the world. As God's Own Self needed to pause after six days of Creation in order to seal the acts of making with a non-act of not-making....so do we.

The modern era, with its works of production, must pause and make Shabbat if the very brilliance of its productivity is not to burn up the earth. It must celebrate Mystery instead of trying to conquer it. Must learn from Mystery that the dark is light enough— is joy, not frightening.

Why is the celebration of Mystery crucial? It is not that Super-Hitler will necessarily come as Hitler came, with full deadly, murderous intention. The idolatry of death may come this time not with deliberate intention, but by putting into a place a potentially lethal system—and then insisting that we can keep it totally under control. *No mistakes, never* a mistake. *All* is known, *all* is controlled. The total rejection of Mystery.

We, the human race, have painted an extraordinary picture. The picture was completed, but we kept on painting. Hiroshima was a brush-stroke too many. The Holocaust was a dozen, a human brush-strokes too many. The painting is marred. It is on the verge of ruination. We must stop our painting, take it off the easel. We must recognize that *we do not know* what to do next, we must celebrate that mystery, stop doing, make Shabbat, and fine a new clean canvas. Then we will hear the new teaching from within us; we will uncover what to do.

We are the generation that stands between the fires. *If we see this,* we can make where we stand into a Shabbat. We can, like Abram, receive the Covenant of the Generations—that there *will* be future generations, despite our deep dread that it will end with us. And our future generations—those of all humanity—will get to live in the land that lies between the rivers and the oceans of space: all earth.

If we do *not* see the two fires in relation to each other, then the fire behind us will lose all meaning, and the one that is yet to come will consume us.

Between the fires is the place of thick darkness, of impenetrable mystery. Will we celebrate this Mystery and live, or scorn it and die?

The Holocaust Now

REFLECTIVE CHALLENGES

The Holocaust Now

The Holocaust: A Summing Up After Two Decades of Reflection

Emil Fackenheim, whose seminal influence upon both post-Auschwitz philosophical and theological thought speaks for itself, as always, raises issues profound in their implication in his essay included here. Preferring the term "unprecedented" to "unique" as regards the Shoah, he reminds us that, now, both philosophy and theology must be rethought in light of the historical *fact* of the Shoah[1], and, subsequent to it, the whole notion of missionizing the Jews on the part of Christians is "a theological obscenity." Then, too, the very idea of human nature must equally be rethought, now confronted with a humanity "infinitely deparavable." Lastly, in traditional Jewish terms, the Shoah took place in *Galut* [Exile], and is, therefore, an experience of "Galut-Judaism." The lesson: Shoah has now come to its end; it is time for the Jew to take leave of his/her Exile and return to Zion. Hence, *because* of the Shoah, Fackenheim now supplies a new rationale, both philosophical and theological, for Zionism, yet echoing both Jewish traditional religious thought and the experience of Jewish history succeeding the Roman destruction of the Second Temple in the year 70.

SLJ

The Holocaust Now

THE HOLOCAUST: A SUMMING UP AFTER TWO DECADES OF REFLECTION[1]

Emil L. Fackenheim

I. Preamble

My preamble consists of two quotations. The first is from Peter Demetz, *Postwar German Literature:*

> In West Germany [where, according to the revised statute of limitations, concentration camp murderers who did not act from base motives can no longer be prosecuted] Celan's "Fugue of Death" has become a popular textbook piece, and one of the academic commentators admonishes the classroom teacher to stick to the text lest "student discussion deviate from the work of art to the persecution of the Jews."

My second text is taken from the Proceedings of the Nuremberg trials and consists of the interrogation of a Polish Auschwitz guard by the Russian prosecutor and reads as follows:

> Witness: Women carrying children were always sent with them to the crematorium. The children were then torn from their parents outside the crematorium and sent to the gas-chambers separately. When the extermination of the Jews in the gas-chambers was at its height, orders were issued to the effect that the children were to be thrown into the crematorium furnaces or into the pit near the crematorium, without being gassed first.

"Holocaust" by Emil L. Fackenheim. Reprinted with permission of Charles Scribner's Sons, an imprint of Simon & Schuster Macmillian, from CONTEMPORARY JEWISH RELIGIOUS THOUGHT, Arthur A. Cohen and Paul Mendes-Flohr, Editors, pp. 399-408. Copyright © 1987 by Charles Scribner's Sons.

The Holocaust Now

> Smirnow [Russian prosecutor]: How am I to understand this? Did they throw them into the fire alive, or did they kill them first?
> Witness: They threw them in alive. Their screams could be heard at the camp.
> Smirnov: Why did they do this?
> Witness: It is very difficult to say. We do not know whether they wanted to economize on gas, or if it was because there was not enough room in the gas-chambers.

II. The Term *Holocaust*

"Holocaust" is the term currently most widely employed for the persecution of the Jewish people by Nazi Germany [1933-1945], first in Germany itself and subsequently in Nazi-occupied Europe, culminating in "extermination" camps and resulting in the murder of nearly six million Jews. However, "Shoa" ["total destruction"] would be more fitting since "Holocaust" connotes, in addition, "burnt sacrifice." It is true that, like ancient Moloch-worshippers, German Nazis and their non-German henchmen at Auschwitz threw children into the flames alive. It was not, however, their own children, in acts of sacrifice, but those of Jews, in acts of murder.

III. The Holocaust and History

Is the Holocaust unique? The concept "unprecedented" is preferable as it refers to the same facts but avoids not only well-known difficulties about the concept "unique" but also the temptation of taking the event out of history and thus "mystifying" it. [See the warnings voiced especially by Yehuda Bauer.] To be sure, Auschwitz was "like another planet" ["Ka-tzetnik 135683," the pen name of the novelist Yechiel Dinur], i.e. a world of its own, with laws, modes of behavior and even a language of its own. Even so, as "unprecedented" rather than "unique" it is placed firmly into history. Historians are obliged, so far as possible, to search for precedents; and thoughtful people—by no means historians only—are obliged to ask if the Holocaust itself may become a precedent for future processes, whether as yet only possible or already actual. Manes Sperber has written: "encouraged by the way Hitler had practiced genocide without encountering resistance, the Arabs [in 1948] surged in upon the nascent Israeli nation, to exterminate it and make themselves its immediate heirs."

The most obvious recent precedent of the Holocaust is the Turkish genocide of the Armenians in World War I. Like the Nazi genocide of the Jews in World War II, this was [i] an attempt to destroy a whole people, [ii] carried out under the cover of a war, [iii] with maximum secrecy and [iv] with the victims being deported to isolated places

The Holocaust: A Summing Up After Two Decades of Reflection

prior to their murder, [v] all this provoking few countermeasures or even verbal protests on the part of the civilized world. Doubtless the Nazis both learned from, and were encouraged by, the Armenian process.

But unlike the Armenian genocide the Holocaust was intended, planned and executed as the "final solution" of a "problem." Thus whereas e.g. the Armenians in Istanbul, the very heart of the Turkish Empire, were left almost untouched, Nazi Germany, had she won the war or even man-aged to prolong it a little, would have murdered every last Jew available. [North American Indians have survived in reservations; Jewish reservations in a victorious Nazi Empire are inconceivable.] Thus the Holocaust may be said to belong, with other catastrophes, into the species "genocide." Within the species "intended, planned, and largely executed extermination," it is without precedent and, thus far at least, without sequel. It is—here the term really must be employed—unique.

Equally unique are the means without which this project could not have been planned or carried out. These include: [i] a scholastically precise definition of the victims; [ii] juridical procedures, enlisting the finest minds of the legal profession, aimed at the total elimination of the victims' rights; [iii] a technical apparatus including murder trains and gas chambers; [iv] most importantly, a veritable army not only of actual murderers but also of managers, army officers, railway conductors, entrepreneurs, and an endless list of others.

All these were required for the "how" of the "Final Solution." Its "why" required an army of historians, philosophers and theologians. The historians rewrote history. The philosophers refuted the idea that man-kind is human before it is "Aryan" or "non-Aryan." And the theologians were divided into Christians who made Jesus into an "Aryan," and neo-pagans who rejected Christianity itself as "non-Aryan." [Their differences were slight compared to their shared commitments." Such were the shock troops of this army. Equally necessary, however, was its remainder: historians, philosophers, and theologians who knew differently but betrayed their calling by holding their peace.

What *was* the "why" of the Holocaust? Even the shock troops never quite faced it, though having no reason or excuse for not doing so. As early as in 1936 Julius Streicher was on record, to the effect that "who fights the Jew fights the devil," and that "who masters the devil conquers heaven." And this basest, most pornographic Nazi expressed only most succinctly the philosophy of the most authoritative one, to the effect that "if the Jew will be victorious" in his cosmic struggle with mankind, his "crown" will be the "funeral wreath of humanity, and this planet will, as it did millions of years ago, move through the ether devoid of human beings" [Hitler in *Mein Kampf*].

Planet Auschwitz was as good as Streicher's word. When the Third Reich was at the height of its power, the conquest of heaven seemed to lie in the apotheosis of the master race; even then, however, the "mastery" of the Jewish "devil" was a necessary condition of it. And when the Third Reich came crashing down and the apocalypse was at hand, "Planet Auschwitz" continued to operate till the end, and Hitler's last will and testament made the fight against the Jewish people mandatory for future generations. The "mastery" of the Jewish "devil," it seems, had become *sufficient* condition for the "conquest of heaven," if indeed not identical with it.

To be sure, this advent of salvation in the Auschwitz gas chambers was but for relatively few eyes to see. What could be heard by all, however, was the promise of it years earlier, when the streets of Germany resounded to the stormtroopers' hymn: "When Jewish blood spurts from our knives, our well-being will redouble."

Never in history has a state attempted to make a whole country—indeed, in this case, a whole continent—*rein* of every single member of a whole people, man, woman, and child. Never have attempts resembling the Holocaust even somewhat been pursued with methods so thorough and with such unswerving goal-directedness. It is difficult to imagine, and impossible to believe that, this having happened, world history can ever be the same. The Holocaust is not only an unprecedented event. It is also of an as yet unfathomable magnitude. It is world-historical.

IV. The Holocaust and Philosophy

As such it poses new problems for philosophical thought. To begin with reflections on historiography, if, by near-common philosophical consent, historically to explain an event is to show how it was possible then, to the philosopher, the Holocaust-historian emerges sooner or later as asserting the possibility of the Holocaust solely because it was actual—as moving in circles. This impasse, to be sure, is often evaded, most obviously when, as in many histories of World War II, the Holocaust is relegated to a few footnotes. An impasse is even explicitly denied when, as in Marxist ideological history, Nazism-equals-fascism-equals-the-last-stage-of-capitalism; or when, as in liberalistic ideological history, the Holocaust is flattened out into man's-inhumanity-to-man-especially-in-wartime. [For Arnold Toynbee, "what the Nazis did was nothing peculiar"]. The philosopher, however, must penetrate beyond these evasions and ideological distortions. And when he finds a solid historian state, correctly enough, that "the extermination grew out of the biologistic insanity of Nazi ideology, and for that reason is completely unlike the terrors of revolutions and wars of the past" [K. D. Bracher], he must ponder whether "biologistic insanity," in this case, has explanatory force, or is rather a metaphor, the chief meaning of which is that explanation has come to an end. And, as he does ponder this, the philosopher, and indeed the historian also, may well be led to wonder "whether even in a thousand years people will understand Hitler, Auschwitz, Maidanek and Treblinka better than we do now....Posterity may understand it even less than we do. [Isaac Deutscher].

Such questions turn philosophical thought from methodological to substantive issues, and above all to the subject of Man. Premodern philosophy was prepared to posit a permanent human "nature" that was uneffected by all historical change. More deeply immersed in the varieties and vicissitudes of history, modern philosophy generally has perceived, in abstraction from historical change, only a human "condition," and this was considered permanent only insofar as beyond it was the humanly impossible. At Auschwitz, however, "more was real than is possible" [Hans Jonas], and the impossible was done by some and suffered by others. Thus, prior to the Holocaust, the human condition, while including the necessity of dying, was seen as also including at least one inalienable freedom—that of each individual dying his own death [Martin Heidegger]. "With the administrative murder of millions" in the death camps, however, "death has become something that was never to be feared in this way before....The individual is robbed of the last and poorest that until then still remained his own. In the camps it was no longer the individual that died; he was made into a specimen" [Theodor Adorno].

As well as of dying, the Auschwitz administrators also manufactured a new way of living. Prior to the Holocaust no aspect of the human condition could make so strong a claim to permanency as the distinction between life and death, between still-being-here and being-no-more. The Holocaust, however, produced the *Muselmann*, the skin-and-bone walking corpse, or living dead, the vast "anonymous mass, continuously renewed and always identical, of non-men who march and labor in silence, the divine spark dead within them, already too empty really to suffer. One hesitates to call them living. One hesitates to call their death death" [Primo Levi]. The Muselmann may be called the most truly original contribution of the Third Reich to civilization.

From the new ways of being human—those of the victims—philosophical thought is turned to another new way of being human, that of the victimizers. Philosophy has all along been acquainted with the quasi-evil of sadism [a mere sickness], the semi-evil of moral weakness, the superficial evil of ignorance, and even-hardest to understand and therefore often ignored or denied—the "radical" or "demonic" evil that is done and celebrated for its own sake. Prior to the Holocaust, however, it was unacquainted with the "banal evil" [Hannah Arendt] practiced by dime-a-dozen individuals who, having been ordinary or even respected citizens, committed at Auschwitz crimes on a scale previously unimaginable, only to become, after it was all over, ordinary and respectable again—without showing signs of suffering sleepless nights.

The evil is banal by dint, not of course of the nature of the crimes but of the people that committed them: these, it is said, were *made* to do by the system what they did. This, however, is only half a philosophical thought, for who made the system—conceived, planned, created, perpetuated, escalated it—if not such as Himmler and

The Holocaust Now

Eichmann, Stangl and Hoess, to say nothing of the unknown-solder-become S.S. murderer? Already in difficulties with "radical" or "demonic" evil, philosophical thought is driven by the "banal" evil of the Holocaust from the operators to the system, and from the system back to the operators. In this circular movement, to be sure, "banal" evil, except for ceasing to be banal, does not become intelligible. Yet the thought-movement is not without result, far from it the Holocaust emerges as *a* world or, rather, as the *anti*-world *par excellence*. The human condition does not dwell in a vacuum. It always-already-is within a world, i.e., within a structured whole that [i] exists at all be cause it is geared to life and that [ii] is structured because it is governed by laws of life. [Innocent so long as they obey the law, the inhabitants of a world have a right to live, and forfeit it, if at all, only by an act of will—the breach of the law]. The Holocaust anti-world, while structured, to be sure, was governed by a law of death. For the victims—mostly Jews—existence *itself* was a capital crime—an unheard of proposition!—and the sole raison d'etre of the others was to mete out their punishment. In this world, the degradation, torture, and eventual murder of some human beings at the hands of others was not a by-product of, or means to, some higher, more ultimate purpose. They were its whole essence.

Modern philosophers, we have said previously, were able to conceive of a "human condition" because not all things were considered humanly possible. Even so, some of their number—possibly with modern history in mind—have not hesitated to ascribe to Man a "perfectibility" that is "infinite." Auschwitz exacts a new concession from future philosophy: whether or not Man is infinitely perfectible he is in any case infinitely depravable. The Holocaust is not only a world-historical even. It is also a "watershed" [Franklin Littell], or "caesura" [Arthur Cohen] or "rupture" [Emil Fackenheim] in Man's history on earth.

V. The Holocaust and Theology

Is the Holocaust a rupture in the sight of theology? This question requires a separate inquiry. Theology, to be sure—at least if it is Jewish or Christian—is bound up with history. But it can be, and has been, argued that this is a Heilsgeschichte immune to all "merely secular" historical events. Thus for Franz Rosenzweig nothing crucial could happen for Jews between Sinai and the Messianic days. And for Karl Barth it was "always Good Friday *after* Easter," the implication being that the crucial saving event of Christianity has already occurred—and is unassailable ever after.

Is the Holocaust a rupture for Christianity? German Christians [and possibly Christians as a whole] "can no longer speak evangelically to Jews" [Dietrich Bonhoeffer]. They cannot "get behind Auschwitz, beyond it" if at all only "in company with the victims," and this only if they identify with the State of Israel, as being a Jewish "house

The Holocaust: A Summing Up After Two Decades of Reflection

against death" and the "last Jewish refuge" [Johann Baptist Metz]. Christians must relate "positively" to Jews, not "despite" Jewish non-acceptance of the Christ but "because" of it [H. H. Henrix, F. M. Marquardt, M. Stoehr]. Even to go only this far and no further with their theologians—it seems fitting in this context to cite German theologians only—is for Christians to recognize a post-Holocaust rupture in their faith, for the step demanded—renunciation of Christian missions-to-the-Jews, as such and in principle—is, within Christian history, without precedent. [Of the Christian theologians who find it necessary to go much further Roy Eckardt is, perhaps, the most theologically-oriented]. To refuse even this one step—for Christians to stay with the idea of missions-to-the-Jews in principle, even if suspending it altogether in practice—is either to ignore the Holocaust or else sooner or later to reach some such view as that missions-to-the-Jews "is the sole possibility of a genuine and meaningful restitution [*Wiedergutmachtung*] on the part of German Christendom" [Martin Wittenberg, a German Lutheran]. Can Christians view such a stance as other than a theological obscenity? The Jewish stance toward Christian missionizing attempts directed at them, in any case, cannot be what it once was. Prior to the Holocaust, Jews could respect such attempts, though of course considering them misguided. After the Holocaust, they can only view them as trying in one way what Hitler did in another.

It would seem, then, that for Christians Good Friday can no longer be *always* after Easter. As for Jews, was the Holocaust a crucial event, happen though it did *between* Sinai and the Messianic days? Franz Rosenzweig's Jewish truth, it emerges in our time, was a truth not of Judaism but of Galut-Judaism only. [Of this latter, his thought was the most profound modern statement]. Galut-Judaism, however, has ceased to be tenable.

"Galut"—or "exile"—Judaism may be defined as follows:

[i] a Jew can appease or bribe, hide or flee from an enemy and, having succeeded, can thank God for having been saved.

[ii] when in *extremis* such salvation is impossible—when death can be staved off only though apostasy—he can still choose death, thus becoming a martyr; and then he is secure in the knowledge that, while no Jew should seek death, *kiddush hashem* [sanctifying God's name by dying for it] is the "highest stage" of which he can be worthy [Maimonides].

[iii] Exile, though painful, is bearable, for it is meaningful—whether its meaning is punishment for Jewish sins, vicarious suffering for the sins of others, or whether it is simply inscrutable—a meaning known only to God.

The Holocaust Now

[iv] Galut or exile will not last forever. If not he or his children's children, so at any rate some Jews' distant offspring will live to see the Messianic end.

These are the chief conditions and commitments of Galut-Judaism. Existing in these conditions and armed by these commitments, a Jew in past centuries was able to survive the poverty, deliberately engineered, of the East European Ghetto; the slander, ideologically embellished and em-broidered, of antisemitism in modern Germany and France; the medieval expulsions; the Roman Emperor Hadrian's attempts once and for all to extirpate the Jewish faith; and, of course, the fateful destruction of the Jerusalem Temple in 70 C.E., to which Galut-Judaism was able to survive. The Holocaust, however, already shown by us to be unprecedented simply as an historical event, is unprecedented also as a threat to the Jewish faith—and Galut-Judaism is unable to meet it.

[i] The Holocaust was not a gigantic pogrom from which one could hide until the visitation of the drunken cossacks had passed. *This* enemy was coldly sober, and systematic rather than haphazard: except for the lucky few, there was no hiding.

[ii] The Holocaust was not a vast expulsion, with the necessity [but also possibility] arising of, yet once again, resorting to wandering, with the Torah as "portable fatherland" [Heinrich Heine]. Even when the Third Reich was still satisfied with expelling Jews there was, except for the fortunate or prescient, no place to go; and when the Reich became dissatisfied with mere expulsions, a place of refuge, had such been available, would have been beyond reach.

[iii] The Holocaust was not an assault calling for bribing or appeasing the enemy. *This* enemy was an "idealist" who could not be bribed; and he remained unappeasable until the last Jew's death.

[iv] The Holocaust was not a challenge to Jewish martyrdom but, on the contrary, an attempt to destroy it forever. Once Hadrian had decreed death for Jews for the crime of practicing Judaism—and inspired the martyrdom of such as Rabbi Akiba, which in turn inspired countless Jewish generations. [According to legend, it was not lost even on his Roman executioner; unable to forget Akiba's steadfastness he at length became a convert to Judaism.] Hitler, who unlike Hadrian sought to destroy Jews but also, like Hadrian, Judaism was too cunning to repeat the ancient emperor's folly. He decreed death for Jews, not for a doing or even believing, but rather for *being*—for the crime of possessing Jewish ancestors. Thus Jewish martyrdom was made irrelevant. Moreover, no

The Holocaust: A Summing Up After Two Decades of Reflection

effort was spared to make it impossible as well, and the supreme effort in this direction was the manufacture of Muselmaenner. A martyr *chooses* to die; as regards the Muselmaenner, "one hesitates to call them living; one hesitates to call their death death."

It cannot be stressed enough that, despite these unprecedented, superhuman efforts to murder Jewish martyrdom, countless, nameless Akibas managed to sanctify God's name by choosing how to die, even though robbed of the choice of whether to die: their memory must have a special sacredness to God and Man. Such memory is abused, however, if used to blot out, to minimize, or even just divert attention from, the death of the children as yet unable to choose, and the death of the Muselmaenner who could choose no more.

That these four *nova* made Galut-Judaism untenable has found an admirable expression in an ancient Midrash that was originally meant to expound it. In this Midrash God, at the beginning of the great exile initiated by the destruction of the Temple in 70 C.E., exacts three oaths, one from the Gentiles and two from the Jews. The Gentiles are made to swear not to persecute the Jews, now stateless and helpless, excessively. The Jews are made to swear not to resist their persecutors, and not to "climb the wall," i.e. prematurely to return to Jerusalem.

But what, one must ask, if not Auschwitz, is "excessive persecution"? In response, some have said that the Jews broke their oath by climbing the wall, i.e. by committing the sin of Zionism, and that in consequence God at Auschwitz released the Gentiles from theirs. Any such attempt to save Galut-Judaism, however, reflects mere desperation, for it lapses into two blasphemies—toward the innocent children and the guiltless Muselmaenner, and toward a God who is pictured as deliberately callously, consigning them to their fate. There remains, therefore, only a bold and forthright taking leave from Galut-Judaism: it was the Gentiles who, at Auschwitz, broke their oath, and the Jews in consequence are released from theirs.

A "post-Galut-Judaism" Judaism is, unmistakably, in the making in our time. Its most obvious aspects are these, that "resisting" the persecutors and "climbing the wall" have become not only rights but also ineluctable duties. After the Holocaust, Jews owe antisemites [as well as, of course, their own children] the duty of not encouraging their murderous instincts by their own powerlessness. And after the *absolute* homelessness of the twelve Nazi years that were equal to a thousand, they owe the whole world [as well as, of course, their own children] the duty to say "no" to Jewish wandering, to return home, to rebuild a Jewish state.

These aspects of the Judaism-in-the-making are moral and political. Their inner source is spiritual and religious. In the Warsaw Ghetto Rabbi Yitzhak Nissenbaum, a famous and respected orthodox rabbi, made the statement—much quoted at the time

The Holocaust Now

by Jews of all persuasions in their desperate efforts to defend, preserve, hallow Jewish life against an enemy sworn to destroy it all—that this was not a time for *kiddush hashem* [martyrdom] but rather for *kiddush ha-chayyim* [the sanctification of life]. It is a time for kiddush ha-chayyim still. The Jewish people has passed through the Nazi anti-world of death; thereafter, by any standard, religious or secular, Jewish life ranks higher than Jewish death, even if it is for the sake of the divine name. This people has experienced exile in a form more horrendous than ever dreamt of by the apocalyptic imagination: thereafter, to have ended exile bespeaks a fidelity and a will-to-live that, taken together, give a new dimension to piety. The product of this fidelity—the Jewish state—is fragile still, and embattled wherever the world is hostile or does not understand. Yet Jews both religious and secular known in their hearts that Israel—the renewed people, the reborn language, the replanted land, the rebuilt city, the state itself—is a new and unique celebration of life. There are many reasons why Israel has become the center of the Jewish people in our time; not least is that it is indispensable to a future Judaism. If a Jewish state had not arisen in the wake of the Holocaust, it would be a religious necessity—although, one fears, a political near-impossibility—to create it now.

VI. Epilogue: The Holocaust and Poetry

Theodor Adorno has written that to write poetry after Auschwitz is barbaric, presumably on the grounds that it presupposes stopping one's ears to the cries of the murdered children. Such poetry, like philosophy carrying on its business at the same price, is, to cite Adorno again, comparable to the music by which the SS customarily drowned out the cries of their victims. Subsequently Adorno mitigated the harshness of his statement about writing poetry after Auschwitz. However, so far as I know, he never withdrew it.

But what about writing poetry *about* Auschwitz? To cite Adorno yet again, the "metaphysical capacity," once confronting Auschwitz and self-exposed to it, is "paralyzed." What is a poetry that is self-exposed to Auschwitz, and therefore self-paralyzed? And what is its role in, and effect upon, the writing of future poetry?

I confess I do not know. I do not even know the effect upon the future *reading* of poetry—of a poetry written long before Auschwitz became part of our world. There is no greater poem in the German language that Goethe's "Wandering Nachtlied." Few poems have so timeless, spaceless a validity. It reads as follows:

> Uber allen Gipfeln
> Ist Ruh.
> In allen Wipfeln
> Spurest Du

The Holocaust: A Summing Up After Two Decades of Reflection

Kaum einen Hauch.
Die Vogelein schweigen im Walde.
Warte nur, balde.
Ruhest Due auch.

On the peaks of all mountains-
Tranquility.
On all treetops
You feel
Barely a breath.
The birds in the forest are silent.
Hush, soon for you too-
Tranquility.

[The translation is mine.—ELF]

Under no circumstances can we allow this poem to be destroyed for us by the Holocaust. But can we read it now as before, i.e., partake of its spaceless, timeless quality? The mountain peaks and treetops looked at by Goethe are the same that were looked at by the murderers of Buchenwald. Doubtless not a few of them were of aesthetic cast of mind and steeped in German poetry. Possibly some of them may have read Goethe's poem of an evening, so as to regain tranquility after a hard day's work, and strength for the work of the day to come. For us to read Goethe's poem as timeless and spaceless would be comparable to the music by which the SS customarily drowned out the cries of their victims.

The Holocaust Now

Apocalyptic Rationality and the Shoah

For Richard Rubenstein, whose book *After Auschwitz: Radical Theology and Contemporary Judaism*[1], may correctly be understood as the harbinger of the "second phase" of Shoah studies, as Professor Haas correctly notes—that of thinking *about* the Shoah—his essay, like that of Fackenheim, is a "summing up" of more than two decades of reflecting on the theological enormity of the Shoah. Many of the themes which have occupied him in his writings over the years are likewise found here: the essential modernity of the Shoah building upon the past; concern with "superfluous populations" as existing "outside the universe of moral obligation;" parallel phenomena to the Shoah existing in other cultures, notably the Australian; and what, for him, may be in fact the most profoundly religious question of all: "Who is to have a voice in the political community?"[2]

The Holocaust Now

APOCALYPTIC RATIONALITY AND THE SHOAH[3]

Richard L. Rubenstein

I. The Modernity of the Shoah

From the time of the National Socialist seizure of power, liberal thinkers in the West, imbued with the spirit of the Enlightenment, have tended to view both Nazism and its most characteristic expression, the Shoah, as anti-modern and irrational in its hatred, paranoia and quest for *volkisch* homogeneity.[4] While there can be no doubt about its hatred, paranoia or aims, the Shoah was a thoroughly modern event in both its method of implementation and in the "problem" it sought to "solve." The Shoah was also an apocalyptic event. Far from being an aberration, regression from, or rejection of modern Western civilization, the Shoah was in reality an expression of some of its most significant demographic, economic, political, moral and religious tendencies.[5] The Greek word apocalypsis means "an uncovering." In ancient times, apocalyptic characterized a movement within Judaism and early Christianity which claimed that God had revealed secrets of the imminent end of the world.[6] The Shoah's ultimate objective was to bring the entire Jewish world to an end; as we know, it succeeded in utterly destroying Eastern European Judaism. *Unlike the ancients' today's Jews, whether in Israel or the Diaspora, do not await an imminent cataclysm. We stand in its terrible shadow.* Moreover, if history is any teacher, were Jews faced with yet another apocalypse, such as the destruction of the State of Israel, many governments, both East and West, would in all likelihood regard the event as a convenient excuse in problem solving.

The modernity of the Shoah is best understood when the elements of continuity linking that event to other instances of catastrophic misfortune in the modern period are understood. It is, however, important to stress that the uniqueness of the Shoah is by no means diminished when it is viewed in historical context. No matter what continuities can be discerned between the Shoah and other destructive events, there is one way in which it is absolutely unique. *In no other twentieth-century instance of mass extermination has the fate of the victims been so profoundly linked to the religio-mythic inheritance of the perpetrators,* whether we look to Christianity or to National Socialist neo-paganism.

The Holocaust Now

For German neo-paganism, the Jews were the *Wiedergeist*, the counter-power that must be exterminated root and branch. For Christianity, the inherited religion of the perpetrators, the Jews, alone among the twentieth century's victims of mass murder, have been depicted as the God-bearing and the God-murdering people *par excellence*. No other religion is thus portrayed in the classic literature of a rival tradition. Moreover, starting with the fall of Jerusalem in 70 C.E., Christianity has taken the disasters of the Jewish people as a principal historical confirmation of its own truth. As we know, Jewish misfortune has been interpreted in the classical Christian sources to be God's punishment of a sinful and deicidal Israel. The practical consequence of this view has been to facilitate the exclusion of Jews from a common universe of moral obligation with the Christians among whom they were domiciled. In times of acute political and social stress, this view has had the effect of decriminalizing any assault, no matter how obscene, visited upon them, as Hitler and the leading National Socialists fully understood. The implementation of the Shoah was greatly facilitated by the deicidal and demonological interpretation of the Jewish people in the Christian religious imagination.

If we wish to comprehend the Shoah as a phenomenon of modernization, we must keep in mind the question, *"Why did it happen in the twentieth century and not before, given the radical demonization of the Jews and their powerless-ness within Christendom?"* Moreover, our inquiry must commence with the beginnings of the modernization process in England, the world's first country to undergo the wrenching dislocation of the "great transformation."[7] Those beginnings are to be found in the acts of Enclosure of the Tudor and Stuart periods which transformed the agrarian subsistence economy of pre-modern England into the depersonalized market economy of the modern era. In the process, the customary rights to land usage of the economically unproductive English peasant class were abrogated and that class was largely transformed into a congery of dispossessed individuals whose survival was dependent upon their ability to find wage labor. Many turned to vagabondage or outright crime. A tragic social by-product of the beginnings of England's modernization was the creation of a large class of people who were superfluous to the new economic system.

The acts of Enclosure can be understood as the first modern, state-sponsored program of population elimination. The Shoah was, of course, the most radical such program. All such schemes share a common objective, the elimination of a target population from its habitual place of domicile. They differ, however, in their methods of implemen
tation which range from dispossession, to encouragement of immigration, to outright expulsion, and finally to outright extermination. In the case of the Enclosures, a large portion of England's peasant population was no longer needed or wanted where they and their ancestors had lived and worked for centuries. The decision was taken to

remove them from their place of habitation. Little or no thought was given to what was to become of them.

A class of more or less permanently superfluous people is a potential source of acute social instability and is more likely to be the object of fear than compassion. Having no hope of receiving society's normal rewards, such a class has little incentive, save fear of punishment, to abide by society's customary behavioral constraints. Even if such a group is tied to the rest of the population by common ethnicity and religion, it is likely to be perceived and to perceive itself as having been cast outside of society's *universe of moral obligation*. A measure of self-sacrificing altruism rather than self-regarding egoism will normally characterize the behavior of members of such a universe towards each other. At a minimum, members will not normally regard other members as potential sources of injury or even personal destruction. To the extent that trust is possible between human beings, the actors within a shared universe of moral obligation are more likely to trust each other than those whom they regard as alien. Such attitudes have less to do with the moral virtuosity of individuals than with the way social relations are structured.

As England modernized, it was confronted with a growing shortage of food and a growing surplus of men. As early as 1597 England passed "An Acte for Punyshment of Rogues, Vagabonds and Sturdy Beggars" [39 Eliz. c. 4] which provided that such "Rogues....be banished out of this Realm....and shall be conveyed to such parts beyond the seas as shall be assigned by the Privy Council." If a banished "rogue" returned to England without permission, he or she would be hanged. In 1717 a new act [4 Geo. I, c. II] provided that the sentences of offenders subject to branding or flogging could be commuted to transportation to America for seven years while capital offenders who were recipients of "the King's Mercy" could be transported for fourteen years. The "rogues" and vagabonds trans-ported overseas were very largely displaced peasants, or their descendants, who had been rendered both redundant and desperate by the acts of Enclosure. Between 1717 and 1776, some 30,000 people from Great Britain and 10,000 from Ireland were transported overseas compelled to work at jobs no free settler would accept.[8]

II. The Case of Australia and Beyond

The American Revolution crated a crisis for England's transportation system. England could no longer use that country as its dumping grounds for its unwanted human beings. In 1788, five years after the signing of the treaty of peace between England and the United States, the first group of 736 men and women convicts were transported from England to Botany Bay, Australia.

According to Professor Tony Barta of La Trobe University, Melbourne, Australia,

The Holocaust Now

the basic fact of Australia's history has been the conquest of the country by one people and the dispossession "with ruthless destructiveness" of another people, the Aborigines, those who were there *ab origine*.[9] While it was by no means the initial intention of the British government to destroy the Aborigines, Barta contends that Australia is a "nation founded on genocide" which was the inevitable, though unintended, consequence of the European colonization. Far from being a consequence of the actions of isolated men acting out their aggressions on a lawless and distant frontier, the destruction of Australia's Aboriginal population was very largely the *projected outcome of modernizing transformations in the mother country.*

Neither North America nor Australia were unsettled territories when white settlers arrived. In the case of Australia, the aboriginal people had developed a viable human ecology which was altogether incomprehensible to the settlers. Moreover, sheep raising and the settlers' rationalized and desacralized agrarian economy were incompatible with Aborigine land use which was deeply rooted in the Aborigines' sacred cosmos. Since both sides were unconditionally dependent upon the land, each in its own way, loss of the land necessarily entailed the complete destruction of the defeated way of life. Coexistence was impossible.

The issue was decided, as it almost always is, by superior arms and power. With their survival at stake, the Aborigines had no choice but to resist. As in North America, the predictable settler response was to root out the menace. There were bloody massacres. There were also government-sponsored attempts to diminish settler violence, but even without overt violence the Aborigines were destined to perish. Deprived of a meaningful future, most of the Aborigines who survived white aggression "faded away." Between 1839 and 1849 there were only twenty births recorded among the seven aboriginal tribes around Melbourne. Barta concludes that, whatever the official British intent, the encounter between the white settlers and the Blacks was one of *living out a relationship of genocide that was structured into the very nature of the encounter.*

The basic colonizing pattern described by Barta, namely, white settlement, native resistance, violent settler victory, and, finally, the disappearance of most if not all of the natives, was played out in North and South America as well.[10] If Australian society was built upon a genocidal relationship with that of the indigenous cultures, so too was American society. There was a time not so long ago when it was taken for granted that "the only good Indian was a dead Indian."

Barta distinguishes between a genocidal society and a genocidal state. National Socialist Germany was a genocidal state. The latter's genocidal project was deliberate and intended. Settler Australia was a genocidal society. It had no genocidal project. Nevertheless, its very existence had genocidal consequences for the original population. The basic pattern of the colonization of Australia was everywhere the same. It consisted of white pastoral invasion, Black resistance, violent victory of the whites, and

Apocalyptic Rationality and the Shoah

finally the mysterious disappearance of the Blacks.

Although Barta confines his description to Australia, the process he describes was repeated in other European colonial settlements. In his biography of Oliver Cromwell [1599-1658], the English historian Christopher Hill comments,

> A great many civilized Englishmen of the propertied class in the seventeenth century spoke of Irishmen in tones not far removed from those which the Nazis used about the Slavs, or white South Africans use about the original inhabitants of their country. In each case the contempt rationalized a desire to exploit.[11]

What Hill could have added was the Cromwell was fully prepared to exterminate those Irish Catholics who resisted exploitation and refused to turn their lands over to Protestant colonizers. When the towns of Drogheda and Wexford refused to surrender to Cromwell in 1649, they were sacked and those inhabitants unable to flee were massacred. In the case of Wexford, after all the inhabitants had been killed, Cromwell reported that the town was available for colonization by English settlers. An English clergyman commended the place for settlement: "It is a fine spot for some godly congregation where house and land wait for inhabitants and occupiers."[12] Even in the seventeenth century, it was clear to England's leaders that the more Ireland was cleared of its original Catholic inhabitants the more available it would be for Protestant English settlement.

The extremes to which England was prepared to go to empty Ireland of its original inhabitants became clear during the famine years of 1846-48. It is estimated that within the period the population of Ireland was reduced by about 2,500,000 out of an estimated 1845 population of 9,000,000. Approximately 1,250,000 perished in the famine. About the same number were compelled to emigrate in order to survive.[13]

The famine relief given by the English government to the Irish, who were technically speaking British subjects at the time, was deliberately kept at levels guaranteed to produce the demographic result it did. Moreover, the deaths by famine and the removal by emigration were welcomed by leading members of England's society and government as doing for Ireland what the Enclosure had done for England: The land had been cleared of uneconomic subsistence producers and made available for rationalized agricultural enterprise.[14] The candor of an 1853 editorial in *The Economist* on the benefits of the elimination of redundant Irish and Scots is instructive:

> It is consequent on the breaking down of the system of society founded on small holdings and potato cultivation....*The departure of the redundant part of the population of Ireland and Scotland is an indispensable*

preliminary to every kind of improvement. [Emphases added.][15]

Unfortunately, the "departure" entailed mass death by famine and disease for a very significant proportion of Ireland's peasant class. In the eyes of the British decision-making class of the period, Catholic Ireland was an inferior civilization with a primitive, superstitious religion.[16] An upper class that was indifferent to the fate of its own peasants was hardly likely to be concerned with that of the Irish.

Just as the rationalization of the English economy from the sixteenth to the twentieth century resulted in the rise of both surplus people and experiments aimed at their elimination, so too the nineteenth-century rationalization of the German economy had a comparable result. Germany's predicament was succinctly summarized in 1891 by Bismarck's successor as Chancellor of the Reich, Leo von Caprivi, who declared: "Germany must export either goods or people."[17] Hitler, however, was determined that the people who left the Reich would not be Germans. He sought to solve what he regarded as Germany's "population problem" through his *Lebensraum* program. He was determined that there would be no surplus German population even if Europe's Jewish population and a significant portion of Germany's Slavic neighbors were exterminated to provide the "living space" for German settlers. Hitler proposed to repeat in Europe, albeit with infinitely intensified viciousness, the exploitative colonialism practiced by other Europeans overseas. They were to be displaced, uprooted, enslaved and, if necessary, annihilated, to make way for Germany's surplus population.

Unlike the earlier European colonizers, Hitler had no illusions concerning the genocidal nature of such an undertaking. He had the historical precedents of earlier European efforts at colonization and imperial domination. He regarded the defeat of native cultures by white settlers and colonists as evidence of the truth of his version of Social Darwinism. As is well known, the same Social Darwinism became an important component in the legitimating ideology for the extermination of Europe's Jews during World War II. In Hitler's eyes, the Jews were the most contemptible of all of the inferior races destined by fate and German strength for destruction.

Unlike the destruction of the Australian Aborigines, the extermination of the Jews was fully intended. Nevertheless, the behavior of the English in Ireland and Australia, as well as that of other Europeans in the New World, shows that the destruction of the indigenous population never constituted a reason for calling colonial and imperial ventures to a halt. Nor ought the difference between intended and unintended extermination obscure the fact that both were attempts at population riddance aimed at solving a similar problem, the relatively humane elimination from the mother country of a sector of its own population rendered redundant or threatened with redundancy by the rationalization of the economy. The very success of the earlier experiments in population-elimination invited their repetition. One's own surplus population problem was to be solved by a combination of emigration, colonization and expulsion. Those who inhabited the lands selected as dumping grounds were threatened by an infinitely harsher fate.

Nor ought we to forget the millions of Europeans considered expendable by their own governments during World War I. The modernization of hygiene and medicine permitted an unprecedented number of Europeans to survive to young adulthood; the modernization and industrialization of military technology made possible their slaughter by the millions in battles such as Verdun, the Second Battle of the Somme and Gallipoli. *Can anyone believe that governments that permitted the killing on so monumental a scale of their own men would be disturbed by the elimination of people for whom they felt neither moral nor political responsibility?* There is thus historical continuity between the unintended genocides of Europe's demo-graphic projection beyond its original territorial limits, Europe's auto-cannibalization during World War I, and the Shoah.

Some may object that, at least in Western Europe before World War II, the Jews were not a surplus population. True enough, but they were a surplus people in the East, as is evident by the massive emigration of Eastern European Jews westward after 1881. Moreover, the Jews of the West occupied slots which surplus members of the majority were prepared to take from them. The question, *Who is to have a voice in the political order?* is fundamental to the decision to initiate a state-sponsored program of population elimination. That decision is in turn related to the question of the universe of moral obligation. In ancient Greece, members of the polis [city-state—Ed.] belonged to a common universe of obligation. This was especially evident in war. Only those who shared common origins belonged by *inherited right* to the same community, and saw themselves as partaking of a common fate could be trusted in a life-and-death struggle with their community's enemies. Neither the slave nor the stranger could be so trusted. Hence, they were regarded as outside of the shared universe of obligation.

A very grave problem arises when, for any reason, a community regards itself as having within its midst a group who are perceived, rightly or wrongly, to be untrustworthy. The problem is urgent in wartime. It is even more urgent when a community has experienced a humiliating national defeat. The perception of disloyalty may be mistaken, as was the case with Germany's Jews in World War I and Japanese-Americans during World War II. Nevertheless, the majority's perceptions are politically decisive.

Sometimes the issue of a voice in the political community takes on a class rather than an ethnic dimension. When Kampuchea fell to the Pol Pot regime in 1975, the victors had a very clear idea of the kind of agrarian communist society they proposed to establish. They regarded Kampuchea's entire urban population as objectively hostile to the creation of the new political order. This perception was consistent with the Marxist idea that the bourgeois class is destined to disappear with the coming of true socialism. Not content to let this process take its course non-violently, the regime determined upon the immediate elimination of all who were regarded as either incapable of fitting into the new system or of being objectively committed to its destruction.[18] In the aftermath of the Russian Revolution, a very similar logic compelled the departure from the Soviet Union of millions of "objective enemies" of the new system. Similarly, the Cuban revolution resulted in the enforced emigration of over a million Cubans who would not fit into Castro's system, primarily to the State of Florida.

The question, "Who is to have a voice in the political community?" was absolutely decisive for National Socialism. It was also important for the Vichy government of Marshal Henri Phillippe Petain. The antisemitic *Statut des Juifs* of 3 October 1940 required no encouragement from the Germans.[19] The political emancipation of the Jews in Europe in the late eighteenth and nineteenth centuries gave to the Jews a voice in the political communities in which they were domiciled. With the sad wisdom of hindsight, the extermination of the Jews can be seen as in part an unintended consequence of their emancipation. Emancipation made membership of the Jews in Europe's political communities both a fact and a political issue for the first time. Emancipation was opposed by those who believed such membership should be restricted to Christians. It was, as we know, also opposed by those who sought to restrict membership to those who regarded themselves as bound together by ties of blood. *An important reason why so little was done to assist the Jews during World War II, both in Germany and throughout occupied Europe, was the almost universal European acceptance of the Mational Socialist objective of excluding the Jews from membership in the political communities in which they were domiciled.* This was certainly true of most mainstream Protestant and Catholic churches, which tended to regard the denial of political rights to the Jews as a beneficial step toward the creation of a Europe that was culturally, intellectually and political Christian.[20] The fundamental difference between Hitler and the churches was that Hitler had no illusions concerning the extreme measures necessary to implement such a program. The churches never faced openly the question of implementation. Having no direct responsibility for carrying out the process of elimination, they preferred to leave the question of implementation to others. In any event, it is now clear that early National Socialist calls for elimination of the Jews from membership in the body politic was in fact a demand for their extermination.

III. Middleman-Minority

An important economic aspect of antisemitic hostility was the fact that Europe's Jews were largely a middleman-minority.[21] Sociologist Walter P. Zenner has observed that, under certain circumstances, middleman-minority status can be a precondition for genocide. Like the Jews, the Armenians were also a middleman-minority. In the

Apocalyptic Rationality and the Shoah

aftermath of the war in Vietnam, yet another middleman-minority, the Hoa or ethnic Chinese of Vietnam, were the object of a large-scale, state-sponsored program of population elimination.[22] Middleman-minorities are usually permitted domicile in a community in order to do work that, for some reason, is not being done by the indigenous population. Their presence as strangers is tolerated because they constitute an *economically* or *vocationally complimentary* population. They are most like to be targeted for elimination when their roles can be filled either by the state or by members of the indigenous population. When this development takes place, the minority members become competitors of the majority. Usually, they compete against one of the most dangerous and potentially unstable groups within the larger population, the majority middle class.

In pre-modern societies it was not socially or economically functional for middleman-minorities to share a common religion with the majority. The objective, impersonal attitudes necessary for successful commerce were less likely to develop between people who considered themselves to be kin worshipping the same god. The flow of commerce often depended upon a depersonalized in-group, out-group double standard. With the rise of Protestantism the personalized ethics of tribal brotherhood gave way to the modern, depersonalized attitude of universal otherhood. It was then possible for a universal money economy to come into being.[23]

As an economy modernizes, the situation of middleman-minorities tends to become increasingly precarious. Thus, the condition of Europe's Jews became progressively more difficult as the economies of Western and Eastern Europe were modernized.[24] As the agriculture of Eastern Europe was progressively rationalized during the second half of the nineteenth century, large numbers of Polish and Russian peasants were dispossessed of their holdings and forced to seek scarce wage labor in the towns and cities of Eastern Europe and later Western Europe and America. The peasants' predicament was further aggravated by yet another aspect of modernization: improved medicine and hygiene which yielded an unprecedented rate of population increase. Desperate for any kind of work under conditions of mass unemployment and underemployment, newly urbanized members of the former peasant class began to compete with the Jews for wage labor and those middleman-minority slots which had previously been predominantly Jewish. In seeking to displace the Jews, the dispossessed peasants and their urbanized offspring had the support of the Tsarist government, which, after the pogroms [riots—Ed.] of 1881 and the May Laws of 1882, made the Jews the target of one of the most highly successful state-sponsored programs of population elimination in all history. Moreover, the beginnings of political antisemitism in Austria and Germany coincide with the beginnings of the westward emigration of Eastern Europe's Jews. From 1881 to 1917, the fundamental objective of the Tsarist government vis-a-vis the Jews differed little from that of the National Socialist regime in Germany. Both sought the elimination of the Jews as a demographic presence in the areas under their control. Most American Jews are alive today because the two regimes did not share a common method of implementation.

Many of the peasants and artisans from Germany and Eastern Europe responded to the demographic crisis by emigrating to the New World. By so doing they unintentionally intensified resentment at those Jews who remained in Europe. Even as a young man in Vienna, Hitler was keenly interested in the problem of emigration. One of the books in Hitler's library whose marginal notes attest to the young Hitler's strong interest was *Auswanderungs-Moglichkeiten in Argentinien*.[25] In *Mein Kampf* Hitler wrote of the need for land to the east to absorb Germany's population surplus. He came to regard emigration as a poor solution for the emigrant was lost to the Fatherland as a human resource. As we know, his solution was conquest, colonization to the east, and extermination.

IV. The Importance of Military Defeat

Frequently, programs of genocide such as the Shoah are initiated in the aftermath of military defeat, especially under the devastating conditions of modern warfare.[26] An important element in the decision of the Young Turk regime to initiate the program of extermination against its Armenian Christian minority was Turkey's defeat by Bulgaria in 1912. Similarly, Germany's defeat in World War I created the conditions in which a radically antisemitic, revolutionary, revisionist National Socialist movement could come to dominate German politics. As a consequence of defeat, the fringe became the center. In addition to the role of a defenseless minority as surrogate object of revenge for the victorious enemy, military defeat can intensify the urgency with which the question of membership in the community is posed. Who can doubt that France's defeat in 1870 contributed to the atmosphere that made the Dreyfus affair possible? As noted, a fundamental issue in population elimination programs is the question of who can be trusted in a life-and-death struggle. All minorities suffer some discrimination and experience some degree of resentment and incomplete identification with the majority, a situation which is as obvious to the majority as to the minority. In normal times, such tensions can be held in check. In the aftermath of catastrophic military defeat, they can get out of hand. Aggressive energies can achieve cheap victories over a defenseless minority. The reality of defeat itself can be denied and responsibility for the misfortunes of war ascribed to the minority's hidden "stab in the back." The accusation of secret treachery can legitimate genocide against the minority. If such a group is perceived as bringing about national catastrophe, *while appearing to be loyal*, it can become a matter of the greatest public urgency to eliminate them from the body politic.

Almost from the moment Germany lost World War I, the Jews were accused of being about her defeat through treachery, an accusation that appeared ludicrous in view of the extremely high proportion of German Jews who had served as front-line soldiers and who had made the ultimate sacrifice for what they regarded as their Fatherland. Elsewhere, this writer has argued that the tradition of Judas betraying Jesus with a *token of love*, a kiss, provided an enormously potent religio-mythic identification of the Jew with betrayal in the minds of Christians.[27] A similar identification was influential in the Dreyfus affair. Commenting on Captain Dreyfus' conduct on the occasion of his public degradation on 4 January 1885, the antisemitic newspaper, *La Croix*, declared, "His cry of 'Vive la France!' was the kiss of Judas Iscariot."[28] Since the identification of the Jew with Judas takes place in earliest childhood and is constantly reinforced by religious tradition, it is more deeply rooted and less subject to rational criticism than beliefs acquired at a later stage in the life cycle. When Hitler and the German right ascribed Germany's defeat to the Jews, they had working for them this immensely powerful, pre-theological archetype. Here, too, we discern a unique religio-mythic element that sets the Shoah apart from other instances of genocide in our times.

V. The Rationality of the Shoah

Given the presence of religio-mythic elements in the Shoah, it is not surprising that many scholars have argued that the Shoah was irrational in its objective if not in its methods. By contrast, this writer has argued against Lucy Dawidowicz and others that the Shoah was, in a nightmarish way, rational in both its objective and its methods.[29] In contrast to spontaneous outbursts of inter-group hatred and violence, modern, systematic, bureaucratically administered genocide can be understood as a form of instrumentally rational [*zweckrational*] action in contrast to value-rational [*wertrational*] action. Max Weber, to whom we are indebted for this distinction, has observed that instrumental rationality is a matter of ends.[30] Above all, it is important not to confuse humane action and instrumentally rational action. The experience of our era should leave no doubt concerning the enormous potential for inhumanity present in morally autonomous instrumental rationality. The perfection of this mode of political and social action is indeed one of the most problematic aspects of both the legacy of the Enlightenment and the modernization process.

The idea that the Shoah could in any sense be regarded as rational has been rejected by Marxist scholar Ronald Aronson. In his book, *The Dialectics of Disaster*, Aronson argues that the Shoah systematically outraged the norms of the "normal world."[31] He insists that it was a product of madness, which he defines as a systematic derangement of perception, a seeing what is not there. The National Socialists saw the Jews as the source of Germany's problems and regarded their riddance as a major element in the solution. Aronson argues that when rulers organize a society against false enemies and falsely propagate the view that society is mortally threatened by them, we may speak of madness as much as when a paranoid individual behaves in a similar delusionary manner. Aronson insists that the Nazi attempt wholly to eliminate the Jews as a demographic presence first in Germany and then in all of Europe was insane because the Jews in no way constituted the threat the National Socialists alleged them to be.

Aronson fails to deal with the underlying reason why the question of "Who shall have a voice in the community?" is raised in the first place. As noted, genocide is a violent means of determining who is to have a voice in a community whose members may have to sacrifice their lives in a life-and-death struggle with external enemies in a crisis. When a group regards itself as secure, it can afford to take a relatively benign view of the presence of a limited number of strangers in its midst. However, in times of acute national stress, such as economic dislocation, modern warfare or military defeat, insiders are likely to view outsiders with intensified suspicion and hostility. Even in relatively tranquil times, the growing presence of those regarded as strangers can be destabilizing. In the case of middleman-minority groups specializing in commerce, insiders may suspect that the outsiders' love of gain will outweigh their loyalty to the homeland. Moreover, when minority intellectuals acquire the ability effectively to communicate in the language of the majority, they can become the object of resentment and hostility. In an extreme situation, leaders of the majority may decide upon the total elimination of the outsiders.

Contrary to Aronson, the patent untruth of National Socialist defamations is irrelevant to the critical fact that the overwhelming majority of Germans regarded even the most assimilated Jews as aliens whose elimination would be a positive benefit to the nation. The Germans wanted the *volkisch* homogeneity Hitler promised them. When it was all over, many regretted the *method of implementation* employed by their government but not the fact that Europe was largely empty of Jews.

Unfortunately, one cannot even say that it is irrational to want an ethnically or religiously homogenous community consisting of those with whom one shares a sense of common faith, values, kinship and trust. After all, that has been an important element in the establishment of the State of Israel. Admittedly, in the urbanized sections of much of the modern world, pluralism is a given. Nevertheless, there is nothing irrational about the desire for a community of moral trust and mutual obligation. An important reason for the astounding success of contemporary Japan has been its ethnic homogeneity. It is not the irrationality of non-pluralistic communities that is the problem, but the extreme cruelty and inhumanity which must be practiced by the modern state in order to transform a pluralistic, multi-ethnic or multi-religious political entity into a homogenous community. Hitler's program of genocide was not irrational in the sense of *Zweckrationalitat* [instrumental rationality]. It was obscenely cruel.

VI. The Role of the Modern State

Finally, we must consider the issue of the modern state, national sovereignty and genocide, an issue which has become ever more urgent with the attainment of sovereignty by so many of the peoples of the world. With the radical secularization of politics in modern times, there is no longer any credible or effective higher authority that the state. *In spite of its persistent one-sided, even obscene hostility to the State of Israel, the United Nations has been singularly indifferent to mass murder and genocide when practiced by favored member nations against their own citizens.* The genocidal Pol Pot regime remains the officially recognized government of Kampuchea in the United Nations.[32] States have accepted limitations upon their actions with regard to those reckoned as possessing a legitimate voice in the nation's political affairs. The problem arises with those who have been deliberately cast outside of the social contract. It is an unfortunate fact that such men and women can be rendered utterly rightless when confronted with a ruthless state apparatus. As long as the leaders of National Socialist Germany were free to exercise sovereignty, no superordinate system of norms constituted any kind of restraint on their behavior. In reality, absent a communal consensus on belief in God and an unconditional willingness to abide by Divine Law, there are only political rights. Human rights exist only insofar as they are guaranteed by a political community with the power to enforce its guarantee. That is why the question, "Who is to have a voice in the political community?" is today one of the most important human questions. Citizenship in a sovereign political community is no absolute guarantee of safety. Nevertheless, to the extent that men and women have any rights whatsoever, it is as members of a political community with the power to guarantee those rights. It is the dolorous fact that made the State of Israel a political imperative in the aftermath of the Shoah. *Genocide is the ultimate expression of absolute rightlessness.*

Thus, the Shoah cannot be understood apart from the distinctive conditions and culture we identify as modernity. The Shoah was thoroughly modern both in the "problem" it attempted to "solve" and in its value-neutral, rational, bureaucratic methods of implementation.

Let us conclude with a few observations on the Jewish situation in the face of modernity and the apocalypse. The philosopher-theologian, Emil L. Fackenheim, has taught us that the Jewish people has experienced both "root experiences" such as the Exodus and Sinai and "epochmaking events" which challenged the "root experiences" with new and terrible situations.[33] The "epochmaking events have included the destruction of Jerusalem first by the Babylonians and then by the Romans, and the most radically disorienting epochmaking event, the Holocaust." Rabbi Yohanan ben Zakkai played a crucial role in responding to the "epochmaking event" of the Roman destruction of Jerusalem. Given the choice of resistance unto death on the part of the Jewish people or submission to Caesar, Yohanan chose submission as the only way Torah and Israel could survive. Even Yohanan's theology of history, which God's hand in the *churban* [destructive devastation—Ed.], made political sense. If the destruction was ultimately due to Israel's sins, then defeat was not the final word. With God's help and mercy, Israel would someday experience a better world.

Nevertheless, Rabbi Yohanan's submission to Caesar made sense only as long as Caesar could be trusted to refrain from using his power to obliterate the Torah and Israel. One of the Shoah's most important lessons is that under conditions of modernity Caesar can no longer be trusted, especially in a time of radical stress. Even Caligula did not have at his disposal the instruments of propaganda and rationalized mass murder available to a modern Caesar. That is why Masada, the name of the other option available to Israel in the aftermath of the ancient Judaeo-Roman War, is once again being uttered with renewed frequency. *Let us, however, be mindful of the fact that the Masada option is an apocalyptic strategy which only makes sense if it includes a credible way of radically escalating the cost of killing Jews.*

A Masada option can either be a suicidal strategy for an honorable national death or a variant of the Mutually Assured Destruction [MAD] strategy which until recently kept the Superpowers at bay from the time the Soviet Union acquired the capacity for intercontinental delivery of its nuclear weapons. At Masada the Jewish people fought with stones, spears, and swords. Today, there is every likelihood that an apocalyptic threat to Israel's existence will be met with the use of the most modern and the most apocalyptic weapons as a deterrent threat. In the long run, the willingness and the capability to bring on the apocalypse may constitute an important element in Israel chances for survival.

Indeed, it may be possible for us to learn from one who, at least for a time, counted himself among Israel's enemies and who remained stonily indifferent to the apocalypse of the Shoah throughout his life, the German philosopher Martin Heidegger.[34] Heidegger reminds us that "Being-towards-death [*Zein zum Tode*] belongs primordially and essentially to Dasein's Being."[35] In the aftermath of the our apocalypse, we cannot dismiss the possibility that Zein zum Tode may belong primordially and essentially to Israel as a people. This, of course, was not the view of Heidegger's contemporary, Franz Rosenzweig, who saw Israel as an "eternal people" which "knows nothing of war."[36] In an era when the utter destruction of Israel remains a passionately desired objective of so many in the Middle East and elsewhere, there may be greater wisdom in seeing Jewish existence in apocalyptic terms than with the calm assurance of the indwelling of eternity which permeates Rosenzweig's *Denken*. He was mercifully spared the apocalypse; we were not.

Half a century after *Kristallnacht* ["The Night of the Broken Glass," Germany, November 9-10, 1938—Ed.], the situation of world Jewry can be likened to that of the city of Oran as described by Albert Camus at the very end of his novel, *La Peste* [*The Plague*—

Apocalyptic Rationality and the Shoah

Ed.], when the crowd rejoices at the lifting of the plague. Dr. Rieux, the novel's protagonist, is unable to join in rejoicing that the death-threat to the city has been lifted. He knows better and so should we. We would do well to give heed to his response:

> And, indeed, as he listened to the cries of joy rising from the town, Rieux remembered that such joy is always imperiled. He knew what those jubilant crowds did not know but could never have learned from books; that the plague bacillus never dies or disappears for good; that it can lie dormant for years in furniture and linen-closets; that it bides its time in bedrooms, cellars, trunks, handkerchiefs, and bookshelves; and that perhaps the day would come when, for the bane and the enlightening of men, it would rouse up its rats again and send them forth to die in a happy city.

The Holocaust Now

Academia and the Holocaust

All those who have contributed to this volume have a university or college connection, either full-time or part-time. Those who will read and ponder these essays, primarily, will be teachers and students in our institutions of higher learning. Alan Berger's essay reminds us that individual and collective ethical responsibility cannot be divorced from such teaching, and, by extension, from learning--not only in those courses which deal centrally with the Shoah, but, equally, with those in the humanities and sciences as well. He further reminds us that academic objectivity, long a hallmark of scholarly work, is, like rationalism itself, a casualty of the Second World War. "Practically speaking, the question is: What is the relationship between teaching and being human?" In so asking the question and framing his critique, he returns us, once again, to a contemporary religious response to the Shoah, invites a re-thinking of the process of learning as presently structured, and suggests a new direction for the future.[1]

The Holocaust Now

ACADEMIA AND THE HOLOCAUST[1]

Alan L. Berger

I. Introduction

This essay is a reflection on the relationship of Hitler's years of slaughter--what is infelicitously termed Holocaust[2]--to the assumptions of university life and its methods of teaching. I am convinced that universities are at best marginal and, in certain cases, poor places to discover and to teach values and I wish, therefore, to argue that academics need to reexamine the foundations of their scholarship. Moreover, the Holocaust, having become grist for the academic mill, is now threatened with death by a thousand qualifications. For example, Elie Wiesel has observed that "yesterday people said, 'Auschwitz, never heard of it.'" "Now they say, 'Oh yes, we know all about it.'" The second statement underscores the perils involved in attempting to teach about the annihilation of the Jews.

Technological sophistication coupled with linguistic impoverishment has left academics ethical unmusical. Like the inhabitants of Plato's cave, university professors are transfixed by illusions. Academia's shadow idols are abstraction and generalization, professionalism and objectivity. The academy strives to understand while simultaneously shunning the particularity which alone can grant access to broader areas of knowledge. Scholarship which loses sight of the human ends as intellectual fascism.

The two poles around which Holocaust studies revolve have been articulated by Elie Wiesel and Richard Rubenstein. Wiesel, the survivor, views the Holocaust as a sacred subject. "One should take off one's shoes," he observes, "when entering its domain, one should tremble each time one pronounces the word."[3] However, there is another and frequently unexplored dimension to Holocaust implications. Rubenstein writes:

> Until ethical theorists and theologians are prepared to face
> without sentimentality the kind of action it is possible freely to perpe-

---

Reprinted from *JUDAISM*, 31:2, Spring, 1982, 166-176. Permission granted.

trate under conditions of utter respectibility in an advanced, contemporary society, none of their assertions about the existence of moral norms will have much credibility. To repeat, no laws were broken and no crimes were committed at Auschwitz....no credible punishment was meted out--Truly, the twentieth century has been the century par excellence that is beyond good and evil.[4]

Both Wiesel and Rubenstein, despite their vastly different conclusions view the Holocaust as a *novum*. Wiesel compares the enormity of Auschwitz to the revelation at Sinai. Rubenstein, on his part, demystifies the Holocaust, claiming that the Nazis successfully breached a hitherto unbreachable moral and political barrier [exterminating the Jews] owing to their highly developed bureaucracy and their superior technology. Both positions form part of the total event. Rather than struggle with this tension, academics, apparently embarrassed by notions of holiness, stress social science categories, finding them more amenable to objectivity.

II. Academica and Objectivity

Academic rightly distinguishes itself from society at large by refraining from the easy temptations of sloganeering and provincialism when dealing with crucial civilizational issues. Dispassionate research broadens the horizon, enabling new constellations of possibilities to emerge. Removed from the intense passions of the moment, academics are able to supply analogies, furnish historical antecedents and, most important, lend perspective. But, too often, this dispassionate condition results in a kind of moral abstentionism. University professors frequently end as bystanders forever tentative, fearing a moral stance as an assault upon their professional status.

Objectivity, learned from Greek culture, heralded by seventeenth-century science and carefully nurtured in succeeding centuries, has attained a semi-sacred status not only among academics, but is, as well, a societal norm, having become the guideline for attorneys, bureaucrats, corporate executives, and physicians, among others. However, objectivity is based upon a presumption of rationality which is, itself, another victim of the gas chambers and ovens. Ethically unanchored objectivity frequently metamorphosizes into moral betrayal. In short, universities uphold objectivity--which is dignified as professionalism--but which is, in reality, only pseudo-professionalism, without a similar stress on compassion.

Elitism, another unspoken assumption of university existence, may be equally culpable. Universities have a right to demand excellence and, if this is what is meant by elitism, there can be little definitional quarrel. However, elitism among intellectuals frequently breeds indifference. Commitment and concern for community are the first casualties of intellectual fascism.

Man has increasingly become the measure of all things. His pro-methean arrogance, coupled with great technological skill, has produced power but not compassion, order without meaning, and progress instead of salvation. Somewhere along the way universities began producing parts for the societal machine, at the expense of living the "examined life." Congratulating themselves on attaining objectivity, the universities have admitted a Trojan Horse. It needs to be recognized that what apostasy is to theology, elitist objectivity [pseudo-professionalism] is to teaching.

Writing in *The Origins of Totalitarianism*, Hannah Arendt reports the emergence of a nineteenth-century tendency which is distressingly contemporary among academics:

> The cynical or bored indifference in the face of death or other personal catastrophes, the passionate inclination toward the most abstract notions as guides for life, [and a] general contempt for even the most obvious rules of common sense.[5]

Specifically concerning the Holocaust, Bruno Bettel- heim reflects on the guilt of physicians in the so-called medical experiments in various death camps, lamenting their pride in professional skill and knowledge irrespective of moral implication. He views this as dangerous. "Auschwitz is gone," observes Bettelheim, "but as long as this attitude remains with us we shall not be safe from the indifference to life at its core."[6] His utterance is, I fear, prophetic. Universities accentuate and multiply skills courses while regularly deemphasizing and eliminating courses in ethics. Although frequently performed as ethically neutral acts [a course's fate typically depends upon enrollment], the results are disastrous. Skills are refined without any moral limit on their use.

III. A Literary Perspective

The need for academics to engage in a prolonged period of soul-searching is urgent, but is expression appears muted. For example, only two fictional Jewish professors react to the Holocaust--Moses E. Herzog and the less well-known Sol Nazerman. Saul Bellow's Herzog is an academic unimpressed by the "commonplaces of the Wasteland outlook, the cheap mental stimulants of Alienation, the can and rant of pipsqueaks about Inauthenticity and Forlornness." Herzog does not enjoy the respect of his academic colleagues. They are upset by his emotionalism which is perceived as an irrelevant concern from everyday truths, and by his refusal to engage in chic apocalypticism. Herzog, for his part, is bitterly critical of spurious elitism. Writing to Professor Shapiro, he denounces such elitism, holding it at least partly responsible for European totalitarianism and....reaching at last the point of denying the humanity of the industrialized "banalized" masses. It was easy for the Wastelanders to be assimilated, to be assimilated to totalitarianism. Here the responsibility of artists remains to be assessed. To have assumed....that the deteriorization of langauge and its debasement was tantamount to dehumanization led straight to cultural fascism. [page 76]

Few academics recognize the validity of Herzog's warning: "How quickly the visions of genius become the canned goods of the intellectuals."

Sol Nazerman, the Pawnbroker, is, like Herzog, a victim. Unlike him, Nazerman is a death camp survivor. Edward Lewis Wallant employs the figure of a displaced academic, professor of history of ideas prior to the cataclysm, who metamorphosizes after the war as front man for a major crime figure. Nazerman has abandoned, and been abandoned by, the morally corrupt and ideologically bankrupt university value system. He bitterly warns his assistant against the seductions of so-called culture: "I do not trust God or politics or newspapers or movies or art." He is most suspicious of "people and their talk, for they have created hell with their talk...." Although failing to pursue the implications for academics, is Wallant [perhaps subconsciously] portraying the role played by academics in Nazi Germany? What are the ethical moorings of scholars and teachers who, when faced with the choice of losing their university positions or supporting the Nazis, chose, in the vast majority, the latter course.[7] Would contemporary academics act differently?

IV. Pseudo-Professionalism and Objectivity in Nazi Germany

Pseudo-professionalism and objectivity were commonplace in Nazi Germany. How they came about and what they resulted in are questions of more than passing interest. If the past is but prologue, we owe to our present, and stake to our future existence, the obligation not only of learning history's lessons, but determining their contemporary implications. Only one generation separates us from the Holocaust. Surely that is too soon to forget the lessons of perverted professionalism. The preponderance of academics, corporate executives and physicians among the murderers raises the most fundamental questions about modernity. Civilizational assumptions in modernity, owing, no doubt, to the fact that man inhabits a desacralized world--Herzog laments the "decay of the religious foundations of civilization"--have less to do with illumination and are more concerned with attaining technological competence. Value-free performance is a hallmark of modernity. It is instructive to recall Raul Hilberg's description of the murderous *Einsatzgruppen* [SS] leadership:

Academia and the Holocaust

These men were in no sense hoodlums, delinquents, common criminals, or sex maniacs. Most were intellectuals. All we know is they brought to their new task all the skills and training which, as men of thought, they were capable of contributing. These men, in short, became efficient killers.[8]

V. Three Examples

Dr. Joseph Mengele, the infamous "angel of death" at Auschwitz, attended a pregnant woman prisoner. According to an eye-witness account, Mengele:

> took all correct medical precautions during childbirth, rigorously observing all aseptic principles, cutting the umbilical cord with greatest care, etc. But only half an hour later he sent mother and infant to be burned in the crematorium.[9]

The corporate elite also had no difficulty divorcing skills from values. Five of I. G. Farben's top executives inspected I. G. Auschwitz, the firm's slave labor factory.[10] Passing two Jewish scientist inmates, one of the directors said to an SS man, "This Jewish swine could work a little faster." Another director, not to be outdone by his companion, added, "If they can't work, let them perish in the gas chamber." Dr. Lohner-Beda, one of the Jewish scientists, was pulled from his group, then beaten and kicked to death.[11]

The record of German academics, nowhere systematically report-ed, is equally appalling. Max Weinrich writes that "German scholarship provided the ideas and techniques which led to and justified this unparalleled slaughter."[12] It is a pity that there was no Nuremberg Trial against professors as such.[13] Few academics and intellectuals have learned to accept responsibility for the consequences [political and otherwise] of their ideological preachments. This divorce of academia from reality is nowhere clearer than in the statement of Martin Heidegger, one of the ranking philosophers in the world. His scholarship is read, studied, and pondered with great care in contemporary universities. Yet how many professors assigning Heidegger's works know, or care, about his actions as Rector of Freiburg University? In that capacity, Heidegger wrote to his students admonishing them:

> Not doctrines and "ideas" be the rules of your being. The Fuhrer himself and alone is the present and future German reality and its law. Learn ever deeper to know: that from now on each and everything demands decision and every action responsibility. Heil Hitler![14]

Ironically, Heidegger's call for decision and responsibility was made to those who had been barred from all possibility of self-responsibility and freedom of choice.[15]

The above record appears to suggest rather strongly that education has abandoned its humanizing task. The new product is described by Franklin H. Littell as a technically competent barbarian, whose education has "trained him to think in ways that eliminate questions of ultimate responsibility."[16] The aphorist, Elias Canetti, states the problem in its fundamental terms: "We have no standard any more for anything, ever since human life is no longer the standard." Is this situation reversible? Dare we think of values in a radically disenchanted world, a world in which there appears to be no restraint upon man's actions?

Values imply standards. Ideally, education is training in human potential and responsibility. What possible meaning could this goal have in the post-Holocaust world? Wiesel reports seeing himself in a mirror after the war, for the first time since he had been taken from the ghetto. "From the depths of the mirror," he writes, "a corpse gazed back at me." Is this the contemporary image of man?

Practically speaking, the question is: What is the relationship between teaching and being human? Professors and students must constantly ask what values are illuminated by the application of skills. The dissonance between what is taught and the world we live in seems overwhelming.

VI. Holocaust Specificity

Wiesel correctly notes that the Holocaust has become a "desanctified theme." Perhaps this was inevitable. Though I do not completely share his view that the Holocaust is "Holy History," I do emphatically agree that the murdered demand respect. What is done with the data reveals much about the nature of society. For example, at Babi Yar, where the earth opened to receive the bodies of 30,000 Jews whom the Nazis had machine gunned to death, the Soviets have put a plaque commemorating not the Jews, but the "victims of fascism."

Distortion of the Holocaust occurs with the very use of that term to describe what happened to Europe's Jews. Derived from the Greek *holocaustoma*, "burnt offering," Holocaust came into use sometime in the late 1950s. This antiseptic word implies a Christian understanding of Jewish history. Six million sacrifices to God Almighty; no grosser falsification of Isaiah was ever proposed. Judaism, for its part, speaks of the trauma differently and in its own idiom. *Hurban* [day of awe] is a Yiddish word which carries with it memories of the destruction[s] of the Jerusalem Temple. Shoah is Hebrew. It means desolation of cosmic proportion. Theologically, the Holocaust remains a mystery. Wiesel has written that "perhaps some day someone will explain how, on the level of man, Auschwitz was possible; but on the level of God, it will forever remain the most disturbing of mysteries."[17]

Two pedagogical goals are elimination of ignorance and a striving for clarity of understanding. The Holocaust, an irrational act implemented in a highly rational bureaucratic manner, challenges at least the second goal. This is not to invalidate further research nor does it denigrate the enormous quantity of post-World War II documents which are coming to light. In fact, scholars continually penetrate ever deeper into the *how* of mass murder, including the reactions of victim and victimizer, but the *why* remains elusive. It is for this reason, I suggest, that Wiesel contends that "....the Holocaust teaching nothing." But there *is* much to learn from it. The Holocaust is a looking glass which reflects civilization and ourselves, simultaneously revealing and unraveling the fabric of our civilization. Post-Holocaust requires us, at the very least, seriously to question any *a priori* comparison of Holocaust to other tragedies. On the other hand, while scrupulously particular in nature [ridding the world of Jews], the Holocaust does have universal implications, especially for the survival of civilization itself. Rabbi Irving Greenberg analogizes the Holocaust to an early warning system, the treatment of Jews serving as a harbinger.

The Holocaust was an advance warning of the demonic potential in the very power and magnetism of modern culture. If one could conceive of Hitler's coming to power not in 1933 but in 1963, after the invention of hydrogen bombs, then the Holocaust would have been truly universal. It is a kind of last warning that if humanity will perceive and overcome the demonism unleashed in modern culture, the world may survive. Otherwise, the next Holocaust will embrace the whole world.[18]

VII. Uniqueness: Particularity and Universalism

Academics have a penchant for classifying which tends to obscure rather than illumine issues, seeking always that which is most general while stumbling over the unique. How, then, will they teach the Holocaust? Does one quantify an abyss? Language itself is a victim of the disaster. In teaching and learning about the Holocaust one needs to steer a course between the Scylla of mystification and the Charybdis of business as usual. Yehuda Bauer argues persuasively against mystification, noting a two-fold danger:

> If what happened to the Jews was unique, then it took place outside history, and it becomes a mysterious event, an upside-down miracle, so to speak, an event of religious significance in the sense that it is not man-made as the term is normally understood.[19]

This is mystification. On the other hand, Bauer warns of the historical and moral failure, or refusal, to confront the Holocaust. For example, Holocaust must be distinguished from genocide. Although there is no difference for the victims, more than semantics is at stake here. Genocide means ruthless, "even murderous, denationalization." Holocaust is systemic and total destruction: complete eradication from the face of the earth. Jews were the only group so designated for this fate.[20] Failure to realize the uniqueness of the Jewish situation is obscuring history.

The attempt to subsume the Holocaust as one example of man's inhumanity to man, thereby making it comparable to Hiroshima, Wounded Knee, Mai Lai, Cambodia, among others, is at best a misreading of history which generalizes human suffering and easily lends itself to distortion. Academics would render more service to genuine objectivity if they re-called Wiesel's admonition: "Every tragedy deserves its own name." However, neither false universalism nor bad faith can sidestep what the Nazis themselves called the *Endlosung*. Elimination of Jews was viewed by Hitler and his devotees in eschatological terms. The question for professors is how to avoid the pitfalls of singularity and mystification, both of which place the Holocaust beyond the realm of human responsibility.

VIII. Contemporary Pseudo-Objectivity and the Holocaust

Two examples of pseudo-objectivity--one personal and the other organizational--have surfaced recently in association with so-called revisionist history and the Holocaust.[21] Noam Chomsky, pioneer in meta-linguistics, influential academic, and selective defender of human rights, recently signed an appeal defending the civil rights of Robert Faurrison, a former professor of French Literature in Lyon. Faurrison has made a career out of "debunking" the Holocaust. Lecturing and publishing on two continents, he denies the reality of the gas chambers, charging that the Holocaust is a lie of Zionist doing. Anne Frank, argues Faurrison, was a fake. Yet Chomsky, in a letter to Professor Dawidowicz, expressed complete agnosticism on the validity of Faurrison's views, claiming that he [Chomsky] was insufficiently involved in the issue to evaluate or pursue it.[22]

The Organization of American Historians [OAH] received protests from some members over the sale of the OAH mailing list to the neo-Nazi *Journal of Historical Review*; other members defended the sale, citing academic objectivity. To resolve the issue, well-qualified historians were to analyze the JHR concerning its use of evidence and its contributors' credentials. Then the OAH's Executive Board would report to the membership. Dawidowicz asks the key question.

Academia and the Holocaust

Report what is not quite clear. Perhaps that the Neo-Nazis did not have proper academic credentials, or that they failed to use primary sources? Again one wonders: Would the OAH have reacted the same way to a pseudoscholarly journal publishing KKK propaganda?[23]

It is tempting to dismiss these reports as merely exempla of endemic anti-Semitism. There have always been, and there always will be, anti-Semites. Self-hating Jews are, likewise and unfortunately, all too frequent a part of the post-Enlightenment landscape. Moreover, the existence of evil is hardly news. But there is, I think, more to the matter. Does academia itself not only encourage but institutionalize attitudes of indifference? Students are urged to eliminate or suspend ["bracket"] their own feelings and opinions while researching and writing papers. Those who most completely remove their attitudes, feelings, and values from their work receive A's. Universities reward indifference and neutrality in areas where an expression of concern would make students more fully human. Consequently, university training frequently leads to moral numbness and the dulling of personal responsibility. Accurate reporting [true objectivity] has, in our time, become confused with ethical objectivity.

IX. The Task Before Us--Types of Instruction

Western education is at a pedagogical as well as financial cross-road. The ancient Greek struggle between spiritual learning and technological skills is today, post-Holocaust, more intense even if less articulated. Our technological society is devoted to models and prototypes in areas outside of academia; why not within? Ananda Coomaraswamy remarks, somewhere, on the difference between Eastern and Western models of teaching. Eastern education requires a harmony between the thinker and his mode of living. Westerners deem sufficient the production of an internally coherent worldview, disregarding or downgrading the manner in which one's life is lead. My own view is that this is a contributing factor to the emergence in the East of the master-disciple rela-tionship with its emphasis upon instructor as personal ideal and disciples as "representatives of humanity." For example, Gandhi's way was unexceptional--in terms of method--whereas Martin Luther King, Jr., seemed so exotic to us. Master-disciple also is a specifically religious mode of instruction, requiring a cosmic orientation and self-understanding. Know-ledge and being are inextricably linked.

On the other hand, we in the West have adopted the teacher-student model. The teacher's skill or knowledge exercises prestige. He is irreplaceable only if, in Joachim Wach's words, "It is merely that none can actually be found to take his place." The teacher's life is irrelevant to, and may actually compete with, the skills that he wishes to communicate. Contemporary universities are built upon the teacher-student model.

The Holocaust Now

The danger is that frequently we confuse the two models, mistaking an accumulation of knowledge for a foretaste of salvation. Knowledge need not be wisdom. Educational schizophrenia can result in civilizational disaster.

Values are learned. While German professors were upholding the Fuhrer--and maintaining their jobs--Dr. Janusz Korczak, educator and physician, chose to accompany the orphans in his care to the gas chambers. Social scientists and psychologists may speculate on differences in behavior. But one thing is certain: when personal obligations and human compassion are sacrificed for utilitarian goals and job enhancement, society is in peril. Ideally, the Holocaust is a course in civic responsibility and personal virtue. Therefore, teaching such a course involves not only history, but equally important, its stress upon current events.

X. Conclusion

One seeks in vain a clear societal signal. Reduced financial support of arts, education, and the humanities are pervasive, ranging from drastic curtailment of federal funding to the elimination of courses in art and music at the secondary level. In universities, skills and vocational courses attract students but minimize ethical concerns. A journalism major reports that her news writing course spend one day--the last session of the semester--on the ethical aspects of reporting. Class responses to the query, "What would you do if the subject of your story threatened suicide upon the story's publication?" were mixed. There was greater clarity in response to the question, "What is the publication of your story would lead to its subject's dismissal?" All class members said they would refrain from publishing. On the other hand, there are more Holocaust courses, seminars, and institutes than at any other time since 1945. Jewish-Christian interchange is also a topic of great interest and scholarly concern. The answer to the question: "Where is our society headed?" is unclear. Numbers alone reveal little. The Holocaust shows the ease with which people may be desensitized to critical moral and ethical concerns.[24] Awareness of the blunting of aesthetic sensibilities is not high on the national agenda.

If teaching and learning are once again to become humanizing experiences, then professors must reconceive their goals and how to achieve them without doing irreparable violence to personal virtue and human responsibility. Students, for their part, must not be content merely to train for a vocation but should prepare themselves to ennoble their chosen field. What constitutes the ethical life? Old definitions pale before the enormity of Auschwitz. Recall the Nazi practice of giving three yellow work permits [which entitled the bearer to live an extra day] to a married father of four children, telling him to distribute those permits.

Honesty compels the admission that after Auschwitz the world is not the same.

Academia and the Holocaust

The task of renewal is urgent and the state of the world is unredeemed. Professional competence is necessary, but so is the realization that being human requires its own full measure of competence. Professors and students could benefit in their soul-searching from the advice given in *Pirke Avot*: "Be deliberate in judgment [thoroughly study an issue from all angles], raise up disciples [teach and be what you know], and made a hedge for the Torah" [protect the divine from assault, making higher values accessible for contemplation].

The Holocaust Now

NOTES

JUDAISM AND CHRISTIANITY AFTER AUSCHWITZ

Steven L. Jacobs

1. First presented at the Second Interdisplinary Conference on the Holocaust, 30-31 March 1987, at the University of Alabama, Tuscaloosa, AL.

2. Irving Greenberg, "Judaism and Christianity After the Holocaust," in Journal of Ecumenical Studies, 12:4, Fall, 1975, 529. This seminal article was reworked and published under the title "Cloud of Smoke, Pillar of Fire: Judaism, Christianity, and Modernity after the Holocaust!" in Eva Fleischner, Editor, Auschwitz: Beginning of a New Era? Reflections on the Holocaust [New York: Ktav Publishing House, 1977], 7-55.

3. Arthur Cohen, The Tremendum: A Theological Interpretation of the Holocaust [New York: Continuum, 1981], 39.

4. Robert Sherwin, "The Impotence of Explanation and the European Holocaust," in Tradition: A Journal of Orthodox Jewish Thought, XII, 1972, 99.

5. Arthur Cohen, Op. Cit., 86.

6. Raul Hilberg, The Destructionof European Jews [Chicago: Quadrangle Books, 1961], 3 ff. Philosopher Emil Fackenheim sees the recreation of the State of israel as a response to this schemata when he writes:

    > For it [i.e. the State of Israel] responses to the three-fold prohibition so well formulated by Hilberg. "You have no right to live"—the Jewish State, although it is impossible to discount a second Masada, will never permit a second Auschwitz. "You have no right to live

among us"—the Jewish State cannot end the persecution of Jews, but through its Law of Return it gives a home to such Jews as the persecutors permit to leave. "You have no right to live among us as Jews"—the very name of the Jewish State in effect replies to Christianity, Paul's "new" Israel, and to its secularist successors, that the "old" Israel is not a defunct people of a non-people, but alive.

Emil L. Fackenheim, "Concerning Authentic and Unauthentic Responses to the Holocaust" in Holocaust and Genocide Studies, 1:1, 1986, 116.

7. Israeli Shoah scholar Yehuda Bauer sees the Shoah as unique for two additional reasons: [1] The annihilation of the Jewish people was to be a total planned annihilation, and [2] Its orchestration possessed a quasi-religious apocalyptic meaning. Reported in Michael Berenbaum, "Our ancient covenant has been shattered," in Sh'ma: A Journal of Jewish Responsibility, 14/272, April 13, 1984, 92.

8. Daniel Polish, "Witnessing God after Auschwitz," in Helga Croner and Leon Klenicki, Editors, Issues in the Jewish-Christian Dialogue: Jewish Perspectives on Covenant, Mission, and Witness [New York: Paulist Press, 1979], 150. Certainly there is no more poignant expression of the latter than Richard Rubenstein's interview with Dean Heinrich Gruber of the Evangelical Free Church in West Berlin: "The Dean and the Chosen People," in After Auschwitz: Radical Theology and Contemporary Judaism [Indianapolis: Bobbs-Merrill, 1986], 47-58, and noted in the present essay.

9. David W. Weiss, "After the Holocaust another covenant?" in Sh'ma: A Journal of Jewish Responsibility, 14/272, April 13, 1984, 88-91.

10. Martin Cohen, "The Mission of Israel after Auschwitz," in Helga Croner and Leon Klenicki, Editors, Issues in the Jewish-Christian Dialogue: Jewish Perspectives on Covenant, Mission, and Witness [New York: Paulist Press, 1979], 159.

11. Here, Greenberg's reference to "burning children" is particularly relevant.

12. Richard L. Rubenstein, "Some Perspectives on Religious Faith After Auschwitz," in Franklin H. Littell and Hubert G. Locke, Editors, The German Church Struggle and the Holocaust [Detroit: Wayne State University Press, 1974], 261. Even so eminent a friend of the Jewish People as the late Paul Tillich was theologically of a similar mindset to Dean Gruber. Se, for example, Albert Friedlander's "A Final Conversation with Paul Tillich," in Albert H. Friedlander, Editor, Out of the Whirlwind: A

Notes

Reader of Holocaust Literature [New York: Union of American Hebrew Congregations, 1968], 515-521.

13. See, especially, The Cunning of History: Mass Death and the American Future [New York: Harper & Row, 1975]; and The Age of Triage: Fear and Hope in an Overcrowded World [Boston: Beacon Press, 1983].

14. Comments taken from lecture notes for a course entitled "The Holocaust in Historical Perspective," taught at the University of Alabama in Birmingham, AL, 1985-1990.

15. Michael Novak, Toward a Theology of the Corporation [Washington, DC: American Enterprise Institute for Public Policy Research, 1981].

16. Elie Wiesel, Night [New York: Hill and Wang, 1960], 71.

17. Seymour Cain, "The Question and the Answers After Auschwitz," in Judaism, 20:3, Summer, 1971, 263-278.

18. Michael Wyschogrod, "Faith and the Holocaust: A Review Essay of Emil Fackenheim's God's Presence in History," in Judaism, 20:3, Summer, 1971, 288.

19. Richard L. Rubenstein, "Some Perspectives on Religious Faith After Auschwitz," in Franklin H. Littell and Hubert G. Locke, Editors, The German Church Struggle and the Holocaust [Detroit: Wayne State University Press, 1974], 267.

20. Among the many books which deal with Wiesel's writings are the following: Ellen Norman Stern, Elie Wiesel: Witness for Life [New York: Ktav Publishing House, 1982]; Ellen S. Fine, Legacy of Night: The Literary Universe of Elie Wiesel [Albany: State University of New York Press, 1982]; Ted L. Estess, Elie Wiesel [New York: Fredrick Unger Publishing Copany, 1980]; Harry James Cargas, Editor, Responses to Elie Wiesel: Critical Essays by Major Jewish and Christian Scholars [New York: Persea Books, 1978]; Harry James Cargas, Harry James Cargas in Conversation with Elie Wiesel [New York: Paulist Press, 1976]; and John K. Roth, A Consuming Fire: Encounters with Elie Wiesel and the Holocaust [Atlanta: John Knox Press, 1979]. A fine literary-critical essay is that of Irving Abrahamson in the first volume of the three-volume set edited by him, Against Silence: The Voice and Vision of Elie Wiesel [New York: Holocaust Library, 1985].

For a discussion of Cargas and his writings, see my essay "Harry James Cargas: Appreciation and Response," in Journal of Reform Judaism, XXXII:2, Spring, 1985, 33-43.

My review of Roth's work appeared in The New Review of Books and Religion, IV:2, September, 1979, 13-14.

21. Eliezer Berkovits, Faith After Auschwits [New York: Ktav Publishing House, 1973].

22. A position somewhat similar to that of Berkovits is that held by philosopher Martin Buber in his Eclipse of God: Studies in the Relation between Religion and Philosophy [New York: Harper & Row, 1942]. See, also, the masterful study by Maurice Friedman, Martin Buber's Life and Work [New York: E. P. Dutton]: The Early Years 1878-1923 [1981]; The Middle Years 1923-1945 [1983]; and The Later Years 1945-1965 [1983].

23. Emil L. Fackenheim, Quest for Past and Future [Bloomington: Indiana University Press, 1968], 19. Repeated in God's Presence in History [New York: New York University Press, 1970], 86.

24. Gerald S. Sloyan, "Some Theological Implications of the Holocaust," in Interpretation, XXXIX:4, October, 1985, 408. Emphasis mine.—SLJ

25. Irving Greenberg, "Judaism and Christianity after the Holocaust," in Journal of Ecumenical Studies, 12:4, Fall, 1975, 544.

26. John T. Pawlikowski, "The Holocaust and Catholic Theology," in Shoah, 2:4, 1979, 6 ff.

27. Quoted in Steven L. Jacobs, "Harry James Cargas: Appreciation and Response," in Journal of Reform Judaism, 32:2, Spring, 1985, 43. Perhaps because of the radical nature of what he is suggesting, Cargas appears to have little, if any, impact on the organized Catholic Church to any appreciable degree. Indeed, one wold hazard the guess whether, in fact, many within that community have ever heard of him or his writings.

28. Rosemary Radford Ruether, Faith and Fratricide: The Theological Roots of Anti-Semitism [New York: The Seabury Press, 1974].

29. Michael B. McGarry, Christology After Auschwitz [New York: Paulist Press, 1977].

Notes

30. Alan Ecclestone, Night Sky of the Lord [New York: Schocken Books, 1980]. See, also, my review in the Anglican Theological Review, LXII:3, Summer, 1989, 331-333.

31. Franklin H. Littell, The Crucifixion of the Jews: The Failure of Christians to Understand the Jewish Experience [New York: Harper & Row, 1975].

32. David A. Rausch, A Legacy of Hatred: Why Christians Must Not Forget the Holocaust [Chicago: Moody Press, 1984]. Significantly, this volume was published by a conservative, evangelical, fundamentalist Christian publishing house, and, to the best of my knowledge, stands alone and unique because of that.

33. A. Roy Eckardt, Elder and Younger Brothers: The Encounter of Jews and Christians [New York: Charles Scribner's Sons, 1967].

34. A. Roy Eckardt and Alice Lyons Eckardt, Long Night's Journey into Day: Life and Faith After the Holocaust [Detoit: Wayne State University Press, 1982].

35. Alice Lyons Eckardt, "Post-Holocaust Theology: A Journey Out of the Kingdom of Night," in Holocaust and Genocide Studies, 1:2, 1986, 229-240.

36. Ibid., 229-230.

37. John Roth, A Consuming Fire: Encounters with Elie Wiesel and the Holocaust [Atlanta: John Knox Press, 1979].

38. Steven L. Jacobs, "Review of A Consuming Fire," in The New Review of Books and Religion, IV:1, September, 1979, 13-14. Emphasis mine.—SLJ

39. Alice Lyons Eckardt, Op. Cit., 230-231. A contempoary evolution of these nightmarish examples is that contained in a footnote to Emil Fackenheim's article, "Concerning Authentic and Unauthentic Reponses to the Holocaust:"

36. Consider among counter instances illustrating this point the fundamentalist Canadian Christian minister who sought out Eichmann in Jerusalem, equally sure that a converted Eichmann would find salvation and that his unconverted Jewish victims would not. Or the famous American liberal Protestant theologian who urged his Jewish audience to forgive the German people, but was left speechless when

asked by a Jewish layman why Christians could expect Jews to forgive the murder of six million Jews, committed a single generation ago, when Christians had yet to forgive the murder of one Jew, committed two thousand years ago.

Emil L. Fackenheim, "Concerning Authentic and Unauthentic Responses to the Holocaust," in Holocaust and Genocide Studies, 1:1, 1986, 119.

40. Alice Lyons Eckardt, Op. Cit., 232-237.

41. Samuel Pisar, Of Blood and Hope [Boston: Little, Brown and Company, 1979].

42. Steven L. Jacobs, "[If] There is No 'Commander'?....There are No 'Commandments!" Originally presented at the Third Annual Conference on Spirituality of the Atlanta, GA, Reform Synagogue Council on Sunday, 21 September 1986, under the title, "Reform Jews in Search of God: The Mitzvot—Law or Lore?" Published in Judaism, 37:3, Summer, 1988, 323-327. See, also, "A Response to the Critiques," in Judaism, 38:2, Spring, 1989, 245-252.

AUSCHWITZ: RE-ENVISIONING THE ROLE OF GOD

Peter J. Haas

1. A parallel discussion to Haas' thinking may be found in Harold Schulweis' notion of predicate theology. See his Evil and the Morality of God [Cincinnati: Hebrew Union College Press, 1984], as well as my briefreview "Theodicy Forces Us to Seek Simplicity and Distrust It," in Books & Religion, 14:10, December, 1986, 13.

2. The most represntative Jewish thinker along these lines is, in my view, Eliezer Berkovits. His concept of hester panim ["the Hidden Face of God"—Editor] draws directly on miedieval Jewish conceptualizations. The result of using medieval concepts to explain God to modern people is that God becomes incomprehensible and so dismissable. One example of this is Amos Funkenstein, "Theological Interpretations of the Holocaust: A Balance," in Francois Furet, Editor, Unanswered Questions: Nazi Germany and the Genocide of the Jews [New York: Schocken Books, 1989], 275-303.

3. Irving Greenberg makes the point on several occasions that Heinrich Himmler insisted that the members of the SS have a belief in God so that they might be different from the Marxists [for example, in his "Religious Values after the Holocaust: A

Notes

Jewish Perspective," in Abraham Peck, Editor, Jews and Christians after the Holocaust [Philadelphia: Fortress Press, 1982], 76. This is simply a formal gesture, and not what I have in mind here. The mere invocation of God's name or the use of certain rituals does not amount to religious faith, as the actions of so many "church people" in Nazi Germany shows.

4. The original edition was copyright in 1961 by Quadrangle Books, New York.

5. Indianapolis: Bobbs-Merrill, 1966. The book is subtitled "Radical Theology and Contemporary Judaism."

6. Hanover: University Press of New England, 1987. See, especially, 2 ff.

7. Rubenstein's writings in After Auschwitz are linked to the "God is Dead" theology associated with, among others, Thomas Altizer. Rubenstein avoids the phrase "God is Dead" as too clsoely linked to Christian imagery. His phrasing throughout is more passive: "....time of the death of God" and the like. See his discussion of this 243-246.

8. The Tremendum: A Theological Interpretation of the Holocaust [New York: Crossroads, 1988].

9. Spelled out in his God's Presence in History: Jewish Affirmations and Philosophical Reflections [New York: New York University Press, 1970]. Also, Part Two of The Jewish Return into History [New York: Schocken Books, 1978].

10. Thus, he talks of the "614th commandment," the original revelation of 613 [as portrayed in traditional Rabbinic Judaism] having been increased, not replaced, after Auschwitz. See Return, 22-23.

11. From her book A Report on the Banality of Evil: Eichmann in Jerusalem [New York: Penguin Books, 1963].

12. This has tended to be a more conservative Christian perspective. The most egregious Jewish example is Joel Teitelbaum in his Vajoel Moshe [New York: 1957].

13. Related I Night, 60-62, in the Bantam Books edition.

14. A Legacy of Hatred: Why Christians Must Not Forget the Holocaust [Chicago:

Moody Press, 1984]. The books is specifically aimed at combatting white supremacists who portray themselves as "true Christians."

15. As in his Faith After the Holocaust [New York: Ktav Publishing House, 1973].

16. There is no doubt that Arendt did regard Eichmann as personally banal. This is clear from her reaction to his final words [252], as well as from her comment that she could not "extract any diabolical or demonic profundity from Eichmann...." [288]. Yet, she also seems to see Eichmann as only an example of a deeper "interdependence of thoughtlessness and evil [288]. Eichmann acted, she concludes, in a wholly meaningful way within the larger framework of which he was a part. Cf. 288 ff.

17. Much of what follows is covered in Hannah Arendt's ground-breaking The Origins of Totalitarianism.

18. A good overall treatment is Vamberto Morais, A Short History of Anti-Semitism [New York: W. W. Norton and Company, 1976]. The Church's attitude is the central concern of Edward W. Flannery's The Anguish of the Jews: A Catholic Priest Writes of Twenty-three Centuries of Anti-Semitism [New York: Macmillan, 1964].

19. "Concerning the Amelioration of the Civil Status of the Jews." A translated and abridged version is in Robert Chaza and Marc Lee Raphael, Editors, Modern Jewish History: A Reader [New York: Schocken Books, 1969], 1-13.

20. George L. Mosse, Toward the Final Solution: A History of Racism [New York: Howard Fertig, 1978].

21. The most articulate nineteenth-century racial theorist of this type is probably Count J. A. de Gobineau. The full confluence of his theoriest with Hegel and Social Darwinism is illustrated in the writings of Houston Steward Chamberlain. Chamberlain championed the idea of the Aryan "race."

22. Published by Harper & Row, New York, 1978. The cited document is on 56.

23. Source, Sanction, and Salvation: Religion and Morality in Judaic and Christian Traditions [Englewood Cliffs: Prentice Hall, 1988], 1.

24. Irving Greenberg makes a similar observation in his paper delivered to a sympo-

Notes

sium on the Shoah hosted by the Cathedral of St. John the Divine in New York. "No assessment of modern culture can ignore the fact that science and technology—the accepted flower and glory of modernity—now climaxed in the factories of death....There is the shock of recognition that the humanistic revolt, celebrated as the liberation of humankind in freeding man from centuries of dependence upon God and nature, is now reverted....to sustain a capacity for death and demonic evil." In Eva Fleischner, Editor, Auschwitz: Beginning of a New Era? [New York: Ktav Publishing House, 1977], 15.

25. The classic work on this is Thomas Kuhn, The Structure of Scientific Revolutions [Chicago: University of Chicago Press, 1962]. Curiously, the work of Kuhn was anticipated in its essential insight by Karl Mannheim, who wrote on the eve of the Nazi ascent to power. See, especially, his article "Wissenssoziologie," in Alfred Vierkandt, Editor, Handwoertebuch der Soziologie [Stuttgart: F. Enke, 1931].

26. Mannheim comes close to saying the same thing in "Wissenssoziologie:" "We will bring with the fact that the same word, or the same concept in most cases, means very different things when used by differently situated persons." He then goes on to use as a concrete example the word [or concept] "freedom." Karl Mannehim, Ideology and Utopia: An Introduction to the Sociology of Knowledge [New York: Harcourt, Brace & World, 1936. Translated by Louis Wirth and Edward Shils.], 273 ff.

27. Alasdair MacIntyre, After Virtue [Notre Dame: University of Notre Dame Press, 1984. Second Edition.], 27 ff.

28. MacIntyre, Op. Cit., 74-75.

29. I recognize that the extermination of the Jews was implicit in Nazi thinking from the beginning, but, it seems to me, that it became fully conceptualized and shaped over time. I thus take a functionalist view of the development of the Nazi war against the Jews. For my arguments, see my Morality after Auschwitz: The Radical Challenge of the Nazi Ethic [Philadelphia: Fortress Press, 1988].

30. See Irving Greenberg's comments, cited above.

The Holocaust Now

EVIL AND EXISTENCE:
Karl Barth, Paul Tillich and Reinhold Niebuhr
Revisited in Light of the Shoah

Alan Davies

1. Arthur A. Cohen, The Tremendum: A Theological Interpretation of the Holocaust [New York: Crossroads, 1988].

2. For example, in his December 13, 1949, radio address on antisemitism, later translated and published as "The Jewish Problem and the Christian Answer" in Against the Stream: Shorter Post-War Writings, 1946-52 [London: SCM Press, 1954], 195-201, Barth describes the contemporary Jewish situation following as "the greatest tragedy in their history" [196].

3. Cited in Eberhard Busch, Karl Barth: His Life from Letters and Autobiographical Texts [Philadelphia: Fortress Press, 1975. Translated by Jim Bowden.], 200.

4. Karl Barth, Community, State and Church: Three Essays [New York: Anchor Books, 1960], 143.

5. Otto Weber, Karl Barth's Church Dogmatics: An Introductory Report [Philadelphia: Westminster Press, 1953. Translated by Arthur C. Cochrane.], 187.

6. Immanuel Kant, Religion Within the Limits of Reason Alone, Book I.

7. Karl Barth, "The Doctrine of Creation," Church Dogmatics [Edinburgh: T. & T. Clark, 1961. Volume III, Part 3. Translated by G. W. Bromley and R. J. Ehrlich.], 295 ff.

8. Ibid., 349.

9. Ibid., 353.

10. Ibid., 523.

11. See John Hick, Evil and the God of Love [New York: Harper & Row, 1966], 141-150.

12. Karl Barth, "The Christian Community in the Midst of Poltiical Change," Against the Stream, 115.

Notes

13. Church Dogmatics, Volume III, Part 3, 343.

14. Ibid., 347.

15. Emil L. Fackenheim, Encounters Between Judaism and Modern Philosophy: A Preface to Future Jewish Thought [New York: Basic Books, 1973], 223.

16. Ernst Zundel, a neo-Nazi propagandist of major proportions, is the author of various tracts, including Did Six Million Really Die? And [under a pseudonym] The Hitler We Loved and Why. He has been tried and convicted twice in Canada for publishing and circulating information that he knew was false and inimical to the public interest [under Section 177 of the Criminal Code of Canada]. For further details of his career, see my article "A Tale of Two Trials: Antisemitism in Canada, 1985" in Holocaust and Genocide Studies, 4:1, 1989, 77-88. Arthur Butz, a professor of electrical engineering at Northwestern University, Evanston, IL, is the author of the new antisemitic classic The Hoax of the Twentieth Century, a work that belongs on the same shelf as Edouard Drumont, La France Juive, etc.

17. For a critique of Barth's theological anti-Judaism, see my book Anti-Semitism and the Christian Mind: The Crisis of Conscience After Auschwitz [New York: Herder and Herder, 1969], 113-126.

18. Church Dogmatics, Volume III, Part 3, 363.

19. Ibid., 364.

20. Ibid.

21. Ibid., 367.

22. Karl Barth, The German Church Conflict [London, Lutterworth Press, 1965. Translated by P. T. A. Parker], 30. Hirsch is cited in Gunda Schneider-Flume, Die politische Theologie Emanuel Hirsch, 1918-1933 [Berne: Herbant Lang, 1971], 160.

23. Cf. Heinz Zahrnt, The Question of God: Protestant Theology in the Twentieth Century [New York: Harcourt, Brace and World, 1966. Translated by R. A. Wilson.], 112-122.

24. Cf. Wilhelm and Marion Pauck, Paul Tillich: His Life and Thought [New York: Harper & Row, 1976. Volume I.], 108.

25. Paul Tillich, "The Demonic," in The Interpretation of History [New York: Charles Scribner's Sons, 1936], 78.

26. Ibid., 79-80.

27. Ibid., 81.

28. Ibid.

29. Ibid., 80.

30. Ibid., 120. See, also, Ronald H. Stone, Paul Tillich's Radical Social Thought [Atlanta: John Knox Press, 1980], 58-61.

31. Ibid., 120-121.

32. Cf. James Luther Adams, Paul Tillich's Philosophy of Culture, Science, and Religion [New York: Harper & Row, 1965], 32, #26.

33. Paul Tillich, The Interpretation of History, 94.

34. Ibid., 95.

35. Paul Tillich, The Courage to Be [New Haven: Yale University Press, 1952], 57-63.

36. Wilhelm and Marion Pauck, Op. Cit., 127.

37. Paul Tillich, The Socialist Decision [New York: harper and Row, 1977. Translated by Franklin Sherman.], Chapter 2.

38. Ibid., 30.

39. Ibid., 22.

40. Wilhelm and Marion Pauck, Op. Cit., 127.

Notes

41. Paul Tillich, Op. Cit., 160-161. See the careful discussion of Tillich on this subject in A. James Reimar, The Emanuel Hirsch and Paul Tillich Debate: A Study in the Political Ramifications of Theology [Lewison/Queenstown: The Edwin Mellen Press, 1989], 223 ff.

42. Cited in D. Mackenzie Brown, Ultimate Concerns: Tillich in Dialogue [New York: Harper & Row, 1965], 59.

43. See Hannah Arendt, Eichmann in Jerusalem: A Report on the Banality of Evil [New York: Viking Press, 1963], 135-136.

44. D. Mackenzie Brown, Loc. Cit.

45. Ibid., 180.

46. See Paul Tillich, "The Jewish Question: Christian and German Problem," in Jewish Social Studies, XXXIII:4, 1971, 253-271.

47. Jacob Boehme [1575-1624]; Friedrich Schelling [1775-1854. Tillich, it should be noted, wrote a dissertation on Schelling, now available in English: Mysticism and Guilt-consciousness in Schelling's Philosophical Development [Lewisburg: Bucknell University Press, 1974. Translated by Victor Nuovo.].

48. Heinz Zahrnt, Op. Cit., 336.

49. For a good account of this issue, see Michael Marrus, The Holocaust in History [Toronto: Lester and Orpen Dennys, 1987], 40 ff.

50. Reinhold Niebuhr, The Nature and Destiny of Man: A Christian Interpretation [New York: Charles Scribner's Sons, 1941. Volume I.], 254, #4.

51. See, for example, his polemic against the use of Kantian, Hegelian, and Whiteheadian analogies in modern Protestant theology in his post-World War II book The Self and the Dramas of History [New York: Charles Scribner's Sons, 1955], 96-97.

52. Ibid., 181.

53. Ibid., 182.

54. Ibid., 184.

55. Ibid., 180.

56. Ibid., 120, #12.

57. Ibid., 263.

58. Ibid.

59. "In modern international life Great Britain with its too strong sense of security....and Germany with its maniacal will-to-power, are perfect symbols of the different forms which pride takes among the established and the advancing social forces. The inner stability and eternal security of Great Britain has been of such long duration that she may be said to have committed the sins of Babylonia and declared, "I shall be no widow and I shall never know sorrow." Germany on the other hand suffered from an accentuated form of inferiority long before her defeat in the World War. Her boundless contemporary self-assertion which literally transgresses all bounds previously known in religion, culture and law is a very accentuated form of the power impulse which betrays a marked inner insecurity."

60. Ibid., 219.

61. Cf. Richard Wightman Fox, Reinhold Niebuhr: A Biography [New York: Pantheon Books, 1985], 191.

62. Reinhold Niebuhr, Man's Nature and His Communities: essays on the Dynamics and Enigmas of Man's Personal and Social Existence [New York: Charles Scribner's Sons, 1965], 19.

63. Reinhold Niebuhr, "Jews After the War," reprinted in Love and Justice: Selections from the shorter writings of Reinhold Niebuhr [Philadelphia: Westminster Press, 1957. Edited by Dr. B. Robertson.], 133.

64. Reinhold Niebuhr, The Children of Light and the Children of Darkness: A Vindication of Democracy and a Critique of its Traditional Defense [New York: Charles Scribner's Sons, 1944], 142,

65. Ibid., 143.

Notes

66. Reinhold Niebuhr, "Jews After the War," 135.

67. Reinhold Niebuhr, Faith and History: A Comparison of Christian and Modern Views of History [New York: Charles Scribner's Sons, 1949], 132.

68. See, for example, his comments in his essay, "The Relations of Christians and Jews in Western Civilization," in Pious and Secular America [New York: Charles Scribner's Sons, 1958], 109-111.

69. Reinhold Niebuhr, Man's Nature and His Communities, 23-24.

70. Ibid.; Niebuhr was actually quoting from the Lond Times Literary Supplement.

71. Will Herberg, Judaism and Modern Man: An Interpretation of Jewish Religion [New York: Meridian Books, 1959], 77.

72. Reinhold Niebuhr, Faith and History, 162.

73. Kurt Gerstein, officer in the SS, attempted to inform the free world of the Nazi atrocities, with, unfortunately, little success.

SUFFERING, THEOLOGY AND THE SHOAH

Alice Lyons Eckardt

1. The use of the term "extermination" is extremely problematic since we normally restrict its use to animal or insect vermin. But that is exactly how the Nazis were using the German equivalent term, catagorizing Jews as vermin, non-human, or more precisely, anti-human, which had to be exterminated for the good of the "real" human race. By using the term do we fall into the Nazi way of thinking just slightly? Or may we reinforce an unconscious attitude in this direction in others? Yet if we use a more innocent term such as "killing," we obscure the radical nature of the Nazis "Final Solution." Even "annihilate," which is an accurate term as far as totality is concerned, removes the odiousness of the prey that is associated with the word exterminate.

2. This particular incident took place [probably not by accident but by Nazi design] on

The Holocaust Now

Rosh Ha-Shanah [Jewish New Year—Editor] when the story of the Akedah [Binding of Isaac] is read in the synagogue services. [Cf. Later discussion of the Akedah.] For a fuller account, see H. Zimmels, The Echo of the Holocaust in Rabbinic Literature [New York: Ktav Publishing House, 1972], 112-113; and Irving Rosenbaum, Holocaust and Halakah [New York: Ktav Publishing House, 1976], 3-5.

3. Hannah Arendt, "Radical Evil: Total Domination," in Roger W. Smith, Editor, Guilt: Man and Society [New York: Doubleday and Company, 1971], 227. Arendt insists that "there are no parallels to life in the concentration camps. Its horror can never be fully embraced by the imagination for the very reason that it stands outside of life and death."

4. Many survivors have sought to express this incomprehensibility. Andre Stein's essay, "A Chronicle: The Necessity and Impossibility of 'Making Sense' at and of Auschwitz," is a masterful attempt to probe the world of the extermination camps as the victims experienced it and tried to take it in. They ahd to recognize that there was no continuity between Auschwitz or Sobibor and any previous existence, even that of the Nazi ghettos. Their previous life came to seem more like hallucinations or fantasies than remembrances of real places and people. [See Jewish Social Studies, XLV:3-4, 1983, 323-336.] Elie Wiesel describes his discovery that the SS could always devise a more naked and refined cruelty than that which the prisoners had already experienced and which they had assumed was the ultimate in suffering. [See One Generation After, New York: Random House, 1970, 46-47.] Wiesel has frequently spoken and written about the total "otherness" of the world of the camps, which he calls the "Kingdom of Night." Can scholars and philosophers encompass this Kingdom in their schemas? "Auschwitz, by definition, is beyond their vocabulary." [See Legends of Our Time, New York: Avon Books, 1968, 19.] Emil Fackenheim comments, "We cannot comprehend [the Holocaust] but only comprehend its comprehensibility." [See To Mend the World, New York: Schocken Books, 1982, 238.]

5. Thomas Indiopulos, "Art and the Inhuman: A Reflection on the Holocaust," in The Christian Century, XCI:35, October 16, 1974, 955.

6. The Nazi camp system was extremely complex, encompassing concentration, labor, exchange, transit, and extermination camps, as well as a few that combined the functions of labor and death camps. [Auschwitz and Maidanek in particular.] But the concentration camp system had gradations with Category III being the most brutal and lethal. [Mauthausen is the prime example of such a camp. For Jews and

Notes

"protective custody" prisoners—whose return was "not desired"—Mauthausen was a virtual death sentence.] Furthermore, the camps underwent frequent transformations from one type to another and experienced different conditions that radically altered the possibilities of survival. Labor camps were often as deadly as the worst of the concentration camps.

7. Reinhold Niebuhr was a firm advocate of the second of these.

8. Haas proposes than any formal system that enables people to make evaluations of what is right and wrong is an ethic, regardless of its content. "Moral" indicates the values "we think an ethic ought to incorporate or develop...."but that content is shaped by language and culture and can be remolded. [See "The Morality of Auschwitz: Moral Language and the Nazi Ethic," in Holocaust and Genocide Studies, 3:4, 1988, 383-384; and Morality After Auschwitz, Philadelphia: Fortress Press, 1988, 2-3, and passim.]

9. Jacob Katz, Exclusiveness and Tolerance [New York: Behrman House, 1983], 86-87.

10. Elie Wiesel, Somewhere a Master [New York: Summit Books, 1982], 42. Lurianc Kabbalah differed from Spanish Kabbalah in that it put much more emphasis on human initiative and responsibility.

11. See Paul's Epistle to the Romans, 5:3-5.

12. See J. Christopher Baker, Suffering and Hope [Philadelphia: Fortress Press, 1988], 47-48.

13. Cited in W. H. C. Frend, Martyrdom and Persecution in the Early Church [Oxford: Basic Blackwell, 1965], 196.

14. Points 11-13 are to be found in Irenaeus, Schleiermacher, and liberal Protestantism. In the Irenaean-Schleiermachian-liberal Protestant theological tradition, the justification of God's goodness and omnipotence along with the existence of evil and the inflicting and experiencing of suffering depend on humanity's "capacity not to sin and God's capacity to bring about good out of all evil—perhaps even to permit or ordain evil so that good may be experienced, by contrast, in human life....[Hence], evil is not 'damnable....but a calling forth of God's compassion on account of [humanity's] weakness and vulnerability'....all evil remains mysteriously under the subjection of God's providential creativity and foreknowledge, and is functionally

vital to humanity's moral growth." [See Carter Heyward, The Redemption of God, Washington, DC, University Press of America, 1982, 112-116. Emphases added.]

15. Heyward, Op. Cit., 125.

16. Heyward, Op. Cit., 107-108.

17. See Face to Face, XIV, Spring, 1989, for a number of very helpful articles on Christian and Jews views of redemption and salvation which are relevant to our present topic.

18. Traditionally, they are always identifiend as "Just Men." I have not seen any Jewish feminist develop the theme as related to "Just Women." The number is not always given as thirty-six; the numbers thirty, forty-five, and 330 have been mentioned by various rabbis. Kabbalah gave widest acceptance to the number thirty-six.

19. In fact, the Akedah became the foundation for the wide-ranging attack on the remnants of idolatry in Biblical Israel.

20. The Akedah received much attention in the crisis the Jewish people faced following the first war against Rome [after 70 C.E.]. For more on this, see Robert Hayward, "The Present State of Research into the Targumic Account of the Sacrifice of Isaac," in Journal of Jewish Studies, XXXII:2, 1981.

21. God's directive threatened to abrogate the promise God had made to Abraham regarding his future progeny, and undercut the commandment not to kill that was subsequently issued on Mount Sinai.

22. These stories are the only account that have survived from the many that have been recorded by Jason of Cyrene about those heroes of faith. See II Maccabees 6:18-31 and 7:1-41 in The Apocrypha, and Shalom Spiegel, The Last Trial [New York: Behrman House, 1979], 13-14.

23. A poetic version of their martyrdom was made part of the synagogue liturgy for Yom Kippur [Day of Atonement—Editor] and the Tisha B'Av [Ninth of Av, Day of Mourning—Editor].

24. Cited in Spiegel, Op. Cit., 15, from Yalkut [Midrashic anthology—Editor], Deuteronomy 26, #938; also city by Alexander Feinsilver, from Babylonian Talmud

Notes

Gittin 57b, The Talmud for Today [New York: St. Martin's Press, 1980], 179-180.

25. Nathan Hanover, The Abyss of Despair [New Brunswick and London: Transaction Books, 1983. Translated by Abraham J. Mesch.], 52, 55, and 64. One rabbi forbade Jewish fighters to attack the Polish nobles of Tulczyn, who had betrayed the community to the Cossacks because such an attack would result in Catholic kings in other nations taking vengeance on Jews in their domain.
Hanover reported that rabbis of the threatened communities exhorted Jews to take all appropriate measures to prevent catastrophe: to escape or bribe their enemies if possible; to remain constant to Judaism depsite their fear; to "indulge in sincere repentance so that the evil decree would not come to pass," but to be prepared for martyrdom if necessary.

26. Abraham Ibn Ezra's twelfth century commentary on Genesis 22:19 calls attention to the fact that Abraham "acted 'contrary to Scripture,' for he slaughtered and abandoned Isaac on the altar." See Speigel, Op. Cit., 47.

27. Spiegel, Ibid., 46, 49, 35, 38, 43-44, and 57; emphasis added. In some accounts, God was said to have used "the dew of resurrecton" to revive Isaac after he had been killed. This also provided assurance that the Holy One will revive the dead in the future because of the merit of Isaac [47, 130, 48, and 111]. Spiegel's full length study should be seen in its entirety; there is no way to do justice to its extensive scholarship in a summary fashion.

28. Spiegel, Ibid., 22, 23, 26-27, and 47. The poem is translated and published on 141-151.

29. As with most Christian themes, there were Jewish antecedents for this idea as well, apart from the Isaac story. In the Graeco-Roman period a number of Jewish writings and sects came to emphasize the value of the martyr's blood to expiate sin and "to guarantee that God would avenge the death of His servant....This was a strong tradition, and it was to influence the Christian theology of righteous suffering...." See Frend, Op. Cit., 57.

30. Frend, Ibid., 81. Cf. Isaiah 53: he was "despised and rejected by men" yet "he has borne our griefs and carried our sorrows; ....he was wounded for our transgressions....was bruised for our iniquities; upon him was the chastisement that made us whole, and with his stripes we are healed....he bore the sin of many, and made intercession for the transgressors."

31. The Interpreter's Bible, 5:631.

32. In Alexandria during the fourth-fifth centuries Bishop Cyril wrote "Christ willingly submitted to suffering and through suffering was led to triumph....The cross itself is a glorious moment." See Robert Wilken, Judaism and the Early Christian Mind [New Haven: Yale University Press, 1971], 199.

33. Frend, Op. Cit., 81 and 197, citing II Clement.

34. Cited in Alice L. Eckardt, "The Reformation and the Jews," in Shofar, 7:4, Summer, 1989, 39.

35. W. H. C. Frend sums up the whole theology of martyrdom in this early period of the church:

> They were seeking by their death to attain to the closest possible imitation of Christ's Passion and death....Christ himself suffered in the martyr. The martyr was a "true disciple of Christ"....one who "followed the Lamb wheresoever he goes," namely to death....Death was the beginning of true discipleship [and its crown] was the climax of the Christian's earthy life, a reward which all should "earnestly desire," but it was a reward to be accepted "in meekness," not grasped at, and by implication, not provoked...." [197-199].

> Nevertheless, there were some "who deliberately courted death." As Ignatius of Antioch travelled to Rome as a prisoner to be executed, he wrote to the churches of Asia Minor in "a state of exaltation bordering on mania." Not only would death make him a true disciple of Christ, and bind him to his Master, but it would serve as expiatory suffering to help overthrow Satan in the Last Times [197-199].

36. Frend, Ibid., 14-15 and 19-20. Othmar Perler's comments on the influence of IV Maccabees are cited: from the third century on, "in both East and West the Maccabees were regarded....as the prototypes of martyrdom and a source of inspiration to confessors....Christians....regarded themselves as the Maccabees' descendants" [20]. The Shepherd of Hermas was regarded as scripture by the church at Lyon, and he made the Jewish martyrdom tradition his ideal, even without including the imitation of Christ's passion [196-197].

37. Epistle to Barnabas; Irenaeus; Tertullian; Augustine; see Spiegel, Op. Cit., 84-85 and

Notes

38. There are other parallels as well: the role of Satan, and the theme of resurrection of the dead [103-108 and 109-113].

38. Spiegel, Ibid., 114, 115, 116. An addiitional difference is that the church held Jesus' sacrifice to be made on behalf of individuals; the synagogue held Isaac's sacrifice" [or merit] to be on behalf of the entire people Israel.

39. See Heyward, Op. Cit., 122-123 and 121-122.

40. Compare views in Acts of the Apostles and Pauline letters that not only express expectation of persecution but also acceptance with rejoicing: e.g. the disciples rejoice that they have been found worthy to suffer for the name [Acts 5:41]; Paul believed that suffering and death were the basis of his right to be called an apostle [II Corinthians 4;11; 6:9; and 11:23]; Paul preached that only through afflictions did one attain the kingdom of God [Acts 14:22; I Thessalonians 3:4].

41. Almost everyone of the apostolic Fathers has something to say regarding the suffering of the Jews as deserved. Origen [185-254] claimed "that Jews suffer here and will hereafter 'on account of their unbelief and other insults which they hepaed upon Jesus'." Hippolytus [179]236] concludes that "the trail of Jewish crimes leadning to deicide is 'the cause of their presnt condition involved in these myriad troubles'." [See Clark Williamson, Has God Rejected His People? Nashville: Abingdon Press, 1982, 98 and 104.] John Chrysostom [c. 344-407] vehemently asserted that for the "odious assassination of Christ" there is "no expiation possible....no pardon;" the loss of Temple and nation, and the dispersion of the people was God's work. [See Edward Flannery, The Anguish of the Jews, New York/Mahwah: Paulist Press, 1985, 51.] Cyril, Bishop of Alexandria [385-412] saw the Jewish exile, destruction of Temple, Jerusalem, and the land as punishment for disobedience to God, specifically their failure to "understand the shadow of the Old Testament" [See Wilken, Op. Cit., 86-87].
In the East, Jacob of Sarug [ca. 449-521] argued that the Cross was the turning point in Jewish history; while previously they had been most favored of peoples, afterwards they became the most rejected. Jerusalem's fall was a result of their rejecting the Son and willingly continuing to do so. [See Homily V; translation from the Syriac by Alison Salveson.]

42. Jacob Katz, Exclusiveness and Tolerance, Chapter VII.

43. Cited in Encounter Today, Paris, VII:2, November 2, 1972, 84. The date and occa-

sion of this quotation [along with its sources] are, unfortunately, not given.

44. Gershon Greenberg, "Orthodox Theological Responses to Kristallnacht," paper presented to the Eighteenth Annual Scholars' Conference on the Church Struggle and the Holocaust, Washington, DC, March, 1988.

45. A Jew of Poland recalled all too vividly how, as a youngster, he pleased with his father to take the whole family to Palestine. The father, not knowing what he should do, asked his rabbi. The rabbi advised him to wait—wait until the Messiah would lead them all to Eretz Yisrael [Land of Israel—Editor]. All but the boy perished while waiting. [Personal conversation, 1979.]

46. Gershon Greenberg, Op. Cit. Wasserman followed his teacher Chofetz Chaim in maintaining that settlement of the land by apostates was a destruction [a churban] of Eretz Yisrael. He held these views until his death.

47. Cited by Pesach Schindler, "Faith During Auschwitz and the Paradox of Tikkun [Mending—Editor] in Hasidic Documents," in Conservative Judaism, XXXI:4, Summer, 1977, 31 & 32. A sixteen year old Dutch Jew, living in Brussels with papers identifying him as a Gentile, came to very similar conclusions, although with much more anguish and uncertainty as he did so. Although he did not see the agony of those years as the end of the Jewish exile, he nevertheless did anticipate that the return to Zion would be "the raising of a banner for the future...." [See Moshe Flinker, Young Moshe's Diary, Jerusalem: Yad Vashem, 1976, 56, 108, & 112.]

48. Ignatz Maybaum, The Face of God After Auschwitz [Amsterdam: Polak and Van Gennep, 1965], 61-67; passim; and Dov Marmur, "Holocaust as Progress: Reflections on the Thought of Ignaz Maybaum," Remembering the Future, I [Oxford: Pergamon Press, 1989], 956.

49. Reeve Robert Brenner, The Faith and Doubt of Holocaust Survivors [New York: The Free Press/London: Collier Macmillan, 1980], 226, 206-207, & 229. Compare, also, the letter a survivor wrote to the Jewish Chronicle of London to denouncde the "thoughtless dayanim [rabbinical judges—Editor] and rabbanim [rabbis—Editor] who claimed that the Holocaust was retribution for the sins of the Jewish people" [24 November 1989].

50. Albert Friedlander, "The Misuses of the Holocaust," in European Judaism, 17:1, Summer, 1983, 61; and "Destiny and Fate," in Arthur A. Cohen and Paul Mendes-

Notes

Flohr, Editors, Contemporary Jewish Relgious Thought [New York: The Free Press/ London: Collier Macmillan, 1988], 139-140.

51. Richard L. Rubenstein and John K. Roth, Approaches to Auschwitz [Atlanta: John Knox Press, 1987], 280.

52. Andre Neher, The Exile of the Word [Philadelphia: The Jewish Publication Society of America, 1981], 132 & 135.

53. Reeve Robert Brenner, Op. Cit., 207.

54. Andre Neher, Op. Cit., 191 & 196. According to Talmudic tradition, Nahor's son Uz was Job. [Genesis 22:20]

55. Andre Neher, Op. Cit., 132, 178, & 179.

56. Martin Buber was led to ask: "Can one still speak to God after Oswiecim and Auschwitz? Can one still, as an individual and as a people, enter into a dialogue relationship with Him?....Dare we recommend to the survivors....'Call to Him,f or He is kind, for His mercy endureth forever'?" [Cited by Harold Schulweis, in Abraham Ezra Milgrom, Editor, Great Jewish Ideas, New York: B'nai B'rith, 1964, 212.]

57. Emil Fackenheim, The Human Condition After Auschwitz [The B. G. Rudolph Lectures in Judaic Studies, Syracuse University, 1971], 10; and "Commanded to Hope," in Michael A. Ryan, Editor, The Contemporary Explosion in Theology [Metuchen: Scarecrow Press, 1975], 59, emphases added. See also Emil Fackenheim, "From Bergen-Belsen to Jerusalem" [Jerusalem: Institute of Contemporary Jewry and World Jewish Congress, 1975, 14].

58. Pesach Schindler, consultation, Jerusalem, June 18, 1976. Irving Greenberg stresses the voluntary nature of the covenant in the age after Auschwitz. Though Jews now know the possible lethal consequences of being identified with the covenant people, they have chosen voluntarily to resume the covenant relationship because of their love affair with God and the covenant. [See The Voluntary Covenant, New York: National Jewish Resource Center, 1982]. But see also Irving Greenberg, "The Ethics of Jewish Power," Perspectives [New York: NJRC, January, 1984].

59. See Alice Lyons Eckardt, "Power and Powerlessness: The Jewish Experience," in

Israel Charny, Editor, Toward the Understanding and Prevention of Genocide [Boulder/London: The Westview Press, 1984], 190-191.

60. Tucker further arges that "all redemptions are destined to be partial redemptions, challenging us to further work as 'God's partners in creation'." [See Gordon Tucker, "Contemporary Jewish Thought on the Messianic Idea," in Face to Face, XIV, Spring, 1989, 28-29 & 30.] John Macquarrie points out that "when the end is removed to the distant future....it shared in the negativity of the 'not yet' and it becomes neutralized and ineffective." [See his "Eschatology and Time" in Frederick Herzog, Editor, The Future of Hope, 115; and cited by Baker, Op. Cit., 89.]

61. Elie Wiesel, Messengers of God: Biblical Portraits and Legends [New York: Random House, 1976].

62. See Note #2. Albert Friedlander asks, "Can we understand this [father]? Should we understand....?" [See his "Stations Along the Way: Christian and Jewish Post-Holocaust Theology," in Common Ground, London, #2, 1978, 13.]

63. Elie Wiesel, Messengers of God, 233-234; Andre Neher, The Exile of the Word, 219-220.

64. Wiesel reminds us of a Jewish legend in which God points out that the difference between a group of pure and a group of impure people is that the pure oes had protested. God says tat the others should have protested "against Me, against Man, against everyting wrong. Because protest in itself contains a spark of truth, a spark of holiness, a spark of God." [See his Jewish Legends: Teachers Study Guide, New York: Archdiocese of New York and Anti-Defamation League of B'nai B'rith, n.d., 8.]

65. Irving Abrahamson, Editor, Against Silence: The Voice and Vision of Elie Wiesel [New York: Holocaust Library, 1985], Volume II, 310, 93, and 267. Wiesel wrote elsewhere, "....there comes a time when only those who do not believe in God will not cry out to him in wrath and anguish. ["Why I Write," The New York Times Book Review, April 14, 1985, 14.]

66. Neher comments that Wiesel's work has wrought a "Copernican revolution in the realm of the Bible." [See The Exile of the Word, 215.]

67. Interview with Harold Flender, March/April, 1979, reprinted in Against Silence,

Notes

Volume III, 198 & 199.

68. See, for example, how Jurgen Moltmann uses Wiesel's account of the young boy hanging on the gallows as "a shattering expression of theologia crucis," [See The Crucified God, New York: Harper & Row, 1974, 273-274]. For an extensive surve and critique of Moltmann's theology and of the continuation of pre-Shoah Christian theology, see Alice L. Eckardt and A. Roy Eckardt, Long Night's Journey into Day: A Revised Retrospective on the Holocaust [Detroit: Wayne State University Press, and Oxford: Pergamon Press, 1988]. See, also, Charlotte Klein, Editor, Judaism in Christian Theology [Philadelphia: Fortress Press, 1978].

69. Johannes Baptist Metz, The Emergent Church [New York: Crossroad, 1981], 19; and "Facing the Jews: Christian Theology After Auschwtiz," in Elisabeth Schussler-Fiorenza and David Tracy, Editors, The Holocaust as Interruption [Edinburgh: T. & T. Clark, 1984], 27 and 28; emphases added.

70. Robert McAfee Brown, "The Holocaust: The Crisis of Indifference," in Conservative Judaism, XXXI:1-2, 1976-1977, 18.

71. Eugene Fisher bravely suggest that,since, "Jesus' death is a divine gift bringing all humanity closer to God's love, [and since the] sense of hope amidst despair is true because of the death of [that] one Jew long ago, Christians will inevitably ask themselves, might it not be also true, and much more so, of the deaths of six million Jewish women, men, and children....?" [See "Mysterium Tremendum: Catholic Grapplings with the Holocaust and its Theological Implications," in SIDIC, XXII:1 & 2, 1989, 13.

    I find two difficulties here: [1] Traditionally, Jesus' death atones for human sin because he is the Messiah/Christos: he does not become Messiah because he is crucified. Thus to try to read any atoning or redemptive function into the death of the six million requires making them a predetermined messianic people, for only then could their deaths have salvational power. But is that what the church really believes about the Jewish people? Is that what even those Jews who are willing to talk about "chosenness" mean by that term? [2] What about all the Jews who are ready to tell God to find another people for that role if it involves Shoah-like suffering? Would Christians be reimposing a special status on Jews who no longer desire this? Gordon Tucker warns that "when you honor a person or a nation with supernatural status, the fate of their natural form, their bodies, their history on earth, becomes less and less objects of concern" [Gordon Tucker, Op. Cit., 28].

72. John Paul II, in "John Paul II: On the Holocaust," [Washington, DC: National Conference of Catholic Bishops, 1988], 8; and cited by Sergio Minerbi, "The Kidnapping of the Holocaust," in The Jerusalem Post, 25 August 1989, 6.

73. John Cardinal O'Connor, "Yad Vashem Revisited," in Face to Face, XIV, Spring, 1988, 47-48; emphases added. O'Connor writes that he was influenced by Richard Cardinal Cushing with regard to the "potential of suffering." O"Connor lists two other ways by which suffering can be a power for good apart from "supernaturalizing: it: Jews can inspire others through their endurance of their suffering [in and since the Shoah] with patience, resignation, hope, faith, and love; and can humanize suffering and turn it into dialogue rather than a sword. [The second of these he attributes to having learned from Elie Wiesel.]

    Professor Ulrich Simon of King's Colege, London, argues in a very similiar way to O'Conoor: While the "martyrs" of the Nazi era have "paid a debt," taking our place, "their heroism could not satisfy the tragic desolation of our existence" without their being "offered by the eternal high priest to the Father." "If the death of Christ is the universal sacrifice for sin which 'takes away' the sin, then expiation and reconciliation have an objective and infinite value." [See Atonement, Cambridge: James Clark and Company, 1987], 96.

74. If we cnclude it ought not, then we are free to question whether our assumptions regarding an ethic of suffering really represents eternal morality/divine reality.

75. True, the idea of sacrificial suffering can lead individuals to endanger themselves and even give up their lives on behalf of someone else. This kind of voluntary sacrificial action merits the highest respect and praise. But no such action should be commanded or demanded or involuntarily imposed. It then ceases to be genuinely sacrificial.

76. Lawrence Langer, "Beyond Theodicy: Jewish Victims and the Holocaust," in Religious Education, 84:1, Winter, 1989, 50-51 and 52.

77. Terrence Des Pres, The Survivor [New York/Oxford: Oxford University Press, 1976], 100.

78. Cf. Eliezer Berkovits, Faith After the Holocaust [New York: Ktav Publishing House, 1973], Chapters IV and V.

Notes

79. I did not list the Palestinian Arabs here out of lack of sympathy for their situation, but because I think there situation is far more complex and even more ambiguous that most of the other disinherited.

80. Consider: Any theodicy that makes blacks "God contemporary suffering servant has to be rejected." "....any theodicy that breeds quietism thereby sustains oppression." "....[A] morally viable and defensible theodicy [must] become the foundation of a moral commitment to human liberation from the plague of unjust suffering. This is the only road along which the divine righteouness can be saved, sustained, and honored." [See William Jones, Is God a White Racist? Garden City: Doubleday/Anchor, 1973, as cited and paraphrased in A. Roy Eckardt, Black-Woman-Jew: Three Wars for Human Liberation, Bloomington: Indiana University Press, 1989, 23 and 24.]

    In this volume, Eckardt provides extensive coverage of these liberation movements' views. For other considerations of this discussion, see Alice L. Eckardt and A. Roy Eckardt, Long Night's Journey into Day, Revised Edition, 1988, 116 and passim.

81. Terrence Des Pres, Op. Cit., 6.

82. Hans Jonas, "The Concept of God After Auschwitz," in Albert Friedlander, Editor, Out of the Whirlwind: A Reader of the Holocaust [New York: Schocken Books, 1976], 470-476 passim.

    Jonas' views offer quite a contrast to Cardinal O'Connor's conviction. Which is closer to the truth? We do not know. All we can do is to consider what the ethical, behaviorial and other consequences of either persuasion will be—on the large scale, that is.

83. J. Christaan Baker, Suffering and Hope, 16; and Lawrence Langer, 53, 54, and 52.

ASKING AND LISTENING, UNDERSTANDING AND DOING:
Some Conditions for Responding to the Shoah Religiously

John K. Roth

The Holocaust Now

1. Primo Levi, Survival in Auschwitz: The Nazi Assault on Humanity [New York: Collier Books, 1976. Translated by Stuart Woolf.], 13.

2. Ibid., 116

3. Ibid., 116-117.

4. Ibid., 117.

5. Elie Wiesel, Night [New York: Bantam Books, 1986. Translated by Stella Rodway.], 3.

6. Elie Wiesel, A Jew Today [New york: Random House, 1978. Translated by Marion Wiesel.], 144-145.

7. Irving Greenberg, "Cloud of Smoke, Pillar of Fire: Judaism, Christianity, and Modernity After the Holocaust," in Eva Fleischner, Editor, Auschwitz: Beginning of a New Era? Reflections on the Holocaust [New York: Ktav Publishing House, 1977], 23. This important essay is reprinted in John K. Roth and Michael Berenbaum, Editors, Holocaust: Religious and Philosophical Implications [New York: Paragon Publishers, 1989].

8. See, for example, Emil L. Fackenheim, God's Presence in History: Jewish Affirmations and Philosophical Reflections [New York: Harper & Row, 1972], 67-98.

9. See Emil L. Fackenheim, To Mend the World: Foundations of Future Jewish Thought [New York: Schocken Books, 1982], 278-294.

10. Rainer Maria Rilke, Poems from the Book of Hours [New York: New Directions, 1975. Translated by Babette Deutsch.], 3.

11. Elie Wiesel, A Jew Today, 164.

12. Elie Wiesel, Twilight [New York: Summit Books, 1988. Translated by Marion Wiesel, 202 & 209.

13. Ibid., 179.

14. Ibid., 118.

Notes

15. Ibid., 37.

16. Ibid., 11.

17. Ibid., 201.

18. Ibid., 202.

19. See Elie Wiesel, The Town Beyond the Wall [New York: Avon Books, 1970. Translated by Stephen Becker.], 3.

20. Ibid., 182.

21. See Elie Wiesel's review of Auschwitz by Bernd Naumann. The review first appeared in Hadassah Magazine, January, 1967, and is reprinted in Irving Abrahamson, Editor, Against Silence: The Voice and Vision of Elie Wiesel [New York: Holocaust Library, 1985. Three Volumes.], Volume II, 293.

22. Elie Wiesel, The Town Beyond the Wall, 189.

23. Elie Wiesel, Twilight, 217.

24. Elie Wiesel, "Forward," in Harry James Cargas, A Christian Response to the Holocaust [Denver: Stonehenge Books, 1981], iii.

25. Elie Wiesel, "Telling the Tale," in Irving Abrahamson, Editor, Op. Cit., Volume I, 1983. This text is from an address to the Forty-ninth General Assembly of the Union of American Hebrew Congregations, November, 1967.

26. Elie Wiesel, "Exile and the Human Condition," Ibid., Volume I, 1983. This text is from a lecture to the International Young Presidents Organization, Madrid, Spain, 1980.

27. Ibid., 182.

28. Elie Wiesel, "The Use of Words and the Weight of Silence," in Irving Abrahamson, Editor, Ibid., Volume II, 79. This text is from an interview conducted by Lily Edelman which appeared in the National Jewish Monthly, November, 1973.

29. Elie Wiesel, "Freedom of Conscience: A Jewish Commentary," in Ibid., Volume I,

210. This text is from an address at the Bicentennial Conference on Religious Liberty, Philadelphia, 27 April 1976.

30. Elie Wiesel, Messengers of God: Biblical Portraits and Legends [New York: Random House, 1976. Translated by Marion Wiesel.], 235.

31. Elie Wiesel, One Generation After [New York: Avon Books, 1972. Translated by Lily Edelman.], 95. See also Elie Wiesel, The Testament [New York: Summit Books, 1981. Translated by Marion Wiesel.], 9.

32. Elie Wiesel, "The Trial of Man," in Irving Abrahamson, Editor, Op. Cit., Volume I, 176. This text is from a lecture at Loyola University, Chicago, which Wiesel delivered on 12 April 1980.

33. Elie Wiesel, Souls on Fire: Portraits and Legends of Hasidic Masters [New York: Random House, 1972. Translated by Marion Wiesel.], 133.

34. Ibid., 198.

35. Ibid., 245.

36. Ibid., 254.

37. Elie Wiesel, The Oath [New York: Random House, 1973. Translated by Marion Wiesel.], 16.

38. Ibid., 239.

39. Ibid., 241.

WHY?

Bernard Maza

1. Hoboken: Ktav Publishing House, 1986. See, also, my review of it in Holocaust and Genocide Studies, 4:2, 1989, 239-241.

2. Ecclesiastes 1:5: "The sun rises and the sun sets, and hurries back to where it rises."

Notes

3. Ritual baths.

4. Schools of higher Jewish learning.

5. The Hasidic Movement During the Time of the Shoah.

6. Book of Testimony.

7. Fall festival of "Booths," remembering the harvest in ancient Israel, as well as the temporary dwellings erected by the Israelites when they went out of Egypt.

8. Holiday songs and hymns.

9. The Destruction of Lita.

10. Deans of these Talmludical academies.

11. Eastern European Jewish ghettos, primarily in Russia and Poland.

12. In Orthodox Jewish Religious Tradition, King Solomon is understood to be the author of the Biblical Book of Ecclesiastes.

13. Annual Day of Atonement, ten days after the start of the Jewish New Year [Rosh Ha-Shanah].

14. Hebrew name of Moses.

15. Aramaic translation of the Pentateuch [Five Books of Moses] by Onkelos, First Century of the Common Era.

16. Rabbi Samuel Eliezer Edels [1555-1631], Polish commentator on the Talmud.

17. Blessings.

18. Heart of the Jewish Worship Service, consisting of eighteen paragraphs devoted to the various types and forms of prayers—e.g. petitions, thanksgiving, praise of God, etc.

The SHOAH: CONTINUING CHALLENGE TO CHRISTIANITY

John T. Pawlikowski

1. Uriel Tal, Christians and Jews in Germany: Religion, Poltiics, aand Ideology in the Second Reich, 1870-1914 [Ithaca: Cornell University Press, 1975], 305.

2. Alexander Donat, The Holocaust Kingdom [New York: Holt, Rinehart and Winston, 1965], 230-231.

3. Cf. John T. Pawlikowski, The Challenge of the Holocaust for Christian Theology [New York: Anti-Defamation League, 1982]; "Christian Perspectives and Moral Implications," in Henry Friedlander and Sybil Milton, Editors, The Holocaust: Ideology, Bureaucracy, and Genocide [Millwood: Kraus International Publications, 1980], 295-308; "The Holocaust: Its Implications for the Church and Society Problematic," in Richard W. Rosseau, S.J., Editor, Christianity and Judaism: The Deepening Dialogue [Scranton: Ridge Row Press, 1983], 95-106; "The Holocaust: Its Implications for Public Morality," in Franklin H. Littell, Irene G. Shur, and Claude Foster, Jr., Editors, The Holocaust: In Answer.... [West Chester: Sylvan Publishers, 1988], 287-297; and "Implications of the Holocaust for the Christian Churches," in Alex Grobman and Daniel Landes, Editors, Genocide: Critical Issues of the Holocaust [Chappaqua: Rossel Books, 1983], 410-418.

4. Emil Fackenheim, The Jewish Return into History [New York: Schocken Books, 1978], 246.

5. On non-Jewish victims, cf. Bohdan Whywycky, The Other Holocaust: Many Circles of Hell [Washington, DC: The Novak Report, 1980]; Frank Rector, The Nazi Extermination of Homosexuals [New York: Stein and Day, 1981]; Richard S. Lukas, Forgotten Holocaust: The Poles Under German Occupation, 1939-1944 [Lexington: University Press of Kentucky, 1986]; Gabrielle Tyrnauer, "The Gypsy Awakening," in Reform Judaism, 14;3, Spring, 1986, 6-8; Richard Plant, The Pink Triangle: The Nazi War Against Homosexuals [New York: Henry Holt, 1986]; Ian Hancock, The Pariah Syndrome [Ann Arbor: Karoma Publishers, 1987].

6. Uriel Tal, "Forms of Pseudo-Religion in the German Kultur-bereich Prior to the Holocaust," in Immanuel, 3, Winter, 1973-1974, 69.

Notes

7. Uriel Tal, Christians and Jews in Germany, 302-303.

8. Michael Ryan, "Hitler's Challenge to the Churches: A Theological Analysis of Mein Kampf," in Franklin H. Littell and Hubert G. Locke, Editors, The German Church Struggle and the Holocaust [Detroit: Wayne State University Press, 1974], 160-161.

9. David Tracy, "Religious Values After the Holocaust: A Catholic View," in Abraham J. Peck, Editor, Jews and Christians After the Holocaust [Philadelphia: Fortress Press, 1982], 101.

10. David Hartman, A Living Covenant: The Innovative Spirit in Traditional Judaism [New York: The Free Press, 1985].

11. David Hartman, "New Jewish Religious Voices II: Auschwitz or Sinai?" in The Ecumenist, 21:1, November/December, 1982, 8.

12. Richard L. Rubenstein, After Auschwitz: Radical Theology and Contemporary Judaism [Indianapolis: Bobbs-Merrill, 1966]; also, cf. "Some Perspectives on Religious Faith After Auschwitz," in Franklin H. Littell and Hubert G. Locke, Editors, Op. Cit., 256-268.

13. Ricahrd L. Rubenstein and John K. Roth, Approaches to Auschwitz: The Holocaust and Its Legacy [Atlanta: John Knox Press, 1987], 311-312.

14. Steven Katz, Post-Holocaust Dialogues: Critical Studies in Modern Jewish Thought [New York: New York University Press, 1983], '76.

15. Emil Fackenheim, The Jewish Return into History [New York: Schocken Books, 1978].

16. Arthur Cohen, The Tremendum: A Theological Interpretation of the Holocaust [New York: Crossroad, 1981].

17. Ibid., 97.

18. Irving Greenberg, "The Voluntary Covenant," in Perspectives #3 [New York: National Jewish Resource Center, 1982], 14.

19. Ibid., 15.

20. Ibid.

21. Ibid., 16.

22. Ibid., 17-18.

23. D. H. Lawrence, Selected Poems [London: Penguin Books, 1967], 144.

24. Robert McAfee Brown, "The Holocaust as a Problem in Moral Choice," in Harry James Cargas, Editor, When God and Man Failed: Non-Jewish Views of the Holocaust [New York: Macmillan Publishing Company, 1981], 94.

25. Elie Wiesel, Messengers of God [New York: Random House, 1976], 235.

26. Robert Heilbroner, An Inquiry into the Human Prospect [New York: W. W. Norton and Company, 1980].

27. John T. Pawlikowski, Christ in Light of the Christian-Jewish Dialogue [Wilmington: Michael Glazier, 1989].

28. John T. Pawlikowski, Jesus and the Theology of Israel [Wilmington: Michael Glazier, 1989].

29. Johannes Baptist Metz, "Facing the Jews: Christian Theology After Auschwitz," in Elisabeth Schussler-Fiorenza and David Tracy, Editors, The Holocaust as Interruption [Edinburgh: T. & T. Clark, 1984], 43-52.

30. Paul van Buren, A Theology of the Jewish-Christian Reality, Part 3: Christ in Context [San Francisco: Harper & Row, 1988].

31. Richard L. Rubenstein and John K. Roth, Op. Cit., 297.

32. Franklin Sherman, "Speaking of God After Auschwitz," in Worldview, 17:9, September, 1974, 29. Also cf. Shermn's essay on the same theme in Paul D. Opsahl and Marc H. Tanenbaum, Editors, Speaking of God Today [Philadelphia: Fortress Press, 1974].

33. Marcel Dubois, "Christian Reflections on the Holocaust," in SIDIC, 7:2, 1974, 15.

Notes

34. Ibid.

35. Douglas Hall, "Rethinking Christ," in Alan T. Davies, Editor, Antisemitism and the Foundations of Christianity [New York: Paulist Press, 1979], 183.

36. Jurgen Moltmann, "The Crucified God," in Theology Today, 31:1, April 1974, 9.

37. A. Roy Eckardt, "Christians and Jews: Along a Theological Frontier," in Encounter, 40:2, Spring, 1979, 102.

38. Stanley Hauerwas, "Jews and Christians Among the Nations," in Cross Currents, 31, Spring, 1981, 34.

39. David Tracy, "The Interpretation of Theological Texts," unpublished lecture, Indiana University, 1984, 16-17.
40. Johannes Baptist Metz, The Emergent Church [New York: Crossroad, 1981], 19-20.

41. Elisabeth Schussler-Fiorenza and David Tracy, "The Holocaust as Interruption and the Christian Return to History," in Elisabeth Schussler-Fiorenza and David Tracy, Editors, Op. Cit., 86.

42. Rebecca Chopp, "The Interruption of the Forgotten," in Elisabeth Schussler-Fiorenza and David Tracy, Editors, Op. Cit., 20.

43.. Fredrich Heer, God's First Love [New York: Weybright and Talley, 1970], 406.

44. Fredrich Heer, "The Catholic Church and the Jews Today," in Midstream, 17:5, May, 1971, 29.

45. Darrell J. Fasching, "Faith and Ethics After the Holocaust: What Christians Can Learn from Jews," in Remembering the Future: Jews and Christians During and After the Holocaust: Theme I, Papers Presented at an International Scholars' Conference, Oxford, England, 10-13 July 1988 [Oxford: Pergamon Press, 1988], 606.

46. Irving Greenberg, "The Third Great Cycle in Jewish History," in Perspectives, September, 1981, 24-25.

47. Stanley Hauerwas, Op. Cit., 34.

48. Marc H. Ellis, Toward a Jewish Theology of Liberation [Maryknoll: Orbis Books, 1987]; "From Holocaust to Solidarity: Perspectives on a Jewish Theology of Liberation," in Christian-Jewish Relations, 21:1, Spring, 1988, 31-36.

49. Marc H. Ellis, Toward a Jewish Theology of Liberation, 37.

50. David Hollenbach, Justice, Peace & Human Rights: American Catholic Social Ethics in a Pluralistic Context [New York: Crossroad, 1988], 115.

51. Irving Greenberg and David Elcott, "The Ethics of Jewish Power: Two Views," in Perspectives [New York: National Jewish Center for Learning and Leadership, April, 1988].

52. Irving Greenberg, "The Third Great Cycle," 24-25.

53. Romano Guardini, Power and Responsibility [Chicago: Henry Regnery, 1961], xiii.

54. Cf. Franklin H. Littell, "Foundations and Traditions of Religious Liberty," in Journal of Ecumenical Studies, 14:4, Fall, 1977, 10; Clyde L. Manschreck, "Church-State Relations: A Question of Sovereignty," in Clyde L. Manschreck and Barbara Brown, Editors, The American Religious Experiment: Piety and Practicality [Chicago: Exploration Press, 1976], 121.

55. Franklin H. Littell, "Early Warning," in Remembering the Future, Theme II, 2125-2133.

56. Cf., John F. Pawlikowski, "The Vatican and the Holocaust: Unresolved Issues," Paper presented at Baruch College, The City University of New York, March, 1989; Helen Fein, Accounting for Genocide: National Responses and Jewish Victimization [Chicago: University of Chicago Press, 1984], 33; Nora Levin, The Holocaust [New York: Schocken Books, 1973], 693; and Otto Kulka and Paul Mendes-Flohr, Editors, Judaism and Christianity Under the Impact of National Socialism [Jerusalem: The Historical Society of Israel and the Zalman Shazar Center for Jewish History, 1987].

Notes

HOW THE SHOAH AFFECTS CHRISTIAN BELIEF

Thomas A. Idinopulos

1. The view of Henry Wieman, cited in Bernard M. Loomer, "Christian Faith and Process Philosophy," in The Journal of Religion, XXIX:3, July, 1949.

2. Jacques Maritain, A Christian Looks at the Jewish Question [New York: 1939], 87.

3. Jacques Maritain, "The Mystery of Israel," reprinted in Joseph Evans and Leo Ward, Editors, The Social and Political Philosophy of Jacques Maritain [New York: 1965], 194-212.

4, Jacques Maritain, "Blessed are the Persecuted," reprinted in The Range of Reason [New York: 1952], 219-226.

5. Thomas Lask, The New York Times, 15 December 1970.

6. David Magarshak, Dostoevsky [New York: 1962], 32.

7. Cited in Lawrence Langer, The Holocaust and the Literary Imagination [New Haven: Yale University Press, 1975], 1.

8. George Steiner, Language and Silence [New York: 1966], 123.

9. Cited in Langer, Op. Cit., 74.

VOLUNTARY COVENANT

Irving Greenberg

1. This text may be read without referring to the notes which are included. A different version of this paper was read at the conference, "God, Covenant and Community," co-sponsored by the Conference on Learning and Leadership/CLAL [then National Jewish Resource Center/NJRC] and the University of Denver Center for Judaic Studies in June, 1981, as part of our joing program: CHEVRA: Society for the Advancement of Jewish Thought, Dialogue and Community. I am grateful to my colleagues and their critique and to the Center for Judaic Studies for permission to

use this essay in the Perspectives series.

2. Genesis, Chapter 1, especially verses 25, 26, 27; 28. An image of God has infinite value, equality and uniqueness. Sanhedrin 37a. On the soul quality of animals, see Proverbs 12:10; Nachmanides on Leviticus 22:28; J. Pederson, Israel [London: Oxford University Press, 1946], 100; Cf. Maimonides, Guide to the Perplexed [New York: Hebrew Publishing Company, n.d.], Part I, Chapter 1, 32, that intellectual perception is the key breakthrough in the human.

3. Rav Abraham Isaac HaCohen Kook wrote: "Only He who is actually Infinite [Ein Sof] can actualize that which is potentially infinite." See "The Doctrine of Evolution," in A. I. Kook, Orot HaKodesh [Jerusalem: Mossad HaRav Kook, 1964], Volume 2, Part 5, Section 19, 537.

4. If people are granted freedom they remain dependent. After being given their freedom, slaves remain psychologically enslaved until they take full responsibility for their own fate and daily life. Thus the Bible portrays the behavior of the Hebrews in the desert, and after the Exodus, as classical slave behavior. The Israelites often turned regressive, were easily thwarted by obstacles, often sought to return to the womb of slavery. See Exodus, Chapters 16, 17, 32; Numbers, Chapters 11, 13, 14, 20; 21.

5. Exodus 19:5-6.

6. See Irving Greenberg, "Jewish Tradition and Contemporary Problems," in Relationships Between Jewish Tradition and Contemporary Issues [New York: Yeshiva University Press, n.d.], 11-13.

7. Deuteronomy 29:14.

8. Deuteronomy 7:7.

9. Reward and punishment are visited on other people, too, especially in the Land of Israel, but the Jews are held on a tighter rein. See Genesis 15:16; Leviticus 22:22-26; Amos, Chapters 1, 2, and 3:1-2.

10. Though they do not carry the makr of the covenant in their felsh, Jewish women also experienced the inescapability of being Jewish as a determinant of their fate. Seen through twentieth century eyes, the fact that the central symbol of covenant is

Notes

carried only by men creates some moral and cultural problematic, i.e., it is gender linked. On another level, however, the special mark on men is the biological analogue of the special status of men in Jewish tradition. For some comments on possible equalization and a new importance to voluntary symbols of covenant, see Note #89.

11. Cf. "To walk in all His ways" [Deuteronomy 11:22], "as He is merciful, so you be merciful" [Sifre to Deuteronomy, Section 49, 85a]. See Ronald Green's extended development of this idea in his Religious Reason [New York: Oxford University Press, 1978].

12. See "The Third Great Cycle of Jewish History," 1-26.

13. In Ezekiel's lacerating words [20:32 ff.], the Destruction is God's "poured out fury," calling Israel to judgment; in order words, holding the people to the covenant—sifting out the rebellious Jews and recalling the others to covenantal relationship with God. Ibid., Chapters 36-38.

14. Hosea 11:8. Cf. Isaiah 50;1, where the prophet, manifestly replying to those Jews who argue that God has rejected israel, quotes God as saying, "Show me a bill of divorce that I sent your mother [Israel."

15. See Irving Greenberg, "Judaism and History: Historical Events and Religious Change," in Jerry Diller, Editor, Ancient Roots and Modern Meaning [New York: Block Publishing Company, 1978], 146-156.

16. It is not just particular texts that can be offered as evidence for this change; the very method and role of the Rabbis was based on this assumption. Cf. Note #15 above.

17. Mekhilta de Rabbi Ishmael, Section "Bachodesh," Chapter 6, 298. Sota, 17a; Genesis Rabbah, "Toledot," Chapter 63, Section 6.

18. Mekhilta, loc. cit.

19. Sifra Bamidbar, Section 161, 221.

20. Sifra Kedoshim, Section 2, Chapter 2, 86a.

21. Mishnah, Peah, 1:1.

The Holocaust Now

22. Menachot, 110a, views of Rabbi Samuel Bar Nachmani, Rabbi Yochanan, and especially Resh Lakish and Rabbi Yitzchak.

23. Yalkut Shimoni, Isaiah, Section 454 [New York: Pardes Publishing Company, n.d.], Volume 2, 795, Column II, "Amar Rabbi Yehudah amar Rav...."

24. Ibid.

25. Consider the Rabbinic interpretation of hocheah tocheach, "thou shalt surely correct," [Leviticus 19:17]. The Rabbis qualify the mitzvah [commandment]; do not correct the other unless he is prepared to listen; one who is open to the same criticism should not correct another; one who does not know how to speak gently and acceptably should not correct [Arachin 14b]. The divine instruction and the divine correction cannot be purely mechanical.

26. "Since the Temple was destroyed, there is no laughter before the Holy One, Blessed be He" [Yalkut Shimoni, Section 454]. "I am with Him in trouble" [Psalms 91:13]. When a human being is in pain, what does the Shechinah [Indwelling Presence of God—Editor] say? "My head is heavy [aches]; my arms are heavy [ache] [Sanhedrin 46a].

27. Megillah, 29a.

28. Yalkut Shimoni, Isaiah, Section 455 [Pardes edition], 795.

29. Lamentations Rabbah, Portion 1, Section 33.

30. The Talmud refers to Masters of the precedents at Sinai [i.e. those who remember the record of the past Revelation which began at Sinai].

31. This involved knowing the past commandments, deciding what is foreground and background in the Tradition in relation to this case and deciding what is the salient similarity in the present situation. The Talmud calls this the capacity L'damia Milta L'milta —to establish the appropriate anaology or similarity in the two situations.

32. Shabbat 23a.

33. Deuteronomy 21:18 ff.

Notes

34. Baba Batra 121b.

35. Makkot 7a.

36. Gittin 3a; Yevmot 88a; Ketubot 10 ff. See on these and other improvements in the legal condition of wives, "Jewish Attitudes Towards Divorce, in Blu Greenberg, On Women and Judaism [Philadelphia: The Jewish Publication Society of America, 1982], 125 ff.

37. Jacob Neusner, Rabbi Yochanan ben Zakkai: Development of a Legend [Leiden: E. J. Brill, 1970], 50. The discontinuance of the ordeal is comparable to the end of prophecy and to the passing of the scapegoat ceremony. Through the scapegoat, the sins of the Jewish people were "sacramentally" removed. See Leviticus, Chapter 16, and Maimonides, Mishneh Torah, Hilchot Teshuvah, Chapter 1, Paragraph 2.

38. Rosh Ha-Shanah 25b.

39. Baba Metzia 86a; Midrash Shohar Tov Tehillim 4; Deuteronomoy Rabbah, Parashat V'Etchanan, Parasha B, Section 14. On this, see Joseph B. Soloveitchik's essay "Ish Halacha," in Talpiot, New York, 1944, Volume I, 700 ff.

40. Deuteronomy 17:11; Berachot 19b.

41. Cf. Moses' argument to the angels to release the Torah to humanity which needs it: "Is there jealousy among you? Is there hatred among you?" Berachot 17a.

42. Joseph B. Soloveitchik, "Ish Halacha," Op. Cit., 702.

43. Cf. Ecclesiastes Rabbah, Parasah 1, v. 10, Section B; Peah 9b, Chapter 2 h. 4; Megillah 19b. Everyone who innovates words of Torah by his own mouth is like one who is being informed from heaven and they are telling him: Thus said the Holy One, Blessed be He. Yalkut Shimoni, Shofetim, Section 49 [Pardes edition], Volume 2, 707, Column B.

44. Saul Lieberman's view is that the middot, rhetorical analytic devices used by the Rabbis to devise laws from Scripture, are based on Hellenic rhetorical modes. Cf. Lieberman, Jews in Hellenistic Palestine [New York: Jewish Theological Seminary, 1962]. This view has been denounced by traditionalists. In the spirit of my inter-

pretation, Lieberman's views would be compatible with the Rabbinic statement that their teachings are halalacha l'Moshe miSinai.

45. Emphasis supplied. Matthew 5:18.

46. The Jewish and Christian heremeneutic of the Destruction of the Temple, the consequences of those views, and the implications for Jewish-Christian relationships today are discussed at length in an essay of mine, presented at a conference entitled "Transformations: Judaism and Christianity After the Holocaust," sponsored by CLAL and Indiana University. See, also, my "Judaism and History: Historic Events and Religious Change," in Jerrry Diller, Editor, Ancient Roots and Modern Meanings [New York: Bloch Publishing Company, 1978], 139-155.

47. Shabbat 88a.

48. Exodus 24:7; Deuteronomy 27:10 ff.

49. Tosafot d. h. Moda'a Rabbah; Shabbat iia.

50. Shavuot 39a.

51. Jeremiah 31:30; Jeremiah 16:14-15.

52. See my "Lessons to be Learned from the Holocaust." Paper presented at the Hamburg Conference, 1975.

53. A. Roy Eckardt, "The Recantation of the Covenant," in Alvin Rosenfeld and Irving Greenberg, Editors, Confronting the Holocaust: The Work of Elie Wiesel [Bloomington: Indiana University Press, 1980], 163.

54. Elie Wiesel, "Jewish Values in the Post-Holocaust Future," in Judaism, 16:3, Summer, 1967, 28.

55. Jacob Glatstein, "Dean Men Don't Praise God," in Selected Poems of Jacob Glatstein [New York: October House, 1972. Translated by Ruth Whitman.], 68-70.

56. Gittin 56b. This is a commentary/critique based on Exodus 15:11.

57. Cf. A. Roy Eckardt, "The Recantation of the Covenant," Op. Cit., 164-165.

Notes

58. In a public lecture, Wiesel has used the image that, in light of the evil revealed in the Shoah, the risk in the Jewish mission to the world can be compared to a collective suicide mission. Conversation with the author, May 12, 1982.

59. Note that by Nazi decree, grandchildren of people who were Jewish but had converted to Christianity or assimilated were also identified as Jews and killed. Cf. Emil Fackenheim, "Jewish Faith and the Holocaust," in Commentary, August, 1967; Emil Fackenheim, God's Presence in History [New York: New York University Press, 1979], 70-71. Compare Irving Greenberg, "Confronting the Holocaust and Israel" [New York: United Jewish Appeal, n.d.], 16-17 and 20-22.

60 Irving Greenberg, "Cloud of Smoke, Pillar of Fire: Judaism, Christianity, and Modernity After the Holocaust," in Eva Fleischner, Editor, Auschwitz: Beginning of a New Era? [New York: Ktav Publishing House, 1977], 43.

61. The term "broken covenant" must be properly understood. A broken covenant may still exercise a powerful magnetism. While its brokenness reflects the wound inflicted on the covenantal people and the damage done to the credibility of hope and redemption, paradoxically enough, the shattering also witnesses the to profound bond between the covenant and the Jewish people. The covenant shares Jewish fate; the Torah is not insulated from Jewish suffering. Thus its brokenness makes the covenant more adequate insofar as it related more totally to the human condition. This helps account for the extraordinary pull it exerts on this generation of Jews. Elsewhere, I have cited Rabbi Nachman of Bratislav's famous dictum that "nothing is so whole as a broken heart," and I argued that, after the Shoah, "no faith is so whole as a broken faith." By this logic, no covenant is so complete as a broekn covenant.

62. Exodus 24:7. The Jews' response—na'aseh v'nishma—implies commitment before hearing all the risks.

63. The Talmud tells a story which illuminates the faith underlying the response. An opponent once saw Raba so engrossed in learning that he ignored a wound in his hand. The Sadducee exclaimed: "You rash people [You Jews!]! You put your mouth ahead of your ears! And you still persist in your recklessness. [You continue to make incredible commitments!] First you should have heard out [the covenant terms in detail]. If it is within your powers, then accept. If not, you should not have accepted." Raba answered: "We walked [with God] with our whole being

[Rashi: "We walked....as those who serve God in love. We relied on Him not to burden us with somehting we could not carry."]. Of us it is written, "The wholeness of the righteous shall guide them" [Proverbs 11:3]; Shabbat 88a-b.

64. Joseph B. Soloveitchik, "The Lonely Man of Faith," in Tradition, 7:2, 1965, 23, 24, 27, 28-30, 33 ff.

65. Michael Berenbaum has powerfully and convincingly argued that, in his writings, Elie Wiesel has developed a doctrine of "an additional covenant forged at Auschwitz, a covenant that renews Israel's mission despite the void....[a covenant] between Israel and its memories of pain and death, God and meaning." Berenbaum finds three elements in Wiesel's addiitonal covenant doctrine: sodality, witness,a nd the sanctification of life. See Michael Berenbaum, "The Additional Covenant," in Alvin Rosenfeld and Irving Greenberg, Editors, Confronting the Holocaust, 169,171 ff. Berebaum has placed these reflections in the context of his important and comprehensive analysis of Wiesel's and others' Shoah theology in The Vision of the Void: Theological Reflections on the Works of Elie Wiesel [Middletown: Wesleyan University Press, 1979]. While I differ somewhat from Berenbaum's assessment as to how much Wiesel comes down on the side of theological void after the Shoah, and while my thesis of the voluntary reassumption of the covenant differs from the additional covenant model, I am indebted to Michael Berenbaum for opening my eyes to the concept of an additional covenant in Wiesel's writings. A. Roy Eckardt's concept of divine repentance at giving the covenant [See Note #53.] particularly, and Berenbaum's formulation of the adiditional covenant as well, were fruitful intellectual stimulants at the time I was struggling to articulate this paradigm of the voluntary covenant.

66. See Michael Wyschogrod's review of Eva Fleischner, Editor, Auschwitz: Beginning of a New Era? [New York: Ktav Publishing House, 1977] in Tradition, 17;1, Fall, 1977, 63-78.

67. "Out of the fire, came forth sweetness," Judges 14;14.

68. One may offer the analogy of talk about God. Any explanation or description of God may be useful or valid as long as it recognizes its metaphoric essence and its inability to portray the Divine exhaustively or even in its actual essence. Any portrait that "captures" the Divine is an idol, not a representation of God.

69. Cf. Joseph B. Soloveitchik, "The Lonely Man of Faith," Op. Cit., 29.

Notes

70. When the Rabbis said, "Do not be like servants who serve the Master for the sake of reward, but be like servants who serve the Master not for the sake of reward" [Ethics of the Fathers, 1:3], they were more prophetic than was realized at the time. Continual divine rewards [or punishments] are in tension with the goal of a relationship based on love.

71. Based on Rabbi Joshua ben Levi's views in Yoma 69b.

72. Cf. Irving Greenberg, "Cloud of Smoke," Op. Cit., 41 ff.

73. That resettlement of the land is proof of the ongoing vitality of the covenant is a central theme in Isaiah, Jeremiah, and other prophetic books.

74. For the format of the classical ceremony of conversion, see Yevamot 74a-b.

75. Cf. "Every controversy for the sake of heaven will have a lasting result" [Ethics of the Fathers 5:20].

76. Eruvin 13b.

77. See "The Theoretical Basis of Women's Equality in Judaism," in Blu Greenberg, Op. Cit., 39-55.

78. Cf. Irving Greenberg, "Toward Jewish Religious Unity," in Judaism, 15;2, Spring, 1966, 135.

79. Cf. Elie Wiesel, Gates of the Forest [New York: Avon Books, n. D.], 41 ff.; 215; cf. 42-43, and 223.

80. Elsewhere I have struggled that this ia a Messiah who limps even as Jacob did after his struggle with the Angel of the Night left him wounded—but unbowed. See Shlomo Shamir, "HaShutafim," [The Partners] in Haaretz Weekly Magazine, 29.

81. Irving Greenberg, "Jewish Tradition and Contemporary Problems," in Relationship Between Jewish Tradition and Contemporary Issues [New York: Yeshiva University Press, n.d.], 11; and Samuel Dresner and Seymour Siegel, The Jewish Dietary Laws [New York: Burning Bush Press, 1959], 21-30.

82. See above.

83. See Guide to the Shabbat [New York: CLAL, 1981], 8-12.

84. Leviticus 19:2.

85. The Talmudic phrase is found in Yevamot 20a.

86. See Nachmanides' analysis in his commentary on Leviticus 19;2, d.h. kedoshim tih'ua.

87. Jeremiah 31:30.

88. The Rabbinic analogue to this concept is the ruling that one who is commanded and performs the act is at a higher level that one who is not commanded but does the act. Cf. Kiddushin 31a. This distinction comes to serve as an obstacle to the admission of women into liturgical roles. Cf. Blu Greenberg, Op. Cit., 82-85.

89. Genesis 15:5-18.

90. The Third Era analogue to this concept may be that "greater is the one who is not commanded but voluntarily comes forward than the one who acts only out of command."

91. The author wishes to thank Jonathan Javitch who is much more than the editor of this publication. He assayed, clarified, redirected, and shaped this essay. My thanks, also, to Deborah Greenberg who served as research assistant for this paper.

A CONTEMPORARY RELIGIOUS RESPONSE TO THE SHOAH:
The Crisis of Prayer

Michael McGarry

1. On the subject of God's silence, see, also, Andre Neher, The Exile of the Word: From the Silence of the Bible to the Silence of Auschwitz [Phiadelphia: The Jewish Publication Society of America, 1981. Translated by David Maisel.].

2. Pope John Paul II, "To the Jewish Community of Australia," November 26, 1986, and reprinted in Eugene Fisher and Leon Klenicki, Editors, Pope John Paul II on Jews

Notes

and Judaism [Washington, DC: United States Catholic Conference, 1987], 96. Shoah is the Vatican's and others' preferred term for the "Holocaust," and so it will be used throughout this essay. Literally, shoah is Hebrew for "catastrophe" or "disaster." "Holocaust" bears connotations of a holy offering made to God....the exact opposite of that to which it refers. On this point, see Zev Garber and Bruce Zuckerman, "Why Do We Call the Holocaust 'the Holocaust'? An Inquiry into the Psychology of Labels," in Proceedings, Remembering for the Future: The Impact of the Holocaust on the Contemporary World [Oxford: Pergamon Press, 1988], Volume II, 1879-1892. [Hereafter referred to RF.]

3. See Arthur A. Cohen, The Tremendum: A Theological Interpretation of the Holocaust [New York: Crossroad, 1981].

4. See the excellent treatment and summary in Richard L. Rubenstein and John K. Roth, Approaches to Auschwitz: The Holocaust and Its Legacy [Atlanta: John Knox Press, 1987], 199-338; John T. Pawlikowski, "Christian Ethics and the Holocaust: A Dialogue with Post-Auschwitz Judaism," in Theological Studies, 49, 1988, 649-669; Abraham J. Peck, Editor, Jews and Christians After the Holocaust [Philadelphia: Fortress Press, 1982]; James E. Moore, "A Spectrum of Views: Traditional Responses to the Holocaust," in Journal of Ecumenical Studies, 26, 1988, 212-224 [Hereafter referred to as JES.]; Alan L. Berger, "Holocaust and History: A Theological Reflection," in JES, 25, 1988, 194-211.

5. See Phillip Lopate, "Resistance to the Holocaust," in Tikkun, 4, May/June, 1989, 55-64, and the responses in the same issue. See S. T. Merhavi, "Remembrance of Things Past," in The Jerusalem Post International Edition, 2 June 1989, 13, for the incipient discussion on the multiplication, taste, and meaning of Shoah memorials. This discussion is only beginning.

6. See Rose Thering, O.P., Ph.D., Jews, Judaism, and Catholic Education [South Orange, NJ: Seton Hall University Press, 1986], 71. See, also, Eugene Fisher, Seminary Education and Christian-Jewish Relations: A Curriculum and Resource Handbook [Washington, DC: National Catholic Education Associaton, 1983].

7. See Michael McGarry, "Problems American Catholics Have in Dealing with the Holocaust," in RF, Volume I, 417-428.

8. See Robert N. Bellah and others, Habits of the Heart: Individualism and Commitment in American Life [Berkeley: University of California Press, 1985].

9. "Notes on the Correct Way to Present the Jews and Judaism in Preaching and Catechesis in the Roman Catholic Church," Paragraph #25 in Helga Croner, Editor, More Stepping Stones to Jewish-Christian Relations: An Unabridged Collection of Christian Documents, 1975-1983 [New York: Paulist Press, 1985], 231.

10. "A Catholic document on the Shoah and anti-Semitism will be fothcoming, resulting from....serious [joint Catholic-Jewish] studies." Pope John Paul II, "The Miami Address to Jewish Leaders," Origins, 17, September 24, 1987, 243.

11. Emil L. Fackenheim, To Mend the World: Foundations of Future Jewish Thought [New York: Schocken Books, 1982], 256.

12. By "prayer," I mean here the believer's personal and communal communication to God of praise, gratitude, contrition for sins, and petition. These four attitudes form the outline of most traditional Christian understandings of prayer.

13. See Michael McGarry, "The Revelance of the Shoah for Christians Today," in Ecumenism, 94, June, 1989, 20-22.

14. Richard L. Rubenstein and John K. Roth, Op. Cit., 285.

15. Emil L. Fackenheim, Op. Cit., 218-219.

16. Ibid., 254.

17. Ibid., 289-291.

18. See David Wyman, The Abandonment of the Jews: America and the Holocaust, 1941-1945 [New York: Pantheon Books, 1984]; Robert W. Ross, So It Was True: The American Protestant Press and the Nazi Persecution of the Jews [Minneapolis: University of Minnesota Press, 1980]; Deborah Lipstadt, "Finessing the Truth: The Press and the Holocaust," in Dimensions, 4, 1989, 3 and 10-15.

19. See Frederick C. Holmgren, "The God of History: Biblical Realism and the Lectionary," in RF, Volume I, 799-811.

20. For a survey of some traditional Jewish interpretations of the Shoah as somehow God's punishemnt "upon the Jewish people on account of its lack of faith and its

Notes

laxity in the observance of God's commandments," see the fine survey by Norman Solomon, "Does the Shoah Require a Radically New Jewish Theology?" in RF, Volume I, 1053-1068, especially pages 1058-1061. For an analysis of Christian applications of the "punishment theory," see Richard V. Pierard, "Varieties of Antisemitic Responses to the Holocaust Within American Conservative Protestantism," in RF, Volume I, 447-460.

21. See Irving Greenberg's still watershed article, "Cloud of Smoke, Pillar of Fire: Judaism, Christianity and Modernity After the Holocaust," in Eva Fleischner, Editor, Auschwitz: Beginnings of a New Era? Reflections on the Holocaust [New York: Ktav Publishing House, 1977], 7-56.

22. Rosemary Radford Ruether, Faith and Fratricide: The Theological Roots of Anti-Semitism [New York: The Seabury Press, 1974], 230.

23. For a Catholic-Jewish discussion on the uniqueness of Jesus' intimacy with the Father, his "Abba experience," see Father John T. Pawlikowski, O.S.M. and Rabbi Eugene B. Borowitz, 1987 Lecture Series: Proceedings of the Center for Jewish-Christian Learning [St. Paul: College of Saint Thomas: 1987].

24. Luke 22:39-44.

25. See Samuel Terrien, The Elusive Presence: Toward a New Biblical Theology [New York: Harper & Row: 1978], 361-372.

26. Paul M. van Buren, A Theology of the Jewish-Christian Reality, Part I: Discerning the Way [San Francisco: Harper & Row, 1980], 116.

27. Etty Hillesum, An Interrupted Life: The Diaries of Etty Hillesum, 1941-1943 [New York: Pantheon Books, 1983. Translated by Arno Pomerans.], 127 and 146-147.

28. See Ellis Rivkin, What Crucified Jesus? The Political Execution of a Charismatic [Nashville: Abingdon Press, 1984].

29. Richard L. Rubenstein and John K. Roth, Op. Cit., 290-338.

30. Elie Wiesel, Night [New York: Hill and Wang, 1960; Bantam Books, 1982. Translated by Stella Rodway.], 61-62.

31. Jurgen Moltmann, The Crucified God: The Cross of Christ as the Foundation and Criticism of Christian Theology [New York: Harper & Row, 1974], 275.

32. The theme of God's suffering in found throughout theological literature on the Shoah. See, for example, Marcus Braybrooke, "The Suffering of God: New Perspectives in the Christian Understanding of God since the Holocaust," in RF, Volume I, 702-708; Robert S. Frey, "The Holocaust and the Suffering of God," in RF, Volume I, 613-621; Dorothee Solle, "God's Pain and Our Pain: How Theology has to Change After Auschwitz," in RF, Supplementary Volume, 448-464. See also Jurgen Moltmann, "Op. Cit.; David Tracy, "Religious Values After the Holocaust: A Catholic View," in Abraham Peck, Editor, Op. Cit., 87-107.

33. John Shea, Stories of God: An Unauthorized Biography [Chicago: Thomas Moore Press, 1979], 89-116, especially 102.

34. Suppmenting John Shea's helpful categories is the suggestion of the creative retrieval fo the hutzpah k'lapei Shamaya [the tradition of arguing with God]. On this, see Belden Lane, "Hutzpah K'lapei Shamaya: A Christian Response to the Jewish Tradition of Arguing with God," in RF, Supplementary Volume, 233-247. Of course, this theme grounds many of Elie Wiesel's writings; see, for example, The Trial of God [New York: Random House, 1978. Translated by Marion Wiesel.].

35. Elie Wiesel, A Jew Today [New York: Random House, 1978. Translated by Marion Wiesel.], 144-145. Quoted in Richard L. Rubenstein and John K. Roth, Op. Cit., 287.

36. Jacques Ellul, Prayer and Modern Man [New York: Seabury Press, 1970].

37. Ibid., 99.

38. Ibid., 102.

39. Quoted in Emil L. Fackenheim, Op. Cit., 289-290.

40. Paul van Buren, Op. Cit., 118.

41. This draws on what Fackenheim has identified as "the commanding voice of Auschwitz, the 614th commandment," that the Jews survive as Jews. See his The Jewish Return into History [New York: Schocken Books, 1979], Chapter 2.

42. Good Liturgy, Intercession.

Notes

MYSTERIUM TREMENDUM:
Catholic Grapplings with the Shoah and Its Theological Implications

Eugene J. Fisher

1. Portions of this work were previously published in the journals: SIDIC, 2:1, 1989, 10-15, and Ecumenical Trends, 17:2, 1988, 24-27.

2. Helga Croner and Leon Klenicki, Editors, Issues in the Jewish-Christian Dialogue [New York: Paulist Stimulus Books], 135; David Tracy, "Religious Values After the Holocaust: A Catholic View," in Abraham Peck, Editor, Jews and Christians After the Holocaust [Philadelphia: Fortress Press, 1982], 87; Arthur Cohen, The Tremendum: A Theological Interpretation of the Holocaust [New York: Crossroad, 1981].

3. For a survey from a Catholic point of view of this literature, now quite extensive, see John T. Pawlikowski, O.S.M., What Are They Saying About Christian-Jewish Relations [New York: Paulist Press, 1980]; Michael McGarry, C.S.P., Christology After Auschwitz [New York: Paulist Pres, 1977]; and Eugene Fisher, "Ani Ma'amin: Theolgoical Responses to the Holocaust," in Interface, December, 1980, National Conference of Catholic Bishops, 1-8.

4. Commission of the Holy See for Religious Relations with the Jewish People, "Guidelines for the Implementation of the Concilar Declaration Nostre Aetate, Number 4," Rome, December 1, 1974.

5. Cf. Pinhas E. Lapide, "The Sermon on the Mount: A Jewish Reading," in Christianity and Crisis, May 24, 1982, 139-142.

6. Even the details of Jesus' Sermon to "turn the other cheek" [Matthew 5:39] draws on the Hebrew Scriptures: "It is good for a person to bear the yoke....let him give his cheek to the smither and be filled with insults. For the Lord will not cast off forever, but....have compassion according to the abundance of steadfast love" [Lamentations 3;27-31]. The context of this saying in the Babylonian exile makes it all the more strong.

7. It needs to be recalled, of course, that Lieutenant Waldheim's commanding officer

was executed after the Second World War for the massive atrocities his unit committed against Jews and Yugoslav partisans.

8. John Paul II, "To the Jewish Community of Australia," Sidney, November 26, 1988. Reprinted in Eugene Fisher and Leon Klenicki, Editors, Pope John Paul II on Jews and Judaism [Washington, DC: United States Catholic Conference Publication Number 151-2], 96.

9. See, for example, the results of my 1976 analysis of Catholic teaching materials regarding Jews and Judaism, summarized in Faith Without Prejudice: Rebuilding Christian Attitudes [New York: Paulist Press, 1977], 9.

10. H. Vogrimler, Editor, Commentary on the Documents of Vatican II, Volume II [New York and London: 1967], 76 and 77.

11. March 6, 1982.

12. Elie Wiesel, Ani Ma'amin: A Song Lost and Found Again [New York: Random House, 1973].

13. Emil Fackenheim, God's Presence in History [New York: Harper & Row, 1970], 87.

14. Bishop James Malone, "The State of Christian-Jewish Relations," in Origins, December 6, 1984.

15. For exampe, see Fackenheim, Op. Cit., 96. Fackenheim's notion of the Shoah as a revelatory moment has been sharply criticized by some Jewish thinkers. Michael Wyschogrod, for example, maintains: "There is no salvation to be extracted from the Holocaust....If there is hope after the Holocaust, it is because to those who believe....the divine promise sweeps away the crematoria and silences the voice of Auschwitz." [See, "Faith and the Holocaust," in Judaism, 20, Summer, 1971, 294.] Jacob Neusner declares flatly: "Jews find in the Holocaust no new defintion of Jewish identity because we need none. Nothing has changed. The tradition endures." [See, "The Implications of the Holocaust," in The Journal of Religion, 53:3, July, 1973, 308.]

16. Irving Greenberg, "Cloud of Smoke, Pillar of Fire: Judaism, Christianity and Modernity After the Holocaust," in Eva Fleischner, Editor, Auschwitz: Beginning of a New Era? [New York: Ktav Publishing House, 1973], 43, 48, and 49.

Notes

17. Press communique on the meeting with Jewish leaders. Rome, September 1, 1987, 3.

18. Pope John Paul II, "Address to Jewish Leaders," Miami: September 11, 1987.

19. One will note, in the above, that I do not deal with the theology of the emergence of a Jewish State in the Holy Land as a "fulfillment" of Biblical prophecies, but, rather, as a "sing of the times," a statement of the Jewish people's faith in God which should evoke in Christians a similar spiriutal affirmation of hope out of despair of our age. While I acknowledge that there are those in both the Christian and Jewish communities who would see in the modern State of Israel such a fulfillment, my own approach to Israel as historical event ["sign of the times"] does not require that view. Neither does such a fundamentalist approach to the Biblical text appeal to Catholic Biblical scholarship.

20. Daniel Polish, "A Painful Legacy," in Ecumenical Trends, 16:9, October, 1987, 153-155.

21. Bishops' Conference for Ecumenical and Interrelgious Relations, National Conference of Catholic Bishops, April 24, 1987.

22. Ibid.

23. Interview with Stanislau Musial, S.J., in 30 Days, July-August, 1989, 9.

24. Ibid.

25. Michael McGarry, C.S.P., conveniently summarizes the historical, theological, ethical, and definitional "Relevance of the Shoah," in Ecumenism, 94, June, 1989, 20-23.

26. See my "The Evolution of a Tradition: From Nostre Aetate to the Notes," in Fifteen Years of Catholic-Jewish Dialogue, 1970-1985 [Rome: Liberia Editrice Lateraneuse, 1988], 239-254.

27. Pontifical Commission for Religious Relations with the Jews, "Guidelines and Suggestions for Implementing Nostre Aetate, Number 4," December 1, 1974, contained in Ibid., 293-298.

28. Ibid., 294.

29. Text and commentary in Ibid., 306-318.

30. For collections of the papal texts, with commentary, see Eugene Fisher, John Paul II and the Holocaust [Washington, DC: United States Cathlic Conference Publications, 1988], and Eugene Fisher and Leon Klenicki, Editors, John Paul II on Jews and Judaism [Washington, DC: United States Catholic Conference Publications, 1987].

31. Ibid., 10.
32. Ibid.

33. Copies are available from the United States Catholic Conference Office of Pubishing and Promotion Services, Washington, DC, Publication Number 211-X.

34. God's Mercy Endures Forever [Washington, DC: United States Catholic Conference Publication and Promotion Services, 1989, Publication Number 247-0], 1.

35. Ibid.

IN THE PRESENCE OF BURING CHILDREN:
The Reformation of Christianity After the Shoah

Douglas K. Huneke

1. Adolf Hitler, Mein Kampf [Boston: Houghton, Mifflin Company, 1971. Translated by Ralph Mannheim.], 640.

2. Paul Althaus, from a lecture presented at the Univesity o Leipzig, May 28, 1937. Quoted in Robert P. Ericksen, Theologians Under Hitler [New Haven: Yale University Press, 1985], 103.

3. Quoted in P. Ericksen, Ibid., 87.

4. Raul Hilberg, The Destruction of the European Jews [New York: New Viewpoints, 1973], 188.

Notes

5. Elie Wiesel, Night [New York: Hill and Wang, 1972], 41 and 43.

6. Irving Greenberg, "Cloud of Smoke, Pillar of Fire: Judaism, Christianity, and Modernity After the Holocaust," in Eva Fleischner, Editor, Auschwitz: Beginning of a New Era? Reflections on the Holocauast [New York: Ktav Publishing House, 1977], 23.

7. Jules Isaac, Jesus and Israel [New York: Holt, Rinehart and Winston, 1971. Edited by Clare Huchet-Bishop and transalted by Sally Gran.], 401-404.

8. Cited as an "Appendix and Practical Conclusion," in Ibid., 404-405.

9. Paul van Buren, "The Status and Prospects for Theology," an address to the Theology Section of the American Academy of Religion, Chicago, November 1, 1975.

10. Regrettably, the first Seelisberg Poijnt actually speaks of "the Old and New Testaments," thereby fueling the triumphalist misconception that the new supplants the old; that the new is superior to and the completion of the old. Only in recent years have there been challenges and some changes to the artificially imposed and archaic use of "Old" and "New" to distinguish between the Hebrew and Christian Scriptures.

11. Richard L. Rubenstein and John K. Roth, Approaches to Auschwitz: The Holocaust and Its Legacy [Atlanta: John Knox Press, 1987], 205.

12. Elie Wiesel, Op. Cit., 71-72.

13. Elie Wiesel, The Oath [New York: Random House, 1973], 138.

14. Helmut Gollwitzer, Editor, Dying We Live: The Final Messages and Records of the Resistance [New York: Pantheon Books, 1956], xiv.

15. Perry London conducted pioneering research on Nazi era resucers. I have expanded his first two findings on adventurousness and moral parental role models. His findings are contained in "The Rescuers: Motivational Hypotheses About Christians Who Rescued Jews from the Nazis," in J. Macaulay and L. Berkowitz, Editors, Altruism and Helping Behavior [New York: Doubleday and Company, 1975].

16. Henri J. M. Nouwen, Reaching Out: Three Movements of the Sprirtual Life [New York: Doubleday and Company, 1975], 46-47.

17. Jules Isaac, Op. Cit., 402.

18. Adolf Hitler, Op. Cit., 307.

19. Ibid., 402.

20. Ellis Rivkin, What Crucified Jesus? [Nashville: Abingdon Press, 1984], 124.

21. Ibid.

22. Stanley Milgram, Obedience to Authority: An Experimental View [New York: Harper Colophon, 1969], 6.

23. Ibid., 8.

24. Dietrich Bonhoeffer, The Cost of Discipleship [New York: Macmillan Publishing Company, 1974], 45.

25. Ibid., 47.

26. Helmut Thielke, "Why the Holocaust," in Christianity Today, 27 January 1978, 521.

27. Ibid.

28. Wendell Berry, Sabbaths [San Francisco: North Point Press, 1987], 83.

IN A WORLD WITHOUT A REDEEMER, REDEEM!

Michael Berenbaum

1. I am convinced that the Jewish community plays a similar role with respect to Soviet Communism as Jews did in Christianity, i.e. Jews helped to bring the Christ and now deny him. By virtue of wanting to leave, Jews deny that community is the kingdom of God on earth and are resented for it.

2. See Yehoshafat Harkabi, The Bar Kochba Syndrome [Chappaqua: Rossel Books, 1983] for a fascinating discussion of the perils of the 132-135 Messianic uprising and the implications of nationalistic historical revisionism surrounding the revolt today.

Notes

3. Gershom Scholem, Sabbatai Sevi: The Mystical Messiah [Princeton: Princeton University Press, 1973].

4. Arthur Hertzberg, Editor, The Zionist Idea [Philadelphia: The Jewish Publication Society of America, 1959], 1-103.

5. Joseph B. Soloveitchik, In Aloneness, In Togetherness: A Selection of Hebrew Writings [Jerusalem: Orot, 1976. Edited by Pinchas Peli.], 331-400.

6. Ehud Sprinzak, "Fundamentalism, Terrorism and Democracy: The Case of Gush Emunim Underground," in Occasional Papers [Washington, DC: The Wilson Center]. This paper was originally delivered on September 16, 1986.

7. Zvi Yaron, The Teachings of Rav Kook [Jerusalem: The world Zionist Organization, 1979. Hebrew.].

8. Ibid.

9. Michael Berenbaum, The Vision of the Void [Middletown: Wesleyan University Press, 1979].

10. Yonina Talmon, "The Pursuit of the Millenium: The Relations Between Religion and Social Change," in Norman Birnbaum and Gertrude Lenzer, Editors, Sociology and Religion [Englewood Cliffs: Prentice Hall, 1969], 238-254.

11. See Michael Berenbaum, "Religion and Politics in Contemporary Israel," in Richard L. Rubenstein, Editor, Spirit Matters: The World-wide Impact of Religion in Contemporary Politics [New York: Paragon House Publishers, 1987].

12. Ibid.

13. Yehuda Amitai, Ascent from the Depths [Jerusalem: Alon Shevut, 1974. Hebrew.].

14. Gershom Scholem, Op. Cit., 11-14.

15. Gershom Scholem, The Messianic Idea in Judaism and Other Essays on Jewish Spirituality [New York: Schocken Books, 1971], 35.

16. Ehud Sprinzak, Op. Cit., 11-14.

17. Emil Fackenheim, To Mend the World: Foundations of Future Jewish Thought [New York: Schocken Books, 1982], 250-313.

18. Elie Wiesel, "Jewish Values in the Post-Holocaust Future," in Judaism, 16:3, Summer, 1967.

19. Richard L. Rubenstein, After Auschwitz: Radical Theology and Contemporary Judaism [Indianapolis: Bobbs-Merrill, 1966].

20. Michael Berenbaum, Op. Cit.

21. Maurice Friedman, Abraham Joshua Heschel and Elie Wiesel: You Are My Witnesses [New York: Farrar, Straus and Giroux, 1987], 229-259.

22. Elie Wiesel, The Town Beyond the Wall [New York: Holt, Rinehart and Winston, 1964], 118.

23. Elie Wiesel, "Jewish Values in the Post-Holocaust Future," 299.

24. See Maurice Friedman, Op. Cit., 247-248, 267-268; and Michael Berenbaum, The Vision of the Void, 15-16, 79, 148.

25. Michael Berenbaum, Ibid., 148.

AFTER AUSCHWITZ AND THE PALESTINIAN UPRISING

Marc H. Ellis

1. For an extended analysis of the themes in Shoah theology, see Marc H. Ellis, Toward a Jewish Theology of Liberation: The Uprising and the Future [Maryknoll: Orbis, 1989], 7-24.

2. For an early, radical, and controversial analysis of these themes, see Richard L. Rubenstein, After Auschwitz: Radical Theology and Contemporary Judaism [Indianapolis: Bobbs-Merrill, 1966]; and The Cunning of History: Mass Death and the American Future [New York: Harper & Row, 1975].

3. Of course, the first priority was to survive as a people so that a future was possible to imagine. The question of survival was described by Emil Fackenheim as the "com-

Notes

manding voice of Auschwitz." See Emil Fackenheim, God's Presence in History: Jewish Affirmations and Philosophical Reflections [New York: New York University Press, 1970].

4. For an interesting exploration of this new framework, see Irving Greenberg, Cloud of Smoke, Pillar of Fire: Judaism, Christianity and Modernity After Auschwitz," in Eva Fleischner, Editor, Auschwitz: Beginning of a New Era? Reflections on the Holocaust [New York: Ktav Publishing House, 1977], 7-55; and "On the Third Era of Jewish History: Power and Politics," in Perspectives [New York: National Jewish Resource Center, 1980].

5. Richard L. Rubenstein, The Cunning of History, 28; Irving Greenberg, "Cloud of Smoke, Pillar of Fire," 29.

6. For an extended discussion of Shoah theology's inability to analyze the case of empowerment, see Marc H. Ellis, Jewish Theology of Liberation, 25-37.

7. In effect, a new pragmatism is stressed that allows the "occasional use of immoral strength to achieve moral ends." With this understanding, the memory of the Shoah enables Israel to be a "responsible and restrained conqueror." See Irving Greenberg, "The Third Great Cycle in Jewish History," in Perspectives [New York: National Jewish Resource Center, 1981], 25-26. The recent uprising in the occupied territories and the response of Israeli authorities exemplify the difficult position Diaspora Jews are in relative to Israel.

8. Ibid., 25. Also, see, "On the Third Era in Jewish History," 6; and "Power and Peace," in Perspectives [New York: National Jewish Resource Center, 1985], 3 and 5.

9. Phillip Lopate, "Resistance to the Holocaust," Tikkun, 4, May/June, 1989, 56.

10. Ibid. Lopate adds, "A good deal of suspicion and touchiness resides around this issue of maintaining the Holocaust's privileged status in the pantheon of genocides. It is not enough that the Holocaust was dreadful; it must be seen as uniquely dreadful," 57.

11. Avishai Margalit, "The Kitsch of Israel," New York Review of Books, 35, November 24, 1988, 23.

12. Ibid.

13. Ibid., 24. All of this is also crucial for the marketing of Israel to the American Jewish community. See Ibid., 22. For Elie Wiesel's response to the trivilization of the Shoah, see his "Art and the Holocaust: Trivializing Memory," in The New York Times, June 11, 1989. To the question of how one transmits the message without trivializing it, Wiesel responds, "Listen to the survivors and respect their wounded sensibility. Open yourselves to their scarred memory, and mingle your tears with theirs. And stop insulting the dead," 38.

14. Boaz Evron, "The Holocaust: Learning the Wrong Lessons," in Journal of Palestinian Studies, 10, Spring, 1981, 16.

15. Ibid., 17 and 18. For an illustration of the need for common struggle with the Shoah, see Helen Fein, Accounting for Genocide: National Responses and Jewish Victimization During the Holocaust [Chicago: University of Chicago Press, 1979].

16. Boaz Evron, "The Holocaust: Learning the Wrong Lessons," 17 and 18.

17. Ibid., 19 and 20. Evron claims that before the Eichmann trial, Shoah consciousness was waning andthe ritualistic system of Shoah commemoration was undeveloped. To immigrants from Arab lands and for Israeli-born youths, "the extermination was a matter of the Jewish of Europe, not of Israelis," 19.

18. Ibid., 21.

19. Ibid., 23.

20. Ibid., 26. For a fascinating response to Evron's article linking the so-called Biblical right of the Jews to Israel and the expulsion of the Palestinians from the land, see Israel Shahak, "The 'Historic Right' and the Other Holocaust," in Journal of Palestinian Studies, 10, Spring, 1981, 27-34.

21. A. B. Yehoshua, Between Right and Right: israel, Problem or Solution? [Garden City: Doubleday and Company, 1981. Translated by Arnold Schwartz.], 101 and 105.

22. Ibid., 107-147.

23. These theme are enunciated most clearly as a consensus progressive Jewish position by Michael Lerner, Editor of the journal Tikkun. See Michael Lerner, "The

Notes

Occupation: Immoral and Stupid," Tikkun, 3, March/April, 1988, 7-12.

24. Amos Oz, "Granting a Divorce," in American-Israeli Civil Liberties Coalition, 10, Summer, 1990, 15.

25. For the development of this theme, see Muhammed Hallaj, "The Palestinian Dream: The Democratic Secular State," in Rosemary Radford Ruether and Marc H. Ellis, Editors, Beyond Occupation: American Jewish, Christian, and Palestinian Voices for Peace [Boston: Beacon Press, 1990], 220-230.

26. On the diversity and complexity of Jewish behavior in the ghettos of Eastern Europe, see Isaiah Trunk, Judenrat: The Jewish Councils in Eastern Europe Under Nazi Occupation [New York: Stein and Day, 1977]. For a dialogue on the shifting of the burden onto Palestinians, see "Special Focus on Iraq," in Tikkun, 5, November/December, 1990, 48-78.

27. Johann Baptist Metz, The Emergent Church: The Future of Christianity in a Postbourgeois World [New York: Crossroad, 1981. Translated by Peter Mann.], 19.

28. For a discussion of these themes, see Robert Gordis, The Dynamics of Judaism: A Study in Jewish Law [Bloomington: Indiana University Press, 1990]. See, also, Norman Gottwald, The Tribes of Yahweh: A Sociology of the Religion of Liberated israel, 1250-1050 B.C.E. [Maryknoll: Orbis Books, 1979].

29. For earlier discussion of this theme, see Georges Friedman, The End of the Jewish People? [Garden City: Doubleday and Company, 1967. Translated by Eric Mosbacher.]; and Earl Shorris, Jews Without Mercy: A Lament [Garden City: Doublday and Company, 1982].

30. A way of confronting Jewish self-perception with reality is by reading Punishing a Nation: Human Rights Violation during the Palestinian Uprising, December, 1987-1988 [Ramallah: Al-Haq/Law in the Service of Man, 1988].

31. For an extended discussion of the themes of innocence and redemption, see Marc H. Ellis, Beyond Innocence and Redemption: Confront the Holocaust and Israeli Power [San Francisco: Harper & Row, 1990]. My review appears in Judaica Book News, 22:1, Fall, 1991, 46-47.

32. The transformation of segments of Christianity is an important focus of my own

work. See, especially, Marc H. Ellis, Jewish Theology of Liberation, 66-90; and Beyond Innocence and Redemption, 177-186. For comments on the ecumenical dialogue, see my "End the Dialogue," in Tablet, 244, June 30, 1990, 810.

33. Roberta Strauss Feuerlicht, The Fate of the Jews: A People Torn Between Israeli Power and Jewish Ethics [New York: Time Books, 1983], 281-282.

34. Etty Hillesum, An Interrupted Life: The Diaries of Etty Hillesum, 1941-43 [New York: Pocket Books, 1985. Edited by J. G. Caarlandt and translated by Jonathan Cape.], 99-101.

35. Ibid., 122.

THEOLOGICAL AND ETHICAL REFLECTIONS ON THE SHOAH:
Getting Beyond the Victim-Victimizer Relationship

Rosemary Radford Ruether

1. See, also, a critique of her position by David Biale in his review of The Wrath of Jonah by Rosemary Radford Ruether and Herman J. Ruether [New York: Harper & Row, 1989] in Tikkun, 4:3, 99-102, under the title "The Philo-Semitic Face of Christian Anti-Semitism."

2. Arthur C. Cochrane, The Church's Confession Under Hitler [Philadelphia: Westminster Press, 1962], 206-208.

3. Emil L. Fackenheim, "The People of Israel Lives," in The Christian Century, 6 May 1970, 563.

4. Reader's Response: Richard L. Rubenstein, The Christian Century, 29 July 1970, 919-921.

5. The Jewish speakers at this conference were Irving Greenberg, Alfred kazin, Yosef Yerushalmi, Emil Fackenheim, Seymour Siegel, Shlomo Avineri, Paul Jacobs, Milton Himmelfarb, Arthur Waskow, Edith Wyschogrod, Lionel Rubinoff, Paul Ritterband, Charles Silverman, and Elie Wiesel. The Christians were Alan T. Davies, Rosemary Radford Ruether, Walter Burghardt, Gregory Baum, Johannes Hoekendijk, Aarne Sirala, John T. Pawlikowski, Claire Huchet-Bishop, Thomas Hopko, Eva Fleischner, Michael Ryan, and Charles Long. Gabriel Habib of the Middle East Council of

Notes

Churches sent a statement. The talks are printed in Eva Fleischner, Editor, Auschwitz: Beginning of a New Era? Reflections on the Holocaust [New York: Ktav Publishing House, 1977].

6. For the idea of a suffering prophet or teacher in First Century Judaism, see H. A. Fischel, "Martyr and Prophet," in Jewish Quarterly Review, 37, 1946/47, 265 ff. and 363 ff.

7. Richard L. Rubenstein, After Auschwitz: Radical Theology and Contemporary Judaism [Indianapolis: Bobbs-Merrill Company, 1966], 9-11, 56-58, 85 and passim.

8. Richard L. Rubenstein, The Cunning of History: Mass Death and the American Future [New York: Harper & Row, 1975], 21.

9. Ibid., 95-97.

10. Richard Rubenstein, After Auschwitz, 131-142 and 154. On the Canaanite Movement in the Jewish Yishuv [Settlement—Editor] in the early 1940's, see Akiva Orr, The UnJewish State: The Politics of Jewish Identity in Israel [London: Ithaca Press, 1983], 95.

11. Richard L. Rubenstein, My Brother Paul [New York: Harper & Row, 1972].

12. Richard L. Rubenstein, After Auschwitz, 196 and 22.

13. See Note #2 above.

14. In Rubenstein's reply to Fackenheim [Note #3 above], he points out, somewhat nastily, that raising Jewish children is indeed an ethical decision for Fackenheim, since his wife is a Christian, and, so, according to Jewish law, his children are not Jews and must be converted to Judaism in order to become Jews.
15. Emil L. Fackenheim, "The Holocaust and the State of Israel: Their Relation," in Eva Fleischner, Editor, Op. Cit., 205-214.

16. The phrase is found in a prayer for the State of Israel by the Israeli Chief Rabbi, quoted by Emil L. Fackenheim, Ibid., 205.

17. See Abraham Isaac Kook, "The Land of Israel," in Arthur Hertzberg, Editor, The Zionist Idea: An Historical Analysis and Reader [New York: Meridian, 1960], 190.

18. Emil L. Fackenheim, Op. Cit., 208.

19. Ibid., 212-214.

20. Ibid., 214.

21. Eva Fleischner, Editor, Op. Cit., 7-55.

22. For the relation of American Jewish organizations to the rescue of European Jewry during World War II, see the study by Shoah survivor Leon Wells, Who Speaks fo rthe Vanquished? American Judaism and the Holocaust [New York: Peter Lang, 1987].

23. Irving Greenberg, "Cloud of Smoke, Pillar of Fire: Judaism, Christianity, and Modernity After the Holocaust," in Eva Fleischner, Editor, Op. Cit., 44.

24. Eliezer Berkovits, Faith After the Holocaust [New York: Ktav Publishing House, 1973].

25. Arthur Waskow, "Between the Fires," in Tikkun, 2:5, 84-86.

26. See my reply to Waskow's article in Tikkun, 2:5, 5-6.

27. "Declaration on the Relationship of the Church to Non-Christian Religions," in Walter Abbott, Editor, Documents of Vatican II [New York: America Press, 1966], 663-666.

28. "Rat der Evangelischen Kirche in Deutschland," in Christen und Juden: Eine Studie des Rates der Evangelischen Kirche in Duetschland [Gutersich: Guterslohe Verlagshaus Gerd Mohn, 1975].

29. For the history and ideology of Christian Zionism, see Regina Sharif, Non-Jewish Zioism: Its Roots in Western History [London: ZED Press, 1983]; and Rosemary Radforde Ruether and Herman J. Ruether, The Wrath of Jonah: The Crisis of Religious Nationalism in the Israeli-Palestinian Debate [San Francisco: Harper & Row, 1989], 74-9.

30. For Christian documents on Jewish-Christian relations published between 1963

Notes

and 1976, see Helga Croner, Editor, Stepping Stones to Further Jewish-Christian Relations: An Unabridged Collection of Christian Documents [London: Stimulus Books, 1977].

31. New York: Seabury Press, 1974.

32. Ibid., 64-66.

33. Long Night's Journey into Day [Detroit: Wayne State University Press, 1982]; and Jews and Christians: The Contemporary Meeting [Bloomington: Indiana University Press, 1986].

34. Long Night's Journey into Day, 125-133.

35. Jews and Christians, 79-81.

36. Ibid., 78.

37. Long Night's Journey into Day, 134.

38. Franklin H. Littell, The Crucifixion of the Jews [New York: Harper & Row, 1975].

39. Franklin H. Littell, The Anabaptist Concept of the Church [Hartford: American Society of Church History, 1952].

40. Franklin H. Littell, The German Phoenix [New York: Doubleday and Company, 1960].

41. Franklin H. Littell, The Crucifixion of the Jews, 68.

42. Ibid., 95-96.

43. Ibid., 88.

44. Ibid., 83-84.

45. All three volumes published by Harper & Row.

46. See Karl Barth, Christ and Adam: Man and Humanity in Romans 5 [New York:

Macmillan Publishing Company, 1956].

47. Paul van Buren, Christian Theology of the People Israel, 70-76 and 116-128.

48. See Rosemary Radford Ruether and Herman J. Ruether, The Wrath of Jonah, 43-47.

49. Paul van Buren, Op. Cit., 350.

50. Ibid., 268-294.

51. Ibid., 33-37.

52. Ibid., 161-162 and 195-197.

53. Ibid., 272-274.

54. Paul van Buren, Christ in Context, 176-183.

55. Ibid., 179.

56. Paul van Buren, Christian Theology of the People Israel, 316-319.

57. Ibid., 127-128 and 312-313.

58. Ibid., 338-341.

59. Ibid., 337.

60. One example of such an effort to provide international standards of human rights is the Universal Declaration of Human Rights, adopted by the United Nations General Assembly, December 10, 1948. Two additional covenants, one dealing with economic, social, and cultural rights and the second with civil and political rights, were adopted December 16, 1966. Ratified by 46 and 44 nations respectively, the covenants went into force in 1976. See The International Bill of Human Rights, Introducton by Peter Mayer [Glen Ellen: Entwhistle Books, 1981].

61. An example of such a construction of criticism of Israel is the view of the book by Rosemary Radford Ruether and Herman J. Ruether, The Wrath of Jonah, by David Biale in Tikkun, 4;3, 1989, 99-102.

Notes

62. A report on Shomron's statement appeared in The Los Angeles Times, 18 June 1989, 1.

63. Maryknoll: Orbis Books, 1987; New Edition with Postscript on the Palestinian Uprising and the Future of the Jewish People, 1989.

64. Irving Greenberg, "On the Third Era of Jewish History: Power and Politics," in Perspectives [New York: National Jewish Resource Center, 1980]; and "The Third Great Cycle in Jewish History," in Perspectives [New York: National Jewish Resource Center, 1981]. Marc Ellis' critique of Irving Greenberg's more recent views are in his book Toward a Jewish Theology of Liberation, 26-36.

65. Johannes Baptist Metz, The Emergent Church: The Future of Christianity in a Postbourgeois World [New York: Crossroads, 1981], 19; quoted in Marc Ellis, Ibid., 24 and 123-124.

66. Ibid., 124.

67. Ibid., 132-136.

68. Maryknoll: Orbis Books, 1989.

REVISIONISM AND THEOLOGY:
Two Sides of the Same Coin

Harry James Cargas

1. On Cargas himself and his attempts to foster Jewish-Christian dialogue, see my "Harry James Cargas: Appreciation and Response," in Journal of Reform Judaism, Spring, 1985, 33-43. On the subject of ritual murder, see R. Po-Hsia, The Myth of Ritual Murder [New Haven: Yale University Press, 1988].

2. Arthur R. Butz, The Hoax of the Twentieth Century [Torrance: Institute for Historical Review, 1976].

3. Edward R. Flannery, The Anguish of the Jews: Twenty-three Centuries of Anti-Semitism [New York: The Macmillan Company, 1965].

4. Rosemary Radford Ruether, Faith and Fratricide: The Theological Roots of Anti-

Semitism [New York: Seabury Press, 1974].

5. Count Arthur de Gobineau, The Inequality of the Races [Los Angeles: The Noontide Press, 1966. Translated by Adrian Collins, M.A.]

6. John F. Morley, Vatican Diplomacy and the Jews During the Holocaust, 1939-1943 [New York: Ktav Publishing House, 1980].

BETWEEN THE FIRES

Arthur Waskow

1. Reprinted from *Tikkun*, Volume 2, Number 1, pages 84-86. Permission granted.

THE HOLOCAUST:
A Summing Up After More than Two Decades of Reflection

Emil L. Fackenheim

1. On the question of uniqueness itself, see Alan Rosenberg, "Was the Holocaust Unique: A Peculiar Question," in Isidor Wallimann and Michaek N. Dobkowski, Editors, Genocide and the Modern Age: Etiology and Case Studies of Mass Death [New York: Greenwood Press, 1987], 145-161; and my review "Genocidal Civilization," in Judaica Book News, 18:2, Spring/Summer, 1988/5748, 29-33.

APOCALYPTIC RATIONALITY AND THE SHOAH

Richard L. Rubenstein

1. Indianapolis: Bobbs-Merrill Company, 1966.

2. That conclusion is likewise in evidence in his "Afterword: Genocide and Civilization," in Isidor Wallimann and Michael N. Dobkowski, Editors, Genocide and the Modern Age: Etiology and Case Studies of Mass Death [New York: Greenwood Press, 1987], 283-298, especially 297. See, also, my review "Genocidal Civilization," in Judaica Book News, 18:2, Spring/Summer, 1988/5748, 29-33.

3. An earlier version of this paper was presented in Paris, November, 1988, at the conference "Penser Auschwitz," by the Alliance Israelite Universelle, and commemo-

Notes

rating the Fiftieth Anniversary of Kristallnacht.

4. See, for example, Lucy S. Dawidowicz, The War Against the Jews, 1933-1945 [New York: Holt, Rinehart and Winston, 1975].

5. This is the author's fundamental thesis concerning the Shoah as expressed in Richard L. Rubenstein, The Cunning of History [New York: Harper & Row, 1975]. See, especially, 6.

6. Norman Perrin, The New Testament: An Introduction [New York: Harcourt, Brace and Jovanovich, 1974], 65.

7. This thesis is spelled out by the author in Richard L. Rubenstein, The Age of Triage: Fear and Hope in an Overcrowded World [Boston: Beacon Press, 1983], 34-59. See Karl Polanyi, The Great Transformation: The Political and Economic Origin of Our Times [Boston: Beacon Press, 1957].

8. Robert Hughes, The Fatal Shore: The Epic of Australia's Founding [New York: Alfred A. Knopf, 1987], 40-41.

9. Tony Barta, "Relations of Genocide: Land and Lives in the Colonization of Australia," in Isidor Wallimann and Michael N. Dobkowksi, Editors, Genocide and the Modern Age: Etiology and Case Studies of Mass Death, 237-252.

10. For a study of the fate of the Indians of North America, see Bernard W. Sheehan, Seeds of Extinction: Jeffersonian Philanthropy and the American Indian [Chapel Hill: University of North Carolina Press, 1973].

11. Christopher Hill, God's Englishman: Oliver Cromwell and the English Revolution [New York: Harper Torchbooks, 1972], 113.

12. R. P. Stearns, Hugh Peter: The Strenuous Puritan, 1598-1660 [Champagne and Urbana: Illinois University Press, 1954], 356; cited by Hill, Op. Cit., 117.

13. Cecil Woodham-Smith, The Great Hunger: Ireland, 1845-1849 [New York: E. P. Dutton, 1980], 411-412.

14. Richard L. Rubenstein, The Age of Triage, 120-127.

15. "Effects of Emigration on Production and Consumption," in The Economist, Febru-

ary 12, 1853, 168-169. See this author's comments in Richard L. Rubenstein, The Age of Triage, 122.

16. See "The Irish Priesthood and the Irish Laity," in The Economist, June 18, 1852.

17. A. J. Ryder, Twentieth-Century Germany: From Bismarck to Brandt [New York: Columbia University Press, 1972], 40.

18. See Richard L. Rubenstein, The Age of Triage, 165-194.

19. Michael R. Marrus and Robert O. Paxton, Vichy France and the Jews [New York: Basic Books, 1981], 3-8.

20. See, for example, J. S. Conway, The Persecution of the Churches, 1933-1945 [New York: Basic Books, 1968], 261-266.

21. The question of the proneness of middlemen to genocidal assault has been raised by Walter P. Zenner and a number of other social theorists. See Walter P. Zenner, "Middleman Minorities and Genocide," in Isidor Wallimann and Michael N. Dobknowski, Editors, Genocide and the Modern Age: Etiology and Case Studies of Mass Death, 253-281; Walter P. Zenner, Middleman Minority Theories and the Jews: An Historical Assessment [New York: YIVO Working Papers in Yiddish and Eastern European Jewish Studies Series, Number 31, 1978]; Edna Bonacich and J. Modell, The Economic Basis of Ethnic Solidarity: The Case of Japanese Americans [Berkeley and Los Angeles: University of California Press, 1981].

22. For a discussion of the elimination of the ethnic Chinese from Vietnam, see Richard L. Rubenstein, The Age of Triage, 165-194.

23. See Benjamin Nelson, The Idea of Usury: From Tribal Brotherhood to Universal Otherhood [Chicago: University of Chicago Press, 1969. Second Edition.].

24. Richard L. Rubenstein, The Age of Triage, 128-164.

25. Robert G. L. Waite, The Psychopathic God: Adolf Hitler [New York: New American Library, 1978], 73.

26. See Irving Louis Horowitz, "Genocide and the Reconstruction of Social Theory: Observations on the Exclusivity of Social Death," in Isidor Wallimann and Michael

Notes

N. Dobkowski, Editors, Op. Cit., 61-80.

27. Richard L. Rubenstein, After Auschwitz: Radical Theology and Contemporary Judaism, 30 ff.

28. Cited by Nicholas Halasz, Captain Dreyfus: The Story of a Mass Hysteria [New York: Simon and Schuster, 1957], 57.

29. This assessment acords with the judgment of political scientist Roger Smith, that genocide is a "rational instrument to achieve an end." See Roger Smith, "Human Destructiveness and Politics: The Twentieth Century as an Age of Genocide," in Isidor Wallimann and Michael N. Dobkowski, Editors, Op. Cit., 21-40.

30. Max Weber, Economy and Society: An Outline of Interpretive Sociology [New York: Bedminster Press, 1968. Edited by Guenther Roth and Claus Wittich.], Volume I, 24-26.

31. Ronald Aronson, The Dialectics of Disaster [London: Verso, 1983].

32. Richard L. Rubenstein, The Cunning of History, 90.

33. Emil L. Fackenheim, God's Presence in History: Jewish Affirmations and Philosophical Reflections [New York: Harper and Row, 1972], 11.

34. See Victor Farias, Heidegger et le Nazisme [Paris: Verdier, 1987]; and Richard L. Rubenstein, "Philosopher and the Jews: The Case of Martin Heidegger," in Modern Judaism, 9:2, May, 1989, 179-196.

35. Martin Heidegger, Being and Time [New York: Harper and Row, 1962. Translated by John Macquarrie and Edward Robinson.], 296. German Edition, Sein und Zeit [Tubingen: Niemeyer, 1953. Seventh Edition.], 252.

36. Franz Rosenzweig, The Star of Redemption [New York: Holt, Rinehart and Winston, 1970. Translated by William W. Hallo.], 329.

ACADEMIA AND THE HOLOCAUST

Alan L. Berger

The Holocaust Now

1. See, also, Zev Garber, Alan L. Berger, and Richard Libowitz, Editors, Methodology in the Academic Teaching of the Holocaust [Lanham: University Press of America, 1988]. My review of this important text appeared in The National Jewish Post and Opinion, 19 April 1989, 10.

2. "Holocaust" is a sanitized word which has entered the public vocabulary. Both inaccurate and inadequate [see below], Holocaust is the name given to Nazi Germany's murder of European Jewry. More appropriate to the horror is its designation as "Auschwitzm," largest of the Nazi death factories. This essay utilizes the term Holocaust only because of its public recognition.

3. Lily Edelman, "A Conversation with Elie Wiesel," in Harry James Cargas, Editor, Resposnes to Elie Wiesel [New York: Persea Books, 1978].

4. Richard L. Rubenstein, The Cunning of History [New York: Harper Colophon Books, 1978], 67.

5. Hannah Arendt, The Origins of Totalitarianism [New York: Harcourt, Brace & World, 1966], III, 316.

6. Bruno Bettelheim, The Informed Heart [Glencoe: The Free Press, 1960], 262.

7. Arendt notes that the general mentality of modern German scholars was heavily influenced by intellectuals of German romanticism. This dubious heritage yielded actions which "proved more than once that hardly an ideology can be found to which they[modern German scholars] would not willingly submit if the only reality—which even a romantic can hardly afford to overlook—is at stake, the reality of their position." The Origins of Totalitarianism, II, 168.

8. Raul Hilberg, The Destruction of European Jews [Chicago: Quadrangle Books, 1967], 189.

9. Bruno Bettelheim, Op. Cit., utilizes O. Lengyel's account from her Five Chimneys: The Story of Auschwitz [Chicago: Ziff Davis, 1947], 147.

10. I. G. Auschwitz was actually located at Buna, the slave center directly adjacent to Auschwitz.

11. Raul Hilberg, Op. Cit., 396.

Notes

12. Max Weinreich, Hitler's Professors [New York: YIVO, 1946], 6.

13. The Nuremberg Trials had specific categories for physicians [most of whom were university professors], attorneys, high ranking military officers, politicians, and for corporate executives. Law professors had spent the war years condemning to death Jews and other opponents of Hitler. Professor Doctor Reinhard Maurach, teacher of Criminal Law at Munich, testified that SS General Otto Ohlendorf [holder of a doctorate in Jurisprudence, who had studied at three German universities], commander of Einsatzgruppe D, which murdered 90,000 people, the overwhelming majority of whom were Jews, had not committed any criminal offense. Ohlendorf, asserted Maurach, had been furthering the aims of the Reich. Maurach continues to be a highly respected law professor. For a vivid and sobering account of Nuremberg and its aftermath, see Benjamin B. Ferencz, Less Than Slaves [Canbridge: Harvard University Press, 1979].

14. Cited by Hans Jonas in "Heidegger and Theology," in Hans Jonas, The Phenomenon of Life [New York: Harper & Row, 1966], 247. Jonas employs the ruport of Guido Schneeberger, Nachlese zu Heidegger: Dokumente zu seinem Leben und Denken [Bern: 1962].

15. Hans Jonas has written, "Neither then nor now did Heidegger's thought provide a norm by which to answer such calls [the call of being]—linguistically or otherwise." "The devil," concludes Jonas, "is also part of the voice of being." Hans Jonas, Ibid., 247.

16. Franklin H. Littell's study The Crucifixion of the Jews [New York: Harper & Row, 1975] contains one of the most lucide and perceptive analyses of university shortcomings. See, especially, Chapter I, "The Language of Events," and Chapter IV, "The Meaning of the Holocaust." See, also, Littell's chapter "Church Struggle and the Holocaust," especially 19-26, "The Treason of the Intellectuals," in Franklin H. Littell and Hubert G. Locke, Editors, The Church Struggle and the Holocaust [Detroit: Wayne State University Press, 1974].

17. Elie Wiesel, Legends of Our Time [New York: Holt, Rinehart and Winston, 1968], 6. Arthur A. Cohen has suggested that the Holocaust be viewed as a Tremendum, a caesura in Jewish history. See his lucid, provocative and richly suggestive book The Tremendum: A Theological Interpretation of the Holocaust [New York: Crossroad, 1981].

18. Irving Greenberg, "Cloud of Smoke, Pillar of Fire: Judaism, Christianity and Modernity After the Holocaust," in Journal of Ecumenical Studies, 12:4, Fall, 1975, 542-543.

19. Yehuda Bauer, The Holocaust in Historical Perspective [Seattle: University of Washington Press, 1978], 31.

20. Bauer notes that while certain Gypsy tribes were murdered, others were protected. Moreoever, many individual Gypsies served in the German Army. Turning to the Turkish massacre of Armenian citizens in World War I, Bauer observes that, while half of the Armenian population in Anatolia was murdered, the Armenians at Istanbul, the heart of the Ottoman Empire, were not killed. Op. Cit., 36.

21. Professor Lucy S. Dawidowicz reports the sordid affair in her article, "Lies About the Holocaust," in Commentary, December, 1980. The article should be requried reading for all those interested in the correct usage of academic objectivity. Dawidowicz analyzes the bizarre career of The Journal of Historical Review [JHR] which is attempting to kill the Jews a second time. Nazis physically eradicated Jews; revisionist historians wish to deny their memory. Academics are in the forefront of this ghoulish assault. For example, Arthur R. Butz, Professor of Engineering at Northwestern University and author of The Hoax of the Twentieth Century, in which he reveals the "Holocaust legend," is a leading contributor.

22. Lucy S. Dawidowicz, Ibid., 35.

23. Ibid., 37.

24. Yehuda Bauer, Op. Cit., specifically warns against the danger of moral anaesthesia when writing a "seminar paper about murder," 43, 44, and 47.

GLOSSARY

Aggadah: [Hebrew] Post-Biblical Jewish literature which includes stories, chronicles, sayings, moral instructions, admonitions and chastisements, as well as consolations.

Akedah: [Hebrew] Reference to the Binding of Isaac as depicted in Bereshit [Genesis], Chapter 22. Oft-times mistakenly referred to in Christian literature as the "Sacrifice" of Isaac, precursor to the death of Jesus.

Aliyah: [Hebrew] Immigration to Israel. Literally a "going up" to the Land of Israel. [Its opposite if yeridah, literally a "going down" from the Land of Israel.]

Anamnesis: [Greek] Literally "remembering." Its Hebrew equivalent is zikkaron. For Eugene Fisher, Volume II, both Judaism and Christianity are religions of remembering.

Ani Ma'amin: [Hebrew] Literally "I believe...." The opening words to Maimonides' [1135-1204] "Thirteen Articles of Faith," traditional included in the Jewish siddur, prayer book.

Antinomianism: An early Christian interpretation which held that salvation is directly contingent upon faith only rather than obedience to any moral law.

Antisemitism: Hated of the Jewish People and the Jewish Religious Faith, Heritage, and Tradition. Throughout history, the forms antisemitism has taken have included expulsion, ghettoization, forced religious conversion, denial of civil rights, and extermination/annihilation. [Preferred spelling here is without the hyphen; to use it is to imply its opposite: That there is such a thing as "S/semitism," which is non-existent.]

Apocalypse: The idea of the revelation of the End of Days as well as the Day[s] of Judgment. Important to all three monotheistic religious traditions, Judaism, Christianity, and Islam.

Apostasy: The abandonment of the beliefs of one's faith community.

Aryan: The term wrongly employed by the Nazis to designate any "pure-blooded" Caucasian, male or female, possessing no Jewish ancestors, primarily, but, also, one possessing neither Polish or Slavic "blood."

Ashkenazim: German Jews and their descendants. Though the term can be found in the Scriptures [Genesis 10:3; Jeremiah 51:27], it has been used since the ninth century in the above way.

Atheism: The philosophical position that either there is no God or that the proofs which have thus far been presented to prove the existence of God are themselves faulty.

Auschwitz: [German; Polish: Oswiecim; Yiddish: Ushpitzin]. Town thirty miles west of Cracow, Poland. Premier Nazi concentration camp which saw the extermination of between four and five million prisoners, more than one and one-half million of them Jews. It has, also, become the symbolic reference to the entire concentration/extermination camp system of the Nazis.

Bat Kol: [Hebrew] Literally, "daughter of a voice." The term is found in rabbinic literature, especially the Talmud to denote the Divine Voice, available to be heard by anyone.

Bayt Ha-Knesset: [Hebrew] One of the primary functions/roles of the synagogue—to be a "House of Assembly and Gathering."

Bayt Ha-Midrash: [Hebrew] One of the primary functions/roles of the synagogue—to be a "House of Study and Learning."

Bayt Ha-Tefillah: [Hebrew] One of the primary functions/roles of the synagogue—to be a "House of Prayer and Worship."

Bayt Ha-Mikdash: [Hebrew] Literally, "House of the Holy." Reference to the ancient Temple in Jerusalem. Destroyed once by the Babylonians in 586 B.C.E., and, again, by the Romans in 70 C.E.

Beviat Ha-Mashiach: [Hebrew] Literally, the "coming of the Messiah." This term is taken from Maimonides "Thirteen Articles of Faith," and is the general referent to that future moment when, according to Jewish Religious Tradition, he will make his appearance known to the House of Israel. [See above, Ani Ma'amin.]

Bureaucracy: According to Webster's New World Dictionary of the American Language, College Edition, [c] 1959, "the administration of government through departments and subdivisions managed by sets of officials following an inflexible routine....the concentration of authority in administrative bureaus." Particularly relevant in understanding the Nazi administration of the Shoah.

Christology: Christianity's unique faith-claim of the distinctiveness of Jesus as the Christ according to the New Testament texts, and, thus, the very heart and essence of the Christian religious tradition.

Glossary

Churban: [Hebrew] Literally, "destruction." One of the possibly appropriate words used to describe the wanton murder and callous slaughter of the Jews by the Nazis and their minions during the years 1939-1945.

Chutzpah: [Hebrew] Literally, "brazenness" or "audacity." Sometimes regarded as a uniquely Jewish trait, though in point of fact, not specifically applicable to only one group or individual.

Conservative Judaism: Also known as "Positive-Historical Judaism," this Jewish Religious Movement represents the so-called "middle of the road" approach to religious questions and practices.

Covenant Theology: That theological understanding, originally, of the unique relationship between God and the Children of Israel/Jewish People, first entered into at Mount Sinai, whereby the Jews agreed to observe God's laws as set forth in the Torah in return for Divine protection and favor. Today, there are those theologians who speak of the Jewish Covenant at Sinai and the Christian Covenant through Jesus at Golgotha.

Creed: An authoritative statement of religious belief describing the essence of the group's and/or individual's faith.

Das Nichtige: [German] Literally, "The Nothingness;" a theological reference by Swiss thinker Karl Barth, with far broader religious and philosophical implications. [See the essay by Alan Davies.]

Deicide: Literally, "God killer." The ages-old charge against the Jewish People, over which so much innocent blood has been shed, that the Jewish People and its leaders were primarily responsible for the death of Jesus at the hands of the Romans who were only their willing tools. Its roots lie in the New Testament accounts of the events themselves and the invidious statement, "His blood be upon us and upon our children." Despite serious scholarship to the contrary, and the contemporary Roman Catholic position that the death of the Christ was attributable to no one group alone, either historically or since, this charge continues to rear its ugly head even in our own day.

Diaspora: One of the terms, without value-judgment, used to describe the world-wide Jewish communities living outside the Land of Israel.

Die Endlosung: [German] Literally, the "Final Solution," that is, the Nazis' "Final Solution to the Jewish Problem"—extermination or annihilation of approximately six million Jewish men, women, and children, with a world plan to obliterate the Jewish People from the face of the earth.

Displacement Theology: The idea, still prevalent in some Christian denominations, that, with the appearance of Jesus as the Christ, and the rise of Christianity, both Judaism and the Jewish People have been "displaced" from their position as God's favored elect.

Dogma: The authoritative affirmation of the beliefs and principles of one's faith community.

Einsatzgruppe [pl. en]: [German] The "Mobile Killing Units" of the SS under the direct authority of Heinrich Himmler, Chief of the SS, responsible for the murder of those Jews found in areas conquered by the Wehrmacht. Oft-times, the Jews themselves were forced to dig their own graves, strip themselves naked, lie down in the trenches and pits and wait to be machine-gunned to death. No regard whatsoever was shown for men, women, children, the aged or the very young.

Einsatzkommando: [German] One of the SS men who considered it their "honorable duty" to put an end to the Jews by such "special operations" as described above.

El Mistater: [Hebrew] Literally, the "Hidden Face of God." Following the idea of German-Jewish philosopher Martin Buber [1878-1965] concerning the "eclipse of God" during the Shoah, for one awful moment in history, God "chose" to "turn His face away" from humankind with the Shoah as result. This concept, interestingly enough, is also found in Jewish rabbinic literature during earlier historical epochs.

En Sof: [Hebrew] Literally, "infinity" or "nothingness." In Jewish mystical literature and tradition, it is the "expanse of God" or "holy nothingness" beyond humanity's full ability to comprehend and understand—the "realm of God."

Eretz Yisrael: [Hebrew] Literally, the "Land of Israel" as distinct from the state and/or government and/or people of Israel. Sacred to all three religious traditions, Judaism, Christianity, and Islam.

Ethics: The system or code by which the morality of a nation-state or any group is put into practice.

Ethnocide: The effort to destroy a people as a cultural entity. [See the essay by Rosemary Radford Reuther.]

Evil: That which causes harm to an individual or group usually innocent. In religious circles, the most difficult questions revolve around the role/place/function of evil in a God-controlled world.

Existentialism: That philosophical understanding usually associated with such thinkers as Jean-Paul Sartre and Albert Camus that our world is one of random accident and chance, that whatever happens happens, and we make our way in the world as best we can. Though some have attempted to develop a "religious existentialism," incorporating both the concept of randomness with an interactive God, others feel they are both

Glossary

mutually-exclusive and mutually incompatible.

Fascism: A political system, usually run by a dictator, supported by one party which brooks no dissent, and characterized by intense nationalistic fervor and oppression of both dissidents and minorities.

Galut: [Hebrew] Literally, "exile." That Jewish understanding usually associated with both religious and secular Zionism which regards those Jews who choose to live outside the Land of Israel as living in exile."

Gemilut Hasadim: [Hebrew] Literally, "deeds of loving-kindness." One of the goals of the Jewish Religious Tradition is to heighten human consciousness to better look for ways to perform such deeds.

Genocide: Term coined by the late Raphael Lemkin [1901-1959] Polish-American jurist and "father" of the United Nations Treaty on Genocide to describe the conscious attempt to destroy a people's identity culturally, spiritually, and physically.

Geulah: [Hebrew] Literally, "redemption." That moment in the Jewish journey when universal peace will be achieved and the Jews will have returned to their homeland to dwell in harmony with their neighbors.

Ghetto: Originally from the Italian word 'giotto', that restricted area of settlement, usually in the worst section of the city. Jews were forced into such environments starting in Italy in the Middle Ages, though the term has expanded to include other groups as well.

Gog & Magog: According to the New Testament Book of Revelations [20:8], those nations, under the leadership of Satan, who will contend against God in the coming cataclysm.

Grace: The fullest expression of Divine love and blessing for all of humanity, largely unmerited, and not always understandable by human beings.

Halakhah: [Hebrew] Literally, "The Way." The system of Jewish Law as culled by the Rabbis from the Torah itself and elaborated upon in the Talmud and subsequent and additional Jewish resource literatures. For the Orthodox Jew, Jewish Law governs all facets and aspects of daily and religious living, coming as it does directly from God and interpreted authoritatively by rabbinic spokesmen. Conservative Judaism likewise affirms its sanctity, but attempts to give it a more human cast through its Law and Standards Committee of the Rabbinical Assembly. Reform Judaism has long rejected its sovereignty, acknowledging, instead, that "the past shall exercise a vote, not a veto."

Hallel Psalms: Specifically, Psalms 113-118. Recited in the Jewish worship services for

Passover, Shavuot, Sukkot, and Hanukkah.

Heilsgeschichte: [German] According to both Jewish and Christian religious traditions, the working out of human history understood as moving towards an ultimate salvation/redemption.

Hesed: [Hebrew] Literally, "lovingkindness." [See Gemilut Hasadim.]

Heshbon Ha-Nefesh: [Hebrew] Literally, "the accounting of the soul." When one's life's journey is at its end, according to Jewish religious tradition, one's good and bad deeds are judged by God and the scale tips one way or the other in terms of admittance into the afterlife.

Hester Panim: [Hebrew] Literally, "[God's] Hidden Face." [See El Mistater.]

Higher Criticism: The so-called "scientific study of the Bible," using the best insights of the various academic disciplines. Growing originally out of 19th Century German Protestant scholarship, it was understood by Jews as "higher antisemitism" and an attack on their own religious legitimacy. Roman Catholics, too, saw it in a similar light.

Historikerstreit: [German] Literally, the "historians fight." The movement, among a small circle of contemporary German historians [e.g. Ernest Nolte and Michael Sturmer, among others], to view the Shoah in a far broader context and thus diminish both its uniqueness and minimize an overall sense of German guilt.

Holocaust: Up until recently, the universally-acknowledged English word used to describe the wanton murder of nearly six million Jews by the Nazis and their collaborators. Said to have first been used by the noted writer and Nobel Prize winner Elie Wiesel. Its origin is an Anglicization of the Greek translation of the Hebrew word 'olah, the totally-consumable offering by fire to God as depicted in the Torah. In recent years, the term itself has become increasingly problematic for obvious reasons. Current thinking is to use the Hebrew term Shoah instead.

Hubris: [Greek] Literally, "pride." The excessive, ego-inflating pride that enables one both to perceive himself/herself and to act as if he/she were as God. Understood to be sinful in all three Western religious traditions.

Ideology: Strongly held beliefs, opinions, ideas, values, etc. whether of an individual, group, nation-state, or religious community.

Immanent: The religious belief that the God who is addressed in prayer is close at hand and responsive to human concerns.

Incarnation: The religious belief, primarily of Christianity, following the New Testament, that out of God's love for humanity, He sent His divine son, Jesus, to earth giving

Glossary

him both human form and human nature.

Intifada: [Arabic] Literally, "uprising." The militant response of Palestinians living in the West Bank of Israel to Israeli military and political rule. Begun in December, 1987, it has witnessed the deaths of hundreds of innocent men, women, and children, both Palestinian and Israeli. Perceived by some as a national liberation movement and by others as a terrorist campaign, it continues to be one of the major stalemates to a lasting peace in the Middle East.

Judenrein: [German] Literally, "Jew-free." The ultimate objective of Hitler's extermination policies towards Jews was to free the world of all physical, cultural, and religious evidence of the presence of the Jewish People and Faith.

K'lal Yisrael: [Hebrew] Literally, "all Israel." That term used to designate the worldwide Jewish People in its collective presentation.

Kabbalah: [Hebrew] Literally, "received tradition." The mystical tradition and literature of religious Judaism, arising, perhaps, as early as the 1st Century of the Common Era, and continually influencing all streams of religious expression.

Kabbalat Shabbat: [Hebrew] Literally, "reception of the Sabbath." The onset of the Sabbath according to Jewish religious tradition occurs on Friday Evening at sundown with appropriate blessings, customs, and festive meal.

Kaddish: [Hebrew] Literally, "holy prayer." Aramaicized prayer usually understood to be the "Mourner's Prayer" recited by survivors after the funeral of a loved one either during the Worship Service or at home.

Kadoshim: [Hebrew] Literally, "holy ones," plural form. Reference to the near six million Jews murdered and slaughtered by the Nazis and their cohorts. The use of this religiously-relevant term raises anew the theological problems with which these two volumes are ultimately concerned.

Kibbutz: [Hebrew] Literally, "collective, gathering." The collective farming settlement begun in Palestine in the 1920's prior to the re-creation of the State of Israel in 1948.

Kiddush Ha-Shem: [Hebrew] Literally, "sanctification of the [Divine] Name." The term applied to those Jews who died a martyr's death. Understood now as applicable to all who died as a result of the Shoah.

Kiddush Ha-Hayyim: [Hebrew] Literally, "sanctification of life." The very opposite of the above Kiddush Ha-Shem. Understood in the contemporary Jewish world both as an historic Jewish value and a post-Shoah Jewish imperative.

Kristallnacht: [German] Literally, "Night of the Broken Glass/Crystal." On November

9-10, 1938, the Nazis attacked Jewish businesses [844], homes [171], and synagogues [267] as well as the Jews themselves [72 killed or severely injured] while the state police did nothing to intervene and the government closed its eyes. This "pogrom" was presumably a spontaneous response to the assassination of the Third Secretary of the German Embassy in Paris, Ernst Vom Rath, by a Polish Jew Hershel Grynszpan. A fine of $1,000,000,000 RM [Reich Marks] was imposed upon the Jews of Germany to pay for the damages and clean up operations.

Lebensraum: [German] Literally, "living room." The German understanding, actually given voice prior to World War I, and furthered by Adolf Hitler, that the German people had a/the "natural right" to claim/reclaim those territories both needed for expansion as well as those areas where the majority of the population was German-speaking and, thus, Aryans.

Lebensunwerte Leben: [German] Literally, "life unworthy of life." That German/Nazi understanding that there existed those sub-populations—the aged, infirm, feeble-minded, handicapped, as well as Jews, Gypsies, homosexuals, and others—who usefulness to the State [economically, politically, militarily, etc.] was nil and thus could be destroyed.

Lecha Dode: [Hebrew] Literally, "Come, my beloved." Title of a popular hymn sung in the synagogue on Friday Evening welcoming the Sabbath.

Limpieza de Sangre: [Spanish] Literally, "purity of blood." A concept which arose in the 15th Century in both Spain and Portugal that only those who were "pure Christians" could perform even the most humble of societal tasks, but especially the more important ones. Its relevance to Nazi ideology is obvious.

Lubavitch Hasidim: Hasidic sect who trace their origins to the town of Lubavitch in Russia. Also known as Habad Hasidim, their understanding of traditional Orthodox Judaism is a merging of the intellectual of normative Judaism with the emotional ecstasy of Hasidic Judaism.

Lurianic Kabbalah: An interpretation of the Jewish mystical tradition based on the writings and teachings of Isaac ben Solomon Luria [1534-1572], also known as "Ha-Ari," the sacred lion. His interpretations of the mystical were infused with a hungering for the advent of the Messiah.

Marranos: [Spanish] Literally, "pigs." Term used to designate those new converts to Christianity who were formerly Jews during the Middle Ages. From the Christian perspective, they were not to be trusted as true and sincere converts. From the Jewish perspective, they were equally understood to be "secret Jews" who converted for their physical survival as well as their children, but secretly practiced the rituals of Judaism.

Glossary

Masada: The summer palace of King Herod in the Judean desert which saw the ultimate suicide of 960 Zealot defenders, men, women, and children. against the Romans at the end of a protracted four-year struggle [66-70].

Medinat Yisrael: [Hebrew] Literally, the "State of Israel." The official term for the contemporary nation-state founded in 1948. Distinguished from Eretz Yisrael, the Land of Israel. [See above.]

Megillah: [Hebrew] Literally, "scroll." Generally, any scroll of ancient Jewish text. Ha-Megillah or Megillat Esther is that associated with the festival of Purim and tells the story of the Book of Esther found in the Torah.

Messianism: That religious strain in both Judaism and Christianity which gives voice to the community's yearning for the appearance of the Messiah in Judaism or the return of the Messiah in Christianity. Jewish and Christian thinking on this subject, however, are substantively different.

Metaphysics: A branch of the discipline of philosophy concerned with both first causes and ultimate reality.

Midrash: [Hebrew] Literally, "that which is drawn out." Jewish interpretive literature of a non-legal nature. Commentary on the Torah as well as additional sermonic and story literature "filling in the gaps," so to speak, in the literary record. Some of it is quite fanciful—allowing the Rabbis, the creators of the literature, to give free rein to their imaginations. Others of it are quite insightful morally, ethically, spiritually, psychologically, as well as intellectually.

Mikveh: [Hebrew] [Pl.: Mikvaot] Jewish ritual baths used for a variety of religious occasions [e.g. after menstruation, prior to a wedding, conversion, etc.] Early mikvaot have been found at Masada.

Minhag: [Hebrew] [Pl. Minhagim] Jewish religious customs of a given Jewish community at a given historical moment. It is said in Jewish religious life that "the minhag of one generation becomes the law of the next."

Mitzvah: [Hebrew] [Pl. Mitzvot] Literally, "commanded act" by God to the Jewish People. According to the Rabbis, there are 613 mitzvot found through the Torah of both a moral-ethical and ritual-ceremonial nature, of equal sanctity. The mitzvot of the Torah given by God ultimately become in the eyes of the Rabbis the legal system—Halakhah—of the Jewish Religious Tradition. The word has also taken on a popular form in describing any "good deed."

Monism: The philosophical-theological idea or concept that there exists only one ultimate thing—in religious thought, obviously God.

The Holocaust Now

Morality: Actions which are in accord with the principles of right conduct of a given group, community, religion, or nation-state

Moshav: [Hebrew] Literally, a "settlement." Existing in Israel and distinct from the kibbutz, the members of the agricultural moshav own their own homes but pool their resources for the purchase of needed farming items and the sale of whatever they produce.

Mussellmann [er]: [German] Literally, "muscleman/men." German Nazi term of irony to describe the zombie-like slaves in the concentration and extermination camps, more often than not prior to their murder.

Mysterium Tremendum: [Latin] Literally, "tremendous mystery." Term made "popular" by the late Arthur Cohen [and others] to, somehow, label the Shoah and extend its implications into both the philosophical and theological realms. [A parallel term also used is caesura, indicating a break in the natural order and rhythm of things.]

Mystery: That thing, event, idea, etc., for which past and present explanations are not satisfactory. In theological terms, a mystery may very well be beyond human comprehension.

Mysticism: That branch of religious expression which sees it as possible to commune with and experience God without recourse to the intellectual and verbal.

Mythology: The collected "stories" of a given religious tradition and/or community often shrouded in the past and expressed in "larger than life" personages.

National Socialism: The "politically correct" term to describe the political philosophy of the Nazis.

Nationalism: Intense patriotic devotion to one's nation-state and its ideals, beliefs, and practices perceived as beyond reproach.

Nazi: Contraction of the German Nationalsozialistiche Deutsche Arbeiterpartei [National Socialist German Workers Party]; also abbreviated as NSDAP. Founded in 1919 and ultimately given free rein under the organizing genius of Adolf Hitler later to become Fuhrer of Germany. It was formally abolished and declared outlawed by the Nuremberg Trials in 1945.

Neturei Karta: [Aramaic] Literally, "guardians of the city." Orthodox Jews already in Jerusalem in Palestine prior to the founding of the State of Israel in 1948. They are intensely opposed to the political rebirth of Israel believing its contravenes the work of the coming Messiah to bring it about.

Nihilism: In philosophical and theological thought, the belief that there is no objective

Glossary

basis for either knowledge or truth. In politics, the belief that all currently-existing political institutions must be destroyed to make way for new ones.

Nostre Aetate: [Latin] Literally, "In Our Time." The 1965 Vatican Declaration on the Roman Catholic Church and the Jewish People which has led to a strengthening and furthering of the inter-religious dialogue between these two faith communities.

Oleh: [Hebrew] [Pl. Olim] Literally, "one who ascends." The term used to describe someone who makes aliyah, immigration, to Israel and becomes a citizen of that country.

Ontology: The philosophical and metaphysical concern with the nature of being and reality.

Original Sin: The theological concept, found in both Judaism and Christianity, that, as a result of the sin of Adam and Eve in the Garden of Eden, subsequent humanity is born with a "taint" and must work diligently to return to a state of grace in God's favor.

Orthodox Judaism: The most traditional and fundamentalist expression of religious Judaism. Orthodox Jews believe the Torah is literally the Word of God and only those who are its authentic and authoritative spokesmen, the Rabbis, can interpret those words for succeeding generations. Orthodox Jews equally claim their religious practices are the only authentic Jewish ritual and ceremonial practices.

Paganism: Religious expression, polytheistic in origin, nature-god oriented, predating Judaism, and today describing a philosophy which is neither Jewish, Christian or Muslim.

Passion of Christ: The suffering of Jesus on the Cross prior to his death. Said to be freely chosen and substitutionary for all humanity.

Pentateuch: [Greek] Literally, "Five Books." Reference to the First Five Books of the Torah: Bereshit [Genesis], Shemot [Exodus], Vayikra [Leviticus], Bamidbar [Numbers], and Devarim [Deuteronomy].

Pharisees: Anglicization of the Hebrew Perushim, "separatists." Religious and political party of the Second Temple Period whose interpretations of the Jewish religious tradition emphasized a "liberal" approach and emphasis on teaching, prayer, ethical behavior, and legal norms. The forerunners of the Rabbis.

Philosophy: The intellectual and academic discipline concerned with such "ultimate questions" as good and evil, knowledge, aesthetics, etc.

Pintele Yid: [Yiddish] Literally, "point Jew." A term of compliment for the Jew who attempts to scrupulously observe all the myriad practices of the Jewish religious tradition.

Pirke Avot: [Hebrew] Literally, "Sayings of the Fathers." Ethical tractate of moral maxims of the Rabbis from the 3rd Century B.C.E. [Before the Common Era] to the 3rd Century C.E. included in the Talmud and studied by Jewish religious families on Sabbath afternoons.

Pogrom: [Russian] Literally, "destruction." Historically, in Russia, used to describe an attack, organized, abetted, and oft-times inspired by the authorities which pitted the serfs against the small Jewish enclaves in their midst. More often than not, the Jews witnessed the wanton slaughter and deaths of their own without any retribution whatsoever.

Predicate Theology: A rethinking and re-focusing of theological questions from the author or subject of an act to the act or object itself. For example, the question is not whether God is good, but what is the nature of goodness. [See, for example, Harold Schulweis, Evil and the Morality of God, Cincinnati: Hebrew Union College Press, 1984, as well as the essay by Peter J. Haas.]

Race: An anthropological term used to categorize the different biological divisions of humankind, based on specific characteristics, for example, skin pigmentation. Adapted by the Nazis to the plane of history.

Racism: Discrimination—and worse—against a given biological sub-population based on the above specific characteristics.

Reconstructionist Judaism: The newest Jewish religious movement based upon the philosophy of Rabbi Mordecai Kaplan's [1881-1984] major work Judaism as A Civilization, which called for a "reconstruction" of American Jewish life in all areas, with religious Judaism serving as the hub of a wheel which spokes radiated to all facets and aspects of Jewish living. Kaplan was a professor at the [Conservative] Jewish Theological Seminary of America and was influenced by the writings of American pragmatic philosopher John Dewey [1859-1952].

Reform Judaism: Perhaps the most "liberal" wing of the Jewish religious tradition. Having its start in Sessen, Germany, in 1810 as a movement for liturgical change, it has flowered in the United States and today numbers almost two million adherents. It is also the most welcoming of non-Jews and has pioneered in the area of interfaith dialogue.

Refusenik: [Russian/English] Literally, "one who has been refused." Term used to described those Jews who were refused permission to emigrate to either Israel or the United States by the previous Soviet Union.

Glossary

Resurrection: The belief, central to Christianity, thought originally brought to it from the Pharisees, that Jesus was resurrected three days after his death on the cross.

Revelation: The belief of Judaism, Christianity, and Islam that, out of God's love for humanity, he chooses to reveal himself to us: Though Moses, Sinai, and the prophets for Jews, through Jesus for Christians, and through Mahomet for Muslims. The Hebrew Scriptures, Christian Bible, and Qur'an are the setting down of those revealing moments.

Revisionism: The pseudo-scholarly, antisemitic attempt to "prove" that the Shoah never took place as it has been reported, that it is a "fiction" of the Zionist Jews, who continue to manipulate others, non-Jews, as well as the historical record to win support and allegiance for the beleaguered State of Israel.

Ritual Murder: Already at play in the Middle Ages, the utterly false notion that Jews periodically kidnap and murder Christian children to drain their blood for the making of the matzot [unleavened cakes] need for Passover. This libel has been a mainstay of the antisemites up to and including our own day.

SA: [German] Stormabteilung or "Storm Troopers." The original Nazi "goon squads," which later become eclipsed into the Gestapo [Geheime Statspolizei] or "Secret State Police." The Gestapo were the original persecutors of Jews and played a central role in their annihilation and extermination during the Shoah.

Sadducees: The conservative, priestly party of the Second Temple/Roman Period who wished to support and maintain that status quo of Judaism as a cultic religious community. Opposed to the Pharisees.

Salvation: The religious belief that the ultimate goal of faith is to be redeemed from death and/or everlasting hell and attain freedom, grace, and eternal afterlife in God's presence.

Sanhedrin: Hebrew word derived from Greek origin which identifies the Supreme Court of ancient Israel during the Roman period. Composed of 71 Rabbis, it has headed by a Presiding Judge and rendered both civil and religious decisions and solutions to complexities of the developing Jewish legal tradition. No longer extent in Jewish life after the 4th Century C.E.

Satan: The ultimate personification of evil in Christian religious tradition. Said to have originally been an angel in the heavenly court who found disfavor in God's eyes.

Scylla & Charybdis: Taken from Greek mythology and understood to have been two sea monsters who lured sailors and ships to their death and destruction. The idiom "between Scylla & Charybdis" is equivalent to "between a rock and a hard place" [i.e.

between two difficult choices, both of which have both positive and negative consequences].

Second Generation: The term now used to describe the children of Shoah survivors, children of severely-diminished families who are now adults themselves. Many of them continue to struggle with the Shoah, some psychologically, others religiously.

Sefirot: [Hebrew] Literally, "numbers." An essential term in Jewish Kabbalistic and mystical literature to denote the various emanations from God which ultimately become his attributes.

Sephardim: [Hebrew] Literally, "Spaniards." Since the onset of the Middle Ages, the term used by Jews to designate those Jews who trace their ancestry to Spain, Morocco, Italy, Egypt, Palestine, and Syria, as well as the Balkans, Greece, and Turkey.

Shearith Yisrael: [Hebrew] Literally, the "Saving Remnant of Israel." That community of Jews who survives the tragic destruction of large numbers of its own people, and because of its commitments, religious and other, rebuilds itself. After the Shoah, all contemporary Jewish communities throughout the world are "saving remnants."

Shechinah: [Hebrew] Literally, the "Presence." Term used to denote the "Indwelling Presence of God." That is, God's immanence, nearness, to humanity; approachable and reachable.

Shema Yisrael: [Hebrew] Literally, "Hear, Israel!" Taken from Devarim [Deuteronomy] 6:4, "Hear, Israel! Adonai is our God, Adonai alone," this sentence has become the Affirmation of God's Unity and is included in all Jewish worship services. It is as close as the Jewish religious tradition comes to a creedal formulation.

Shevirat Ha-Kelim: [Hebrew] Literally, the "breaking of the vessels." Term taken from Jewish Kabbalistic mystical literature to describe the human condition in its estrangement from God. These vessels which held the divine sparks or emanations have been shattered because of human error and can only be put back together through human commitment to God.

Shoah: [Hebrew] Literally, "Destruction, Devastation." The Hebrew, Biblical term now preferred more and more to describe the wanton murder and callous slaughter of almost six million Jewish men, women, and children during the years 1939 and 1945 by the Nazis and their assistants. A singularly unique event in the history of the Jewish People as well as all humankind.

Shofar: [Hebrew] Literally, "ram's horn." Reminder of the Bereshit [Genesis] story whereby Abraham sacrificed a ram rather than his son Isaac. Used in ancient Israel as both a military instrument and a call to gather the community. Associated today with

Glossary

the High Holy Days of Rosh Ha-Shanah [New Year] and Yom Kippur [Day of Atonement].

Shtetl: [Yiddish] Literally, "small town." Term used to denote the village where Jewish lived in Eastern Europe, primarily Russia and Poland.

Shulchan Aruch: [Hebrew] Literally, "Set/Prepared Table." The abstracted and organized Code of Jewish Laws taken from the Talmud and elsewhere, originally prepared and added to by Joseph Caro [1488-1575]. Together with the commentary of Moses Isserles [1525-1572], it has become authoritative in Orthodox Jewish religious life.

Shutafut: [Hebrew] Literally, "partnership." The classical rabbinic idea in Jewish religious life that God and humanity are co-partners in the very process of creation. God needs us every bit as much as we need God to bring about a world of which he would be proud.

Sitz im Leben: [German] Literally, "seat in life." Term used to denote one's "situation in life," that is, description of reality as it is, not as we would like it to be.

Social Darwinism: Philosophy popular in the 1920's in both America and Europe where Charles Darwin's twin emphasis on survival of the fittest and evolution of the species were adapted onto the plane of history. The Nazis perverted even this questionable understanding and saw all of history as a battleground between the Aryan, of whom they were its finest representatives, and the Jews, the most evil and lowest ordered among the species.

Socialism: Political philosophy whereby ownership, production, and distribution of goods are held by the collective rather than the individual.

Sonderkommando: [German] Literally, "special commando." Those Jews assigned the grisly task of removing the bodies from the various gas chambers and taking them either to the crematoria or for burial. Their own life expectancy was less than three months, after which they themselves were murdered to prevent witnesses.

SS: [German] Contraction of Schutzstaffeln, "Protection Squad." Originally organized as a body guard unit for the Fuhrer, it became one of the primary instruments under Heinrich Himmler's direction of the implementation of the Shoah.

Surplus Population: Term used in the writings of Helen Fein, Richard Rubenstein, and others to designate those groups "falling outside the universe of moral obligation," and, thus, liable for Shoah in the case of the Jews and genocide in the case of others.

Synoptic Gospels: Reference to the first three Gospel accounts of Jesus life and death—Matthew, Mark, and Luke—governed primarily by a similar point of view.

Talmud: [Hebrew] Literally, "Teaching." The encyclopedic collection of rabbinic literature following several centuries after the close of the Mishnah [the first compilation of Jewish laws completed around 200 C.E.] covering all aspects of Jewish life, based on both discussions in the various rabbinic academies as well as rendered legal decisions. There are both a Babylonian and Palestinian versions, the former ultimately becoming more authoritative in subsequent Jewish religious life.

Talmud Torah: [Hebrew] Literally, "study of the Torah." Term used to designate both the intensive Jewish religious study, especially the Talmud itself, as well as a unique educational system of schools set up for such a purpose.

Teaching of Contempt: Term first suggested by the late French Jewish historian Jules Isaac [1877-1963] to describe the anti-Jewish and antisemitic teachings of Christianity over the course of the centuries. Isaac believed, and rightly so, that such "teaching of contempt" was an indirect contributor to the Shoah which he himself experienced firsthand. His monumental work Jesus et Israel and Genese de l'antisemitisme were said to have influenced directly Pope John XXIII and led directly to the Vatican Declaration Nostre Aetate.

Teleology: The philosophical study of the final cause of things and events.

Teshuvah: [Hebrew] Literally, "return." The religious belief of Judaism that the sincere penitent who recognizes the error of his/her ways and returns to the path of Jewish life will be accepted by God with open heart and open arms. One finds such an expression in the classic statement, "The gates of repentance are always open."

Theodicy: The religious and philosophical position which attempts to reconcile the goodness of God with the existence of evil in the world.

Theology: The study of the nature of God, God's relationship with the world, and matters pertaining to both.

Theophany: A religious event characterized by the appearance of God to humanity. Jews speak of the theophany at Sinai, not necessarily indicating the physical appearance of God.

Tifutzah: [Hebrew] Literally, "dispersion." Parallel term for the Diaspora of Jews living throughout the world outside the Land of Israel. Term itself is value-neutral.

Tikkun Olam B'Malchut Shaddai: [Hebrew] Literally, "repairing the world beneath the sovereignty of God." The ethical ideal of Jewish life which impels social action and demands that Jews involve themselves in improving society wherever they find themselves.

Glossary

Torah She B'al Peh: [Hebrew] Literally, "Torah which is upon the mouth." The Oral Tradition of Rabbinic interpretation later set down in such primary texts as the Mishnah and Talmud. The so-called "Oral Tradition" continues to be authoritative today for Orthodox Jews, less so for Conservative, Reform, and Reconstructionist Jews.

Torah She B'michtav: [Hebrew] Literally, "Torah which is written down." The written text of the Hebrew Scriptures which begins with Bereshit and ends with Divre Hayamim Bet [II Chronicles].

Tosafot: [Hebrew] Literally, "addenda." The additional rabbinic commentaries on the Talmud compiled by the French Rabbis from the 12th to the 14th Centuries.

Totalitarianism: The political philosophy which has as its goal the complete domination of all aspects of the life of its citizens, usually under the leadership of a dictator, benevolent or otherwise.

Transcendence: The religious belief that God is above and beyond the realm of human approachability.

Tzaddik: [Hebrew] [Pl. Tzaddikim] Literally, "righteous or holy man." According to Jewish literary and mystical tradition, in each and every generation, the world is sustained by "thirty-six righteous men" [Hebrew: Lamed-Vav Tzaddikim] who, by virtue of their goodness and holiness, bring joy to God. They are, however, unknown to themselves as well as to the rest of humankind.

Unique: Singularly distinct. The issue with regard to the Shoah is whether or not this historical event is unique in both Jewish and world history, calling forth new and different responses, or "simply" another in a long list of antisemitic and genocidal world events not mandating significantly different responses.

Untermensch: [German] Literally, "underman." Term of opprobrium used to designate Jews, Poles, Gypsies, Slavs, and others, as "sub-human"—to be disposed of by the Nazis at will and to be enslaved as necessity dictated.

Volk: [German] Literally, "people." The almost mystical reverence shown by the Nazis for the "purely German person and people," the Aryan. The German term *blut und boden* ["blood and soil"] equally stresses this idea and its impact upon a generation of Germans willing to do Hitler's bidding.

Weltanschauung: [German] Literally, "worldview." A perspective on the human condition from one's own individual or collective viewpoint, taking into consideration political, economic, religious, and other factors.

Xenophobia: The psychological fear of the different. Said to be at the root of antisemitism in particular and all prejudice in general. Part of the psychological make-up of most human beings, though its conscious manifestation and translation into acts of hatred is a learned response.

Yad Vashem: [Hebrew] Literally, "a hand and a name." Refer-ence taken from the Biblical book of Yishayahu [Isaiah], Yad Vashem is the Israeli Shoah Memorial Authority created in 1953 to memorialize this tragedy of the Jewish People as well as to do significant archival gathering and research into these events.

Yahadut: [Hebrew] Literally, "Judaism." The Hebrew term for the religious expression of those committed to the belief in the One God of Israel.

Yeshiva: [Hebrew] [Pl. Yeshivot] A traditional Jewish parochial school whose primary curriculum consists of the study of the Talmud together with other rabbinic literatures.

Yiddish: A cognate, folk language of Hebrew, consisting of linguistic elements of Hebrew, French, Italian, German, and Slavic. Spoken primarily by those Jews coming from Eastern Europe [Poland and Russia] and their descendants. A significant literature also arose using Yiddish beginning in the late 18th and early 19th Centuries.

Yishuv: [Hebrew] Literally, "settlement." Term used to designate the Jewish community of Palestine prior to 1948 and Israel subsequent to it.

Yordeh: [Hebrew] [Pl. Yordim] Literally, "one who goes down, emigre." Term used to indicate that citizen of Israel who leaves Israel, settles somewhere else, and may or may not become a citizen of her/his adopted country.

Zikkaron: [Hebrew] Literally, "remembering." Its Greek equivalent is anamnesis. For Eugene Fisher, Volume II, both Judaism and Christianity are religions of remembering.

Zykon B: [German] The trade name of the actual crystalline gas pellets used in the gas chambers in the concentration and extermination camps. Upon contact with the air, Zykon B, a pesticide, becomes gaseous suffocating those in its immediate confined space. Death was said to take place within fifteen to forty-five minutes depending upon the size of the gas chamber.

Glossary

THE BOOKS OF THE TORAH
The Five Books of Moses

Bereshit	Genesis
Shemot	Exodus
Vayikra	Leviticus
Bamidbar	Deuteronomy

Nevi'im: The Prophets

Yehoshua	Joshua
Shofetim	Judges
Shmuel Alef	I Samuel
Shmuel Bet	II Samuel
Melachim Alef	I Kings
Melachim Bet	II Kings
Yishayahu	Isaiah
Yirmiyahu	Jeremiah
Yehezkel	Ezekiel

"The Twelve"

Hoshai'ah	Hosea
Yoel	Joel
Amos	Amos
Ovadiah	Obadiah
Yonah	Jonah
Micha	Micah
Nachum	Nahum
Havakkuk	Habakkuk
Tzfaniah	Zephaniah
Haggai	Haggai
Zechariah	Zechariah
Malachi	Malachi

The Holocaust Now

Ketuvim: The Writings

Tehillim	Psalms
Mishlei	Proverbs
Iyov	Job
Shir Ha-Shirim	Song of Songs/Canticles
Rut	Ruth
Aicha	Lamentations
Kohelet	Ecclesiastes
Esther	Esther
Daniel	Daniel
Ezra	Ezra
Nehemiah	Nehemiah
Divrei Ha-Yamim Alef	I Chronicles
Divrei Ha-Yamim BetI	I Chronicles

THE JEWISH HOLIDAYS

Biblical—Major

Shabbat	Sabbath
Pesach	Passover
Sefirat Ha-Omer	Counting of the Omer
Shavuot	Weeks
Rosh Ha-Shanah	New Year
Yom Kippur	Day of Atonement
Sukkot	Booths
Shemini Atzeret	8th Day of Solemn Assembly
Rosh Hodesh	New Moon

Biblical—Minor

Hanukkah	Festival of Dedication
Purim	Festival of Esther/Lots

518

Glossary

Rabbinic

Lag B'Omer	33rd Day of the Omer
Tisha B'Av	9th Day of Av/Collective Day of Mourning
Simchat Torah	Celebration of the Torah
Tu B'Shevat	15th Day of Shevat/Jewish Arbor Day

Contemporary

Yom Ha-Shoah	Shoah Remembrance Day
Yom Ha-Atzmaut	Israeli Independence Day

THE MONTHS OF THE JEWISH CALENDAR

Tishri	September-October
Heshvan	October-November
Kislev	November-December
Tevet	December-January
Shevat	January-February
Adar [& Adar Bet/II]	February-March
Nisan	March-April
Iyar	April-May
Sivan	May-June
Tammuz	June-July
Av	July-August
Elul	August-September

The Holocaust Now

BIBLIOGRAPHY

Abrahamson, Irving, Editor, Against Silence: The Voice and Vision of Elie Wiesel [New York: Holocaust Library, 1985].

Arendt, Hannah, A Report on the Banality of Evil: Eichmann in Jerusalem [New York: Penguin Books, 1963].

Arendt, Hannah, *The Origins of Totalitarianism* [New York: Harcourt, Brace and World, 1966].

Aronson, Ronald, *The Dialectics of Disaster* [London: Verso, 1983].

Ateek, Naim, *Justice and Only Justice: A Palestinian Theology of Liberation* [Maryknoll: Orbis Books, 1989].

Barth, Karl, *The German Church Conflict* [London: Lutterworth Press, 1965].

Barth, Karl, *Church Dogmatics* [Edinburgh: T. & T. Clark, 1961].

Bekker, J. Christaan, *Suffering and Hope* [Philadelphia: Fortress Press, 1987].

Bonhoeffer, Dietrich, *The Cost of Discipleship* [New York: Macmillan Publishing Company, 1974].

Berenbaum, Michael, *The Vision of the Void* [Middletown: Wesleyan University Press, 1979].

Berger, Alan L., *Crisis and Covenant: The Holocaust in American Jewish Fiction* [Albany: State University of New York Press, 1985].

Berkowits, Eliezer, *Faith After Auschwitz* [New York: Ktav Publishing House, 1973].

The Holocaust Now

Bettleheim, Bruno, *The Informed Heart* [Glencoe: The Free Press, 1960].

Birnbaum, Norman and Gertrude Lenzer, Editors, *Sociology and Religion* [Englewood Cliffs: Prentice Hall, 1969].

Brenner, Reeve Robert, *The Faith and Doubt of Holocaust Survivors* [New York: The Free Press, 1980].

Buber, Martin, *Eclipse of God: Studies in the Relation between Religion and Philosophy* [New York: Harper & Row, 1952].

Cargas, Harry James, Editor, *Responses to Elie Wiesel: Critical Essays by Major Jewish and Christian Scholars* [New York: Persea Books, 1978].

Cargas, Harry James, *Harry James Cargas in Conversation with Elie Wiesel* [New York: Paulist Press, 1976].

Charny, Israel, Editor, *Toward the Understanding and Prevention of Genocide* [Boulder: Westview Press, 1984].

Chazan, Robert and Marc Lee Raphael, Editors, *Modern Jewish History: A Source Reader* [New York: Schocken Books, 1969].

Cochrane, Arthur C., *The Church's Confession Under Hitler* [Philadelphia: Westminster Press, 1962].

Cohen, Arthur, *The Tremendum: A Theological Interpretation of the Holocaust* [New York: Crossroad Publishing Company, 1981].

Conway, J. S., *The Persecution of the Churches, 1933-1945* [New York: Basic Books, 1968].

Davies, Alan T., Editor, *Antisemitism and the Foundations of Christianity* [New York: Paulist Press, 1979].

Dawidowicz, Lucy S., *The War Against the Jews, 1933-1945* [New York: Holt, Rinehart and Winston, 1975].

Des Pres, Terrence, *The Survivor: An Anatomy of Life in the Death Camps* [New York: Oxford University Press, 1976].

Bibliography

Diller, Jerry, Editor, *Ancient Roots and Modern Meanings* [New York: Bloch Publishing Company, 1978].

Donat, Alexandre, *The Holocaust Kingdom* [New York: Holt Rinehart and Winston, 1965].

Ecclestone, Alan, *Night Sky of the Lord* [New York: Schocken Books, 1980].

Eckardt, Alice and A. Roy, *Jews and Christians: The Contemporary Meaning* [Bloomington: Indiana University Press, 1976].

Eckardt, Alice and A. Roy, *Long Night's Journey into Day: Life and Faith After the Holocaust* [Detroit: Wayne State University Press, 1982].

Eckardt, A. Roy, *Elder and Younger Brothers: The Encounter of Jews and Christians* [New York: Charles Scribner's Sons, 1967].

Ellis, Marc H. *Beyond Innocence and Redemption: Confronting the Holocaust and Israeli Power* [San Francisco: Harper & Row, 1990].

Ellis, Marc H., *Toward a Jewish Theology of Liberation* [Maryknoll: Orbis Books, 1987].

Ellul, Jacques, *Prayer and Modern Man* [New York: Seabury Press, 1970].

Ericksen, Robert P., *Theologians Under Hitler* [New Haven: Yale University Press, 1985].

Estess, Ted L., *Elie Wiesel* [New York: Frederick Ungar Publishing Company, 1980].

Fackenheim, Emil L., *Encounters Between Judaism and Modern Philosophy: A Preface to Future Jewish Thought* [New York: Schocken Books, 1973].

Fackenheim, Emil L., *From Bergen Belsen to Jerusalem: Contemporary Implications of the Holocaust* [Jerusalem: Hebrew University Institute of Contemporary Jewry, 1975].

Fackenheim, Emil L. *God's Presence in History* [New York: New York University Press, 1970].

Fackenheim, Emil L., *The Human Condition After Auschwitz* [Syracuse: Syracuse University Press, 1971].

The Holocaust Now

Fackenheim, Emil L., *The Jewish Return into History: Reflections in the Age of Auschwitz and a New Jerusalem* [New York: Schocken Books, 1978].

Fackenheim, Emil L., *Quest for Past and Future*[Bloomington: Indiana University Press, 1968].

Fackenheim, Emil L., *The Religious Dimension in Hegel's Thought* [Chicago: University of Chicago Press, 1967].

Fackenheim, Emil L., *To Mend the World: Foundations of Future Jewish Thought* [New York: Schocken Books, 1982].

Fackenheim, Emil L., *What is Judaism? An Intepretation for the Present Age* [New York: Summit Books, 1987].

Fein, Helen, *Accounting for Genocide: National Responses and Jewish Victimization During the Holocaust* [Chicago: University of Chicago Press, 1979].

Feuerlicht, Robert Strauss, *The Fate of the Jews: People Torn Between Israeli Power and Jewish Ethics* [New York: Times Books, 1983].

Fine, Ellen S., *Legacy of Night: The Literary University of Elie Wiesel* [Albany: State University of New York Press, 1982].

Fisher, Eugene, *Faith Without Prejudice: Rebuilding Christian Attitudes* [New York: Paulist Press, 1977].

Flannery, Edward M., *The Anguish of the Jews: A Catholic Priest Writes of Twenty-three Centuries of Anti-Semitism* [New York: Macmillan Publishing Company, 1964].

Fleischner, Eva, Editor, *Auschwitz: Beginning of a New Era? Reflections on the Holocaust* [New York: Ktav Publishing House, 1977].

Flinker, Moshe, *Young Moshe's Diary* [Jerusalem: Yad Vashem, 1976].

Friedlander, Albert, Editor, *Out of the Whirlwind* [New York: Schocken Books, 1976].

Friedlander, Henry and Sybil Milton, Editors, *The Holocaust: Ideology, Bureaucracy, and*

Bibliography

Genocide [Millwood: Kraus International Publications, 1980].

Friedman, Georges, *The End of the Jewish People?* [Garden City: Doubleday and Company, 1967. Translated by Eric Mossbacher.]

Friedman, Maurice, *Abraham Joshua Heschel and Elie Wiesel: You Are My Witnesses* [New York: Farrar, Straus and Giroux, 1987].

Furet, Francois, Editor, *Unanswered Questions: Nazi Germany and the Genocide of the Jews* [New York: Schocken Books, 1989].

Garber, Zev, Alan L. Berger, and Richard Libowitz, Editors, *Methodology in the Academic Teaching of the Holocaust* [Lanham: University Press of America, 1989].

Gollwitzer, Helmut, Editor, *Dying We Live: The Final Messages of the Resistance* [New York: Pantheon Books, 1956].

Grobman, Alex and Daniel Landes, Editors, *Genocide: Critical Issues of the Holocaust* [Chappaqua: Rossel Books, 1983].

Guardini, Romano, *Power and Responsibility* [Chicago: Henry Regnery, 1961].

Haas, Peter, *Morality After Auschwitz* [Philadelphia: Fortress Press, 1988].

Halasz, Nicolas, *Captain Dreyfus: The Story of a Mass Hysteria* [New York: Simon and Schuster, 1957].

Hancock, Ian, *The Pariah Syndrome* [Ann Arbor: Karoma Publishers, 1987].

Harkabi, Yehoshafat, *The Bar Kochba Syndrome* [Chappaqua: Rossel Books, 1983].

Hartman, David, *A Living Covenant: The Innovative Spirit in Traditional Judaism* [New York: The Free Press, 1985].

Heer, Fredrich, *God's First Love* [New York: Weybright and Talley, 1970].

Herberg, Will, *Judaism and Modern Man: An Interpretation of the Jewish Religion* [New York: Macmillan Publishing Company, 1959].

Hertzberg, Arthur, Editor, *The Zionist Idea* [Philadelphia: The Jewish Publication Society of America, 1959].

Heywood, Carter, *The Redemption of God* [Washington, DC: University Press of America, 1982].

Hick, John, *Evil and the God of Love* [New York: Harper and Row, 1966].

Hilberg, Raul, *The Destruction of the European Jews* [Chicago & New York: Quadrangle and Holmes & Meier, 1961 1985].

Hillesum, Etty, *An Interrupted Life: The Diaries of Etty Hillesum* [New York: Pocket Books, 1985. Edited by J. G. Gaarlandt and translated by Jonathan Cape.]

Hughes, Robert, *The Fatal Shore: The Epic of Australia's Founding* [New York: Alfred A. Knopf, 1987].

Isaac, Jules, *Jesus and Israel* [New York: Holt, Rinehart and Winston, 1971].

Jacobs, Steven L., Editor, *Contemporary Christian Religious Respones to the Shoah* [Lanham: University Press of America, 1994].

Jacobs, Steven L., Editor, *Contemporary Jewish Religious Responses to the Shoah* [Lanham: University Press of America, 1994].

Jacobs, Steven L., *Rethinking Jewish Faith: The Child of A Survivor Responds* [Albany: State University of New York Press, 1995].

Katz, Jacob, *Exclusiveness and Tolerance* [New York: Behrman House, 1983].

Katz, Steven, *Post-Holocaust Dialogues: Critical Studies in Modern Jewish Thought* [New York: New York University Press, 1983].

Klein, Charlotte, *Anti-Judaism in Christian Theology* [Philadelphia: Fortress Press, 1978].

Kuhn, Thomas, *The Structure of Scientific Revolutions* [Chicago: University of Chicago Press, 1962].

Langer, Lawrence, *The Holocaust and the Literary Imagination* [New Haven: Yale University Press, 1975].

Bibliography

Levi, Primo, *Survival in Auschwitz: The Nazi Assault on Humanity* [New York: Collier Books, 1976].

Levin, Nora, *The Holocaust* [New York: Schocken Books, 1973].

Littell, Franklin H., *The Crucifixion of the Jews: The Failure of Christians to Understand the Jewish Experience* [New York: Harper & Row, 1975].

Littell, Franklin H. and Hubert G. Locke, Editors, *The German Church Struggle and the Holocaust* [Detroit: Wayne State University Press, 1974].

Littell, Franklin H., Irene G. Shur, and Claude Foster, Jr., Editors, *The Holocaust: In Answer....* [West Chester: Sylvan Publishers, 1988].

Lukas, Richard S., *Forgotten Holocaust: The Poles Under German Occupation* [Lexington: University of Kentucky Press, 1986].

Macaulay, J. and L. Berkowitz, *Altruism and Human Behavior* [New York: Doubleday and Company, 1975].

MacIntyre, Alasdair, *After Virtue* [Notre Dame: University of Notre Dame Press, 1984. Second Edition.].

Marrus, Michael. *The Holocaust in History* [Hanover: University Press of New England, 1987].

Marrus, Michael and Robert O. Paxton, *Vichy France and the Jews* [New York: Basic Books, 1981].

Maybaum, Ignaz, *The Face of God After Auschwitz* [Amsterdam: Polak & Van Gennep, Ltd., 1965].

McGarry, Michael B., *Christology After Auschwitz* [New York: Paulist Press, 1977].

Milgram, Stanley, *Obedience to Authority: An Experimental View* [New York: Harper and Row, 1969].

Morais, Vamberto, *A Short History of Anti-Semitism* [New York: W. W. Norton and Company, 1976].

Morgan, Michael, Editor, *The Jewish Thought of Emil Fackenheim: A Reader* [Detroit: Wayne State University Press, 1987].

Morley, John F., *Vatican Diplomacy and the Jews during the Holocaust, 1939-1943* [New York: Ktav Publishing House, 1980].

Mosse, George L., *Toward the Final Solution: A History of Racism* [New York: Howard Fertig, 1976].

Neher, Andre, *The Exile of the Word: From the Silence of the Bible to the Silence of Auschwitz* [Philadelphia: The Jewish Publication of America, 1981. Translated by David Maisel.]

Nelson, Benjamin, *The Idea of Usury: From Tribal Brotherhood to Universal Otherhood* [Chicago: University of Chicago Press, 1969. Second Edition.]

Niebuhr, Reinhold, *The Nature and Destiny of Man: A Christian Interpretation* [New York: Charles Scribner's Sons, 1941].

Pauck, Wilhelm and Marion. *Paul Tillich: His Life and Thought* [New York: Harper & Row, 1976].

Pawlikowski, John T., *Jesus and the Theology of Israel* [Wilmington: Michael Glazier, 1989].

Peck, Abraham, Editor, *Jews and Christians After the Holocaust* [Philadelphia: Fortress Press, 1982].

Pisar, Samuel, *Of Blood and Hope* [Boston: Little, Brown and Company, 1979].

Plant, Richard, *The Pink Triangle: The Nazi War Against Homosexuals* [New York: Henry Holt, 1986].

Po-Hsia, R., *The Myth of Ritual Murder: Jews and Magic in Reformation Germany* [New Haven: Yale University Press, 1988].

Rausch, David A., *A Legacy of Hatred: Why Christians Must Not Forget the Holocaust* [Chicago: Moody Press, 1984].

Bibliography

Rector, Frank, *The Nazi Extermination of Homosexuals* [New York: Stein and Day, 1981].

Remembering for the Future: The Impact of the Holocaust on the Contemporary World [Oxford: Pergamon Press, 1988].

Rivkin, Ellis, What Crucified Jesus? [Nashville: Abingdon Press, 1984].

Rosenbaum, Irving, *Holocaust and Halakhah* [New York: Ktav Publishing House, 1976].

Rosenberg, Alan and Gerald E. Myers, Editors, *Echoes from the Holocaust: Philosophical Reflections on a Dark Time* [Philadelphia: Temple University Press, 1988].

Rosenfeld, Alvina and Irving Greenberg, Editors, *Confronting the Holocaust: The Work of Elie Wiesel* [Bloomington: Indiana University Press, 1980].

Ross, Robert W., *So It Was True: The American Protestant Press and the Nazi Persecution of the Jews* [Minneapolis: University of Minnesota Press, 1980].

Roth, John K., *A Consuming Fire: Encounters with Elie Wiesel and the Holocaust* [Atlanta: John Knox Press, 1979].

Roth, John K. And Michael Berenbaum, Editors, *The Holocaust: Religious and Philosophical Implications* [New York: Paragon Hosue Publishers, 1989].

Rubenstein, Richard L., *After Auschwitz: Radical Theology and Contemporary Judaism* [Indianapolis: Bobbs-Merrill, 1966].

Rubenstein, Richard L., *The Age of Triage: Fear and Hope in an Overcrowded World* [Boston: Beacon Press, 1983].

Rubenstein, Richard L., *The Cunning of History: Mass Death and the American Future* [New York: Harper & Row, 1975].

Rubenstein, Richard L., *My Brother Paul* [New York: Harper & Row, 1972].

Rubenstein, Ricahrd L., Editor, *Spirit Matters: The Worldwide Impact of Religion in Contemporary Politics* [New York: Paragon House Publishers, 1987].

The Holocaust Now

Rubenstein, Richard L. and John K. Roth, *Approaches to Auschwitz: The Legacy of the Holocaust* [Atlanta: John Knox Press, 1987].

Ruether, Rosemary Radford, *Faith and Fratricide: The Theological Roots of Anti-Semitism* [New York: The Seabury Press, 1974].

Ruether, Rosemary Radford and Marc H. Ellis, Editors, *Beyond Occupation: American Jewish, Christian, and Palestinian Voices for Peace* [Boston: Beacon Press, 1990].

Ruether, Rosemary Radford and Herman J. Ruether, *The Wrath of Jonah: The Crisis of Religious Nationalism in the Israeli-Palestinian Conflict* [San Francisco: Harper & Row, 1989].

Scholem, Gershom, *The Messianic Idea in Judaism and Other Essays on Jewish Spirituality* [New York: Schocken Books, 1971].

Scholem, Gershom, *Sabbatai Sevi: The Mystical Messiah* [Princeton: Princeton University Press, 1973].

Schulweis, Harold, *Evil and the Morality of God* [Cincinnati: Hebrew Union College Press, 1984].

Schussler-Fiorenza and David Tracy, Editors, *The Holocaust as Interruption* [Edinburg: T. & T. Clark, 1984].

Sheehan, Bernard W., *Seeds of Extinction: Jeffersonian Philanthropy and the American Indian* [Chapel Hill: University of North Carolina Press, 1973].

Shorris, Earl, *Jews Without Mercy: A Lament* [Garden City: Doubleday & Company, 1982].

Spiegel, Shalom, *The Last Trial* [Philadelphia: The Jewish Publication Society of America, 1967].

Stern, Ellen Norman, *Elie Wiesel: Witness for Life* [New York: Ktav Publishing House, 1982].

Tal, Uriel, *Christians and Jews in Germany: Religion, Politics, and Ideology in the Second Reich, 1870-1914* [Ithaca: Cornell University Press, 1975].

Bibliography

Tillich, Paul, *The Socialist Decision* [New York: Harper & Row, 1977].

Tillich, Paul, *The Interpretation of History* [New York: Charles Scribner's Sons, 1936].

Trunk, Isaiah, *Judenrat: The Jewish Councils in Eastern Europe Under Nazi Occupation* [New York: Stein and Day, 1977].

van Buren, Paul, *A Christian Theology of the People Israel* [New York: Harper & Row, 1983

van Buren, Paul, *Christ in Context* [New York: Harper & Row,1988].

van Buren, Paul, *Discerning the Way* [New York: Harper & Row, 1980].

Waite, Robert G. L., *The Psychopathic God: Adolf Hitler* [New York: New American Library, 1978].

Wallimann, Isidor and Michal N. Dobkowski, Editors, *Genocide and the Modern Age: Etiology and Case Studies of Mass Death* [New York: Greenwood Press, 1987].

Waskow, Arthur, *Before There Was a Before* [New York: Adama Books, 1984].

Waskow, Arthur, *Godwrestling* [New York: Schocken Books, 1978].

Waskow, Arthur, Co-Author, *The Shalom Seders* [New York: Adama Books, 1984].

Waskow, Arthur, *Seasons of Our Joy* [New York: Bantam Books, 1982].

Waskow, Arthur, *These Holy Sparks: The Rebirth of the Jewish People* [New York: Harper & Row, 1983].

Weinreich, Max, *Hitler's Professors* [New York: YIVO, 1966].

Wells, Leon, *Who Speaks for the Vanquished? American Judaism and the Holocaust* [New York: Peter Lang, 1987].

Wiesel, Elie, *Ani Ma'amin: A Song Lost and Found Again* [New York: Random House, 1973].

Wiesel, Elie, *The Gates of the Forest* [New York: Avon Books, 1966].

The Holocaust Now

Wiesel, Elie, *A Jew Today* [New York: Random House, 1978].

Wiesel, Elie, *Legends of Our Time* [New York: Avon Books, 1968].

Wiesel, Elie, *Messengers of God: Biblical Portraits and Legends* [New York: Random House, 1976].

Elie Wiesel, *Night* [New York: Bantam Books, 1960].

Elie Wiesel, *The Oath* [New York: Random House, 1973].

Elie Wiesel, *One Generation After* [New York: Avon Books, 1972].

Elie Wiesel, *Somewhere a Master* [New York: Summit Books, 1982].

Elie Wiesel, *Souls on Fire* [New York: Vintage Books, 1973].

Elie Wiesel, *The Testament* [New York: Summit Books, 1981].

Elie Wiesel, *The Town Beyond the Wall* [New York: Avon Books, 1970].

Elie Wiesel, *The Trial of God* [New York: Random House, 1978].

Elie Wiesel, *Twilight* [New York: Summit Books, 1988].

Woodham-Smith, Cecil, *The Great Hunger: Ireland, 1845-1849* [New York: E. P. Dutton, 1980].

Wyman, David, *The Abandonment of the Jews: American and the Holocaust, 1941-1945* [New York: Pantheon Books, 1984].

Wytwycky, Bohdan, *The Other Holocaust: Many Circles of Hell* [Washington, DC: The Novak Report, 1980].

Yehoshua, A. B., *Between Right and Right: Israel, Problem or Solution?* [Garden City: Doubleday and Company, 1981. Translated by Arnold Schwartz.]

Zehrnt, Heinz, *The Question of God: Protestant Theology in the Twentieth Century* [New

Bibliography

York: Harcourt, Brace and World, 1966].

Zenner, Walter P., *Middleman Minority Theories and the Jews: An Historical Assessment* [New York: YIVO, 1978].

Zimmels, H., *The Echo of the Nazi Holocaust in Rabbinic Literature* [New York: Ktav Publishing House, 1977].

The Holocaust Now

ABOUT THE CONTRIBUTORS

ALAN L. BERGER: Alan L. Berger occupies the Raddock Eminent Scholar Chair of Holocaust Studies and directs the Jewish Studies Program at Florida Atlantic University, Boca Raton, FL. Prior to his current position, he chaired the Jewish Studies Program and taught in the Department of Religious Studies at Syracuse University. In 1988-1989, he was the Visiting Gumenick Professor of Judaica at the College of William and Mary. He has lectured onthe Shoah in Oxford, in Israel at Yad Vashem, in Paris, and throughout America. His articles deal mainly with literature, pedagogy, and the theory of post-Auschwitz Jewish thought. Among his books are Crisis and Covenant: The Holocaust in American Jewish Fiction and Methodology in the Academic Teaching of the Holocaust [Associate Editor].

MICHAEL BEREBAUM: Michael Berenbaum is the Project Director of the United States Holocaust Memorial Museum,Director of its Research Institute, and the Hymen Goldman Adjunct Associate Professor of Theology at Georgetown University, Washington, DC. In the past he has served as Director of the Jewish Community Council of Greater Washington, Editor of The Washington Jewish Week, and Deputy Director of the President's Commission on the Holocaust, where he authored its Report to the President. The author of more than six books, more than 100 scholarly articles, and hundreds of journalistic pieces, his writings include The Vision of the Void; After Tragedy and Triumph: Essays in Modern Jewish Thought and the American Experience; A Mosaic of Victims: Non-Jews Persecuted and Murdered by the Nazis; and, together with John Roth, The Holocaust: Religious and Philosophical Implications.

RAHEL FELDHAY BRENNER: Rahel Feldhay Brenner is Associate Professor at the University of Wisconsin-Madison. She received her B.A. from Hebrew University and her M.A. from Tl Aviv University. Her Ph.D. is from York University, Toronto. She has publsihed numerous articles on the literary responses to the Shoah in Jewish Jewish literature and israeli fiction. Her published books are on the Canadian Jewish authors Mordecai Richler and A.M. Klein. Her forthcoming book, Writing as Resistance: Four Women Confronting the Holocaust, will be published in the Spring of 1997 by Penn

The Holocaust Now

State University Press.

HARRY JAMES CARGAS: Harry James Cargas recently retired as Professor of Literature and Language and of Religion at Webster University, St. Lous, MO. He is the author of more than twenty-four books, including five on the Shoah. Among them are Harry James Cargas in Conversation with Elie Wiesel; A Christian Response to the Holocaust; and Reflections of a Post-Auschwitz Christian. He serves on numerous boards, including the Catholic Institute for Holocaust Studies, the Anne Institute, the Simon Wisenthal Center, and is the only Catholic ever appointed to the International Advisory Board at Yad Vashem in Jerusalem. He also serves on the Executive Council, International Philosophers for the Prevention of Nuclear Omnicide, on the Advisory Board of the Institute for Ultimate Reality and Meaning, and is the Executive Secretary of Canine Assistance for the Disabled.

ALAN DAVIES: Alan Davies is a member of the Department of Religious Studies, Victoria College, University of Toronto. He is the author of Anti-Semitism and the Christian Mind [1969]; Infected Christianity: A Study of Modern Racism [1988]; and the Editor of Antisemitism and the Foundations of Christianity [1979]. Currently, he is editing a volume on antisemitism in Canada.

ALICE L. ECKARDT: Alice Lyons Eckardt was Maxwell Fellow in Holocaust Studies at the Oxford Centre for Postgraduate Hebrew Studies, 1989-1990, and is Professor Emerita of Religious Studies, Lehigh University, Bethlehem, PA. Her books include Long Night's Journey into Day: A Revised Retrospective on the Holocaust [1988, with A. Roy Eckardt]; and Jerusalem: City of the Ages [1987]. She served on the Executive Committee of the international conference "Remembering the Future," held at Oxford and London in July, 1988; on the Editorial Advisory Board of the three volumes of papers from that conference published by Pergamon Press [1989]. She is a member and past Chairperson of the Christian Study Group on Judaism and the Jewish People; the Executive Editorial Review Board of Holocaust and Genocide Studies; the Editorial Board of the Holocaust Library; the Board of Directors of the Anne Frank Institute of Philadelphia, PA.; and the National Advisory Board of the Foundation to Sustain Righteous Gentiles.

MARC ELLIS: Marc H. Ellis received his B.A. and M.A. degrees from Florida State University, where he studied with the eminent Shoah theologian Richard Rubenstein, and his Ph.D. from Marquette University in Contemporary Religious Thought. He has written more than five books, including Towards a Jewish Theology of Liberation [1987]; and Beyond Innocence and Redemption: Confronting the Holocaust and Israeli Power [1990]. He has lectured extensively in North America, Europe, Africa, Asia, Latin

Contributors

America, and the Middle East. Currently he is Professor of Religion, Culture, and Society Studies at Maryknoll School of Theology.

EMIL L. FACKENHEIM: Emil L. Fackenheim was born in Halle, Germany, in 1916, and studied at the Liberal Seminary in Berlin before World War II. He received his ordination in the year following his release from Sachsenhausen concentration camp. Emigrating first to Scotland and then to Canada, he received his Ph.D. in philosophy and was a member of the Philosophy Department of the University of Toronto where he served until his retirement in 1983 as a University Professor. He is the author of many distinguished books including The Religious Dimensions of Hegel's Thought [1967]; Quest for Past and Future: Essays in Jewish Theology [1968]; God's Presence in History: Jewish Affirmations and Philosophical Reflections [1970]; Encounters between Jewish and Modern Philosophy: A Preface to Future Jewish Thought [1973]; The Jewish Return into History: Reflections in the Age of Auschwitz and a New Jerusalem [1978]; To Mend the World: Foundations of Future Jewish Thought [1982]; What is Judaism? An Interpretation for the Present Age [1987]; and The Jewish Bible after the Holocaust: A Re-Reading [1990]. He now lives in Israel with his family and is a Fellow of the Institute of Contemporary Jewry at Hebrew University in Jerusalem.

EUGENE J. FISHER: Dr. Eugene J. Fisher is the Executive Secretary for Catholic-Jewish Relations of the National Conference of Catholic Bishops [NCCB] and Consultor to the Vatican Commission for Religious Relatins with the Jews, the only American on the Commission. He received his Ph.D. from New York University in Hebrew Culture and Education, where his dissertation was entitled, "The Treatment of Jews and Judaism in Current Roman Catholic Teaching." He is the author or editor of several books, including Faith Without Prejudice: Rebuilding Christian Attitudes Toward Judaism [1977]; The Formation of Social Policy in the Catholic and Jewish Traditions and Liturgical Foundations of Social Policy in the Catholic and Jewish Traditions [1980 and 1983; co-edited with Rabbi Daniel Polish]; Homework for Christians Preparing for Christian-Jewish Dialogue [1982]; and Seminary Education and Catholic-Jewish Relations [1983]. His memberships include the Catholic Bible Association; the National Association of Professors of Hebrew; the Society of Biblical Literature; and the National Conference of Christians and Jews.

ZEV GARBER: Zev Garber is Professor and Chair of Jewish Studies at Los Angeles Valley College, and taught as Visiting Professor in the Religious Studies at the University of California at Riverside. He has written extensively in the fields of Judaism and Shoah, and is the Editor-in-Chief of Studies in the Shoah. His Shoah: The Paradigmatic Genocide [1994] has been published in the series. Among his edited publications are

Methodology in the Academic Teaching of Judaism [1986]; Methodology in the Academic Teaching of the Holocaust [1988]; Teaching Hebrew Language and Literature at the College Level [1991]; Perspectives on Zionism [1994]; and Consulting Editor to What Kind of God? Essays in Honor of Richard L. Rubenstein [1995]. He is the new Associate Editor of Shofar, and has served as President of the National Association of Professors of Hebrew.

IRVING GREENBERG: Rabbi Irving Greenberg is President of the National Jewish Center for Learning and Leadership [CLAL]. He has served as Professor and Chair of the Department of Jewish Studies at the City College of New York, and Rabbi of the Riverdale Jewish Center. He has explored the religious and ethical implications of the Shoah and the rebirth of Israel in a series of essays and monographs including "Cloud of Smoke, Pillar of Fire: [1977]; "Judaism, Christianity, and Modernity After the Holocaust" [1976]; "The Third Great Cycle in Jewish History" [1981]; and "Voluntary Covenant" included here. He is the author of The Jewish Way [1988], an interpretation of the relationship of the Jewish religion and Jewish history.

PETER J. HAAS: Peter J. Haas, the son of Shoah survivors, teaches Judaism and ethics in the Religious Studies Department at Vanderbilt University, Nashville, TN. After receiving rabbinic ordination from the Hebrew Union College-Jewish Institute of Religion, Cincinnati, OH, in 1974, he served as a United States Army Chaplain for three years, going on to earn his Ph.D. in Jewish Studies from Brown University in 1980. He has published several books and articles in early rabbinic legal and moral discourse. His most recent book Morality After Auschwitz: The Radical Challenge of the Nazi Ethic examines how the Shoah affects our understanding of ethical discourse in the modern world.

DOUGLAS K. HUNEKE: Douglas K. Huneke, D.D., is the Pastor of Westminster Presbyterian Church, Tiburon, CA. He served for eight years as the Presbyterian University Pastor at the University of Oregon, Eugene, OR. For five years he was a member of the Honors College faculty at that university. In 1976-1977, he was granted a sabbatical leave to study and write on the implications of the Shoah and on the life and writings of Elie Wiesel. He spent a major portion of his leave at the former extermination camps in Poland and East Germany, and studied at Yad Vashem in Jerusalem. He is Visiting Lecturer at San Francisco Theological Seminary. In 1980, he was awarded a Faculty Research Grant by the Oregon Committee for the Humanities [NEH] to research the moral and spiritual development of Christians who rescued Jews and other endangered persons during the Nazi era. In 1981, he was awarded an additional grant from the Memorial Foundation for Jewish Culture to continue gathering the accounts of res-

Contributors

cuers. He is the author of The Moses of Rovno, the biography of the German Nazi-era rescuer Herman Graebe [1986].

THOMAS A. IDINOPULOS: Thomas A. Idinopulos, Ph.D. University of Chicago, is Professor of Religious Studies at Miami University, Oxford, OH, writing and teaching on the politics and religion of Jewish, Christian, and Muslim communities of the Middle East. He also serves as Consulting Editor to the Middle East Review, and is the author of The Erosion of Faith: An Inquiry into the Origins of the Contemporary Crisis in Religious Thought [1971]; and Co-Editor of Mysticism, Nihilism, Feminism: New Critical Essays in the Theology of Simone Weil [1984]. In 1986, he received the Associated Church Press Excellence Award for his writing in The Christian Century, and, in 1988, in recognition of his work in Israel, was nominated as a Fellow to the Patriarchal Institute for Patristic Studies, Vlatadon Monastery, Thessaloniki, Greece.

BERNARD MAZA: Bernard Maza received his rabbinic ordination at Mesivta Tiferet Jerusalem from the famous Rosh Yeshiva Moshe Feinstein, of blessed memory. He also recieved his M.A. degree from Brooklyn College. He is today the Dean of Bais Midrash REM, and the Rabbi of Congregation Emunah Shleima in Kew Gardens, NY. Rabbi Maza is the author of two books of Talmudic commentary; a two-volume work of Biblical commentary entitled Insights into the Sedra of the Week; and a book on the Shoah entitled With Fury Poured Out: A Torah Perspective on the Holocaust [1986], the sequel to which Holocaust Messengers to Mankind is in publication.

MICHAEL MCGARY: Revered Michael McGary, C.S.P., has served as the Rector of the Paulist Father's Seminary in Washington, DC, and serves today in Berkeley, CA. He writes frequently on Jewish-Christian relations, theology after the Shoah, and the meaning of the Shoah for Christians today. He is the author of Christology After Auschwitz. Father McGarry serves on the Advisory Committee to the Secretariat for Catholic-Jewish Relations of the National Conference of Catholic Bishops, and is host of the nationally syndicated program "Religious Book World."

JOHN T. PAWLIKOWSKI: John T. Pawlikowski, O.S.M., a Servite priest, is Professor of Social Ethics at the Catholic Theological Union in Chicago, a constituent of the cluster of theological schools at the University of Chicago. He was appointed a member of the United States Holocaust Memorial Council by then President Jimmy Carter in 1980, a position he still holds. He has authored numerous books and articles on Christian-Jewish relations, the Shoah, and social ethics, including The Challenge of the Holocaust for Christian Theology [1982]; and Jesus and the Theology of Israel [1989]. In 1986, he received the "Righteous Among the Nations Award" from the Holocaust Museum in

Detroit. He has also been active in the Polish-Jewish dialogue as well as the Christian-Jewish-Muslim trialogue.

JOHN K. ROTH: John K. Roth is the Pitzer Professor of Philosophy at Claremont McKenna College, where he was taught since 1966. His more than seventeen books include A Consuming Fire: Encounters with Elie Wiesel and the Holocaust; Approaches to Auschwitz: The Holocaust and Its Legacy [with Richard L. Rubenstein]; and The Holocaust: Religious and Philosophical Implications [with Michael Berenbaum]. In 1988, he was named Professor of the Year in the United States by the Council for the Advancement and Support of Education [CASE] and the Carnegie Foundation for the Advancement of Teaching.

RICHARD L. RUBENSTEIN: Richard L. Rubenstein currently serves as the President of the University of Bridgeport, Bridgeport, CN. He has served as the Robert O. Lawton Distinguished Professor in Religion at Florida State University, Tallahassee, FL, and the President of the Washington Institute for Values in Public Policy, a public policy research institute based in Washington, DC. He is the author or editor of more than eleven books, including After Auschwitz: Radical Theology and Contemporary Judaism [1966]; The Religious Imagination [1968]; The Cunning of History [1975]; The Age of Triage [1983]; Approaches to Auschwitz: The Holocaust and Its Legacy [1987; co-authored with John K. Roth]. In 1988, the Jewish Theological Seminary of America confererd the degree of Doctor of Hebrew Letters, Honoris Causa, upon him at its Centennial Convocation.

ROSEMARY RADFORD RUETHER: Rosemary Radford Ruether is a Christian liberation theologian teaching at Garrett-Evangelical Theological Seminary and Northwestern University, Evanston, IL. She holds the B.A. in Religion and Philosophy from Scripps College, and an M.A. and Ph.D. from Claremont Graduate School in Claremont, CA., in Classics and Early Christianity. She is the author or editor of more than twenty-one books and numerous articles on religion and social justice, among them Faith and Fratricide: The Theological Roots of Anti-Semitism [1974]; and The Wrath of Jonah: The Crisis of Religious Nationalism in the Israeli-Palestinian Conflict [1989; with Herman J. Ruether].

ARTHUR WASKOW: Arthur Waskow has served as the Director of the Shalom Center and Fellow of the Institute for Jewish Renewal. He founded and co-edited the journal The New Menorah, and is the author of The Freedom Seder [1969]; Godwrestling [1978]; and Seasons of Our Joy [1982]. He is also the co-author of The Shalom Seders [1984]; and Before There was a Before [1984], a book of midrashic tales of the Creation for children and adults. His book These Holy Sparks: The Rebirth of the Jewish People [1983] examines the history and meaning of the Jewish renewal movement during the last several decades. He helped found the National Havurah Committee, and has served as a member of the Board of P'nai Or Religious Fellowship and the editorial boards of The Reconstructionist, Genesis 2, and Tikkun.

The Holocaust Now

ABOUT THE EDITOR

Steven L. Jacobs serves as the Rabbi of Temple B'nai Sholom, Huntsville, AL, and teaches or has taught Jewish and Shoah [Holocaust] Studies at Oakwood College and the University of Alabama in Huntsville; Mississippi State University, Starkville, MS; and Martin College, Pulaski, TN. He received his B.A. [With Distinction] from the Pennsylvania State University, University Park, PA, and his B.H.L., M.A.H.L., D.H.L., and Rabbinic Ordination from the Hebrew Union College-Jewish Institute of Religion, Cincinnati, OH. In addition to serving congregations in Steubenville, OH, Niagara Falls, NY, Birmingham and Mobile, AL, and Dallas, TX, he has taught at Spring Hill College, Mobile, AL, where he served as the Herbert P. Feibelman, Jr., Chautauqua Professor Jewish Studies; University of Alabama, Tuscaloosa, AL, as Adjunct Professor of Religious Studies; University of Alabama at Birmingham, Birmingham-Southern College, and Samford University, Birmingham, AL.

Author of more than fifty scholarly articles and reviews dealing primarily with the Shoah, his books include *Shirot Bialik: A New and Annotated Translation of Chaim Nachman Bialik's Epic Poems* [Columbus, OH: Alpha Publishing Company, 1987]; *Raphael Lemkin's Thoughts on Nazi Genocide: Not Guilty?* [Lewiston, NY: The Edwin Mellen Press, 1992]; *Contemporary Jewish Religious Responses to the Shoah and Contemporary Christian Religious Responses to the Shoah* [Lanham, MD: University Press of America, 1993]. His latest book is *Rethinking Jewish Faith: The Child of A Survivor Responds* [Albany, NY: State University of New York Press, 1994]; a January, 1995, selection of *Jewish Book News*.

He serves on the Alabama State Holocaust Advisory Council; the International Council of the Institute on the Holocaust and Genocide, Jerusalem, Israel; the Editorial Board of "Studies in the Shoah" of the University Press of America; the Editorial Board of *Bridges: An Interdisciplinary Journal of Theology; Philosophy, History, and Science*; and as an Educational Consultant to the Center on the Holocaust, Genocide and Human Rights, Philadelphia, PA. He is, also, the Editor of the papers of the late Dr. Raphael Lemkin, author of the term "genocide" and "Father" of the United Nations Treaty on Genocide; and serves on the Board of Directors of the Post-Holocaust Dialogue Group, New York, NY. For the Spring Semester, 1996, he was named the first Zimmerman Scholar-in-Residence at Martin College, Pulaski, TN. Steven L. Jacobs is married to the former Louanne Clayton; they have three children, Hannah Beth, Naomi Rachel, and Shea Clayton.

[1/96]